The Palgrave Handbook of the Hashemite Kingdom of Jordan

P. R. Kumaraswamy
Editor

The Palgrave Handbook of the Hashemite Kingdom of Jordan

palgrave
macmillan

Editor
P. R. Kumaraswamy
School of International Studies, CWAS
Jawaharlal Nehru University
New Delhi, India

ISBN 978-981-13-9165-1   ISBN 978-981-13-9166-8 (eBook)
https://doi.org/10.1007/978-981-13-9166-8

© The Editor(s) (if applicable) and The Author(s), under exclusive licence to Springer Nature Singapore Pte Ltd. 2019

This work is subject to copyright. All rights are solely and exclusively licensed by the Publisher, whether the whole or part of the material is concerned, specifically the rights of translation, reprinting, reuse of illustrations, recitation, broadcasting, reproduction on microfilms or in any other physical way, and transmission or information storage and retrieval, electronic adaptation, computer software, or by similar or dissimilar methodology now known or hereafter developed.

The use of general descriptive names, registered names, trademarks, service marks, etc. in this publication does not imply, even in the absence of a specific statement, that such names are exempt from the relevant protective laws and regulations and therefore free for general use.

The publisher, the authors and the editors are safe to assume that the advice and information in this book are believed to be true and accurate at the date of publication. Neither the publisher nor the authors or the editors give a warranty, express or implied, with respect to the material contained herein or for any errors or omissions that may have been made. The publisher remains neutral with regard to jurisdictional claims in published maps and institutional affiliations.

Cover illustration: Maram_shutterstock.com
Cover design: eStudio Calamar

This Palgrave Macmillan imprint is published by the registered company Springer Nature Singapore Pte Ltd.
The registered company address is: 152 Beach Road, #21-01/04 Gateway East, Singapore 189721, Singapore

*To the memory of
King Hussein
Who built and personified modern Jordan*

Acknowledgements

I have survived. This profound reflection of Emmanuel-Joseph Sieyes on the French Revolution sums up one's life during turbulent times. Staying under the radar is often the only option. In so doing, the Middle East offers immense opportunities, challenges, and above all ideas. This Handbook on the Hashemite Kingdom of Jordan is one such fruitful outcome.

The authors of the Handbook are the primary force behind its successful completion within 15 months. Their passion for Jordan enabled many to take time off from their other pressing commitments. I am moved by their commitment and dedication to the study of the Kingdom.

In the 1980s, Professor Subramanian Swamy sparked my interest in the Middle East, and my Guru, Professor M.S. Agwani, trained me as a good student of the region. I owe immensely to these two personalities for everything that has happened since then.

The style of Bernard Lewis influenced and shaped my writings, though one can only be a local imitation of his indomitable scholarship.

For nearly two decades and with endless passion and tireless dedication, Honourable Shri Mohammed Hamid Ansari has shared his understanding, wisdom, and nuances of the Middle East.

Fortune favoured with inspiring teachers in the form of Professors K.R. Singh, Gopalji Malviya, Sadanand Patra, and A.H.H. Abidi, who showered boundless patience, encouragement, and blessings.

The academic journey has been enriching thanks to scores of scholar friends, especially Ammon Ben-Ariyah, C. Raja Mohan, Csaba Nikoleni, D. Shyam Babu, Daniel Pipes, David Shulman, Edy Kaufman, Efraim Inbar, Efraim Karsh, Girijesh Pant, Gulshan Dietl, Hayat Alvi, Hussein

Solomon, Irene Eber, Jasjit Singh, M.L. Sondhi, Meena Singh Roy, Rajesh Rajagopalan, Santishree Pandit, Sean Foley, Sima Baidya, Sreeradha Datta, Steve Cohen, Uday C. Bhaskar, Yezid Sayigh, and Yitzhak Shichor. Ambassadors Chinmaya Gharekhan, K.P. Fabian, R. Dayakar, Ranjit Gupta, and Sanjay Singh have been generous with their knowledge and time.

Very dear Avraham Sela untied many knots and patiently went over and improved the introduction. D. Shyam Babu has been a source of inspiration, intellectual honesty, and professionalism.

Directly and indirectly, much of the work has been supported by Jawaharlal Nehru University (JNU), first as a doctoral candidate and in later years as faculty, and a special mention is reserved for colleagues, friends, and well-wishers like S.D. Muni, Rajeshwari Pillai-Rajagopalan, G.V.C. Naidu, Jayati Srivastava, Alka Acharya, and Srabani Roy Choudhury.

When I was down and out, numerous friends provided encouragement, especially the ever-cheerful Alvite, street-smart Atul, tech-savvy Dipanwita, and the ever-optimistic Sameena Hameed.

I wish to convey my gratitude to my valuable colleagues in the Centre, namely, A.K. Pasha, A.K. Ramakrishnan, A.K. Mohapatra, Bansidhar Pradhan, Sima Baidya, Mahendra Pratap Rana, and Vrushal Ghoble for enabling me to engage with my academic pursuits.

The students of the Jawaharlal Nehru University gave the comfort and stimulation necessary for a sharpened understanding of the complex region. I am also thankful to the Institute for Defence Studies and Analyses, Indian Council of World Affairs, Knowledge World, and Sage (India) for their institutional support. The Harry S. Truman Research Institute for the Advancement of Peace of the Hebrew University of Jerusalem has been my academic home in the 1990s.

Special word is reserved for a few friends who made the Handbook possible: Manjari Singh, who inspired the volume; Rashmi, who bailed out glitches in the bibliography; and the ever dependable Md. Muddassir Quamar, who ensured the successful completion of the Handbook.

It is the persuasive power of Sagarika Ghosh and her team at Palgrave Macmillan, especially Sundeep Kaur, which resulted in this work reaching its logical conclusion.

All along, I have been blessed with the unconditional love and affection of my parents, Jayanti, Ravi Mama, Sreedhar, and Jayashree. My parents-in-law and brothers-in-law have been generous in showering their warmth.

Ever since I first met her in Jerusalem in the summer of 1988, my wife Lin Qian has smilingly endured my eccentricities and saying YES to her is the only sensible thing I did in my life.

For most of its citizens and foreigners alike, the late King Hussein personified the Hashemite Kingdom of Jordan, and this volume is dedicated with humility to his memory.

As the Bhagavad Gita says, *You are your friend, and you are your own enemy*. All errors and omissions are mine.

Contents

Introduction 1
P. R. Kumaraswamy

Part I   Society 27

From Small Sheikhdom to Over-Population 29
Onn Winckler

The Foreign Workers 49
Françoise De Bel-Air

Minorities 69
Miranda Egan Langley

Christians in Jordan 81
Nanneke Wisman

Circassians 93
Chen Bram and Yasmine Shawwaf

Part II Economy and Environment — 115

Political Economy — 117
Imad El-Anis

Environmental Challenges — 135
Moshe Terdiman

Sustainable Development — 151
Manjari Singh

Smoking — 165
Sean Foley

Part III Politics and Identity — 179

Citizenship — 181
Paul Esber

Composite Nationalism Re-visited — 195
Alexander Bligh and Gadi Hitman

King Abdullah I — 215
Ronen Yitzhak

King Hussein (1935–99) — 233
Md. Muddassir Quamar

The Arab Legion — 243
Graham Jevon

Muslim Brotherhood and Salafism — 257
Joas Wagemakers

The West Bank Under Jordan — 277
Avraham Sela

Jerusalem: Hashemite Quest for Legitimacy 295
Yitzhak Reiter

Jordan-Hamas Relations 311
Hillel Frisch

Political Reforms 323
Artur Malantowicz

The Palestinians 341
Donna Robinson Divine

Part IV Foreign Policy and Security 355

Foreign Policy Under King Hussein 357
Victoria Silva Sánchez

Foreign Policy Under King Abdullah II 373
Faisal Odeh Al-Rfouh

Relations with Saudi Arabia 393
Md. Muddassir Quamar

A Century of Israel-Jordan Relations 407
Meron Medzini

Jordanian-Israeli Relations Under King Hussein 421
Russell E. Lucas

Rabin and Hussein: From Enemies at War to Partners in Peace 435
Meron Medzini

The ISIS 447
Tally Helfont

National Security Priorities 463
Hayat Alvi

Annexure 477

Bibliography 479

Index 521

Notes on Contributors

Faisal Odeh Al-Rfouh is Professor of Political Science at the University of Jordan, Amman and he is now avisiting Professor at Glendon Political Science, York University, Toronto, Canada. He was the dean of Prince Al-Hussein Bin Abdullah II School of International Studies, and the chairman of Political Science Department, University of Jordan. He is a former Minister of Social Development, Administrative Development, and Culture of Jordan. He is the president of Orient Center for Studies and Cultural Dialogue and was a visiting professor at Brigham Young University, Eastern Michigan University, York University, Toronto University, and McGill University. He was a Fulbright scholar during 2009–10. In 2002, he was conferred the title of *Ambassador for Peace* by the Interreligious and International Federation for World Peace. He has authored over 20 books and 65 research articles in both Arabic and English. He has supervised over 100 master's and doctoral theses. He is also the President of India-Jordan Friendship Society.

Hayat Alvi is an associate professor in the National Security Affairs Department at the US Naval War College. She has served as the director of International Studies at Arcadia University and has taught political science at the American University in Cairo, Egypt (2001–05). She also spent a year in Damascus, Syria, as a Fulbright Fellow (1993–94). Her specialisations include international relations, political economy, security and strategic studies, terrorism, conflict resolution, genocide studies, Middle East and South Asian studies, and Islamic studies. She is an international advisory board member at the Middle East Institute in New

Delhi, India. She is currently writing a book entitled *The Political Economy of the Middle East: The Case of Tunisia* (Palgrave Macmillan). She is the author of numerous books, articles, and chapters, including *Regional Integration in the Middle East: An Analysis of Inter-Arab Cooperation* (2007); "The Post-Secular Republic: Turkey's Experiments with Islamism" in *Air & Space Power Journal (USAF)* (2015); and "Women's Rights Movements in the 'Arab Spring': Major Victories or Failures for Human Rights?" in *Journal of International Women's Studies* (2015).

Alexander Bligh is the Chief Scientist, Ministry of Science and Technology, Israel, and research associate, National Knowledge and Research Center for Emergency Readiness, Haifa University. Formerly, he was the acting dean of Faculty of Social Sciences and Humanities and director of the Middle East Research Center, Ariel University. He was a founding chair of the Department of Political Science and Middle Eastern Studies at Ariel University and visiting professor at Columbia University, University of Toronto, University of Notre Dame, and others. He was president of *Strategic Objects*, an international strategic consulting firm dealing with risk analysis and civilian infrastructure projects. He served with the prime minister of Israel (1987–92) and during the last couple of years of his tenure as prime minister's advisor for Arab Affairs. He has studied the field of ethnic relations within multi-cultural societies, and his most recent books are *The Political History of POW Issues in Israel Foreign and Security Relations, 1956–2011* (2017), and *National Schism and Civil Integration: Mutual Relations between the Israeli Central Government and the Israeli Arab Palestinian Minority.* (2018, co-authored with G. Hitman). His book, the *Political Legacy of King Hussein* (2002), and his articles on Jordan have been enthusiastically accepted by scholars of Jordanian affairs.

Chen Bram is an anthropologist and educationalist, with training in organisational studies, sociology, and comparative religion. He is a research fellow at the Truman Institute of the Hebrew University and a senior lecturer at the Department for Behavioural Science at Hadassah Academic College, Jerusalem. He also teaches at the Israel studies graduate programme of the Rothberg International School and the School of Education, the Hebrew University. His work focuses on inter-group relations, ethnicity and religion, and Diaspora and immigration, especially the cases of Circassians and Caucasus "Mountain" Jews; and Holocaust and Genocide studies. His research relates mainly to the Caucasus and Central Asia, Israeli society, and minorities in the Middle East. Combining his academic interests with practical applications, he previously worked as an applied anthropologist. He conducted fieldwork in the Caucasus, Central Asia, Israel, and among post-Soviet immigrant communities in New York City. He served as academic manager of the research group "Anthropological knowledge: relevance, use and potential" at the Van Leer Institute, and as a visiting professor at the University of Florida; at James Madison College of Public Affairs, MSU; and at the Strassler Center for Holocaust and Genocide Studies, at Clark University. He was a research fellow at the International Research Institute, Yad Vashem, and a visiting scholar at the Herbert D. Katz Center, University of Pennsylvania. He also has many years of experience in leading cultural and geographical tours and expeditions in different parts of Asia and Israel.

Françoise De Bel-Air (PhD) is a researcher and consultant based in Paris, France. A socio-demographer by training, she specializes in the demography of Arab countries. Since 2013, she has been a senior fellow and scientific coordinator for Demography within the Gulf Labour Markets, Migration and Population Program (GLMM) (http://gulfmigration.eu/), coordinated by the Gulf Research Centre in Geneva and the Migration Policy Centre of the European University Institute in Florence, Italy. She has been a research fellow at the French Institute for the Near East (IFPO) in Amman, Jordan for several years and a part-time professor at the Migration Policy Centre, EUI, as well as a Jordan and Arab-EU migration expert for ICMPD (EUROMED Migration IV) and others. Her research focusses on youth, family structures, labor and forced migration, migration and population policies in the Arab region. Her recent writings include Chapter 7 "Exclusion, Mobility and Migration" in the Arab Human Development Report 2016 on Youth and "'Blocked Youth': The Politics of Migration from the SEM Countries Before and After the Arab Uprisings." The International Spectator (53): 2018.

Donna Robinson Divine is the Morningstar Family Professor of Jewish Studies and Professor of Government, Emerita at Smith College where she taught a variety of courses on Middle East politics. Her books include *Women Living Change: Cross-Cultural Perspectives-Essays from the Smith College Research Project on Women and Social Change*; *Politics and Society in Ottoman Palestine: The Arab Struggle for Survival and Power*; *Postcolonial Theory and the Arab-Israeli Conflict*; and *Exiled in the Homeland: Zionism and the Return to Mandate Palestine*. She was named the Katharine Asher Engel lecturer at Smith College for 2012–13 in recognition of her scholarly achievements; she was also designated as Smith's

Honoured Professor for the excellence of her teaching. She is currently serving as president of the Association for Israel Studies and as an affiliate professor at the University of Haifa.

Imad El-Anis is Senior Lecturer in International Relations at Nottingham Trent University, UK. He holds a BA (Hons.) in international relations, an MA in international political economy, and a PhD in international political economy. He has authored several books, including *Jordan and the United States: The Political Economy of Trade and Economic Reform in the Middle East* (2011), *A New A-Z of International Relations Theory* (2015), and *International Political Economy in the 21st Century: Contemporary Issues and Analyses* (2017). He has also authored several articles on various aspects of the political economy of the Middle East and North Africa, including work on economic integration and political cooperation, freshwater scarcity, and energy security and nuclear energy proliferation.

Paul Esber is a researcher at the University of Sydney, Australia, where he completed his doctoral studies in 2018 in the Department of Arabic Language and Cultures. A former recipient of the Australian Postgraduate Award scholarship, he is a country expert contributor to the Bertelsmann Transformation Index (BTI). He has been a visiting researcher at the Identity Center for Human Development in Amman, Jordan, focusing on legislative and regulatory electoral developments. His current research interests coalesce around citizenship and its evolving practical and theoretical facets in Jordan and across the Arab states more generally.

Sean Foley is Professor of History at Middle Tennessee State University and specialises in the Middle East, Southeast Asia, and religious and political trends in the broader Islamic world. He holds an MA in Arab studies (2000) and a PhD in history (2005) from Georgetown University (US), where he also taught. He has held Fulbright fellowships at Damascus University (Syria), Istanbul University (Turkey), and the International Islamic University (Malaysia). Besides, he has held research fellowships at King Saud University (Saudi Arabia) and the Australian National University (Australia). He speaks Arabic and Bahasa Malaysia. His work on the Middle East and Islamic history, Gulf politics, the arts, smoking, Sufism, and Muslims in American and European history has been widely published. His works include *The Arab Gulf States: Beyond Oil and Islam* (2010) and *Changing Saudi Arabia: Art, Culture, and Society in the Kingdom* (2019). He has also delivered papers to international conferences and universities throughout Asia, Australasia, the Middle East, North America, South Asia, and Southeast Asia.

Hillel Frisch is Professor of Political Studies and Middle East Studies in Bar-Ilan University, Israel, and senior researcher in the BESA Center for Strategic Studies. His latest books are *Israeli Security and Its Arab Citizens* (2011) and *Palestinian Armies and Militias* (2008). He has written numerous articles on Palestinian and Arab politics and security issues in the Middle East in leading political science and regional journals. He edited a special issue of *Journal of Strategic Studies* (2013) on the role of Arab armies in the recent Arab revolutions, to which he contributed an article on the Egyptian military. His other works include "Choosing the Right Strategy: Why the Palestinians Were More Successful in the First Intifada than in the Second?" in *Contemporary Review of the Middle East* (2015); *Hamas: A Social Welfare Government or War Machine?* (BESA, 2015); and *The ISIS Challenge in Syria: Implications for Israeli Security* (BESA, 2016).

Tally Helfont provides analysis support to the Defense Security Cooperation Agency's Institute for Security Governance (ISG) in Monterey, CA. She was the founding director of the Foreign Policy Research Institute's Program on the Middle East (2011–2018) as well as the Project Lead for its After the Caliphate Project. Her research has focused on regional balance of power, Jordan and the Gulf States, and US policy therein.

The views expressed in the book are those of the author and do not reflect the official policy or position of the U.S. Department of Defense or the U.S. Government.

Gadi Hitman is a faculty member in the Middle East Department and Political Science at Ariel University. He holds a PhD from Bar-Ilan University and his dissertation analyses mutual relations between the Arab Israeli minority and the state of Israel. His research topics include national minorities, protests, and political violence; leadership in the Middle East and Arab Spring; nationalism and ethnicity; and army-state interactions. His works include *Israel and Its Arab Minority: Dialogue, Protest and Violence 1948–2008* (2016) and *National Schism and Civil Integration: Mutual Relations between the Israeli Central Government and the Israeli Arab Palestinian Minority* (2018, co-authored with Alexander Bligh). His recent articles focus on aspects of nationalism in different Middle East countries, like Saudi Arabia, Libya, and Syria.

Graham Jevon is a historian and author of *Glubb Pasha and the Arab Legion: Britain, Jordan, and the End of Empire in the Middle East* (2017), which is based on unprecedented access to Glubb's private papers and papers of Lieutenant Colonel Robert K. Melville, who ran the Arab Legion Staff Liaison Office in London. His work has also been published in the *English Historical Review* and the *Journal of Imperial and Commonwealth History*. A graduate of the University of Salford and the London School of Economics and Political Science, Jevon holds a DPhil in history from St. Antony's College at the University of Oxford, thanks to scholarships from the Arts and Humanities Research Council and the British Society of Middle Eastern Studies. He has previously taught third-year undergraduates visiting Oxford from Stanford University and recently worked on a project related to the history of the Arabian Gulf, at The National Archives in London. Currently, Jevon is part of the British Library's Endangered Archives Programme, which seeks to preserve and make available culturally important archives from around the world that are at risk due to general neglect, poor storage, damaging environmental conditions, or wanton destruction.

Chetna Kuanr is a graduate student of international relations at University of Chicago. She has completed her MA in international relations from Jawaharlal Nehru University, and bachelor's in economics from University of Delhi. She has previously worked as a research assistant at UNDP and interned at Institute for Defence Studies and Analyses. Her research interests include comparative economics of Maghreb and Middle East, with special focus on inter-linkages of ideology with welfare, redistribution and social movements, and IR theories of the region.

P. R. Kumaraswamy is Professor of Contemporary Middle Eastern studies at Jawaharlal Nehru University (JNU), New Delhi. From 1992 to 1999, he was a research fellow at the Harry S. Truman Research Institute for the Advancement of Peace of the Hebrew University of Jerusalem. Since joining JNU in September 1999, he has been researching, teaching, and writing on various aspects of the contemporary Middle East. His academic works include *India's Israel Policy* (2010); *Historical Dictionary of the Arab Israeli Conflict* (2015, second edition); *Squaring the Circle: Mahatma Gandhi and the Jewish National Home* (2018); and *India's Saudi Policy: Bridge to the Future* (Palgrave Macmillan, 2019, co-authored).

Kumaraswamy has edited many volumes and published research articles in numerous refereed and non-refereed international journals and regularly contributes to Indian as well as international media outlets. In February 2010, he set up the virtual *Middle East Institute, New Delhi* (www.mei.org.in) and serves as its honorary director. He is the editor of *Contemporary Review of the Middle East* and the series editor of *Persian Gulf: India's Relations with the Region* (Palgrave Macmillan).

Miranda Egan Langley is an Ireland-based Barrister at Law practising for the last six years, primarily in criminal law, asylum and immigration, and family law with a focus on human rights—specifically access to justice and minority rights issues. She also works at the International Protection Office of the Department of Justice as a legal panel member. She has a keen interest in the Middle East having completed her undergraduate studies in ancient history, archaeology, and Jewish studies at Trinity College, Dublin. After this, she went on to complete a master's in education from the University of London focussing on conflict resolution methodologies in Rwanda and the former Yugoslavia. She then spent time with various NGOs in human rights and advocacy before returning to Dublin to complete her training as a barrister at the Honourable Society of Kings Inns. She recently qualified from University College Dublin with a distinction in international human rights law.

Russell E. Lucas is the director of the Global Studies in Arts and Humanities program and Associate Professor of International Relations (James Madison College of Public Affairs) and Arab Studies (College of Arts and Letters) at Michigan State University. His book *Institutions and the Politics of Survival in Jordan: Domestic Responses to External Challenges, 1988–2001* was published by SUNY Press. His articles have appeared in a range of journals, including *Journal of Democracy, International Studies Quarterly, International Journal of Middle East Studies, Journal of Arabian Studies, International Interactions, Journal of Middle East Culture and Communication*, and *the Middle East Journal*. His current research focuses on conceptions of public opinion in the Arab World and on the politics of Arab monarchies.

Artur Malantowicz is a geographer and political scientist, with his research interests focussed on the Middle East and its socio-political and humanitarian crises. He has worked in academic, governmental, and NGO settings and since 2012 is professionally involved in the humanitarian sector. He serves as the Middle East Expert at the Warsaw-based think tank Centre for International Initiatives. Artur is a member of the British Society for Middle Eastern Studies, European International Studies

Association, and International Humanitarian Studies Association. His work has been published extensively on Jordan's domestic and foreign policy, as well as the regional security dynamics in the Middle East.

Meron Medzini is Adjunct Associate Professor of History (emeritus) in the Department of Asian Studies of the Hebrew University of Jerusalem. He holds a BA degree from City College of New York, an MA degree from Georgetown University, and a PhD from Harvard University where he specialised in East Asia civilisations and languages. The author of six books and scores of articles, he taught at the Hebrew University for almost half a century. He specialised in modern Japanese history as well as Israel-Asia relations and Israeli foreign policy. His recent works are *Japan and the Jews during the Holocaust Era* (2016) and *Golda—A Political Biography* (2017). During 1962–78, he was the director of the Israel Government Press Office, and in that capacity, was the spokesperson for Prime Ministers Levi Eshkol (1966–69), Golda Meir (1973–74), and Yitzhak Rabin (1974–75). He is the editor of the 18-volume series *Israel's Foreign Relations—Selected Documents* published by the Israel Ministry for Foreign Affairs.

Rashmi Muraleedhar is a research assistant at the Institute of Chinese Studies, New Delhi. She is part of a project that looks into the political, military, and economic implications of US-China strategic engagement for India. She completed her master's in international relations from Jawaharlal Nehru University and her bachelor's in chemical engineering from Indian Institute of Technology, Guwahati. Her interest lies in the cross-section of Indian foreign policy, nationalism, great power politics, and globalisation.

Md. Muddassir Quamar is an associate fellow at the Institute for Defence Studies and Analyses (IDSA), New Delhi. He got his doctorate in 2016 from Jawaharlal Nehru University for his thesis on social reforms in Saudi Arabia. His research papers have appeared in leading international journals such as *Asian Affairs, Contemporary Arab Affairs, Journal of Arabian Studies, Digest of Middle East Studies, India Quarterly, and Journal of South Asian and Middle Eastern Studies.* He has co-authored two books, *India's Saudi Policy: Bridge to the Gulf* (2019) and *Persian Gulf 2018: India's Relations with the Region* (2019)—both published by Palgrave Macmillan—and co-edited an anthology, *Contemporary Persian Gulf: Essays in Honour of Gulshan Dietl, Prakash C. Jain and Girijesh Pant* (2016). He regularly contributes media commentaries for IDSA, All

India Radio, and other institutions in India. He was a visiting fellow in King Faisal Center for Research and Islamic Studies, Riyadh, and serves as the associate editor of *Contemporary Review of the Middle East.*

Yitzhak Reiter is a Professor of Islam, Middle East History, and Politics and Israel Studies at Ashkelon Academic College. He also chairs the Department of Israel Studies and is the head of the Research Authority at Ashkelon Academic College. He is also a senior researcher at the Jerusalem Institute for Israel Studies and at the Harry S. Truman Research Institute for the Advancement of Peace of the Hebrew University of Jerusalem. Yitzhak is the author of 13 books (and editor or co-editor of another five books) and numerous articles. Reiter is active in track-two meetings regarding the Arab-Israeli conflict and Jewish-Arab relations inside Israel, and media interviews cover his expertise. He taught at the University of Minnesota and Emory University. Reiter was a visiting scholar at St. Antony's College, University of Oxford (2001); Middle East Institute, Washington D.C. (2003); and the University of Sydney (2003–04). His most recent books are *Contested Holy Places in Israel-Palestine: Sharing and Conflict Resolution* (2017) and *The Eroding Status Quo: Power Struggles on the Temple Mount* (2016).

Victoria Silva Sánchez is an independent journalist and researcher based in Amman and Spain. She holds a master's degree in international relations and African studies and a master's degree in peace, security and defence. As a journalist, her work has been published in *Esglobal, Política Exterior, The Jordan Times, Aquí Europa, Because.bz* and *Algiers Herald.* Her writings and research focus on geo-politics, security, terrorism, extremism, refugees and gender in the Middle East and North Africa and the Sahel. She is a contributor at the Institute of Studies on Conflict and Humanitarian Action (IECAH), the Spanish Institute of Strategic Studies (IEEE), the International Observatory of Studies on Terrorism (OIET) and an analyst at the Jordan Expert Hub of Wikistrat. She is a Junior Research Fellow at the European Institute of the Mediterranean (IEMed). Her articles have appeared in the journals *Relaciones Internacionales* and *Critical Studies on Terrorism* and she has also featured a chapter in the book *Asia-Pacific and Sahel: Emerging Perspectives.* She is a member of the editorial team of the journal *Relaciones Internacionales* of the Universidad Autónoma de Madrid.

Avraham Sela is Professor Emeritus of International Relations and a senior research fellow at the Truman Institute of the Hebrew University of

Jerusalem. His research interests are contemporary Middle East, political history, and foreign fighters in comparative perspective. He is the author of many works, including *The Decline of the Arab Israeli Conflict* (1998) and *The Palestinian Hamas*, co-authored with Shaul Mishal (2000 & 2006). He is co-editor of, and contributor to, two recently published volumes: *Popular Contention, Regime, and Transition: The Arab Revolts in Comparative Global Perspective* (2016), with Eitan Alimi and Mario Sznajder; and *Representations of Israeli and Palestinian Memories and Narratives of the 1948 War* (2016), with Alon Kadish.

Yasmine Shawwaf holds a master's degree in community development and planning. She has studied and written about the identities of Circassians living in the diaspora, including an auto-ethnographic work focused on her experiences and research. Recently, she presented on this work at the conference "Circassians in the 21st Century: Identity and Survival" hosted at the University of Malmö in Sweden. In 2016, she visited Jordan where she studied Arabic and engaged with the Circassian community in Amman. She works in the housing field in New England and continues to independently research intersectional Middle Eastern and Circassian identities.

Manjari Singh is an associate fellow at Centre for Land Warfare Studies (CLAWS) and she obtained her doctorate from the Jawaharlal Nehru University, New Delhi, for her thesis on Sustainable Development in Jordan: A Study of Social, Economic and Environmental Dimensions.
Singh is a Ryoichi Sasakawa Young Leaders Fellowship Fund (SYLFF) Fellow and is specializing in sustainable development and the Middle East. Her research papers have appeared in international journals such as Contemporary Review of the Middle East, Mediterranean Quarterly and Migration and Development. She has co-authored Persian Gulf 2018: India's Relations with the Region (Palgrave Macmillan) and has co-edited Islamic Movements in the Middle East: Ideologies, Practices and Political Participation. She also serves as Assistant Editor of Contemporary Review of the Middle East (Sage) and Managing Editor of CLAWS Journal.

Moshe Terdiman is an expert on Islam in Africa, environmental issues in the Arab and Muslim world, environmental security, environmental refugees, Islam, environment, and interfaith environmental cooperation. He is the founder and director of the Think Tank for the Research of Islam and Muslims in Africa which deals with Islam and Muslim communities in Africa and the Diaspora. He is a research fellow in the Ezri Center for Iran and

Persian Gulf Studies in the University of Haifa dealing with environmental issues in the Arab and Muslim world and the links between the Arabian Peninsula and Africa. He is also a research fellow at the Forum for Regional Thinking dealing with environmental issues in the Middle East. Earlier, he taught courses on environmental policy in the Middle East, Islam and environment, and interfaith environmental cooperation in the Department of Geography and Environmental Development and the Conflict Management and Resolution Program in the Ben-Gurion University and the Arava Institute for Environmental Studies in Kibbutz Keturah.

Joas Wagemakers is Assistant Professor of Islamic and Arabic Studies in the Department of Philosophy and Religious Studies at Utrecht University, the Netherlands. His research focuses on Salafism, Islamism (particularly the ideological sides of these phenomena), and Islamic political thought. Regionally, he concentrates on Jordan, Saudi Arabia, and the Palestinian territories. His work on these subjects has been published widely, including many articles in peer-reviewed international journals as well as books, such as *The Transmission and Dynamics of the Textual Sources of Islam: Essays in Honour of Harald Motzki* (2011; edited with Nicolet Boekhoff-van der Voort and Kees Versteegh); *A Quietist Jihadi: The Ideology and Influence of Abu Muhammad al-Maqdisi* (2012); *Salafism: Utopian Ideals in a Stubborn Reality* (Parthenon, 2014; in Dutch, with Martijn de Koning and Carmen Becker); and *Salafism in Jordan: Political Islam in a Quietist Community* (2016). He also co-edits *ZemZem*, a Dutch-language journal on the Middle East, North Africa, and Islam and blogs at Jihadica.com, a weblog on developments in jihad.

Onn Winckler is an associate professor in the Department of Middle Eastern and Islamic Studies, University of Haifa. His major fields of academic research are the political demography and economic history of the modern Middle East. His recent works include *Behind the Numbers: Israel Political Demography* (Haifa: University of Haifa, Reuven Chaikin Chair in Geostrategy, 2015, Hebrew); *Arab Political Demography: Population Growth, Labor Migration and Natalist Policies*, third edition (2017); with Elie Podeh (ed.), *The Third Wave: Protest and Revolution in the Middle East* (Jerusalem: Carmel, 2017, Hebrew); "The Arab Spring: Socioeconomic Aspects" in *Middle East Policy* (2013); "How Many Qatari Nationals Are There?" in *Middle East Quarterly* (2015); and "Can this be Spring? Assessing the Impact of the Arab Spring on the Arab Tourism Industry" in *Tourism* (2015, co-authored).

Nanneke Wisman is working as country expert (Libya) at the African Cabinet and Political Elite Data (ACPED) Project based at the University of Sussex, UK. In her current function, she successfully built up and maintained a network of local stakeholders and academics to conduct research in both a horizontal and vertical manner. Prior to that, she worked for the International Criminal Court (both for the Office of the Prosecutor and the Registry) for several years as an analyst, mainly focusing on political and security dynamics in different countries providing contextual analysis, threat and security risk assessments, and background papers. Her knowledge and professional experience working on Libya led to her current function where she is mainly focusing on political dynamics after 2011. Nanneke holds an LLM in public international law and an LLM in criminal law and law of criminal procedure, both from Leiden University, the Netherlands. During her studies, she volunteered with the Dutch Council of Refugees as a language coach, supporting refugees in their integration in the Netherlands. She is currently living in and working in Amman.

Ronen Yitzhak is the chair of the Department of Middle Eastern Studies at Western Galilee College in Acre, Israel. His academic interests include the modern history of Jordan, military intelligence, and terror and the 1948 War. He served as the co-editor of *The New East* (Hamizrah Hehadash)—the Hebrew journal of the Middle East and Islamic Studies Association of Israel (MEISAI)—between the years 2012 and 2015, and now he is the member of its editorial board. Since 2012, he has served as a member of MEISAI's executive committee. He has published over 20 articles in refereed journals and 3 books. His book *Abdullah al-Tall—Arab Legion Officer: Arab Nationalism and Opposition to the Hashemite Regime* (2012) was published in an Arabic version in Amman in 2016.

LIST OF FIGURES

From Small Sheikhdom to Over-Population

Fig. 1	Jordan's national population, 1952–2015	32
Fig. 2	Jordan's natural increase rate, 1950–2014	36
Fig. 3	Jordan's age-specific fertility rate, 1965–2012	37

The Foreign Workers

Fig. 1	Registered foreign workers by nationality (selected nationalities, 2004–2016). (Source: Ministry of Labour's Yearbooks, given years, work permits data)	59
Fig. 2	Distribution of work permits by workers' main activity sector and sex (selected nationalities, 2016). (Source: Ministry of Labour's Yearbooks, work permits data)	60

Sustainable Development

Fig. 1	Seventeen Sustainable Development Goals. (Source: Adapted from UNDESA 2017)	152
Fig. 2	Data available for each goal. (Source: Adapted from Jordan Voluntary National Review report 2017)	161

List of Tables

Introduction

Table 1	Monarchs of Jordan	15
Table 2	Parliamentary elections	16
Table 3	Governorates of Jordan	17
Table 4	Palestinian refugee camps in Jordan, 2018	20

From Small Sheikhdom to Over-Population

Table 1	Jordan's national population, 1952–2015	32
Table 2	Jordan's natural increase rate and total fertility rate, 1950–2014	35
Table 3	Jordan's age-specific fertility rate, 1965–2012	36
Table 4	Infant mortality rate and life expectancy in Jordan, 1930–2016	37
Table 5	Percentage of Jordanian ever-married women by age (15–49), 1961–2012	45

Political Economy

Table 1	Macroeconomic indicators (budget deficit, trade deficit, and external aid and grant income)	122
Table 2	Jordanian exports, imports, and trade deficit values (US$) since 2000	133

Introduction

P. R. Kumaraswamy

The Hashemite Kingdom of Jordan has been an oasis of peace and stability in the Middle East. Some might argue otherwise due to the frequent bouts of domestic and regional crises facing the country. If one were to take a holistic approach towards the post-Ottoman Middle East, Jordan has been more stable and secure than many of its neighbours and rivals. In 2021, Jordan is entering its second century of existence since Britain carved out territories east of the River Jordan to establish the Emirate of Transjordan, which became independent in 1946 and was renamed the Hashemite Kingdom of Jordan in 1949.

During the past century, the broader Middle East had faced unprecedented upheavals in the form of military coups, revolutions, external interventions, overthrowing of monarchies, territorial divisions, statelessness, and consistent domestic contest for power among different sections of the population. Beginning with Egypt in 1952, monarchies were overthrown in Iraq, Libya, and Iran. If Sudan was partitioned along ethno-religious lines, the Yemeni unification did not last. Since the end of World War I, the Kurds and Palestinians have been fighting for their statehood. Within a century after the demise of the Ottoman Empire, the Turkish Republic witnessed as many as four military coups. The death or

---

P. R. Kumaraswamy (✉)
School of International Studies, CWAS, Jawaharlal Nehru University, New Delhi, India

© The Author(s) 2019
P. R. Kumaraswamy (ed.), *The Palgrave Handbook of the Hashemite Kingdom of Jordan*, https://doi.org/10.1007/978-981-13-9166-8_1

removal of strong leaders unravelled the "artificiality" of Iraq, Libya, and Yemen. Some states have questioned the sanctity of the colonial borders and, in the process, coveted, captured, or annexed the territories of their weaker neighbours. Until recently, most Arab leaders either died in office or were forcibly removed from power. Iran and Turkey had their share of political violence. Existential threat and four comprehensive wars marked and marred the seven decades of Israel's existence.

Seen in this broader regional canvas, Jordan has disproved many doomsday predictions and has survived and flourished as a distinct, important, and stable political entity. Indeed, since 1921, not only the Hashemite rule continued, the country has witnessed only four rulers.

The resilience of the Kingdom becomes apparent when one looks at its physico-climatic features and natural resources. Covering an area of just under 90,000 square kilometres, it is an arid and semi-arid country as deserts cover nearly 90 per cent of its territory. It is almost a landlocked country with 26-kilometre-long coastline in the Gulf of Aqaba being its only access to the sea. The inadequate rainfall is accompanied by the near absence of forest cover, thereby leaving only a limited arable land for cultivation as well as human habitation. The economic challenges of Jordan are compounded by a higher population growth due to both natural increase and periodic influx of refugees from its neighbours. At present, refugees or non-citizens make up nearly a third of Jordan's population, one of the highest in the world. Confronted with resource crunch and population pressures, the Hashemite Kingdom relies heavily upon remittances of its workers abroad and foreign aid and assistance to maintain a highly subsidised welfare mechanism to feed its population, citizens, and residents. Under such circumstances, the Hashemites have perfected survival as an art and this is manifest in their political survival and economic sustenance.

Land, Ecology, and Natural Resources

In terms of natural resources, Jordan is a resource-starved country and lacks the most essential requirement for human subsistence and development, namely, water. In 2017, it became the second driest country in the world. Due to periodic droughts, rising temperature, salinity, urbanisation, poor agricultural practices, population pressures, and wastage, its water security has become precarious. As against the standard international poverty line of 500 cubic metres of water per person per year, Jordanians got only 145 cubic metres in 2010, and this is expected to drop further in the coming years. Over 90 per cent of the landmass receives less than 200 millimetres of rainfall annually. The flow of River Jordan, the primary source of freshwater, has been dwindling over the years and groundwater level is receding. The peace treaty with Israel resulted in Jordan getting 50 million cubic metres of additional waters in River Jordan, but this is inadequate to meet the growing demands.

Minerals from the Dead Sea are its only naturally available resource and even this is shared with Israel and Palestine. Over the years, the inflow of the Jordan River into the Sea has dwindled leading to dropping of the water level to 430 metres below the sea level and the formation of sink-holes around the Dead Sea.

Oil forms the major component of Jordan's imports and, for long, it has depended upon Iraq for its energy needs. The Iraqi civil war after the US invasion led to the Kingdom looking for Egypt as an alternative. The post-Mubarak domestic unrest saw gas pipelines in the Sinai Peninsula being periodically blown up and this created a fuel crisis. This compelled Jordan to explore non-conventional options such as nuclear energy, and exploratory talks are being conducted with countries such as Russia, South Korea, and Australia. Overcoming domestic opposition in September 2016, Jordan Electric Power Company signed a US$10 billion agreement with an Israeli consortium for the supply of natural gas for 15 years. Despite its vast potential, solar energy has not become a commercially viable option mainly due to massive capital cost and a longer gestation period.

Evolution of Jordan

The Emirate of Transjordan and later on the Hashemite Kingdom of Jordan are mostly a British construct. The exigencies of the World War I and the need to confront the Ottoman Empire resulted in Britain propping up the Sharif Hussein Bin Ali of Mecca as an alternate power in the region. Through the Hussein-McMahon Correspondence of 1915–16, London endorsed Hussein's rebellion against the Ottoman Sultan who also held the office of Caliph. In return for the Arab Revolt against the Ottoman Turks, Britain promised an independent Kingdom of Arabia under Sharif Hussein. As later events proved, this pledge ran counter not only to the Sykes-Picot understanding of post-Ottoman cartography but also to the Balfour Declaration of 1917.

The military victories of Abdulaziz Bin Abdulrahman al-Saud or Ibn Saud, the ruler of Najd and the founder of the third Saudi state, scuttled the British plans in the Arabian Peninsula, especially after the al-Saud capture of the Hejaz region that ended centuries-old Hashemite control of Mecca and Medina in 1925. Forced to choose between the emerging Saudi state and its commitments to Hussein, Britain sought alternative plans. When the French foiled the efforts of Faisal—the third son of Hussein—to be the King of Syria, the British installed him as the monarch of the newly formed Iraqi state. Since this arrangement did not satisfy the Hashemites, in 1921, Britain carved out territories east of River Jordan and installed Hussein's second son Abdullah as the ruler of the Emirate of Transjordan.

Much of the post-Ottoman Middle Eastern states have been imperial legacies whose borders and territorial limits were defined according to colonialism, but Jordan is unique. If its formation was rooted in the British promises to the Sharif Hussein, its leadership was not indigenous. However, when he was installed as the Emir of Transjordan, Abdullah positioned himself as the arbiter of the warring Bedouin tribes, and in the process, secured their loyalty and support towards the transformation of Jordan.

Devoid of natural resources, the British aid and subsidy was critical for the nascent Emirate. Initially, it received an annual financial assistance to the tune of £50,000 and it was gradually increased to 2 million pounds by 1948. The formation of the Mobile Force in 1920 became the forerunner of the Arab Legion, which was trained, armed, funded, and eventually commanded by the British. What was conceived as a security apparatus to reign in warring tribes and consolidate the Hashemite rule transformed into being the most powerful military force in the region. The Arab Legion played a crucial role in the Arab-Israeli War of 1948 in capturing the old city of Jerusalem and in preventing the Jewish forces from capturing the eastern part of Mandate Palestine or the West Bank.

At the end of the World War II, Britain granted independence to Transjordan, and on 25 May 1946, the latter became the Kingdom of Transjordan with Emir Abdullah I becoming the king. In the wake of the capture and subsequent annexation of the West Bank following the 1948 War, Abdullah renamed the country as the Hashemite Kingdom of Jordan.

The British support and strength of the Arab Legion emboldened the territorial ambitions of the newly crowned Abdullah. He was not opposed to a Jewish State in Palestine if it were to satisfy his expansionist dreams. As other Arab leaders and Palestinians opposed the UN partition plan,

Abdullah was favourable and secretly conveyed it to the Zionist leadership. The Abdullah-Meir understanding during the run-up to the British departure survived and remains the basis of not only Jordan's relations with Israel but also the bedrock of Jordanian policies, both domestic and foreign.

However, perceived collaboration with the Zionist enemy proved fatal for Abdullah. With his grandson and future ruler Hussein standing next to him, the King was assassinated by a Palestinian at the steps of the Al-Aqsa Mosque on 20 July 1951 after Friday prayers. After a brief tenure, Abdullah's son Talal was removed due to health concerns and his grandson Hussein was appointed the crown prince on 9 September 1951; he ruled through the council of regents from August 1952 and assumed the title of King on 2 May 1953.

The spate of assassination attempts on his life by elements within and outside Jordan resulted in King Hussein changing the line of succession in March 1965 from his one-year-old son Abdullah to his brother Hasan. This arrangement enabled the infant to lead a normal life, go abroad for higher studies, and eventually become a senior commander of an elite unit in the Jordanian army. However, on 24 January 1999, literally days before his impending death, King Hussein suddenly changed the line of succession. Accusing his brother—who managed the affairs of the state during his periodic absence from the country—of impropriety, Hussein settled for the primogenital succession and renamed Abdullah as his designated successor. Upon the death of Hussein on 9 February 1999, Abdullah became the ruler and as per the deathbed wishes of Hussein, named his half-brother Hamza as the crown prince. This arrangement, however, did not last long and on 28 November 2004, the King removed Hamza and eventually named his son Hussein as the crown prince on 2 July 2009 and in line for the throne. Despite the sudden change of fortunes and public insult by his brother, Prince Hasan handled the situation with great dignity, poise, and forbearance, and has remained a strong pillar of support of his nephew.

Externally, the territorial ambitions of the Hashemites were not confined to Palestine, and in the early years, Jordan coveted parts of its neighbours towards realising the United Arab Kingdom promised to Sharif Hussein of Mecca. These were overtaken by the July 1958 coup which toppled the Hashemite rule in Baghdad and the Lebanese civil war which spurred the Syrian territorial ambitions. However, for long, Hussein aspired to regain full or parts of the West Bank which he lost in 1967 through political understandings with Israel and the local Palestinian leadership. His idea of Jordanian-Palestinian confederation in 1972 evoked sympathetic noises in Israel but since the early 1970s, following the expulsion of the Palestinian *Fedayeen*, having a stronger and effective control over the East bank became far more important for the Hashemites than any expansionist dreams.

The evolution of Transjordan/Jordan was accompanied by other monarchies falling like a house of cards in the broader Middle East. The overthrowing of dynasties in Egypt (1952), Iraq (1958), Libya (1969), and Iran (1979) and the ascendance of the US in the Middle East brought Jordan closer to Washington. The decline and eventual demise of the British Empire after the World War II had a cascading effect upon the British-Jordanian ties. While Britain continued to play an essential role in the Hashemite family and social engagements, reflecting the post-War American preponderance, Jordan also moved closer to the US and emerged as a significant player in the American strategic calculations in the Middle East. Some of the principal American foreign policy initiatives had a direct bearing upon Jordan.

Historical Legacy

The Hashemite Kingdom of Jordan is a rare state whose historical claims and legacies are closely intertwined with the three Abrahamic faiths—Judaism, Christianity, and Islam. More importantly, River Jordan was being linked to some of the critical events of Judaism and Christianity. According to the Old Testament, Moses led the Israelites from Egypt and crossed the Red Sea to reach Jordan. While God had commanded Moses to lead the Israelites to the Promised Land, He had forbidden Moses from crossing the Jordan River. Hence, standing on Mount Nuevo, Moses urged Joshua to lead the Jews to Eretz Israel and the burial cave of Moses is located in Mount Nebo in present-day Jordan.

Bethany is said to be the birthplace of Christianity and according to New Testament, Jesus Christ was baptised by John the Baptist in "Bethany beyond Jordan" (Book of John 1:28 and Matthew 3.13). The Christian historiography refers to pilgrims visiting the site through the centuries but after the fourteenth century, the pilgrims mainly comprised of Christians from the region. In the late nineteenth century, it regained attention and at the end of World War I, a small church was built in Bethany and this more or less coincided with the formation of the Emirate of Transjordan.

Gradually, the site of baptism and its tourism potential became a bone of contention among the riparian states of River Jordan. Bethany became entangled in the Arab-Israeli War of 1948 and became a no-go zone as both Israel and Jordan mined the areas under their control. The June 1967 War saw the entire West Bank coming under the Israeli military control and this resulted in Israel identifying Qasr al-Yahud or Yardenit as the baptism site. This situation changed after the signing of the Israel-Jordan peace treaty in 1994 and Bethany re-emerged as a major attraction for Christian pilgrimage in the region.

This move spurred a politico-economic tussle between Jordan and the Palestinian leadership and the latter sought to popularise Qasr al-Yahud as the baptism site. The visit of Pope John Paul II shifted the balance in favour of Jordan, and him attending prayers in Bethany on 22 March 2000 strengthened the Hashemite claims; Pope Francis followed this tradition when he visited the Holy Land in May 2014. Besides Bethany, Jordan has many sites, including monasteries, churches, and places which are identified with Christian historiography. As would be discussed, Jordan often uses its Christian legacy to buttress its liberal and inclusive societal position.

Likewise, the Hashemites trace their lineage to the Hashem clan of Prophet Mohammed. These linkages are critical for the evolution of the Jordanian state and to dispel its relative modern origin. Monarchy is integral to Jordan's emergence, foundation, evolution, and progress. Close to a century of existence, the Hashemite monarchy has become synonymous with Jordan.

Society and Population

Jordan is a heterogeneous society marked by many inbuilt cleavages. The Palestinians are a significant component of its population. While Jordan remains the only Arab country to grant full citizenship to them, the Palestinians form its toughest challenge concerning national identity, demographic distribution, and foreign policy priorities. Palestinians are also a major portion of the refugees that the Kingdom has been hosting since the late 1940s.

Regarding religious groups, Jordan has a significant number of Christians and Druze population as well as ethnic groups, such as Circassians, Chechens, and Bedouins. Among these groups, the Bedouins from the most critical group concerning political power and social presence as they are seen as the backbone of the Hashemite regime.

The small but significant Christian population has dwindled over time, from about 200,000 in the 1930s or 20 per cent of the population, it came down to 250,000 or 4 per cent in 2014. The decline is primarily due to the low growth rate among the Christians and their emigration to the West for economic reasons. Despite the smaller number, the Christian community is diverse and has about 15 sub-sects. The largest one is Greek Orthodox with about 125,000 adherents, but Catholicism is more prominent and conducts some of the largest congregations. Christian holidays are commemorated in public, and Christmas is a national holiday. Though Lebanon and Palestine also officially celebrate the birth of Christ, the Jordanian situation is different and there is a public recognition of Christianity and an affirmation of its multicultural character.

Primarily because of the historicity, Christianity survived and continued even before Jordan's formation. Free access to Jerusalem and Bethlehem until 1967 also enhanced Christian presence in the polity. The inclusive nature of the Kingdom is reflected in Christians securing senior positions in the government, including ministership. Interestingly, while members belonging to other minorities have headed the government, no Christian has ever become prime minister since Jordan was formed in 1921.

At the same time, Christians have flourished economically and are seen as one of the prosperous communities and are primarily concentrated in urban centres such as Amman. Though the demographic picture is muddled in controversies, it is safe to assume that the bulk of the Christians of Jordan are of Transjordanian origin, that is, the residents of the East Bank before 1948 or the Jordanian-Jordanians.

The inclusive attitude of the Hashemites towards the non-Muslim population manifests in greater cooperation between the two. The liberal state policies resulted in the regime enjoying their loyalty of and proximity to the rulers. As a result, Christians enjoy greater public space in Jordan than in many other countries in the Middle East. Christians have been elected to the parliament even before Jordanian independence, and when the affirmative action was formalised in 2003, they were the primary beneficiaries. They constituted about 4 per cent of the population but were given 9 seats in the 130-member house. The strength of the parliament was increased to 150 in 2013 and reduced to 130 in 2016, but on both occasions, the number of seats reserved for Christians remained the same. In other words, in 2018, Christians makeup about 4 per cent of the population, but they enjoy 7.5 per cent representation in the lower house of Jordanian parliament. This is in addition to many Christians being appointed to the Upper House which has a strength of 65 members.

Besides, there is a small Baha'i community, estimated to be around 1000. They are not formally recognised as Muslims or non-Muslims but enjoy a degree of non-intrusive private practices. Concerning the personal law, however, their disputes are adjudicated within the Sharia framework. This is a far better treatment than they face in Iran, the birthplace of the Baha'i faith, where their non-recognition by the Islamic Republic has institutionalised their exclusion, discrimination, marginalisation, and persecution.

Jordan is also a multi-ethnic country. It has a significant Bedouin population whose number is estimated at 200,000 and comprises a substantial portion of the Jordanian-Jordanians and is integral to the broader debate involving the Palestinian-Jordanians. They are the backbone of the regime and contribute to its longevity. The political arrangement manifests in the gerrymandering of electoral districts in favour of the Bedouin-inhabited rural areas. Agricultural subsidies for water and electricity, procurement prices, and cultivation pattern are linked to the Bedouin-Hashemite patronage system (Kumaraswamy and Singh 2018). Some of the Bedouin tribes are also large landowners whose support is critical for the survival of the regime. The Ma'an governorate, which is mainly tribal, witnessed the worst food riots in 1989 when King Hussein reduced food subsidies in line with the diktats of the International Monetary Fund (IMF). The unviable agricultural pattern which contributes neither to the gross domestic product (GDP) nor to the employment is primarily an outcome of this Hashemite-Bedouin political arrangement and impedes the regime from pushing forward reforms and modernisation.

There are other ethnic minorities in Jordan, and the most prominent are the Circassians, Chechens, Druze, and Armenians. Circassians and Chechens fled to the then Ottoman Empire in the late nineteenth century following their violent persecution by the Czarist Russia. Though Muslims, they did not become Arab or were not Arabised in the ethno-national sense of the word. Their identification with the state enabled members of both the communities gaining visible positions in the establishment, including prime ministership. The security establishment has the most visible presence of the Circassians where they make up about 4 per cent, while their share in Jordan's population is much smaller. Circassians and Chechens jointly have three seats reserved for them in the lower house of Jordanian parliament.

The presence of Druze and Armenians is smaller and is estimated to be around 32,000 and 3000, respectively. Both are also religious communities;

while the Druze have a distinct ethno-religious identity, the Armenians are predominantly Christians and they adhere to the Armenian Apostolic Church.

The greater visibility and disproportionately higher representation of minorities in the parliament come against the backdrop of a general marginalisation of the minorities in much of the Middle East. Unlike the Islamic Republic of Iran, the minorities are full citizens of Jordan and have progressed socially, politically, and militarily.

Islam

Islam plays an important role in the Jordanian society, polity, and foreign policy. Though surrounded by not-so-liberal states, Jordanian Islam is accommodative of diversities. While declaring Islam to be the religion of the state, the constitution adopted in January 1952 admits and recognises the rights, privileges, and obligations of non-Islamic faiths and their personal laws. Unlike much of the Middle East, Jordan provides for a non-religious civil route to adjudicate differences. The implementation of sharia in some of its brutal forms is not uncommon in Iran and Saudi Arabia. The Hashemites seek legitimacy as the direct descendants of Prophet Mohammed through the Hashem clan. Them being the rulers of Hejaz until 1925, which included Mecca and Medina since the early days of Islam, emboldens that claim.

Since the early 1950s, the palace had maintained a flexible approach towards the Muslim Brotherhood, and after 1992, its political wing, the Islamic Action Front (IAF). The Islamists were helpful to King Hussein when he was confronted with the revolutionary fervour in the 1950s and 1960s in the form of pan-Arabism championed by Gamal Abdul Nasser. For its part, the Muslim Brotherhood was a positive and regime-supporting opposition and bestowed popular support for the regime when regional undercurrents were against Jordan.

Religious pluralism exists both at the official and societal levels. Public display of Christian symbols and celebrations add to Jordan's diversity. Interfaith respect and dialogue in the Kingdom predated the September 11 attacks when such exchanges became fashionable for Gulf Arab countries. At the same time, as would be discussed, the palace-Brotherhood relations have not always been smooth and often flared up before parliamentary elections. While prepared to coexist with and accommodate the Islamists, the regime has been wary of the latter gaining a greater say in governance. Hence, through electoral laws and gerrymandering, the regime has periodically sought to restrict the electoral gains of the IAF.

Demography

The population is the most complex issue facing Jordan as it includes citizens, residents, refugees, migrant labourers, non-citizen spouses, and stateless children of Jordanian women. Since its founding as an Emirate and its transformation as a state, Jordan has had a high population growth rate. From 225,000 in 1922, it nearly doubled to 433,000 at the time of independence and has been growing exponentially since then. Its population reached 1.2 million in 1950; 895,000 in 1960; 1.67 million in 1970; 2.29 million in 1980; 3.4 million in 1990; 4.8 million in 2000; and 6.1 million in 2010 (World Bank 2014). In the wake of the annexation of the West Bank and the granting of citizenship to its Palestinian residents, in 1952, Jordan had 1.3 million people under its control (UNCTAD 1994). As of 2018, Jordan's population stands at 9.5 million and it is the tenth most populated country in the Middle East and seventh in the Arab world.

High birth rate along with increased life expectancy and drop in infant mortality have largely contributed to the population increase. Jordan has one of the highest birth rates in the world. As against 2 per cent in the Middle East and 1.13 per cent globally, the Kingdom's population through births is increasing at the rate of 2.3 per cent (World Bank 2014). At the same time, the Jordanian population growth rate is higher than the natural growth, that is, higher than 2.3 per cent (World Bank 2014). This is the result of Jordan being a safe haven for refugees from the neighbouring countries since the late 1940s.

The process began with the annexation of the Arab parts of Mandate Palestine in the wake of the Arab-Israel War of 1948 which brought in an estimated 400,000 Palestinians as Jordanian subjects and about the same number as refugees. The loss of the West Bank in the June War created a precarious situation for the Kingdom. While it lost the Palestinian territories, Jordan was burdened with the Palestinian population who held Jordanian citizenship or a "people-without-land" syndrome.

Controversies over King Hussein's position during the Kuwait crisis resulted in the expulsion of about 400,000 Palestinians from Kuwait and its Arab allies and most were holding Jordanian travel documents (Lesch 1991). In the wake of the US-led invasion of Iraq in 2003, Jordan hosted about 450,000–500,000 refugees from that country. Following the emergence of the Islamic State of Iraq and Syria (ISIS) and subsequent violence in Iraq, Jordan witnessed a new wave of refugees, and by May 2015, it hosted more than 47,000 Iraqi refugees. In between, the Israel-Hezbollah Second Lebanon War in 2006 saw a small number of Lebanese citizens coming into Jordan via Syria and taking temporary refuge.

The Syrian civil war has opened a floodgate of a fresh round of refugee influx, but there is a huge discrepancy regarding their number. In December 2014, the Jordanian Interior Ministry claimed that there were 1.4 million Syrian refugees in the country (*The Jordan Times* 2014) and at that time, the UNHCR put the number of "registered" just over 600,000. This discrepancy between the UN and Jordanian figures is attributed to refugee fears over possible "reprisal" actions against their families left behind in Syria and integration of the refugees with the host society (Kumaraswamy and Singh 2017). At the end of 2014, there were about 4.1 million refugees who were living in Jordan, while the citizen population stood at 6.6 million. In other words, over 10 million were residing in the Kingdom on a semi-permanent basis. If one accepts the Jordanian, not the UN figures, then about one-sixth of the total resident population in the Kingdom is Syrian refugees.

The continuing presence of the Syrian refugees has intensified some of the traditional problems related to population pressures and added new ones. Increase in unemployment, drop in real wages, housing crisis, cuts in subsidies, decrease in the availability of water, urban congestion, drop in GDP, challenges to food security, growing food imports, decline in agricultural exports, and increasing cost of imports are directly linked to the Syrian crisis and the resultant refugees influx into Jordan (Kumaraswamy and Singh 2017).

The second category of non-citizen residents is foreign workers. A high rate of domestic unemployment is accompanied by a significant number of migrant labourers in critical sectors of the economy, like agriculture and the service industry. In 2010, the Ministry of Labour put the number at over 335,000, and a few years later, Swiss Agency for Development and Cooperation (SDC) estimated the migrant workforce in the Kingdom to be around 1.5 million, including about half a million "undocumented" workers (SDC 2014, p. 1). The migrant labourers are the replacement for Jordanians who emigrated to the Gulf Arab countries in the wake of the oil boom in the early 1970s. At the same time, a significant portion of the foreign workforce is also required in the low-paying sector, like domestic workers, which the honour-conscious tribes consider to be demeaning.

The non-citizen residents, both refugees and foreign workers, compete with the citizenry in consuming Jordan's limited natural resources, especially water and adding to its demographic composition, social tension, and economic challenges.

Economy

Inflation in Jordan is very high and this makes the Kingdom one of the costliest places to live in the Middle East. With a per capita income of US$3700 in 2018, it is bracketed as a lower income country. Its GDP stands at US$40 billion and its total foreign trade is relatively small and stands at US$26 billion. Regarding human development indexes, Jordanian achievements are commendable.

At the same time, it is not easy to categorise the Jordanian economy. It is often seen as a semi-rentier state, that is, a state that heavily depends upon the "rent" it receives from abroad and not through domestic economic activities or taxation. The "rent" comes from two principal sources: remittances from its citizens and residents who are working abroad, mainly in the energy-rich Gulf Arab countries and aid and assistance from friendly countries. During the heydays of the oil boom, the Kingdom annually received about US$3.5 billion from its workers abroad, but this has dwindled due to low oil price and competition from other labour-exporting countries. Controversies over King Hussein's position during the Kuwait crisis resulted in the expulsion of about 400,000 Palestinians from the Gulf and this added to its financial burden.

Likewise, international aid and assistance make up a substantial portion of the Jordanian budget and gross national product. The vast subsidies and the resultant budget deficits are met mainly through overseas aid and assistance. Amidst domestic protests in 2011, four richer members of the Gulf Cooperation Countries (GCC), namely, Kuwait, Qatar, Saudi Arabia, and the United Arab Emirates (UAE) pledged US$5 billion as financial assistance and an additional US$2.5 billion was pledged by these countries when Jordan faced a fresh round of domestic protests in early 2018 over tax reforms.

Dependence upon external aid and assistance considerably limits Jordan's political manoeuvre in regional affairs and impedes its reforms process. Direct or indirect (the IMF route) American assistance is invariably linked to greater Jordan accommodation with Israel over the peace process, a not-so-popular option domestically, especially among the Palestinian-Jordanians and the Muslim Brotherhood. The financial largesse from the

Gulf Arab countries is not unconditional either and is accompanied by a demand for a slower pace of political reforms. Donor countries are afraid of the cascading effect of Jordanian reforms upon their societies. Thus, external aid, either from the West or Arab neighbours, imposes a political price that is not in sync with the popular sentiments in the country. At the same time, having accustomed to a high degree of subsidies, the citizens are not prepared for burden sharing, especially during the financial crisis.

The domestic economic problems are compounded by the continuous influx of refugees into the country. As of 2018, nearly 20 per cent of the residents of Jordan are refugees or foreign workers. Presenting itself as a safe haven for refugees from its neighbours has often become a precondition for Jordan receiving international attention and aid. Prolonged financial help was often linked to the Kingdom hosting a large Palestinian refugee population and its acceptance of the Syrian refugees. These financial supports are not commensurate with the cost of hosting the refugees, and of late, refugee camps with modern amenities generate hostile reactions from ordinary Jordanians who face impoverished living conditions. While the Jordanian acceptance of the Palestinian refugees in 1948 and 1967 was a political choice, the influx of other refugees in later years was a geostrategic compulsion; hosting of refugees had become a precondition for Western aid, even when the latter was insufficient and has a cascading effect upon the Jordanian economy.

Over the years, some of the sectors of the economy are facing competition from its neighbours. For long, Amman functioned as a major transit hub with *Royal Jordanian* ferrying passengers between Asia and Europe and North America. It was also a major transit point for Gulf-bound migrant workers. In recent years, competition from *Etihad*, *Emirates*, and *Qatar Air* had dented the market forcing *Royal Jordanian* to cancel some of its lucrative routes to Asia, especially India. This came amidst the Queen Alia International Airport in Amman undergoing massive modernisation in 2013. While the number of passengers using the airport almost reached 8 million in 2017, the national carrier is not out of the woods.

Domestic Politics

Since its founding as an Emirate in 1921, Jordan has remained a hereditary monarchy and founder ruler Abdullah I was followed by primogenital succession. Until his assassination in July 1951, Abdullah was at the helm of affairs, first as emir and then as king (Table 1). He was briefly succeeded

Table 1 Monarchs of Jordan

Monarch	From	To
Emir Abdullah-I	1 April 1921	25 May 1946
King Abdullah-I	25 May 1947	20 July 1951 (assassinated)
King Talal	20 July 1951	11 August 1952 (abdicated)
Hussein (Regent)	11 August 1952	2 May 1953 (through a regent council)
King Hussein	2 May 1953	7 February 1999 (natural death)
King Abdullah-II	7 February 1999	Till date

by his eldest son Bin-Talal who was forced to abdicate in August 1952 due to health issues. The country was ruled by a regency council, and Hussein took over as king in May 1953 upon attaining the age of 17. He ruled the kingdom for over four decades and became the longest reigning king in the world since the end of the World War II. During Hussein's rule, for example, the US had seen as many as ten presidents. Upon his death in February 1999, Hussein was succeeded by his eldest son Abdullah. In short, in its century-long existence, Jordan had seen only four rulers.

Though monarchical, Jordan has been in the forefront of electoral politics. Partly because of his own inclination and partly due to his desire to secure popular legitimacy, elections became a key component of Abdullah's rule. Being a British protégé from Hejaz with no roots in the territory over which he ruled weighed heavily upon Abdullah. The first election to the parliament was held in April 1929, a few years after the formation of the Emirate of Transjordan. The 22-member unicameral legislature was based on the constitution that was adopted in the previous year. Elections were sporadic, without time-bound regularity. The first election after independence was held in October 1947 and, since then, Jordan has held 18 elections to the parliament (Table 2).

Moreover, the composition of the elected lower house or *Majlis al-Nuwab* has been flexible and changing. When the first elections were held in 1929, it had 16 members and this was raised to 40 for the newly elected parliament in 1950 with equal representation for East and West Banks. The number was increased to 80 in 1989 when the first multiparty elections were held and to 110 in 2003 when seats were reserved for the minorities. The strength rose to 150 in 2013 but came down to 130 three years later. The fluctuation does not appear to be exclusively linked to population growth but to the political expediency of the times.

Table 2 Parliamentary elections

Parliament	Date of elections
1	2 April 1929
2	10 June 1931
3	16 October 1934
4	16 October 1937
5	20 October 1942
6	20 October 1947
7	11 April 1950
8	29 august 1951
9	16 October 1954
10	21 October 1956
11	19 October 1961
12	24–25 November 1962
13	6 July 1963
14	27 April 1967
15	8 November 1989
16	8 November 1993
17	4 November 1997
18	17 June 2003
19	20 November 2007
20	9 November 2010
21	23 January 2013
22	20 September 2016

Source: Hashemite Kingdom of Jordan, *Majlis al-Umma*, http://www.parliament.jo/en/node/146; Inter-Parliamentary Union, http://archive.ipu.org/parline/reports/2163_arc.htm; and Dieter Nohlen, Florian Grotz & Christof Hartmann (2001) *Elections in Asia: A data handbook, Volume I*, p. 148 ISBN 0-19-924958-X

In a significant step towards gender equality, in 2013, 15 out of 150 seats were reserved for women and the proportion was maintained even when the strength of the parliament was reduced to 130 in 2013. In a significant move, in 2016, the reserved seats for women were equally distributed to the 12 governorates and 3 tribal-dominated Badia districts (Table 3). The affirmative action for minorities was formalised in 2003 when nine seats were reserved for the Christians and three for Circassians and Chechens. This number did not change even when the strength of the parliament was increased to 150 in 2013 or reduced to 130 three years later.

Under the constitution adopted in 1952, the parliament became bicameral with the formation of the Senate (Majlis al-Aayan), or the Upper

Table 3 Governorates of Jordan

Governorates	Capital	Area (sq. km)	Population (2015)
Irbid	Irbid	1572	1,770,158
Ajloun	Ajloun	420	176,080
Jerash	Jerash	410	237,059
Mafraq	Mafraq	26,551	549,948
Balqa	Salt	1120	491,709
Amman	Amman	7579	4,007,526
Zarqa	Zarqa	4761	1,364,878
Madaba	Madaba	940	189,192
Karaq	Al-Karaq	3495	316,629
Tafilah	Tafilah	2209	96,291
Ma'an	Ma'an	32,832	144,082
Aqaba	Aqaba	6905	188,160
Total			9,531,712

Source: Hashemite Kingdom of Jordan, Population and Social Statistics, Directorate Department of Population Statistics, https://web.archive.org/web/20171013221522/http://web.dos.gov.jo:80/wp-content/uploads/2016/04/No_of_pop_depand_on_GOV.pdf

House, with nominated members. Senior political leaders, social figures, and retired military officials, often close to the palace, have been nominated for a four-year term, and at present, the Senate has 65 members.

Since the late 1950s, Jordan faced a host of domestic and regional tensions and wars. Pan-Arabism and the anti-monarchical rhetoric threatened Jordan severely, especially when Nasserism had strong support among the Jordanians. The fall of Hashemite Iraq, periodic Arab conflicts with Israel, the ascendance of the PLO as an independent player, loss of the West Bank in the June War, and realignment of the region under the Saudi domination had a cascading effect upon Jordan and its ability to pursue participatory politics. Thus, political parties were suspended between 1961 and 1989 and a political reopening became inevitable following the bread riots in Ma'an on 18 April 1989. Considered the stronghold of the pro-regime tribal loyalists, the riots were sparked off by the reduction of food subsidies as part of the structural adjustment programme of the IMF.

Partly to alleviate the social tension and violence, King Hussein opened up the political space and political parties were allowed under a new law. The most significant beneficiary of this limited political openness was the Muslim Brotherhood which has been cooperating and collaborating with the palace for decades. Its prolonged presence in the society and extensive grassroots network enabled the Brotherhood to announce the formation of the Islamic Action Front which took part in the 1993 election. At the same time, the electoral participation of the IAF has been erratic; it contested the elections held in 1993, 2003, 2007, and 2016 but boycotted the polls in 1997, 2010, and 2013.

There is a cat-and-mouse game between the palace and the Islamists. The participation of the latter, the most visible political group in the country, is critical to making the electoral process credible and legitimate. At the same time, the palace was not prepared to grant greater leeway to the electoral system whereby the Muslim Brotherhood could emerge as the dominant force in parliament and the polity. Hence, through gerrymandering, the palace has periodically slanted electoral districts in favour of the tribal-dominated rural areas; under the notionally democratic one-person-one-vote arrangement, more parliamentary seats are earmarked for the less populated tribal-dominated areas than for urban centres like Amman. Thus, electoral districts with smaller population send more lawmakers than bigger cities do.

The regularity of elections does not ensure a greater popular say in the Kingdom's governance. The prime minister is nominated by the palace and is not chosen by the lawmakers. Both Hussein and Abdullah II promised that the heads of governments would be elected, but this has not happened. Frequent changes in the electoral laws and gerrymandering have ensured that political parties never secure a sufficient number of seats in parliament to influence the choice of the candidate for prime minister. In the first multiparty election held in 1989, the candidates backed by the Muslim Brotherhood secured 32 out of 80 seats in parliament and this was the highest number of seats ever obtained by a political party in Jordan. In the 18th elections held in September 2016, the coalition that included a faction of IAF secured merely 15 out of 130 seats. This was the largest bloc in parliament and independent candidates won the rest of the seats. Such dismal performance of political parties eliminates the prospects of an elected government.

As a result, assigning the responsibility to form a government is the primary responsibility and function of the monarchy and the incumbent holds office only at the "pleasure" of the monarch and not at the trust of the elected representatives. This, in practice, means the frequent changes and dismissals of government whenever a policy decision becomes domestically unpopular or controversial. During his 46-year reign, King Hussein, for example, had as many as 44 governments and often the same person was asked to form the next government. Likewise, since ascending to the throne in February 1999, King Abdullah II had 13 governments until he asked Omar al-Razzaz to form the government after widespread protests over income taxes in June 2018.

As a result of the limited role of political parties in governance, popular participation in parliamentary elections has declined over the years. Only 36 per cent of the electorates chose to take part in the 2016 elections and this was despite the voting age being reduced to 17 years, the lowest in the Middle East.

When the Arab Spring-linked popular protests began in the region in late 2010, some of the Jordanian protesters, especially the Islamists, were demanding the transformation of the Kingdom into a constitutional monarchy. Such a course would have considerably limited the freedom enjoyed by the palace in determining not only the composition of the government but also some of the critical policies of the state, both domestic and foreign. Given the delicate demography, social cleavages, and tension in its immediate neighbourhood, Jordan is not yet ready to embark on that road. On the contrary, these challenges have transformed the Hashemites as the personification of the Jordanian society and collective identity.

The Palestinian Dimension

The Palestinians are a significant component of the Jordanian population. While Jordan remains the only Arab country to grant full citizenship to them, the Palestinians form its toughest challenge concerning national identity, demographic distribution, and foreign policy priorities. Palestinians are also a major portion of the refugees that the Kingdom has been hosting since the late 1940s.

The annexation of the West Bank in early 1950 was accompanied by Jordan granting full citizenship rights to the Palestinians estimated at 800,000, including 400,000 residents of the West Bank. Most of the Palestinians were integrated into the Jordanian society, but tensions persisted. As the regime was seeking to integrate them, events such as Abdullah's assassination and support for anti-monarchical Nasser and his pan-Arabism highlighted the differences between the Jordanians of Transjordanian origin and the Jordanians of Palestinian origin—commonly known as East Bankers and West Bankers, respectively.

If the formation of the PLO in 1964 presented a political challenge to the Jordanian claim to speak for and represent the Palestinians, the Black

September was a decisive moment for the Jordanian-Palestinian relations. The willingness of the Palestinian Fedayeen led by Yasser Arafat to challenge the Hashemite rule within Jordan irreversibly poisoned the two segments of the Jordanian population. Coming in the wake of the loss of the West Bank, the civil war situation resulted in the government becoming more cautious towards the Palestinians and their position. Gradually, sensitive positions and security establishment became off limits to the Jordanian-Palestinians.

After protracted hopes and behind-the-scene negotiations with Israel, in July 1988, in the midst of the first Intifada, Hussein gave up hopes of regaining the West Bank and announced a formal Jordanian "disengagement" from the West Bank. This was accompanied by the government revoking the citizenship rights of a large number of Palestinians who either did not reside in the country or whose status became questionable in the wake of the loss the West Bank. The Kuwait crisis also saw the return of a large number of Palestinians who were holding temporary Jordanian travel documents.

Until recently, the Kingdom does not publish its demographic profile and this has contributed to an intense debate over the size of the Palestinian population. Two types of Palestinians reside in the country; the citizens who enjoy full rights like the rest of the population and the refugees who reside in camps run by the UNRWA. As of 2018, there are about 2.1 million registered Palestinian refugees in the Kingdom, out of whom, 370,000 or 18 per cent live in the ten refugee camps run by the UNRWA (Table 4).

Table 4 Palestinian refugee camps in Jordan, 2018

Refugees camp	Established in	Number of registered refugees
Amman New Camp	1955	57,000
Baq'a Camp	1968	119,000
Husn Camp	1968	25,000
Irbid Camp	1951	28,000
Jabal el-Hussein Camp	1952	32,000
Jarash Camp	1968	29,000
Marka Camp	1968	53,000
Souf Camp	1967	19,000
Talbieh Camp	1968	8000
Zarqa Camp	1949	29,000
Total refugees in camps	–	370,000
Total registered refugees in Jordan	–	2,174.491

Source: UNRWA https://www.unrwa.org/where-we-work/jordan

Without identifying the share, the UNRWA declares that "(m)ost Palestinian refugees in Jordan, but not all, have full citizenship" (UNRWA 2014). Six out of the ten camps were established in the wake of the June War, thereby highlighting its cascading impact upon the refugee population.

If one takes the UNRWA statement at its face value, a considerable portion of Palestinian refugees also has citizenship rights. For long, the Department of Statistics did not clearly spell out the population breakups, but the magnitude of the Syrian refugee influx resulted in the government observing that the population figures "excludes" Syrian refugees.

The discrepancy in the estimates of the Palestinian-Jordanians is a demographic as well as a political issue (Chatelard 2010) and raises questions over the actual size of the Palestinian-Jordanians. Forecasts by the Palestine National Authority (PNA) and Western and Israel scholars suggest that the Palestinians, both citizens and refugees, make up a numerical majority in Jordan. In 2001, the PNA declared that 2,560,000 Palestinians were living in Jordan when the population of Jordan was officially put at 5,182,000 (Kumaraswamy 2006). Some assessments present a bleaker picture; in the words of one, the Palestinian component of the Jordanian population was "more than 80 per cent prior to 1967, some 65 per cent thereafter and perhaps 75 per cent after the exodus of Palestinians from Kuwait during the Second Gulf War (1990–91)" (Israeli 2003, p. 49).

The periodic gerrymandering of electoral districts is seen as an attempt "to reduce" the Palestinian representation in parliament (Majed 2005). There are apprehensions that creating "a more equitable distribution of districts might produce a huge increase in the representation of Jordanians of Palestinian origin, which might in time threaten the identity of the Jordanian state" (Sweiss 2005). These concerns came to the fore when Jordan restricted the flow of Palestinian refugees from Syria (IFRCJRC 2012). For their part, the Jordanian authorities reject any claims of Palestinians being the majority in the country and maintain that they form about 40 per cent of the total Jordanian population and maintain that all are Jordanians, without any discrimination or differentiation. Irrespective of the actual number, it is undeniable that Palestinian-Jordanians form a sizeable portion of the Jordanian population.

This demographic composition affects Jordanian nationalism and its identity. In the early years of the state, an inclusive approach was the dominant discourse and manifested in the Hashemites projecting themselves as representatives of the Palestinians. This claim was undermined by the formation of the PLO in 1964 and its gradual emergence as a distinct and independent entity. The diasporic existence of the Palestinians meant that the PLO was increasingly seen as the representative of the Palestinians everywhere, including those residing in Jordan. Much of the Palestinian-Jordanians remained aloof during the civil war in September 1970 that followed the expulsion of the PLO and its Fedayeen fighters from the Kingdom. The roller-coaster Hussein-Arafat relations and the Jordanian interference in the Fatah-Hamas contest were partly linked to the demographic genie. As discussed elsewhere, some of the foreign policy choices of King Hussein were associated with the Palestinian dimension.

Relations with Israel

The Arab-Israeli conflict hangs as a large shadow over Jordan's existence as an independent political entity and a key determinant of its domestic and foreign policies. At one level, Jordan was a primary beneficiary of the formation of the State of Israel in terms of territorial expansion (until 1967), regional leadership aspirations (until the emergence of Nasserism in the mid-1950), as the representative of the Palestinians (until the Arab League's endorsement of the PLO in 1974), access to the US, and its emergence as a principal interlocutor in the Israeli-Palestinian negotiations. Their opposition to an independent Palestinian state as visualised by the UN partition plan brought the Hashemites and the Jewish leadership closer. While collusion is factually inaccurate, the interest convergence was real and enduring.

At the same time, Jordan's politico-geographic proximity with Israel came with a host of problems and complications. Abdullah's territorial aspirations were not the only reason for the non-realisation of the Palestinian state in 1948. Despite widespread support from neighbouring Arab countries and Muslim communities elsewhere, the Palestinian leadership led by Haj Amin Al-Husseini could not evolve into being an inclusive and effective Palestinian national movement against Zionism. The Palestinian reliance on external dependence, guidance, and military support proved fatal, especially when King Abdullah was not averse to accepting the Jewish State if it were to result in him acquiring parts of Mandate Palestine. His stand vis-à-vis Palestine in 1948 sowed the seed of an irreconcilable difference between the Hashemites and the wider Arab world. The perceived betrayal and collaboration with Israel became a constant theme in challenging the legitimacy of the Hashemite rule and its stability. Other Arab rulers have equally, if not more, exploited the Palestinians for their narrow interests but the Jordanian-Israeli linkages became a constant theme for various anti-Jordanian forces and situations. The assassination of King Abdullah I in July 1951, scores of assassination attempts on King Hussein, the Black September events of 1970, and periodic domestic upheavals were directly linked to the Palestinian anger over the Hashemite approach towards the Arab-Israeli conflict.

The original Jordanian claims to be the representative of the Palestinians and speak on their behalf proved to be a double-edged sword. Initially, this assertion enabled the Hashemites to overcome the immediate challenge posed by the formation of the All Palestine Government in the Gaza Strip in October 1948. Controlling a more substantial portion of Mandate Palestine, King Abdullah outmanoeuvred the Arab League and its prominent member Egypt and annexed the West Bank. The formation of the PLO in East Jerusalem in May 1964, then held by Jordan, was supposed to be a symbolic gesture of President Nasser to silence its detractors for his "inaction" vis-à-vis the Palestinian cause. It also reflected the broader Arab frustrations over the international apathy.

The June War, however, fundamentally altered Jordan's claims to the West Bank, its geography, demography, as well as its strategic worldview. Dragged into the hostilities due to domestic pressures in favour of Nasser's war coalition, Jordan lost East Jerusalem, including the al-Haram al-Sharif, Islam's holiest site after Mecca and Medina. Had he continued his anti-Nasser rhetoric or stayed neutral, King Hussein would have lost the throne. The capture of the old city in the 1948 War was also a symbolic compensation for the Hashemites who had lost control over the Hejaz region to the al-Saud in the 1920s. Thus, control over al-Haram al-Sharif added a religious legitimacy not only to the Hashemite rule but also to its claims to the Palestinian West Bank. More than the West Bank, the loss of East Jerusalem in 1967 was devastating to King Hussein. This was partly remedied through the Israel-Jordan Peace Treaty of 1994 which guaranteed a "special role" for the Hashemites over Islamic holy sites in Jerusalem.

Moreover, the loss of the West Bank shrunk the territory of Jordan and deprived it of the more fertile Jordan Valley which contributed to agricultural production, employment, and economy of the country and the Jordanian food security situation began deteriorating after 1967. The rapid fall in agriculture's contribution to the national economy became noticeable after the loss of the West Bank. The loss of tourism, especially to Islamic holy sites in East Jerusalem, also dented the Jordanian economy.

Above all, the loss of the West Bank meant that Jordan was left with the Palestinian people without any Palestinian territory. The citizenship rights of many Palestinians have been revoked especially in the wake of the 1988 decision to "disengage" from the West Bank. Still Jordan faces a demographic nightmare in the form of Palestinian-Jordanians who make up a large, if not the majority, population in the Kingdom. The Jordanisation of the Palestinians was a prudent strategy when King Abdullah I annexed the West Bank, but this became problematic after 1967 when Jordan was left with the Palestinian population without the West Bank.

While the peace camp in Israel represented by the Labour Party favoured a Jordanian-Palestinian confederation under the Hashemites, the Likud and its allied viewed the Kingdom itself as the Palestinian state without a Palestinian head of state. Installing Yasser Arafat as the King of Jordan, according to the right, would resolve the Palestinian statelessness. Using the Kingdom to resolve the Palestinian issue fashioned a love-hate relationship between Jordan and Israel. At the same time, the Hashemite-Israeli interest convergence has been significant and explains the prolonged meetings, engagements, and understanding between the two. Except for David Ben-Gurion and Menachem Begin, every Israeli Prime Minister, including a hardliner like Yitzhak Shamir, had met the Jordanian monarchs.

The Israeli willingness to intercede on behalf of Jordan with Washington and its desire to checkmate a possible Syrian intervention during the Black September events were some of the notable examples. At the same time, both countries found at opposite ends during the June War and the Kuwait crisis when domestic Palestinian pressures resulted in King Hussein departing from neutrality and sided with Nasser and appeared to be siding with Iraq over the Kuwait crisis. The consequences of both were negative; Jordan lost the West Bank in 1967 and its leverage vis-à-vis the Gulf Arab countries was weakened in the early 1990s over the Kuwait crisis.

Much of the anti-normalisation campaign against Israel since the 1994 peace agreement is also led by the Palestinian segment of the Jordanian population. The lack of progress in the Red Sea-Dead Sea linkage is primarily due to the absence of progress in the Middle East Peace Process and its cascading effects upon the Israeli-Jordanian relations.

Conclusion

Close to a century, the Hashemites have dispelled much scepticism and many misgivings about their political survival, and seen in the broader context of the Middle East and the Arab world, their accomplishments are not inconsiderable. Despite the economic hurdles, the Kingdom has remained relatively liberal and accommodative of the religious and national other. When resourceful and naturally well-endowed states have questions over their political trajectory, the Hashemites and the people of Jordan can be reasonably proud of their accomplishments. None should underestimate the political and economic challenges facing Jordan, but going by its trajectory since the early part of the twentieth century, Jordan can be described an oasis of peace and stability in the otherwise volatile and turbulent Middle East.

References

Chatelard, G. (2010). Jordan: A Refugee Haven. *Migration Policy Institute*. http://www.migrationpolicy.org/article/jordan-refugee-haven/. Accessed 17 Sept 2015.

IFRCJRC (International Federation of Red Cross and Red Crescent Societies & Jordan Red Crescent). (2012). Syrian Refugees living in the community in Jordan. *Assessment Report by IFRCJRC* (pp. 1–55). Retrieved from https://www.google.co.in/url?sa=t&rct=j&q=&esrc=s&source=web&cd=1&cad=rja&uact=8&ved=0CBwQFjAAahUKEwj4-8uo5b_IAhWDVo4KHTbfADc&url=https%3A%2F%2Fdata.unhcr.org%2Fsyrianrefugees%2Fdownload.php%3Fid%3D1168&usg=AFQjCNFRFWoh65EVuL-rLhppxyeIJ-Cfhw

Israeli, R. (2003). Is Jordan Palestine? In E. Karsh & P. R. Kumaraswamy (Eds.), *Israel, the Hashemites and the Palestinians: The fateful triangle* (pp. 49–66). London: Frank Cass.

Kumaraswamy, P. R. (2006). Who am I? Identity crisis in the Middle East. *MERIA*, *10*(1), 66–76. http://www.rubincenter.org/2006/03/kumaraswamy-2006-03-05/

Kumaraswamy, P. R., & Singh, M. (2017). Population pressure in Jordan: Role of Syrian Refugees. *Migration and Development*, *6*(3), 412–427. http://www.tandfonline.com/doi/full/10.1080/21632324.2016.1141500

Kumaraswamy, P. R., & Singh, M. (2018). Jordanian's food security challenges. *Mediterranean Quarterly*, *27*(1), 70–95. (co-authored with Manjari Singh).

Lesch, A. M. (1991). Palestinians in Kuwait. *Journal of Palestine Studies*, *20*(4), 42–54.

Majed, Z. (2005). Introduction and executive summary. In I. al-Attiyat, M. Shteiwi, & S. Sweiss (Eds.), *Building democracy in Jordan: Women's political participation, political party life and democratic elections* (pp. 13–22). Stockholm: International Institute for Democracy and Electoral Assistance (IDEA) & the Arab NGO Network for Development (ANND). Retrieved from http://www.idea.int/publications/dem_jordan/upload/Jordan_country_report_English.pdf

Sweiss, S. (2005). Electoral System in Jordan. In I. al-Attiyat, M. Shteiwi, & S. Sweiss (Eds.), *Building democracy in Jordan: Women's political participation, political party life and democratic elections* (pp. 103–130). Stockholm: International Institute for Democracy and Electoral Assistance (IDEA) & the Arab NGO Network for Development (ANND). Retrieved from http://www.idea.int/publications/dem_jordan/upload/Jordan_country_report_English.pdf

Swiss Agency for Development and Cooperation (SDC). (2014). *Labour migration in Jordan*. Amman: SDC Regional Cooperation Office. Retrieved from https://www.dfae.admin.ch/content/dam/countries/countries-content/jordan/en/GPMD-Jordan-Dec.%202014_EN.pdf

The Jordan Times. (2014, December 29). *Syrians constitute one-fifth of Amman population: Official figures*. Retrieved from http://www.jordantimes.com/news/local/syrians-constitute-one-fifthamman-population-%E2%80%94-official-figures

United Nations Conference on Trade and Development. (1994, June 28). *Population and demographic developments in the West Bank and Gaza strip until 1990*. https://unctad.org/en/docs/poecdcseud1.en.pdf

UNRWA. (2014, July 1). *Where we work*. Retrieved from http://www.unrwa.org/where-we-work/jordan

World Bank. (2014). *Population growth definition*. Retrieved from http://data.worldbank.org/

PART I

Society

From Small Sheikhdom to Over-Population

Onn Winckler

Two factors, geography and politics, have strongly influenced Jordan's demographic history. Geography has played a role since more than 80 per cent of its total area is desert, the majority of the population being concentrated in the northern and central highlands. Politics has had an effect: first, due to Jordan's need to absorb large numbers of Palestinian refugees from the 1948 War and the June 1967 War; and second, since Jordan controlled the West Bank (including Arab Jerusalem) from 1948, and up to the June 1967 War, it also absorbed non-refugee Palestinians who had immigrated from the West Bank to the East Bank between and after the wars.

Hence, Jordan's national population is comprised of two components: the original population of the East Bank, namely those who lived in the East Bank before the 1948 War and their descendants, and the Palestinians. Since the mid-1970s, two non-national groups were added to the Jordanian population: foreign workers and their accompanying family members, and since 1991, non-Palestinian refugees.

The aim of this chapter is twofold: first to describe the population growth in Jordan which, with the exception of the Gulf Cooperation Council (GCC) countries, was the fastest growing among the Middle

O. Winckler (✉)
Department of Middle Eastern and Islamic Studies, University of Haifa, Haifa, Israel
e-mail: owinkler@univ.haifa.ac.il

Eastern countries. The second aim is to examine the Jordanian natalist policy. This is because, despite a large number of non-nationals in the Kingdom, the most prominent factor for Jordan's rapid population growth since its establishment has been the high fertility rate of the national population.

The chapter is organised as follows: following a brief description of the ethno-religious composition of the Jordanian citizenry population, the chapter examines the components of the rapid population growth, namely the influx of Palestinians, the natural increase rate (NIR) of the Jordanian national population, the increase in the number of foreign workers, and lastly, the transformation of the Kingdom into a shelter—first for Iraqi refugees, and since mid-2011, for "Arab Spring refugees" as well. Finally, the chapter examines the Jordanian natalist policy since the 1950s.

ETHNO-RELIGIOUS COMPOSITION OF THE JORDANIAN CITIZENRY POPULATION

From a religious viewpoint, Jordan is almost homogenous with Arab Sunni Muslims constituting approximately 97 per cent of its citizens. The largest religious minority group is that of the Christians. According to the 1961 census, Christians represented 6.4 per cent of the total population of the East Bank, and their percentage declined to 4.0 per cent as reported in the 1979 census.[1] According to the 2015 census, their percentage declined further to 2.3 per cent.[2] There is also a small Druze community in Jordan, estimated at 0.5 per cent of the Jordanian citizens.

From an ethnic viewpoint, there are two significant minorities in Jordan. One is the Circassians, who were deliberately planted in the area of current Jordan by the Ottomans during the late nineteenth and early twentieth centuries. In the late 2000s, their number was estimated at approximately 45,000, and they were concentrated in Amman and some villages around the capital. The second ethnic minority is the Chechens (sometimes called Shishanis), most of whom arrived in Jordan during and following World War I. In the late 2000s, their number was estimated at 15,000.[3]

---

[1] The Hashemite Kingdom of Jordan, Department of Statistics, *Results of Housing and Population Census, East Bank-1979*, Vol. 2, part 1 (Amman, 1983), p. 44, table P.1.10.
[2] CIA, *The World Factbook-2015*.
[3] Colbert C. Held, John V. Cotter and John Thomas Cummings, *Middle East Patterns: Places, Peoples, and Politics, fifth edition* (Boulder: Westview Press, 2011), p. 325.

The Components of Population Growth

In 1922, as Transjordan was being established, it was estimated that 122,430 people were living in villages and another 102,950 were living as nomads, bringing the total population of Transjordan to 225,380. By late 1930, this figure had grown to 300,214, including 31,500 who were added when the southern border of Transjordan was extended beyond Ma'an and 'Aqaba. In 1946, the population was estimated to be 433,659.[4] According to the first population census which was conducted in 1952, the East Bank population numbered 586,885, and according to the second census in November 1961, it amounted to 900,776. This number increased to 2.133 million in November 1979. The December 1994 census measured 4.096 million, among them 3.779 million Jordanian citizens and the remaining foreigners, the vast majority of whom were foreign workers.[5] According to the 2004 census, the population numbered 5.104 million; among them, 4.682 million were Jordanian citizens. According to the latest census, which was carried out in November 2015, the national population numbered 6.579 million (see Table 1). The total number of the Jordanian population, including both foreign workers and refugees, amounted to 9.532 million.[6] In mid-2019, the population numbered 10.4 million.[7] Thus, within less than a century, Jordan's population increased 44 times! (Fig. 1).

Four components led to this unprecedented growth rate of the Jordanian population during the past century, and they are being examined in the following sections.

The Influx of Palestinians into the East Bank

The incursion of Palestinians into the East Bank started in late 1947 with the beginning of the armed struggle in Palestine. According to the UN estimate, in 1949, following the end of the Palestine War, the number of Palestinian refugees in the East Bank was approximately 70,000.[8] It should

---

[4] Peter Gubser, *Jordan: Crossroad of Middle Eastern Events* (Boulder: Westview Press and London: Croom Helm, 1983), p. 12; Mary C. Wilson, *King Abdullah, Britain and the Making of Jordan* (Cambridge: Cambridge University Press, 1987), p. 56.

[5] Al-Mamlaka al-Urdunia al Hashimiyya, Da'irat al-Ihsa'iyyat al-'Amma, *Al-Ta'dad al-'Amm lil-Sukan wal-Masakin-1994* (Amman, October 1995), p. 19, table 1 (Arabic).

[6] Jordan, Department of Statistics (DoS), Housing and Population Census 2015 [http://www.dos.gov.jo/dos_home_e/main/population/census2015/index.htm].

[7] Jordan, DoS [http://web.dos.gov.jo].

[8] IBRD, *The Economic Development of Jordan* (Washington, DC, 1956), p. 49, table 1; Mustafa Kabha, *The Palestinians: A People Dispersed* (Ra'anna: The Open University, 2010), p. 154 (Hebrew).

Table 1 Jordan's national population, 1952–2015

Year	Population (thousands)
1952 (c)[a]	586.2
1961 (c)[a]	900.8
1965[a]	1028.0
1970	1508.2
1975	1810.5
1979 (c)	2133.0
1985	2700.0
1990	3268.0
1994 (c)	3795.0
2004	4682.0
2010	6113.0
2015 (c)	6578.6

(c) = Census

[a]East Bank only

Sources: The Hashemite Kingdom of Jordan, Department of Statistics (DoS), *Statistical Yearbook*, various issues; idem, *Housing and Population Census* of 1994, 2004, 2015

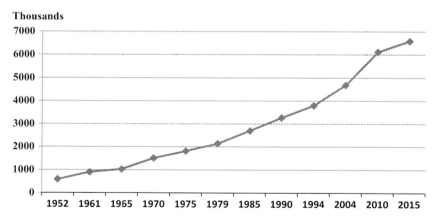

Fig. 1 Jordan's national population, 1952–2015

be noted that the only Arab country which granted citizenship to the Palestinian refugees was Jordan. Following the annexation of the West Bank, including Arab Jerusalem, to Jordan in 1949, there was large-scale emigration from the West Bank to the East Bank, and this was welcomed by the Jordanian authorities who aspired to develop the East Bank. The third wave of migration from the West Bank to the East Bank occurred following the June 1967 War. The overall number of Palestinian refugees (including internal refugees from the West Bank), which found refuge in the East Bank as a result of the occupation by Israel of the West Bank and the Gaza Strip in the June 1967 War, was estimated at between 310,000[9] and 360,000.[10] Overall, the number of Palestinians in the West Bank in late 1987, on the eve of the onset of the first Palestinian *Intifada*, was estimated at 1.2 million.[11] The continuation of emigration from the West Bank to the East Bank, together with the continuation of the high NIR, led to the rapid growth in the percentage of the Palestinian composition in Jordan.

Since the Jordanian authorities do not publish any official data regarding the distribution of the citizenry population according to origin of nationality, the only option to evaluate the percentage of the "Jordanians," that is, those who were living on the East Bank of the Jordan River before the 1948 War and their offsprings, as a total of the Kingdom's citizenry population, is to add the NIR to the number of the East Bank population before 1948, assuming a zero net migration balance. This is because there are neither official nor unofficial figures regarding the scale of Jordanian citizens who emigrated from the Kingdom according to their nationality "origin." The population of Transjordan in 1946, namely the last British figure, was 433,659. Assuming a net population growth[12] of 3 per cent on an annual average since 1948, by 2017, the number of "original Jordanians" in Jordan is about 3.2 million. Taking into consideration that according to the November 2015 census, the number of Jordanian citizens was 6.578 million, this means that the "original Jordanians" and their offsprings represented some 47–48 per cent of the total Jordanian citizens. If we add the 634,182 Palestinians refugees who do not have Jordanian nationality but are living permanently in Jordan, then the percentage of the "original Jordanians" of the total Jordanian population (not including the foreign workers and the non-Palestinian refugees) is reduced to about 44 per cent.

---

[9] Asher Susser, "Demography and Politics in Jordan," in Gad G. Gilbar and Ami Ayalon (eds.), *Demography and Politics in the Arab States* (Tel Aviv: Hakibbutz Hameuchad, 1995), p. 133 (Hebrew).

[10] Bichara Khader, "Jordan's Economy: 1952–1989: Past Achievements and Future Challenges," *Journal of Arab Affairs*, Vol. 9, No. 2 (Fall 1990), p. 87.

[11] Gad G. Gilbar, *Population Dilemmas in the Middle East* (London: Frank Cass, 1997), p. 12, table 1.1.

[12] Population growth is the sum of the NIR and the net migration balance.

High Natural Increase Rate (NIR) of the Jordanian National Population

Throughout the period under discussion, the fertility rates of Jordanian women were among the highest in the Arab region. In the early 1950s, Jordan's crude birth rate (CBR) was estimated at 47.4 per 1000 people and peaked to almost 50 during the second half of the 1960s and the early 1970s, while the total fertility rate (TFR)[13] was more than seven children per woman (see Table 2). As one can see in Table 3, in 1965, the average age-specific fertility rate (ASFR) of the women in the age group of 20–34 was 337 per 1000. This means that one of three Jordanian women in this age group gave birth during that year. The ASFR for women in the age group of 15–19 was also extremely high at the rate of 123 per 1000 women. Although the ASFR for women less than 20 years substantially declined during the late 1960s and the early 1970s, it significantly increased among women in the older age group of 35–49 years, thus producing a peak of TFR at a rate of 7.4 in 1976. According to the *1976 Jordan Fertility Survey*, the average number of children ever born for women in the age group of 45–49 was 8.42—one of the highest rates ever measured in any given society.[14]

Despite the high fertility rates, Jordan's NIR until the mid-1970s was less than 3 per cent due to the extremely high crude death rates (CDR), mainly because of the high infant mortality rate and relatively low life expectancy. By 1960, Jordan's infant mortality rate was 135 per 1000 live births and somewhat declined to 90 in 1970. The life expectancy in 1960 was 47 years (for both sexes) and increased slightly to 52 years in 1970 (see Table 4).

The rapid socio-economic development following the oil boom of October 1973 led to a sharp decline of Jordan's CDR to 10.0 in 1980 and only 6.0 in 1990 (see Table 2). This rapid decline of the CDR resulted in a sharp decline of infant mortality rates in line with a severe increase in life expectancy. By 1980, Jordan's infant mortality rate was 58 per 1000 live births and further declined to 40 in 1990. The under-5 mortality rate fell accordingly from an average of 139 per 1000 live births during 1960–64,

---

[13] The total fertility rate (TFR) is the average number of children a woman would have if she survives and passes all her reproductive years (15–49). The TFR is the most widely used fertility measure.

[14] Abdullah Abdel-Aziz, *Evaluation of the Jordan Fertility Survey-1976*, Scientific Reports, No. 42 (March 1983), p. 17, table 11.

Table 2 Jordan's natural increase rate and total fertility rate, 1950–2014

Year	CBR	CDR	NIR	TFR
1950–55	47.4	20.4	27.0	7.4
1960	47.4	19.9	27.5	7.2
1965	49.2	17.9	31.3	7.1
1970	47.5	15.7	31.8	7.1
1975	46.9	13.8	33.1	7.0
1980	46.9	10.0	36.9	7.2
1984	41.5	6.7	34.8	7.2
1986	34.7	5.8	28.9	6.6
1990	39.0	6.0	33.0	5.8
1992	37.9	5.3	32.6	5.9
1994	33.0	5.2	27.8	4.7
1996	33.3	6.4	26.9	4.2
1998	34.3	4.7	29.6	4.7
2000	28.9	4.7	28.9	3.8
2007	32.3	7.0	22.6	3.8
2009	30.1	7.0	23.1	3.8
2010	30.1	7.0	23.1	3.8
2011	28.6	7.0	21.6	3.8
2012	28.1	7.0	21.1	3.5
2013	28.1	7.0	21.1	3.5
2014	26.7	6.0	20.7	3.5

CBR = Crude Birth Rate

CDR = Crude Death Rate

NIR = Natural Increase Rate

TFR = Total Fertility Rate

Sources: The Hashemite Kingdom of Jordan, Department of Statistics (DoS), *Statistical Yearbook*, various issues (Amman); idem, *Vital Statistics* [http://www.dos.gov.jo/dos_home_e/main/vitality/vital_index1.htm]; ECWA/ESCWA, *Demographic and Related Socio-Economic Data Sheets for Countries of the Economic and Social Commission for Western Asia*, various issues (Beirut, Baghdad and Amman); UN, *Demographic Yearbook*, various issues (New York)

to 26 on an average during the 1995–99, and to 18 only in 2015.[15] Life expectancy increased from 52 years in 1970 to 69 years in 1990 (see Table 4). Since the decline of the CDR was faster than the drop of the CBR, the NIR peaked at more than 3 per cent on an annual average during the 1970s and the 1980s (see Fig. 2).

---

[15] Omar B. Ahmad, Alan D. Lopez and Mie Inoue, "The Decline in Child Mortality: A Reappraisal," *Bulletin of the World Health Organization*, Vol. 78, No. 10 (2000), p. 1180, table 1; UNDP, *Human Development Report-2006*, pp. 315–318, table 10; UNDP, *Human Development Report-2016*, p. 227, table 8.

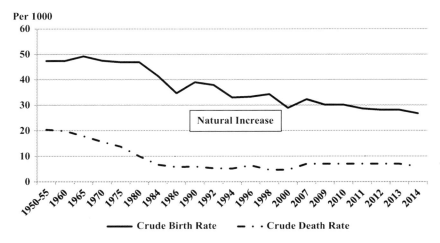

Fig. 2 Jordan's natural increase rate, 1950–2014

Table 3 Jordan's age-specific fertility rate, 1965–2012

Age group Year	15–19	20–24	25–29	30–34	35–39	40–44	45–49	TFR
1965	123	310	364	336	207	64	17	7.1
1976	71	300	367	332	240	112	47	7.4
1981	87	252	340	316	239	134	49	7.1
1983	49	228	335	305	233	127	40	6.6
1990	49	219	296	264	188	79	19	5.6
1997	43	172	246	206	144	48	11	4.4
2002	28	150	202	184	122	43	5	3.7
2007	28	148	212	162	121	41	6	3.6
2009	32	152	238	182	126	37	3	3.8
2012	26	139	209	180	111	34	3	3.5

Sources: A. Thavarajah, "Mid-Decade Demographic Parameters of Jordan and Population Growth," in Cairo Demographic Center, *Demographic Measures and Population Growth in Arab Countries*, Research Monograph Series, No. 1 (Cairo, 1970), p. 72; Borham N. Shrydeh, "Population Situation in Jordan," proceedings of the *Symposium held at Cairo Demographic Centre*, 3–7 November 1985, CDC, Research Monograph Series, No. 14, Special Issue, p. 91, table 1; *Jordan Population and Family Health Survey-1990*, p. 22, table 3.1; *JPFHS-1997*, p. 27, table 3.2; *JPFHS-2012*, p. 51, table 5.4

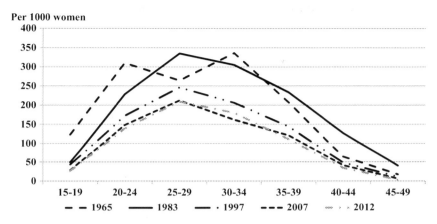

Fig. 3 Jordan's age-specific fertility rate, 1965–2012

Table 4 Infant mortality rate and life expectancy in Jordan, 1930–2016

Year	IMR	LE
1930	222	38
1960	135	47
1970	90	52
1980	58	63
1990	40	69
2000	30	70
2014	17	74
2016	17	74

IMR = Infant Mortality Rate (per 1000 live-births)

LE = Life Expectancy (years, average females/males)

Sources: The Hashemite Kingdom of Jordan, DoS, *Statistical Yearbook*, various issues (Amman); Allan G. Hill, "Population Growth in the Middle East Since 1945 with Special Reference to the Arab Countries of West Asia," in J.I. Clarke and H. Bowen-Jones (eds.), *Change and Development in the Middle East* (London and New York: Methuen, 1981), 132, table 8.1; *Survey of Economic and Social Developments in the ECWA/ESCWA Region*, various issues (Baghdad, Amman and Beirut); idem, *Demographic and Related Socio-Economic Data Sheets for Countries of the Economic and Social Commission for Western Asia*, 1978–2001, various issues (Baghdad, Amman and Beirut); UN, *Demographic Yearbook*, various issues (New York)

From the mid-1980s and until the early 2000s, however, Jordan's fertility rate, similar to the process which occurred in all of the other Arab countries at that time, sharply declined. By 2000, Jordan's TFR was 3.8 as compared to 5.8 in 1990 and 7.2 in 1980. Since the CDR remained stable at the rate of 6–7, the result was a sharp decline of the NIR from more than 3 per cent on an annual average during the 1970s and the first half of the 1980s to about 2.5 per cent in the mid-2000s. From the early 2000s, however, Jordan's TFR remained stuck at 3.8 and slightly declined to 3.5 in recent years. Consequently, the CBR only slightly decreased from about 30 to 27–28, leaving the NIR at a level of a little more than 2 per cent (see Fig. 2).

From Labour Surplus to Labour Shortage: The Influx of the Foreign Labour

Due to the extremes of both rapid population growth as a result of the combination of high NIR and the influx of Palestinians and resulting high unemployment rates, since the 1950s, Jordan has adopted the most supportive labour emigration policy among all of the non-oil Arab countries. This policy rested on two fundamental assumptions: the first was that without extensive labour emigration to the GCC countries, the Jordanian economy, especially the labour market, would not be able to deal with the massive influx of Palestinians.[16] The second was that the workers' remittances would be the most accessible source for hard currency.[17] According to the 1961 census, the number of Jordanian workers in other Arab countries was 15,901.[18] In 1970, the number of East Bank Jordanians which were employed in the GCC countries was estimated at 54,263.[19] Their number dramatically increased following the oil boom, amounting to 139,000 in 1975,[20] and reached 271,200 in 1983,[21] namely more than 30 per cent of the total Jordanian civilian workforce at that time—the highest rate among all of the Arab labour-exporting countries ever.

[16] By 1959, unemployment in Jordan (both banks) was almost 30 per cent. See: Salem O. Ghawi, "The Manpower Situation in Jordan," paper prepared for seminar on Manpower in Jordan, National Planning Council, Amman, April 1972, p. 8, table 1.
[17] John M. Wardwell, "Jordan," in William J. Serow *et al.* (eds.), *Handbook of International Migration* (New York and London: Greenwood Press, 1990), p. 168.
[18] M.A.J. Share, "The Use of Jordanian Workers' Remittances," in Bichara Khader and Adnan Badran (eds.), *The Economic Development of Jordan* (London: Croom Helm, 1987), p. 33, table 3.1.
[19] Nazli Choucri, "Migration in the Middle East: Transformation and Change," *Middle East Review*, Vol. 16, No. 2 (Winter 1983/4), p. 18, table 1.
[20] J.S. Birks and C.A. Sinclair, *International Migration Project: Country Case Study: The Hashemite Kingdom of Jordan* (Durham: The University of Durham, Department of Economics, November 1978), p. 9, table 3.
[21] Jordan, *Statistical Abstract-1989*, p. 83, table 4/2/3.

The massive inflow of Jordanian workers to the GCC countries following the oil boom, combined with the rapid economic development which amounted to a cumulative GDP (gross domestic product) growth rate of 62 per cent during the years 1976–80[22]—the highest rate ever in Jordanian history—led to the elimination of the acutest socio-economic problem, namely a high unemployment rate. By 1976, the unemployment rate was as low as 1.2 per cent,[23] which is even less than the frictional unemployment which exists in any given economy even under conditions of rapid economic expansion, as compared to 14 per cent in 1972.[24]

Hence, in the mid-1970s, a new problem emerged in Jordan—a labour shortage. Consequently, the Jordanian authorities decided to implement an "open door" policy for labour immigration. The underlying assumption of the Jordanian authorities was that cheap foreign workers would replace the Jordanian nationals who had migrated to the GCC countries and that the economy would benefit from the gap between the much higher remittances of the workers abroad compared to the low salaries of the foreign workers in the Kingdom. The phenomenon of replacement migration, it should be noted, was widespread during the 1970s, such as in Greece and Spain, where a large number of nationals emigrated to the more developed Western European economies, while at the same time, workers from less developed economies replaced them. Thus, by 1975, the number of foreign workers in Jordan was estimated at 32,800,[25] increasing to 186,506 in 1985.[26]

During the second half of the 1980s, however, due to the intensification of the socio-economic problems in the GCC countries, combined with the new employment policy of the GCC authorities which favoured non-Arab workers at the expense of Arabs, the number of Jordanian workers in these countries stopped increasing and remained more or less stable.

---

[22] *Middle East International*, 22 February 1985, p. 16.
[23] Muhammad Sa'ad 'Amirah, "Waqi'al-Bitala fil-Urdun wa-Nazara Nahwa al-Mustaqbal," in Mustafa al-Hamarneh (ed.), *al-Iqtisad al-Urduni: al-Mushkilat wal-Afaqa* (Amman: Markaz al-Dirasat al-Istratigiyya, 1994), p. 224, table 2 (Arabic).
[24] Tayseer Abdel Jaber, "Jordanian Labour Migration: Social, Political and Economic Effects," in Mohammad Shtayyeh (ed.), *Labour Migration: Palestine, Jordan, Egypt and Israel* (Jerusalem: Palestine Center for Regional Studies, 1998), p. 85.
[25] J.S. Birks and C.A. Sinclair, *International Migration and Development in the Arab Region* (Geneva, 1980), p. 135, table 10.
[26] HRD base Ltd., Lloyds Bank Chambers, *Socio-Demographic Profiles of Key Arab Countries* (Newcastle, May 1987), p. 44, table 3.2.

Following the expulsion of some 350,000 Jordanians from Kuwait and Saudi Arabia during the Kuwaiti Crisis of 1990–91 and the consequent intensification of employment pressures in Jordan, the authorities tried to tighten control of the flow of foreign labour. These efforts, however, were without success. Thus, during the 1990s, a new phenomenon emerged in Jordan: a parallel increase in the unemployment rates of the nationals and the number of foreign workers. In late 1991, unemployment skyrocketed to above 20 per cent.[27]

Although the peace treaty with Israel (October 1994) did provide some benefits to the Jordanian economy, these were not enough to bring relief in the employment pressure, and unemployment continued to increase. Despite the substantial unemployment rate, however, the number of foreign workers not only did not decline but instead continued to rise. According to the 1994 census, the number of non-nationals amounted to 314,965, with the vast majority of them being foreign workers.[28]

The opening of the Jordanian private sector to an effect an unlimited number of foreign labour, led, naturally, to the concentration of the nationals in the public sector—a similar process which occurred in the GCC labour markets. Thus, it is not surprising that the attempts of the Jordanian authorities to reverse the process by replacing the foreign workers in the private sector with nationals almost failed utterly. There is not a single instance worldwide of a successful attempt of the reversal of this process.

Thus, as long as the Jordanian nationals found employment either abroad or in the public sector, unemployment was relatively low. With the decline of these two prominent employment options, unemployment steadily increased. By 1998, Jordan's official unemployment rate was 15.2 per cent. According to unofficial estimates, the real unemployment rate was about 21 per cent.[29] The number of foreign workers, however, continued to increase. According to the 2004 census data, they amounted to 392,273[30] or about 77,000 more than their number according to the 1994 census data.

Even the harsh socio-economic situation, a result of the Arab Spring events which led, *inter alia*, to increased unemployment of Jordanian nationals, did not bring about a decline in the number of the foreign

---

[27] *The Jordan Times*, 14 October 1991.
[28] Jordan, DoS, *Housing and Population Census-1994*.
[29] ESCWA, *Survey, 1998–1999*, p. 51; *The Jordan Times*, 18 November 1999.
[30] Jordan, DoS, *Housing and Population Census-2004*.

labour. By mid-2016, Jordan's Minister of Labour Ali Ghezawi declared that there were some 750,000 foreign workers in the Kingdom, among them only 300,000 had valid work permits.[31] The number of Jordanian workers abroad, however, remained stable, estimated in the mid-2000s at approximately 350,000, with the vast majority in the GCC countries.[32] This number remained stable during the decade that followed and was estimated at 346,000 in 2011.[33] Thus, by 2016, the number of foreign workers in the country, not including the Arab Spring refugees, was more than twice the number of Jordanian workers abroad.

Non-Palestinian Refugees in Jordan

Aside from the Palestinian refugees, there are two other groups of refugees in Jordan. The first is the Iraqis who started to flee in 1991, following Saddam Hussein's brutal repression of the Shias. By 1996, their number was estimated at 100,000 and reached 250,000–300,000 in 2003.[34] The flood of Iraqi refugees rapidly intensified following the US invasion of Iraq in March 2003. Many of the Iraqi refugees, however, used Jordan only as a transit country to their final destination in one of the EU countries. Overall, according to the November 2015 census, the number of Iraqis living in Jordan amounted to 130,911 (42,941 of whom were classified as refugees).

The second wave of non-Palestinian refugees into Jordan was made up of Arab Spring refugees. According to the November 2015 census, the number of these totalled 1.305 million; 953,289 of whom were Syrians, 31,163 Yemenis, and 22,700 Libyans.[35] Overall, in mid-2018, Jordan had the second highest refugee-to-nationals ratio among all of the Arab countries, following Lebanon.

---

[31] *The Jordan Times*, 11 July 2016.
[32] Riad al Khouri, "Aspects of Migration and Development in Jordan," paper prepared for the *Migration and Refugee Movements in the Middle East and North Africa*, The Forced Migration & Refugee Studies Program, The American University in Cairo, Egypt 23–25 October 2007, p. 17.
[33] Migration Policy Centre, *Migration Facts-Jordan* (April 2013).
[34] Joseph Sasson, *The Iraqi Refugees: The New Crisis in the Middle East* (London and New York: I.B. Tauris, 2009), p. 33.
[35] Jordan, DoS, *2015 Census data*, table 7.7; *Jordan Times*, 30 January 2016.

Jordan's Natalist Policy

The issue of family planning first arose in Jordan in the late 1950s with the first attempts to set up a Jordan Family Planning and Protection Association (JFPPA) which eventually was established in 1963. The JFPPA received governmental financial support until the June 1967 War.[36] The establishment of the JFPPA, however, was accompanied neither by increased governmental or other anti-natalist measures nor even by increasing politician and public awareness to the steady intensification of the demographic pressure. Hence, family planning services were available in the Kingdom, but only in the major cities where the JFPPA operated.

In 1972, due to the rising demographic pressure because of both the steady increase of the NIR and the influx of Palestinian refugees following the June 1967 War, the Department of Statistics initiated a conference of demographic experts with the intention of drawing up a demographic policy for the Kingdom.[37] Consequently, in 1973, the National Population Commission (NPC) was established with the aim of advising the authorities of population policies.

However, despite the warnings of the professional bodies on the intensified demographic pressure, in practice, nothing was done. In 1974, during the *Economic Commission for Western Asia (ECWA) First Regional Population Conference*, Wasef Azar[38] described Jordan's natalist approach as follows: "The general public and the politicians are not yet aware that Jordan is facing a situation of population explosion."[39] The reason for ignoring the "demographic issue" was the combined result of a number of things: rapid economic expansion following the October 1973 oil boom; common belief that the high fertility rates would decline naturally without direct government involvement due to the substantial socio-economic improvements; sensitivity of the family planning issue from a political viewpoint due to the harsh resistance of the Islamic fundamentalist groups; and lastly, the feeling among the decision makers that the short-term demographic trends, namely for the coming gen-

---

[36] Fouzi Sahawneh, "Demographic and Social Characteristics of Family Planning in Jordan," *Population Bulletin of ECWA*, No. 22/23 (June & December 1982), p. 119.

[37] Charles W. Warren *et al.*, "Fertility and Family Planning in Jordan: Results from the 1985 Jordan Husbands' Fertility Survey," *Studies in Family Planning*, Vol. 21, No. 1 (1990), pp. 33–34.

[38] The Director of the Economic Data Bank (Amman).

[39] Wasef Y. Azar, "The Population Position of Jordan," paper presented at the *First Regional Population Conference of ECWA*, Beirut, 18 February–1 March 1974, p. 6.

eration, were already set and that the ability to change them, even through an extensive national family planning programme, was quite limited. Abbdul-Razaq Badran claimed that "no well-defined population policy has been declared in Jordan because of the sensitivity of the population situation in the occupied territories,"[40] namely the "demographic battle" between the Palestinians in the occupied territories and Israel.

Whatever the cause or causes for ignoring the intensified demographic pressure, it is clear that the Jordanian authorities did nothing in the area of family planning during the 1970s and the 1980s except for some financial assistance to NGO (non-governmental organisation) activities and availability of family planning services in the governmental maternal and child health clinics.[41] In the *2002 Jordan Population & Family Health Survey* (JPFHS), it was written that:

Because of the sensitive nature of the topic, the NPC took no distinct actions or steps. The Ministry of Health, through its Maternal and Child Health Centres, provided optional and predominantly free family planning services as [an] unofficial and indirect intervention in the population policy.[42]

The result of the Jordanian "vague anti-natalist policy" during the 1970s and the 1980s was only a moderate increase in the contraceptive use rate among married women from 23 per cent in 1976 to 26 per cent in 1983 and 35 per cent in 1990; among them, only 26.9 per cent were using modern contraceptives.[43] This means that by 1990, two-thirds of the currently married Jordanian women did not use any contraceptives and only one-fourth used modern contraceptives. Consequently, in 1990, fertility rate remained very high by any international comparison with a TFR of 5.8 (see Table 2).

Following the return of 350,000 Jordanian citizens from the GCC countries in the early 1990s, the authorities realised that the only viable option for reducing the socio-economic burden was through a sharp fertility decline. Hence, in 1993, within the framework of the Five-Year Development Plan (1993–97), the government approved the Birth

---

[40] Badran Abbdul-Razaq Badran, "Features of the Population Situation and Policies in Jordan," *Population Bulletin of ESCWA*, No. 40 (1992), p. 83.

[41] On the Jordanian anti-natalist measures, see: Gilbar, *Population Dilemmas*, pp. 73–76; Onn Winckler, *Population Growth and Migration in Jordan, 1950–1994* (Brighton and Portland: Sussex Academic Press, 1997), pp. 82–84.

[42] *JPFHS-2002*, p. 3.

[43] *JPFHS-1990*, p. 37.

Spacing National Programme. The focus of the programme was to achieve fertility decline through enhancing spaced pregnancies. The target set by the plan was to reduce the CBR by one point each year.[44]

Due to the steadily increasing burden of the rapid population growth, in 2000, the NPC declared the National Population Strategy that comprised four dimensions: (a) reproductive health; (b) population and sustainable development; (c) gender equality and the empowerment of women; and (d) population and enhancing advocacy. This strategy was activated from 2002 by the Higher Population Council (HPC), headed by the prime minister.[45] The overall aim of the Jordanian National Population Strategy, 2000–20 was to reduce the TFR to 2.9 in 2010 and 2.5 by 2017 and to reach the replacement level (2.1) by 2020.[46] However, this action plan as well as the next two Reproductive Health Action Plans, the first for 2003–07 and the second for 2008–12, failed as the TFR remained stable at 3.5–3.8 during the 2002–12 period.

Why did Jordan's TFR "stick" at around 3.5 and not decline in recent years despite intensified anti-natalist activities? Why was the contraceptive use rate among married women only 61 per cent in 2012,[47] even though the awareness of Jordanian women of modern contraceptives was universal since the early 1990s at least? The HPC strategy for the period of 2013–17 indicated this contradiction:

Despite the high education rates among Jordanians [women] in all age groups and the spread of all means of communication and media and the availability of accurate information about the use of family planning [FP] methods at the national level, widespread social concepts still hinder the use of family planning methods.[48]

It seems that there are three main reasons for this fundamental contradiction:

---

[44] *Jordan Population and Family Health Survey-2002*, p. 3; Jordan, Ministry of Planning, *Plan for Economic and Social Development, 1993–1997* (Amman, 1993), p. 155.

[45] *JPFHS-2012*, pp. 3–4.

[46] Ebba Augustin, "Demographic Transition and Gender Systems: The Case of Jordan and Yemen," in Hans Groth and Alfonzo Sousa-Poza (eds.), *Population Dynamics in the Muslim Countries* (London and New York: Springer, 2012), p. 167.

[47] Jordan Higher Population Council, *National Reproductive Health/Family Planning Strategy, 2013–2017*, p. 11, figure 4.

[48] Ibid., p. iv.

Table 5 Percentage of Jordanian ever-married women by age (15–49), 1961–2012

Year Age group	1961	1972	1976	1983	1990	1997	2002	2007	2012
15–19	31.2	30.5	19.5	9.4	10.6	8.2	6.2	5.8	6.3
20–24	77.0	73.0	64.1	42.0	45.2	38.8	34.1	36.7	33.6
25–29	91.0	92.9	87.4	76.3	73.7	66.2	65.3	69.3	69.8
30–34	95.6	96.4	95.3	90.1	89.1	80.7	79.6	79.4	82.7
35–39	97.6	97.4	92.4	94.9	94.6	89.9	87.3	85.4	86.3
40–44	97.9	98.2	98.0	96.8	97.3	94.4	92.6	91.6	89.5
45–49	97.3	98.4	98.3	97.1	98.0	96.0	95.4	95.9	92.0

Sources: Jordan, DoS, *Evaluation of the Jordan Fertility Survey-1976*, by Abdallah Abdel-Aziz, Scientific Reports, No. 42 (Amman, March 1983), p. 13, table 3; idem, *Jordan Fertility & Family Health Survey-1983*, p. 60, tables 3–6; idem, *JPFHS-2012*, p. 40, table 4.2

(a) **Early age of marriage for women, mainly in the countryside and the remote areas**. As one can see in Table 5, although the very early marriage (less than 20 years), substantially declined since the 1970s, still, in 2012, one-third of Jordanian women married before the age of 24. At the age of 29, almost 70 per cent of the Jordanian women were married. Thus, the vast majority of the Jordanian women are married during most of their reproductive age. The early marriage is most common in the more traditional areas. Thus, while the TFR in Amman was measured by the *JPFHS-2012* at 3.2, it was as high as 4.1 in Ma'an and Mafraq and 4.3 in Jerash.[49]

(b) **Low labour force participation rate of women**. Despite the rapid improvement of the educational level of Jordanian women who achieved a literacy rate of 99 per cent in the early 2010s, their labour force participation rate remained very low, even by Middle Eastern standards. In 2013, only 10 per cent of women of the working age group (15–65) were formally employed.[50] Not only was the women's labour force participation rate meagre, but unemployment among women who were in the workforce was extremely high, amounting to more than 20 per cent in 2014.[51]

---

[49] *JPFHS-2012*, p. 49, table 5.2.
[50] IMF, *Jordan: 2014 Article IV Consultation*, IMF Country Report No. 14/152 (June 2014), p. 5.
[51] ESCWA, *Survey, 2014–2015*, pp. 60–61.

The intensified competition with the foreign workers and with the Arab Spring refugees since 2011 made it extremely hard for Jordanians, both male and female, to find employment in the private sector.[52]

(c) **Low governmental commitment to the family planning issue.** Since the mid-1970s until the present, the most prominent characteristic of the Hashemite regime in the area of family planning is its unwillingness to "pay the political price" for implementing an extensive national family planning programme. Until the present day, the issue of family planning is marginal for socio-economic and political priorities. There have been no declarations by King Hussein and later by King Abdullah on the issue of family planning. It was, and still is, "a technical issue" which should be treated by the professionals in the governmental ministries, but not by the King himself. Moreover, the Hashemite regime did not even recruit the prominent *'ulama* to the issue, as was the case in Mubarak's Egypt. Thus, it is not surprising that according to a study conducted by the United States Agency for International Development (USAID) in late 2015, the majority of participants continue to think that "Islam forbids family planning."[53]

In 2012, the HPC, financially aided by the USAID, set out to establish a new reproductive health strategy aimed at reducing the TFR from 3.5 in 2012 to 3.0 in 2017 and 2.1 in 2030 through increasing availability of family planning services, in line with raising the awareness of the public to the importance of declining fertility through media campaigns focussing on the benefits of family planning to the families themselves.[54] However, due to the short period since the launching of the programme, it is, of course, impossible to evaluate its efficiency at this point.

[52] IMF, *Jordan: Selected Issues*, IMF Country Report No. 17/232 (July 2017), pp. 4–5.

[53] USAID, JCAP, *Exploring Gender Norms and Family Planning in Jordan: A Qualitative Study*, Final Report (Amman, January 2016), p. 4.

[54] Jordan HPC, *National Reproductive Health/Family Planning Strategy, 2013–2017*, p. 1; USAID, "Population and Family Health in Jordan" [https://www.usaid.gov/jordan/family-planning-reproductive-health]; USAID, "A New Roadmap to Guide Family Planning in Jordan," 7 August 2013; USAID, *Jordan Family Planning Assessment: Final Report*, April 2016, p. 8.

What Next?

Despite the decline of the NIR to 2.1 per cent in recent years, however, in nominal numbers, the natural increase of the Jordanian citizenry population steadily increased from 142,575 in 2006 to 191,378 in 2015.[55] This is the true meaning of the "Population Momentum" phenomenon as a result of the current wide-based age pyramid. This trend of nominal increase of Jordan's natural increase will continue in the coming two decades at least, even if the TFR will indeed decline to 2.5, due to the nominal rise in the number of women in the main reproductive age (20–39). Thus, Jordan's citizenry population is projected to increase to 10.7 million in mid-2030 and to reach 12.7 million in mid-2050.[56]

The projected rapid population growth combined with the anticipated low economic growth rate as a result of the global economic stagnation and the political instability in the Middle East will force Jordan to require an ongoing increase of financial aid. By 2016, the foreign aid to Jordan totalled $2.18 billion.[57] The US aid was the highest, amounting to $1.6 billion, not including almost $800 million in humanitarian assistance for the Syrian refugees in Jordan. This aid was the highest US civilian aid to any other Arab country.[58] However, this aid is projected to decline in 2018.[59] Due to the continuation of low oil prices, it seems that the GCC aid to Jordan will also decline soon.

Can the Jordanian economy bear both continued rapid population growth and declining foreign aid?

---

[55] Jordan, DoS, *Vital Statistics* [http://web.dos.gov.jo/sectors/social/vital-statistics].
[56] PRB, *2017 World Population Data Sheet* (New York, 2017), p. 11.
[57] Zawya, 5 December 2016.
[58] *Al-Monitor*, 22 August 2016.
[59] *Jordan Times*, 4 July 2017; *The Guardian*, 27 February 2017.

The Foreign Workers

Françoise De Bel-Air

According to the last census in November 2015, Jordan's population was 9.5 million, and out of this, nearly 3 million (31 per cent) were foreign nationals, up from 392,300 recorded during the previous population census held in 2004. The country's population was thus multiplied by 7.5 in one decade. Foreign nationals included some 1,265,000 Syrians and 636,000 Egyptians. This reflects the impact of immigration, forced and labour-related, on Jordan's astonishing population growth rates, as well as pressure on its labour market. Waves of forced migrants channelled to Jordan by repeated and unending regional conflicts (Palestinians, Iraqis, Syrians, and other nationalities) needed to earn a living and are now part of an estimated 1.4 million foreign workforce, of whom less than 400,000 are holding a work permit.

Out of a working-age population of over 4 million, only 40 per cent of Jordanian nationals were economically active in 2017 and only 13.4 per cent among women. Besides such low participation rates, Jordan suffers from growing unemployment, rising from 13 per cent in 2015 to 18.3 per cent in 2017. Highly educated women are particularly affected; 33 per cent were unemployed, and as much as 54 per cent among university graduates in 2017. Nonetheless, over half of the jobs created in the private sector, predominantly low skilled and low paid, go to migrant workers.

F. De Bel-Air (✉)
Paris, France

Moreover, international pressure led to the planned incorporation of 200,000 Syrian nationals within the country's workforce.

The chapter describes the history of Jordan's labour immigration and analyses its current immigration policies. These are confronted with the characteristics and dynamics of the foreign workforce. Socio-political factors could explain the persistent concomitance of high levels of unemployment among Jordanians and large labour migrants' pools, most of them in the irregular administrative situation.

Labour Immigration Since the 1970s

Supporting the Rentier Welfare State

Jordan's economic growth rates went markedly up after the 1973 oil boom. These were first boosted by a hike in public revenues collected by the government. The oil-rich Gulf States allocated large amounts of development aid and other revenues in return for Jordan's "frontline" position at the border with Israel. Private funds also increased the country's gross domestic product (GDP), as about 300,000 Jordanian citizens (one-third of Jordan's labour force), who had found employment in the Gulf following the oil boom, were sending remittances back to their families at home. Such external revenues, not resulting from productive activities, made up as much as half of Jordan's GDP around 1980, thus consolidating Jordan's "rentier State" (Beblawi 1987) or "rentier economy" (Brand 1995). This situation defined the patterns of Jordan's future labour immigration.

First, a large share of the country's workforce being expatriated in the Gulf States, Jordan opened its labour market to foreign immigrants. This process was officially designated as "replacement migration." However, a large share of the foreign nationals employed in Jordan was in fact "secondary labour," and the inflows of semi-skilled and unskilled foreign casual labourers were indeed stimulated by a "job-ladder effect" (Seccombe 1987). Following the waves of emigration of mostly urban, skilled Jordanian labourers to the Gulf States, residents of rural areas emigrated to urban centres to take up "white-collar," governmental positions. Meanwhile, immigrants were filling jobs in low-status, low-paying occupations, for example, in the construction and agricultural sectors. The private remittances from expatriate citizens, thus, raised Jordanian labourers' reservation wages, while rentier public revenues and low-skilled immigration upgraded nationals' professional opportunities, including for the less educated and less qualified among them.

Second, resident population's growth, ambitious sectoral development projects (for instance, in the agricultural sector), and the advent of the rent-based economic prosperity in the country stimulated the development of the sectors employing foreigners from the mid-1970s onwards. Expatriates' remittances to households also created a private wealth, which spurred the emergence of new economic sectors. Domestic employment, for instance, was previously reserved for wealthy households and was performed by poor women from Palestinian refugee camps and the Jordan Valley. After 1973, the growing inflows of expatriates' remittances to Jordanian households made domestic labourers more affordable to families. Local domestics were replaced by Asian live-in immigrants.

Third, in the name of Pan-Arabism, citizens of Arab states were guaranteed some privileges over non-Arabs and could enter Jordan as well as reside in the country without a permit.[1] Such preferential provisions, however, did not extend to employment, and holding a labour permit was required from all foreign nationals, Arabs and non-Arabs alike, to access the Jordanian labour market. Nonetheless, the many employment opportunities offered by the booming economy, as well as weak law enforcement, swelled the numbers of expatriate workers in Jordan. Egyptians were the biggest community of Arab expatriates in the country (80 per cent of the 153,519 registered foreign workers in 1984). Syrian labourers were also employed in seasonal activities, especially in agriculture in northern Jordan.

This period of the rentier state had critical outcomes on the economy and socio-political makeup, which are lasting until today. It laid the ground for the consumer society in the absence of a productive economy and high dependency on the external financial input at the domestic (remittances) and public levels (foreign aid and loans). The decade also set the basis of the socio-political stakes of labour in Jordan. The labour market became segmented to the privilege of Jordanian nationals, between labour-intensive sectors (agriculture, construction, and services) dominated by foreigners—hence characterised by low wages, high turnover, and no legal protection for workers—and the mainly unproductive and overstaffed governmental sector, offering "white-collar" jobs, better pay, and social protection to nationals (retirement schemes, paid vacations, and health insurance). The segmentation of the labour market became part of the socio-political "contract" binding the citizens to the regime.

[1] Law 24 (art. 30) of 1973.

The Reform Process Since the 1990s

At the same time, labour migration policies had to be reformed in the late 1980s. Slumping oil prices and changes in immigration policies in the oil-producing states (a replacement of Arab workers by Asians) compelled many Jordanian expatriates to return, which progressively dried out remittances' flows. The Arab aid to Jordan also declined. Following the Kuwait crisis of 1990–1991, about 300,000 Jordanian nationals employed in the Gulf Cooperation Council (GCC) countries, most of them of Palestinian descent, were deported to Jordan. Unemployment levels consequently skyrocketed to about 30 per cent of the active population after the crisis. To reschedule its expanding public debt, Jordan was forced into a process of drastic socio-economic reforms, negotiated with the World Bank and the International Monetary Fund (IMF). Agreements passed under the umbrella of successive Structural Adjustment Plans (SAPs) imposed a number of economic reform measures, such as trade liberalisation, financial deregulation as well as the privatisation of state assets. The severe limitations of public expenditures and, especially, the downsizing of public employment restricted the job opportunities available to Jordanian youth.

Jordan eventually mended relations with Gulf countries, and large numbers of educated Jordanians resumed migration to the oil-producing States during the 2000s. However, Jordan's economy still suffers from low productivity. Unemployment rates are also very high, up to 18 per cent in 2017. Jordanian jobseekers remain reluctant to engage in low-skilled activities, for instance, construction. The manufacturing sector, the spearhead of the socio-economic reform process, also struggles to attract the local workforce. For these reasons, business owners continue hiring foreign labourers, whom they consider cheaper to employ, more flexible, easier to lay off, and available for short-term contracts. Local labourers, therefore, see themselves as competing with foreigners, whom unemployed Jordanians accuse of taking up available jobs and of accepting unattractive conditions prevailing in the private sector[2] deemed unsuitable for the nationals. Foreign labour immigration has thus become a central

---

[2] Economic activity sectors employing large numbers of migrant labourers are usually characterised by longer work hours and less generous social packages (in terms of social security, health insurance and other allowances, maternity leaves, etc.) than governmental jobs. Unlawful practices, for example, delayed payment of wages, unpaid overtime, and unpredictable work hours, may also occur. The so-called 3D jobs ("dirty, dangerous, difficult") are the less paid and lowest status jobs.

political issue, and immigration policies must reconcile two objectives: increase employment opportunities for Jordanians, especially the young and middle- to low-skilled, less able to emigrate; and comply with economic reforms' requirements by supplying business people with a suitable and cheap workforce.

Concerns, Policies, and Regulations Governing the Entry and Recruitment of Foreign Labourers

The National Employment Strategy (NES) was formally endorsed in May 2011. The policy seeks to gradually reduce the number of migrant workers and plans for their replacement with Jordanian workers to address structural unemployment aimed at tightening the management of foreign immigration by governmental authorities. These include, most notably, a closure of most economic sectors to foreign applicants to the exception of the construction, domestic services, cleaning, and agriculture sectors. Another range of measures looks to increase the costs of employing foreigners. This comprises increasing recruitment-related fees and expenditures, as well as improving labour conditions and compliance with the international labour standards, to avoid international criticisms and attract Jordanian jobseekers into the sectors staffed by foreigners. The third range of measures targets irregular migration.

Until today, foreign residents in Jordan are bound to their employer by the *kafala* (sponsorship) system, which imposes foreign workers to depend on a local guarantor. However, the monitoring of labour immigration policies has been increasingly confined to the highest political authorities. The King provides the general outlook and retains the upper hand on the decision-making process regarding immigration and employment policies. Governmental bodies (chiefly, the Ministry of Labour) implement the policies in coordination with relevant public sector institutions and semi-public corporations involved in promoting local and foreign investment (investors and business owners). Bilateral agreements between Jordan and labour-sending countries rule over the entry, stay, and employment conditions applied to each nationality.

The entry and sojourn of foreigners in Jordan are governed by the 1973 Law on Residence and Foreigners' Affairs (amended in 1998) and the By-Law number 3 of 1997, which regulate visa requirements. Some nationalities can enter the country without a visa, such as Egyptian nationals, but can only stay for one month. Citizens from most labour-exporting

Asian nations (Sri Lanka, the Philippines, and Bangladesh, for instance) have to obtain their entry visa before entering Jordan. A valid residence permit (renewable every year) is now mandatory for all legal workers.

The 1996 Labour Law organises the recruitment of foreign workers. These have to secure their labour contracts before leaving the origin country through the Jordanian economic and diplomatic missions abroad. Sponsors-employers must settle recruitment and work permit fees before workers enter Jordan. Labour permits are delivered by the Labour Migration Directorate of the Ministry of Labour. To promote the employment of Jordanians, nationals have to be hired in priority over foreign applicants. Some occupational sectors have been recently closed to non-nationals, such as the medical, engineering, administrative, and accounting professions, clerical professions that include typing and secretarial functions, telecommunications, warehouse work, sales, interior decoration, teaching professions, electricians, car repair professions, gas selling in main cities, drivers, and guards, unless no Jordanian candidate would be suitable.[3] In this case, a clearance from the Public Employment Service and, if applicable, the concerned professional union is required. In professions and sectors open to foreigners, some quotas are set for the maximum share of admitted non-nationals. These can reach up to 60–70 per cent of the workforce in physically challenging, unhealthy occupations or for professions imposing night shifts, such as bakeries and certain industries.[4]

Over the years, fees imposed on foreign workers seeking work permits went markedly up to increase the costs of foreign labourers for business owners as well as to raise funds for the training of the local labour force. Since 2012, JD100 (US$141) have been added to the cost of work permits for that purpose. As of 2017, the basic work permit fee was set at JD400 (US$564), but costs of permits for domestic labourers, gardeners, and workers on small private farms (JD500 or US$705) were significantly higher than for the garment manufacturing sector (JD175 or US$247), for instance. An additional fee of JD100 applies for each new non-Jordanian worker brought into Jordan (Razzaz 2017, 35).

Until 2003, the agriculture and domestic services[5] were exempted from the provisions of the 1996 Labour Law. However, under international

---

[3] http://www.mol.gov.jo/Pages/viewpage.aspx?pageID=206.

[4] http://www.mol.gov.jo/Pages/viewpage.aspx?pageID=205.

[5] This sector includes all household services functions (cleaners, nannies, cooks, private drivers and guards, private gardeners, etc.).

pressure to limit abuses and to enhance control over informal employment, Jordan was the first country in the Middle East to endorse a unified standard contract for migrant domestic workers (MDWs) in 2003. The *Special Working Contract for Non-Jordanian Domestic Workers* guarantees every domestic worker the right to benefit from life insurance, to be covered by medical insurance, to be granted one day of rest a week, and to be repatriated at the employer's expenses after the expiration of the employment contract. In 2006, the United Nations Development Fund for Women (UNIFEM) and the Ministry of Labour drafted the *Booklet for Migrant Women Workers in Jordan*, which informed foreign employees about Jordan's Labour Law, living conditions in the country, and so on. The booklet was made available to workers in embassies and in licensed recruitment agencies, and was distributed to employers. Domestic labour and agricultural employment were finally incorporated within the provisions of the Labour Law in 2008 after the Jordanian Parliament amended the Law. Regulations still favour Jordanians over foreigners and, in 2016, the minimum salary was raised to JD220 per month for nationals (about US$300), while foreigners' minimum wage remained at JD110.

Nonetheless, compliance with international labour standards and the Jordanian Labour Law, workers' well-being, and fair recruitment practices were addressed by the government of Jordan in partnership with International Labour Organization (ILO) and other agencies. The Better Work Jordan (BWJ) programme, for instance, a joint initiative of the International Labour Organization and the International Finance Corporation, targeted the apparel industry. It was launched in 2008 and is now in its second phase. ILO's Integrated Programme on Fair Recruitment (FAIR) is currently being implemented to recruit Nepalese workers for the garment sector in a fair way, namely, through procedures free from deceptive and coercive recruitment practices. The FAIRWAY project (Regional Fair Migration in the Middle East Project) is focused on supporting the improvement of working and living conditions of migrant labourers in Jordan, particularly domestic and construction workers.[6] Other initiatives also target MDWs and involve local and international civil society organisations, such as Adaleh (*Justice*) Center for Human Rights studies, Tamkeen (*Empowerment*) for legal assistance, and Caritas or the Jordanian Women's Union.

---

[6] ETF (European Training Foundation), *Migrant Support Measures from an Employment and Skills Perspective (MISMES): Jordan* (Turin: ETF, 2017).

In 2009, the Parliament also endorsed a legislation forbidding human trafficking, which is enforceable through the enhanced monitoring of immigration channels into Jordan and the employment contracts and working conditions of immigrant workers. It established a National Anti-Trafficking Committee. Chaired by the Ministry of Justice, the Committee is a multi-sectoral committee composed of officials from the various ministries and government departments that play a role in combatting human trafficking. At the executive level, an Anti-Trafficking Unit was established within the Public Security Department of the Interior Ministry. The Ministry of Social Development also set up shelters (that it also runs) for the victims of trafficking. Within this realm, the legality and practices of private agencies brokering the recruitment of MDWs, for instance, in Jordan and the sending countries, were also better scrutinised by the Ministry of Labour. It led to the closure of non-law-abiding or unregistered agencies. It is notable, nonetheless, that live-in domestic labourers, staying within households, remain out of reach of labour and anti-trafficking inspections and often suffer financial, physical, and psychological abuses.

Labour and Interior ministries also tightened up control operations conducted on worksites and areas inhabited by immigrants. Under the umbrella of the Ministry of Labour's Strategic Plan for 2006–2010, inspection teams were strengthened. They operated jointly with the Borders and Residence Department of the Interior Ministry's Directorate of Public Security to conduct periodic raids to workplaces to verify foreign labourers' documents. Ministry inspection teams apprehended 29,221 migrants in irregular administrative situations in 2014 and deported 6467 of them.[7] The Labour Ministry's inspection teams conducted 94,136 field visits in 2015, arrested 28,341 workers, fined 13,908 establishments, and issued warnings to 14,497 others.[8] The ministry also deported 5735 illegal workers and closed 1635 institutions violating the law during that year. In 2017, raids by Ministry of Interior (MoI) and Ministry of Labour's (MoL's) teams intensified. A two-month amnesty period spanning from February to April 2017 allowed 11,200 workers to rectify their status and secure work permits. However, 9448 migrant

---

[7] Arab Trade Union Confederation, *Jordan-Ministry of Labour Deported 6467 Migrant Workers Last Year*, 2015-02-08, http://arabtradeunion.org/en/content/jordan-ministry-labor-deported-6467-migrant-workers-last-year (last accessed: 3 April 2018).

[8] *The Jordan Times*, "5,735 Illegal Workers Deported in 2015," *The Jordan Times*, 10 January 2016, http://www.jordantimes.com/news/local/5735-illegal-workers-deported-2015%E2%80%99 (last accessed: 3 April 2018).

workers were deported in 2017.[9] Most deportations targeted migrants with expired work permits or working in professions reserved for nationals.

A significant policy development concerns Syrian refugees in Jordan. The Kingdom is not a signatory of the 1951 Geneva Convention on Refugees. The terms of the 1998 Memorandum of Understanding between the Government of Jordan and United Nations High Commissioner for Refugees (UNHCR), which consequently regulates the entry and sojourn of non-Palestinian refugees in the country, stated that registered refugees, especially Syrians residing in camps, were not permitted to work in Jordan (ILO 2015, 5–6). Non-refugee Syrians, Iraqis, or other nationals could legally join the labour market, under the condition that they would abide by the rules set out for foreigners' employment: holding a valid labour permit for a profession opened to non-Jordanians and a valid residency under the sponsorship of the employer—the latter being expected to secure permit fees' payment and other administrative procedures.

However, as increasing numbers of Syrians were taking up low-paid jobs, often irregularly, in the informal sector, the Syria donors conference held in London, 4 February 2016, under the umbrella of the Jordan-European Union (EU) Mobility Partnership signed in October 2014, had Jordan commit to incorporate 200,000 Syrian refugees into the country's workforce within five years, especially within the Special Economic Zones or Qualifying Industrial Zones (QIZs).[10] As compensation, the foreign and international donors, such as the EU and the World Bank, committed to granting 2 billion dollars aid packages ("compacts") as well as grants

---

[9] Ibáñez Prieto, A.V., "9,448 Migrant Workers Deported in 2017—Labour Ministry," *The Jordan Times*, 23 January 2018, http://www.jordantimes.com/news/local/9448-migrant-workers-deported-2017-%E2%80%94-labour-ministry (last accessed: 3 April 2018).

[10] The Qualifying Industrial Zones (QIZs) are special economic zones set up in Jordan in the aftermath of the peace process with Israel in 1994 and the signing of a Free Trade Agreement (FTA) between Jordan and the US in 2001. They were seen as an incubator of the reforms' implementation process and, especially, of the development of export-led, labour-intensive industrial plants, mainly in the sector of textile and garment. QIZs offer duty- and quota-free access to the US and EU markets for products manufactured by "qualifying" enterprises located in those enclaves, which must meet certain quota regarding foreign participation to qualify under the programme. Its declared aim is to serve as a tool of regional integration with Israel, as well as to attract and channel foreign direct investments, mainly towards rural, poverty-stricken areas of the country and provide job opportunities for local unskilled workers (see De Bel-Air, F., "Migration Profile: Jordan," *Policy Brief 2016/06*, Robert Schuman Center for Advanced Studies/European University Institute, November 2016, endnote 20).

and cheap loans to Jordan. Partners also guaranteed privileged access to European markets for Jordanian products. The aim of the compact was to "transform the Syrian refugee crisis into a development opportunity,"[11] which was expected to raise consumer spending and drive wages up. For undocumented Syrians to apply for labour permits, an amnesty period was decided. Penalties for the lack of documentation or overstaying were waived and the payment of new visa fees was postponed to the end of 2016.

FOREIGN WORKERS IN JORDAN: A SNAPSHOT

From 110,580 in 2000, the number of work permit holders has been increasing until the end of the 2000s and has been stalling since then. Foreign nationals holding a valid labour permit numbered 318,883 in 2016. Of these, 76 per cent were men. Most had a low education level, with 95 per cent being recorded with below secondary education. Workers are, indeed, mostly low skilled. More than a half of permit holders were Egyptian nationals or 53 per cent of all foreign labourers. Seventy per cent of Egyptian workers were men. Labour permits granted to Syrian nationals amounted to 33,485; Syrians, thus, made up 11 per cent of the total legal foreign workforce, up from a mere 1.8 per cent of all recorded foreign labourers in 2014. Nationals from Bangladesh accounted for 16 per cent of all labour permit holders. Women made up 53 per cent of these workers. Filipinos and Sri Lankans had, respectively, 21 and 9 per cent of legal female workers among them.[12]

Figure 1 points out the large numeric domination of Egyptian nationals among foreign workers in Jordan, even though their numbers significantly went down since 2009 from 250,000 to 170,000 in 2016. One can also notice a diversification of Asian nationalities. In the late 2000s, Indonesian female nationals had outnumbered Filipinas and Sri Lankans. However, a hiring ban was applied, which later stopped the employment of Indonesians.[13] Bangladeshis only came recently to Jordan. The increase in

---

[11] Government of the UK, *Final: Supporting Syria & the Region, London 2016—4 February*, https://www.gov.uk/government/uploads/system/uploads/attachment_data/file/498021/Supporting_Syria__the_Region_London_2016_-_Jordan_Statement.pdf, p. 1 (last accessed: 3 April 2018).

[12] Ministry of Labour, *Statistical Yearbooks*, given years. Data quoted refer to labour permits' statistics.

[13] In retaliation for Indonesia's protest against the abuses suffered by its female nationals in Middle Eastern countries, where they are usually employed as live-in domestics.

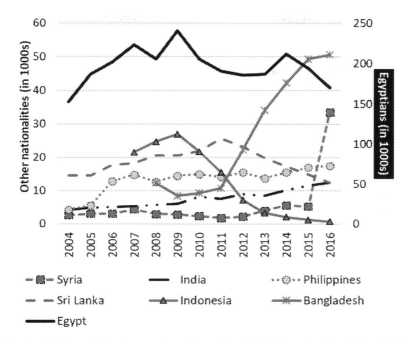

Fig. 1 Registered foreign workers by nationality (selected nationalities, 2004–2016). (Source: Ministry of Labour's Yearbooks, given years, work permits data)

their numbers is due to the expansion of the manufacturing sector among industries located in QIZs. Syrians received only 5700 work permits in 2014, 5307 in 2015, and 33,485 in 2016; however, the World Bank estimated, in 2016, that between 42,000 and 150,000 Syrian nationals were irregularly employed in the informal sector. Other estimates released by the Jordanian Labour Ministry ranged from 160,000 to 200,000 for 2015. Before February 2016 London Conference, non-refugee Syrians could legally access employment in Jordan under the conditions set out to other foreign nationals, but most of them were driven to low-paid jobs in the informal economy, as many did not have residency documents and only few could afford labour permit fees.

Figure 2 is indicative of the selectivity of employment by nationality and gender in Jordan; Egyptians, as well as Syrians, are mostly employed

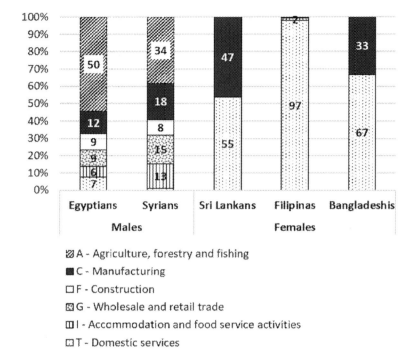

Fig. 2 Distribution of work permits by workers' main activity sector and sex (selected nationalities, 2016). (Source: Ministry of Labour's Yearbooks, work permits data)

in the agriculture and construction sectors as well as in the trade and hospitality sectors. Syrian men are absent from the domestic service sector, whereas Egyptian men are often employed as gardeners or private guardians. Women, mostly Asians from the three selected countries, were predominantly engaged in domestic household work, while many women from Sri Lanka and Bangladesh were also employed in manufacturing activities, in the apparel assembly, and garment industries.

The manufacturing sector employed 35 per cent of foreign female legal workers (27,217) and a quarter (83,052) of all foreign labourers. The sector ranks third in importance after the agricultural sector (91,363 permit holders or 29 per cent of the total) and the domestic services sector (19 per cent of all registered workers in 2016 and 60 per cent of all women among them). Manufacturing industries are usually located within the Qualifying Industrial Zones (QIZs). These comprise closed housing compounds to accommodate foreign employees, who are most often recruited in bulk from their country of origin. Soon after QIZ's inception in the early 2000s, human resource shortages were felt. Investors in textile and apparel assembly manufactures, indeed, considered the Jordanian workforce, initially meant to fill these jobs, to be lacking the necessary skills as well as reliability and "work ethics."

Jordan authorities, thus, had no alternative but to resort to hiring foreign labourers to guarantee that these productive, export-led activities could expand successfully. Foreign labourers made up 39 per cent of QIZs' workforce in 2001; their share went up to 66 per cent in 2005 (De Bel-Air and Dergarabedian 2006). For several years, it has been oscillating around 75 per cent (74 per cent as of December 2017 or 54,215 foreign labourers). From the onset, QIZs' foreign workers were from South Asian countries. However, the channelling of (male) Syrian refugees to jobs in the QIZs' manufacturing industries is underway and could significantly affect the number of opportunities available there for Asian labourers.

The increase in the numbers of foreign workers in QIZs may also be due to attempts at regularising undocumented labourers employed in the Zones, a privileged target for police raids (De Bel-Air 2008). The scale of irregular labour is, indeed, vast in Jordan. Government officials estimated in mid-2016 that foreign labourers in the country could be around 800,000. The figure included about 300,000 holders of regular labour permits only.[14] In specific sectors like agriculture, especially, it was estimated that only 40 per cent were holding valid permits. Of these, moreover, about 70 per cent were supposed to have moved to other sectors in order to work illegally. Other estimates released by the Minister of Labour even suggested that figures of employed foreigners were as high as 1.4 million in early 2017 in Jordan, and this would imply (after the subtraction of about 350,000 work permit holders) that over 1 million foreign workers would be undocumented (Nemeh 2017; Razzaz 2017).

Irregularity is more frequent in economic sectors offering short-term, project-based assignments (construction), away from cities (agriculture) and, especially, away from the public sphere (domestic household labour).

---

[14] *The Jordan Times*, "800,000 Guest Workers Are in Jordan—Ministry", *The Jordan Times*, 16 August 2016, http://www.jordantimes.com/news/local/800000-guest-workers-are-jordan-%E2%80%94-ministry.

A study conducted on a sample of 303 domestic workers (live-in, live-out, and freelance)[15] showed that only 54 per cent of workers were holding work and a residency permit (Tamkeen 2015). Estimates of the total numbers of female household domestic workers were in the range of 100,000 in 2016, according to the Domestic Helpers Recruitment Agencies Association (DHRAA), of whom 35,000 had no work permit.

The high prevalence of irregularity among foreign workers in Jordan, however, does not relegate these workers to a specific category, clearly separated from "legal" labourers. Becoming irregular is a process, and the status is transient in time. A migrant may enter with a valid visa and acquire legal labour documents, but after these expire, he/she would later be compelled to take up a job for an employer who is not his/her sponsor or work in an industry or profession different from the one stated on the labour document. The legal sponsor may also fail to renew the employee's documents on time. Yet, migrants in an irregular situation may, sometimes, take advantage of amnesty operations to regularise their status or fix their situation by paying fines. Irregularity is also multifaceted, and there exist different levels of compliance to laws and different categories of irregularity: a "regular" resident but a worker in an irregular situation, a holder of a permit employed by a person who is not his/her legal sponsor, and so on. Some categories of residence, namely, that of "refugee" under UNHCR, which applies to half of the Syrian nationals recorded in Jordan, are conducive to irregularity, when refugees need to work to earn a living. Irregularity is thus a "grey area," and categories of residence often overlap de facto.

Socio-political Underpinnings and Stakes of Foreign Labour Migration

Migration patterns and dynamics stand in a stark contrast with the policy goals and the increase in the numbers of foreign workers, especially in the sectors initially designed to supply opportunities to Jordanian jobseekers, such as the manufacturing sector. The Jordanisation of the workforce, that

---

[15] "Freelancers" work independently on an hourly basis for multiple employers and live in their own accommodation, not under the employers' roof. These are often in an irregular situation since it is forbidden to work for other employers than the sponsor. The live-out workers work for one employer but are not housed by the employer. Live-in domestic labourers (officially) work for one employer (their sponsor) and are accommodated by the employer.

is, the replacement of foreign labourers by Jordanians, is far from sight and there has been an increase in irregularity. Does this mean that policies are not enforced efficiently enough to produce significant results? Migration patterns and policies stem from a variety of factors ranging from domestic to international politics, and these are obstacles to implementing policy goals head on, such as compelling unemployed Jordanians to the low-skilled, low-paid, and physically challenging tasks performed by some expatriates. Moreover, non-enforcement or partial enforcement of policy goals points to the divergences of interests between stakeholders, especially the unemployed Jordanians, the Jordanian regime, and the employers and business people among them.

Pan-Arabism's Political Inheritance and Inflows of Refugees to Jordan

As noted earlier, legislation governing the entry, sojourn, and conditions for legally joining the employment market existed in Jordan, but were not applied to the Arab workers (most of them Egyptians) before the mid-1980s. In addition, preferential hiring policies for Arab labourers also existed. The Pan-Arabist stance of Jordan's Hashemite leaders was shared by parts of the national population. These were, and may still be, favourable to the opening of the country's borders to refugees of regional conflicts (Palestinians, Iraqis, and, more recently, Syrians). The relative leniency in enforcing labour control contributed to the formation of large pools of informal labourers, reproduced until today by migrants' networks consolidated over decades of circulation with Jordan. Moreover, the massive deportation of Syrian irregular workers is not an option, as the Syrian civil war is still raging as of early 2019.

The Legacy of the Rentier State: Migrants and the Redistribution Process

The emergence of a rentier state in Jordan spurred demands for additional labourers from abroad. Moreover, the import of cheap labour to perform productive, service, and "3D" activities, namely "dangerous, difficult and dirty," was an important element of the government's redistribution of rentier resources to the citizens in return for their political allegiance to the regime. The process helped to strengthen the state-society bonds. Much like in the Gulf States, the "increasing dominance of domestic house workers is part of an unspoken bargain between the state and the emerging civil society, by which the state provides a leisure life in exchange for complete political control," as stated by Sociologist Rima Sabban.[16] It is important to highlight that Jordan's rentier state was severely hit by economic reforms. Redistribution channels such as generous public employment, free health and education, and other benefits were significantly reduced, especially since the 2000s. The perpetuation of citizenship-based privileges, such as the supply of cheap and docile human commodities to locals, was, thus, a major element of the political bargaining process. Domestic labourers, especially those that are dependent on their sponsor under the *kafala* system and remain confined in employers' houses, away from public gaze, aptly illustrate this notion of human resource commodity.

Human Resource Needs Versus the Segmentation of the Labour Market

Besides the two factors explaining sustained numbers of foreign labourers to Jordan, another factor makes the replacement of foreign labourers by locals unlikely, namely, the high price of local workforce when compared to the foreign one. Jordan's economic reform process demanded the privatisation of governmental assets coupled with financial deregulation, as well as the liberalisation of trade and the development of productive activities. Yet, citizens are unwilling to take up low- and semi-skilled activities, especially in the agriculture, manufacturing, or hospitality sector, which propose employment conditions neither financially nor socially rewarding.

The segmentation of the labour market between labour-intensive sectors (agriculture, construction, and services)—characterised by low wages, high turnover, no legal protection for workers, hence dominated by foreigners—and the governmental sector (offering "white-collar" jobs, better pay, and social protection to nationals) is an essential part of the socio-political "contract" binding Jordanian citizens with the regime. Therefore, official statements emphasise the measures of labour training and improvement of work conditions that are implemented as well as the priority rights and privileges allocated to citizens over foreign labourers,

---

[16] Sabban, R., "Women Domestic Workers in the United Arab Emirates," in International Labour Office (ILO), *Gender and Migration in the Arab States: The Case of Domestic Workers* (Beirut: ILO, 2004), pp. 86–107, (p. 90).

such as the higher minimum salary granted to Jordanians. These measures aim at encouraging Jordanians to take up opportunities in these sectors without feeling downgraded. However, they increase the costs of Jordanian workforce for employers and create a sense of entitlement among citizen job applicants, thereby putting enormous political pressure on the regime to guarantee employment opportunities. More so, business owners and employers prefer employing foreigners, a cheaper and less constraining workforce. The balance is, thus, very delicate for the government to satisfy citizens as well as business owners.

Keeping Migrants in Irregular Situation: A Political Asset

Keeping some of the workforce in an irregular status may, therefore, be a political strategy, despite the large-scale publicity surrounding police operations against undocumented migrants. Tough-looking immigration policies please average citizens who voice anti-immigration feelings, while weak law enforcement satisfies employers' needs for the cheap foreign workforce.

Indeed, unauthorised foreign migrants are among the most vulnerable members of society. Their presence and exploitability have repercussions in domestic politics, as they highlight the existing segmentation between protected workers (the nationals) and unprotected ones (the foreigners) and, more generally, between local and foreign populations. Benefitting from fundamental human rights, thus, appears as a privilege reserved to citizens. More specifically, the undocumented workforce forms pools of hugely flexible labourers that are able to adjust to the demands of a de-regularised economy, thus guaranteeing better profits to investors. More so, business owners in specific sectors, such as construction, work on limited duration projects and these affirm that they cannot afford to grant yearly work permit and sponsorship to foreign employees.

Political and Financial Rent-Seeking in International Relations

Bilateral and international affairs also exerted an influence on the size and composition of immigrants' flows and, consequently, on the balance between local and foreign workforce. The advancement of QIZs, for example, is an important stake in the Jordanian-US relations. It also favourably impresses economic reform-monitoring institutions and stimulates the allocation of international aid and grants to Jordan. However, the availability of a cheap and trained workforce is an important factor in the successful development of QIZs. Foreign labourers, thus, play a crucial role in Jordan's bilateral and international politics (De Bel-Air and Dergarabedian 2006).

Similarly, the incorporation of 200,000 Syrian workers into the legal workforce was negotiated under the umbrella of Jordan-EU Mobility Partnership. Such agreements mostly aim at securing Europe's borders by externalising their control to "Neighbourhood" countries. By providing livelihoods to Syrian refugees on its soil, Jordan, thus, would retain them away from Europe. Cooperation on irregular migration has become a precondition for financial and development support from the EU.

Jordan is strongly dependent on foreign aid, and, therefore, it has very little bargaining power as regards the outcomes of the London Conference and is required to employ Syrians legally, despite the unpopularity of the measure. The decision spurred anxiety among non-Syrian foreign labourers as well as among jobless and employed Jordanians, fearing increased competition in the labour market. Employers also protested the measure. All this highlights the limitations faced by Jordan's government to effectively enforce its stated policies of limiting the size of the foreign workforce and replacing it with Jordanian jobseekers.

Conclusion

The characteristics of the labour migrants in Jordan underline the failure of the stated aims of immigration policies (reducing the number of migrant workers and replacing them with Jordanian labourers) and the apparent inefficiency of the policies taken to that effect (restricting foreign labourers' access to Jordan's labour markets; increasing the costs of employing foreigners for employers; and improving conditions in the labour-intensive sectors to attract Jordanians and fight irregularity). The mandatory incorporation of 200,000 new Syrian workers within the legal workforce pinpoints the extent of the challenges posed by conflicting policy goals.

The continuous expansion of the numbers of foreign labourers can be explained by the long-standing ties between Jordan and Arab labour-exporting countries, sustained by Arab solidarity. It is also due to the political-clientelist policy of supplying large numbers of cheap migrants to enhance the status of citizens. Substituting Jordanian labourers to migrants and fighting irregular employment is also hampered by socio-political obstacles: significant improvements made to the labour conditions in the private sector are meant to attract Jordanians to that sector; yet, this in return increases the costs of hiring locals for entrepreneurs. The domestic political pressure to supply more job opportunities considered suitable by Jordanian jobseekers clashes with the employers' demands for cheap labour. Keeping a share of the foreign workers in irregular status may, therefore, be a strategy to supply cheap labour to employers while also pressuring them to hire locals. Jordan's lack of bargaining power with international donors to control its domestic labour market cannot be ignored. Official policies to streamline the employment of young Jordanians, as well as Syrian refugees, now raise the issue of the future of other nationalities (Egyptians as well as Asian nationals) in Jordan's labour market.

REFERENCES

Arab Trade Union Confederation. (2015, February 8). *Jordan-Ministry of labour deported 6467 migrant workers last year*. http://arabtradeunion.org/en/content/jordan-ministry-labor-deported-6467-migrant-workers-last-year

Beblawi, Hazem. (1987). The rentier state in the Arab world. In Hazem Beblawi & Giacomo Luciani (Eds.), *The rentier state. Nation, state and integration in the Arab World* (Vol. 2). London/New York: Croom Helm.

Brand, Laurie. (1995). *Jordan's inter-Arab relations: The political economy of alliance making*. New York: Columbia University Press.

De Bel-Air, F. Irregular migration in Jordan: Socio-political stakes. *CARIM analytic and synthetic notes* 2008/78, San Domenico di Fiesole (Florence, Italy): Robert Schuman Centre for Advanced Studies (RSCAS), European University Institute (EUI), pp. 1–19. http://hdl.handle.net/1814/10511

De Bel-Air, F. (2016, November). Migration profile: Jordan, *MPC Policy Brief 2016/06*, Robert Schuman Center for Advanced Studies/European University Institute (EUI), pp. 1–17. http://cadmus.eui.eu/handle/1814/44065

De Bel-Air, F., & Dergarabedian, A. (2006). Migrations internationales, globalisation et politique. Les Zones industrielles qualifiantes (QIZs) de Jordanie. In F. De Bel-Air (Ed.), *Migration et politique au Moyen-Orient* (pp. 37–60). Beyrouth: IFPO.

ETF (European Training Foundation). (2017). *Migrant Support Measures from an Employment and Skills Perspective (MISMES): Jordan*. Turin: ETF.

Ibáñez Prieto, A. V. (2018, January 23). 9,448 migrant workers deported in 2017—Labour Ministry. *The Jordan Times*. http://www.jordantimes.com/news/local/9448-migrant-workers-deported-2017-%E2%80%94-labour-ministry

ILO. (2015). *Access to work for Syrian refugees in Jordan: A discussion paper on labour and refugee laws and policies*. ILO. www.ilo.org/beirut/publications/WCMS_357950/lang%2D%2Den/

Nemeh, B. (2017, March 21). How can the kingdom's troubled economy benefit more from Syrian migrant workers? *Diwan*. Carnegie Middle East Centre. http://carnegie-mec.org/diwan/68330

Razzaz, S. (2017). *A challenging market becomes more challenging: Jordanian workers, migrant workers and refugees in the Jordanian labour market* (International Labour Organisation). Beirut: ILO. http://www.ilo.org/wcmsp5/groups/public/%2D%2D-arabstates/%2D%2D-ro-beirut/documents/publication/wcms_556931.pdf

Seccombe, I. (1987). Labour emigration policies and economic development in Jordan: From unemployment to labour shortage. In B. Khader & A. Badran (Eds.), *The economic development of Jordan* (pp. 118–132). Louvain/London: CERMAC/Croom Helm.

Tamkeen. (2015). *Invisible women. The working and living conditions of irregular migrant domestic workers in Jordan*. Amman: Tamkeen Fields for Aid.

The Jordan Times. 800,000 guest workers are in Jordan—Ministry, August 16, 2016. http://www.jordantimes.com/news/local/800000-guest-workers-are-jordan-%E2%80%94-ministry

The Jordan Times. 5,735 illegal workers deported in 2015, January 10, 2016. http://www.jordantimes.com/news/local/5735-illegal-workers-deported-2015%E2%80%99. Statistical publications from the Department of Statistics of Jordan and the Ministry of Labour.

Minorities

Miranda Egan Langley

Jordan is formally recognised as a constitutional monarchy; however, in practice, the government serves at the pleasure of the king, who, throughout the Jordanian history, has displayed a tendency to override their authority at will. This monarchy has had to evolve and adapt to the ever-changing social structure of its region's inhabitants, as minority groups dominate the Kingdom.

It is also a country in which its minority groups can often fall between the gaps as tensions increase with the continuing flow of refugees from the neighbouring countries. The available data on the total number and proportion of ethnic groups appear to be an object of frequent state management and have often resulted in political controversy, where ethnic groups can be a politically sensitive issue and official data on them are not available in public domain. However, acknowledging the rich historical tapestry of minorities which inhabit the region, their origins, and, for many, their continued existence in the Kingdom is the key to the understanding their present status (Alan 2005) in Jordan's social structure.

M. E. Langley (✉)
Honorable Society of Kings Inns, Dublin, Ireland
e-mail: miranda.langley@lawlibrary.ie

The Ottoman Empire, King Abdullah, and Beyond

During the Ottoman rule (1516–1918 CE), the territory now known as the Hashemite Kingdom of Jordan was primarily populated by the Bedouin tribes. The Ottoman administration was fragile and was not in a position to effectively control the tribes. This was evident in the many towns and villages which were abandoned, resulting in the decline of agriculture and subsequently the movement of families and tribes who frequently travelled from one village to another owing to the lack of resources or infrastructure. Jordan was to emerge from the clutches of the Ottoman Empire primarily populated with a foundation of Bedouins, who remained as they were, as masters of the desert, continuing to live much as they had for hundreds of years.

Prior to the British involvement, the region had a small settled population in the north-west that remained largely desert and was inhabited by Bedouin tribes. In 1921, Britain awarded Transjordan, the area east of Palestine and the Jordan River, to Emir Abdullah. The initial attempts at forging a regional state disregarded any previous claims to an exclusive existence that the region might have had (Robins 2004). The tribes were co-opted by the Emir, and he recruited a small armed force predominantly from the southern tribes. It was not until 1946 that Transjordan became an independent state and was formally recognised as the Hashemite Kingdom of Jordan.

During this pivotal time, ethnic minorities were already visible throughout the region. Many Syrians and Palestinians opted to migrate to Jordan in an attempt to escape over-taxation and ongoing feuds, while many Muslim Circassians and Chechens fled the Czarist Russian persecution to settle in Jordan, Syria, Iraq, and Turkey. Before the British involvement, the Ottomans had settled Circassians together with a few Shia Chechens, on the almost completely deserted East Bank between 1878 and 1909. Their intention was to form a barricade against the predatory Bedouin and also to develop the region agriculturally. The result was that they created the first proper settlements at Amman, Zarqa, and Jerash (Zabad 2017). At the time of the independence, Circassians numbered about 6000 and formed an elite and loyal core retinue for Abdullah, well represented in the armed forces and administration. It is clear that from the very foundations of the state, Jordon already had a significant share of minority groups.

In the present context, these groups can be divided into three broad categories of minorities: refugees, religious minorities, and ethnic minorities.

Refugees

Initially, relations between the King and the emerging Israeli state remained amicable; however, in 1948, Transjordan fought Israel to capture the West Bank, part of the putative Palestinian Arab state. When it formally annexed it in 1950, the population of Jordan tripled. Over time, the refugee population increased from about 300,000 in 1967 to over 1.8 million in 2006 with the addition of refugees and West Bank inhabitants (Minority Rights Group International 2008, p. 1).

The 1948 War was the first of several conflicts Jordan was to have with Israel, and the June War of 1967 resulted in Israel occupying the West Bank. In 1970, fierce fighting broke out between the Jordanian military and Palestinian fighters which resulted in King Hussein deciding to attack several of the Palestinian camps by ground and air force and in the crisis at least 400 were killed and over 700 wounded (Morris 2001).

Despite this conflict, Jordan has continued to host Palestinian refugees since 1948, and according to the United Nations Relief and Works Agency (hereinafter, the UNRWA), there were 2.2 million Palestinian refugees in Jordan in 2017. Out of them, more than 440,000 are residing in 13 camps which are spread across the country. The UNEDW goes on to report that over 90 per cent of those individuals were holders of a Jordanian national identification number. This has enabled these individuals to access all state services, leaving them with the same equality as Jordanian citizens and providing the required foundations for successful social integration (The United Nations Committee of the Elimination of Discrimination Against Women UNEDW 2017).

However, this is not the status quo for all Palestinian refugees who are resident within the country and there are significant constraints both in terms of access to basic essentials and education. While essential services were to be provided by the UNRWA to the Palestinian refugees, both residing inside and outside of the camps owing to limited resources and funding, it has only been in a position to provide those essential services to about 3 per cent of the entire population of Palestinian refugees (UNEDW 2017). This has meant that the deficit has fallen upon the Jordanian state, increasing the already strained financial burden. To add to this tension, the relationship between the resident Palestinians and the state remains fragile owing to Jordan's historical relationship with Israel together with the long-held belief by many Palestinians that a secret agreement took place between Jordan and Israel regarding the status of the

West Bank. This is compounded by the Jordanian fear vis-à-vis the Palestinian community within its borders (Castallenio and Cavanaugh 2013, p. 153).

While Palestinian refugees make up the majority of refugees, the country has also absorbed a wave of Iraqi refugees after the US-led invasion of that country in March 2003 and, at one time, the Iraqi refugee population ranged from 750,000 to 1 million and it made up about 17 per cent of Jordan's population (Nanes 2007, p. 1).

The Iraq war indirectly resulted in an economic boom for Jordan (Nanes 2007, p. 1) but the resulting refugee flows have become onerous, and the state was economically stretched. Jordan has admitted more refugees fleeing from the war in Iraq per capita than any other country (Ibid.). The influx has not only placed a heavy burden on the government but has also resulted in an increase in house prices and the cost of essential and basic goods.

The United Nations High Commissioner for Refugees (UNHCR) conducted a survey in 2007, which indicated that the migration of Iraqis to Jordan is predominantly a migration of families; with 77 of them, who arrived in 2003 and later, with the highest volume of movement of the population taking place in 2004 and 2005 (UNHCR 2007, p. 7). The survey also showed that the 68 per cent were Sunni Muslims; 17 per cent Shia Muslims, and 12 per cent Christian. Owing to increased fears over the import of sectarian violence from Iraq, after the 2005 Amman bombings, Jordan has routinely turned away male Iraqi refugees between the ages of 18 and 45 and has further attempted to prevent Shia refugees from entering the country (International Crisis Group 2008, p. 9).

There has been a particular concern raised by the Christian Iraqi refugees as funding dried up for the refugee community and the prohibition against working remained in place. The UNHCR report also showed that a majority of Iraqis were living on savings or received transfers and only 42 per cent received such transfers from Iraq. This has made a large segment of Iraqis in Jordan at risk of becoming vulnerable with the depletion of savings, as the deterioration in the security situation in Iraq has affected the transfers of funds. The result is that a decade later, the number of Iraqis living in Jordan has decreased to about 140,000. This number is significantly smaller when compared with approximately 1.2 million Syrians in the country in addition to about 600,000 Egyptian guest workers. While the Iraqi population of Jordan has shrunk from its high point of about half a million in 2008, more affluent Iraqis continue to play a highly visible role in Jordanian society (Sheldon 2018, p. 1).

Jordan also has a significant number of Syrian refugees, which it is currently acting as a host country to. In November 2017, the Committee on the Elimination of Racial Discrimination stated that Jordan has the largest refugee population per capita in the world and identified 29 per cent of the population as refugees. The UNHCR indicated, as of 1 May 2018, there were 666,596 registered Syrian refugees in the Kingdom (UNHCR 2018). To put this into context, Jordan has received one-in-five of all Syrians fleeing the war. The UNHCR reports that, in 2017, many of these Syrian refugees are living in refugee camps, such as Zaatari and Azraq (Ibid.), where aid groups have converted desert wastelands into cities. *Human Rights Watch* reports that since the beginning of the war in Syria, between 2011 and 2016, Jordan had received over 656,000 Syrian refugees and out of them, approximately 79,000 were housed at the Zaatari Refugee Camp, 54,000 in Azarq Camp, and 7300 in the Emirates Jordan Camp in Zarqa Governorate and the rest have been living in towns and cities without permits (HRW 2016, p. 4). While the refugees have been welcomed warmly, such a large number of people have been taking its toll on the region.

The Committee on the Elimination of Racial Discrimination Jordan indicated that the direct cost of providing for such large numbers has amounted to about 5 per cent of the gross domestic product or in real financial terms about two billion dollars annually (UNEDW 2017). The impact of this is evident particularly in the education system which has witnessed a surge in the number of Syrian pupils who now represent 12 per cent of the student population (UNEDW 2017). Despite ongoing efforts to increase the capacity, 47 per cent of the schools remained seriously overcrowded with the direct cost of this crisis amounting to on an average two billion dollars a year (UNEDW 2017).

Jordan does not receive sufficient international assistance to manage the increased refugee crisis on its infrastructure, particularly in relation to education and health and, by November of 2016, only 57 per cent of the US$1.1 billion budget goal for 2016 had been raised. Furthermore, in 2016, there were at 80,000 Syrian refugee children who were not in formal education, but the Jordanian Ministry of Education has taken significant steps to provide access to education for more than 50,000 children and introduced targeted "catch up" programmes for children who had not had access to education for the past three years (HRW 2016, p. 10). To tide over the crisis, 28,000 work permits had been issued for Syrian Refugees by the Jordanian labour authorities (UNHCR 2018). However, it is clear that despite these significant efforts, the state lacks the requisite means and infrastructure to support the ceaseless flow of refugees into the country.

Ethnic Minorities

Apart from the significant Palestinian, Iraqi, and Syrian refugee population, the country is defined by further minority divisions. While the countries official language is Arabic, English, Circassian, and Armenian are also widely spoken. The main minority and indigenous groups consist of Palestinians 3 million (50 per cent), Bedouins of Jordanian origin (est. 33 per cent), Iraqi refugees 450,000—1 million (7.5–17 per cent), Christians 360,000 (6 per cent), Chechens and Circassians 60,000 (1 per cent), Armenians 60,000 (1 per cent), Druze 12,000–14,000 (0.2 per cent), Baha'i 1000 (0.02 per cent), Kurds 30,000 Shia Muslims (number unknown), and Assyrians (0.8%) (CIA 2007). The Jordan Demographics Profile reported in 2018 that the main ethnic groups present in the Kingdom were Arab (98 per cent), Circassian (1 per cent), and Armenian (1 per cent) (Jordan Demographics Profile 2018).

The World Population Review on Jordon reports that Assyrian Christians make up 0.8 per cent of the population, most of whom are Eastern Aramaic-speaking refugees. There are also 30,000 Kurds, most of which are refugees from Turkey, Iran, and Iraq, and about 5000 Armenians. Jews, who were once prevented in the country, are 300 in number. In addition, it is estimated that there are 1.2 million illegal migrant workers and 500,000 legal migrant workers in Jordan, and thousands of foreign women come to work in hotels or other service sectors (World Population Review 2018).

Currently, the citizen population of Jordan is estimated to be 6 million. The majority of Jordanians, which includes a portion of the large Palestinian refugee population, descend from Bedouin or tribal origins.

However, there are about 60,000 Circassians and Chechens, who have retained their identity, living in Amman and six villages in the north. Circassians are highly integrated into the Arabic-speaking society while retaining community consciousness. The Circassians had been forced out of their homeland by the Czarist Russia, and thousands of them fled to the Ottoman Empire in 1864. Refugees scattered to the four corners of the

Empire: from Turkey to the Suez Canal and from Syria to Palestine. Circassians are one of the invisible expatriate minorities living in the Middle East and the precise number is not known. The census taken in 1933 by the British was the only occasion when people were ethnically identified, and it put the number of the Circassians to be at 5850 (Mackey 1979). However, today that number is closer to 60,000, and the impact that the Circassian community has had is significant. A Circassian became Jordan's first Prime Minister in 1950, an indication of the influential position the community achieved in the Kingdom. The Chechens have also retained a large part of their cultural identity and are more likely to speak their mother tongue (Kailani 2002).

There is no official source for the total number of Palestinians and it is often cited in numerous media reports that they number half or slightly more than half of the population. The UNRWA reports that there are 2,175,491 registered Palestine refugees as of 1 December 2016, and this would tend to suggest that almost 50 per cent of Jordan's population is made up of Palestinians (El-Abed 2014, p. 81) and most of them were refugees who fled the Arab-Israeli wars of 1948 and 1967 and their descendants. The Palestinians are located overwhelmingly in the north-western part of the country, principally in the environs of Amman, Zarqa, and Irbid. The Palestinian refugee community has retained its identity owing to the special management of King Abdullah I during the first exodus of Palestinians whereby full citizenship rights were granted (Amro 2008, p. 66). However, the same cannot be said for the rest of Jordanian minority groups.

Religious Minorities

The Constitution in Jordan guarantees freedom of religious beliefs and that is evident in the presence of religious minorities. In 2007, the main religions in Jordan were divided into Sunni Islam (92 per cent), Christianity (6 per cent), and Druze faith and Shia Islam (together around 2 per cent). In 2018, the religious minority landscape has changed somewhat. The Jordan Demographics Profile (2018) outlines that the majority of the country is Muslim (97.2 per cent), predominantly Sunni, and Islam is the official religion.

There are some Christians, the majority being Greek Orthodox, but there are also some Greek and Roman Catholics, Syrian Orthodox, Coptic Orthodox, Armenian Orthodox, and Protestant denominations. The non-citizen population also include about 0.4 per cent Buddhists, 0.1 per cent

Hindus, and a smaller portion of Jews, folk religionist, unaffiliated, and others (Jordan Demographics Profile 2018).

The overwhelming majority of Jordanians are Sunni Muslims. However, Christians form approximately 6 per cent of the population. Many of the Christians are Palestinians, but some are also from long-established East Bank families in the north-west of the country (USLS 2018). Many Christians in Jordan belong to the Greek Orthodox Church, while the rest are Latin Roman Catholics, Eastern Catholics, and various Protestant communities, including Baptists (USLS 2018).

The main areas of the indigenous Christian communities located in the East Bank were limited to towns such as Karak, Madaba, Salt, and Ajlun, and Christian communities were noted to also reside in Amman and some other major cities. In previous times, Christians were often largely represented among the more educated and affluent classes. As a result, they had increased access to education (USLS 2018).

The non-Christian religious minorities include a small community of Druze who live near the Syrian border. They originally derive from a small sect of the Ismaili branch of Shia Islam. Their belief system is based on the teachings of Imam Muhammad Bin-Ismail (died ca. A.D. 765), the Seventh Imam, whom they consider as the last Imam. This is in conflict with and opposed to other groups who recognised 12 Imams. There is some suggestion that the Druze were in fact a people even before conversion to the faith of al-Hakim, a Muslim (Marshal 2016, p. 2). For example, there are theories that suggest that the Druze are descendants of Persian colonists. Other sources suggest that they are of Christian descent, during the time of the crusades (Ibid., pp. 1–2). However, the latter is most unlikely considering that the first crusade began about 80 years after al-Hakim.

A unique aspect of the Druze identity is that they do not seek to assert their own country and are faithful to the country which governs their territory. As a result of this, they can be found in Israel, Lebanon, and Syria and are said to be great warriors. In 2005, the Druze in Jordan numbered approximately 20,000 (International Religious Freedom Report 2005, p. 1) and, in 2018, the figure rose to 41,000 (The Joshua Project 2018, p. 1). Although the government does not specifically recognise the Druze faith, considering them instead to be Muslims, it does not set out to impede their worship or customs (Ibid., p. 3).

The Shishans, a group whose origins lie in the Caucasus Mountains, are connected to the Circassians and are Shias. Estimates in the early 1980s placed their number at 2000. However, data are unavailable as to their current population. Both the Circassians and the Shishans have adapted to their Arabic environment within a short space of time and both groups have adopted Arabic as their main lingua franca (Shoup 2007, p. 8).

In general, it would appear that there is a higher degree of religious freedom in Jordan with different groups being permitted to practice their faith. For example, in general, Christians do not suffer discrimination, holding high-level positions in the government and private sector and have been represented in the media and academia. However, it is noteworthy that there is a small religious minority of Baha'is, which inhabits the village of Al Adasiyah in the northern Jordan Valley, use Persian dialect (Harris 1958, p. 12) and have faced some societal discrimination (International Religious Freedom Report 2005, p. 6).

It appears that the majority of the indigenous population view religion as a personal choice and central to one's personal identity. This is evident in the fact that relations between Muslims and Christians are generally considered to be amicable (Ibid.).

Conclusion

Three major minority groupings exist in Jordan today, namely, refugees, ethnic minorities, and religious minorities and with the continued influx of refugees, the demography of these groups may continue to alter over time. The constitution which was established under King Talal in 1952 was progressive in many senses but primarily due to its approach in providing representation towards the minorities. The long practice was formalised in 2003 when women and minority groups are represented in parliament through a quota system. Nine seats, or 8 per cent of the Chamber, are reserved for Christians, and three seats are reserved for Chechens and Circassians.

However, while these groups are well represented, the cultural landscape has dramatically altered over time with significant numbers of Palestinians, Syrians, and Iraqis now living within the Kingdom in refugee camps or elsewhere. Furthermore, since February 2017, the UNHCR has reported that over 10,000 Somali, Sudanese, and Yemeni refugees and asylum seekers are registered with UNHCR in Jordan, though many members of these communities live in the country without valid documentation.

Although there have been significant regional and domestic issues which contribute to the constant influx of refugees, Jordan's high rates of population growth will inevitably be linked to its economic fortunes and failures. Amidst this vulnerability and the financial barriers, that many of these minority groups face, in particular, the refugees, there is a growing sense of alienation from the general Jordanian identity. In a media commentary on "*A nation of minorities?*" in March 2018, an author suggests that many of these minorities feel aggrieved and marginalised and often complain of mistreatment by the state system (Murad 2018). While Jordan is committed to the promotion and protection of human rights, it is clear that the battle for true equality for many minority groups living in the Kingdom will be a continued uphill struggle.

References

Alan, G. (2005). *Jordan living in the cross fire*. London: Zed Books.

Amro, R. (2008). Palestinian refugees in Jordan as a successful example of immigrants. In M. Finkelstein & K. Dent-Brown (Eds.), *Psychosocial stress in immigrants and in members of minority groups as a factor of terrorist behavior*. Amsterdam: IOS Press.

Castallenio, J., & Cavanaugh, K. A. (2013). *Minority rights in the Middle East*. Oxford: Oxford University Press.

CIA (Central Intelligence Agency). (2007). *CIA world fact book 2007*. https://www.cia.gov/library/publications/resources/the-world-factbook/geos/jo.html. Accessed 22 June 2018.

El-Abed, A. (2014). The discourse of guesthood: Forced migrants in Jordan. In A. Fabos & R. Isotalo (Eds.), *Managing Muslim mobilities* (Regional and migrational book series) (pp. 81–100). New York: Palgrave Macmillan.

Harris, G. L. (1958). *Jordan, its people, its society, its culture*. New Haven: HRAF Press.

HRW (Human Rights Watch). (2016). *Education for Syrian refugee children: What donors and host countries should do?* New York: HRW. https://www.hrw.org/news/2016/09/16/education-syrian-refugee-children-what-donors-and-host-countries-should-do. Accessed 22 June 2018.

International Crisis Group. (2008, July 10). *Failed responsibility: Iraqi refugees in Syria, Jordan and Lebanon*. Brussels: ICG. https://d2071andvip0wj.cloudfront.net/77-failed-responsibility-iraqi-refugees-in-syria-jordan-and-lebanon.pdf. Accessed 22 June 2018.

International Religious Freedom Report. (2005). *US Department of State*. https://www.state.gov/j/drl/rls/irf/2005/51602.htm. Accessed 22 June 2018.

Jordan Demographics Profile. (2018). https://www.indexmundi.com/jordan/demographics_profile.html. Accessed 22 June 2018.

Kailani, W. (2002). *Chechens in the Middle East: Between original and host cultures.* Caspian Studies Program, Harvard Kennedy School, Belfer Center for Science and International Affairs. https://www.belfercenter.org/publication/chechens-middle-east-between-original-and-host-cultures. Accessed 22 June 2018.

Mackey, B. D. (1979). *The Circassians in Jordan.* M.S. Thesis in National Security Affairs. Monterey: Naval Postgraduate School.

Marshal, S. et al. (2016). Reconstructing Druze Population History. *Scientific reports.* https://www.nature.com/articles/srep35837. Accessed 22 June 2018.

Minority Rights Group International. (2008). *World directory of minorities and indigenous peoples—Jordan: Palestinians.* http://www.refworld.org/docid/49749cfcc.html. Accessed 22 June 2018.

Morris, B. (2001). *Righteous victims: A history of the Zionist Arab conflict, 1881–2001.* New York: Vintage.

Murad, N. (2018, March 24). A nation of minorities? *The Jordan Times.* http://www.jordantimes.com/opinion/nermeen-murad/nation-minorities. Accessed 22 June 2018.

Nanes, S. (2007). *Jordan's unwelcome guests.* https://www.merip.org/mer/mer244/jordans-unwelcome-guests. Accessed 22 June 2018.

Robins, P. (2004). *A history of Jordan.* Cambridge: Cambridge University Press.

Sheldon, Z. (2018, January 2). Nationality, class, and Iraqi migrants in Jordan. *American Center of Oriental Research.* https://www.acorjordan.org/2018/01/02/nationality-class-iraqi-migrants-jordan/. Accessed 22 June 2018.

Shoup, J. A. (2007). *Culture and customs of Jordon.* London: Greenwood Press.

The Joshua Project. (2018). *Druze in Jordan.* https://joshuaproject.net/people_groups/11620/JO. Accessed 22 June 2018.

UNEDW. (2017, November 24). (UN Committee on the Elimination of Discrimination Against Women) (UNEDW) (2017) Committee on the Elimination of Racial Discrimination considers the report of Jordan. https://www.ohchr.org/EN/NewsEvents/Pages/DisplayNews.aspx?NewsID=22450&LangID=E. Accessed 1 June 2018.

UNHCR. (2007). *Iraqi's in Jordan, their numbers and characteristics.* http://www.unhcr.org/47626a232.pdf. Accessed 22 June 2018.

UNHCR. (2018). *Operational portal, situation of refugees.* https://data2.unhcr.org/en/situations/syria. Accessed 22 June 2018.

USLS (US Library of Congress). (2018). *Jordan: Religious minorities. Country studies.* Washington, DC. http://countrystudies.us/jordan/. Accessed 22 June 2018.

World Population Review: Jordan 2018. http://worldpopulationreview.com/countries/jordan-population/. Accessed 22 June 2018.

Zabad, I. (2017). *Middle eastern minorities, the impact of the Arab spring.* New York: Routledge.

Christians in Jordan

Nanneke Wisman

It is estimated that in the Hashemite Kingdom of Jordan, on a population of 10,248,069, Muslims make up 97.2 per cent of the total population while Christians make up 2.2 per cent (CIA World Factbook 2018). The majority of Muslims identify themselves as Sunni (approximately 92 per cent), reported to be the highest percentage in the world. Additional religious demographics include 0.4 per cent of Buddhists and 0.1 per cent of Hindus (Ibid.). Official statistics regarding the percentage of persons who are not adherents to any faith or who identify as atheist are not readily available.

With a few exceptions, the country knows no significant geographic concentrations of particular religious groups (Lipton 2002, p. 54); the cities of Al Husun (located 65 kilometres north of Amman, where one of the oldest Orthodox churches in Jordan was built in the second century) and Fuheis (located 20 kilometres northwest of Amman) are known to include a relatively high number of Christians; approximately 60 per cent of the population in Fuheis identify as Greek Orthodox. Karak (located 140 kilometres south of Amman, known for its crusader castle, Karak Castle) and Madaba (located 30 kilometres southwest of Amman, known as the location where the Madaba map is located in an early Byzantine church) also have significant Christian populations compared to the

---

N. Wisman (✉)
University of Sussex, Brighton, UK

© The Author(s) 2019
P. R. Kumaraswamy (ed.), *The Palgrave Handbook of the Hashemite Kingdom of Jordan*, https://doi.org/10.1007/978-981-13-9166-8_5

national average. Madaba has been described to know a "long tradition of religious tolerance (which) is joyfully—and loudly—expressed on Friday when Imams summon the faithful to pray before dawn, and bells bid Orthodox Christians to rise at first light" (Walker & Clammer 2015). Umm Al-Jamal (located less than 10 kilometres from the Syrian border) is known to have a significant Druze population as does the northern part of Azraq (located 100 kilometres east of Amman). There are also Druze populations in Amman and Zarqa and a smaller number in Irbid and Aqaba (Lipton 2002). Cities in the south of the country have the highest percentage of Muslims as compared to the national average (The Embassy of the Hashemite Kingdom of Jordan in the US 2018).

Official or reliable statistics and exact numbers on the composition of the Christian population are hard to find, but it is noted that the majority of Christians belong to historical churches, most identifying themselves as either Greek Orthodox or Roman Catholic (Latin) (CIA World Factbook 2018), which are both legally and thus officially recognised denominations. Other officially recognised Christian denominations in the Kingdom are the Anglican, Armenian Orthodox, Coptic, Lutheran, Maronite Catholic, Melkite Catholic, Seventh-day Adventist, Syrian Orthodox, and United Pentecostal churches (US Department of State 2017, p. 4). Besides, there are five Christian classifications which are not officially recognised as denominations by the government but which are registered as associations, namely the Assemblies of God, Baptists, Christian and Missionary Alliance, Free Evangelical Church, and Nazarene Church (Ibid., p. 4). Some religious factions, including Jehovah's Witnesses and The Church of Jesus Christ of Latter-day Saints (Mormons), are not officially recognised denominations (Ibid., p. 4), but these groups and factions are allowed to conduct religious services and activities without government or other outside interference.

For a religious institution to become an officially recognised denomination, they must apply for government registration through submitting documentation of its bylaws, its board, and members, budget (including foreign funding) and provide information about its religious doctrine (Ibid., p. 3). Subsequently, these documents are reviewed by the Prime Minister, the Minister of Interior, and the Council of Church Leaders (CCL), a government advisory body representing officially recognised local churches (Ibid., p. 4; see, also, Abu-Nimer et al. 2007, p. 182). The government makes reference to an exhaustive set of criteria when considering official recognition of churches, which are the following: the faith must not contradict the nature of the Constitution, public ethics, customs or traditions; the Middle East Council of Churches must recognise it; the faith must not oppose the national religion (i.e., Islam); and the group must include some (Jordanian) citizen adherents (US Department of State 2017, p. 4). It is noted that groups which the government deems to engage in practices which violate the law and the nature of society or which threaten the stability of public order are prohibited; however, in 2017, no reports were made that any religious associations were banned based on these grounds.

Jordan is famous for its rich religious history, is part of the Holy Land, and contains some of the oldest Christian sites and communities in the world, it generally being stated that Christians have resided in the area since the first century. In June 2008, archaeologists in Jordan discovered a cave under the church of Saint Georgeous in Rihab (northern Jordan), which the archaeologists believe to have been originally used both as a place of worship and a shelter by Jesus Christ's followers who fled Jerusalem following the crucifixion, making it what they believe to be the oldest Christian church in the world. The underground chapel is thought to date from between AD 33 to AD 70 (The Independent 2008). A mosaic inscription on the floor pays tribute to the "70 beloved by God and Divine." In this context, Dr. Abdul Qader Husan, Head of the Rihab Centre for Archaeological Studies, at the time of the discovery said: "We have evidence to believe this church sheltered the early Christians—the 70 disciples of Jesus Christ" (Ibid.) who are believed to have lived and practiced their faith therein secrecy until Christianity became more accepted a few centuries later when Roman Emperor Constantine the Great converted to Christianity in or about AD 312, a major turning point in the history of early Christianity.

As already evinced through events occurring centuries ago, Jordan has welcomed and hosted countless numbers of refugees which have affected the percentage of Christians residing in the country; the Christian population, for example, saw an increase with the influx of Palestinian refugees following the Arab-Israeli wars in 1948 and 1967. In 2017, the country was estimated to host 2,175,491 Palestinian refugees (CIA World Factbook 2018) who have or can avail of Jordanian nationality, due to an amendment of the Citizenship Law No. 56 (1949). Another wave of refugees occurred with the immigration of Iraqi nationals entering Jordan in the 1990s in the aftermath of the 1991 Gulf War and also following the US-led invasion in 2003; the country is currently estimated to host 66,823

Iraqi refugees. More recently, the United Nations High Commissioner for Refugees (UNHCR), as of 31 December 2017, recorded 655,624 registered Syrian refugees in Jordan of whom approximately 10 per cent practices Christianity (Jordan INGO Forum 2018). However, despite these peaks of immigration, numbers have relatively gone down; British mandatory authorities in 1921 estimated the total population to be at 230,000 persons, out of which a little less than 10 per cent identified as Christian (Wilson 1987, p. 56) compared to the current 2.2 per cent. Among reasons mentioned for the decrease in numbers are: the amount of Christians migrating to seek career opportunities abroad and falling birth rates.

It is reported that Christians are very well integrated into society, enjoying social, legal, economic, and political standing, the Jordanian electoral system, for example, confirming the number of parliamentary seats reserved for Christians. Jordan has a bicameral National Assembly which consists of the Senate (whose members are directly appointed by the King) and the House of Representatives. The House of Representatives consists of 130 seats out of which 115 members are directly elected in single- and multi-seat constituencies by open-list proportional representation vote (members serve a four-year term) (CIA World Factbook 2018). Out of the directly elected members, 21 seats are reserved for minorities: 9 for Christians, 9 for Bedouins, and 3 for Chechens and Circassians (Ibid.). Given that their demographic weight is estimated at 2.2 per cent, the Jordanian state granting Christian communities a (directly elected) representation of 7.8 per cent shows a real interest in establishing an inclusive society and ensuring that Christian community life is not only recognised but also guaranteed through institutionalisation. An example can be found in Marwan Jameel Essa al-Muasher, a Christian, who served as the country's Foreign Minister from 2002 to 2004 and as deputy Prime Minister from 2004 to 2005. From 2006 to 2007, he served as a member of the Jordanian Senate. Additionally, al-Muasher was Jordan's first ambassador to Israel and served as ambassador to the US from 1997 to 2002. Christians hold important ministerial portfolios, are appointed to serve as ambassadors and hold positions of high military rank as the government traditionally reserves a certain percentage of upper-level positions in the military for Christians. Besides, Christians hold high-level private sector positions and are represented in the media and academic world, generally more than what would be in proportion to their demographic presence. As to employment, it has been noted that employment applications for positions in government sporadically contained questions about an applicants' religious status; however, passports as well as national ID cards issued since May 2016 reportedly no longer list an individual's religion (US Department of State 2017).

Legal Framework

The Constitutional Charter of 1952 states that Islam is the religion of the State (Article 2), and Article 28(e), among other things, states that the King must be Muslim (The Constitution of the Hashemite Kingdom of Jordan 1952). Despite Islam being the country's official religion, Article 6 (i) of the Constitution specifies that "Jordanians shall be equal before the law. There shall be no discrimination between them as regards to their rights and duties on ground of ... religion" (Ibid.). More specifically, Article 14 of the Constitution stipulates that the State shall safeguard the free exercise of all forms of worship and religious rites in accordance with the customs observed in the Kingdom, "unless such is inconsistent with public order or morality" (Ibid.).

As in every country, the concept of what exactly would be considered a breach of the public order or morality is subject to change over time; one of the clearest examples of this in Jordan concerns the Islamic fasting of Ramadan. In 1960, publicly breaking fast during the holy month of Ramadan (the ninth month of the Islamic calendar) was made a criminal offence (Article 274 Penal Code 1960) punishable by up to one month in prison and/or a fine of up to 25 Jordanian Dinar (US$35). However, there is a grey area when it concerns public and private spaces, specifically when regarding the premises of private businesses and hotels frequented by tourists. In May 2018, the Ministry of Tourism announced instructions which allowed tourist facilities to work during Ramadan and provide services, but without violating the "sanctity" of the fasting month. Minister of Tourism and Antiquities Lina Annab said that the annual instructions allowed the serving of food and beverages to visitors of tourist restaurants during Ramadan, provided that such facilities are fully closed and cannot be seen from the outside (*The Jordan Times* 2018). In practice, a significant number of restaurants and hotels (including those with tourist licences) serve breakfast and lunch in Amman; when visiting as a tourist during Ramadan, it is mainly a matter of doing some internet research before going out as many restaurants appear closed from the outside.

Jordan knows a civil legal system influenced by the Ottoman and Napoleonic codes. Articles 108 and 109 of the Constitution guarantee religious communities—which are officially recognised denominations—the right to establish community courts to adjudicate issues relating to personal and family status. More specifically, judicial authority is vested in three categories of courts which are laid down in Article 97 of the Constitution, stating that the judiciary shall be divided into civil, religious, and special courts. Article 104 of the Constitution further specifies: "Religious Courts shall be divided into: (i) The Sharia Courts; (ii) The Tribunals of other Religious Communities." Matters of personal status (which includes marriage, divorce, child custody, and inheritance), in which the parties are Muslim, fall under the exclusive jurisdiction of Sharia Courts, whereas matters of personal status of officially recognised religious denominations fall under the jurisdiction of their respective courts. Civil courts have jurisdiction in cases where parties have different religions. Sharia Courts follow the Hanafi School of jurisprudence and comprise primary and appellate courts. In addition to having jurisdiction over family matters, they exercise jurisdiction over *aldiyeh* (compensation paid to the family of a murdered or man-slaughtered person) and Islamic *waqf* (religious endowment). Denomination-specific courts which have jurisdiction over personal and family status matters for non-Muslims exist for those communities whose religion is officially recognised; such courts exist for the Greek Orthodox, Roman Catholic Latin, Melkite Catholic, Armenian Orthodox, Coptic, Syrian Orthodox, and Anglican communities (US Department of State 2017, p. 6). Members of recognised religious denominations lacking their own courts must take their cases to civil courts, which, in principle, follow the rules and beliefs of the litigants' denomination in deciding cases (Ibid.). There is no concept such as a registered partnership or civil marriage, and there are no tribunals for atheists or adherents of non-recognised religious groups; these individuals have to request a civil court to hear their case (Ibid.).

Both legally and in practice, the Jordanian government is overwhelmingly tolerant of the Christian minority. One exception and repeatedly mentioned issue within the pluralistic system of different courts addressing matters of personal and family status remains the topic of inheritance matters. In this area, only Sharia (Islamic law) applies, and Sharia inheritance law is binding on the jurisdiction of the various Christian courts. Another noteworthy topic is that individuals (including Christians) are prohibited from proselytizing Muslims; the 2017 US *International Religious Freedom Report* indicates that individuals who proselytise Muslims *may* be prosecuted in the State Security Court under the Penal

Code's provisions against "inciting sectarian conflict" or "harming the national unity" (Ibid., p. 3). These offences are punishable by imprisonment of up to two years or a fine of up to 50 Jordanian Dinar (US$71) (Ibid.). Moreover, the same report states that "the Constitution and the law accord primacy to Sharia, which includes a prohibition against Muslims from converting to another religion; although conversions of Muslims continued to occur" (Ibid., p. 1). This, in practice, means that the government does not recognise conversion from Islam, and for legal purposes, such as family law and property, continues to consider individuals as being Muslim. It has been argued that, although the act of conversion out of Islam itself is not criminalised or punishable by law in any way, civil law implications of such conversions have punitive effects as conversion from Islam can lead to the dissolution of marriage, loss of custody, and exclusion from inheritance.

The generally amicable relationships among different religions in society contribute to religious freedom and vice versa. Although (an unspecified number of) incidents were reported in 2017 (US Department of State 2017, p. 11), it is noted that Christians generally do not suffer from discrimination.

Social Landscape

Jordan is a party to many human rights treaties and has signed the International Covenant on Civil and Political Rights (ICCPR) on 30 June 1972 which was subsequently ratified on 28 May 1975. Article 18(1) ICCPR states that everyone shall have the right to freedom of thought, conscience, and religion while for example subparagraph 4 of the same Article regulates that States party to the Covenant shall "(…) ensure the religious and moral education of (…) children in conformity with their own convictions" (UN GA, ICCPR 1966). Furthermore, when it comes to education, the Constitution guarantees (in Article 19) that "Congregations shall have the right to establish and maintain their own schools for the education of their own members (…)." Public schools provide Islamic religious courses as part of the basic national educational curriculum, however for non-Muslims, they are not compulsory, and they are allowed to not follow these classes (which does not mean that every non-Muslim student automatically does not follow these courses—it is really considered an individual choice). Islamic religious studies are an optional subject for university entrance exams for non-Muslim students who are enrolled in the standard curriculum or for Muslim students who are enrolled in international curricula (US Department of State 2017, p. 5).

Private schools are allowed to offer religious instruction; in several cities, including Amman, recognised Christian denominations have been operating numerous private schools and teaching religious classes with, for example, Baptist schools having been established in 1950. To set up or run a private school, religious institutions must request and receive permission from the Jordanian Ministry of Education, which ensures the curriculum given is in accordance with national rules and standards (Ibid.). By decree, Christian schools have been allowed to close on Sundays instead of Saturdays and in addition to Fridays, the national official weekly holiday (Chatelard, p. 6). Moreover, Christian civil servants are authorised to arrive at office later on Sunday to enable them to attend their respective church services. National holidays in the country are either religious (Islamic or Christian) or celebrations of important historical events. Islam being the state religion, Eid al-Adha, Eid al-Fitr, the Birth of the Prophet, the Prophet's Ascension, and the Islamic New Year are recognised as national public holidays. As to Christian celebrations, Christmas and the Gregorian calendar New Year are recognised as national public holidays.

When doing research about spending Christmas time in Jordan, all reactions of Christians being interviewed are positive with interviewees stating relations between Muslims and Christians are "positive," explaining that much of the country taps into the "secular spirit" and with many stories being shared of Christians welcoming friends and families of different religions into their households during their special events. Vice versa, many similar stories are found of Muslim families inviting Christian friends over to join their special events, with many interviewees stating these invites have nothing to do with religion, as it's all about "warmth and friendship" and "genuine Middle Eastern hospitality." Easter is a government-recognised holiday and Christians may request leave for other Christian holidays or feasts. Successive monarchs have conveyed their best wishes to the Christian communities at, for example, Easter and Christmas, King Abdullah II stating in a 2016 Christmas and New Year's speech that those occasions embodied the values of tolerance and love among followers of different religions, noting that Christians are an integral part of the Kingdom's social fabric.

There are two major institutions, sponsored by the government, which promote interfaith dialogue and understanding: the Royal Institute for Inter-Faith Studies (RIIFS) and the Royal Academy for Islamic Civilisation

Research (the Al al-Bayt Foundation). The RIIFS, established in Amman in 1994, is a non-profit non-governmental organisation (NGO) which provides a venue "for the interdisciplinary study of intercultural and interreligious issues with the aim of defusing tensions and promoting peace, regionally and globally" (RIIFS 2018). The Al al-Bayt Foundation, as one of its initiatives, has been holding Muslim-Christian dialogues since 1984 aiming to exchange "ideas and conceptions on the Arab, local and global levels, its strong impact in building bridges of confidence among the people of the dialogue, and in strengthening understanding (...)" (Al-Bayt Foundation 2018). Further evidencing the inclusive approach implemented by the state and its bodies are the efforts made by the Royal Family through actively pursuing interaction and dialogue with religious leaders and community members.

An influential and powerful example of Jordan's integrated society is found in King Abdullah II who for example in December 2017 visited baptism site "Bethany Beyond the Jordan" (or *Al-Maghtas* as it is known in Arabic, a Christian pilgrimage site commemorating the location where Jesus of Nazareth is thought to have been baptised by his cousin, John the Baptist, which is described in John 1:28-29 and 10:40 in the Christian Bible) and "affirmed the strong values of interfaith harmony and brotherhood among Muslims and Christians" in the country during the Christmas period (King Abdullah II personal website 2017). In 2015, the baptism site was added to UNESCO's (United Nations Educational, Scientific and Cultural Organization's) World Heritage list to become the fifth site in Jordan to make it to the list after Petra (1985), Quseir Amra (1985), Um er-Rasas (2004), and the Wadi Rum Protected Area (2011).

Religious Sites

The land of modern-day Jordan has been the site of significant events in the history of Christianity, as evidenced by events written throughout the Bible. Reminders of Christianity are scattered all across contemporary Jordan; the country knows more than 100 Christian and around 40 Islamic holy sites. In 2000, the Vatican officially recognised five Christian pilgrimage sites: Bethany Beyond the Jordan (Al-Maghtas), Mount Nebo (also known as Siyagha, which comes from the Aramaic word for monastery), Mukawir (also known as the Fortress of Mukawir, the site where John the Baptist was beheaded), Our Lady of the Mountain in Anjara, and Mar Elijah (Elias) (Jordan Tourism Board 2018). Jordan has subsequently been visited by Pope Paul VI (1964), Pope John Paul II

(2000), and Pope Benedict XVI (2009), with Pope Francis visiting for three days in May 2014. The official purpose of Pope Francis' tour was to improve ties with the Orthodox Church. On his trip, the Pope invited Rabbi Abraham Skorka and Omar Abboud, a leader of Argentina's Islamic community, to come with him, which can be seen as a clear message of unity and respect for each other and each other's religion. Upon arrival, Pope Francis' first appointment was al-Husseini Royal Palace in Amman, where he met with King Abdullah II (whom he already met twice before at the Vatican). In televised remarks after the meeting, the Pope paid tribute to Jordan's efforts to promote interfaith tolerance and to the fact that the relatively small nation has welcomed Palestinian refugees, and, more recently, those fleeing Syria. In his speech, he moreover called for more respect for religious freedom, calling it "a fundamental human right."

Being a country which is dedicated to religious coexistence, many holy sites are maintained for the use of pilgrims from all around the world. In recent years, the Jordanian government has been actively promoting tourism, including through highlighting religious locations and venues; as a consequence, religious tourism is one of the main drivers of tourism in general in the country. As described above, one of the foremost biblical sites includes Bethany Beyond the Jordan, lying at the end of the Jordan Valley, located approximately 9 kilometres north of the Dead Sea. In 1996, through archaeological discoveries such as pottery, coins, and architectural remains, (as well as through tales told by locals) archaeologists believed the site had been used in the early first century. It was subsequently identified as the exact site where John lived and carried out his baptisms for about 20 years, and where the first five apostles met, thus being an important location for the early foundations of Christianity. On the Baptism site, the remains of five different churches built at different times were discovered, having been built one on top of the other. Steps nearby leading down to the original water level mark the likely site of Jesus' baptism. Other remains were found, including Byzantine churches built during the fifth and sixth centuries AD. Records of different churches having remained and being rebuild throughout the Islamic periods show a history and sign of continued Muslim-Christian coexistence in the country.

Another significant site which is revered as a holy place and of vital religious importance to all three monotheistic religions is Mount Nebo, the final location in Moses' journey from Egypt to the Holy Land. From there (at 820 metres high), Moses viewed the Holy Land of Canaan which God had said he would not enter. He is said to have died there (reportedly at the age of 120 years) and has been buried in the area though the location of his burial site has never been discovered. Mount Nebo became a place for pilgrimage for early Christians from Jerusalem, and a small church was built on one of its peaks in the third or fourth century (by Egyptian monks) to commemorate the end of Moses' life. Another site worth mentioning is Madaba; the region around Madaba has been inhabited for approximately 4500 years and was one of the locations shared among the 12 tribes of Israel (said to have descended from the 12 sons of Jacob) at the time of the Exodus. After power in the region passed through different tribes, eventually, by AD 106, Romans started building streets as well as remarkable public buildings. Prosperity continued during the Christian Byzantine period, which is evidenced through the construction of churches and other facilities decorated by elaborate mosaics. Following an earthquake in AD 747, the town was deserted which remained the case until the late nineteenth century, when approximately 2000 Christians migrated from Karak to Madaba. In 1884, the new inhabitants from Karak came across the remnants of a Byzantine church when they started digging to build foundations for their houses and other buildings. Among the rubble, they discovered what is now known as the Madaba map, which is part of a floor mosaic estimated to have been crafted in AD 560. The map contains 157 captions (in Greek) depicting all the major biblical sites in the Middle East, spanning from Egypt to Palestine, thus providing many historical insights into the region. It was not until an 1896 visit of the librarian of the Greek Orthodox Patriarchate in Jerusalem that the relevance and value of the map were acknowledged; the librarian published a document with his findings following his trip which brought and continues to bring international attention to the riches of Madaba.

Though most of the sites are either explicitly Islamic or Christian, Muslims visit Christian holy sites and vice versa, and many of the sites are of relevance to different religions due to a common (religious) heritage. People of all faiths, as well as interested tourists, visit the holy sites which are related to prophets, messengers, and saints to pray, ask for blessings or support, or to obtain a deeper level of knowledge and understanding. The manner in which these sites have been and are continued to be amicably shared is yet again a powerful testament to Jordan's interfaith society and its levels of coexistence and acceptance.

References

Abu-Nimer, M., Khoury, A., & Welty, E. (2007). *Unity in diversity: Interfaith dialogue in the Middle East*. Washington, DC: US Institute of Peace Press.

Al al-Bayt Foundation, Muslim-Christian dialogue. (2018). Available at https://www.aalalbayt.org/muslim-christian-dialogue/

Central Intelligence Agency World Factbook, Jordan. (2018). Available at https://www.cia.gov/library/publications/the-world-factbook/geos/jo.html

Jordan INGO Forum, Syrian refugees in Jordan, a protection overview. (2018). Available at https://reliefweb.int/sites/reliefweb.int/files/resources/JIF-ProtectionBrief-2017-Final.pdf

Jordan Tourism Board, Religion & Faith. (2018). Available at http://international.visitjordan.com/Whattodo/ReligionFaith.aspx

King Abdullah II personal website. (2017). Available at https://kingabdullah.jo/en/news/king-meets-christian-leaders-figures-jordan-jerusalem

Lipton, E. P. (2002). *Religious freedom in the near East, Northern Africa and the former Soviet States*. New York: Nova Science Publishers, Inc.

Penal Code for the Year 1960, Law No. 16 of 1960, 1 January 1960. Available at https://www.scribd.com/document/265701032/Jordan-Penal-Code-1960

RIIFS, About us. (2018). Available at http://www.riifs.org/index.php/en/

The Constitution of the Hashemite Kingdom of Jordan [Jordan], 1 January 1952. Available at http://www.refworld.org/docid/3ae6b53310.html

The Embassy of the Hashemite Kingdom of Jordan in the US, About Jordan, Culture and Religion. (2018). Available at http://www.jordanembassyus.org/page/culture-and-religion

The Independent, World's oldest church unearthed in Jordan, 14 June 2008. Available at https://www.independent.co.uk/news/world/middle-east/worlds-oldest-church-unearthed-in-jordan-846952.html

The Jordan Times, Tourism Ministry announces Ramadan regulations for tourist facilities, 10 May 2018. Available at http://www.jordantimes.com/news/local/tourism-ministry-announces-ramadan-regulations-tourist-facilities

UN General Assembly, *International Covenant on Civil and Political Rights*, 16 December 1966, United Nations, Treaty Series, vol. 999, p. 171. Available at http://www.refworld.org/docid/3ae6b3aa0.html

US Department of State, Jordan 2017 International Religious Freedom Report. Available at https://www.state.gov/documents/organization/281234.pdf

Walker, J., & Clammer, P. (2015). *Lonely planet Jordan*. Shanghai: Lonely Planet Publications Pty Ltd.

Wilson, M. C. (1987). *King Abdullah, Britain and the making of Jordan*. Cambridge: Cambridge University Press.

Circassians

Chen Bram and Yasmine Shawwaf

The Circassians (*Sharkas* in Arabic) are an important and exceptional ethnic group in Jordan and a non-Arab Muslim elite group that is fully integrated with the wider Jordanian society and has a salient presence in civil service, army, police, as well as in free professions (law, accounting, engineering, and so on). Although a rather small minority (approximately 1 per cent of the total population), the Circassian contribution to the Hashemite Kingdom and its stability, their historical role as the founders of modern Amman and their alliance with the Hashemite court make them an emblem of modern urban Jordanian identity. At the same time, Circassians are a non-Arab minority originally from the Caucasus, who strive to maintain their cultural and national heritage and are highly involved in trans-national connections with the wider Circassian diaspora. The Jordanian Circassians are an outstanding group also from a comparative perspective: their high

---

We would like to give gratitude to Alex Kukuk and Hadas Bram for their contribution to this article.

C. Bram (✉)
Truman Institute for the Advancement of Peace, Hebrew University of Jerusalem, and Hadassah Academic College, Jerusalem, Israel
e-mail: chen.bram@mail.huji.ac.il

Y. Shawwaf
Independent Researcher, Worcester, MA, USA

© The Author(s) 2019
P. R. Kumaraswamy (ed.), *The Palgrave Handbook of the Hashemite Kingdom of Jordan*, https://doi.org/10.1007/978-981-13-9166-8_6

position in the State and society, and especially in the armed forces,[1] makes them a compelling case for minorities in the Middle East and a useful prism on modern Jordan. Their situation is different from the position of other Circassian diasporas.

This chapter will survey the historical, social, and political processes that have enabled this unusual position of the Circassians in Jordan and examine current developments and challenges that derive from their "dual" characteristics, namely being fully Jordanian but also being part of the Circassian people.

CIRCASSIANS IN JORDAN AND BEYOND

Originally native to the North-West Caucasus, the Circassians were expelled from their native homeland following the Russian colonisation of the Caucasus, and presently the majority of them live throughout the Middle East. The largest concentration of them is in Turkey, and a sizeable community is also in Syria, with many becoming refugees recently. There are very different figures as for the number of Circassians in the world. Estimations are around 3.7–5 million, with varying degree of assimilation, with the majority of them in Turkey. Jordan is one of the most important centres of Circassians in the region, and according to some estimates, there are around 80,000–100,000 Circassians in the country; while there are no credible figures, others suggest a smaller number.[2] Other small communities can also be found in Iraq and Israel. In the Caucasus, there are around 800,000 Circassians, and most of them reside in three semi-autonomous regions of the Russian Federation where the Circassian language and identity had some symbolic presence during the Soviet era, but the continuing processes of Russification have endangered this position today (Bram and Gammer 2013; Hansen 2018).

"Circassian" is a term coined by outsiders to the group that has different meanings in different contexts. The most common use of the term refers to the indigenous inhabitants of North-West and North-Central Caucasus, who call themselves *Adyghe* and *Apsua*. These are two separate people who speak differently related but not intelligible languages (the latter made up of *Abkhaz* and *Abaza*). In Turkey and other Middle Eastern

[1] For example, four Circassians had served as Chief of Staff of the army, four served as the Commanders of the Royal Jordanian Air Force, and six as the heads of the public security directorate, along with many in other high-rank positions (see also Hedges 2018, p. 34).

[2] Different estimations range from 30,000 to more than 100,000 Circassians living in the Kingdom. See Rannut (2011, pp. 6–13) for a detailed discussion of different estimates and of the motivations behind them.

locations, the term "Circassians" sometimes also refers to other Caucasian groups. In Jordan, most of the Circassians are *Adyghe*, although there are some Abaza who have lived for centuries among the *Adyghe*. The "Caucasian" minority in Jordan also consists of a smaller group of Chechens estimated at 10–20,000,[3] who maintain their different Chechen identity (Kailani and Haddad 2002).[4]

The *Adyghe* originally speak a North-West Caucasian language (Adyghe or "Circassian") which is famous for its many consonants (between 50 and 70 consonants in different dialects). As Arabic became the main language of Circassians in Jordan, they are the only minority that speaks in their native *Adyghe* language. The Circassians in Jordan, like most Circassians worldwide, are Muslims (Circassians adopted the Hanafi school of Islam, while the majority of Jordanians are Shafi'is, but these distinctions are minor).[5]

Originally, Circassians were divided into various sub-groups ("tribes"), who spoke different dialects. The most important distinction is between the various groups of the North-West Caucasus (such as *Sha'psu*, *Abzakh*, and *Bzhadugh*) and the Kabardian (*Kabartai*), a big group from Central-North Caucasus. These sub-groups brought with them different traditions, such as a class-based hierarchy among Kabardians versus a more "egalitarian" ethos among sub-groups of the North-West Caucasus. Although many of the specific differences are less relevant today, sub-divisions were, and still are, prominent among the Circassians, including the Circassians of Jordan. Different historical concentrations in Jordan are associated with specific sub-groups, and alongside cooperation, there is also an internal competition.

Circassians can be found today in all urban concentrations in Jordan. However, their historical concentrations were in a few major settlements that they founded between 1878 and 1906, namely Amman, Wadi Seer, Sweileh, Jerash, Na'ur, Sweileh, and Russeifa (Shami 2009; Watts 1984). The main concentrations of Chechens are in Al-Zarqa, Al-Sukhnah, Sweileh, and Al-Azraq (Kailani 1998).

---

[3] This number is based on Kailani (1998). It seems that most of the estimations of Circassians in Jordan also include the Chechens. Some estimations give even higher numbers, while according to Al-Bashayer (1997, cited in Dweik 2000), they are only 8776 Chechens in Jordan.

[4] Unless noted specifically, this chapter deals mostly with the Circassians. Much of the analysis—but not all of it—is relevant also to the Chechens. For this chapter, "Circassian" can be understood as Adyghe (or Abaza who live among the Adyghe).

[5] Circassians once were pagans, then adopted Christianity, and then later embraced Islam. Islamisation process started in the sixteenth century but culminated only after the colonisation and the struggle with Christian Russia.

Forced Migration and Settlement

In the second half of the nineteenth century, vast areas of the present-day Kingdom of Jordan were marginal and comparatively economically undeveloped, populated mainly by Bedouin tribes, with minimal control of the Ottoman Empire. Events that took place far away in the Caucasus created new opportunities for the Ottomans to settle the new loyal Muslim inhabitants in the area, as part of a larger attempt to develop and govern strategic peripheral areas and to consolidate and centralise the empire (Rogan 1994). This process led to the settlement of the Circassians and later influenced the impact Circassians had on the development of the State of Jordan.

A harsh resistance of the locals followed the Russian colonisation of the Caucasus in the nineteenth century. The Circassians continued their struggle even after the defeat of Imam Shamil in the North-East Caucasus in 1859. The Russian's attempt to pacify the Circassians eventually led to a genocide of Circassians and expulsion of those who were left (Richmond 2013).

Following the final battles in May 1864, mass expulsion of the Circassian population to the Ottoman Empire began (Shami 2009). The number of victims and the dynamics of these events are debated. A recent study by Walter Richmond states that around three-quarters of a million died and a similar number were expelled (Richmond 2013). An agreement was signed between Russia and the Ottoman Empire in 1864, showing that the latter was willing to accept around 50,000 Circassian refugees (Ibid). The Ottoman Empire was given more Circassian refugees than they had expected, and approximately 800,000 Circassians made their way out of the Caucasus, many of them losing their lives on the journey. While most Circassians were forced to leave their homeland, some left voluntarily in different waves of migrations; there were also various economic, political, and religious "pull factors" on the Ottoman's side that influenced this migration (Shami 2009).

The first years following the exodus from the Caucasus were characterised as a harsh situation for the refugees with plagues and death in the landing areas in Anatolia, and soon, the empire systemically settled them; first in the Balkans and Anatolia, and then, following the Balkan war and the 1878 Berlin Treaty, in the Arab part of the Middle East. The vast majority of them were settled as farmers in agricultural communities, and some men were recruited for the military which continued the Circassian tradition of Middle Eastern Empires to employ Circassians in their military that existed since the Mamluk and Ottoman periods.

Among the most concentrated areas of settlement were the Balqa region in Transjordan and the Golan Heights. These were frontier areas that were practically controlled by native Bedouin tribes who often did not obey the Ottoman rulers (Abd-el-Jawad 2006; Patai 1958). The Circassians brought with them a mixed agricultural economy with advanced techniques. They also introduced the use of bull carts and more advanced agricultural tools, and in a short time, they had changed the landscape of these semi-arid areas and built successful agrarian settlements. Following the Ottoman loss of highly critical agrarian region in the Balkans in 1878, the mobilisation of the Circassian labour force to cultivate land in Transjordan helped the Ottomans to even out their losses (Karpat 1972, cited in Jaimoukha 2001).

Initially, the relations between the Circassian settlers and the local Bedouin tribes were tense, and conflicts arose mostly around harvest time over the use of land and water. The Circassians, however, were persistent and had a high degree of social cohesion, and over time they managed to establish relatively peaceful relationships with Bedouins and brought law, order, and security to the main regions of their settlement, stabilising the Transjordan area as part of the Ottoman Empire (Lewise 1987, Shami 2009). Step by step, the Ottomans had given the Circassians settlers more critical tasks, and in 1905, the Circassian cavalry was founded. One of its functions was to protect the strategically crucial Hejaz railway, and the Circassian had a significant role in the construction of the railway.

Amman, the modern capital of Jordan, was established by the Circassians near the ruins of ancient Philadelphia. The ability of the Circassians to bring security to the area was highly relevant. The rise of Amman as the most critical urban merchant and urban centre in Jordan benefitted the Circassian population greatly (Hamed-Troyansky 2017; Abu Assab 2011). In certain areas of Amman, and in towns where they settled, the population was predominantly Circassian. Under the Ottoman era and in the early days of the Hashemite Kingdom, in many of those homogenous settlements, contacts with non-Circassians were limited and this enabled the preservation of their culture and language.[6]

---

[6] There were even some local Arabs who became quite fluent in Circassian language, which was needed for them to trade with the Circassians.

Construction of Emirate of Transjordan

The Circassian position in the Ottoman Middle East was based on their background as warriors and on their loyalty to the Sultan. Following World War I, this loyalty was replaced by an alliance between the Circassian and the Hashemite family. Two Circassian leaders–Mirza Pasha and Othman Hichmat–were among the first supporters of Emir and later King Abdullah, when he first established his rule in Transjordan in cooperation with the British.

Pasha had close connections with the Ottoman government and held high positions in the service of the empire. His shift to the Hashemites after the downfall of the Ottoman Empire paved the way for the Circassian influence in Jordanian politics. Abdullah trusted Pasha and the Circassians and granted them higher authority, status, and power in the emerging Emirate of Transjordan (Abd-el-Jawad 2006). Mirza Pasha was appointed commander over the cavalry force in 1921 (Mackey 1979) and Omar Hichmat later become minister of justice.

In the following years, the Circassians were overrepresented in the government and more so in the military forces. The decision to give the Circassians a priority and to create a special Circassian unit in the Arab Legion (*al-Jaysh al-ʿArabi-*, founded in 1923) was another critical step in building a close relationship between the Circassians and the Hashemite court. Out of the 1000 men, about 30 per cent were Circassians, showing how Emir Abdullah trusted them and used them strategically.

While being "nominally" Muslims when they arrived, they were also highly influenced by various pre-Muslim traditions in the Caucasus. During their settlement in the Middle East, the Circassians gained a more profound Muslim identity. Their loyalty to Jordan also stems from the belief that the Hashemites are descendants of Prophet Mohammed and hence are legitimate rulers. However, looking from the outside, the alliance was also based on the similarities of their structural position, which differentiate them from the local Bedouin tribes. The Hashemites had claims for historic and religious legitimacy to rule but were outsiders who migrated from Hejaz, while the Circassians were a foreign group who settled in the area, transformed it, and became locals after a struggle and even gained recognition from the local Bedouin tribes.

The 1928, numerous laws formalised these relations and symbolic statuses and strengthened the Circassian position even further. The new constitution divided Transjordan into four districts, and one autonomous territory of Circassian villages. This status established their direct connection with the monarch. Following a land survey, the Circassian ownership over their properties was secured. These steps created feelings of political security and social acceptance. Their political participation also rose, and the Hashemites had granted them with special minority status: one seat per 5000 inhabitants was reserved for Circassians in the parliament, compared to one seat per 27,000 for other groups (Mackey 1979). By 1937, 7 per cent of the government positions were held by ethnic Circassians, while they only made up for 2 per cent of the total population in Transjordan (Ibid.).

Circassians in the Hashemite Kingdom

In 1946, the Emirate of Transjordan became the independent Hashemite Kingdom of Jordan. Under King Abdullah-I, the Circassians' central position in the military and government had become even more salient. In 1950, this was manifested in the nomination of Said al-Mufti, the leader of the Karbadey Circassians, to become the first Circassian-Jordanian prime minister. Mufti, who was active as the first Circassian representative in Legislative council since 1929, was known for being loyal but still independent—meaning he would at times support the opposition against the government. His nomination was also connected to the broader political and demographic changes. Mufti thrice served as the prime minister from 1950 to 1956 and later held other posts such as the president of the Senate (1963).

The massive inflow of Palestinians into Jordan after the 1948 war with Israel had an enormous impact on the society and economy. Many Circassians became prosperous due to the dramatic increase in estate prices. Politically, the Palestinian immigrants supported Circassian political leaders, especially Said-al Mufti, and his nomination was also a strategic move by Abdullah to please the Palestinian population (Mackey 1979). The demographic changes, with waves of immigration, first from Palestine and later from Iraq and Syria, had an impact on the Circassian settlements and their neighbourhoods in Amman and they became ethnically mixed areas, where the Circassians became a minority (Abd-el-Jawad 2006). These developments intensified processes of social and cultural integration.

Anthropologist Seteney Shami has shown that presenting the Circassians as another "tribe" has enabled them to integrate into Jordanian society, which is based on Bedouin tribalism. This allowed Circassians to preserve their ethnic boundaries and distinctiveness while also integrating with the dominant Jordanian Arab culture based on tribes (Shami 1994).

In comparison to the Bedouin tribes, the Circassians are "under tribal code," and this enabled them to form different cultural organisations and to highlight the *Adyghe Khabze*—the Circassian ethos that combines customary law and social and educational codes. In this way, Circassians were not viewed as an ethnic minority but were considered full citizens with equal rights and duties but were also guaranteed freedom of cultural expression (Jaimoukha 2001). Until today, most of the Jordanian writers name the Circassians "'Asha'ir" (عشائر), which can be translated as "tribes" or "clans," rather than using the most common word for the ethnic group "Ta'ifah" (طائفة).[7] The close bond of Circassian to the regime continued under King Hussein, and many Circassians had important duties. Circassians made up 10 per cent of the whole officer corps (Hedges 2018), and in the Commando Unit, a Jordanian elite unit, they consisted of seventy to eighty per cent. Fawaz Maher, a Circassian-Jordan military commander in the 1960s, was a prominent figure who is still talked about in public discourse (Tal 2002). However, gradually, the Circassians increasingly turned towards the economic sphere and away from politics.

During the conflict with the Palestinian organisations in September 1970, the Circassians took an important role in securing the Hashemites' power. The tension between the two groups rose following the detention of two Circassian General Intelligence Directorate (GID-Jordanian intelligence) officers in 1970 near Zarqa. One of the two captives, Awni Yervas, later became the Minister of Interior (MOI) (Mackey 1979; Hedges 2018). This period still had a symbolic impact on the relations between the Circassians and Palestinians in Jordan, although in everyday life many Circassians and Palestinians have close ties and cooperation in various areas. In the 1990s, General Tahseen H. Shurdom, who was Head of Military Intelligence, Chief of Staff, and Director of Public Security, took a central position in the negotiations that led to the peace treaty with Israel. His brother, Major General Ihsan Shurdom, former Chief of the Jordanian air force and later an advisor to King Hussein, was also highly involved in forming the relations with Israel and promoting negotiations between Israel and the Palestinians (Shehori 2018).

In addition to the actual central positions that many Circassians had in the army and governmental services, their special position in the Kingdom is manifested in ceremonial guards of the Hashemites, which consist of ethnic Circassians in their traditional customs. Hussein's reign was a

---

[7] See, for example, recent article in Arabic on Circassian marriage customs in the Jordanian website "Al-Ain": https://al-ain.com/article/circassians-jordan-girl-marriage-custom

"golden age" for the Circassians in Jordan, a period when they were often described as an influential, loyal, patriotic, and wealthy group in society (Mackey 1979). Due to their apolitical stance throughout King Hussein's rule, the monarchy could rely on the Circassians and Chechens for support at critical junctures. They also encouraged Hussein during his negotiations with Israel and other international actors. Because of these negotiations, Jordan could benefit from financial packages and thus further the continuation of Hashemite rule (Hedges 2018, p. 35).

CURRENT TRENDS

The last two decades saw both continuity and changes. The Circassians still keep their privileged position, and many of them are still incorporated in prominent positions, including in the army and civil services. However, there are new developments such as the struggle of the Kingdom to adapt to the changing demography caused by the growing percentage of Palestinians and of late the Syrian refugees, which have specific impacts on the Circassians (El-Abed, 2014).

King Abdullah II pursued a policy of better integrating Palestinians into Jordanian society, and this included their integration to the civil service and even into service in the Royal Court. This came at the expense of many Circassians losing their jobs. These developments did not break the ties of the Circassian community with the Hashemites as they remained loyal to the crown (Abu Assab 2011). These new policies, however, were accompanied by new tendencies among the Circassians, and many young Circassians have tended to prefer prospective careers in the private sector, such as engineering, medicine, and business, rather than in the civil or military services (Jaimoukha 2001, p. 108).[8] Many Circassians seek advanced degrees outside Jordan, especially in fields that lead to careers in the private sectors. These economic and professional shifts also give them mobility beyond the traditional economic fields and professions that they use to hold in Jordan.

The results can be seen in the higher number of young Circassians who migrate to other states, following work opportunities, some temporarily and some leaving the Kingdom permanently. Although these trends signal a change amongst younger generations of Circassians in Jordan, it is also a persistent trend amongst other young people in Jordan who are not

---

[8] According to the interviews that we conducted, this tendency became even more salient in the last two decades.

Circassian but belong to higher and middle-class backgrounds. This can be attributed to the continuous economic difficulties in Jordan in recent decades. In the case of Circassians, many of these migrants are heading towards other diaspora Circassian communities outside of the Middle East, such as the two sizable communities in New Jersey and California in the US (Bram 2017).

These changes are still gradual, and many Circassians are still actively involved and employed by the government, especially the royal family. Politically, Circassians and Chechens also preserve their reserved seats in the parliament, which constitute of three deputies in the lower house and two senators in the upper house.[9] Their role in the economy is still much higher than their actual size as a group, and they keep the symbolic position as the allies of the ruling dynasty. Moreover, Circassians and Chechens are still overrepresented in the armed forces. "Since the Armed Forces will remain a long and trusted ally of the Hashemite monarchy, the Circassians and Chechens play a significant role within this and thus cannot be overlooked in the evaluation of the stability of the monarchy in Jordan" (Hedges 2018, p. 35). At the same time, different changes and development in Jordan–as well as in the Circassian world–bring with them new developments and dilemmas. The following sections will analyse various aspects of the current developments and characteristics of Jordanian Circassians in the twenty-first century.

COLLECTIVE IDENTITY

The Circassians in Jordan are an example of a minority that was able to build a multifaceted identity: to become fully Jordanian while maintaining their ethno-cultural and even ethno-national Circassian identity and distinctiveness. While these identities are primarily complimentary and live side by side, there are also tensions and dilemmas.

Circassians are a widely accepted and acknowledged group, fully integrated into the Jordanian society. Many Circassians describe great feelings of gratitude towards Jordan and its people as a place that welcomed them following the atrocities in the Caucasus. The agricultural background of the community led to a special connection and attachment to the land, and most Circassians view Jordan as their homeland (Abu Assab 2011),

[9] This system of representation is based on principles that were formed already in the proclamation of numerous laws in 1928.

and many even stress the role of Circassians in the foundation of modern Jordan. However, there are still complexities and tensions Circassians face regarding their multifaceted identities.

According to Anastasia Ganich (2003), most Circassians first identify themselves as Muslims and then as Circassians. Although they are a non-Arab community in an Arab State, through religion, they can feel closely connected to the rest of the population. Circassians, from this point of view, can be even described as "real Jordanians." While the bigger sectors of society (Bedouins and Palestinians) sometimes stress their affinity to their groups, Jordanian Circassians stress their loyalty and belonging first and foremost to the Kingdom itself (Ganich 2003).

At the same time, Circassians are different from the majority of Arab groups in the Kingdom, and they want to keep their separate identity. They enjoy the freedom of culture and expression, and their efforts to maintain their cultural heritage even get support from the Kingdom. One example for this support can be seen in the close relations between Prince Ali, son of the late King Hussein, and the Circassian community. The prince is known as a patron of Circassian culture and language (Jaimoukha 2001, p. 110). This attitude of the Hashemite court contributes to the appreciation of Circassians to their status in Jordan.

While the Arab majority and non-Arab Circassian minority share significant values, there are cultural differences that have led to tensions between them. Circassians, unlike Arabs in Jordan, have significant differences regarding gender relations and cultural practices. Generally, the Arab majority do not approve of gender mixing at social gatherings, especially with dancing. The Circassian cultural dances include men and women dancing with one another. Due to such practices, many Arab Jordanians believe that these events go against the values of Islam, while Circassians argue that the separation of the sexes is cultural and not a religious requirement (Ganich 2003).[10]

Many Circassians negotiate these potential tensions of their "dual-identity" by differentiating between public life, where they describe themselves as Muslim Jordanians and in private spheres as non-Arab Circassians. Nour Abu Assab claims that sometimes these two identities can lead to a

---

[10] These issues came out also in the interviews and conversations that we conducted with Jordanian Circassians.

confliction of feelings (Abu Assab 2011).[11] Ganich argued that regarding national identity, Jordanian-Circassians view themselves as Circassians who have a homeland in the Caucasus but that many identify that their future is in Jordan and that Arabic cultural identity is also inevitable (Ganich 2003).

Given the existence of confliction of identity and feelings, there are different approaches among the Circassians as for the relations between their Jordanian and Circassian identity. Circassian memory and historiography of the migration to Jordan mirrored these differences. Retrospectively, many Circassians claim that religious reasons were the primary force that drove Circassians to the area to live in a Muslim society. This religious narrative helps them to embellish the history of their community. Furthermore, the narrative of a "hijra," a religious exodus, explains why so many Circassians refer to Jordan as their homeland—a phenomenon that can be found less among other Circassian diasporas.[12]

However, other Circassians oppose the narrative and point out that the Ottoman used the Circassians as settlers and warriors solely to pursue their interest, which should not be forgotten in today's debate about Circassian identity (Shami 2009). These different trajectories among Circassians became vivid in the last decades, with the rise of a trans-national Circassian ethno-national movement.

Education, Culture, and the Ethno-cultural Identity

The Circassians in Jordan, like many other diaspora Circassians communities, developed various organisations that served to preserve their ethnic identity and avoid assimilation into Arab culture. The Circassian Charity Association, founded in 1932, was designed to be an educational and cultural organisation, operating clubs for elders and youth, a women's department, the Ahili Sports Club, a library, and an archive (Jaimoukha 2001,

---

[11] The situation among the smaller Chechen group approach is somehow different: their concentration in specific localities allows them to preserve a bigger degree of "cultural enclave."

[12] For a recent example to this approach, see recent interview (in Arabic) with the Circassian Jordanian historian Umran Khamsh, in 137 years to the immigration of Circassians to Jordan and the Middle East, an article in the website of the magazine *Raya* (written on 12 December 2015): http://www.raya.com/home/print/f6451603-4dff-4ca1-9c10-122741d17432/8e5fd30b-8e82-4234-a353-1293e34f06f7. Retrieved 26-4-2018).

pp. 109–110). The association also offers support for young Circassians to study in the Caucasus and publishes a magazine called *Nart* (named after the Circassian epic sagas) and other publications on Circassian matters, all in Arabic. The Ladies' Branch runs a school (Emir Hamza) in Amman, which aims to preserve Circassian language and culture. The Al-Jeel Al-Jadeed club was established in 1950 and patronised by Prince Ali Bin-Hussein; it promotes cultural activities, including a successful Circassian dance group (ibid.). The Jordanian *Adyghe Khase* (Xase) or Circassian association is an important social "umbrella organisation," which represent Jordanian Circassians in International Circassian organisations, such as the International Circassian Association (ICA).

While the activity of various organisations has supplied an important framework for the maintenance of Circassian society and culture, the education and the ethno-cultural identity are based foremost on the transmission of the *Adyghe Khabze*, the Circassian ethos, and code of behaviour and manners. In the past, Jordanian Circassians have excelled at maintaining the *Khabze*, and current social dynamics raise questions on its future.

The Circassians were able to keep their ethnic distinctiveness while at the same time being fully integrated to Jordanian society. However, with the geographical and generational distance from their homeland in the Caucasus, as well as social changes of late modernity, new dilemmas arise over ethnic maintenance and "management" of their multi-layer identity. Younger generations have a greater distance to their mother tongue and their cultural heritage. The exposure of younger generations to current processes of globalisation and the westernised culture that they share with other middle/higher class Jordanians of elite groups pose challenge for ethnic and cultural preservation. And indeed, although most of the marriages are still endogamous, there is an increase in inter-ethnic marriages.

The use of *Adyghe* (Circassian) language is steadily declining. There is a gap between declerations regarding the importance of the language for ethnic preservation and the linguistic behaviour and choices. *Adyghe* was mainly a spoken language (only a few intellectuals could read and write it), but currently it is principally spoken among the older generations. There are language lessons at the Emir Hamza School, but the Circassian language is not a compulsory subject, and most of the teachings are in Arabic.

Circassian activists and educators are well aware of these processes. There are different attempts to respond to these social changes. The emergence of a trans-national Circassian movement and the struggle for recognition of the Circassian genocide (see below) give an essential arena to stress Circassian identity and heritage. At the same time, in recent years, new initiatives brought to the establishment of new organisations. One example is the International Circassian Cultural Academy (ICCA) established in 2010; the ICCA aims to preserve and promote Circassian culture and heritage in Jordan. The organisation provides language classes and cultural activities, employing teachers and artists from the Caucasus. Its primary focus, however, is Circassian dance (Rannut 2011). Its establishment under the auspices of the Ministry of Culture exemplifies the ability of the Circassians to mobilise State agencies to their cause.

Another critical agent of Circassian culture is the Circassian National Adiga Radio and Television, or *Nart TV* established in 2007. Its broadcasting went through different changes in the last decade. In its beginning, the number of Arabic broadcasts was higher, but following appeals including from Circassians outside Jordan, its broadcasts now have more programmes in the *Adyghe* language, and it also has some broadcasts in Turkish, English, and Russian. Israeli Circassians are also among the audience of the broadcasting. These changes reflect the continuing emergence of a trans-national Circassian diaspora and the vital role of Jordanian Circassians in this process (Rannut 2009; Bram 2017).

Circassian Ethno-nationalism

The Circassian ethno-national movement emerged during the disintegration of the Soviet Union. The Jordanian Circassians took an active part in it, and at the same time, they were influenced by various developments that re-shaped the collective identities of Circassians and their connections to their historical motherland over the last decades (Shami 1995, 2001).

During the 1990s, the International Circassian Association (ICA) was founded, and Circassians from the various Republics in the Caucasus and different diasporas gathered in a series of national congresses in the Caucasus. The agendas included a project for cultural and linguistic revival; a struggle for more autonomy within the Russian Federation; recognition of the nineteenth-century Circassian genocide and expulsion; and the right for repatriation to the Caucasus. Russian President Boris Yeltsin's less centralistic policy enabled a political atmosphere that generated some possibilities to advance the Circassian ethno-national project. The centre of the Congress was in the Caucasus, and the leaders took a pragmatic approach, looking for ways to promote within the framework of the Russian Federation. Delegations representing Jordanian Circassian organisations took a central part in this process (Bram 2004). At the beginning of the 1990s, until the first Chechen War (1995), many diaspora Circassians had visited their homeland, and new relations were formed between the Circassians in Jordan and their counterparts in the Caucasus.

With the new political circumstances, the idea of "repatriation to Circassia" arose, and some Circassians from various Middle Eastern countries even migrated and started the processes of naturalisation in the Caucasus. Soon, however, the ideals were re-shaped by reality encounter in the Caucasus: the severe economic situation, the ethno-national tension in the region, and the degree of Russification of the homeland. Diaspora Circassians also had to admit the influence of years of separation that created silent cultural differences between them and their kin in the Caucasus. Hence, the idea of permanent return was replaced by the constitution of mutual connections. This process influenced the Jordanian identity in various ways: on the one hand, for many Circassians, it strengthened their Jordanian identity and their appreciation of their position in the Kingdom. At the same time, these processes also created a growing and salient awareness of a diaspora people, which was more covert before. The new relations with the Caucasus, however, as we will see below, were developed in coordination with the Hashemite court.

Jordanian Prince Ali was an honourable guest in the ICA Congress held in Cherkessk (North Caucasus) in 1996. Later, in September 1998, the Prince led Circassian horsemen on a journey from Jordan to the Caucasus, "to draw attention to the Circassians and their unique culture" (Jaimoukha 2001, p. 110). Jordan's involvement in Circassian affairs, however, went beyond symbolic gestures: at the late 1990s, Circassians in Jordan, and Prince Ali personally, have initiated cooperation and coordination among Circassian leaders in Jordan, Syria, Turkey, and Israel and organised a preparatory meeting in Amman between Circassian leaders in the region, in anticipation of the fourth congress of the ICA in Krasnodar in 1998. In 1999, Circassian leaders from the Middle East met again in Amman to condole with the royal family on the demise of King Hussein.[13]

---

[13] The developments among the smaller Chechen community in Jordan went to different directions, following the chaos there after the first Chechen war and even more following the second Chechen war and the fractions also among Chechens themselves. Chechens in Jordan were split between supporters of different fractions (and later supporters of Kadirov and opposition), and the problematic situation in the Caucasus had a harsh impact also on the diaspora. While analysing the court involvement, the more fragile—and hence sensitive—and even potentially danger (especially when terrorism became the last refuge of Chechen struggle) should also be taken into account.

The dynamic was dramatically changed, however, following the second Chechnya War (started in 1999) and the rise of Vladimir Putin in Russia. His centralist policy involved harsh treatment towards the local people of the Caucasus, with little differentiation between Islamic revivalism, ethno-national, and/or ethno-cultural initiatives (Bram and Gammer 2013). The Circassian republics in the Caucasus faced the difficult political and economic situation, as well as a crisis of leadership. The International Circassian Association lost its central role, and Moscow co-opted its leaders in the Caucasus. New laws and regulations practically stopped any advancement or negotiations regarding the Circassians' ethno-national aspirations (Bram 2017).

Moreover, new regulations imposed by Russia also banned the option of returning to the Caucasus for diaspora Circassian people. In this context, history and memory became the main arenas that were left for the national activists. The 21 May, already announced earlier as the Memorial Day for the Commemoration of the Circassian Genocide, became central among all the Circassian communities, including Jordan. Circassian activism started to focus more on the Russian recognition of the Genocide and activists from the various diaspora, including Jordanian Circassians, led this struggle for recognition (Hansen 2014).

Two events shaped the Circassian struggle for recognition. Following the Russian-Georgian War in 2008, Georgia opened the Tsarist archives in Tbilisi and invited historians and Circassian activists to explore their past. For the first time, Circassians now had documents showing the genocidal violence inflicted upon them by the Czarist Russian forces during the nineteenth century (Richmond 2013). The Jordanian and other diaspora Circassian activists took part in a few conventions in Georgia, culminating with the 20 May 2011 resolution of the Georgian parliament on the recognition of the Circassian genocide. A conference on the question of Genocide planned in Amman in 2012 was cancelled after Russia put political pressure on the Jordanian government (Hansen 2014).

The struggle over the question of the Circassian Genocide gained additional attention during the preparations for the 2014 Sochi Winter Olympics. Sochi was a critical Circassian centre and the last site of resistance in their struggle against the Russian colonialism. The Circassian activists in the diaspora launched the "No Sochi" campaign, with slogans such as *You'll be skiing over mass graves (of our ancestors)*, accompanied by salient graphics. This campaign enables a resurgence of ethno-national sentiments and awareness which highly influenced Jordanian Circassians.

Advocacy groups such as "Jordanian Friends of Circassians in the Caucasus" were organised and protesters gathered in front of the Russian embassy in Amman (Whitman 2014).

The Russian responses to this struggle, which involved pressures on Circassian leaders in the Caucasus and other measures, brought some disagreements among the Circassians themselves. While activists pushed the struggle against Russian approach and policy, more conservative leaders were more hesitant and feared the loss of close relations with the Circassian republics in the Russian-controlled Caucasus. The Syrian refugee crisis added more complexity; tens of thousands of Circassians became refugees, and leaders of Circassian diaspora hoped that some of them would be granted refuge in their ancestral homeland.[14] Russian policy, at the same time, seems to put pressure on Circassian leadership—by the acceptance of a minimal number of refugees and refusal to any others (Hansen 2017).

The "post-Sochi" period was marked with a downfall in the activities of the Circassian ethno-national movement, and a search for new directions. The question of the Syrian Circassian refugees became an issue on focus, but at the same time, the 21 May events continue to be central among Jordanian Circassians as it incorporates a renewed historic consciousness of their shared history. However, it is difficult to evaluate its impact beyond the circle of activists. Another outcome is growing cooperation and engagement between Circassians in Jordan and other diasporas, such as Turkey and Israel (Rannut 2009; Bram 2017). Examples are a new innovative summer camp for Circassian children from these communities, organised in different locations each year, and the performance of Jordanian Circassian dance groups in Circassian events in Israel and in Turkey. Lastly, there are increasing relations between the virtual sphere and social media.

Conclusions

The Circassians had a central and unusual position in Jordan and actively contributed to the foundation of the Kingdom. Since its early days, the Circassians were intertwined in the Jordanian politics, government, and security and are heavily concentrated in the army, police, and civil service.

---

[14] There was also a precedent—the ICA organised a "rescue" operation for Circassians in Kosovo during the war there—with Russian permit. They were brought to the Adyghe republic in the Caucasus (Bram 2004).

With time, many of them became prominent also in the private sector. The Circassians stress their Jordanian identity and loyalty to the Hashemite court. They were the founders of modern Amman, and they still constitute a significant segment in Jordanian urban society.

While these basic characteristics of the community are generally stable, there are also some developments that raise questions on current trends regarding their position in Jordan. Some commentators argue that with the demographic changes in Jordan, many Jordanian Circassians have expressed feelings of exclusion and distance from governmental positions and decision making (Slackman 2006). While Circassians are still close to the Hashemite court, some of these changes are also reflected in the response of the Royal court to the demographic changes.

At the same time, while there are some signs of influence on Circassian's position due to the changes in Jordanian society, in the last decades, they were also influenced by the emergence of Circassian ethno-nationalism and the emergence of a worldwide Circassian trans-national diaspora. To some extent, Jordanian Circassians were a part of a wider diaspora, and they never lost their symbolic connection to their homeland. However, these features of the community became much more salient. At the same time, the emergence of a "diasporic consciousness" stresses both the symbolic connection to the ancestral homeland and the strong and actual connections to Jordan.

The Circassians enjoy an exceptional status and position in Jordan considering the combination of being "fully Jordanian" in a respected position while also highlighting their specific ethno-cultural identity. At the same time, the Circassians in the twenty-first century also face challenges of ethnic and cultural preservation. The combination of increased economic success and inclusive relationships with other Jordanians has led to the social prosperity of Circassians in Jordanian society but has also raised challenges of maintaining ethnic boundaries, especially for younger generations of Circassians. The Circassian activists and leaders have launched new initiatives to resolve these challenges, and it is interesting—although not surprising—that they do it in coordination and with support from the State and the Hashemite court. Although the challenges they face are not simple, it is still too early to predict where it will lead. Finally, it is important to stress that although Circassians nowadays are part of a transnational diaspora people, they are first and foremost Jordanians, and in many respects, their history in Jordan and their place in the establishment of modern Jordan can grant them the title of "real Jordanians" not less than any other group in the Kingdom.

The close alliance and identification between the Jordanian Circassians and the Kingdom can also be a starting point to farther explorations that go beyond the specific case of this group. To some degree, it seems that the dilemmas and the processes that the Jordanian Circassians face tell us something also about broader dilemmas of collective identity and belonging, as well as of continuity and change in the Jordanian Kingdom.

References

Abd-el-Jawad, H. R. (2006). Why do minority languages persist? The case of Circassian in Jordan. *International Journal of Bilingual Education and Bilingualism, 9*(1), 51–74.

Abu Assab, N. (2011). *Narratives of ethnicity and nationalism: A case study of Circassians in Jordan*. Thesis (Ph.D.), University of Warwick.

Abu Jaber, R. S. (1989). *Pioneers over Jordan: The frontier of settlement in Transjordan, 1850–1914*. London: I.B. Tauris & Co Ltd.

Bram, C. (2004). The Circassian World Congress: Dilemmas of ethnic identity and the making of an ethno-national movement. In M. Gammer (Ed.), *The Caspian region* (Vol. 3, pp. 63–103). London: Routledge.

Bram, C. (2017, November 23–24). *Identity challenges of a diaspora minority: Lessons from the case studies of Circassians in Israel and in the U.S.A*. Paper presented at the conference: Circassians in the 21st century: Identity and survival. RUCARR at Malmö University.

Bram, C., & Gammer, M. (2013). Radical Islamism, traditional Islam and ethno-nationalism in the north-western Caucasus. *Middle Eastern Studies, 49*, 1.

Dweik, B. S. (2000). Linguistic and cultural maintenance among the Chechens of Jordan. *Language Culture and Curriculum, 13*, 184–195.

El-Abed, O. (2014). The discourse of guesthood: Forced migrants in Jordan. In A. Fabos & R. Osotalo (Eds.), *Managing Muslim mobilities* (1st ed., pp. 81–100). London: Palgrave Macmillan.

Ganich, A. (2003). *Circassian diaspora in Jordan: Self-identification, ideas about historical homeland and impact on North Caucasian developments*. Central Asia and the Caucasus. Available from http://www.ca-c.org/journal/2003/journal_eng/cac01/03.ganeng.shtml

Hamed-Troyansky, V. (2017) Circassian Refugees and the Making of Amman, 1878-1914. *International Journal of Middle East Studies* 49 (4): 605–623

Hansen, L. F. (2014). *The Circassian revival: A quest for recognition: Mediated transnational mobilisation and memorialisation among a geographically dispersed people from the Caucasus*. Københavns Universitet, Det Humanistiske Fakultet.

Hansen, L. F. (2018, May 13–14). *Ethnicity and education: Towards a renewed arena of conflict in the North Caucasus?* Paper presented at the conference "Russia in the Muslim world", Truman Institute, The Hebrew University of Jerusalem.

Hedges, M. (2018). *The role of minorities in regime security; case study of the Circassians and Chechens in King Hussein's Jordan* (Durham Middle East papers, no. 95). Durham: Institute for Middle Eastern and Islamic Studies. Retrieved June 21, 2018, from http://dro.dur.ac.uk/24395/1/24395.pdf?DDD35

Jaimoukha, A. (2001). *The Circassians: A handbook* (Vol. 6, 1st ed.). London: Curzon Press.

Kailani, W. (1998). *The Jordanian Chechens' identity between the original and host cultures: A field work among the Chechens in al-Sukhnah-al-Zarqa Districts.* Irbid: Yarmouk University.

Kailani, W., & Haddad, M. (2002). Chechen identity, culture and citizenship in Jordan. In M. Ma'oz & G. Sheffer (Eds.), *Middle Eastern minorities and diasporas*. Brighton: Sussex Academic Press.

Lewis, N. (1987). Nomads and Settlers in Syria and Jordan, 1800–1980, Cambridge: Cambridge University Press

Mackey, B. D. (1979). *The Circassians in Jordan*. Doctoral dissertation. Ft. Belvoir: Defense Technical Information Center.

Patai, R. (1958). The Kingdom of Jordan. Princeton University Press.

Rannut, U. (2009). Circassian language maintenance in Jordan. *Journal of Multilingual and Multicultural Development, 30*(4), 297–310.

Rannut, U. (2011). *Maintenance of the Circassian Language in Jordan*. IRI Language Policy Publications.

Richmond, W. (2013). *The Circassian genocide*. New Brunswick: Rutgers University Press.

Rogan, E. 1994. Bringing the State Back: The Limits of Ottoman Rule in Jordan, 1840–1910. In: Rogan, E. L. & Tell, T. (eds.) *Village, Steppe and State: The Social Origins of Modern Jordan*. London: British Academic Press.

Shami, S. K. (1994). Displacement, historical memory and identity: The Circassians in Jordan. In S. K. Shami (Ed.), *Mobility, modernity and misery: Population displacement and resettlement in The Middle East* (pp. 189–201). New York: Centre for Migration Studies.

Shami, S. K. (1995). Disjuncture in ethnicity: Negotiating Circassian identity in Jordan, Turkey and the Caucasus. *New Perspective on Turkey, 12*, 79–96.

Shami, S. K. (2001). The little nation. Minorities and majorities in the context of shifting geographies. In A. Goldman et al. (Eds.), *Nationalism and internationalism in the post-Cold War era* (pp. 103–127). London: Routledge.

Shami, S. K. (2009). Historical processes of identity formation: Displacement, settlement and self-representations of the Circassians in Jordan. *Iran & the Caucasus, 13*(1), 141–159.

Shehori, D. (2018, June 26). Peace and quiet and exports. *Ha'aretz*. Retrieved June 26, 2018, from https://www.haaretz.com/1.4727156

Slackman, M. (2006, August 10). *Seeking roots beyond the nation they helped establish*. Retrieved from https://www.nytimes.com/2006/08/10/world/middleeast/10circassians.html

Tal, L. (2002). *Politics, the military and national security in Jordan, 1955–1967*. Basingstoke: Palgrave Macmillan.

Watts, D. (1984). A Circassian quarter in Jerash, Jordan. *Urbanism Past & Present*, *9*(1), 21–29.

Whitman, E. (2014, February 22). *Jordan's Circassians balk at Sochi Olympics*. Retrieved from https://www.aljazeera.com/indepth/features/2014/02/jordan-circassians-balk-at-sochi-olympics-201421972329112257.html

PART II

Economy and Environment

Political Economy

Imad El-Anis

Jordan's survival and emergence as a stable and peaceful country have surprised many observers. Since its creation, this small desert kingdom has been regarded as less powerful, less capable, and less significant than almost all other states in the Middle East. Most of these observations have been predicated on an assessment of Jordan's political and military standing in the region. A complete evaluation of contemporary Jordan needs to take into account its political economy—indeed doing so might help to explain just how it has managed to grow into the established state that it is, albeit one that still faces many developmental and security challenges. Jordan is an important country, and it offers a fascinating case of how modern global political and economic processes interact with local political economy to shape individual states/markets. It is a small country by most interpretations and faces immense structural limitations, yet under King Abdullah II (as under his father, the late King Hussein) Jordan endures as its political economy evolves in response to an ever-dynamic set of challenges.

This chapter first discusses relevant concepts used to explain the most common challenges and limitations to Jordan's economic development. This allows us to contextualise the discussion on the critical features of Jordan's political economy in the twenty-first century. It then outlines

I. El-Anis (✉)
School of Social Sciences, Nottingham Trent University, Nottingham, UK
e-mail: imad.el-anis@ntu.ac.uk

how national policymaking is made in Jordan and how this is impacted by and in turn impacts on the main political and economic issues facing the kingdom. As a discussion of the political economy of modern Jordan would not be complete without considering energy insecurity and freshwater scarcity, the chapter then turns to these areas. Energy insecurity and freshwater scarcity demonstrate a great deal about the nature of Jordan's political economy, representing Jordan's most pressing security concerns and demonstrating the state's pragmatism in its policy responses to developmental challenges. It then moves on to a discussion of the embedding of economic neoliberalism, led by the government and King Abdullah II in particular. Neoliberal policies have become prevalent in Jordanian decision-making circles and have transformed Jordan's political economy. Final thoughts on Jordan's prospects conclude the chapter.

STRUCTURAL CHALLENGES AND LIMITATIONS TO DEVELOPMENT

For the most part, Jordan is generally regarded as a small state, and this often leads to assumptions about its economic, political, and military capabilities. Usually, this means that Jordan is a vulnerable and rather weak state that has limited domestic capacities and is primarily restricted in its ability to act on the international scene. It is essential to note that there are several ways of defining *smallness* in the context of states, and there are many competing approaches to identifying which states should be classed as small, and different ways of explaining what this means for their behaviour. One can distinguish two broad categories that are relevant to a study of the political economy of Jordan. In the first instance, scholars working in various fields, including international relations, international political economy, comparative politics, and security studies, have used material realities-based methodologies to define smallness. Here, the nature of a state is measured by focussing on observable factors such as the size of a country's territory, its overall population, size of its gross domestic product (GDP), number and technological advancement of military forces, and so on. Using this approach, one can conclude that Jordan is a small state. Jordan's total sovereign territory is only 89,341 square kilometres (for comparison, the entire sovereign territory of the US is 9,833,520 square kilometres). At the end of 2017, Jordan's population is approximately 10 million (including significant numbers of Syrian and Iraqi refugees that may add up to 1.5 million), and its GDP is approximately US$39.5 billion—only good enough to rank 91st out of 191 countries according to the International Monetary Fund (IMF). The World Bank classifies Jordan as a lower middle-income country, as is demonstrated by its relatively low US$5092 per capita income (which has remained mostly unchanged since the 2008–09 financial crisis). The Jordanian Ministry of Defence states that the Jordan Armed Forces total a little over 110,000 active personnel with approximately 65,000 personnel in reserve. Furthermore, Jordan's military capabilities are modest in terms of its equipment, although Jordan is well-regarded in the region for its counter-terrorism expertise.

The second approach to assessing smallness focuses on non-material factors including the discursive roots of smallness and the social constructs of what this means for national capabilities. Here, how national characteristics (including the material realities mentioned above) are identified and interpreted is important. If Jordan is compared with Israel using a material realities-based approach, for example, one might regard both as small states (Israel is, after all, far smaller geographically at 20,770 square kilometres and has a population of less than 9 million), yet it appears far more confident and internationally capable in its policymaking. Jordan is a small state, not necessarily because of its small geographical size, population, and economy. It is a small state because these material realities are perceived by Jordanian decision makers (and perhaps the broader population) as posing significant challenges to its development and as placing severe limitations on what Jordan as a national polity and market can achieve. Any consideration of its political economy must take this into account alongside the following structural challenges.

Jordan possesses minimal reserves of almost all of the natural resources that are essential for a modern economy to thrive. Created out of a mostly empty and barren stretch of land between the Syrian Desert and the Arabian Peninsula, this small kingdom has had to rely on supplies of fuel, food, chemicals, and metals among other products from external sources. Unlike all of its neighbours (apart from Palestine) which possess significant amounts of crude oil and/or natural gas, no such reserves have ever been found in Jordanian territory—an unfortunate and unintended outcome of how Jordan's borders were formalised under the UN mandate (Joffé 2002). Therefore, the country has had to rely on the importation of approximately 97 per cent of its energy demands from neighbouring countries throughout its history. Recent imports of oil and gas have tended to cost Jordan approximately US$3.5 billion per year—the government is the initial purchaser of fuel, which it then sells on to the domestic market.

Crude oil, totalling approximately 108,000 barrels per day, has traditionally been imported from Iraq, Saudi Arabia, and Kuwait (with Iraq being the most significant supplier of oil in the 1990s and early 2000s until Iraqi production was halted after the US-led invasion and occupation). In more recent years, natural gas from Egypt has formed the mainstay of Jordanian energy imports and has amounted to 2.72 billion cubic metres per year. Energy security and its role in the broader political economy of Jordan are discussed further below.

Perhaps the most pressing resource scarcity faced by Jordanians is the lack of freshwater (Cammett et al. 2015, pp. 199–229). The UN designated freshwater poverty line is 1000 cubic metres per person per year, yet Jordan only possesses 123.4 cubic metres per person per year of renewable freshwater resources. In other words, the amount of renewable freshwater supplies available for drinking, food production, industry, and household use is not enough to maintain a high quality of life. The UN's Food and Agriculture Organisation ranks Jordan as one of the five most freshwater poor countries in the world. Most precipitation and all of the major river systems (for example, the Jordan River) are found in the north-west of Jordan, and approximately 85 per cent of Jordan's territory receives very little or no rainfall at all. This limits the amount of arable land available for use, and that which is available is increasingly being lost to urban sprawl (with the majority of people living in Jordan found in the north-west, mainly because that is where the limited freshwater sources are located) and degradation due to overuse and pollution. Industrial production is also hindered by the lack of available freshwater for manufacturing processes.

An oft-overlooked or downplayed structural limitation to Jordan's development is unemployment *and* underemployment. The official unemployment rate recorded by the Jordanian government is 16.5 per cent (2017) of the total working-age population. This is a relatively high rate in itself and results in two profound and seemingly insurmountable problems. First, a significant proportion of the population is unable to earn a living wage to support themselves and their dependents which hinder efforts at both poverty alleviation and human development. And second, it means that the Jordanian labour market is saturated which drives down salaries—this inescapable fact is evident around the world where there is a surplus of labour. One can also question the official government figures on unemployment as it may be advantageous to report lower than real levels of unemployment as observers in Jordan form opinions on governmental performance. Unofficial estimates put the unemployment rate at closer to 30 per cent.

Furthermore, the problem of underemployment is rarely considered and is not often reported. Out of the 83.5 per cent of the working-age population (2017) that are regarded as being employed, a significant number (although no official figures exist) are likely to be employed in only seasonal, casual (day-to-day), or part-time work, meaning they have little job security, and more often than not, meagre incomes. These dual problems of unemployment and underemployment are compounded by the lack of social welfare in Jordan. The government does not offer those who are unemployed, for example, sufficient support, and because of the very constrained national budget, as Jordan has long run a budget deficit, which in 2017 stood at US$2.653 billion, equivalent to 6.5 per cent of GDP. In other words, the Jordanian state is not rich enough to provide its citizens with a sufficient social welfare safety net. Unemployment and underemployment pose even more serious obstacles to development when, in 2017, the age of approximately 55 per cent of the population was recorded as below 25 years, and unemployment and underemployment are most prevalent in the 15–30 year age range. Jordan has an expanding, young, and educated population that faces increasingly inadequate avenues for employment.

Poverty in Jordan is an enduring problem, with 2017 estimates suggesting that 14.2 per cent of the population lives below the poverty line (which the World Bank puts at US$1.90 per person per day). Again, this already high figure is likely to be slightly conservative. A significant proportion of Syrian refugees in Jordan are unlikely to be recorded in official surveys of household poverty, for example. A large proportion of the population remaining below the poverty line leads to significant structural limitations of the economy. In the first instance, those living below the poverty line are primarily restricted from developing their human capital, for example, by not having access to suitable education and training. Furthermore, a substantial proportion of the population lives just above the poverty line and can be severely impacted by economic turbulence both at the domestic level and in the broader global economy. This happened in the aftermath of both the 1989 Jordanian financial crisis and the 2008–09 global financial crisis and recession, where spikes in households living below the poverty line were witnessed.

Since the 1970s, the government has attempted to reduce poverty levels, but Jordan has an enduring budgetary deficit problem leaving little resources to combat the root causes of poverty effectively. The government's budget has been further affected by the adoption of neoliberal economic policies and their accompanying macroeconomic structural adjustments (such as cutting subsidies on basic foodstuffs and fuel). They have been driven both by domestic factors (King Abdullah II, for example, has been supportive of Washington Consensus neoliberal economic policies) and external forces (for example, the IMF and World Bank which have supported the Jordanian government financially since 1989 but have demanded wide-ranging reforms in return that focus on reducing government expenditures).

Jordan's situation is also problematic due to its persistent trade deficit which it has experienced for much of the past few decades. Since 2000, each year has seen a significant deficit in Jordan's current account with year-on-year growth in this deficit seen between 2002 and 2014. Increases in hydrocarbon prices, as well as many consumer prices on the global market, have seen Jordan's trade deficit climb to over US$8.05 billion in 2016, up from US$2.26 billion in 2000 (see Table 1 below). These two deficits (budget and trade) have been offset to an extent by official external aid and grant support coming from donor states and international organisations. This form of external income has grown from US$550 mil-

Table 1 Macroeconomic indicators (budget deficit, trade deficit, and external aid and grant income)

Year	Budget deficit (percentage of GDP)	Trade deficit (US$ billions)	Aid and grant income (US$ billions)
2000	+1.14	−2.26	0.55
2001	+1.04	−2.25	0.45
2002	−0.67	−1.83	0.56
2003	+1.41	−2.14	1.32
2004	+1.49	−3.4	0.6
2005	−2.79	−5.15	0.71
2006	−4.2	−5.01	0.57
2007	−5.1	−6.31	0.63
2008	−2.2	−6.53	0.73
2009	−8.9	−5.4	0.74
2010	−5.6	−5.49	0.95
2011	−6.8	−7.56	0.97
2012	−8.3	−8.67	1.58
2013	−5.5	−9.94	1.4
2014	−2.3	−9.46	2.7
2015	−3.5	−8.6	2.15
2016	−3.2	−8.05	2.74

Source: World Bank Data Bank; IMF; Government Finance Statistics Yearbook

lion in 2000 to over US$2.74 billion in 2016 (growth that has somewhat mirrored the government's growing budget deficit). The US is the largest donor to the Jordanian government with US aid totalling US$1.522 billion in 2017 (the US aid to Jordan has consistently topped US$1 billion in recent years). Overall, the twin deficit problem coupled with high levels of foreign assistance has increased Jordan's dependence on external actors for its economic well-being.

POLITICAL AND ECONOMIC POLICYMAKING IN A REFORMIST MONARCHY

Since independence, Jordanian politics have ebbed and flowed in different directions with national interests, national institutions, foreign and domestic policies, and the politics of decision-making changing over time. In some ways, governance in Jordan has also been remarkably consistent. King Abdullah I (ruled 1946–51) oversaw the emergence of Jordan as an absolute monarch (Salibi 1998, pp. 73–91), but governance in the early era was also characterised by an appreciation of the importance of dialogue with established communities (namely the East Bank tribes and small Circassian community centred around Amman) that would come to form the backbone of monarchical support (Ryan 2002). By no means did engaging with local communities equate to a transparent and accountable government, although Jordan did have a functioning parliament in the 1940s and 1950s which had, by the regional standards of the time, relatively significant powers and functions.

Governance has continued to reflect this original structure, and since the late 1980s, in particular, the Jordanian government has engaged with political reforms aimed at satisfying an increasingly restless and demanding population that seeks greater governmental accountability and greater representation for the masses. These attempts at *democratisation* (there are many forms of democratic governance, and the Jordanian conception of democracy may differ to that of other communities) have had a mixed record and have taken place at varying speeds and with significantly different levels of governmental sincerity. In 1989, for example, in the wake of the most damaging economic downturn in Jordan's history up to that point King Hussein orchestrated essential reforms allowing for the legalisation of more political parties, the holding of free and fair elections, and the re-establishment of parliament. However, these reforms were almost entirely rolled back by the mid-1990s in the wake of the Iraqi invasion of Kuwait on 2 August

1990, the subsequent UN-sanctioned war to liberate Kuwait in 1991, and the emergence of the Palestinian-Israeli and broader Arab-Israeli peace process. These events had a galvanising effect on large parts of Jordanian society which subsequently meant that politics in Jordan became less predictable. Under these circumstances, King Hussein and most of those in government argued (Robins 2004, pp. 187–190) that greater political stability was needed to steer the country through such a difficult time.

By the time King Abdullah II ascended to the throne in February 1999, there was once again significant pressure from the street for political reform that would allow for ordinary Jordanians to participate in governance at the local and national levels. King Abdullah II has been regarded as a *reformist* leader who has pursued political reform. However, his democratic credentials have not been free from criticism and observers have claimed that under his reign Jordan has at best formed a democratic façade, and at worst, become an entrenched police state with the discourse of political reform used to placate external backers like the US and European Union members (Ryan 2014). King Abdullah II inherited a kingdom that, for the first time since the 1940s, had engaged in political reform (during 1989–91) and which had a population that had gained significant experience in civil society activities through the 1990s. Given the domestic and international political and economic challenges discussed above and later in this chapter, political reform in Jordan has faced many obstacles and there has been a great deal of uncertainty in Jordanian politics.

As stated above, one can identify some consistencies in governance in Jordan. In particular, virtually since independence, budgetary stability has been directly tied to regime survival. In short, securing sufficient funds to pay the government's bills year-on-year has perhaps been the most immediate consideration of consecutive governments and the monarchy itself (Brand 1994). It is quite easy to argue that socio-economic interests have been subservient to more traditional notions of national security, regime survival, and regional stability. However, it is more accurate to note that—especially given the accelerating processes of globalisation, regional economic transformation, and the changing socio-economic characteristics of society itself—the regime has long been focused on political economy-oriented domestic and foreign policymaking that has at its heart, budgetary security and regime survival. Directly informing these two considerations are energy security, freshwater security, and the modernisation of the Jordanian economy through the creation of a *business-friendly* and competitive environment.

Energy Insecurity and Policy Responses

Jordan's lack of resources has made it energy insecure. Soon after King Abdullah II ascended the throne in 1999, the government began to formulate policies to diversify its energy supplies by importing its fuel needs from several sources at one time, rather than maintaining the long-standing policy of relying on bilateral agreements with neighbouring states. This change in policy has mostly been unsuccessful. Iraq through the 1990s, for example, supplied Jordan with almost all of its crude oil needs at heavily discounted prices well below market prices in return for Jordanian political and economic support. Aqaba, Jordan's only port, for example, was used as the main entry point for goods destined for the Iraqi market while Basra, Iraq's main port, was inoperable.

Jordan's energy vulnerability stems not only from its lack of domestic energy sources but also from its over-reliance on single external sources in which the Jordanian government has had very little ability to influence the stability of its energy supplies. The government vociferously protested against the build-up to the 2003 Iraq war on humanitarian and legal grounds. At the same time, rather quietly, but more whole-heartedly, it protested because such a war would likely severely damage the Jordanian economy, not the least through cutting off its energy supply and forcing consumers in Jordan to pay global market prices for fuel. Of course, the government was unable to affect the outbreak of the war, and the economy was subsequently negatively impacted by soaring fuel bills.

Within a few years, the government had signed an agreement with Cairo for the purchase of Egyptian natural gas in large quantities through the so-called Arab Peace Pipeline that runs through the Sinai Peninsula and branches out to Israel and Jordan. The government also invested heavily in converting Jordan's power plants from oil-based to gas-based power generation.

But this attempt to switch from Iraqi oil to Egyptian gas also proved fragile and did little to alleviate Jordan's energy insecurity. The preferential agreement signed between Jordan and Egypt came under heavy scrutiny following the fall of the Mubarak regime in February 2011. At the heart of the matter was the concern Egyptians had about the fact that Jordanians were paying less for Egyptian gas than Egyptians themselves were being charged. Through the first half of 2011, the Jordanian and Egyptian (transitional) governments sought to renegotiate the terms of the agreement, concluding in July 2011 a new deal stipulating that Jordan would receive supplies of Egyptian gas for 12 years, but at a higher price than had been agreed in the previous treaty. However, Jordan's vulnerability to external shocks was once again demonstrated following the new agreement when a series of bomb attacks on the gas pipeline in the Sinai Peninsula led to persistent halts in gas supplies to Jordan—which the government estimated cost the economy upwards of US$3 million for each day that the supply was shut off. Since 2012, Egyptian natural gas supplies have been somewhat more stable, but confidence in Egypt as a stable supplier of energy has dwindled because of instability in the Sinai Peninsula which has repeatedly hindered gas supplies through the pipe network there. The post-2011 Egyptian governments' reneging on previous agreements encouraged the Jordanian government to pursue other ways to secure its energy needs.

Jordan's experiences of the Arab Spring in 2011 also affected energy security. While Jordan did not face the same levels of instability experienced in Tunisia, Egypt, Libya, and Syria, the pro-democracy/opposition movement did place sufficient pressure on the government to encourage it to act on political and economic reforms. King Abdullah II was compelled to engage in serious dialogue with a wide range of segments of Jordanian society. At the very centre of the Jordanian Arab Spring experience was the demand for better living conditions, better pay, more jobs, and a better general economic situation. These demands remain and are evident in the concerns of ordinary Jordanians is the rising price of food and fuel. The government finds itself between the proverbial rock and hard place, faced with pressure for lower fuel prices (from electricity to fuel for cars) from a restless population, and the high cost of externally-sourced fuel.

King Abdullah II views securing Jordan's energy supplies as of the greatest importance. He has consistently directed the government to develop policy responses that will ensure Jordan has stable, reliable, and reasonably priced supplies of energy for the long-term (El-Anis 2016, pp. 528–547). The resulting policy direction has been to develop domestic sources of energy. Jordan is hugely resource scarce and does not possess any crude oil and has negligible reserves of natural gas. While there are some supplies of shale oil, estimated at over 65 billion tons, these are currently not readily recoverable in large quantities at viable prices. Renewable energy initiatives have been developed and both the public and private sectors have shown some encouraging signs; for example, in November 2017, the government coordinated with the German government to oversee the completion of the world's largest solar power plant within a refugee camp. When the 12.9 megawatts solar plant became operational, the Zaatari refugee camp housed over 80,000 Syrian refugees. In the same month, the technology group Wartsila signed an agreement to build Jordan's largest photovoltaic solar plant—a 52-megawatt plant just to the East of Amman. Overall, renewable energy is set to constitute 10 per cent of Jordan's total energy mix by 2020.

Wind energy is still in relative infancy, but there are plans to expand on the country's three current wind farms. These are located at Ibrahimya (a 0.32-megawatt plant 80 kilometres north of Amman), Hofa (a 1.125-megawatt plant 92 kilometres north of Amman), and Tafila (a 117-megawatt plant south of the Dead Sea that provides energy for approximately 83,000 homes). Solar power in Jordan is more developed with many smaller settlements and rural communities using off-grid photovoltaic systems for household use (for example, electricity, water pumping and heating) and a substantial number of private and public residential and business buildings are equipped with solar water heating systems. Highlights from the government's current Energy Master Plan include a plan to ensure that up to one-third of all residences in Jordan will have solar water heating systems by 2020; all mosques in the country are to be fitted with solar panels; and seawater desalination using solar power will be established.

Even though Jordan's renewable energy sector is expanding, King Abdullah II has strongly advocated the development of nuclear energy to meet Jordan's needs in the coming decades. The atomic energy policy began in earnest on the 1 April 2007 with the announcement by then-Energy Minister Khaled Sharida that Jordan was going to tender bids to build its first nuclear power plant to produce electricity. The programme has since developed a pace and the government now plans to build five nuclear reactors by 2040. Committee for Nuclear Strategy established in 2007 plans for nuclear energy to account for 30 per cent of the total energy mix by 2030, but with current production plans and estimations for energy demand, Jordan could produce almost half of its electricity demand in the coming decades by nuclear power. By 2019, however, Jordan's nuclear energy programme was suspended despite significant progress being made in its development.

In 2015, the government signed an agreement with the Russian government to contract the latter's Rosatom State Nuclear Energy Corporation to build a US$10 billion twin-reactor power plant. The plant is set to be completed by 2025 at which point it will supply Jordan with 2000 megawatts of electricity (out of an estimated total demand of 8000 megawatts). The nuclear energy programme was buoyed by the discovery of at least

40,000 tons of uranium ore in central Jordan (a figure that the Jordan Atomic Energy Commission estimates may be as high as 300,000 tons). It was anticipated that the excavation of this ore along with the operation of nuclear power plants could make the country more energy independent and secure by not having to rely on external sources of energy entirely.

Freshwater Scarcity

As mentioned above, resource scarcity is a fundamental feature of Jordan's political economy, and freshwater scarcity is the most pressing issue facing Jordanian decision-makers and ordinary citizens on a daily basis. Jordan's freshwater supplies stand at approximately 1.62 billion cubic metres per year of internal and external renewable freshwater which equates to 123.4 cubic metres per person per year (down from around 164 cubic metres in the mid-2000s). Freshwater scarcity is worsened by the fact that the limited available resources are, for the most part, not sovereign and are instead shared with neighbouring states. The Jordan River system, for example, is one of the most significant above-ground sources of freshwater and is shared with Israel and Palestine. The river's over-use upstream has reduced its flow downstream to the extent that, by August each year, it virtually dries up before it reaches the Dead Sea. Since the 1960s, rapidly growing demand due to population growth and increased agricultural and industrial activity has resulted in the River's over-exploitation (Venot et al. 2008, pp. 247–263). For Jordan's part, the creation of a series of dams on the smaller tributaries has unsustainably reduced the size and flow of the River and contributed to the lowering of the Dead Sea by up to a metre per year. This experience is being repeated across Jordan where above-ground and below-ground freshwater resources are being unsustainably exploited.

The government does seem to acknowledge that current practices are leading to the exhaustion of available freshwater sources (many of which are non-renewable) yet given the severe shortage of this resource and the already well-below global average consumption of freshwater, there seems little option but to seek ways of making freshwater consumption more efficient and finding alternative supplies. Through the Ministry of Water and Irrigation, the government has developed a set of policy responses to its freshwater scarcity problem. Some policies are entirely domestic in focus and centre on increasing efficiency of use and maximizing the availability of existing freshwater sources in Jordan. These have a direct impact on both household and private sector consumption practices. For example, since the mid-2000s, the government has increased efforts to improve wastewater management and reuse. By collaborating with national and foreign private sector actors, the government has developed the use of modern technologies to collect and treat wastewater from urban, industrial, and domestic use. The Wastewater Management Policy calls for the use of treated wastewater rather than unused freshwater for agricultural and industrial processes, freeing up higher quality freshwater sources for domestic and urban use.

In a similar approach to Jordan's energy security problems, the government is also developing long-term and large-scale infrastructural projects to increase its freshwater supply. Central to these plans is the principle of maximising sovereign control of these freshwater sources. Two central tenets are evident in these plans: first, the exploitation of large underground aquifers, and second, desalination of seawater to produce freshwater. In the case of the former, the Disi Aquifer water conveyance project is useful to consider. The Aquifer is in the south of Jordan and stretches underneath the border with Saudi Arabia. It is an ancient fossilised aquifer and Jordan's share, as agreed with Saudi Arabia, is an estimated 2.2 billion cubic metres of freshwater. The conveyance project was inaugurated in 2013 and consists of a pipeline system with pumping stations to take the freshwater from the south up to Amman and its surroundings. The project cost over US$1.1 billion to complete and supplies Amman with 100,000 cubic metres of freshwater per year. Turkey's GAMA, a large private sector construction firm, constructed the project given a lack of technical know-how and capabilities in the Jordanian private sector. It must be noted that as a fossilised aquifer and a non-renewable source, it does not represent a long-term solution to Jordan's freshwater scarcity problem.

The government's focus on desalination of seawater may offer a more sustainable response. As part of the 1994 Treaty of Peace between Israel and Jordan, an integrated plan for the development of the Jordan Rift Valley was agreed upon. This plan included the creation of a water conveyance system to take seawater from the Red Sea at the Gulf of Aqaba, desalinate it, and pump freshwater to the primary population centres in Jordan, Israel, and the West Bank. This plan has not materialised; however, there has been a great deal of groundwork completed to date. Feasibility studies have been completed, design plans have been developed, and funding sought. Given the political tensions that remain between Israel and Palestine and the failure to fully normalise relations between Jordan and Israel, the multilateral project has mostly stalled. In its place, Jordan has begun construction of its own, somewhat smaller, desalination facility—the project which involves intake of seawater at Aqaba—with a projected capacity of 65–85 million cubic metres per year, a conveyance system and hydropower plant (to help power the energy-intensive desalination process). While the desalination of seawater will add to Jordan's overall energy demand, the government sees the sustainable domestic production of freshwater as essential to the country's future.

Neoliberal Economic Policies

In the 1970s and 1980s, King Hussein was slightly hesitant to implement neoliberal economic reforms and preferred instead to balance capitalism with a form of Arabist patrimonialism. He was also never focussed on economic policies, dedicating his adept abilities towards foreign policy (Shlaim 2008, pp. 63–64). At times, he played a pivotal role in domestic financial affairs when needed, and he was eventually encouraged to adopt neoliberal economic policies bringing the economy more in-line with global capitalist practices. This move came with the decline of oil prices in the early 1980s and the subsequent economic downturn in Jordan. In the 1980s, much like today, the economy relied substantially on worker remittances, investments, aid, and other forms of financial support from the hydrocarbon-rich Gulf monarchies (Robins 2004, pp. 141–146). When the price of oil declined, so too did the flow of financial resources coming into Jordan from these states.

By 1989, the budget crisis had worsened to the extent that Jordan had defaulted on its international debt repayments leading King Hussein to approve the implementation of a Structural Adjustment Programme (SAP) demanded by the IMF to receive financial support to help Jordan balance its books. This SAP signalled the embedding of neoliberal economic policies, and in effect, King Hussein had set the path towards neoclassical economic policies, and these have shaped the economy ever since. Since 1999, King Abdullah II has deepened economic neoliberalisation, and unlike his father, who approached policymaking in a more creative manner, relying on charisma and his own experiences, King Abdullah II has placed more emphasis on neoliberal economic practices inspired in part by the time he spent being educated and working in the UK and the US before his ascension, and by a range of Jordanian and foreign advisors. Under his reign, successive Jordanian governments have advocated making Jordan a *business-friendly* environment and encouraging businesses to become more competitive to help the Kingdom to modernise, industrialise, and develop into a more prosperous and affluent society.

During the first decade of his reign, King Abdullah II proposed several economic reforms that built on the neoliberal project begun in the latter stages of his father's reign. Since 1999, there have been three main thrusts of neoliberal economic reform pursued in Jordan (Knowles 2005, pp. 163–205); these are, macroeconomic structural adjustment; privatisation of national assets; and liberalisation of foreign trade. The macroeconomic restructuring has been guided by SAPs designed by the IMF and World Bank as part of the conditions for financial assistance to Jordan. These adjustments have allowed Jordan to service its external debt, although overall debt remains high at US$27.72 billion (2017), equivalent to over 86 per cent of GDP. Jordan is committed to reducing its external debts, and under King Abdullah II, further economic restructuring has taken place to pursue this goal.

Unlike the SAP and macroeconomic reforms implemented in the early 1990s which sought economic stability rather than growth, more recent policy reforms have aimed at achieving the latter. Reducing subsidies for food and fuel and replacing them with subsidisation that targets those most in need of it, for example, has allowed the government to reduce its budget deficit while at the same time promote local market growth through higher profits for food and fuel producers. The government has traditionally maintained relatively high rates of subsidisation for fuel (primarily petroleum) and basic foods (in particular, bread, through wheat flour subsidies) for all consumers. In recent years, petroleum subsidies cost Jordan between 6.8 per cent (2007) and 8.8 per cent (2012) of the government budget, while food subsidies have approximately accounted for a further 18.9 per cent (2005) and 3.8 per cent (2010) of the budget.

In early 2018, the government ended subsidies on flour to help stabilise the country's finances. The price of bread products subsequently increased by 60–100 per cent in the first quarter of 2018. Fuel subsidies were cancelled in 2012 helping to lead to an increase of one-third in fuel prices paid by consumers. Previous attempts at liberalising Jordan's government expenditures led to "bread riots" in 1996 and a large number of anti-government demonstrations in 2011–12. The privatisation of government-owned enterprises and service industries has been widespread since the early 2000s and has helped the government to raise revenue to service external debts and to rebalance the role and scale of the public sector in the economy (El-Said and Becker 2001). The Executive Privatisation Commission was established in 1996 to oversee the sale of national assets in several sectors, including construction, telecommunications, transport, energy and agriculture. Among the most important goals of the programme have been increasing efficiency and productivity, attracting FDI (foreign direct investment), and reducing the government's role in the economy to that of a regulator. The privatisation programme has led to over 70 transactions, including the sale of the government's shares in over 50 companies. By the end of 2017, the total proceeds of the privatisation programme are approximately US$3 billion, and total domestic and foreign investment had surpassed US$1 billion.

In addition to designing SAPs, the IMF, World Bank and World Trade Organisation (WTO) have also encouraged the government to liberalise its foreign trade. Free trade has been popular from the King down. Since the late 1990s, Jordan has liberalised its international trade to attract investment, increase Jordanian exports, and reduce domestic consumer prices. King Abdullah II has been a strong advocate of free trade and has overseen six main facets to the government's programme of trade liberalisation; accession to the WTO in 2000; Jordan-Europe Free Trade Association free trade agreement (FTA) of 2002; Jordan-EU Association Agreement (JEUAA) of 2002; the implementation of the 1997 Greater Arab Free Trade Area agreement (GAFTA); Mediterranean Arab Free Trade Area agreement (MAFTA), also known as the Agadir Agreement of 2004; and several bilateral free trade agreements such as the Jordan-USA FTA (2000) (El-Anis 2011), Jordan-Singapore FTA (2004), Jordan-Turkey FTA (2011) and Jordan-Canada FTA (2012). Their impact on foreign trade has been mixed with gains seen in some sectors and with some trade partners (especially increases in textiles and apparel exports to the US, pharmaceutical exports to Saudi Arabia, Egypt and Libya, and increases in machinery imports from Germany, Italy, and the US), little change seen in other cases (for example, Jordan's Association Agreement with the EU has had limited impact with trade remaining under US$4.2 billion in 2007 and US$5.8 billion in 2016), and declines in trade with some partners (for example, trade with Singapore declined from US$132.86 million in 2015 to US$118.3 million in 2016).

On the whole, however, data from Jordan's Ministry of Industry, Trade and Supply shows that Jordan's exports of textiles and clothing, pharmaceuticals, and phosphates have increased dramatically, while its imports of machinery, transportation equipment, and high-tech consumer products

Table 2 Jordanian exports, imports, and trade deficit values (US$) since 2000

Year	Exports (millions of US$)	Imports (millions of US$)	Deficit (millions of US$)
1990	922	2581	1658
1995	1444	3721	2277
2000	1265	4597	3331
2005	4301	10,492	6191
2010	5939	15,562	9623
2015	6757	20,466	13,709

Source: IMF Direction of Trade Statistics database. http://www.imf.org/en/Data

have also increased. Free marketeering has not resolved Jordan's persistent trade deficit problem. It has, perhaps, contributed to it with the Kingdom now running an annual trade deficit of just under US$10 billion in 2017 (Table 2).

Conclusion

Given the challenges facing Jordan's political economy in the twenty-first century, it is safe to say that it will remain a small state that will have to continue to respond to processes which are mainly out of its control. From budgetary insecurity and high unemployment levels to energy security and freshwater scarcity, Jordan's policymakers, as well as the ordinary citizen on the streets, will have to constantly create solutions to problems that are not necessarily of their making. Macroeconomic restructuring and neoliberalisation in Jordan have had mixed results and are not universally popular. While some have benefitted from the economic transformation since the 1990s, many more have been left behind—an experience noticeable around the world, and demonstrated at the national level by Jordan's budget and trade deficits. Poverty levels remain stubbornly high, per capita incomes have stagnated since 2008–09, and Jordan's youthful population is increasingly frustrated and restless due to a lack of job and other opportunities. The scarcity of the most critical resources in Jordan is a long-term challenge and the government's responses entail long-term and large-scale infrastructural projects which will not bear fruit for some time. And even when they do, growth in the demands for energy and freshwater, for example, may have surpassed even the most pessimistic current estimates, leaving Jordan perennially facing insecurity in these areas. With all of these considerations in mind, the political economy of modern Jordan also tells us that it is an enduring country, one that is faced with what may appear to be insurmountable obstacles, only for it to continue to survive and evolve. In some ways, therefore, the story of Jordan's political economy is one of resilience as much as it is one of challenges.

References

Brand, L. (1994). *Jordan's inter-Arab relations: The political economy of alliance making*. New York: Columbia University Press.

Cammett, M., Diwan, I., Richards, A., & Waterbury, J. (2015). *A political economy of the Middle East* (4th ed.). Boulder: Westview.

El-Anis, I. (2011). *Jordan and the United States: The political economy of trade and economic reform in the Middle East*. London: I.B. Tauris.

El-Anis, I. (2016). Explaining the behaviour of small states: An analysis of Jordan's nuclear energy policy. *Cambridge Review of International Affairs, 29*(2), 528–547.

El-Said, H., & Becker, K. (2001). *Management and international business issues in Jordan*. Binghamton: International Business Press.

Joffé, G. (Ed.). (2002). *Jordan in transition: 1990–2000*. London: Macmillan Press.

Knowles, W. (2005). *Jordan: A study in political economy*. London: I.B. Tauris.

Robins, P. (2004). *A history of Jordan*. Cambridge: Cambridge University Press.

Ryan, C. (2002). *Jordan in transition: From Hussein to Abdullah*. London: Lynne Rienner Publishers.

Ryan, C. (2014). Jordanian foreign policy and the Arab Spring. *Middle East Policy, 21*(1), 144–153.

Salibi, K. (1998). *The modern history of Jordan*. London: I. B. Tauris.

Shlaim, A. (2008). *The Lion of Jordan: The life of King Hussein in war and peace*. London: Penguin.

Venot, J., Molle, F., & Courcier, R. (2008). Dealing with closed basins: The case of the lower Jordan River Basin. *International Journal of Water Resources Development, 24*(2), 247–263.

Environmental Challenges

Moshe Terdiman

At present, the Middle East is facing five main environmental security challenges, namely, water security, energy security, food security, desertification, and land degradation. These challenges are exacerbated by the rapid population growth and severe droughts. All these factors together make life in the Middle East more difficult and harder to deal with. Jordan is no exception, and Jordan has been facing all these environmental challenges which were exacerbated by the flow of hundreds of thousands of refugees from Iraq following the US-led invasion in 2003 and from Syria following the breakout of the civil war in March 2011. This chapter focuses on the environmental challenges faced by Jordan and on the development of environmental activism in the country from the 1960s.

A lot has been written about the environmental challenges faced by Jordan, but not much about environmental activism in the country, not to speak about environmental protest movements during the last decade, which is a new phenomenon in Jordan and the Arab world.

M. Terdiman (✉)
Think Tank for the Research of Islam, Jerusalem, Israel
e-mail: terdmana@inter.net.il

© The Author(s) 2019
P. R. Kumaraswamy (ed.), *The Palgrave Handbook of the Hashemite Kingdom of Jordan*, https://doi.org/10.1007/978-981-13-9166-8_8

Environmental Challenges Facing Jordan

Jordan is a very arid country. Geographically, it is divided into three areas. Deserts make up 94 per cent of its territory which cover the whole east, south-east, and north-east of the country. They are part of the Syrian Desert and the northern Arabian Desert and are the least populated regions in the country. To the west of these deserts are highlands with an average elevation of 900 metres with few mountainous areas that reach 1200 metres high in the north and 1700 metres in the south. West of the highlands, the land descends into the East Bank of the Jordan Rift Valley which is part of the Great Rift Valley.

Therefore, most of Jordan receives less than 120 millimetres of rain a year. In the highlands, precipitation increases to around 300 millimetres in the south and 500 millimetres or more in the north. The Jordan Valley receives up to 300 millimetres of rain in the northern reaches and less than 120 millimetres in the Dead Sea area. Thus, the agricultural land comprises 11.4 per cent of Jordan's total land area, and this is divided into the arable land (2 per cent), permanent crops (1 per cent), and permanent pasture (8.4 per cent), and only 1.1 per cent of the land consists of forests.[1]

Its population growth also characterises Jordan. As of July 2017, Jordan has a population of 10,248,069 people, including the Syrian refugees. Most of the population is concentrated in the highlands in the west of Jordan, and particularly in the north-west, in and around the capital of Amman. A smaller community is located in the south-west of Jordan along the shores of the Gulf of Aqaba.[2]

Jordan's overall population density is 69 inhabitants per square kilometre. However, Myriam Ababsa contends that it should be taken into account that 80 per cent of the country has fewer than five inhabitants per square kilometre and that the entire population lives in an area of less than 10,000 square kilometres. The three north-western governorates of Amman, Zarqa, and Irbid, with fewer desert areas and more rainfall, accounted for two-thirds of the Kingdom's population, that is, 4.4 million out of 6.3 million in 2010. Their population growth rate is the highest in the country and stands at over 3 per cent per year compared to 2.3 per cent for the country as a whole. They also attract most of the refugees, foreign workers, and internal migrants. Hence, the actual population density is over 650 inhabitants per square kilometre; and in the cities, population

---

[1] CIA World Factbook 2018: Jordan. Available at: https://www.cia.gov/library/publications/the-world-factbook/geos/jo.html/ (5 April 2018).
[2] CIA World Factbook 2018: Jordan.

density reaches over 30,000 inhabitants per square kilometre in the poor areas of Amman and Zarqa.[3] Thus, Jordan's urban population comprises 84.1 per cent of Jordan's total population.[4]

Jordan faces many environmental challenges that are exacerbated by the high population growth, the influx of refugees—nowadays from Syria but before also from Iraq and Israel—and the rapid urbanisation process. These include, "limited natural fresh water resources; deforestation; overgrazing; soil erosion; and desertification."[5] Jordan's *State of Environment Second Report 2016* added a few more environmental challenges including, energy, water, waste management, and the loss of biodiversity.[6]

Water Security

The first and foremost environmental challenge facing Jordan is water security. The water scarcity is so dire that according to *State of Environment Second Report*, the country "is considered one of the four poorest countries in water resources. Jordan's per capita share of water decreased from 3,600 m3 per year during 1946 to 130 m3 in the year 2014, which is significantly lower than the level of the global water poverty line which stands at 1,000 m3 per person a year." For example, water supply in the Jordanian highlands is generally intermittent. Water is delivered once a week in big cities like Amman and once every 12 days in some rural areas.

The same report clarifies the causes for this water scarcity, which are a mix of anthropogenic and natural ones and include:

> limited renewable and non-renewable water resources, a decline in the long-term rainfall due to climate change impacts, the high rates of evaporation where it reaches up to 93 per cent in many areas, years of successive droughts since 1997, illegal pumping from renewable and non-renewable groundwater wells, population increase with an annual natural growth rate up to 2.2 per cent the notable steady increase in the population as a result refugees and migrant workers and the improvement in the living standards causing more water consumption.

---

[3] Myriam Ababsa, "Changes in the Regional Distribution of the Population", in *Atlas of Jordan: History, Territories and Society* (Beyrouth: Presses de l'Ifpo, 2013), pp. 257–267. Available at: http://books.openedition.org/ifpo/5021/ (6 April 2018).
[4] CIA World Factbook 2018: Jordan.
[5] CIA World Factbook 2018: Jordan.
[6] Jordanian Ministry of the Environment, *Jordan's State of Environment Second Report 2016 Technical Summary*. Available at: http://www.moenv.gov.jo/En/Documents/Technical%20Summary.pdf (5 April 2018).

This dire situation is expected to exacerbate in the future as temperatures are supposed to rise and precipitation to decrease. Moreover, water demand for expanding economic sectors, such as industry and tourism, for agriculture and the household will much exceed water supply from minimal water resources, whether surface water (Jordan River, Yarmouk River, and Zarqa River) or groundwater exploited to its maximum capacity or over-exploited.

Energy Security

Another reason for the water scarcity is limited energy sources available for water projects, such as pumping groundwater. Jordan is nearly wholly dependent on imported energy—mostly natural gas—and energy consistently makes up 25–30 per cent of the Kingdom's imports. To diversify its energy mix, it has secured several contracts for liquefied natural gas and is currently exploring nuclear power generation, exploitation of abundant oil shale reserves and renewable technologies, as well as the import of the Israeli offshore gas.[7]

Indeed, Jordan is one of the most dependent countries in the world on foreign energy sources with 97 per cent of its energy needs coming from imported oil and natural gas from neighbouring countries, mainly Egypt and Iraq. This complete reliance on foreign oil imports consumes a significant amount of its gross domestic product (GDP). Moreover, multiple attacks on the Arab Gas Pipeline extending from Al-Arish in the Sinai Peninsula to Jordan forced the country's power plants to use diesel and heavy fuel oil, costing the treasury millions of dinars which necessitates raising the costs of electricity in the country.

Desertification

Another environmental challenge faced by Jordan is desertification. According to *State of Environment Second Report*, 90 per cent of the country's total land area is threatened by desertification, but primarily so 15 per cent of Jordan's entire land area, which is located between the desert and the highlands, where the rainfall is relatively high. The environmental

---

[7] CIA World Factbook 2018: Jordan. Available at: https://www.cia.gov/library/publications/the-world-factbook/geos/jo.html/ (5 April 2018).

impacts of the desertification as experienced in Jordan include, deterioration in flora and fauna, degradation of soil and rangelands, loss of agricultural lands, and decrease in water resources and its quality. Moreover, sandstorms pollute the environment and negatively affect public health and the agricultural production.

Land Degradation

Another environmental challenge is land degradation. Jordan has been facing this challenge for a few decades because of increasing pressures on limited land resources. For example, according *to the State of Environment Second Report 2016*, the Syrian refugees caused an increase in grazing, logging, and hunting in protected areas as well as in open areas. Thus, the increase in the number of grazing animals has increased the pressure on the limited natural resources of the rangelands, decreased the number and size of plants, and accelerated vegetation degradation.

Besides, soil salinisation has also contributed to deepening the problem of land degradation. Thus, for example, around 63 per cent of the Jordan Valley soil is already suffering from salinisation. Moreover, farmers using heavy agricultural tractors, disc ploughs, and salinised water have also led to increasing the percentage of soil salinisation.

Loss of Biodiversity

Jordan also considers the loss of biodiversity to be another essential environmental challenge that it has been facing. According to *the State of Environment Second Report 2016*, natural phenomena, such as snowstorms and floods endanger the forests and the coral reefs, respectively. Besides, human factors such as overgrazing, renovation or building of new roads, fires, construction of new ports and the expansion of the port of Aqaba, mining, and hunting have been responsible for the loss of vegetation and the extinction of many wildlife species, such as the Arabian Oryx and the Dark Deer.

Rapid Urbanisation

The rapid urbanisation process, especially in the north-western governorates, has brought with it more environmental challenges. One is the expansion of the city into agricultural lands, forests, and rangelands.

Another problem is the increasing quantities of waste. According to the *State of Environment Second Report 2016*, Jordan produces 2.5 million tons of solid waste and 45,000 tons of hazardous industrial waste annually. Despite the efforts of the municipalities to collect, transport, and dispose of the waste, some of it still finds its way to water streams and pollutes the Zarqa River. Jordan has been facing an increase in pollution levels as a result of an increase in the number of vehicles and industrial and commercial activities that impact air quality.

Establishment of the Ministry of Environment

Given these environmental security challenges facing Jordan and the growing gap between a rapidly growing population mostly concentrated in the north-western governorates and the dwindling limited natural resources, sustainable development and especially water security has become a key component in its growth and development strategies. The ministries that have been dealing with these most critical issues—water and energy security—were established in the 1980s: the Jordanian Ministry of Energy and Mineral Resources was established in 1984 whereas the Jordanian Ministry of Water and Irrigation was established in 1988. The Ministry of Agriculture and the Ministry of Health were also charged with the protection of the environment. Thus, the laws regulating their work included special clauses providing for the protection of the environment.

It seems like the establishment of a Ministry of Environment was not prioritised by the Jordanian decision makers. The first institutional entity responsible for environmental protection was the Department of Environment which was established in the Ministry of Municipal and Rural Affairs in 1980. In 1996, the General Corporation for Environmental Protection was established as a financially and administratively independent entity and was the official body responsible for environmental protection in the country. The Jordanian Ministry of Environment was established only in 2003 as a result of increased attention to environmental issues and increased pressure from environmental non-governmental organisations (NGOs). It was established under the Environment Protection Law No. 1 of 2003, which was approved by the Parliament to become the Environmental Protection Law No. 52 of 2006.

Environmental NGOs and Activism

The Royal Society for the Conservation of Nature (RSCN)

The first and one of the most critical Jordanian environmental NGO to date, the Royal Society for the Conservation of Nature (RSCN), was established in 1966 with King Hussein as its Honorary President. According to its website, this is an independent national organisation dedicated to "protecting and managing the natural resources of Jordan" and to protecting "wildlife and wild places." It has achieved this mission by establishing seven protected areas covering over 1200 square kilometres; captive breeding of the endangered Arabian Oryx, gazelle, and ibex and their reintroduction into the wilderness; setting up over 1000 Nature Conservation Clubs in schools to raise the environmental awareness among children; and the establishment of Wild Jordan as the RSCN's business arm to develop socio-economic programmes using locally available skills and products in the nature reserves.[8]

The RSCN has been deemed in certain matters as the environmental enforcement branch of the government. Thus, by 1973, it was officially given the responsibility of issuing hunting licenses and establishing hunting patrols to enforce hunting laws. It has also been implementing the Wildlife Protection Act through a special mandate from the Ministry of Agriculture and has been working closely with law enforcement agencies, such as the environmental police unit, to protect biodiversity. In 1991, it took part in drafting the national environmental strategy for Jordan, and in 1995, it worked in cooperation with government agencies to formulate the first Environmental Protection Law for Jordan. In 2004, it received the mandate from the Ministry of Environment to manage the protected areas. It is also designated as the management and enforcement authority for the Convention on International Trade in Endangered Species of Wild Fauna and Flora. The RSCN has also worked with government agencies on the formulation of environmental strategies and laws.

The RSCN has received sufficient and direct royal support, and in 2002, it established a trust fund to ensure its ongoing sustainability—the Jordanian government and the USAID (United States Agency for International Development) fund this. This support has made the RSCN

---

[8] *The website of the Royal Society for the Conservation of Nature.* Available at: http://www.rscn.org.jo/ (6 April 2018).

the most effective environmental NGO in the field of environmental protection and was the only Jordanian NGO that was active since its establishment until the late 1980s. Its activity was accompanied by academic and scientific research conducted mostly by the Royal Scientific Society, which was established in 1970.

The Emergence of Environmental NGOs

The rise of global environmental awareness during the 1980s which led to the 1992 UN Earth Summit Conference on Environment and Development in Rio de Janeiro had an impact on the rise of environmental awareness among Jordanians and, thus, paved the way for the emergence of environmental NGOs. The draft of the Jordanian National Charter in 1990 following the food riots in 1989 and the beginning of a slow democratisation process also enabled the right atmosphere for the establishment and activity of civil society NGOs in general and of environmental NGOs in particular. These environmental NGOs have received funding from abroad and from the local private sector. They have also attracted environmental experts alongside ordinary citizens to join their ranks and take part in their programmes.

The first of these NGOs was the Jordanian Society for Controlling Pollution of the Environment, now called Jordan Environment Society, which was established in 1987 by the former Jordanian Prime Minister, Ahmad 'Ubaydat, who also happened to be Chairman of the Royal Committee for Drafting the National Charter. It has grown to be the largest Jordanian environmental NGO and its primary aims have been to protect the environment, to mobilise all those interested to take part in its programmes and to fight against all types of pollution. It has won the support and cooperation of the government, private sector, and foreign Arab and Western donors. Just like the RSCN, it has good relations with the government. Thus, as of 2003, it has been collaborating with the Ministry of Environment in all environmental issues in the national level. Its achievements include: raising environmental awareness and environmental awareness concerning water issues among local communities throughout the Kingdom, developing an environmental information data and material to share with the public, training local environmental experts in environmental management methods, establishing an environmental theatre, and so on.[9]

---

[9] *The website of the Jordanian Environment Society.* Available at: http://jes.org.jo/ (6 April 2018).

Other environmental NGOs that have been established since the 1990s are active all over the country; some are active in a specific place or governorate while others focus on specific issues, such as water, renewable energy, spreading environmental awareness, protection of the environment, combating pollution and waste, and so on. Most of these NGOs are part of the civil society and a few enjoy royal patronage. Most NGOs are funded by private sectors and foreign donors and have developed collaboration with the Jordanian government.

Impact on Decision Makers

During the last two decades, the environmental NGOs have been very instrumental in exerting pressure on the Jordanian government to prevent it from implementing plans that harm the environment. For example, in 2006, the RSCN launched the "Save Jordan's Trees" campaign in cooperation with several Jordanian environmental NGOs and succeeded in blocking the government's proposal to amend the agricultural law of 2005 to permit investors to instigate business ventures in the forested areas. The RSCN also launched an online campaign to assert more pressure on the decision makers through a mass public campaign.[10] In 2012, environmental NGOs stopped the implementation of a government decision to merge the Ministry of Environment and the Ministry of Municipal Affairs. In March 2014, the same group of environmental NGOs succeeded in stopping plans to establish fish farms in Aqaba by warning against their adverse impact on marine life and coral reefs.[11]

After the environmental NGOs experienced their ability, when united, to stop government policies or acts that they deemed as harmful to the environment, eight environmental NGOs decided in May 2014 to take a step towards making a stronger impact on decision makers by establishing the Jordanian Federation for Environmental NGOs. The eight founding NGOs are Jordan Environment Society, the RSCN, Jordan Royal Marine Conservation Society, Energy Conservation and Environmental Sustainability Society, Arab Group for Protection of Nature, Jordan

---

[10] *The website of the Royal Society for the Conservation of Nature*. Available at: http://www.rscn.org.jo/ (6 April 2018).

[11] Hana Namrouqa, "Environmental NGOs Federation Officially Launched", *The Jordan Times*, May 20, 2014. Available at: http://www.jordantimes.com/news/local/environmental-ngos-federation-officially-launched (7 April 2018).

Society for Combating Desertification, Organic Farming Society, and the Jordan Green Building Society. The Federation aims at raising environmental awareness among the public in the Kingdom, having more weight in the formulation of national environmental policies and legislation, and supporting member organisations.[12]

In May 2017, another dramatic step towards having more impact on decision makers was made. For the first time in the history of the environmental movement in Jordan, representatives of the 124 registered environmental NGOs assembled for a national conference and called on the government to consult with them during the environmental decision-making process since they feel that they are often sidelined. This one-day conference was organised by the Jordanian Federation for Environmental NGOs in cooperation with the Friedrich Ebert Stiftung and was held under the patronage of Princess Basma. It aimed at providing a platform for Jordan's environmental NGOs to collaborate more with each other, to exchange knowledge and expertise in the implementation of projects, to secure funding for their projects, and to explore entrepreneurship opportunities in the environment sector.[13]

These moves can also be understood on the background of the events of the Arab Spring, following which the Jordanian government and King Abdullah II have understood that they need to listen more to their citizens and to take the civil society into account in the decision-making process. At the same time, the environmental NGOs have also recognised that they can be more influential if united.

Environmental Activism Following the Arab Spring

Uprising across the Arab world have encouraged popular and youth activism in Jordan. Instead of demanding socio-political reforms, they have pursued more targeted and achievable single-issue campaigns, such as environmental campaigns. Many of these new forms of activism use social media platforms to mobilise and inform supporters.

---

[12] Hana Namrouqa, "Environmental NGOs Federation Officially Launched", *The Jordan Times*, May 20, 2014. Available at: http://www.jordantimes.com/news/local/environmental-ngos-federation-officially-launched (7 April 2018).

[13] Hana Namrouqa, "Environmental NGOs Urge Seat at the Table for Policymaking", *The Jordan Times*, May 7, 2017. Available at: http://www.jordantimes.com/news/local/environmental-ngos-urge-seat-table-policymaking (7 April 2018).

Save Bergesh Forest Campaign

A good example of the use of online activism in an environmental campaign is the Save Bergesh Forest campaign.[14] In January 2011, the Jordanian government approved plans to construct a new military academy in the Bergesh Forest, near the city of Ajloun in northern Jordan about 90 kilometres north-west of Amman. This decision, if implemented, meant the cutting of 2200 trees but after unprecedented pressure from environmental NGOs and activists, the construction was halted. It was one of the first examples of the Jordanian government yielding to environmental concerns.

However, it was only a temporary victory. In April 2011, a parliamentary committee gave the green light for the construction of the military academy after the Jordan armed forces adjusted their designs so that only 300 trees would be cut down and promised to plant new trees to replace them. Moreover, some of the residents of the city of 'Ajloun, which suffers from unemployment of 15.3 per cent back this project expressing hope that the construction will materialise and new create jobs.

The compromise was not enough for the environmental NGOs, who claimed that they are not against the project but against its location, which should be relocated to an alternative land with no forest or vegetation cover. Another claim made by environmental activists was that the authorities would be violating various environmental laws, such as the ban on allocating, selling, or trading forest land to any person or entity for any reason. Laws also prohibit chopping trees and uprooting wild plants without the consent of the Minister of Agriculture.

Therefore, they intensified their fight and took to the social media to raise public awareness about the environmental hazards of this project. The environmental activists created a new group on 29 April 2011 calling itself the National Campaign to Save Bergesh Forest from Extinction. It managed to attract more than 1600 members in Facebook. Among them were environmental activists, journalists, politicians, lawmakers, academics, Jordanians living abroad as well as the former Minister of Agriculture who was responsible for the approval of the project. During April and May

---

[14] For more details about the online campaign to save the Bergesh Forest, look at: Asma Hussein Malkawi, "Digital Public Sphere within the Jordanian Political Movement: A Case Study for Saving Bergesh Forests through Facebook", *British Journal of Humanities and Social Sciences*, Vol. 8, No. 1 (December 2012), pp. 16–27. Available at: http://www.ajournal.co.uk/HSpdfs/HSvolume8(1)/HSVol.8%20(1)%20Article%203.pdf (7 April 2018).

of 2011, the group organised four protests: one was held in front of the Ministry of Agriculture, another in front of the Prime Minister's office and two were held in the Bergesh Forest itself.

This topic was covered by the mass media channels, including private television satellite channels, newspapers, and radio stations. Academics, economists, and journalists wrote articles against the project. The pressure on the government to halt the project started to bear fruit only when Members of Parliament petitioned the Prime Minister to reconsider the location of the military academy. The Water and Agriculture Committee of the Lower House of parliament sent letters to the Prime Minister and the Chairman of the Jordan Armed Forces, calling on them to halt the construction of the military academy which will entail uprooting hundreds of rare and ageing trees.

Thus, the growing strength of the campaign and the mounting pressure forced the government and the Jordanian Armed Forces to cancel the project in September 2011. This environmental campaign marked the success of the first-ever public advocacy and the civil movement against a government decision in the Kingdom. It succeeded mainly because it could mobilise all sectors of the society using online activism and the mass media, including Members of Parliament and journalists. The constant coverage and the involvement of decision makers alongside environmental activism were paramount for this success.

Following the reports in May 2014 that the Jordan Armed Forces resumed cutting down 2200 trees to establish the military academy and the resumed environmental campaign against it, the Jordanian Minister of Agriculture, Akef Zu'bi, said on 19 August 2014 that "from now on, not one tree will be chopped down and no forest will be abused in the implementation of the military academy". He further said that although the military academy in Bergesh is "a vital and national development project, the construction of the project will be confined to the land appropriated by the Jordan Armed Forces, and those lands are bare."[15] This declaration finally ended the controversy concerning the construction of the military academy in the Bergesh Forest in a sour-sweet taste. The project was eventually halted, but by then 2200 trees were gone.

---

[15] Hana Namrouqa, "No More Bergesh Trees Will Be Cut for Military Academy—Agriculture Minister", *The Jordan Times*, August 19, 2014. Available at: http://www.jordantimes.com/news/local/no-more-bergesh-trees-will-be-cut-military-academy-%E2%80%94-agriculture-minister (7 April 2018).

The environmental activists and NGOs have continued to protect the forests from harmful governmental activities. For example, in June 2017, they expressed anger over a newspaper advertisement offering a plot of land with all its trees and buildings in the Dibbeen Forest in the Jerash Governorate at an auction. The advertisement also specified the description and prices of each tree. The Jordan Agricultural Engineers Association said that offering trees from the Dibbeen Forest for sale at the auction was "a shock to Jordanian society, which values trees." The Jordanian Federation of Environmental NGOs denounced any sale of the land and its trees at auctions and threatened to go to court over this issue. Its President, Omar Shoshan, said that a total of 8000 trees—including Greek juniper, maple, and oak—are offered for sale for JD931,845. Following the outcry, the Jordanian Minister of Agriculture Khaled Hneifat said that "all trees across the Kingdom are the property of the Ministry of Agriculture, whether on private or public lands, and anyone planning to cut down a tree must take the approval of the ministry... we will not allow cutting down any tree in Dibbeen."[16]

The Controversy over Nuclear Energy

Another environmental debate has been raging in Jordan during the last decade concerning the nuclear power and the building of nuclear reactors in the country's territory.[17] Since 2007, the government planned a nuclear plant and towards this endeavour, it established the Jordanian Atomic Energy Commission (JAEC) to be responsible for safety and security, nuclear science and technology as well as safeguards and verifications. In 2012, the Parliament voted to suspend nuclear energy planning fearing the adverse effects a power plant could have on the economy. This suspension was preceded by a huge wave of protests from all Jordanian sectors.

Nevertheless, in October 2013, Jordan and Russia agreed on the construction of a US$10 billion nuclear power plant in Quseir Amra, a town 70 kilometres southeast of Amman, leading to protests from many activ-

---

[16] Hana Namrouqa, "Activists Condemn Plans to Auction Land in Dibbeen Forest Reserve," *The Jordan Times*, June 21, 2017. Available at: http://www.jordantimes.com/news/local/activists-condemn-plans-auction-land-dibbeen-forest-reserve (14 April 2018).

[17] For more details on the controversy over nuclear energy in Jordan see Nicholas Seeley, "The Battle over Nuclear Jordan", *MER 271—Fuel and Water: The Coming Crises*, Vol. 44 (Summer 2014). Available at: http://www.merip.org/mer/mer271/battle-over-nuclear-jordan (8 April 2018).

ists, tribes (especially representatives of the Bani Sakhr tribe who is situated near the site), Members of Parliament and scientists who pointed at the dangers to the environment and the economy. The plant happens to be located directly atop the Azraq aquifer, a significant source of fresh water for the residents of Amman. Environmentalists warn that one accident may instantly poison up to one-third of the country's water networks. A group of 5000 youths established the Bani Sakhr Awakening Group which launched a series of civil disobedience campaigns to prevent construction crews from reaching the site. To keep the pressure, sit-ins in front of the Ministry of Energy, conferences and other events have regularly been organised by the Nuclear Free Jordan collective with the aim of highlighting the unsustainability of nuclear energy and its detrimental effects.

On the other hand, the authorities said that atomic energy is the only way for the country to solve its energy crisis. Thus, in this case, however, the environmental campaign seems to have failed, most likely because of Jordan's need to diversify its energy sources and to be less dependent on other countries for its energy supply. On 20 August 2016, the JAEC said that the country's first nuclear power plant could be operational by 2025 if sufficient financing is secured.[18] Two months later, in December 2016, JAEC in cooperation with a consortium headed by the Korean Atomic Energy Research Institute under the patronage of King Abdullah II inaugurated the 5 MW Jordan Research and Training Reactor. This is the first nuclear reactor in Jordan which is located on the campus of Jordan University of Science and Technology in the city of Al-Ramthain to the north.[19]

Another failed environmental campaign opposed the construction of a 30-megawatt coal-fuelled power plant in the Kerak Governorate, which would be the first coal plant in the Kingdom. In June 2016, the Jordanian Ministry of Energy and Mineral Resources and the Modern Cement and Mining Company (Al-Manaseer) signed a MoU for the construction of the plant, which would start in the following month and would be completed in two years. Once completed, it will supply power to the company's cement factory in Qatraneh using the coal imported from the US,

---

[18] Mohammad Ghazal, "Jordan Seeking Funds for First Nuclear Power Plant—Official", *The Jordan Times*, August 20, 2016. Available at: http://www.jordantimes.com/news/local/jordan-seeking-funds-first-nuclear-power-plant-%E2%80%94-official (8 April 2018).

[19] Jordan Times, "PM Inaugurates Jordan Research and Training Reactor", *The Jordan Times*, December 7, 2016. Available at: http://www.jordantimes.com/news/local/pm-inaugurates-jordan-research-and-training-reactor (8 April 2018).

Russia, and Africa. The environmental NGOs IndyACT and Climate Action Network opposed the construction of the plant, saying an Environmental Impact Assessment should be carried out beforehand to make sure that the proposed plant would not damage the environment and public health. The spokesman of the Ministry of Energy and Mineral resources Haydar Gammaz said in reaction that the "new plant will be built in line with the highest international standards to protect the environment." He further said that the ministry required the company to abide by all the basic conditions for using coal in coordination with the Ministry of Environment and that if the coal-fuelled power plant is successful, other will be built as well.[20]

Conclusion

From all these case studies it is possible to argue that following the Arab Spring, the civil society, including environmental NGOs, has much more say in policy formation and implementation than they were used to in the past. This does not mean that it can stop any government decision or policy that it does not like or that has a negative impact on the environment or Jordan's society or economy. The deciding factor is the civil society's impact on the decision makers. Thus, in the efforts to halt the construction of the military academy in the Bergesh Forest, the civil society won the battle. Part of the reason is that the military academy could be moved to another place and thus, no harm is done. The use of online and mass media means to mobilise people from all walks of the Jordanian society also contributed to this campaign.

More people have taken part in the campaign against the construction of a nuclear reactor than in the campaign to save the Bergesh Forest. However, this controversy seems to be won by the Jordanian government backed by King Abdullah II. The reason is the almost total dependence of the Kingdom upon energy imports from neighbouring countries, which has proved to be not safe because of the instability in Iraq and Egypt. This instability resulted in a few interruptions in the supply of energy to Jordan. Therefore, King Abdullah and the Jordanian government understand that Jordan has to be less dependent on others for the supply of its energy

---

[20] Hana Namrouqa, "Environmentalists Protest Plan for Coal-Fuelled Power Plant," *The Jordan Times*, June 23, 2016. Available at: http://www.jordantimes.com/news/local/environmentalists-protest-plan-coal-fuelled-power-plant (14 April 2018).

needs and has to diversify its energy sources. Hence, in addition to renewable energy sources (solar energy, wind energy, etc.) and oil shale, Jordan feels obliged to resort also to the nuclear option.

These case studies also show that the level of environmental awareness among Jordan's population has risen in a considerable part because of the constant efforts of the environmental NGOs, whose aim is to safeguard Jordan's environment. Hopefully, the environmental NGOs, the Jordanian government, the parliament and civil society would collaborate more to better face the environmental security issues that unless met and treated, can bring about instability in the country. This can be especially true given the future scenario of temperature rise and fall in rainfalls coupled with tremendous population growth and more people moving to the cities and, thus, putting more pressure on dwindling natural resources of the Kingdom.

References

Abasa, M. (2013). Changes in the regional distribution of the population. In *Atlas of Jordan: History, territories and society* (pp. 257–267). Beyrouth: Presses de l'Ifpo. Available at http://books.openedition.org/ifpo/5021. Accessed 6 Apr 2018.

CIA World Factbook 2018: Jordan. Available at https://www.cia.gov/library/publications/the-world-factbook/geos/jo.html. Accessed 5 Apr 2018.

Jordanian Ministry of the Environment. *Jordan's State of Environment Second Report 2016 Technical Summary*. Available at http://www.moenv.gov.jo/En/Documents/Technical%20Summary.pdf. Accessed 5 Apr 2018.

Malkawi, A. H. (2012). Digital public sphere within the Jordanian political movement: A case study for saving Bergesh Forests through Facebook. *British Journal of Humanities and Social Sciences, 8*(1), 16–27. Available at http://www.ajournal.co.uk/HSpdfs/HSvolume8(1)/HSVol.8%20(1)%20Article%203.pdf. Accessed 7 Apr 2018.

Seeley, N. (2014). The battle over nuclear Jordan. *MER 271—Fuel and Water: The Coming Crises, 44*. Available at http://www.merip.org/mer/mer271/battle-over-nuclear-jordan. Accessed 8 Apr 2018.

Sustainable Development

Manjari Singh

Sustainable development seeks to maintain the ecosystem by conserving the environment and bettering the society while pursuing economic development. Three significant components highlighted by the concept are a desirable human condition, an enduring ecosystem, and a balance between the present and future generations and hence, the level of sustainability depends on the stage of development of that particular country. The most widely accepted definition was given by the UN-mandated Brundtland Commission which in 1987 viewed sustainable development as one "that meets the needs of the present without compromising the ability of future generations to meet their own needs" (Brundtland Commission 1987). Over time, the ambiguous nature of the definition was expanded to encompass all aspects of an ecosystem that affect various dimensions of sustainability.

The Kingdom of Jordan has lower economic growth and is a middle-income country. Its pluralistic nature and precarious environment make *Intermediate Sustainability* approach which envisages economic growth along with sustaining the surrounding, more appropriate.

Jordan ratified the Earth Summit or the World Summit on Sustainable Development of 2002, which discussed sustainable development. The summit adopted the eight Millennium Development Goals (MDGs) for

M. Singh (✉)
Centre for Land Warfare Studies (CLAWS), New Delhi, India

© The Author(s) 2019
P. R. Kumaraswamy (ed.), *The Palgrave Handbook of the Hashemite Kingdom of Jordan*, https://doi.org/10.1007/978-981-13-9166-8_9

152 M. SINGH

Fig. 1 Seventeen Sustainable Development Goals. (Source: Adapted from UNDESA 2017)

2000–15. In 2006, Jordan outlined a National Strategy to Combat Desertification (NAP) and established a separate Ministry of Environment (MoE) as part of its drive towards sustainability. Moreover, with the help of United Nations Development Programme (UNDP), in 2015, it came out with *Jordan 2025* as its policy guideline. It is to be noted that *Jordan 2025* was announced before the UN recognised 17 Sustainable Development Goals (SDGs) in January 2016 (Fig. 1). However, there are various hurdles facing Jordan towards achieving sustainable development. In that context, what are the social, economic, and environmental problems facing Jordan?

In 2018, the Kingdom ranked 80th on sustainable development index amongst 157 countries and is 5th in the Middle East. Out of 17 SDGs, gender equality, clean water and sanitation, affordable and clean energy, decent work and economic growth, reduced inequalities, climate action, peace and justice, and regional and international partnership and cooperation are critical for Jordan. This is due to its lower economic growth, lack of natural resources, and growing inequalities due to diverse population structure. Hence, problems facing the country are multi-dimensional requiring a holistic and inclusive policy approach.

Significant problems facing Jordan can be categorised into four parts, namely, environmental issues, social issues, economic challenges, and regional dynamics.

Environmental Issues

Most of the environment-related issues facing Jordan such as desertification, increasing salinity, and land degradation are linked to water scarcity, the biggest challenge facing the country. The Hashemite Kingdom lies in one of the severest arid and semi-arid regions of the world, and almost 90 per cent of its land area is desert. Due to climatic consideration and rapid urbanisation, only 2.54 per cent of the land mass is fertile and available for cultivation.

The amount and frequency of rainfall are very less, and large parts of the country receive less than 200 mm of rain annually. Due to high temperatures and less soil retention capacity, evaporation rates are high, and almost 92 per cent of the water received through rainfall is lost in evaporation; for instance, in 2015 the country received 8884 million cubic metres (MCM) of rain out of which 8154 MCM was lost in evaporation, 245 MCM in floods, and only 485 MCM was available for groundwater recharge (MWI 2015). This has always been the case and means that the availability of surface water budget[1] in the Kingdom is very low.

Jordan has limited freshwater resources in the form of rivers. River Jordan is the primary river system and two of its tributaries, River Yarmouk and River Zarqa, also cater to its water needs. The water available from these rivers is limited owing to Jordan being a lower riparian state and most of the water is controlled and used by upper riparian countries, namely, Syria and Israel. According to Ministry of Water and Irrigation (MWI) estimates, freshwater bodies or the rivers meet only 27.2 per cent of the total water availability, and most of the water supplies come from groundwater recharge (which as pointed out above is itself very low), and about 13.2 per cent water is available through non-conventional sources, primarily from reclaimed wastewater. Desalination and import of water are other possible alternatives, but they are expensive and not conducive owing to unstable regional dynamics.

Due to low rainfall, non-conventional sources are a viable option for generating more water, but in the Jordanian case, there are structural problems and resource constraints. The country has only one outlet to the

---

[1] Is calculated as precipitation—evaporation—runoff.

sea in the form of the Gulf of Aqaba and its only port Aqaba lies in the extreme south-west corner of the country. This makes the transportation cost of desalination of seawater prohibitive to meet the water demands of the urban centres in the middle of the country and the desert prone rural areas. Moreover, regional cooperation needed to generate water face political problems. The Red Sea-Dead Sea linking project has been entangled in the periodic tension between Israel and Jordan over the Middle East peace process.

Added to a lower natural supply of water, several anthropogenic factors contribute to Jordan being a water-scarce country. These include water thefts, leakages, and increasing amount of non-revenue water (NRW), that is, the amount of water lost during production to the distribution process. To combat water thefts, between 2007 and 2015 the country closed down about 1099 illegal wells (MWI 2015). Such measures have only marginally increased the per capita availability of the water because the overall shortage is massive.

These factors resulted in Jordan being an acute water-starved country, and only 108 cubic metre per capita of water is available annually, and this is likely to drop to 90 cubic metres per capita per year by 2025 (MWI 2015). The international water poverty line stands at 500 cubic metres per capita per year (Lawrence et al. 2002) and presently Jordan provides only a fourth of this requirement to its citizens resulting in the Kingdom being identified as the second water-poorest country in the world (Namrouqa 2014).

Social Issues

The changing population dynamics of the country has resulted in more and conflicting identities leading to extra pressures on sharing limited resources. A high birth rate characterises Jordan's population and it stood at 433,000 in 1946, which was double than its population in 1921 when the Emirate was formed. Gradually it increased to 586,000 in 1952 to 895,000 in the 1960s; in 1970, it stood at 1.67 million and got doubled in two decades. It became 6.1 million in 2010; and in 2018 it stands at more than 9.5 million (DoS 1921–2018).

Even though the natural increase hovers around 2.3 per cent (one of the highest in the Middle East), the drastic population increase in Jordan is majorly due to the refugee influx from the neighbouring countries. Since the independence of the country in 1946, the Palestinians make up a majority of its population and in recent times, the percentage of refugees to the total population is high, constituting about one-third of the total resident population. Both steep natural increase and refugee influx have put enormous pressure on its meagre resources.

The proportion of Palestinian-Jordanians to the Jordanian-Jordanians remains highly contested. The Jordanian officials maintain that the former comprises around 40 per cent of the population (Abu-Odeh 1999), while Palestinian sources have often maintained that the Palestinian-origin Jordanians comprise 60 per cent of the population (Brand 1995; Muasher 2017). Either way, the Palestinians make up a substantial portion of Jordan's population. Most of the Palestinians have been accommodated through citizenship rights but the United Nations Relief and Works Agency (UNRWA), maintains that the Kingdom has 2 million Palestinian refugees who have come at different times since 1948.

Moreover, in the wake of the US-led invasion of Iraq in 2003, about a million refugees from that country fled to Jordan, and while most have returned home, the kingdom still has about 500,000 Iraqi refugees. Following the outbreak of civil war in 2011, approximately 1.3 million Syrian refugees have come to Jordan. Thus, in 2017, the Jordanian total resident population stood at 9.5 million and out of which about 3.8 million or 40 per cent are refugees (Kumaraswamy and Singh 2017).

The influx of Syrian refugees rang a warning bell as it came when the country was grappling with its scarcity of resources, especially water and energy, unemployment was increasing, and the economy was getting worse. Moreover, about 83 per cent of the refugees from Syria live outside the refugee camps, and their mixing with the host communities increased the challenge of employment, schooling, housing, etc., and prices of essential commodities for the Jordanians increased, leading to sporadic protests. The grants and aid promised by the international agencies and regional countries were inadequate to meet the welfare of the refugees thereby placing extra pressures on the Kingdom (MoPIC 2013). Concerns were also raised about the refugees succumbing to extremist ideology out of desperation and hence, their well-being is critical to the political stability in the country (Al-Safadi 2018).

The sudden influx of refugees also exerted pressures on some of the on-going developmental projects. For example, Disi-Amman Conveyance Project was visualised as a major project to mitigate the water problems, but the Syrian refugee crisis not only slowed the process but also made it insufficient to meet the water demands of Amman and Aqaba due to a sudden increase in population pressure. As flagged in the Voluntary National Review (VNR) report submitted to the UN, most developmental projects were affected by the Syrian refugee crisis at two levels; namely, by putting extra pressure on the resources and by the diversion of meagre resources for refugee settlement (Jordan VNR 2017).

Gender inequality, rising youth unemployment, lack of quality education, and mainstreaming of the tribal population are some of the other social problems facing Jordan (World Economic Forum 2006–2017). The Kingdom is primarily a tribal society, and in return for its loyalty, the crown provided the tribal population with public sector jobs, higher positions in the military, and accommodation in the political system through gerrymandering. This has upset the Palestinian-Jordanians who often complain of differential treatment (Abu-Odeh 1999; Christopherson 2013).

Over 93 per cent of the population are literates, but Jordan aspires in quality education to make the sector sustainable in the long run (Jordan VNR 2017). Gender differentials concerning literacy are not high, and the Jordanian women enjoy "liberal" education system the same as the men (*Jordan 2025* 2015). More female candidates are enrolled in the secondary education than their male counterparts, but their participation in the job market is comparatively lower; in 2016, for example, 22.5 per cent of the working-age women were unemployed as against 11 per cent males and only 13.3 per cent women were employed as against 60 per cent males. There is gender equality regarding education and health benefits, but women lag far behind men when it comes to political empowerment, employment, and salaries.

The unemployment is a significant problem facing Jordan and it stood at over 18 per cent in the first quarter of 2018, and this was an increase from 12 per cent in 2011 and 14.8 per cent in 2005. Two reasons contributing to this rise in joblessness are: the massive influx of Syrian refugees presents the employers with cheap and skilled labours and the Jordanians are less inclined to work in unorganised sectors and have limited skills for it. This is one of the main reasons for a large number of foreign workers especially Egyptians and Syrians (before the refugee crisis) who are being employed in the unorganised sectors and agriculture.

The unemployment rate amongst the youth is even more alarming. The growth structure of unemployment rate amongst the youth is U-shaped; it stood at 41.7 per cent in 1991, decreased to 28.6 per cent in 2008, and is again increased to 39.7 per cent in 2017. It is to be noted that the youth unemployment rate has always been high in Jordan even after the onset of privatisation as access to that sector requires skilled workers. Owing to the low payment structure, most skilled youth prefer to migrate to rich Gulf Arab countries for work and hence, there is a need for foreign workers for low-paying jobs.

Therefore, social sustainability which refers to the inclusion of all the actors of the society with equal rights, duties, and opportunities towards decreasing disparities, is of utmost importance especially after 2011 when Jordan witnessed widespread protests over unemployment, income differentials, gender disparity, and inequitable distribution of resources. The economic demands were met by some relaxation in terms of more job opportunities in the private and public sectors and through the provision of subsidies on essential amenities such as water, electricity, and bread; for example, in 2015, subsidies comprised 29.84 per cent of Jordan's total expenses. While there has been a 10 per cent reduction in total subsidies since 2011, that is, from above 40 per cent to over 30 per cent in 2017, the unforeseen measures have contributed substantially to lower economic growth which dropped from 18.7 per cent in 1992, that is, two years after privatisation was introduced to 2.6 per cent in 2017. The government has tried to implement austerity measures through subsidy cuts but these have not been successful.

Economic Issues

Economically, Jordan is classified as a lower-middle-income country with lower national GNP (gross national product) and GDP (gross domestic product) per capita. While the GDP stood at US $38.7 billion in 2016, GDP per capita stood at US $4087.9 and both are lower figures in the Middle East. Since the mid-1960s, the economy has been growing at just over 2 per cent but registered a higher growth during the 1990s largely due to privatisation. At the same time, the introduction of the structural adjustment programme as demanded by the IMF (International Monetary Fund) led to social unrest in 1989, 2011, and 2018 and slowed down the pace of economic reforms. Slower economic growth rate, lower GDP, and uneven distribution of wealth have led to the less than optimal performance of various sectors of the economy.

The main sectors namely, agriculture, industries, and services do not contribute substantially to the economy, and there is an excessive reliance on non-traditional sectors such as overseas remittances and foreign aid and assistance. Since the oil boom of the early 1970s, remittances from Jordanians working in the energy-rich Gulf Arab countries make up a sizeable portion of the GDP. During the same period, reliance on external aid and assistance has also increased. For example, personal remittances amount to 11.06 per cent of the GDP and share of foreign aid and assistance offers about 7.1 per cent to the GDP. Even though the percentage of foreign aid and assistance has decreased considerably over the years from 44 per cent in 1979 to 7.1 per cent in 2017, it remains a substantial contributor to GDP. In the wake of widespread protests, in 2011, wealthier Gulf Arab countries pledged US $5 billion to Jordan, and a similar pledge to the tune of $3 billion was made in 2018 the following domestic protests over taxation. Even though the aid from these countries is timely, they also limit Jordan's ability to pursue substantial economic reforms.

Unlike many other developing countries, Jordan is not an agrarian economy. Due to political hurdles, the country never embarked upon significant reforms in this sector. Out of the 10 per cent land available for human activities, only 2.54 per cent is available for agriculture. The critically water-scarce country provides about 58 per cent of the total available water to the agricultural sector which also benefits from subsidies in the form of water and electricity. Despite these, the output is not commensurate, and agriculture contributes only about 3–4 per cent to the GDP, and only 1 per cent of the total Jordanian workforce is employed in the sector. Above all, Jordan has to import nearly 90 per cent of its food items and the sector does not contribute to combating the rising food insecurity challenges in the country (Kumaraswamy and Singh 2018).

Less availability of natural resources limits industrial growth which is confined primarily to fertiliser and cement industries. The industrial contribution to the GDP has been hovering between 10.8 per cent in 1965 and 16 per cent in 2017. The only promising sector of the economy is services, and efforts are on to harness tourism. Though in its infancy, results are visible regarding educational and health tourism and architectural, historical, and environmental tourism.

Regional Dynamics

Political situations in its neighbourhood affect Jordan severely and limit its stability, and hence, its efforts towards sustainability. Periodic regional upheavals not only bring in more refugees into the country but also undermine its foreign trade. Because of near-landlocked status, trade routes are often hampered by tension and violence in its neighbourhood. If the Syrian crisis affected its export of fruits and vegetables, the security situation in the Sinai Peninsula undermined the flow of gas imports from Egypt. The supply of water in the River Yarmouk has been affected because of the civil war in the upper riparian Syrian state. Likewise, tension with Israel has delayed the implementation of the ambitious Dead Sea-Red Sea project which seeks to mitigate the water crisis in the country.

To top it all, any domestic hindrances in the Gulf countries, the potential donors and aid providers to Jordan, affects the Hashemite Kingdom's economic prosperity directly as it is majorly dependent on aid and assistance. This is one of the reasons why the Kingdom has been trying to reduce the share of aid and assistance in GDP, but only a little progress is made on this front. Hence, regional dynamics play a crucial role in the sustainability aspirations of Jordan and will continue to do so until and unless the Hashemite Kingdom manages to lower its dependence on their neighbours.

All of these problems, therefore, need a holistic approach and the solution needs to be multi-dimensional as the problems are interconnected. It was pointed out by the government in 2008 when its single-handed efforts to combat desertification did not yield positive results that such issues can only be solved under the "umbrella of sustainable development" (MoPIC-MoE 2008, p. 59). The United Nations Department of Economic and Social Affairs (UNDESA), the UN agency responsible for sustainable development provided 17 goals, and 169 targets for the countries to follow that are multi-dimensional and are inclusive of all sectors and actors of economy and society, respectively. The environmental, social, and economic challenges facing Jordan manifest in many forms, and the prominent amongst them are:

- Continuous depletion of the availability of water resources, which had dropped from 190 MCM per capita the 2000s to 108 MCM in 2017
- Mounting foreign debts which grew from 18 per cent of the GDP in the 1970s to over 75 per cent in 2017
- Exponential population growth which rose from 433,000 in 1946 to 9.5 million in 2018 or 22 times in seven decades
- Increasing desertification due to environmental conditions as well as rapid urbanisation thereby limiting the land available for agriculture and other forms of economic and industrial activities (MWI 2013)
- Growing dependency upon external aid and assistance to balance the budget as foreign aid still makes up 7.1 per cent of the GDP even though the share had decreased from above 44.1 per cent in 1979 (MoPIC 2015)

- A higher degree of subsidies for food, water, electricity, and other basic amenities which grew from 17 per cent in the 2000s to 29.87 per cent in 2015
- Increasing influx of refugees from neighbouring war-torn countries leading to about 40 per cent of the resident population being non-citizens in 2017

These, in turn, inhibit the kingdom from pursuing meaningful reforms thereby contributing to its political instability and economic fragility.

Response and Policies

The Ministry of Planning and International Cooperation (MoPIC) is responsible for sustainable development in the Kingdom. The ministry has a separate division which collaborates with all the stakeholders such as Ministry of Environment (MoE), MWI, Ministry of Social Development, Ministry of Industries, Ministry of Agriculture, Department of Statistics, etc., as well as non-governmental organisations dealing with private sectors, women, children, youth, etc.

In 2015, along with UNDP, Jordan published its *Jordan 2025* which is a visionary project and deals with a set of guidelines to achieve sustainability. The Kingdom has set up its goals and agendas which are in line with the UN's goals. Moreover, while the global support systems of sustainable development are economy, society, and environment, Jordan has identified its pillars of sustainability as *citizen, society, business,* and *government*. Each of these pillars is crucial for the sustainable development aspirations of the country. While *citizens* refer to the Jordanian citizens and require them to be actively involved and aware of the surrounding, *society* refers to the stability which is possible when there is inclusiveness. *Business* refers to the active participation of the private sector in the development approach and *government* provides a set of laws, which are effective and efficient (*Jordan 2025* 2015).

Jordan 2025 highlights the need to build priority clusters to create more jobs and opportunities and to bring in development. As of 2018, about eight clusters of growth have been identified; they are construction and engineering, tourism and events, transport and logistics, life sciences, healthcare, educational services, financial services, and digital and business services. Various programmes are being undertaken simultaneously and are in line with guidelines set by vision document. Four significant programmes are Executive Development Programme (EDP), Governorate Development Programme, Jordan Response Plan for the Syria Crisis, and Economic

Growth Plan. These are to help in developing Jordan's sustainably. Added to these, the approaches to be followed are active participation, excellence, competitiveness and sustainability, and institutionalisation.

However, in its Voluntary National Review (VNR) submitted to the UN in July 2017, Jordan reported that it is in the stage of collecting data on the 17 goals envisaged by the UN and the data collection is of type Tier I which implies that the country has been collecting only broad data and has not gone to governorate or lower unit levels as the methodology for it is not formulated until early 2018 (*Jordan 2025* 2015; Jordan VNR 2017). Even though a good percentage of primary data has been available for almost all the indicators crucial to Jordan by 2015, the country has not framed any concrete policies to reach these goals. For instance, on gender inequality, Jordan has about 64 per cent Tier 1 data available;

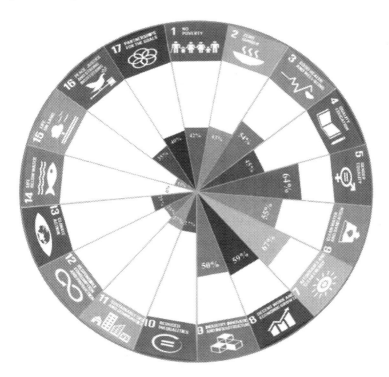

Fig. 2 Data available for each goal. (Source: Adapted from Jordan Voluntary National Review report 2017)

on education the country has collected over 54 per cent of the data; on energy, it has 67 per cent data; and on economic growth, over 59 per cent data is available with the government (See Fig. 2). The country faces many challenges to its sustainable development journey and until and unless these are addressed, the Hashemite Kingdom will have a long way to go before achieving sustainable development.

Challenges

Of the many challenges facing the country, the major ones which affect the sustainable development approach are sudden and frequent influxes of refugees resulting in immense population pressure; over-dependence on foreign aid and external sources of income in terms of remittances and assistance; regional instability; corruption; agriculture as non-performing sector; acute crisis of water and its wrong channelling; lack of data and problems in data acquisition; and frequent change of government. These challenges have slowed the process and these are to be addressed in a holistic manner for Jordan to realise sustainable development.

Therefore, owing to multi-dimensional issues sustainable development is the only answer to Jordan's problems. However, lack of interest and awareness and various other hurdles have limited and challenged the Kingdom's ability to incorporate sustainable development to its full potential. Some of the challenges undermining sustainable development are not under Jordan's control while many of them are. Hence, if Jordan wants to realise the fruits of sustainability, it will have first to address these challenges and until then, sustainable development, and Jordan's journey towards sustainable development would be long and arduous.

References

Abu-Odeh, A. (1999). *Jordanians, Palestinians, and the Hashemite Kingdom in the Middle East peace process.* Washington, DC: United States Institute of Peace Press.
Al-Safadi, A. (2018). Personal interview with Minister of Foreign Affairs and expatriates of Hashemite Kingdom of Jordan in Amman on 10 March 2018.
Brand, L. A. (1995). Palestinians and Jordanians: A crisis of identity. *Journal of Palestine Studies, 24*(4), 46–61.
Brundtland, H. (1987). *Our common future.* Oxford: Oxford University Press (for the World Commission on Environment and Development).

Christopherson, M. (2013). Jordan's 2013 elections: Further boost for tribes. *Norwegian Peace Building Resource Centre*, NOREF report.

DoS (Department of Statistics). (1921–2018). *Population statistics*. The Hashemite Kingdom of Jordan. Available at http://dosweb.dos.gov.jo/population/population-2/

Jordan VNR (Jordan Voluntary National Review). (2017). *Jordan's way to sustainable development, first National Voluntary Review on the implementation of the 2030 Agenda*. The Hashemite Kingdom of Jordan. Available at https://sustainabledevelopment.un.org/content/documents/16289Jordan.pdf

Kumaraswamy, P. R., & Singh, M. (2017). Population pressure in Jordan and the role of Syrian refugees. *Migration and Development*, 6(3), 412–427.

Kumaraswamy, P. R., & Singh, M. (2018). Jordan's food security challenges. *Mediterranean Quarterly*, 29(1), 70–95.

Lawrence, P., Meigh, J., & Sullivan, C. (2002). *The Water Poverty Index: An international comparison*. Keele Economic Research Papers (KERP), Issue 19. Available at: http://econwpa.repec.org/eps/dev/papers/0211/0211003.pdf. Accessed 30 June 2018.

MoPIC (Ministry of Planning and International Cooperation). (2013, November). *Need assessment review of the impact of the Syrian crisis in Jordan*. Host community support platform. Available at https://www.undp.org/content/dam/rbas/doc/SyriaResponse/Jordan%20Needs%20Assessment%20-%20November%202013.pdf. Accessed 29 July 2019.

MoPIC (Ministry of Planning and International Cooperation). (2015). *Jordan 2025: A national vision and strategy*. The Hashemite Kingdom of Jordan. Available at http://inform.gov.jo/Portals/0/Report%20PDFs/0.%20General/jo2025part1.pdf. Accessed 30 June 2018.

MoPIC-MoE (Ministry of Planning and International Cooperation-Ministry of Environment). (2008). *Integrated financing strategy for sustainable land management in Jordan*. Final report. Available at http://moenv.gov.jo/En/EnvImpactAssessmentStudies/Documents/Jordan%20IFS%20Final%20Report.pdf

Muasher, M. (2017, September 8). Palestinian nationalism: Regional perspective. *Carnegie Endowment for International Peace*. Available at https://carnegieendowment.org/2017/09/08/jordanian-palestinian-relations-pub-73006

MWI. (2013). *Jordan water sector: Facts and figures*. Available at http://www.mwi.gov.jo/sites/en-us/Documents/W.%20in%20Fig.E%20FINAL%20E.pdf. Accessed 30 June 2018.

MWI (Ministry of Water and Irrigation). (2015). *Jordan water sector facts and figures*. Available at http://www.mwi.gov.jo/sites/en-us/Hot%20Issues/Jordan%20Water%20Sector%20Facts%20and%20%20Figures%202015.pdf

Namrouqa, H. (2014, October 22). Jordan world's second water-poorest country. *The Jordan Times.* http://www.jordantimes.com/news/local/jordan-world%E2%80%99s-second-water-poorest-country. Accessed 30 June 2018.

UNDESA (United Nations Development for Economic and Social Affairs). (2017). *Sustainable development goals.* Available at: https://www.un.org/development/desa/en/. Accessed 29 July 2019.

World Economic Forum. (2006–2017). *Global Gender Gap Report (GGGR).* Available at http://reports.weforum.org. Accessed 30 June 2018.

Smoking

Sean Foley

> *Everyone here smokes – even women, even children.*
> —Mahmoud Husain, Amman Taxi Driver, 2013

In one of the opening sequences of *Theeb*, the 2014 Jordanian movie set in the Arabian Desert during the Arab Revolt in 1916, Edward, a British army officer, arrives at the remote encampment of the Howeitat Tribe. Edward, who is modelled on T.E. Lawrence, hopes that the tribesmen, who know the Arabian Desert well, will accompany him on a dangerous trip on an abandoned trail to a remote well adjacent to the Hejaz railway for an attack on the railway and the Ottoman army.

To gain the trust of the Howeitat, Edward turns to tobacco, a tool that he and other men like him have used for years to cement new alliances in the Arab World from Oman to North Africa. After the British officer gives a Howeitat sheikh one of his British cigarettes and lights it with his own modern cigarette lighter, the tribe agrees to help him. Hussein, who is the older brother of *Theeb*, the hero of the story, is assigned to accompany Edward on his journey to the remote well. *Theeb* secretly joins the trip and is the only one to survive the expedition.

S. Foley (✉)
Middle Tennessee State University, Murfreesboro, TN, USA

© The Author(s) 2019
P. R. Kumaraswamy (ed.), *The Palgrave Handbook of the Hashemite Kingdom of Jordan*, https://doi.org/10.1007/978-981-13-9166-8_10

Although *Theeb* is not based on real events, the Howeitat were a significant tribe in 1916 in Jordan and played a prominent role in *The Seven Pillars of Wisdom*, Lawrence's account of his time, fighting in the Arab Revolt. The Howeitat also likely greatly valued tobacco and cigarettes in 1916. As *The Times* of London noted in a 1923 story, practically "every tribesman" in what is now Jordan was "a devoted adherent of the long Arab Pipe, and more recently, the cigarette" (Abu Nowar 2006, p. 80).

Nearly a century after *The Times* observed the popularity of cigarettes among the tribesmen of Jordan, tobacco retains a pivotal position in the country. Today, nearly a third of adult men smoke, the highest percentage for any country in the Middle East. In 2015, Jordanians spent close to US \$700 million on cigarettes and other tobacco products—a remarkable number for a middle-income country of fewer than 10 million people (El-Emam 2015). Moreover, for years, the tobacco industry has been one of the most dynamic sectors of the country's economy, deserving special treatment from the state. Since the 1970s, Jordan has also served as a key destination and transit point for networks that smuggle Western cigarettes in the Middle East from Cyprus to the Levant to the Gulf and Iran (World Health Organisation; *Legal Monitor Worldwide*).

This chapter provides an introduction to tobacco and its importance to Jordan and its people. It aims to start to fill a gap in the literature on Jordan, a state that is often overlooked in the scholarship of the Middle East. Despite the centrality of cigarettes and tobacco to Jordan, one would be hard pressed to find more than a few words devoted to the subject in any of the recent scholarly histories of the country.

THE OTTOMAN EMPIRE AND MANDATE JORDAN

The history of tobacco in Jordan extends back to the Ottoman Empire, which ruled what became the modern Kingdom of Jordan from the sixteenth century until the 1920s. Tobacco first reached the Ottoman Empire in the sixteenth century, following the first European voyages to the Americas. It was first planted in Anatolia, in the late sixteenth century, and spread throughout the empire, including to the Levant and the other Arab territories within the empire.

In the seventeenth century, smoking tobacco became popular among all the classes in the Ottoman Empire, earning the wrath of the sultans, such as Sultan Murad IV (r. 1612–1640), who issued an edict making smoking a capital crime. In his eyes, smoking tobacco was the cause of the empire's international and socio-cultural decline at the turn of the seventeenth century. His edict received support from many Islamic jurists, who issued Islamic opinions (singular: *fatwa*; plural: *fatawa*) declaring smoking illegal under Islamic law.

In 1646, however, Shaikh al-Islam Bahai Efendi, who smoked voraciously, lifted the restrictions on smoking in the Empire with a *fatwa* declaring it to be *Halal*, sparking a debate that continues to this day in Jordan and elsewhere among Muslims about whether smoking is permissible under Islamic law. In the subsequent decades, the Ottoman state further legitimised smoking by taxing it, producing a problem that plagues modern Jordan—namely, the smuggling of tobacco products to avoid paying the high taxes on them. Just as in Jordan today, Ottoman men, women, and children smoked in significant numbers from the seventeenth century forward (Birdal 2010, pp. 129–132).

By the nineteenth century, tobacco was one of the most vibrant sectors of the Ottoman economy, much as it has been for over a century in Jordan. Those profits reflected the popularity of Ottoman tobacco products, especially cigarettes, which were introduced to the West by British veterans of the Crimea War (1853–1856). After the Ottoman Bankruptcy in 1876, the Ottoman government and its European partners created the Régie, a tobacco monopoly to help to pay back Istanbul's debts to European creditors.

Over the next four decades, the company came to control virtually all tobacco growing and production in the empire, becoming a magnet for foreign capital, accounting for a quarter of the foreign direct investment in the Ottoman Empire. It became profitable when the government in the early twentieth century agreed to provide substantial assistance dealing with tobacco smuggling, providing a model that both Jordan and the other Arab Ottoman successor states adopted in the twentieth century (Birdal 2010, pp. 155–165).

After World War I, the Ottoman territories east of the river Jordan became a British-administered mandate, Transjordan (later Jordan). The new and sparsely populated state was landlocked and had little rainfall, water, and other natural resources. To address the new state's acute economic needs, Jordanian and British authorities—much like their Ottoman predecessors—looked to agriculture, especially to cash crops. Tobacco was attractive to Jordan's emerging farmers for two reasons.

First, there was a potentially large market for cigarettes and tobacco in Jordan. As noted earlier, Jordanian tribesmen loved smoking cigarettes, especially the English ones that Edward used in *Theeb*. This love of cigarettes and smoking would also have geo-strategic implications. Indeed, it was widely assumed by British officials that the country's tribesmen, although they were very pious Muslims, would never join any state led by King Abdulaziz Ibn Saud because of his and the Wahhabi demand of total abstinence from using any form of tobacco (Abu Nowar 2006, p. 80).

Second, tobacco requires much less water per acreage than wheat and other major crops, while several strands of tobacco, such as Virginia Tobacco (Bright Tobacco), thrive in poor soils in climates that are both hot and receive minimal rainfall. Jordan, with its hot and arid climate, proved to be a good match for tobacco, especially bright tobacco. By the end of the 1930s, Jordan's farmers produced close to 30 tons of tobacco annually on nearly 7400 acres in the country (Abu Nowar 2006, p. 298).

Those totals proved more than enough to allow Jordanians to both export tobacco to other states in the region, such as the Mandate Palestine, and to meet domestic needs. Among the most important domestic customers were two cigarette factories in Jordan opened by British American Tobacco (BAT) in 1935. By that time, Jordanians had become accustomed to BAT's type of flue-cured tobacco cigarettes.

Jordanians' taste in cigarettes reflected BAT's expansion into the Middle East following the collapse of the Ottoman Empire, an event that ended Régie's tobacco monopoly in Jordan and the other former Ottoman territories in the Arab World. In the 1920s and 1930s, BAT bought stakes in regional tobacco companies and built the new cigarette factories in the Middle East. One of BAT's purchases was Osman Sharabai, a successor to Régie in Jordan. In 1931, the cigarette company was incorporated in Amman as the National Tobacco and Cigarette Company (NTC). That same year another cigarette company, the Jordanian Tobacco Company (JTC), was also founded in Amman and the national tobacco industry had been born (Cox 2000, pp. 285–286).

Smoking in Modern Jordan

After Jordan gained its independence from Great Britain in 1946, cigarette consumption in the Kingdom increased rapidly and nearly tripled in the decade between 1954 and 1964 (Parker 1964, pp. 15–16). All classes of Jordan's diverse society smoked—from the Bedouin nomads and farmers to highly paid urban professionals to Palestinian refugees. Although most of Jordan's industries were initially unable to meet the country's basic needs in the 1940s and 1950s, the tobacco industry could meet the domestic demand with what a US Department of Agriculture (USDA) report labelled as "some of the finest cigarettes" in the Middle East. The industry, which *The New York Times*, in 1951, called the "most important" in Jordan received assistance from the US Four Points Programme—a technical programme launched by the Truman Administration to help Jordan and other poor developing countries. By the 1960s, Jordanian consumers could choose from quality cigarettes costing between US $.20 and US $.30 a pack along with cheaper, lower-grade varieties of cigarettes that were "within the reach of a larger number of Jordanians" (Parker 1964, pp. 15–16; Phillips 1957, p. 25).

JTC dominated the cigarette market in Jordan in much the same way that the Régie had dominated the Ottoman market, benefiting from the US assistance and the complete prohibitions on importing cigarettes. The company mainly met Jordan's domestic needs and helped to address the country's growing trade deficit. By 1964, Jordan exported 50,000–100,000 pounds of cigarettes annually to Lebanon and many states in the Gulf. Most of the cigarettes were produced in factories in and around Amman (Parker 1964, p. 16).

The tobacco in Jordan's cigarettes drew from domestic and foreign sources. While Jordan imported a million pounds of unmanufactured tobacco annually before 1964, it produced between 3 and 4 million pounds of tobacco domestically. Most of the Jordanian-grown tobacco was Virginia or flue-cured tobacco popularised by BAT in the 1930s. But Jordanian farmers also grew nearly a million pounds annually of other types of tobacco, including tombac—the type of tobacco used in hookah (narghile) water pipes that are popular in Jordan and other countries in the Middle East.

While Jordanians grew tombac in garden patches wherever arable land was available, flue-cured tobacco was grown in prime farmland within 30 miles (or 48 kilometres) of Amman. Not only were these farmlands close to the cigarette factories in Amman, they were also accessible to natural springs—a critical water source in a dry and desert country with limited rainfall. Some of the new farmers were Bedouins, who had been encouraged to farm tobacco as part of the state's programme, carried out in cooperation with the United Nations, to sedentarise the Kingdom's nomadic peoples between 1960 and 1980. To further aid these new farmers, some of whom lived on territories where water was more than a mile away, the government classified tobacco an essential national crop and provided subsidies to the farmers growing tobacco.

The government policies certainly reflected the widespread popularity of tobacco and its importance to the country's export earnings. But it also reflected the fact that the elites, including the long-time monarch, King Hussein (r. 1952–1999), regularly smoked—long after he publicly pledged to the Jordanian people that he would quit in 1986. Over the years, he reportedly used smoking to relieve stress and to build bridges in the key meetings, he often held with Israeli and Western foreign leaders about the Arab-Israeli conflict and the Palestinians.

Two examples of Hussein's diplomacy and smoking are noteworthy. The first was a secret meeting, held in 1963 at the residence of Hussein's London doctor, between Hussein and Yaakov Herzog, an Israeli bureaucrat. During the meeting, Hussein made a point of offering Herzog a cigarette and insisted on lighting it with his lighter—a gesture of friendship that cemented their decade-long productive relationship as Herzog rose to become a senior official in the Israeli government (Bar-Zohar 2016, p. 718). Three decades later, in 1994, the King turned to smoking to mark Israeli Prime Minister Rabin's visit to Jordan—the first official visit by an Israeli leader to the country and a vital part of the politics tied to a peace treaty signed two weeks earlier between the two countries. At the royal residence in Aqaba, Hussein, a cigarette lit and in his mouth, allowed himself to be photographed lighting up the cigarette for a smiling Rabin. The photo of the two men happily smoking, which became an iconic image of the Oslo Peace Process in the 1990s, signalled the warming ties between the two nations but also reminded them of a moment that they had shared two weeks earlier in Washington. At the time, Hussein and Rabin, who had come to Washington to meet President Clinton and to publicly sign an historic treaty between their nations, were both asked to step outside when they lit up cigarettes in the White House.

The needs of King Hussein's regional diplomacy, however, had negative consequences for Jordan's cigarette industry, especially after the June War of 1967. The Six-Day War, in which Jordan lost East Jerusalem and the West Bank to Israel, devastated JTC, robbing it of more than a third of its old domestic market for cigarettes. At the same time, Hussein's decision to allow the West Bank residents to smuggle goods into Jordan from the West Bank—as a way to retain ties with his former subjects there—also created a surge in cheap, smuggled cigarettes in Jordan (Friendly 1967, B2).

Those smuggled cigarettes eviscerated the market position of both JTC and NTC, with the latter seeing its market position drop from 27 per cent in 1965 to just 13 per cent in 1970. Losses for both JTC and NTC grew even faster, especially after the King ordered the Jordanian military to suppress an armed Palestinian rebellion in September 1970. A May 1971 BAT report flatly stated that JTC losses had reached US $240,000 a year, while NTC's losses had reached US $148,000 annually, a number that was seemingly unsustainable. Seeing no hope for NTC in 1971, BAT executives recommend the company's board of directors liquidate BAT's substantial investments in NTC ("Middle East" 1967, pp. 1–4; Lockhart 1971, pp. 1–4).

As bad as Jordan's domestic politics and cigarette market appeared to be at the start of the 1970s, both the situation in Jordan and the financial health of its tobacco growers and companies rebounded in the later part of the decade. Between 1975 and 1994, the Jordanian cigarette market grew from 1.5 billion units to 4.8 billion units in 1994, with JTC retaining the position of market leader and retaining at least 75 per cent of the market (Maxwell International Estimates 1977, p. 13; "Draft Amendments").

Throughout this era, the tobacco industry was buoyed by rising consumer spending and the Jordanian government's decision in the early 1990s to deregulate the cigarette industry. While four separate companies emerged, the government kept in place its high excise taxes on cigarettes and prohibitions on foreign investment in the trading companies that did not engage in manufacturing. Consequently, virtually all of the legal cigarettes were manufactured in the Kingdom, while international tobacco companies bought stakes in or signed licencing partnerships with Jordanian companies to produce foreign brands to sell in Israel, Jordan, and other Arab states.

The investments more than proved their worth. Between 1990 and 1997 alone, consumption in Jordan and the Middle East increased by 24.3 per cent, making it one of the few new markets in the world for international tobacco that was growing. The numbers of cigarettes sold in the region continued to rise into the twenty-first century, lifted by strong economic growth in Saudi Arabia and its neighbours because of sustained high oil prices. Jordan was no exception, where the cigarette market grew to 6.5 billion units annually by 2003 (Fawaz 2003; Nakkash and Lee 2008, p. 324).

One can see the continued importance of the tobacco industry in Jordan's economy and its leadership in the US-Jordanian Free Trade Agreement. The agreement, which was implemented by both countries in late 2001, differs in one way from the US free-trade agreements with Oman, another Arab state that also grows tobacco—namely, it specifically does not apply to Jordanian cigarettes and other tobacco products. Philip Morris and other American tobacco companies had to choose between either paying very high import duties or establishing partnerships with local companies if they wanted to serve the Jordanian market. Most chose to invest in Jordan.

Cigarette Smuggling

The continued success of Jordan's tobacco industry in the four decades after the crisis of 1970 is all the more remarkable when one considers that it coincided with the rise of (a) tobacco smuggling in Jordan and the region, and (b) initiatives to reduce smoking and to raise the awareness of the health risks associated with tobacco generally.

The most important of these issues was cigarette smuggling, which had a definite impact on Jordan's domestic market and the country's finances. By 1994, a fifth of all cigarettes sold in the country were smuggled, robbing domestic cigarette companies of market share, and depriving the Jordanian state of millions of dinars in cigarette taxes (Draft Amendments). Further exacerbating the situation was the fact that the cigarettes, often Western brands sold at a significant discount, provided a pretext for legal cigarette companies to reduce the prices to compete in the market. Over time, the reduced prices of legal cigarettes led to lower tax rates because cigarette taxes are tied to the price of the cigarette.

Of course, smuggling had long been a challenge for Jordan because of the country's taxes on cigarettes, its prohibition on imported cigarettes, and its geography. The country's porous land and sea borders with the West Bank had already led to widespread cigarette smuggling in the days after the 1967 War. Moreover, Jordan had porous land and sea borders with multiple countries that had cigarette industries—Egypt, Israel, and Syria. Cigarette prices in the governorates bordering Syria have long been lower than in Amman or in governorates that do not directly border Syria, most likely because of smuggling of Syrian cigarettes which are far cheaper than Jordanian ones (Sweis 2012, p. 111).

But in the 1970s, 1980s, and 1990s, the chief problem for Jordan was cigarette smuggling tied to three states that did not directly border Jordan—namely Cyprus, Lebanon, and Iran—and to political changes, first in Lebanon and then in Iran. In Lebanon, the state-run tobacco monopoly, the Régie, collapsed after 1975 under the weight of both the civil war in the country along with the competing interests of the factions that had a stake in the company. Not only did domestic cigarette production cease, but the central government also lost control of the country's borders—opening the way to the smuggling of cigarettes and other goods into Lebanon and to other countries, including Jordan.

At the same time, Iran, which had become the most lucrative export market for American cigarettes in the 1970s during the oil boom, closed its market to the US and other foreign cigarettes. Tehran's decision, which followed the 1979 Islamic Revolution, reflected the desire of Iran's new government to protect the country's domestic industries from foreign competitors, especially US ones.

In response to these challenges at opposite ends of the Middle East, multinational tobacco companies, in cooperation with Cypriot cigarette companies, such as Kental, turned to smuggling as the chief way to gain market share in Lebanon and to regain their old markets in Iran. Between 1981 and 1985, as cigarette imports into Iran collapsed, imports of cigarettes into Cyprus increased from 281 million pieces annually to over 1.8 billion pieces per year—just as Cypriot cigarette exports rose from 1.8 billion to 3 billion pieces annually (*Cigarettes: Imports of Selected Countries*, p. 41).

Many of these cigarettes were shipped to the Levant. This is a region that tobacco executives saw as having "fluid" distribution networks and included Jordan along with Lebanon, Cyprus, and Syria—another country that, like Jordan, banned cigarette imports and had a cigarette monopoly (Sandefur 1992, p. 1). During this era, Lebanon's imports of cigarettes soared, climbing from 4.2 billion pieces in the late 1970s to 7.2 billion pieces by the middle of the 1980s (*Cigarettes: Imports of Selected Countries*, p. 41).

While some of these foreign cigarettes were destined for Lebanon's domestic market, many more were transited through the country to other countries, including Jordan. As Philip Morris executives told the company's board of directors in October 1983, "We dominate Lebanon with an overall market share of 65 per cent... Although there are no direct sales to Syria and Jordan, the overflow from Lebanon generates estimated sales in these two markets of 18 per cent and 9 per cent respectively" ("September EEMA" 1983, p. 5).

Even after the conclusion of Lebanon's civil war and Régie regaining its former position in the country's cigarette market, BAT and other tobacco companies retained the distribution channels in the Levant that they had developed in the 1970s and 1980s. Most of the cigarettes distributed via these networks went to Iran, which saw smuggled cigarettes reach billions of pieces annually in the late 1990s.

But not all smuggled cigarettes travelling through Lebanon were destined for Iran. As has already been noted, smuggled cigarettes accounted for a fifth of Jordan's total tobacco market in the early 1990s—a presence that had tangible impacts on the rest of the industry and only grew in the 2000s. Indeed, in January 2014, Philip Morris justified its decision to significantly cut prices for cigarettes in Jordan by citing the large presence of cheaper smuggled cigarettes in the Kingdom—46 per cent—and the US $190 million in lost tax revenues from smuggled cigarettes (Whitman 2013).

Tobacco Control in Jordan

The decision of tobacco companies to reduce the prices of their cigarettes was widely seen as a blow to Jordan's efforts to curb tobacco use, a programme going back decades. Starting in the late 1960s and early 1970s, Jordan banned advertising of any type of tobacco and strictly regulated distribution and sponsorship deals. Only shops with specific licences from the Ministry of Finance and Customs were legally allowed to sell cigarettes and tobacco. According to a set of regulations passed in the 1970s and then amended in the twenty-first century, smoking was prohibited in airports, government buildings, hospitals, libraries, movie theatres, offices, schools, and all other large public spaces during daylight hours. Smoking was also banned in taxis and public transport—buses, trains, and ships. In 1998, Royal Jordanian Airlines voluntarily banned smoking on its short-haul flights, including its international flights to Damascus ("Public Smoking," pp. 2–3).

Jordan's civil society and government also supported tobacco control initiatives with national and global partners. The Jordanian National Society for Anti-Smoking, which was founded in 1981, has held meetings and pushed to limit tobacco use in the country. In 1988, the Kingdom hosted the first Arab Anti-Smoking Symposium in Amman (Borek 1988). By the early twenty-first century, fines were imposed on both minors who bought cigarettes and those who sold cigarettes to them. New restrictions were introduced for both five-star and fast-food restaurants. In cooperation with the World Health Organisation (WHO), Jordan's government-funded various programmes through the state media to educate the public on the dangers of smoking and of second-hand smoke along with cardiovascular diseases.

In 2003, Jordan became one of the first countries to adopt the WHO's ambitious Framework Convention on Tobacco Control (FCTC), which commits countries to eliminate tobacco advertising within five years, adopt large warning labels on cigarette packs, and to forbid misleading statements about cigarettes. Cigarette packets soon carried large health warnings for both tar and nicotine levels in accordance with FCTC.

However, for decades, the government rarely enforced cigarette and tobacco laws generally. As the Jordanian English-language weekly newspaper, *The Star*, noted in February 1997, while the rest of the world was decreasing its use of cigarettes and tobacco, Jordanians were smoking more than ever in the "heyday for Jordan's smoking cult." The newspaper observed that it was common to see men and women lighting up "even where smoking is prohibited." Among the many Jordanians who smoked were heads of households and authority figures, including 51 per cent of doctors. Even more worrisome was the fact that 28 per cent of all smokers were children and most of the patients admitted to King Hussein Medical City for major conditions smoked (*The Star/GIN* 1997).

In explaining Jordan's attachment to smoking, *The Star* and others have highlighted the paucity of state resources dedicated to enforcing anti-tobacco laws along with a societal acceptance of smoking. Not only are mourners at wakes often given cigarettes, but cigarettes have also been available at business frequented by people of all ages—namely, grocery stores, coffee shops, and street kiosks. Many Jordanians smoked hookah at home and asked their children to light it for them. In the eyes of many, the choice to smoke cigarettes or hookah was a matter for which the state had no right to regulate no less prohibit.

As the Jordanian public debated smoking and its role in society in the 1990s and 2000s, the Kingdom's religious leaders proved to be equally divided—mirroring the debates of Ottoman jurists in the early seventeenth century. While Wahhabi Jurists in Saudi Arabia have ruled for decades that smoking is always forbidden under Islamic law, Jordanian Muslim scholars, who, like Ottomans jurists adhere to the Hanafi vision of Islamic law, have provided a far more nuanced position, one that allows for multiple perspectives on smoking and Islam to exist.

For instance, in 2003, Jordanian jurists ruled that it was permissible for a Muslim to open a coffee shop serving carbonated beverages and hookah provided that it was not used for an "illegal purpose, such as serving alcoholic drinks" (At-Tamimi et al. 2003). While this decision was reversed only three years later, the judicial opinion banning smoking opens by admitting that there is no text that forbids smoking and acknowledging that Muslim scholars have "disagreed as to whether it is forbidden, disliked or allowed" (Helayel et al. 2006). This tone stands in stark contrast to the mood in most decisions banning smoking in Saudi Arabia and other Arab countries in recent years, which include language stating that Muslim jurists universally agree that smoking is forbidden in Islamic law.

Equally importantly, the 2006 decision only bans smoking in specific circumstances in which it threatens public welfare. In particular, the authors ban smoking in public spaces where non-smokers congregate, prohibit smokers from wasting all of their earnings on tobacco at the expense of their familial responsibilities, and forbid advertising encouraging smoking. At the same time, the authors only "recommend" that Muslims *not* sell cigarettes, tobacco, and hookah or rent a property for any of these purposes (Helayel et al. 2006). Indeed, a Muslim is not directly barred from smoking in a private setting or owning a café that sells cigarettes or hookah—provided of course that non-smokers are not adversely affected by the smoke.

Conclusion

The ambiguity of Jordan's Islamic rulings brings into stark relief the challenge facing both activists and policymakers determined to reduce the amount of smoking in the Kingdom—despite additional support from the country's governing institutions in recent years. Not only has the government, since 2008, steadily raised the cigarette taxes, it has also broadened the definition of public spaces where smoking is prohibited. During this same period, the government has increased the penalties for (a) individuals caught smoking illegally (US $300 and three months in jail) and (b) the owners of the premises where people are caught smoking illegally (up to US $4500 and six months in prison). Nonetheless, in 2013, there were just 184 liaison officers authorised to ticket violations of the smoking law in a country of nearly 7 million people (Whitman 2013).

That same year, Dr. Feras Hawari, the head of the Cancer Control Office at King Hussein Cancer Centre, told *Al-Jazeera* that he and others were determined to fight to reduce smoking in Jordan. "It might take us a while," Hawari explained, "but we're not going to quit" (Whitman 2013). Given the importance of tobacco to Jordan's culture, economy, and modern history, Hawari and others will have to carry on that fight for many years to come.

REFERENCES

Abu Nowar, M. (2006). *The development of trans-Jordan 1929–1939: A history of the Hashemite Kingdom of Jordan*. Reading: Ithaca Press.

Anonymous. (1967, June 14). Middle East, pp. 1–4. Tobacco Control Documents, British American Tobacco Records. Retrieved from https://www.industrydocumentslibrary.ucsf.edu/tobacco/docs/#id=qhnk0198.

Anonymous. (1983, September). September EEMA Region Presentation to the Board of Directors of Philip Morris Inc. Tobacco Control Documents, Philip Morris Records. Retrieved from https://www.industrydocumentslibrary.ucsf.edu/tobacco/docs/#id=xfcj0111.

Anonymous. (2014, February 5). Hookah ban causes uproar in Jordan. *Legal Monitor Worldwide*. Retrieved from LexisNexis Academic.

Anonymous. *Cigarettes: Imports of selected countries by country of origin annual 1981–85*. N.D. Tobacco Control Documents, British American Tobacco Records. Retrieved from https://www.industrydocumentslibrary.ucsf.edu/tobacco/docs/#id=npbc0212.

Anonymous. Public smoking: Warning levels in Arab countries. N.D. Tobacco Control Documents, British American Tobacco Records. Retrieved from https://www.industrydocumentslibrary.ucsf.edu/tobacco/docs/#id=rfnk0196.

At-Tamimi, I., al-Abbadi, A., Yahia, M. A., Ghyzan, Y., Mujahid, N., Shewayat, M., al-Bakhri, W., & al-Hijjawi, S. (2003, November 6). Resolution No. (71): Ruling on leasing an endowment as a coffee-shop. *Board of Iftaa, Research, and Islamic Studies, the Hashemite Kingdom of Jordan*. http://aliftaa.jo/DecisionEn.aspx?DecisionId=478#.WkvI2N-nFPY.

Bar-Zohar, M. (2016). *Yaacov Herzog: A biography*. London: Halban Publishers.

Birdal, M. (2010). *Political economy of Ottoman debt*. London/New York: I.B. Tauris.

Borek, A. (1988, May 18). Memo: First Arab anti-smoking symposium. Tobacco Control Documents, British American Tobacco Records. Retrieved from https://www.industrydocumentslibrary.ucsf.edu/tobacco/docs/#id=rmpg0201.

Cox, H. (2000). *The global cigarette: Origins and evolution of British American Tobacco, 1880–1945*. Oxford: Oxford University Press.

El-Emam, D. (2015, February 18). Jordanians spend JD500 million on tobacco every year. *The Jordan Times*. Retrieved from http://www.jordantimes.com/news/local/jordanians-spend-jd500m-tobacco-every-year.

Fawaz, M. (2003, January 23). E-mail letter to Karl Rooke. Tobacco Control Documents, Gallaher Records. Retrieved from https://www.industrydocumentslibrary.ucsf.edu/tobacco/docs/#id=zzpl0189.

Friendly, A. (1967, August 13). Jordan valley harvest time means it's dinar time: Tractor fleet on hand a plus for Hussein profits and peace. *Washington Post*, B2. Retrieved from ProQuest Historical Newspaper Database.

Helayel, A. M., al-Khasawneh, A. K., Ghayithan, Y. A., el-Salaheen, A. M., el-Bakri, W. A. W., Mujahed, N. M., & al-Hajjawi, S. A. H. (2006, May 30). Resolution No. (109): Ruling on smoking and selling cigarettes. *Board of Iftaa, Research, and Islamic Studies, the Hashemite Kingdom of Jordan*. Retrieved from http://aliftaa.jo/DecisionEn.aspx?DecisionId=234#.WkvK19-nFPY.

Lockhart, S. (1971, May 4). Policy Committee: National Tobacco & Cigarette Co, LTD, Jordan, pp. 1–4. Tobacco Control Documents, British American Tobacco Records. Retrieved from https://www.industrydocumentslibrary.ucsf.edu/tobacco/docs/#id=xsmy0196.

Maxwell International Estimates. (1977, July). How the brands ranked. Tobacco Control Documents, Liggett & Myers Records. Retrieved from https://www.industrydocumentslibrary.ucsf.edu/tobacco/docs/#id=ghmw0009.

Nakkash, R., & Lee, K. (2008). Smuggling as the 'Key to a combined market': British American tobacco in Lebanon. *Tobacco Control*, 17 (5), 324–331.

Parker, J. B. (1964). *The tobacco industry of Western Asia*. Washington, DC: United States Department of Agriculture, Foreign Agricultural Service.

Phillips, W. (1957, December 8). Jordan strives to pay her way. *The New York Times*, p. 25. Retrieved from ProQuest Historical Newspaper Database.

Sandefur, T. E., Jr. (1992, September 14). Letter from TE Sandefur to UG Herter regarding recommendations on specific market. Tobacco Control Documents, Brown and Williamson Tobacco Corporation Records. Retrieved from https://www.industrydocumentslibrary.ucsf.edu/tobacco/docs/#id=sfpj0194.

Sweis, N. J. (2012) *The economics of tobacco use in Jordan*. Ph.D. dissertation, University of Illinois Chicago.

The Star/GIN. (1997, February 21) Jordan: Heyday for Jordan's smoking cult. *The Star/GIN*. Tobacco Control Documents, RJ Reynolds Records. Retrieved from https://www.industrydocumentslibrary.ucsf.edu/tobacco/docs/#id=gfph0021.

Whitman, E. (2013, April 19). Cheap tobacco lights up a controversy in Jordan. *Al-Jazeera*. Retrieved from http://www.aljazeera.com/indepth/features/2013/04/2013414101437602592.html.

World Health Organisation. *WHO report on the world tobacco epidemic 2017: Country profile Jordan*. Retrieved from http://www.who.int/tobacco/surveillance/policy/country_profile/jor.pdf.

PART III

Politics and Identity

Citizenship

Paul Esber

> *In many ways, the authoritarian bargain that has been the foundation of society has collapsed and people are searching for a new social contract with the state and between themselves ... one that is founded on a more inclusive and equitable basis, entailing new notions of citizenship.* (Meijer and Butenschøn 2017, p. 3)

The above reflection encapsulates the essence of citizenship's importance to lived politics in contemporary Jordan. Simultaneously, the statement reveals one of the citizenship's central characteristics: its regulative function in the relationship between rulers and ruled. Citizenship, which on a fundamental level denotes membership of an identified political community, is correspondingly a central variable in the practice of politics. It is ergo, of seminal significance to the study and comprehension of politics.

The chapter is divided into five sections addressing the theoretical and practical facets of Jordanian citizenship. It provides a reflection on the question of "what is citizenship?" in which attention is given to three components: extent, depth, and content. This is followed by considering a similar yet distinct question concerning what can be called citizenship. Here the two prevailing concepts, *jinsiyyah* and *muwātanah*, which are

P. Esber (✉)
University of Sydney, Sydney, NSW, Australia
e-mail: paul.esber@sydney.edu.au

utilised in Arabic political discourse, are introduced. Devoting space to these two questions is necessary due to the ready assumptions that discussions about citizenship generate. After establishing the theoretical facets of citizenship, the chapter enunciates the duties and rights of Jordanians as outlined in the Kingdom's constitution. Following from this, the chapter focuses on the actual practice of these rights using four illustrations: freedom of expression, the patriarchal transferal of citizenship, voting patterns, and the influence of non-citizen residents.

What Is Citizenship?

It is impossible to answer this question without ruminating on citizenship's depth, content, and extent in the political community, where it is practised. Extent is concerned with "the who" of citizenship; who is included and by extension, excluded from it and the package of rights and obligations associated by way of inclusion within its ambit (Faulks 2000, p. 7). Because of the dominant role of nation-states in the world politics, there are at least two fundamental dynamics worth referencing here. The first relates to the external other, the non-national who is often but not always a citizen of another state. In this context, the critical point of differentiation between a Jordanian and a Syrian would be the reality of their belonging to two distinct nation-state constructs.

The second dynamic at play of equal if not greater significance for Jordanian citizenship is the presence of refugees and displaced persons across the breadth of the kingdom's history. Many, but not all, became citizens, including Chechens and Circassians in the nineteenth century, Armenians, Palestinians, and Iraqis in the twentieth century, and Syrians fleeing the post-2011 civil war. Among them, the Palestinians are of cardinal importance, as a consequence of their demographic weight, diversity of their experience and their possession of a distinct Palestinian nationalism. While many of them are citizens of the kingdom, others are refugees without access to Jordanian citizenship. Both groups as part of the Palestinian diaspora share identification with Palestine as a font of national identity, which complicates their relationship to Jordanian citizenship, to other Jordanian citizens, and to Jordanian national identity. The politics surrounding the practice of Palestinian identity (let alone other sub-identities) in Jordan are implicated within the country's citizenship regime.

Such raises the value of depth in discussing citizenship. Depth refers to the question of how and when: *how* demanding should citizenship be as an identity requiring an individual and collective actors to behave in particular ways; and *when* should a citizenship-based identity be prioritised above others? (Faulks 2000, p. 7). Depth is seminal because among the three factors it is the one where arguably, the state exerts the most influence. This is a result of the nation-state operating as a site on which the interplay and contestation between nationalism/s as a mode of ideological expression and citizenship as a vessel of rights and obligations (concerning both citizens and the state itself) play out. The relationship between the two is necessarily uneasy. Due to its mixture of duties and rights, citizenship carries embedded within it a promise of reciprocity: that the state will respect and reciprocate the rights of citizens.

The last of Faulk's triumvirate is content, which is primarily associated with questions about the balance between rights and duties. Furthermore, thinking about content additionally asks scholars to consider what trade-offs are implicated in the processes of negotiating alterations to an existing citizenship model (Faulks 2000, p. 7). Conventional reflections on citizenship, therefore, see it defined "as rights, obligations and belonging to the nation-state," with three rights "civil, political and social" traded with three duties "conscription, taxation and franchise" (Isin 2017, p. 512). More recently, scholars have approached citizenship from a more critical perspective, bringing two main points of critique. First, rights (indigenous, environmental, etc.), whose emergence and wide circulation since the end of the Cold War indicate the contestable, rather than stable nature of the political space occupied by citizenship. Second, the role of international and transnational actors in interceding and mediating in citizen-oriented contests. Doing so enables critical scholars to question state-bounded assumptions of citizenship (Isin 2017, p. 512). Subsequently, the study of citizenship becomes less focussed on it being a status, so much as a process.

Jinsiyyah and *Muwātanah*: What Do We Call Citizenship?

In contemporary Arabic political discourse, two keywords are utilised to convey citizenship: *jinsiyyah* (nationality, citizenship) and *muwātanah* (residence, citizenship). The two must be simultaneously considered if the citizenship regime in Jordan is to be better understood. This is because together the terms constitute a dialogic structure that cannot be separated. *Jinsiyyah* refers to a form of top-down categorisation on the part of the nation-state as a means of distinguishing between members and non-members of the political community. Its root j-n-s has no association with pre-existing lingual forms of collective organisation such as *ummah* (community of believers) or *sha'ab* (people), and it is not connected with either individual or collective feelings of attachment to space or territory. Further, its expansion into political discourse came about as a direct consequence of exposure to European experiences with the nation-state and their increasingly felt presence in the Arab territories of the Ottoman Empire (Parolin 2009, p. 116).

An important question emerging from this concerns the power relations embedded within the mechanisms by which individuals are selected and excluded on the basis of citizenship. Who gets to choose statuses of citizen and non-citizen? The state is central in the answer. All Jordanians carry a national identity card with their identity number, citizenship status, name, and family written on it under the umbrella of *jinsiyyah*, not *muwātanah*. *Jinsiyyah*, therefore, refers to a "legal and political association," tied to, yet concomitantly separate from, *muwātanah* (Sha'bān 2017, p. 30).

Muwātanah deals explicitly with the individual and collective attachments to territory that are absent in *jinsiyyah*. Its historical development is especially exciting given that its active participle *muwātin/muwātaneen* predates it. In Butrus al-Bustāni's formative dictionary of modern Arabic: *Muḥīṭ al-Muḥīṭ*, published in the second half of the nineteenth century, *muwātin/muwātanīn* is referenced but not *muwātanah*, which would only come into circulation in the twentieth century (al-Bustāni 1987, pp. 975–976). The direct link to land as an emotive and mobilising entity evident in al-Bustāni's entry derives from its root w-t-n, which in its various verb formulae denotes to reside (I), settle in a place (II, V), and to become naturalised to and in a locality (X). Correspondingly, the noun *watan* is employed in reference to the homeland and nation, alongside which *wataniyyah* becomes synonymous in political discourse with nationalism.

Subsequently, *wataniyyah* conjunctively expresses the *muwātanīns'* collective "feelings of attachment to the nation" (Hussein 2010, p. 3). In this way, it is apparent that the functionality of *muwātin* as a designation "relies on a relation with a place (namely the city) more than an authority" (Parolin 2009, p. 25), which as demonstrated above, is conveyed via *jinsiyyah*. Thus, when *muwātanah* entered popular circulation in the twentieth century, it had to contend with the locus of political authority and institutionalism contained within *jinsiyyah*. In practical terms, this means that unlike the Anglo-European experience which incorporates belonging, attachment with ruling authority and the division of rights and obligations, citizenship in Jordan has evolved on two different foundations: of residing in a particular place on the one hand (*muwātanah*) and the state's recognition, acceptance, and resultant categorisation of this (*jinsiyyah*) on the other.

Textual and Legal Foundations: *The Constitution*

Constitutions shape both institutions and operations of the government via their existence as framing mechanisms structuring political and legal architecture within nation-states, influencing the characteristics of citizenship regimes, and therefore, of citizens. The social influence of constitutions resides in their embodiment of both the facets and ideals supposedly shared by the members of the political community. Jordan's constitution, promulgated in 1952 with amendments in 2011, 2014, and 2016, is no exception. However, it is important to note that the Jordanian constitution does not define *jinsiyyah* and does not refer to *muwātanah*. Therein, it does not delimit the borders of citizen-based membership within the Jordanian political community.

The constitution performs a pivotal role in delineating the space in which citizens may practice their citizenship within the domestic social and political system. Suffice to say that they are comprehensive in their scope. Within Article 6, all citizens are accorded equality before the law without exceptions or exclusions on the basis of language, religion, and race. This is paired with the responsibility of all Jordanians to, as a "sacred duty," safeguard the unity of the political community and defend the nation (The Constitution, Art. 6). The personal freedom of individual citizens is "guaranteed" under the constitution, alongside which, their property and person cannot be detained or have their freedoms delimited "except in accordance with the provisions of the law" (The Constitution, Art. 7).

Resultantly, if the state seizes a Jordanian, their treatment while in custody must preserve their "human dignity" as befitting their citizen status (The Constitution, Art. 7 and 8). To this end, the constitution forbids unauthorised entry into the homes of citizens, which are deemed "inviolable" unless particular laws permit it under specified circumstances (The Constitution, Art. 10). Analogously, if, for public purposes, the state seeks to confiscate the property of citizens, "a just" compensation must be forthcoming (The Constitution, Art. 11). All citizens can choose where they reside within the country, insofar as the state cannot prohibit them from residing in a given part of the Kingdom unless specified by law (The Constitution, Art. 9).

Concerning the public sphere, the constitution similarly provides substantial rights for citizens. Their exercise of religious rites is secured, conditional on their consistency with "public order and morality" (The Constitution, Art. 14). Likewise (or similarly), freedom of expression, research, scientific inquiry, the press, publication, and printing are guaranteed by the state (The Constitution, Art. 15). Each, however, is predicated on the specifics of the relevant laws which govern the day-to-day practice of these freedoms. Hence, the constitution is in and of itself, not a guarantor of rights in the same way that a bill of rights may be in offering un-conditionality to the practice of citizen-based rights. Legislation performs a critical role in framing the ways Jordanians as individuals practice their rights. Legislation functions analogously with rights of collective action and association. Citizens enjoy the right to hold assemblies and meetings and to establish unions, political parties, and societies (The Constitution, Art. 16). All activities must take place within the parameters set by the legislation that governs their practice. For illustration, political parties must be set up and run as per the Political Parties Law; labour unions by the Labour Trade Unions Law 1953 Jordanian Labour Law 1961 (amended 1996 and 2002), especially section 97. Equally, the constitution affords Jordanians protection of their personal communications and correspondence, which are considered immune from censorship, surveillance and or suspension in the absence of a judicial warrant enabling such to be undertaken in-line with legal statutes (The Constitution, Art. 18).

Therefore, the constitution in isolation can do little to unilaterally safeguard citizen rights in all conditions. Furthermore, those which it does protect may, depending on legislation, be circumvented. Ergo, it is the role of the legislature to determine the actual parameters of citizen practice via law and regulation. While not a phenomenon limited to Jordan, the Kingdom as a self-styled democratizing state feels these convolutions acutely.

Textual and Legal Foundations: *The Nationality Law (No. 6 of 1954—Amended 1987)*

Jordan's Nationality Law, *Qanun al-Jinsiyyah al-Urduniyyah*, which replaced the 1929 Organic Law, defines the necessary conditions to be recognised as a Jordanian citizen (and national) ... Individuals holding passports or identification papers under the 1929 law remain citizens under the Nationality Law. A second category eligible for citizenship were those individuals not of the Jewish faith who possessed Palestinian nationality before 15 May 1948 and had been residing in Jordanian territory between 20 December 1949 and 16 February 1954. This was the product of King Abdullah I's desire to establish unity between both banks of the Jordan River following the successful defence of East Jerusalem and the West Bank in the Palestinian *Naqba*/first Arab-Israeli War of 1948. His project of unity included the extension of citizenship to Palestinians fleeing the war. In this manner, Jordan is noticeably different in its treatment of Palestinians than any of its neighbours: Egypt, Lebanon, and Syria.

A third way through which Jordanian nationality is conferred is via patrilineal descent. That is to say that any child whose father is Jordanian will automatically in the eyes of the state be recognised as a Jordanian as well. Matrilineal descent does not analogously bestow citizenship. The specifics of this and its application are not transparent. An on-going campaign "My Mother is Jordanian and Citizenship is My Right" led by the late Nima Habashnah, and Jordanian mothers married to non-Jordanian men is a testament to this reality. As of 2016, the number of women married to non-citizen men was estimated at 89,000, with 52,606 of them married to Palestinian men. The number of children with an uncertain citizen status as a consequence of these unions was in-excess of 355,000 in 2014. These children are non-citizens because their mothers are unable to transmit their citizenship to them owing to the patrilineal nature of Jordanian citizenship transferal.

It is within the authority of the Council of Ministers to rectify this situation, as Article 4 of the Law grants them collective power to grant citizenship to "any Arab" who has been a continuous resident of Jordan for 15 years (Nationality Law, Article 3). As of yet, no such move has been made, although the governments of Abdullah Ensour in 2014 and 2015, and his successor Hani al-Mulki in 2017, expanded the privileges available to the children of foreign fathers and their families. The fifth stipulation in Article 3 recognises as citizens, children born to unknown parents within the territorial demarcations of the Kingdom. Pending the later emergence of evidence to the contrary, these individuals remain citizens. Finally, the members of Bedouin tribes whose *dirah* or tribal land in the north along the Syrian border had been annexed to the territory of the Kingdom in 1930 are granted nationality under the provisions of the Law (Nationality Law, Article 3).

CITIZENSHIP IN PRACTICE

Citizenship is critical for its role in the control and distribution of a society's resources, and the practice of it, therefore, is subject at all times to the politico-legal environment in which it exists. Alterations to this environment accordingly influence the ability of Jordanians to practice their citizenship in the spirit of the constitution. This is observable acutely in the following areas. One of these areas concerns press freedoms, and the subsequent abilities for Jordanians to express opinions and criticisms in the civil sphere. Amendments made to the 1998 Press and Publications Law (PPL) legislated in 2012 are emblematic of the state's acknowledgement of the potential power of citizenship to threaten the established order by the reality of how the state attempts to control and delimit its practice.

One of its key developments was a series of changes to Article 49, which saw the categorisation of web pages providing news content and analysis as analogous with print media; placing new conditions on Jordanian online news providers and bloggers. Now that web pages were considered synonymous with print media, organisations in charge of web pages overnight became responsible not only for content published by the organisation on their pages but, equally, for any posted public commentary. Use of the internet as part of a public sphere outside the direct penetrative agency of the state, therefore, became circumscribed; and with it the ability for citizens to foster cross-coalitional, class, and religious relations with their compatriots.

Previous amendments to the PPL enacted in 2010 enabled charges against journalists, bloggers, and other media industry personnel to be heard by the State Security Court (SSC) instead of a civilian court (Freedom House 2012a). The delimitation of the civilian space—whether online, within the breadth of the judiciary or in this instance both—functions as a controlling device on the practice of citizenship. Decisions made by the SSC cannot be appealed short of a Royal pardon,[1] and therein amounts to a diminishing of civilian power-over government institutions. What were hitherto civil legal cases now become matters of national security. The effect is twofold. Concerning popular perceptions, framing the acceptability of expression and criticism concerning security, favours the status quo, especially given Jordan's location in a turbulent region.

Second, trial by SSC removes civilian judicial oversight in determining what constitutes a security threat. Moreover, amendments made to Articles 48 and 49 bestow upon the Press and Publications Department authority to close offices and block website addresses of those online platforms, who are either unlicensed irrespective of the reason or who have published material interpreted as "defamatory" (Guthrie and Adely 2012). By June 2013, more than 300 websites had been blocked facilitating "a chilling effect on expression online" (Freedom House 2012b, p. 5), as online content writers, bloggers, and news producers complain of direct or indirect interference in their work on a regular basis.

A second way in which the socio-political environment shapes the experience of citizenship is observed in the campaign "My Mother is Jordanian and Her Citizenship is My Right," initiated in 2007 to address the plight of Jordanian women married to non-Jordanian men, whose children do not and cannot acquire citizenship by descent. The state does not recognise them as citizens and subsequently denies them access to public education and healthcare services among others that are available to citizens. The campaign illuminates elements of, and critiques, masculine privilege in the construction of Jordanian citizenship.

While in the civil code "all women are considered ostensibly equal to all men"; according to personal status law genders "are unequal (in terms of rights and duties)" (Massad 2001, p. 50). Within the duality of male/female citizen constructions, there are additional layers of nuance and intersectionality. One illustration concerns the legal and normative construction of Jordan's Bedouin, who historically have been distinguished legally from their urban dwelling co-citizens (Massad 2001, p. 50). Another concerns the role of religious affiliation, which despite the equality extolled in Article 6 of the Constitution, does impact the citizenship

---

[1] As part of the 2011 constitutional amendments, the jurisdiction of the SSC was limited to treason, terrorism, and espionage. Whatever safety-net this provided to journalists, bloggers and other online content builders, it has not stopped charges being laid. This is especially so after the widening of the definition of terrorism in 2014.

regime. Frequently, "family law embodies the clerical imprint of religious law which principles male guardianship over females" (Maktabi 2013, p. 281), revealing the reality of dialogic relationships between institutions—religion, the nation-state, and citizenship—whose various narratives in one context influence developments across institutions in other contexts.

Where a marriage is recognised and children born within it, the state operates on the assumption that the children will become citizens through patrilineal association, foregoing the need for a matrilineal equivalent. To take this a step further, the masculine communitarian principles which shape the socio-political environment in which Jordanian citizenship emerges, facilitate a problematic situation for female citizens. Because of the primacy of patrilineal descent in citizen citizenship transmission, they "can never aspire to be the conduits into family units and therefore to citizenship" (Joseph and Kandiyoti 2000, p. 8).

There is another element or intersection worth a mention here regarding the uneasy triangle of neighbouring nationalisms: Jordanian, Palestinian, and Israeli. Because the majority of the children born to Jordanian mothers and foreign fathers have Palestinian paternity, Jordanian authorities consider them to be Palestinian or at least future citizens of a forthcoming Palestinian state. Resultantly, recognising them as Jordanians would amount to a sharp increase in the number of Jordanians with Palestinian origin (and Palestinian nationalist sympathies) in the country. The struggle for equal citizenship rights for Jordanian mothers to transmit citizenship to their children is, therefore, a thread in the Gordian knot of identity and demography internal to the Kingdom, in particular, in some sectors of the population fear what is known as the *watan al-badil* (alternative homeland) analogy.

Proposed as a solution to the Palestinian-Israeli conflict as early as the 1920s by Ze'ev Jabotinsky, but reaching a degree of maturity in the 1980s with members of the first Likud government, the alternative homeland concept envisages the permanent settlement of the Palestinian population in the Arab states bordering Israel. Jordan is targeted mainly because of the high percentage of its citizens have Palestinian origins and because Kings Abdullah I and Hussein at various times affirmed publicly their commitment to the idea that *Palestine is Jordan and Jordan is Palestine* (see Karsh and Kumaraswamy 2003). Subsequently, some Israeli politicians and ideologues argue that the conflict could be resolved if Jordan becomes Palestine willingly or not. Understandably Jordanians of all persuasions vehemently reject the implication that their country can be turned into an alternative homeland and state for Palestinians displaced in the 1948 *al-Naqba* (the catastrophe) and 1967 *al-Naksa* (the setback). Such is demonstrative of the intertwining of citizenship with narratives of national identity, with the former subordinated by the latter.

A third area in which political expediencies shape citizenship is voting practices. When parliamentary life was reinitiated with the first elections in more than 20 years in 1989, Jordanians could cast as many votes as there were seats in their parliamentary district of residence. The subsequent parliament was diverse with a combination of members affiliated with political currents, and others nominally independent (Ryan 1998, pp. 178–179). Leading up to the next elections in 1993, voting procedures changed, with the introduction of the Single Non-Transferable Vote (SNTV), limiting the number of votes available to citizens to one. This had an immediate effect on the make-up of the parliament, reducing its diversity as voting procedures encouraged citizens to vote along kinship rather than party or ideological lines. The maintenance of the SNTV has had a stymying effect on the development of political parties. In turn, this has restricted the evolution of parliamentary government, and therefore, the ability of citizens to have direct input into the political decision-making.

Single-vote casting remained unchanged until 2012 when the draft elections law introduced a national list to run parallel with the district-bound SNTV. Voters could cast two votes: one for a candidate in their district and another for candidates on the national list. These candidates subsequently could attract votes from across the Kingdom. The SNTV was abolished as part of draft elections law put before parliament in 2015 and approved in time for the 2016 general elections. Voters were once more able to cast as many votes as candidates in their district. However, the stunted development of political parties has meant that the 18th parliament resembles its predecessors, with a majority of members winning seats off the back of kinship and tribal networks.

Jordanian citizenship is additionally impacted upon by Jordan's population of non-citizen residents, primarily Palestinian (from 1948 to 1967), Iraqi (1991, 2003), and now Syrian (2012 to present). The longevity of their residence in the Kingdom, and, depending on class, integration into the fabric of Jordanian society has complicated in material and non-material ways, Jordan's citizenship regime. Employment dynamics are an example of the former, and debate about national identity, an example of the latter. Both are at play when it comes to Jordan's Palestinians, both citizens and non-citizen populations. The latter are the preserve of United Nations Relief and Works Agency (UNRWA), the former of the Jordanian state. Apprehensions about the loyalty and place of Jordan's citizens of Palestinian origin, especially after the 1970/71 conflict between the Jordanian army and Palestine Liberation Organisation (PLO) fighters, contributed to the development of an intriguing division of labour.

The Kingdom consists of a private sector dominated by Jordanians of Palestinian origin, and a public sector monopolised by those of East Bank or Transjordanian roots. Critically, this included the military and security services. Since the ascension of Abdullah II in 1999, Jordan has accelerated its programme of economic liberalisation, which has seen a gradual shrinking of the public sector and greater support for the private sector. Citizenship is implicated in this process owing to the perception that the state (the preserve of citizens in theory if not in practice) is withdrawing in the face of private enterprise, resulting in citizens becoming more vulnerable to the market without sufficient social nets in place. Fears among some sectors of a default Palestinian takeover of the Kingdom only compound this socio-economic situation.

More recently, this contention has combined with trepidation from the population of displaced Syrians since 2011. Numbering in-excess of 661,859 individuals according to the United Nations High Commissioner for Refugees (UNHCR), Jordan hosts one of the largest populations of Syrian refugees. Their influence on Jordanian citizenship is less direct than the Palestinians, revolving at present around the state's distribution of resources, particularly foreign aid. With fluctuating growth (GDP) rates 8.6 per cent in 2004, 5.5 per cent in 2009, 2.8 per cent in 2013, and 2.4 per cent in 2015, Jordan's private sector has been unable to generate enough jobs to absorb the annual graduates from the Kingdom's schools and universities. Consequently, unemployment, registered at 15.8 per cent in 2017, has remained persistently high over the past three decades.

The Syrians are influential in this situation because of the employment privileges some have acquired without becoming members of the political community and in selected Special Economic Zones (SEZs), Syrians are given employment opportunities. Jordan's privileging of the refugee population over civilian and foreign imported labour has been encouraged by a 2016 trade agreement with the EU. Relaxing rules of origin regulation, on the provision that Jordanian companies exporting to the EU, exported goods manufactured by an in-factory workforce, 15 per cent of which were to be Syrians (International Labour Organisation 2017). Given the official unemployment rate, the presence of Syrians with any employment privileges has generated further disconcertion amongst Jordanians.

Conclusion

Dissecting citizenship into depth, content, and extent alongside recognising its unique development in Arabic political discourse enables a more thorough foundational comprehension of its significance in contemporary politics in Jordan. Beginning with the theory and textual foundations, the chapter illuminated the politico-legal wellspring from which citizenship emerges in the Hashemite Kingdom, without which it is impossible to recognise let alone understand the importance of the constitution as an anchor for political action, and of legislation as both interpreter and delimiter of it in Jordanian politics post-2011. The outlining of the rights and duties of Jordanians bestowed by the constitution was contextualised with illustrations coalescing around the press freedoms, the Jordanian mothers' campaign, voting behaviours, and the influence of non-citizen residents. Thus, the Jordanian citizenship is a dynamic concept, whose content, depth, and extent are subject to different forces, both internal and external, which continue to inform its practice.

References

al-Bustānī, B. (1987). *Moḥīt al-Moḥīt Qāmus Muṭawal li-Lughah l-Arabiyyah* (The circumference of the ocean: An extended dictionary of Arabic). Beirut: Maktabah Lubnān.

Faulks, K. (2000). *Citizenship*. London: Routledge.

Freedom House. (2012a). Jordan: Freedom of the Press 2012. https://freedomhouse.org/report/freedom-press/2012/jordan. Accessed 14 Mar 2016.

Freedom House. (2012b). Freedom on the Net 2012. https://freedomhouse.org/report/freedom-net/2012/jordan. Accessed 13 Mar 2016.

Guthrie, B., & Adely, F. (2012, October 31). Is the sky falling? Press and Internet censorship rises in Jordan. *Jadaliyya*. http://www.middleeastdigest.com/pages/index/8102/is-the-sky-falling-press-and-internet-censorship-r. Accessed 7 July 2015.

Hussein, A. a.-S. (2010). Al-Muwātanah fi al-Watan al-Arabi. In H. Ghaṣib (Ed.), *Al-Muwātanah fi al-Watan al-Arabi* (Citizenship in the Arab nation) (pp. 1–30). Amman: Dar Ward.

International Labour Organisation. (2017). *Work permits and employment of Syrian refugees in Jordan: Towards formalizing the work of Syrian refugees*. Beirut: International Labour Organisation. http://www.ilo.org/wcmsp5/groups/public/%2D%2D-arabstates/%2D%2D-ro-beirut/documents/publication/wcms_559151.pdf. Accessed 12 Feb 2018.

Isin, E. (2017). Citizenship studies and the Middle East. In R. Meijer & N. Butenschon (Eds.), *The crisis of citizenship in the Arab world* (pp. 511–534). Leiden: Brill.

Qānun al-Jinsiyyah al-Urduniyyah, (The Jordanian Nationality Law) Law No. 6 (1954).

Qānun al-Muṭbu'āt wa al-Naṣr al-Mu'adl, (Press and Publications Law) Law No. 32 (2012).

Joseph, S., & Kandiyoti, D. (2000). *Gender and citizenship in the Middle East.* New York: Syracuse University Press.

Karsh, E., & Kumaraswamy, P. R. (Eds.). (2003). *Israel, the Hashemites and the Palestinians: The fateful triangle.* London: Frank Cass.

Maktabi, R. (2013). Female citizenship in the Middle East: Comparing family law reform in Morocco, Egypt, Syria and Lebanon. *Middle East Law and Governance, 5,* 280–307.

Massad, J. A. (2001). *Colonial effects: The making of national identity in Jordan.* New York: Columbia University Press.

Meijer, R., & Butenschøn, N. (Eds.). (2017). *The crisis of citizenship in the Arab world.* Leiden: Brill.

Parolin, G. (2009). *Citizenship in the Arab world: Kin, religion and nation-state.* Amsterdam: Amsterdam University Press.

Ryan, C. (1998). Elections and parliamentary democratization in Jordan. *Democratization, 5*(4), 176–196.

Sha'bān, A. H. (2017). *Al-Huwiyyah wa al-Muwātanah: Al-Badā'il al-Multabasah wa al-Ḥadāthah al-Muta'atharah* (Identity and citizenship: Ambiguous alternatives and hampered modernisation). Beirut: Markaz Dirāsāt al-Wiḥdah al-Arabiyyah.

The Constitution of Jordan. (1952). *The Official Gazette,* no. 1093. Amended in 2011. English version available at https://www.constituteproject.org/constitution/Jordan_2011.pdf?lang=ar. Accessed 5 Sept 2015.

Composite Nationalism Re-visited

Alexander Bligh and Gadi Hitman

Since the birth of the two Hashemite Kingdoms in the early 1920s (the other, Iraq, ceased to exist with the 14 July 1958 revolution), their separate existence has produced an appearance of an oxymoron. In 1915–16, the leader of the Hashemite family negotiated with the British the establishment of Arabistan, a country to include all Arabic speaking lands, under one Hashemite flag. Since the mid-1950s, his descendants in Jordan have had to provide an ideological foundation for the existence of a distinct Hashemite Jordanian nation-state, a far cry from the pan-Arab family dream.

Ever since its independence in 1946, Jordan has had to grapple with the issue of its *raison d'être* especially when the call for Arab unity was popular among the Arab grassroots. This theme of Arab unity has been used at least twice against the very existence of Jordan as a separate entity. Egyptian President Gamal Abdul Nasser and Palestine Liberation Organisation (PLO) leader Yasser Arafat, each with a different set of interests and

A. Bligh (✉)
National Knowledge and Research Center for Emergency Readiness,
Haifa University, Haifa, Israel
e-mail: ab1061@columbia.edu

G. Hitman
Middle East and Political Science Department, Ariel University

constraints, attacked the very existence of Jordan as an independent state, let alone as a Hashemite kingdom. In retrospect, both have substantially contributed to the emergence of Jordanian nationalism as a way of justifying its distinct existence as a nation-state. The various sets of political circumstances have captured the attention of many scholars.[1] Some have concentrated their analyses on the Jordanian leadership's attempt to justify its standalone status. Others, like Ryan and Brand,[2] for instance, chose to study the grassroots ideological and public expressions of the way they see the essence of Jordanian nationalism. This chapter endeavours to analyse the main pillars of the development of Jordanian nationalism in light of the changing ruling personality and the regional instability in the aftermath of the Arab Spring.

With the 20th anniversary of the accession of King Abdullah II approaching, it is time not only to present the main components of King Hussein's ideas briefly but also to consider the politically changing times elsewhere. The zeitgeist approach comes in handy.[3] This term defines the dominant set of ideals and beliefs that motivate and eventually shapes the actions of the members of a society in a particular period. In the case study of Jordanian nationalism, zeitgeist may be useful for understanding the evolution of an idea from the royal perspective of the Hashemite family.

What was the heritage of Jordanian nationalism that King Abdullah II inherited from his father? In a nutshell, it was the duty to serve the Arab

---

[1] Cf. for instance some recent articles: Abulof, U. (2017). 'Can't buy me legitimacy': The elusive stability of Mideast rentier regimes. *Journal of International Relations and Development, 20*(1), 55–79; Martínez, J. C. (2017). Jordan's self-fulfilling prophecy: The production of weak political parties and the perceived perils of democracy. *British Journal of Middle Eastern Studies, 44*(3), 356–372; Moore, P. W. (2017). The fiscal politics of rebellious grievance in the Arab world: Egypt and Jordan in comparative perspective. *The Journal of Development Studies, 53*(10), 1634–1649; Oesch, L. (2017). The refugee camp as a space of multiple ambiguities and subjectivities. *Political Geography, 60*, 110–120; Spierings, N. (2017). Trust and tolerance across the Middle East and North Africa: A comparative perspective on the impact of the Arab uprisings. *Politics and Governance, 5*(2), 4–15; Yom, S. (2017). Jordan and Morocco: the palace gambit. *Journal of Democracy, 28*(2), 132–146.

[2] Ryan, C. R. (2010). We are all Jordan, but who is we? *Middle East Research and Information Project* (July 13, 2010); Brand, L. A. (1995). *Jordan's inter-Arab relations: The political economy of alliance making*. New York: Columbia University Press. Ryan, C. R. (2011). Identity politics, reform, and protest in Jordan. *Studies in Ethnicity and Nationalism. 11*(3), 564–578.

[3] Cf. Patrick, T. Y. (2016). The zeitgeist of secession amidst the march towards unification: Scotland, Catalonia and the future of the European Union. *Boston College International and Comparative Law Review, 39*(1), 195.

nation and within that the Palestinian cause. That translated into an obligation to include western Palestine within the Hashemite kingdom until 1967 and to include the Arabs living there within the definition of Jordanian nationalism—that is, until King Hussein realised in the 1960s the potential threat they posed. Consequently, his definition of Jordanian nationalism changed into one that would include only East Bankers and an obligation to care for the basic needs of the Palestinians. This arrangement lasted until Israel took over the West Bank in 1967 and the international community did so after 1988. These stages are the topic of this chapter.

In this context, the term "composite" indicates the amalgamation of ideas and elements of nationalism, which are to be found in other national movements and political entities in addition to many unique ingredients aiming at producing a new ideological approach. Additionally, it means the artificial creation of a national identity and ideology, which in most cases, evolve on their own without any elaborate human touch. This almost laboratory approach has enabled the King to create throughout his reign a model that is supposed to respond to changing circumstances. Jordanian nationalism is not the result of a philosopher's effort to provide his countrymen with some talking points. This is the product of the cumulative effect of bringing forth answers to the daily challenges facing Jordan in the years before and since 1967.

Jordanian nationalism underwent several stages in maturing into the state nationalism as it exists today. On its way, it has undergone four transformational stages. The central themes of the Jordanian identity have dramatically changed in the almost 100 years since the establishment of this geographical and today national, entity. These are the highlights of the four eras analysed:

- Stage 1: 1921/46–51: *We are all Arabs.*
- Stage 2: 1952–63: *All who live under the Hashemite Crown belong to the Jordanian political entity.*
- Stage 3: 1963–88: *All who live under the Hashemite Crown on the East Bank are Jordanian, but Jordan has a special responsibility to its brother people, the Palestinians on the West Bank.*
- Stage 4: 1988–present: *Original East Bankers are Jordanian, but not all of those living on the East Bank are Jordanian by nationality.*

The First Stage: 1921/46–51—Arabism First

Twice in its formative era, in 1921 and in 1946, the Emirate of Transjordan, in the eastern part of the British Mandate over Palestine, needed to devise some justification for its distinct existence. It first occurred in 1921 within the zeitgeist of self-determination, which became an acceptable principle in the aftermath of World War I. However, Palestine, at least according to Zionist and Arab interpretations, had been promised to the Jews, definitely not to the Hashemites.[4] More critical was the Hashemite acceptance of the principle of a divided Arabistan. These issues were added to the Arab agenda with the 1946 Jordanian independence.

Establishing the first stage time frame is almost self-evident. It began with the British decision and implementation of the 1921 decision to remove Transjordan from the Jewish national home believed to be promised by the 1917 Balfour Declaration. It was re-affirmed with Jordanian independence in 1946 and finally ended with the April 1950 annexation of the West Bank and the 1951 assassination of King Abdullah-I. All throughout the first stage King Abdullah-I had to square the circle. On the one hand, Abdullah was committed to the pan-Arab legacy of his father, Sharif Hussein. The elder leader had exchanged several letters with Henry McMahon, the British High Commissioner in Egypt, which ended up with the false understanding by the Hashemites that the British would support a united Arab country under Sharif Hussein's leadership. By signing the Sykes-Picot agreement (1916) with the French, Italians, and Russians, the British practically abandoned any promise to the Hashemites, if there had been any at all. Instead, after several more rounds of diplomacy, they gave the Hashemites Jordan and Iraq after the World War I. Consequently, in the minds of the Hashemites, they were betrayed, and their historical mission continued as the carriers of the Arab unity torch.

However, on the other hand, concurrent with their championing of Arab unity, both the Hashemite kingdoms—had to justify their distinct Hashemite domain and stick to whatever was given them. That was not an easy task. Sir Winston Churchill, the then Secretary of State for the Colonies, insisted on keeping the newly created unit within the mandate

---

[4] See for instance: Bligh, A. (2004). Palestinian and Jordanian views of the Balfour declaration. In: Neguin Yavari *et al.* (eds.), *Views from the edge; Essays in honor of Richard W. Bulliet*. New York: Columbia University Press, 19–26; Gutwein, D. (2016). The politics of the Balfour declaration: Nationalism, imperialism and the limits of Zionist-British cooperation. *Journal of Israeli History*, 35(2), 117–152.

over Palestine; consequently, the people living within that territory were considered Transjordanian Palestinians.[5] Until its 1946 independence, Jordan continued to be included within the annual report on the status of the mandate over Palestine (first, to the League of Nations and later, to the UN). This way, the British were responsible for the security, and foreign relations of the Emirate (the then status of Jordan) and that policy continued after independence as well. The apparent outcome of that approach was that the British authorities had every reason even after 1946 to improve the separate status of Jordan as an ally and as a Middle Eastern outpost in the Cold War days, but they had no interest in the emergence of a local identity and a national movement lest it turn against the British, with Egypt serving as a living reminder.

King Abdullah-I for his part, did not support separate Jordanian nationalism either. With the loss of the Arabistan entity, his zeitgeist and mindset as a leader during the first decades after the World War I was limited to a smaller territory. His leadership vision from the 1920s to the late 1940s was the creation of a Greater Syria under his rule. His Iraqi Hashemite cousins shared the same dream with only one understandable exception—that the crown would be laid on an Iraqi Hashemite head. In a word, none of the Hashemites craved a national leading position, but rather a supranational ideological identity that would be the lesser evil, considering that the bigger Arabistan dream was wholly lost.

There are several reasons for that aspiration. First and probably foremost among them was the fact that the King himself was not of Jordanian origin, if such a thing existed at all since his family did not come until the 1920s to Transjordan from the Hejaz.[6] Additionally, in spite of close relations with the British, the main if not the only backer of the Transjordanian entity, the King harboured ill feelings towards them as well as the French. After all, these two colonial powers were the ones that led to the Hashemite destruction in the Muslim holy places in the Hejaz and to negate what the Hashemites saw as a promise for one united Arab kingdom. These foreign players finally took over Palestine and Syria, kicking the Hashemites out of Syria as well.

However, not only fresh memories were involved. Abdullah-I perceived himself, as well as all Arabs wherever they were, as being Arab, because they all had come to their current locations from the same place, that is,

[5] Cf. Massad (2001, pp. 23–24).
[6] Brand (1995, p. 51).

the Arabian Peninsula.[7] He made his point clear in a unique sentence (1933): "I do not wish to see any among you identify themselves by geographical region; I wish to see everyone rather trace his descent to the Arabian Peninsula."[8]

It is safe to assume that in the early 1930s, sometime around the accession of King Ghazi in Iraq, the Jordanian Greater Syria vision took off in earnest. The timing is strongly suggested by the Iraqi diplomatic and political behaviour at the time. The six years of Ghazi rule were characterised by a weak king and strong military. The latter preferred an Iraqi character to the kingdom rather than a pan-Arab one. That stance was manifested at least twice: first, with the 1933 Assyrian massacre demonstrating that non-Arab, non-Christian people could not become Iraqis and second, with the Iraqi military demand that Kuwait (at the time under British rule) be "returned" to its "legal" owners, namely, the Hashemite Kingdom of Iraq.[9]

With the road clear for Abdullah to take the lead as far as Greater Syria was concerned, he began voicing his new ideology. In 1934, for instance, he met representatives of the Jewish Agency and discussed the option of uniting the two banks of the Jordan River under his rule. Sir Alan Cunningham, the High Commissioner of Palestine from November 1945 to 1948, was fully aware of the King's aspiration to annex Palestine to his Kingdom, as he wrote to the British Ambassador in Cairo.[10]

Those ideas were not alien to the Jewish leadership either. Much research has been devoted to the secret negotiations between King Abdullah and the Zionist leaders in Palestine before the declaration of Israel's independence (1946–48) and even after that (1948–50).[11] The King's primary goal in the former period was to find creative ways to annex the would-be Jewish state territory to his Kingdom as a first step in the realisation of Greater Syria. Moreover, on the eve of the 1948–49

[7] Shlaim, A. (2009). *Lion of Jordan*, 35.

[8] Al-Oudat, M. A. and Ayman, A. (2010). Jordan first: Tribalism, nationalism and legitimacy of power in Jordan. *Intellectual Discourse, 18*(1), 66.

[9] Al-Hamdi, M. (2015). The consistency of the Iraqi claims on Kuwait during the monarchy and the republic: 1921–1963. *International Journal of Contemporary Iraqi Studies, 9*(3), 209–224.

[10] Levenberg, H. (1995). The Interaction between the High Commissioner, Sir Alan Cunningham and King Abdullah, 1945–1948. *Studies of Israel's Resurrection*, 5, 23–36 (Hebrew).

[11] Sela, A. (1990). The relationships of King Abdullah and Israel: Re-examination. *Catedra*, 58, 120–162 [Hebrew].

conflict in Palestine, he was deeply involved in designating the representatives of the Arabs in Palestine for the international forums to discuss the Palestine issue so that they would support his Greater Syria idea. Moreover, two weeks after the United Nations General Assembly endorsed the Partition Plan for Palestine on 29 November 1947, he ordered the Arab Legion (the official name of the Transjordanian army at the time) to remain in Palestine to support its Arab (not Palestinian) inhabitants.

With the conflict over at least in military terms and Abdullah in possession of large parts of Arab Western Palestine, he took several steps to demonstrate the Arab nature of his country, rather than adopting a particular Jordanian identity. The King's policy was partially successful after 1948, when in the aftermath of the Jericho Conference (1 December 1948) for Arabs living under his control West of the Jordan River, he announced in April 1950 the annexation of those territories, re-named the West Bank.

King Abdullah's activities in the years 1946–50 strongly suggest that he was not too fond of the idea of Jordanian nationalism. His citizens were a myriad of different groups (Bedouins, Circassians, Christians/Assyrians, and, after 1948, Palestinians) with no common values, territory, history, or traditions. The main idea connecting them all was perhaps his dream of a larger Arab unit, not the existence of a unique Jordanian entity and ideology. The 1950 unity of the two banks was not for the Hashemites the beginning of the formation of a stronger Jordanian kingdom, but rather the nucleus of a larger "Greater Syria" Hashemite kingdom. These ideas were dashed with the 1951 assassination of the King and in the ensuing year during which King Talal was the titular head of state, but he was used by the commoner ministers to re-shape the Kingdom's political structure, while keeping the unity of the two banks.

THE SECOND STAGE: 1952–63—BUILDING STATE NATIONALISM

King Hussein, with his accession, inherited a complex political and ideological foundation for the Kingdom. However, the 1948–50 hopes for the unity of the two banks to serve as the foundation for a larger Arab entity were dashed; first, by the 1951 assassination of the King; later, by the 1956 pro-Nasserite and anti-monarchy Suleiman Nabulsi cabinet; the mass protest demonstrations that followed; the 1958 post-Iraqi revolution Jordanian unrest; the 1963 riots in the wake of the declaration of a republican union in the Arab world; and by many less dramatic incidents. The 1958 and 1963 disturbances made the possibility of a Hashemite fall almost real, leading the King to military cooperation with the West, as well as with Israel. This was a deviation from the contemporary Arab zeitgeist which centred on resistance to the West, to Israel and every monarchy in the region. Those foreign and domestic constraints dictated a gradual and lengthy process of abandoning the idea of Arab unity and the unity of the banks in the Jordanian context and turning instead to providing the regime with ideological support.

All of the above meant that the years 1952–63 were characterised by a careful movement away from the pillars of Arab unity into something new and unique and yet, Hussein did not abandon the concept of putting together a unique nation-state. Annexing the West Bank in 1950 under his grandfather marked the beginning of a new ideological agenda for the nation-state, built on two distinct identities: one of the East Bank and one of the West Bank. The uniting ideology had therefore to be one that would bring the two together, producing loyalty to the Hashemite ruler. It had to be Arab to the degree that all citizens would accept and yet Jordanian enough to justify the separate existence of a Hashemite kingdom in an Arab world whose declared, but not pursued, the zeitgeist was one of Arab unity.

This ideology's only purpose was the building of legitimacy for the continued Hashemite rule over the East and West Banks of the Jordan River. Transjordanians and Palestinians who lived side by side within the [unrecognised] borders of Jordan comprised the intended audience for that ideology. The Arab zeitgeist of the 1950s was different from the reality of the 1920s. In the aftermath of the World War II, many nation-states were liberated, created, and recognised. Undoubtedly, imperialism was singing its swan song all over the world, leaving behind at times political units, new or reborn, in need of a common cause or uniting slogan that would serve as a calling to the flag tactic for uniting a given entity. Jordan was no different. Between 1946 and 1967, it existed in limbo: it had to pay lip service to the Arab Unity slogan and yet develop its own identity in the face of Egyptian attempts to subvert its regime allegedly on behalf of that Arab unity.

As indicated, having a foreign enemy is one of the best ways of developing national cohesion, ideology, and unity. In the Jordanian context, that paradigm could work only with the East Bankers. The West *Bankers, who only in 1964* officially began to identify themselves as Palestinian with the creation of the Palestine Liberation Organisation (PLO), did not feel like loyal and obedient residents under the Hashemite crown even before that. On several occasions, some of them, later many, demonstrated their displeasure with the regime—usually in the form of demonstrations that at times turned violent and led to clashes with the Jordanian armed forces. Perhaps the assassination of King Abdullah-I (July 1951) by a Palestinian marked the first step in a long process of separation that began with alienation from the Hashemite crown, the most significant attribute of a Jordanian national core of solidarity.

In accessing the throne, King Hussein had to devise a substitute for the "Arabism first" concept. Inheriting from his grandfather the "Jordanian and Palestinian comprise one people" concept, he conceived a plan of building state nationalism. Even during the early period, 1952–63, Hussein's particular version of nationalism was already built on three elements, two of which, perhaps, were rather difficult even for his enemies to refute: pan-Arab-based legitimacy, Arab nation-state legitimacy, and dynasty legitimacy.[12] Even though he never spoke ill of the Palestinians in public, King Hussein gradually realised the danger the Palestinians posed to his rule. A significant part of that population, or at least some of the non-establishment leaders of that community, saw in Nasser after 1952 their hero and in 1963 (as well as later) took their followers to the streets threatening to topple Hussein's rule.

As if that were not enough, the creation of the short-lived United Arab Republic (Syria and Egypt, 1958–61) could be interpreted through Hashemite eyes as one more indication of losing the position of champion of Arab unity. Consequently, the foreign and domestic risks only accentuated the Hashemite need to formulate a new approach to the people living under their rule. Though it was not declared until 1988, it stands to reason that losing the West Bank in the 1967 War perfectly suited the King's need to formulate some East Bank identity that would at least lay the foundation for the rule of that part of the Kingdom.

It is safe to assume that a gradual process of change took place between 1952 and 1963: from a genuine attempt to completely unite the two banks under the Hashemite and Arab double flag to a realisation of the danger that the West Bank posed to the Hashemite regime. The approach proposed here is in contrast to other analyses that espouse the belief that

---

[12] Bligh, A. (2014). Redefining the post-nation-state emergence phase in the Middle East in light of the "Arab Spring." *Journal of the Middle East and Africa, 5*(3), 213.

the Hashemite interest has always been, especially before 1967, in integrating the Palestinians into the Jordanian identity.[13] Especially, when since 1948 the West Bank Palestinians, contrary to their fellow people on the East Bank, saw themselves as separate and unique in relation to all East Bank people.

Being a practical leader rather than an ideologue, King Hussein struggled for the survival of his kingdom until the 1963 crossroads. With danger looming over the existence of the monarchy, he elevated his strategic yet tacit agreement with Israel into one of the pillars of his policy. Concurrent with that, he started voicing in private his displeasure and concern with his West Bank citizens.[14] From 1963 on, his expressions regarding the ingredients of Jordanian nationalism have become stronger. It is evident in retrospect that at that very juncture his words regarding the nature of being Jordanian became clear. At first, he spoke about those emerging approaches within his inner circle, but gradually, until the 1988 culmination of the process, it became clearer that Jordanian nationalism was limited to the East Bank geographically and to the people living there only, whether Palestinian or Transjordanian by origin.

STAGE 3: 1963–88—ALL LIVING UNDER THE HASHEMITE CROWN ON THE EAST BANK ARE JORDANIAN, BUT JORDAN HAS A SPECIAL RESPONSIBILITY TO ITS BROTHER PEOPLE, THE PALESTINIANS ON THE WEST BANK

Perhaps this period in the history of Jordan is the most significant concerning the emergence of Jordanian nationalism. It started with Hussein's realisation in 1963 that the Palestinians on the West Bank are a threat, moved on to the loss of the West Bank and East Jerusalem in 1967, through the Jordanian civil war (1970/71), the 1974 Rabat formula granting the PLO some degree of international status and ended with the 31 July 1988 speech by Hussein in which he renounced all relations with the West Bank and its citizens.

The Arab zeitgeist of 1963, as far as Jordan was concerned, was menacing. Nasser was moving on, the Palestinian issue was beginning to be noticed among the Arab countries, and the Hashemite crown was almost

---

[13] Cf. Brand (1995, pp. 50–51).
[14] Bligh (2002, chapter 3).

helpless in confronting the strong republican winds blowing all over the Middle East. Diplomatic, as well as military steps were needed, but perhaps the most pressing issue was to bring together the loyal citizens of Jordan, who at that point were concentrated on the East Bank. The West Bankers championed Nasser and began taking part in activities against Israel.

Concurrent with speaking publicly in favour of common Arab causes, the king voiced very cautiously the elements of what would become the admitted pillars of Jordanian nationalism. One of the elements to be publicly expressed was the required association of the people living within the Kingdom with the ruling family at large and the King in particular as the central pillar of loyalty. There was a distinct national Jordanian response to the personality cult of Nasser before 1967 that attracted many within the Kingdom. In speaking as described above, Hussein also added primordial essentials, perhaps imagined ones, to build some collective identity under the title "We are all Jordanian." That strategy was so successful that most East Bank Jordanians began to see him, as early as the early 1960s, as the father of the Jordanian nation. That policy was supported by the state TV channels that underlined the primordial elements of the local identity: Bedouin dance and song, references to Muslim history, including Quran programmes and slides of pre-Islamic archaeological sites. The message was clear and was meant to form national feelings among people who traditionally saw the tribe as their reference group.

While voicing support for Arab causes, yet developing through a long process the unique ingredients of the Jordanian identity, the King had to grapple with the Palestinian issue during this stage under worsening inter-Arab and international conditions. He did not want to reintegrate the Palestinians based on the 1952–63 period. That was, as already mentioned above, a result of their political activities and aspirations that included the East Bank, as would be demonstrated by the 1970–71 civil war between Transjordanians represented by the King and Jordanian army and the Palestinians represented to some extent by the PLO, which claimed all of the [former] mandatory Palestine. Even before the civil war and clearly between 1963 and 1970, Hussein was concerned with the possibility that the Palestinians would align themselves with Jordan's enemies and turn the country into a Nasser style republic.[15]

---

[15] Cf. for instance: [UK] National Archives, London/FO371/186830/ER1071/4/ March 23, 1966, From: Tel Aviv; USNA/RG 59/POL 32-1 ISR-JORDAN/22466/ November 24, 1966, From: Amman; USNA/RG 59/POL 23-9 JORDAN /December 6,

That policy—Jordan as a unique nation-state—needed the continued presentation of Jordan and the West Bank as two distinct entities. Consequently, Hussein always underlined his willingness to assist the Palestinians in reaching a solution acceptable to them, provided it did not endanger the existence of the Hashemite entity. That entity could not take on the form of an independent state lest it might serve as a national focal point for a possible irredentist Palestinian movement within the Kingdom.

Simultaneous with the King's watchful stand regarding the Palestinians and acceptance of the 1974 Rabat formula recognising the PLO as the sole and legitimate representative of the Palestinian people, he continued to see the 1948 and 1967 Palestinian refugees as Jordanian citizens (this could be considered a decision out of charity—*zakat*—because Jordan already hosted refugees). During this period, he amalgamated primordial nationalism with instrumentalism to form his version of composite nationalism: one imposed from above without any prior evidence of its existence in the past. That policy saw in all people living on the East Bank full partners in the creation of one national identity. That image exists to this day, even though the post-1948 and 1967 East Bank Palestinians are prohibited from participating in sensitive positions, especially in combat units.[16]

However, piecing together Hussein's references to his beliefs,[17] it is evident that during the period 1963–88, he was already laying out his elements of Jordanian nationalism which is the product of three interwoven processes that took place during that era:

- The evolution of mutual alienation between the Hashemite central government and the West Bankers as the result of the 1963 and 1966 crises.
- The need to put together a coherent national ideology as the basis for the East Bankers to be united for further challenges. With the

1966, From: Amman (1406); USNA/RG59/POL 23-9 JORDAN/9500/December 10, 1966, From: Amman.

[16] Central Intelligence Agency, Directorate of Intelligence, *Jordan: The Palestinian Stake in the East Bank, a research paper*, ([Washington, D.C.], July 1987), 8, https://www.cia.gov/library/readingroom/docs/CIA-RDP88T00096R000600760001-3.pdf, retrieved April 1, 2018; "Jordan: Rights and obligations of Palestinians living in Jordan without Jordanian citizenship, not including Palestinian refugees fleeing Syria since 2011, including employment, mobility and access to social services (2013–May 2014)", Refworld [UNHCR], http://www.refworld.org/docid/53ecc8004.html, retrieved April 1, 2018.

[17] Bligh (2002, chapter 4).

loss of the West Bank, it became imperative to manifest the identification between Jordan and the East Bank.
- The 1974 Rabat formula making the PLO the sole and legitimate representative of the Palestinian people once again raised the question of affiliation and loyalty of the Palestinians living on the East Bank. In spite of the civil war victory and the East Bank Palestinians staying neutral throughout the 1970–71 crisis, some degree of suspicion still lingered on.

The outcome of those processes was a clear national ideology that has been based since the late 1960s on the legitimacy of the dynasty, legitimacy of the nation-state and using attributes of sovereignty (armed forces, local history, national anthem, etc.) to support the former two. A special place within that rational approach is kept for Jerusalem. Most of the elements composing Jordanian nationalism do take their inspiration from the daily harsh political realities. It is no wonder that Jerusalem, the holy city as much as the burial place of the founder of the Arab national movement, Sharif Hussein b. Ali, the great-grandfather of the King, is different. Many times references to Jerusalem are more emotional and religious than political. This attitude cannot hide the meticulous use of Jerusalem as another pillar of Jordanian nationalism. About the centrality of Jerusalem in the minds of his people, Hussein emphasises in line with his grandfather[18] not only the obvious Muslim connection, but also from time to time the Christian connection to the city and the justification for *jihad* that under the present circumstances cannot be declared. Strangely enough, it is one of the few cases in which a source of legitimacy rests outside its national territory, very strongly suggesting an element of irredentism—clearly not part of Jordanian policy towards the territories other than Jerusalem.

The first layer of that composite nationalism has to do with the most crucial political challenge: the legitimacy of the Hashemite dynasty. This broad term includes several elements: Muslim religious legitimacy, Arab historical and current political legitimacy. All three are interwoven, but it is not very difficult to identify all elements and to define them.

---

[18] 1 December 1971, *al-Majmu'ah*, vol. 3, 346–347; 1 September 1980 *Der Spiegel* Interview, *FBIS*, 8 September 1980; *al-Ra'i al-'Amm*, 13 February 1982; *al-Ahram*, 6 May 1982; Miller, A. D. (1986). Jordan and the Palestinian issue: The legacy of the past. *Middle East Insight*, 4(4), 24; 21 March 1988 speech before the conference of the foreign ministers of the Muslim countries, Jordanian press, 22 March 1988; *al-Quds*, 24 April 1994; www.aljazeera.com, 13 December 2007.

The second layer is more specific to the Jordanian entity and deals with issues of territory and national identity. The most crucial components in this respect are the definitions of people in general and the Jordanian people and the relations between them and the Palestinian people—past, present, and possible future contenders for the same territory.

The third layer has to do with symbols of sovereignty. Loyalty to these elements means full acceptance of the kingdom and its nationalism. This layer combines the first two in the sense that it connects the (legitimate) Hashemite kingdom to the (legitimate) Jordanian national and geographical entity. This multi-layered analysis of Jordanian nationalism is based on developments over decades, because of domestic, foreign, and coincidental elements: in short, the zeitgeist.

It appears as though the most significant contribution to the emergence of Jordanian nationalism was made during the 1963–88 period in response to the new zeitgeist in the monarchy, which had to deal almost on a daily basis with the Palestinian issue, practically and ideologically. If anything, the period 1963–88 can be summarised by the phrase "all East Bankers are Jordanian."

Stage 4: 1988–Present—Original East Bankers Are Jordanian, but Not All of Those Living on the East Bank Are Jordanian by Nationality

Hussein's 31 July 1988 disengagement speech marked the conclusion of the most definitive period in the creation of imposed Jordanian nationalism. His ideology survived him and continued well into the rule of his successor, his son, Abdullah II. However, the concept of "all living on the East Bank are Jordanian" has been challenged several times by regional developments affecting the demographic and geographic makeup of the Hashemite Kingdom during the reigns of both the kings. In a nutshell, it is the issue of whether the Arab refugees, most of whom are Syrians, are included within the preponderantly East Bank Jordanian nationalism.

It is evident from a historical perspective that there is a well-defined difference between the 1948 and 1967 Palestinian refugees who, according to the predominant Jordanian nationalism concept, could find their places as loyal citizens of the East Bank Jordanian nation-state and all other refugees who fled to Jordan under different sets of international and regional circumstances. Debating the standing of refugees within the

Jordanian nation-state is as old as the Arab-Israeli War of 1948–49. It has been so problematic dealing with the issue of the future civilian status of refugees within Jordan that Kingdom refrained from joining the parties to the 1951 convention concerning the status of refugees and from the 1967 Protocol. That convention was passed after the unification of the two banks and the granting of citizenship to all Palestinian refugees found at the time in both banks of the Hashemite realm.

Since the Palestinian issue within the process of creating a distinct Jordanian state nationalism has already been discussed, it is time to examine the role of other refugees with that state nationalism. Being the lynchpin holding the Middle East together and a major Arab crossroads within the turbulent region, Jordan has become since its independence the desired destination for people fleeing their countries of residence during times of major crises.

The 1990s influx of Iraqis and Kuwaitis is a case in point. These refugees fled their homes in the wake of the August 1990 Iraqi invasion of Kuwait and the subsequent war. However, the challenge presented to the Jordanian authorities by this influx was minor compared with the next wave. That one included Syrian and Iraqi refugees running away from their homes turned into war zones in the context of the Arab Spring and the civil wars in Iraq and Syria, 2003 and 2011 and after, respectively. The magnitude of that wave has been unprecedented, and according to official Jordanian estimates in December 2015, the country's population had reached a total of 9.5 million people, 2.9 million of whom were refugees (officially defined as guests), 46 per cent of them Syrians.[19] The official use of the term "guests" indicates that Jordan does not see these refugees as future permanent residents or future citizens of the Kingdom.

Furthermore, consistent with this approach, Jordan has no legislation for the protection of asylum seekers and refugees.[20] In its stead, it passed its 1973 "Law No. 24 of 1973 on Residence and Foreigners' Affairs," which does not distinguish between any categories of foreigners.[21] It applies to all foreigners whether refugees and or non-refugees. Article 2 defines a foreigner as anyone who does not have Jordanian nationality.

---

[19] Muhammad Ghazal, Population stands at around 9.5 million, including 2.9 million guests, from http://www.jordantimes.com/news/local/population-stands-around-95-million-including-29-million-guests, http://www.jordantimes.com, 30 January 2016.

[20] www.refworld.org/pdfid/513d90172.pdf, 2013.

[21] http://www.refworld.org/docid/3ae6b4ed4c.html

Indeed, Jordan's policy towards the post-1990 wave of refugees is different than its policy relating to the Palestinian refugees of 1948 (*lajiin*) and even to those of 1967 (*nazihin*). King Abdullah II expressed his policies in unequivocal terms: "I am looking into the eyes of my people and see their anxiety and fatigue as a result of the heavy burden. I am telling you all – Jordan has already maximised its capacities. We will continue to support the needy, but this assistance will not come before our people's interests."[22] This is only an illustration of the current Jordanian policy regarding its own identity and concept of nationalism: there are "us" and "them." "Us" means Jordanian, whereas all the rest are Arab—deserving of temporary shelter ("guests"), but not deserving to be considered Jordanian, despite their belonging to the larger Arab community (*umma*). The opening phrase of the Jordanian constitution, boasts by stating: "Jordan has a constitution that emphasises that all the people belong to one family."[23]

Being fully aware of the possibility that the refugees would continue to stay on Hashemite territory for a long time, King Abdullah II has been clear in explaining that their presence would not constitute any prelude to or excuse for including them within the current Jordanian Kingdom and its definition of "Jordanian." In an Interview with the BBC, he said that Jordanian hospitality for its guests has its reputation, but "whether we want the refugees with us or not, they are here to stay at least 17 years, according to UN estimations. If we receive international support to develop workplaces for the refugees, we will use this money to assist original Jordanians as well."[24]

One of the most important and tangible implications of this policy was the Kingdom's decision to restrict the movement of Syrian refugees and to instruct the United Nations High Commissioner for Refugees (UNHCR) to stop issuing Asylum Seeker Certificates (ASCs), which are "indispensable for obtaining Ministry of Interior Service Cards for refugees' access

---

[22] *al-Rai* newspaper, 4 February 2016.
[23] www.kingabullaah.jo/ar/page/about-jordan, 7 June 2017.
[24] kingabdullah.jo/ar/news/محطة-بي-بي-سي-البريطانية-تجري-مقابلة-مع-الملك, February 4, 2016, King Abdullah's interview to the BBC, 2 February 2016 from the official website of the king: https://kingAbdullah.jo/ar/news/%D9%85%D8%AD%D8%B7%D8%A9-%D8%A8%D9%8A-%D8%A8%D9%8A-%D8%B3%D9%8A-%D8%A7%D9%84%D8%A8%D8%B1%D9%8A%D8%B7%D8%A7%D9%86%D9%8A%D8%A9-%D8%AA%D8%AC%D8%B1%D9%8A-%D9%85%D9%82%D8%A7%D8%A8%D9%84%D8%A9-%D9%85%D8%B9-%D8%A7%D9%84%D9%85%D9%84%D9%83, www.kingabullaah.jo/ar/page/about-jordan

to public health care and education services."[25] That resolution makes it unmistakably clear that no refugee will be treated by the Jordanian authorities as potential future citizens.

That policy has echoed throughout the Kingdom, creating to some extent once more the menace of possible adverse elements that might deprive real Jordanians of their rights within their homeland. Several examples illustrate the reverberating effect of that policy. Parliament member Bassam al-Batush expressed his anxiety lest Jordanian society lose its identity, if the refugees accept Jordanian citizenship.[26] Columnists from various newspapers often wrote about their concern that public services provided by the state would be undermined due to preferring refugees over Jordanians. One commentator mentioned that no unemployed Jordanian would agree to provide refugees with jobs.[27]

Compared with the economic level, the national dimension has at times taken a back seat. However, history is replete with examples of financial hardships turning into the fuel for a national revolution, precisely the situation the Hashemite King tries to avoid. That economic concern is well established. Jordan is a developing country, which has traditionally been supported by wealthy Arab countries and the international community to survive. Jordan alone cannot handle the challenges following the flow of refugees. The fact that Zaatari Camp in northeast Jordan became the fourth biggest city in Jordan is enough to demonstrate the demographic and socio-economic changes. At least one study, conducted in 2015, found that the Syrian refugee crisis has worsened the political, economic, and resource challenges in Jordan.[28] The kingdom's challenges run more profound than the refugee crisis and if left unaddressed what might develop into sources of instability. Jordanian nationalism and steadfastness in the face of such possible eventualities might significantly help in facing the current crisis; however, at a certain undefined point in the near future that might not be enough.

Some ominous signs are already being noticed. Refugees consistently complain that they cannot find jobs and that the Jordanian authorities ignore their requests. Besides, refugee camps, unlike the Palestinian camps

---

[25] Achilli, L. (2015). Syrian refugees in Jordan: A reality check. Migration Policy Centre, EUI, 5.
[26] http://www.allofjo.net, 2 February 2016.
[27] *al-Khitan in al-Ghad*, 30 January 2016.
[28] Francis, A. (2015). *Jordan's refugee crisis*, Vol. 21. Carnegie Endowment for International Peace, 1.

in the past, are located along the border with Syria. That location was intentionally chosen to keep the maximum number of refugees as possible in the geographical margins of the Kingdom and to make it difficult for Syrian and Jordanian populations to mix with each other. That marginalisation is an indication that at least on the official level the central government does not view the Syrian and Iraqi refugees as belonging in any sense to Jordan and perhaps living on the border will be an incentive for Syrians and Iraqis to go back to their homes. This policy is not new in Jordan; Iraqi and Kuwaiti refugees there were being housed along the borders in the 1990s following their escapes caused by the Kuwait crisis.

Jordan, during the period beginning in 1988, is undergoing in the second decade of the twenty-first century its toughest test. Its lessons so far for the rest of the countries in the region is that it is not enough to be part of the Arab community to consolidate a collective identity. The modern history of the new Arab nation-states (even if territorial nationalism is imagined in some countries), made Arab rulers and populations grasp reality through new lenses. The new Jordanian zeitgeist is that Jordan has its own identity and that its citizens since 1988 constitute a closed society that would not welcome newcomers, even if they are Arab.

Deviating from the empirical evidence into a theoretical analysis, it is possible to identify in the current policy and its various expressions a move from instrumental nationalism during the third phase of the emergence of Jordanian nationalism, to a territorial-primordial brand of nationalism. Differently put, that means that whatever began as an imposed from above nationalism in the past did change into one of the pillars of the Jordanian Kingdom.

Conclusion

The emergence of distinct Jordanian nationalism has been the result of several processes, but primarily it was intended to encounter the appearance of Syrian nationalism that aimed at annexing Jordan to Syria and Palestinian nationalism that has claimed possession of the former mandatory Palestine. The national foundation laid by King Hussein is healthy and has survived several domestic and foreign challenges. Perhaps the two outstanding crises involved the 1970–71 civil war and later on the 2003 and 2011 demographic changes triggered by the still on-going ordeals in

Iraq and Syria respectively. However, judging from the public words of Kings Hussein and Abdullah II it is evident that both felt and feel that at least the issue of Jordan's *raison d'être* as an independent and unique country on its own is no longer an issue, at least since 1988.

The concept of Jordanian nationalism and collective identity has moved from "Arabism first" to "Jordan First." The Arab Spring that revolved at times around the issue of national identity missed Jordan and if anything proved its resilience as one national entity. Indeed, it is the result to a large extent of the activities of King Hussein who had brought together several distinct groups within the Jordanian society: Muslim East Bankers, especially those originating from Bedouin tribes; Palestinians—those who moved prior to 1948 are fully integrated into the Jordanian identity; the 1948 refugees (*laji*); and the 1967 refugees (*nazih*), who are part of the Jordanian identity in that they live on the East Bank and manifest full solidarity with the Hashemites. Even the Palestinian refugees who reside in the camps and those who live in the cities, mainly in Amman[29] are no longer threats to the regime, due to a large extent to the Hashemite victory in the civil war. Those who do not belong to the common Jordanian identity are the "foreigners": the refugees who fled from Syria since civil war erupted in March 2011. This group has already changed the demographic reality in Jordan, and its presence has generated a public discourse regarding the need to protect original Jordanian identity.

Jordanian nationalism is the result of the amalgamation of three sources: Islam, Arab history, and family lineage, dating back to the Prophet. The composite Jordanian nationalism that resulted was perhaps the central theme of the late King Hussein. In a sense, he was not only the father of Jordanian nationalism but was also regarded by his people as a father figure.

In the aftermath of the Arab Spring, these ideas are stronger than ever. The Jordanian nation-state already exists and a strong sense of belonging to the nation (*al-Ummah al-Urduniyyah*) is an integral part of the Kingdom's zeitgeist. Those who fled Syria and Iraq are perceived by most Jordanians as a threat. And yet, Jordan did not close its borders to refugees, enabling the Kingdom to present itself as a Muslim society fulfilling the pillar of the Muslim religion related to its charity commandment (*zakat*).

---

[29] Perez, M. V. (2011). *Identifying Palestinians: Palestinians refugee and the politics of ethno-national identity in Jordan*, Michigan State University, 72–74.

King Abdullah I

Ronen Yitzhak

The end of the World War I and the collapse of the Ottoman Empire gave the Hashemite family, then ruling the Hejaz region of the Arabian Peninsula, an important role in the formation of the modern Middle East. The Hashemite family was headed by Sharif Hussein Ben Ali, a descendant of the Prophet Muhammad. As a result of his support and that of his family for Britain during the war, as well as his agreement to launch an Arab revolt against the Ottoman Empire in 1916, the pro-Hashemite movement in London grew. This movement was led by British Lieutenant T.E. Lawrence (*Lawrence of Arabia*), who operated in the Middle East on behalf of the British intelligence before the First World War. As Lawrence grew closer to the Hashemite family, he was able to assist with the execution of the Arab Revolt. Lawrence, like Major General Frederick G. Peake, the first British Commander of the Arab Legion in Transjordan, and other British officers, believed that the Hashemite family should be given a significant role in the formation of the Middle East at the end of the war in recognition of their support for Britain during the war.[1] Although modern research has cast

---

[1] Peake wrote in his memoirs: "We must not forget the assistance given to us by Hussein, King of the Hejaz, and his sons…for service against the Turks…", Frederick G. Peake,

R. Yitzhak (✉)
Department of Middle Eastern Studies, Western Galilee College, Acre, Israel
e-mail: roneni@wgalil.ac.il

© The Author(s) 2019
P. R. Kumaraswamy (ed.), *The Palgrave Handbook of the Hashemite Kingdom of Jordan*, https://doi.org/10.1007/978-981-13-9166-8_13

doubt upon the contribution of the Hashemite family to the success of the Arab Revolt,[2] it was the open and public presence of the Hashemite family alongside Britain which finally led the British to the decision in March 1921, to establish two Hashemite states, Iraq and Transjordan under the rule of Faisal and Abdullah—the two sons of Sharif Hussein—respectively.

The British wanted to give power to Abdullah in Transjordan as a reward for the contribution of the Hashemite family towards the British war effort. The British also sought to build a central government connected to the alliance with it as part of its imperialist policy in the Middle East. Until then, there were three local governments in Karak, Salt, and Irbid, headed by local dignitaries but they did not maintain contact with each other and did not cooperate with the British. The British believed that Abdullah's appointment could establish a regime closely connected with them and in the process would advance the British interests in the Middle East.

Moreover, the British believed that the appointment of Abdullah as Emir Transjordan would block his ambitions to rule Syria and ensure political stability in the region. Shortly before that, Abdullah planned to take revenge on the French for having expelled his brother Faisal from Damascus and wanted to reinstate the Hashemite regime there.[3] Therefore, his appointment in Transjordan was intended to replace his desire to rule Syria, because that was where the French mandate had already been implemented under the decision of the San Remo Conference, which in April 1920 approved the division of the mandates between Britain and France.

Thus, the British established the Emirate of Transjordan without advanced planning. Emir Abdullah, for his part, sought to intertwine his fate with the British as part of a strategic-political belief that the British were the only support for stability in the region. This was in addition to the belief that they could promote the emirate from a previously neglected and insignificant area during the Ottoman Empire. Indeed, the British not only financed the Transjordan to the tune of £150,000 a year, but they also protected it from external and internal threats and contributed to the consolidation of Emir Abdullah's status in the Middle East. The first

---

"Trans-Jordan", *Journal of the Royal Central Asian Society*, Vol. 26 (1939), p. 376.

[2] See for example: Efraim Karsh and Inari Karsh, "Myth in the Desert, or Not the Great Arab Revolt", *Middle Eastern Studies*, Vol. 33, No. 2 (April 1997), pp. 267–312.

[3] Abdullah ibn Hussein, *Muthakarati* (Jerusalem: Beit al-Maqdis, 1945), pp. 190–191.

partition of Palestine resulted in the formation of two separate political entities following Churchill's first White Paper in June 1922. During his visit to Amman on 25 May 1923, British High Commissioner to Palestine Herbert Samuel declared that the British government had agreed to recognise the independent government in Transjordan. Although he emphasised that it recognised only an independent government, Abdullah interpreted this as recognition of Transjordanian independence and 25 May was then declared the official day of independence in Jordan.

In the early years, Bedouin tribes in Transjordan rebelled and renounced Abdullah's rule, refusing to recognise him. They refused to pay taxes, and as a result, cavalry forces raided their villages, meting out punishments. One such was the al-Adwan tribe, which staged a rebellion against Abdullah in September 1923. As the British were heavily involved in defending Abdullah's rule, they not only helped suppress the revolt but also exploited by arresting and expelling all opponents of the regime who refused to accept Abdullah's authority or accept his pro-British policy. Among those arrested was the famous Jordanian poet Mustafa Wahbi al-Tall, who had connections with the al-Adwan tribe and was tried on charges of conspiracy against the state. Abdullah also received British support when Ibn Saud tried to undermine his rule in the summers of 1922 and 1924. The al-Saud raids on the Jordanians resulted in many casualties, and these were repelled after the British Air Force bombed the al-Saud soldiers in the south of Amman.[4]

Relations between Transjordan and Britain were formalised only in February 1928, when a first treaty was signed. The Anglo-Jordanian treaty expressed the total dependence of Transjordan and Emir Abdullah upon the British. Although the treaty recognised Abdullah as Emir of Transjordan, it stated that "The Amir agrees to be guided by the advice of His Britannic Majesty tendered through the High Commissioner for Tran-Jordan in all matters concerning foreign relations of Trans-Jordan, as well as in all important matters affecting the international and financial obligations..." (Article 5). The treaty was made possible for Britain to "maintain armed forces in Trans-Jordan and may raise, organise and

---

[4] Mary C. Wilson, *King Abdullah, Britain, and the Making of Jordan* (Cambridge: Cambridge University Press, 1990), pp. 74–75; Benjamin Shwadran, *Jordan: A State of Tension* (New York: Council for Middle Eastern Affairs Press, 1959), p. 146; Suleiman Musa and Madi Munib, *Ta'arikh al-Urdun fi al-Qarn al-Ishrin* (Amman: Dar al-Muhtasib, 1996), Vol. I, pp. 203–204.

control in Tran-Jordan such armed forces as may in his opinion be necessary for the defence of the country…" (Article 10).[5]

At the same time, the relationship that Abdullah had formed with Britain was shaped by his relations with the Zionist community in Palestine. Abdullah and the Hashemite family were not hostile to the Zionist movement unlike the other Arab nationalists and had even maintained contacts. One of the most prominent and well-known agreements in this context was the Faisal-Weizmann Agreement[6] which aroused the opposition of Arab nationalism not least because the agreement determined that Palestine would be separated from the Arab state and that the Jews could establish a national home there in the spirit of the Balfour Declaration of November 1917.

However, it appears that the reason for Amir Abdullah's closeness to the Zionists was related to his political ambitions. Abdullah was interested in taking control of Palestine at an early stage of his rule and did not hide it. He explicitly asked Winston Churchill, Colonial Secretary in March 1921 to allow him to merge Palestine with Transjordan, but Churchill refused. His political ambitions and rumours of contacts with the British and the Zionists to promote these ambitions led him into conflict with Mufti Amin al-Husseini, the head of Palestinian national movement.

Al-Husseini had wanted to establish an independent Palestinian state under his leadership since the early 1920s and therefore was opposed the annexation of Palestine to Transjordan. He not only opposed the establishment of a Jewish state but also prevented any political agreement with the Jews and incited the Palestinians against them. Therefore, Abdullah assumed that Palestinian resistance to the Zionists would lead them (the Zionists) to agree to a Jordanian annexation of Palestine. This was the basis of the relationship that was created between Abdullah and the Zionist leadership in Palestine in the late 1920s. Political relations between the two sides developed and strengthened economic and intelligence ties. Abdullah was willing to lease lands to the Jewish Agency in the Jordan Valley and gave them intelligence information about what was going on in the Arab world. In return, for example, during the mid-1930s, the Jewish

---

[5] The full text of the agreement see: "Agreement: The United Kingdom and Transjordan", J. C. Hurewitz, *Diplomacy in Near and Middle East: A Documentary Record* (New York: Octagon Books, 1972), pp. 156–159.

[6] Antonius first published the text of the agreement in 1938. George Antonius, *The Arab Awakening* (London: Hamish Hamilton, 1938), pp. 437–439.

Agency paid Abdullah £10,000 a year and provided intelligence information about his political rivals, especially the Palestinians.[7]

At the end of April 1936, the Palestinians rose up against the British Mandate, demanding the establishment of independence and an end to Jewish immigration. The 1936–39 revolt which opened with the general strike against the Jews developed into violence and anarchy in Palestine. The British rejected Palestinian demands and suppressed the Arab Revolt after three years of prolonged suppression and violence. The Arab Revolt led to a temporary rapprochement between the Jewish Agency and Mandate authorities. Abdullah made efforts to keep the revolt out of Transjordan to avoid linking himself to Palestinians violence. He tightened security on the borders of Palestine-Transjordan, prevented the infiltration of Arab nationalists into Palestine, and also averted the smuggling of arms and ammunition to Palestine.

Abdullah's warm relations with Britain were reflected in the recommendations of the Palestine Royal Commission (Peel Commission) of Inquiry. In a report published in July 1937, the committee, which visited Palestine in December 1936, recommended that the solution to the conflict would be a partition of Palestine into two states, Jewish and Arab and mandatory government. Unlike the independent Jewish state, the Arab-Palestinian state would not be independent but would be part of Transjordan under Emir Abdullah. This was the first time that Abdullah had been able to pursue his political ambitions to control Palestine and to further close connection between Transjordan and Britain.

The Second World War, which broke out in September 1939, also illustrated the close ties between the two. Unlike other Arab leaders who supported Germany in their bid to defeat British colonialism from the Middle East and to gain Arab independence, Abdullah wished for Britain's victory. He was the only Arab leader, apart from Hashemite leaders of Iraq, who stood clearly and openly alongside Britain and offered military support. The British saw no need for assistance from the Jordanian Arab Legion because they did not appreciate its military capabilities at the time.

However, at the end of April 1941, an anti-British military coup in Iraq resulted in regime change under the leadership of the Pro-German Prime

---

[7] On the relations between King Abdullah to the Zionists see: Yoav Gelber, *Jewish–Transjordanian Relations 1921–1948* (London: Frank Cass, 1996); Ronen Yitzhak, "A Short History of the Secret Hashemite-Zionist Talks: 1921–1951", *Midstream,* Vol. LIII (2007), pp. 9–12.

Minister Rashid Ali al-Kilani. When the Hashemite Iraqi leaders fled from Iraq, the British feared that they would lose the port of Basra in southern Iraq which they used on for trade with India. Therefore, Britain decided to act against the al-Kilani government with the help of Arab Legion soldiers and allowed them to join the British forces, which had arrived in Iraq in mid-May. They took part in the military campaign to subdue the government of al-Kilani. The Arab Legion continued its military activity in Syria a month later, in cooperation with British forces and the Free French Army, to remove the German supporters from power.

It seems that the support of Transjordan for Britain and its participation in the Second World War left no doubt about the political and strategic ties between the two. Britain appreciated and strengthened the activity of the Arab Legion and trained its members to perform combat duties and armed them with new weapons that it had previously refused. After the war, the Arab Legion became one of the best Arab armies in the Middle East and formed part of the British forces in the Middle East. Conversely, within and beyond Transjordan, there was growing criticism of Emir Abdullah's pro-Western policy and the Palestinian attempts to undermine the Hashemite regime in Jordan increased, resulting in the assassination attempts of senior Jordanian figures including Emir Abdullah and General Glubb Pasha.

As a result of cooperation between Transjordan and Britain during the war, in March 1946, Britain declared Transjordan's independence. This was the result of a change in British policy in the Middle East following the post-war economic crisis, which led to the desire to reduce costs and cut the workforce and to close military bases. There also followed a decision to promote British interests through friendly governments, which in turn served King Abdullah's interests. Two months later, in May, Emir Abdullah declared himself the King of Transjordan.

THE 1948 WAR AND THE REALISATION OF ABDULLAH'S POLITICAL AMBITIONS

In the early 1940s, King Abdullah began to act on his intention to take over Palestine under a new political plan known as the "Greater Syria" Plan whose aim was to unite parts of Syria, Lebanon, and Palestine into Transjordan under his rule. The political situation in Syria was encouraging and in June 1940, France surrendered to Germany and its colonies in the Middle East and North Africa became pro-German regimes. Abdullah thought that he could fill the vacuum in Syria and annex it and to convince the Arabs and the British to grant him power in Syria, he claimed that this was the goal of the Arab Revolt in 1916: "We left the Hejaz for Syria, Transjordan, Palestine, and Lebanon, which are all one unit – Greater Syria."[8] However, both the Arabs and the British objected. British Prime Minister Churchill preferred to tighten his relations with General Charles de Gaulle's "Free France" forces and rejected the demand. The Arabs also opposed it because they favoured independence with the liberation of Syria and Lebanon from the pro-German regime.

It seems that the first opportunity for Abdullah to realise the "Great Syria" plan came during the 1948 war. The 1947 UN partition plan for Palestine, which recommended the end of the British Mandate and the establishment of independent Arab and Jewish states in Palestine, was unacceptable to Arab leaders but not to some Palestinians. While Arab leaders were debating how to respond to the partition resolution and thwart it, King Abdullah's position was clear. His goal was to gain control of the whole or part of Palestine, whether by war or through negotiations. Therefore, Jordan's activity on the eve of the termination of the British Mandate was to reach agreements with all of those concerned, namely, the British, Palestinians, and Zionists, to persuade them to allow King Abdullah to take control of Palestine.

It was important for Abdullah to obtain the consent of the British to realise his political ambitions regarding Palestine. In early February 1948, the Jordanian Prime Minister Tawfiq Abu al-Huda arrived in London for a meeting with the British Foreign Secretary Ernest Bevin and described the possible scenarios when the British withdrew from Palestine: the Jews ignored the UN partition plan, took control whole of Palestine, and established the State of Israel, or Mufti Amin al-Husseini declared the establishment of a Palestinian state and stood at its head. Since those two options were not attractive for Britain or to Jordan, Abu al-Huda suggested that the Arab Legion enter Palestine and take control of the areas allocated to the Palestinian state under the partition plan. "It seems the obvious thing

---

[8] Abdullah ibn Hussein, *al-Takmila min Muthakarat Hadrah Sahib al-Jalalah al-Hashemiya al-Malik Abdullah ibn Hussein* (Amman: n.p., 1951), p. 39.

to do," Bevin agreed but added a warning that the Arab Legion must not enter the areas allocated to the Jewish state, and Abu al-Huda agreed.[9]

Britain's approval of the Legion's takeover of the Arab territories stemmed from the belief that this could reduce the bloodshed in Palestine. "While the riots in Palestine are heading toward a general clash, Abdullah's policy has a chance of preventing chaos," stated the British intelligence report written at the beginning of 1948.

The Palestinian support was essential to King Abdullah, to reduce the influence of the Palestinian nationalist movement. The Palestinian national movement, headed by al-Husseini, ignored the partition plan and did not recognise a Jewish state in Palestine because, according to the Palestinian-Muslim view, the whole of Palestine should have been under Arab rule and this resulted in Palestinians not cooperating with the United Nations. After the adoption of the partition plan, opposition to the Jewish state in the Arab countries grew and they also feared Abdullah's intention to take control of Palestine and created a coalition with Palestinian elements, which sought to prevent Abdullah's plans vis-à-vis Palestine.

Towards this endeavour, the Arab League established the Arab Liberation Army—a volunteer army whose task was to thwart the partition plan and to prevent the Arab Legion's involvement in Palestine. The Arab League assumed that if this army succeeded in its mission, the UN would retract its intention to implement the partition plan as there would be no need for the intervention of regular armies.[10] This, in turn, would prevent the Arab Legion from intervening in Palestine and thus prevent King Abdullah from realising his "Greater Syria" plan.

However, Abdullah succeeded in taking advantage of the split amongst the Palestinians, some of whom opposed the hegemony of the al-Husseini family as they dominated the Palestinian political and religious institutions. Some disgruntled Palestinians even sought to harm this family. Notable Palestinian families, who felt deprived, believed that they could regain their status by cooperating with the Hashemite regime and thereby supported King Abdullah's aspirations in Palestine. In other words, they believed that the solution to the conflict was to annex Palestine to Jordan and to thwart the intention to establish an independent Palestinian state.

---

[9] Bevin to Kirkbride, "Conversation with the Transjordan Prime Minister," 9 February 1948, National Archives (London), FO 371/68366.

[10] "The Greater Syria Movement," 10 January 1948, National Archives (London), FO 371/6149.

To some extent, they were also willing to cooperate with the Zionists in Palestine. Thus, the Ja'bari families from Hebron, Tuqan from Nablus, Nashashibi, and Khalidi from Jerusalem and other important and dominant families in the West Bank promoted Jordanian interests in Palestine on the eve of the termination of the British Mandate and helped Abdullah take control of the Arab territories of Palestine.

As noted, contacts with the Zionists had continued regularly since the 1920s and both had no interest in the establishment of an Arab state in Palestine. In August 1946, Abdullah reached an understanding with the Jewish Agency about the partition of Palestine into two parts: a Jewish section in which a Jewish state would be established and an Arab part annexed to Transjordan. Abdullah explicitly admitted that he intended "to take over Arab Palestine in order to prevent the creation of an unwanted Palestinian state."[11] In November 1947, the two sides again agreed to partition Palestine, ignoring the intention to establish an independent Arab state. According to the understanding reached between Golda Meyerson (Meir) the head of the Political Department of the Jewish Agency and King Abdullah, Abdullah would annex the territories which were allocated to the Palestinian state, and the Jews would be able to establish a Jewish state in the other part of Palestine.[12]

However, in May 1948, when Abdullah was encouraged by the possibility of taking control of the whole of Palestine, he tried to persuade the Jews to cancel the declaration of the State of Israel and to allow him to take over the territories without the need for war. "Why are you so in a hurry to declare your own state?" Abdullah asked Meyerson, and her answer was that a people who waited 2000 years could not be said to be in a hurry.[13] Abdullah warned Golda Meyerson that if the Jews insisted on declaring a state, he would have to join with the Arab states and fight against them. It seemed that after Abdullah had failed to obtain Jewish consent to take control of Palestine, he had no choice but to declare war against them to further his political ambitions. Abdullah did not believe that the Jews were capable of declaring a state under the circumstances, as the Arab League and Arab leaders made threats and warnings against them

---

[11] William W. Haddad and Mary M. Hardy, "Jordan's Alliance with Israel and Its Effects on Jordanian-Arab Relations", in Efraim Karsh and P. R. Kumaraswamy (eds.), *Israel, the Hashemites, and the Palestinians: The Fateful Triangle* (London: Frank Cass, 2003), p. 36.

[12] Avi Shlaim, *Collusion across the Jordan: King Abdullah, the Zionist Movement, and the Partition of Palestine* (Oxford: Clarendon, 1988).

[13] Golda Meir, *My Life* (Jerusalem: Steimatzky, 1975), p. 218.

and were hence surprised by their determination. He believed that the Jews would bow to Arab pressure and he could use this to win the whole of Palestine without the need for a war.

During the period between the UN adoption of the partition plan and the 1948 war (November 1947–May 1948), the Arab Legion did not conduct military activities against the Jews. The commander of the British army in Palestine General Gordon Macmillan unequivocally stated his opposition to any aggression from the Arab Legion against the Jews: "As long as the Arab Legion is in Palestine under our instructions it mustn't fight the Jews."[14] Indeed, the Arab Legion did not intervene in battles and generally maintained neutrality. British instruction was also consistent with King Abdullah's policy as he feared that active intervention of his soldiers against the Jews before the end of the British Mandate would complicate his relations with Britain and thwart his political ambitions to occupy the Arab territories of Palestine.

Despite this, the Arab Legion took part in anti-Jewish activities in many attacks, the largest of which was in Etzion Block (Gush Etzion). The Block included four Jewish settlements (Kfar Etzion, Massuot Yitzhak, Ein Tzurim, and Revadim) located alongside the Hebron-Jerusalem road. Ostensibly, the conquest of the Block on 12 May was intended to remove the Jewish threat to the military supply route, which served the British army for the transfer of military supplies from the British army base in Suez to the Arab Legion forces in Jerusalem. It, however, was part of the Jordanian policy to take control of the Arab territories at the outbreak of the 1948 war and to cleanse them of all Jewish presence. The conquest was also intended to facilitate the Legion in the Jordanian campaign for the conquest of Jerusalem and to ensure that Jewish forces from southern Jerusalem would not assist the Jews in the Old City. The attack took place on 12 May and the day after it ended with the conquest of Kfar Etzion, the largest settlement in the Block and the massacre of its inhabitants. Following this, the rest of the Block surrendered to the Arab Legion and they were transferred as prisoners to the POW camp in Transjordan.

On 15 May, a day after the declaration of the establishment of State of Israel, Arab armies invaded Palestine. The Arab Legion, some of whose forces had already been in Palestine as part of its cooperation with the British, immediately took control of the West Bank and established a

---

[14] Quoted in Yona Bendman, "Haligion Ha'aravi Likrat Milhemet Ha'atzmaut" (The Arab Legion toward the War of Independence, Hebrew), *Ma'archot*, 294–295 (1984), p. 42.

Jordanian military administration within three days. Military governors were appointed in major cities under Jordanian rule, and economic, commercial, and political ties between the occupied territories and Transjordan were forged immediately. Jordan paid the salaries of the workers, opened post offices and banks, invested in infrastructure, roads, and renovation of buildings, undertook rehabilitation of refugees, and more. Concurrently, preparations were made to pave the way for the annexation of these areas to Transjordan after the war.

The principal battles in which the Arab Legion took part in Palestine were fought to further King Abdullah's political ambitions. They focused on the conquest of Jerusalem and Latrun and Bab al-Wad, the main road from Tel Aviv to the Jerusalem sector. Although Jerusalem was designated as an international territory according to the UN partition, King Abdullah sought to take control and wanted it to become the most conquest because of its historical and religious importance. The role of the Hashemite family has been the protector of the Islamic holy sites and the Islamic faith because Jerusalem is considered the third holiest city in Islam (after Mecca and Medina) its conquest became essential.

On 18 May, the battles in Jerusalem began with the control of Latrun and Bab al-Wad by the Arab Legion's forces and the Jordanians sought to block the road from Tel Aviv to Jerusalem, to prevent Jewish reinforcements and supplies from getting into Jerusalem, and to facilitate the conquest of the city by Transjordan. Within ten days, the Arab Legion had conquered the Old City of Jerusalem, including the Jewish Quarter, after the surrender of its Jewish residents. The Legion's attempt to break into the new city of Jerusalem and conquer it, however, failed. Jewish attempts to open the road to Jerusalem and conquer the Jewish Quarter also failed. Two months after the outbreak of the war, in July 1948, the border areas between Israel and Jordan stabilised and the Jordanian government established its rule in the occupied territories. Israel, for its part, took up arms against the Egyptian and Syrian armies to drive them from Palestine and end the war.[15]

---

[15] The Jordanian political position and the military activities in the 1948 war are described in few books which were written by Jordanians. However, the most important is the book written by the Jordanian historian Suleiman Musa, *Ayyam la Tunsa, al-Urdun fi Harb 1948* (Amman: Dar al-Muhtasib, 1997). The commander of the Arab Legion General Glubb Pasha also wrote his memoirs of the war under the title *A Soldier with the Arabs* (London: Hodder and Stoughton, 1957).

Thus, the Arab Legion fulfilled some of King Abdullah's political ambitions. He fought for the territories that were important to him and obtained them, while he gave up areas less politically or strategically important to him such as the Arab towns of Lod and Ramla and the Negev and did not fight for them. For military reasons, Abdullah failed to take control of the whole of Palestine, but he conquered those Arab territories close to Transjordan (i.e., the West Bank) without much Israeli opposition. Thus, the intention to establish a Palestinian state in Palestine or part thereof was thwarted by Transjordan, with the consent of Israel and Britain.

The Palestinians, with the support of the Arab League, tried to prevent King Abdullah from rendering the military occupation to a political achievement. On 20 September, Mufti Amin al-Husseini succeeded in convening the Palestinian National Council in the Gaza Strip, which was under Egyptian military rule, and declared the establishment of Palestinian government—the All Palestine government. Although most of the territories of the All Palestine government were under the rule of Transjordan and the State of Israel, King Abdullah feared the support of the Arab states for the government and therefore decided to take counter-measures. On 1 October, he organised in Amman the first Palestinian Conference with the participation of hundreds of Palestinian notables from the West Bank, who expressed public support for the Hashemite policy in Palestine. Two months later, on 1 December, the second Palestinian Conference was held in Jericho which called on King Abdullah to formally annex the Arab territories of Palestine (the West Bank) to Transjordan and recognised him as King of Transjordan and Palestine. Thus, King Abdullah received official legitimacy from the Palestinians to annex the territories to Transjordan and he had been waiting for the right moment to realise this.

Arab Nationalism and the Assassination of King Abdullah

The end of the 1948 war and the achievement of the objectives of the Arab Legion allowed Israel and Jordan to continue with their negotiations to reach a peace agreement. In fact, at the end of the war, the two countries were isolated. Israel was founded despite the military and political efforts of the Arab states who could not oppose it because the fledgling country gained international recognition when it joined the United Nations in May 1949. Jordan's efforts to conquer the Arab territories of

Palestine and its preparations for the annexation brought about hostility between the Palestinians and the Arab countries and anti-Hashemite propaganda in the Middle East increased. King Abdullah was accused of collusion with Israel and of cooperation with Western imperialism which they maintained prevented the establishment of an Arab state in Palestine.

Under these circumstances, King Abdullah was interested in reaching an understanding with Israel to obtain an agreement for the formal annexation of the West Bank. Israel, for its part, was interested in reaching a peace agreement with any Arab state to dismantle the Arab bloc and bring other Arab countries to ally with it. Although Israel preferred to establish diplomatic relations with Egypt because of its greater political importance, it decided to negotiate with Jordan because of Egypt's refusal to negotiate. It seems that Abdullah's desire to negotiate with Israel was not, in the opinion of the British government, in their own best interests and accordingly the British government opposed this because it believed that a separate peace agreement with Israel would weaken Abdullah's status in the Arab world and thus would harm him.

Negotiations for peace between the two countries took place between November 1949 and March 1950. King Abdullah personally dealt with many issues including territorial questions, issue of the Palestinian refugees, Jordanian access to the Mediterranean Sea, and others. Despite King Abdullah's personal involvement, the negotiations failed because of the lack of flexibility on both sides.[16] Israel was not willing to agree to the Jordanian demands to permit the return of the limited number of Palestinian refugees nor would it agree on the passage to the Mediterranean as requested by the Jordanians. On the other hand, the Jordanians refused to allow Jews free access to the Western Wall, the Jewish Quarter, and Mount Scopus.

Despite Abdullah's personal efforts to establish peace, he failed to impose his will on the Jordanian people. The Prime Ministers appointed by him (Sa'id al-Mufti and Samir al-Rifa'i) not only opposed a peace agreement with Israel but also openly condemned Israel in the Jordanian Parliament for thwarting efforts to broker a peace deal. King Abdullah toured West Bank cities, met with Palestinian dignitaries, and tried to persuade them to agree to negotiate a peace deal with Israel, but his efforts failed. In March 1950, the two sides decided that the situation no longer merited the continuation of the negotiations and in effect, he ruled. The

---

[16] Glubb, *A Soldier with the Arabs*, p. 258.

government of Israel appreciated King Abdullah's efforts to achieve peace and claimed that he was the only Arab leader who made efforts to forge a lasting peace.[17]

Meanwhile, King Abdullah stepped up his efforts to annex the West Bank with Jordan. In November 1949, restrictions on movement between the two banks were abolished, and customs duties on goods transferred between the two were cancelled and a month later, the Jordanian military administration was formally abolished on the West Bank. In the same month, a new citizenship law came into force whereby the residents of the West Bank became Jordanian citizens. At the beginning of January 1950, the Jordanian Parliament was dissolved as a first step towards the establishment of a newly elected parliament, comprising 40 representatives, 20 representatives from each side. On 11 April 1950, the first elections were held for the unified parliament and the next day a new government was formed in Jordan. Approximately two weeks later, on 24 April, the Jordanian government announced the annexation of the West Bank to Jordan and the establishment of the Hashemite Kingdom of Jordan.

At the same time, the process of assimilating the Palestinian population in Jordan increased and the government sought to turn the Palestinians into Jordanians for political and economic reasons. The political motive was the desire to nullify the Palestinian national identity as part of the Jordanianisation process of the West Bank as advocated by King Abdullah, who perceived that he was responsible for the fate of the Palestinians. The economic objective was driven by the belief that their absorption and integration into the Jordanian economy would constitute additional human resources and thereby increase production which in turn would enhance its development and advancement. The Palestinians received passports and were granted freedom of movement towards their integration into the Jordanian economy. The Jordanian government also provided plots of land to the various development organisations, the most important of which was the construction project established by Musa al-Alami to settle the refugees in the Jericho area. In contrast with other countries, the Jordanian government increased cooperation with UNRWA (United Nations Relief and Works Agency) and allocated money to projects proposed by UNRWA. Thus, Jordan was different from other Arab countries,

---

[17] About the peace negotiation between Israel and Jordan in 1949–1950 see: Mordechai Gazit, "The Israel-Jordan Peace Negotiations (1949–1951): King Abdullah's Lonely Effort", *Journal of Contemporary History*, Vol. 23 (1988), pp. 409–424.

which preferred to leave the Palestinian refugees in the refugee camps without granting them political rights or any political status to put the onus of the problem upon Israel and their right to return them to their homes.

Despite this, the Palestinians did not become Jordanians. Not only did they maintain their national identity, they also outnumbered the Jordanians in the Hashemite Kingdom of Jordan (600,000 Palestinians vs. 400,000 Jordanians).[18] The Palestinian residents of Jordan were also more culturally and politically aware than their Jordanian counterparts, wishing to reduce the absolutist regime of King Abdullah. Their demands included the following: the King to sever ties with Britain and Israel; Britain to sever ties with the Arab Legion and finally, the Jordanian constitution to be amended, ensuring that the government would bear responsibility for the parliament instead of the king.[19] Although the king promised to discuss the proposal to amend the constitution, he did not fulfil his promise, and therefore, an opposition majority was formed in the parliament, consisting of both Palestinians and nationalist opposition parties.[20]

During 1951, King Abdullah's status in the Arab world deteriorated and reached an unprecedented low. The situation of the Palestinian refugees was difficult and hostility in the Arab world due to his political moves and anti-Hashemite propaganda was rife, encouraged by the Mufti Amin al-Husseini, the head of Palestinian national movement.

On Friday, 20 July 1951, when King Abdullah entered the Friday prayers at the al-Aqsa mosque on the Temple Mount, he was assassinated. The assassin, Shukri Ashu, a 21-year-old Palestinian from Jerusalem, was killed by King Abdullah's security guards. The assassination shocked the Arab and Western world and there was fear that the murder would bring about the collapse of the regime. However, rapid actions by the Arab Legion, including curfews, arrests of Palestinian activists, and a thorough investigation into the plot, enabled the return of political stability to Jordan.

---

[18] Foreign Office: News to Israeli delegations in the World, 24 July 1951, Israel Defence Forces Archive (Tel Hashomer), 40/68/1955; Laurie A. Brand, "Palestinians and Jordanians: A Crisis of Identity," *Journal of Palestine Studies*, Vol. 24, No. 4 (Summer 1995), pp. 46–61, 47.

[19] Foreign Office: News to Israeli delegations in the World, 24 July 1951, Israel Defence Forces Archive (Tel Hashomer), 40/68/1955; Research Department, 31 August 1951, Israel State Archives (Jerusalem), 2565/11.

[20] Foreign Office: News to Israeli delegations in the World, 24 July 1951, Israel Defence Forces Archive (Tel Hashomer), 40/68/1955.

About three weeks after the assassination, the Jordanian intelligence managed to expose all those involved in the conspiracy. Ten people were tried, and others, initially suspected of involvement in the murder, were released. At the end of a nine-day trial, four of the defendants were acquitted, while the other six, who were charged under the Jordanian Penal Code relating to murder, were sentenced to death. Two of them—Col. Abdullah al-Tall and Musa al-Ayubi—were sentenced to death in their absence. The request for extradition sent to the Egyptian government went unanswered because there was no extradition agreement between the two countries. On 4 September 1951, four defendants were executed.[21]

Conclusions

The death of King Abdullah I ended a critical period in the history of Jordan. With the help of Britain, the regime strengthened, and state institutions were built. The regime was dependent on Britain and the latter protected the Hashemite regime from external and internal threats. The strategic alliance between the two, reflected in the Second World War, enabled Britain to support King Abdullah's political ambitions, leading to the military occupation of the West Bank and annexation later to Jordan to prevent the establishment of an Arab state in Palestine.

The coronation of King Hussein in May 1953, after a brief reign of King Talal (1951–52), ensured not only the continued existence of the Hashemite regime but also the continuation of Jordan's political relations with Western countries in general and Britain in particular.

References

Antonius, G. (1938). *The Arab awakening*. London: Hamish Hamilton.
Bendman, Y. (1984). Haligion Ha'aravi Likrat Milhemet Ha'atzmaut (The Arab Legion toward the War of Independence, Hebrew). *Ma'archot*, 294–295, 36–45.
Brand, L. A. (1995). Palestinians and Jordanians: A crisis of identity. *Journal of Palestine Studies*, 24, 46–61.
Gazit, M. (1988). The Israel-Jordan peace negotiations (1949–1951): King Abdullah's lonely effort. *Journal of Contemporary History*, 23, 409–424.
Gelber, Y. (1996). *Jewish—Transjordanian relations 1921–1948*. London: Frank Cass.

---

[21] *Filastin* (Jerusalem), 24 July 1951; Glubb to Melville, 6 August 1951, National Archives (London), FO 371/91838.

Glubb, J. B. (1957). *A soldier with the Arabs*. London: Hodder and Stoughton.
Haddad, W. W., & Hardy, M. M. (2003). Jordan's alliance with Israel and its effects on Jordanian-Arab relations. In E. Karsh & P. R. Kumaraswamy (Eds.), *Israel, the Hashemites, and the Palestinians: The fateful triangle* (pp. 31–48). London: Frank Cass.
Hurewitz, J. C. (1972). *Diplomacy in near and Middle East: A documentary record*. New York: Octagon Books.
Ibn Hussein, A. (1945). *Muthakarati*. Jerusalem: Beit al-Maqdis.
Ibn Hussein, A. (1951). *Al-Takmila min Muthakarat Hadrah Sahib al-Jalalah al-Hashemiya al-Malik Abdullah ibn Hussein*. Amman: n.p.
Israel, the Hashemites, and the Palestinians: The Fateful Triangle. London: Frank Cass, 2003. 31–48.
Karsh, E., & Karsh, I. (1997). Myth in the desert, or not the Great Arab Revolt. *Middle Eastern Studies, 33*, 267–312.
Meir, G. (1975). *My life*. Jerusalem: Steimatzky.
Musa, S. (1997). *Ayyam la Tunsa, al-Urdun fi Harb 1948*. Amman: Dar al-Muhtasib.
Musa, S., & Munib, M. (1996). *Ta'arikh al-Urdun fi al-Qarn al-Ishrin*. Amman: Dar al-Muhtasib.
Peake, G. F. (1939). Trans-Jordan. *Journal of the Royal Central Asian Society, 26*, 375–396.
Shlaim, A. (1988). *Collusion across the Jordan: King Abdullah, the Zionist movement, and the partition of Palestine*. Oxford: Clarendon.
Shwadran, B. (1959). *Jordan: A state of tension*. New York: Council for Middle Eastern Affairs Press.
Wilson, C. M. (1990). *King Abdullah, Britain, and the making of Jordan*. Cambridge: Cambridge University Press.
Yitzhak, R. (2007). A short history of the secret Hashemite-Zionist talks: 1921–1951. *Midstream, LIII*, 9–12.

King Hussein (1935–99)

Md. Muddassir Quamar

For close to five decades, Hussein Bin-Talal (1952–99) was synonymous with the Hashemite Kingdom of Jordan. He took over the Kingdom at a critical time. Not only was Jordan a young state without critical natural resources, especially water, but it was also situated in one of the world's most turbulent and conflict-ridden areas. Furthermore, the end of World War II had announced the beginning of a new era in global affairs dominated by two powers, the US and the USSR, what came to be defined as a bipolar international order. For the young King Hussein, who for the first nine months ruled through the regency council as he had not yet attained the age of coronation, heading the monarchy was full of challenges. Domestically, he was faced with issues of security, political stability, economic prosperity, and social cohesion, and internationally Jordan was yet to join a political bloc. But even more challenging was the regional environment that was fraught with conflicts, hostility, and power struggle.

Coronation

Hussein succeeded his father King Talal in extraordinary circumstances in August 1952 after the latter was deposed after being declared medically unfit to continue as the ruler, and Hussein was coroneted as King on 2

Md. M. Quamar (✉)
Institute for Defence Studies and Analyses, New Delhi, India

May 1953. The situation within the Hashemite family and among its tribal supporters was not ideal. Hence, for the first ten years of his rule, King Hussein faced a series of crises to the monarchy. Of the most immediate challenge was to manage relations with the Palestinian refugees who had fled their homes in the wake of the 1948 Arab-Israeli War and the tension between the East Bank and West Bank. Second, relation with Britain of which Jordan was a protectorate between 1921 and 1946 was of immediate concern. Domestically, Jordan's proximity with the colonial power was becoming unpopular, and people were demanding that the Kingdom ends all its military and security arrangement with Britain.

The situation was exacerbated by the Qibya massacre on 14 October 1953. During an Israeli military raid on the West Bank village of Qibya, about 50 villagers including women and children were killed. This provoked severe anti-Israeli and anti-British protests in both East and West Banks, and one of the crucial demands was to dismiss British Officers commanding the Jordanian army. While the crisis could be managed with some political manoeuvring, this proved to be an important lesson in the young King's political life, especially in terms of managing relations with Israel.

While the domestic situation was coming to normalcy, the regional situation became a source of trouble. Once again, the British links were at the centre of the problem. Hussein who was keen on joining the US-backed Baghdad Pact (later renamed Central Treaty Organisation, CENTO) could not overcome the domestic opposition to the military relations with Britain. In early 1955, Turkey, Iraq, Pakistan, Iran, and the UK eventually signed the Baghdad Pact without Jordan. The primary objective of the Pact was to counter the influence of the USSR in the Middle East. This was a major conundrum for the young King, and his willingness to join was dampened by at the one level fear of domestic backlash and at other level opposition to the Pact from both the Arab nationalists led by Gamal Abdul Nasser (who at the time was the prime minister and chairman of the Revolutionary Command Council) and Arab traditionalists led by Saudi Arabia.

The Suez Crisis and the Aftermath

Eventually, to placate the domestic opposition, in March 1956, the King dismissed Gen. John Bagot Glubb (Glubb Pasha), the British officer who had commanded the Arab Legion since 1939 and had raised the Jordanian National Guard in 1951 to defend its borders. The move not only targeted the domestic population that was against the continued British presence in the Jordanian military but also neutralised growing regional voice against Jordan's proximity with Britain. The regional situation took another serious turn in the wake of the Suez crisis in October that year when Britain, France, and Israel launched tripartite aggression on Egypt in the wake of Nasser's decision to nationalise the Suez Canal. While the crisis eventually came to an end with the Israeli withdrawal from the Sinai Peninsula and the Gaza Strip and the American political intervention stamping its superiority of the regional affairs, Jordan was in a peculiar situation. Its strong military relations with Britain on the one hand and internal pressure on the other put it in a difficult position. The Suez crisis was one of the first international tests of the leadership of King Hussein and according to Zeid Raad (1994) if not for the political astuteness of the King, Jordan could have easily joined the war from either of the two sides.

With the end of the Suez crisis, the attention of King Hussein became focussed on the internal situation in the Kingdom. Factionalism, opposition, and tensions between the tribes and the restive Palestinian population had become a major headache for the monarch. He was also perturbed by the growing economic demands and the lack of any solution by the governments forcing him to change the prime minister frequently. Indeed, during his 47-year reign, Hussein had as many as 44 prime ministers.

The other issue was the pressure from regional powers to give up the financial aid received from Britain. In many ways, the Kingdom was dependent on this aid for its economic survival. A resource-starved country, Jordan was not in a position to refuse the British aid. In the meanwhile, countries like Saudi Arabia, Egypt, and Syria offered to fill up the financial vacuum that would be created by rejecting the British aid. However, King Hussein was not yet ready to completely end relations with Britain (Ashton 2008). This did not end the problems facing the King in terms of maintaining ties with Britain, even though he asserted the Jordanian right to receive continued British subsidy in his conversations with various Arab leaders.

Nonetheless, the military ties between Jordan and Britain had been severely damaged due to the Suez crisis and the dismissal of General Glubb. This also intensified the struggle between the London and Arab capitals for influence in Amman. The young King, despite his inexperience, did not want to keep anything to chance. Thus, in his effort "to enhance Jordan's security in the face of his uncertain relations with Britain, Hussein explored the avenues open to him for securing Arab military backing" (Ashton 2008, p. 58). The aid arrived in the form of military contingents from Syria, and Egypt, but these were no match for the professional military support provided by the British.

While the regional situation was quiet and neighbours were competing among themselves to establish their hold in Jordan, King Hussein's attention was focussed on the internal situation that was developing into a severe challenge. To avoid factionalism and political tussles, in October 1956, the King decided to hold the parliamentary election after a gap of two years. This was also the time when Hussein was toying with the idea of getting close to the Arab nationalists at the regional level. The election results threw a surprise with the pro-Nasser National Socialist Party (NSP) emerging as the largest party, securing 12 out of the 40 seats. Despite internal opposition both within and outside, the King invited NSP leader Suleiman Nablusi to form the government. With an Arab nationalist government that actively supported the Egyptian stand during the Suez crisis, King Hussein agreed to terminate the Anglo-Jordanian Treaty of Alliance, 1948 with the UK in March 1957. The subsequent political developments created uncertainty over the fate of the monarchy and gave rise to speculations about an impending coup. Eventually, King Hussein was able to establish his hold and in the process also gained close relations with the US.

End of the Fling with Pan-Arabism

After the 1958 military coup in Iraq and the end of the Hashemite rule, Hussein was faced with the challenge of securing his regime. He took severe measures of purging the armed forces of nationalist leaning officers and sought American support. The 1960s brought new regional dynamics that kept the King preoccupied. However, the shape of the things became more evident. By this time, many Arab countries had gone through the revolutions and had been taken over by revolutionary republican regimes. This was an alarm for the two standing monarchies, namely Jordan and Saudi Arabia. Both were concerned with the rising tide of Arab nationalism and the growing rhetoric from Nasser for the overthrow of the monarchies. This led to the consolidation of the partnership between the two monarchies within the framework of external support from the US for security. King Hussein wholeheartedly came out in support of the Saudi stand in Yemen against Egypt and supported the Saudi military aid in favour of the Yemeni Imamate.

Internally, the King became more cautious and managed the political situation by putting loyalists in critical positions in government and military. Domestic challenges were being astutely managed, but it was the fragile regional dynamics that had started to become a significant challenge for the King. The foundation of the Palestine Liberation Organisation

(PLO) in 1964 and its increasing bid to take control of the Palestinian affairs within the League of Arab States were becoming a source of irritation for Jordan. This was also the beginning of tensions between King Hussein and Fatah leader Yasser Arafat. The two leaders shared an uneasy relation for life. This was largely because both to some extent wanted to be recognised as the leader of the Palestinian people. King Hussein continued to hope for retrieving the West Bank that was lost in 1967 June War until 31 July 1988, when in the wake of the First Intifada, he announced the Jordanian disengagement from the West Bank and surrendered all sovereignty claims over the territory. Even this did not allow the relationship between Arafat and King Hussein to be cordial.

In the meanwhile, Jordan was also disturbed by the attempts of the Kennedy administration of courting Nasser (Perra 2017). King Hussein then started secret contacts with Israeli officials and held several meetings with then Deputy Director General in Israel Ministry of Foreign Affairs, Yaacov Herzog. However, the situation was soon about to change as tensions between Israel and Egypt, and Syria has started to escalate.

King Hussein found himself in a peculiar situation in the run-up to the June War of 1967. He was concerned with the military built up on both sides not only because he did not want to take sides but also because he wished to avoid a regional conflict. He was concerned about his restive Palestinian subjects and at the same time did not want to get militarily involved with Israel when consultations on both sides had led to a degree of understanding between Amman and Tel Aviv on managing the borders (Haddad and Hardy 2003). Jordan was to some extent a factor behind the Egyptian move to send military enforcement in Sinai and demand for removal of UN Emergency Force in the Sinai Peninsula. While maintaining ties with Israel, it continued to egg on Nasser to be dependent on international forces (Yitzhak 2017).

Nonetheless, the situation did not take the desirable turn and the events leading up to the June conflict forced Jordan to take sides and led to the disastrous outcome not only for the Palestinian cause and the Arab nationalists but also for Jordan itself. In the June War, King Hussein not only lost the control over the West Bank but Israel also took control of the East Jerusalem. This was a critical situation for the Hashemite monarchy that sought legitimacy through its custodianship of the al-Aqsa Mosque. It was a devastating blow for Jordan and though it later gained some control of the *al-Haram al-Sharif* in the Old City in the 1990s, the 1967 War made Amman dependent on Riyadh for both financial as well as strategic standing.

Reflecting on this Nigel Ashton writes:

> For King Hussein, the disaster of the June war was complete. Haunted by his decision to commit Jordan to battle, the King's physical and emotional condition in the wake of the conflict was fragile. The loss of Jerusalem, the decimation of the Jordanian armed forces, the plight of the refugees and the general economic dislocation within the East Bank all affected him badly. Not only that, but he felt betrayed by all sides. (Ashton 2008, p. 121)

It took some time for the King to deal with the US which he felt betrayed him. It was only after a high-level intervention that the King could be persuaded to come to terms with the new situation. Gradually, with American mediation, he tried to have a peace deal with Israel that did not materialise. This left him further bitter, disheartened, and doubtful of American intentions, even though the Kingdom became more dependent on American economic and military support. According to Ashton, "the failure to reach an agreement during 1967—8, and particularly what Hussein later came to regard as the fiasco of the UN Resolution 242, left a lasting impact on the King" (Ibid., p. 135).

Black September

While Hussein could manage the defeat at the hands of Israel, the internal situation had soon started to go out the control. The already tense Palestinian population in Jordan were becoming more resentful of the King and the Hashemite family. They felt that rather than trying to resolve the issue of Palestinian statelessness, the King was focused more on securing his rule and were agitated by the King's dealings with Israel and the US. Hence, occasional protests inside the refugee camps in Amman have been taking place since 1967. Economic hardships, political hopelessness, and the disaster of 1967 War had put the King and his Palestinian subjects in a peculiar situation. King Hussein, however, was avoiding any direct military action to salvage the situation. He was hoping for the Palestinian anger to subside and his diplomatic overtures to the US and Israel to work. The situation, however, did not go as expected.

In the words of Hussein's biographer Avi Shlaim:

> The arrogance and the indiscipline of the Fedayeen placed Hussein in an acute dilemma. If he used force to crush them, he would alienate his

Palestinian subjects and the Arab world. If he failed to act against them, he would forfeit the respect of his Jordanian subjects and, even more seriously, that of the army the mainstay of his regime. (Shlaim 2008, p. 313)

The King eventually heeded to his advisors to rein in the Palestinian Fedayeen and "the final straws came on 6 September 1970, when George Habash's Popular Front for the Liberation of Palestine (PFLP) hijacked three Western aircrafts" (George 2005, pp. 32–33). After facing threats for weeks and as all efforts for reconciliation failed and many Palestinian factions openly declared their intention to overthrow the Hashemite monarchy, King Hussein decided to take recourse to force. On September 16, the Jordanian army entered the Palestinian refugee camps in Amman and pitched battle between the armed Palestinian Fedayeen and Jordanian security forces broke out. Eventually, the Palestinian Fedayeen were defeated and the PLO was forced to move out of Jordan and take refuge in Lebanon. With the Egyptian and other Arab interventions, the fighting in Jordan came to an end, but not before King Hussein had succeeded in suppressing the most difficult internal challenge the Hashemite Kingdom had faced since its establishment. The PLO's defeat in 1970 and its ouster from Jordan did not spell an end to the Palestinian activities inside Jordan as a substantial Palestinian refugee population continued to live in the refugee camps. However, the Black September event further deteriorated the tense relationship between King Hussein and Arafat. It partially contributed to the eventual recognition of the PLO being the "sole legitimate representative of the Palestinian people" in 1974.

The Middle East conflict again erupted in 1973 with the October War, but King Hussein had learned his lessons hard and decided to keep a minimal involvement in the war by only extending some military support to Syria. However, the 1974 Arab summit brought another surprise for King Hussein who felt betrayed and isolated in the intra-Arab affairs (George 2005). The Rabat Summit recognised the PLO as the "sole legitimate representative of the Palestinian people" and led to the decision to founding "an independent national authority … in any Palestinian territory that is liberated" (Ibid., p. 33). This also challenged the Jordanian claim over the West Bank and to be representatives of the Palestinians.

Sadat's Perfidy

The next major political challenge for King Hussein was the Camp David Accords. Amman like other Arab capitals was angry with Egyptian President Anwar Sadat for "betraying" the Arab/Palestinian cause and securing an independent peace accord with Israel to regain the Sinai Peninsula. The Arab leaders believed that Sadat walked out of the promise he has given them of "explicit commitment before the summit to negotiate a comprehensive settlement in which the rest of the Arabs, including the Palestinians, could join, or that they could at least support, without unacceptable political risk" (Shlaim 2008, p. 402). For King Hussein, it was not only a betrayal of the Arab-Palestinian cause but also personal perfidy. In one of his meetings with the American diplomat and National Security Advisor in the Jimmy Carter administration, Zbigniew Brzezinski, King Hussein said:

> The [Sadat's] visit to Jerusalem under occupation had great religious significance. My grandfather is buried there. He was involved in the Arab revolt against colonial rule and he dies because he would not compromise. We lost Jerusalem in 1967 under Egyptian command. We knew we would lose, but we went into that war anyway. Under Egyptian command and responsibility, the West Bank was lost. The Sadat visit was a very, very big shock. (Cited in Ashton 2008, p. 197)

Despite the disappointment over the Camp David Accords, King Hussein did not give up on the peace process. Even though for some time, especially due to the shift in regional affairs to the Islamic revolution in Iran and the Iran-Iraq war (1980–88), the Palestinian issue and, in turn, the Israeli-Jordan peace process remained in the cold storage. It was only after the eruption of the First Intifada in 1987 that the US and its allies woke up to the need for reviving the peace process. On the part of the Arab leaders including King Hussein, this was an indication to come out of their anger and recognise the need for a revival of the peace process.

For Jordan, the situation was more complicated than others. It had gained control of the West Bank during the 1948 Arab-Israeli War and had announced its annexation on 24 April 1950. The same year Jordanian Parliament had been expanded to accommodate representation from the West Bank. Hence, the loss of West Bank to Israel in 1967 and the Arab League resolution in 1974 to recognise PLO as representative of the Palestinian people not only created political problems for the monarchy but also led to a constitutional crisis. This was one of the reasons that parliamentary elections were not held in the Kingdom between 1967 and 1989. The outbreak of the First Intifada in December 1987 forced Jordan to rethink its policy on the West Bank. On 31 July 1988, King Hussein announced severance of all legal and administrative links with the West Bank. This facilitated renewal of negotiations between the conflicting parties.

Hope for Peace

However, the resumption of the peace process was delayed by the Iraqi intervention and annexation of Kuwait in August 1990 and the Gulf war of 1991. King Hussein was in a difficult position during the Gulf war because of his good relations with Iraq and Saddam Hussein on the one hand and the relations with the US and Gulf monarchies on the other. He was dealing with the situation astutely and he neither completely denounced the Iraqi action for fear of retribution nor take an overtly pro-Saddam stand. Nevertheless, this was enough for him to be isolated in regional affairs. The Gulf monarchies, especially Kuwait, had expected Jordan being a fellow monarchy to denounce Saddam and the Iraqi aggression. But the strong economic and military relations Jordan shared with Iraq and the Palestinian question prevented King Hussein from condemning Iraqi aggression. Saddam had linked his withdrawal from Kuwait to Israeli withdrawal from occupied Palestinian territories making him an instant hero among the Palestinians and global Muslim population. This had also gained him the unequivocal support of Arafat. For King Hussein, the domestic Palestinian population and competition with Arafat contributed to taking a policy that appeared pro-Saddam from the Gulf perspective.

The end of the Iraqi occupation of Kuwait in February 1992 through the US-led and UN-mandated international coalition eased the situation for the King and gave him the motivation to take the lead in the Madrid Middle East Peace Conference in October 1991. The Madrid Conference and the Oslo peace process eventually led to the Oslo Accords in September 1993 between Israel and PLO that provided the framework for peace and the two-state solution. Subsequently, King Hussein and Prime Minister Yitzhak Rabin signed the peace treaty between Israel and Jordan in October 1994. This formally ended the state of enmity between Israel and Jordan and the recognition of the unique role of Jordan over the Islamic holy sites in the Old City of Jerusalem. Though West Bank remained under Israeli occupation, King Hussein agreed to the Oslo process that would eventually lead to self-rule for Palestinians living in the West Bank.

Long Live the King!

On 7 February 1999, King Hussein died in Amman after suffering from Non-Hodgkin lymphoma, a type of blood cancer, which was first diagnosed in May 1998. Since the diagnosis, he was undergoing treatment in the US and had come back to Amman in November 1998 but had to be rushed back due to deterioration in his condition. During the treatment, the succession question had become a major issue. Speculations were rife, both within the palace and outside, that the King is contemplating a change in the line of succession from his younger brother Hassan who had served as the heir apparent since 1965 to the King's eldest son Abdullah. Eventually, on 25 January 1999, the royal decree removing Crown Prince Hassan was issued and Abdullah was appointed the heir apparent. Upon the death of King Hussein, he was coroneted as King Abdullah II on 9 June 1999.

Hussein's funeral on 9 February 1999 saw such a massive outpouring of masses and global leaders that indicated on his popularity enjoyed among both the people and his peers in the world.

Among his lasting legacies are the security, stability, and economic sustenance of the Hashemite Kingdom of Jordan despite the constant challenges that his rule faced both from within and outside. On several occasions such as in the aftermath of the 1967 War and during the Black September events, it appeared that the Kingdom would collapse under the weight of the social, economic, political, and geopolitical challenges but the political astuteness and pragmatism of King Hussein and his ability to deal with friends and adversaries alike saved the day for Jordan.

References

Ashton, N. (2008). *King Hussein of Jordan: A political life*. New Haven: Yale University Press.

George, A. (2005). *Jordan: Living in the crossfire*. London: Zed Books.

Haddad, W. W., & Hardy, M. M. (2003). Jordan's alliance with Israel and its effects on Jordanian-Arab relations. In E. Karsh & P. R. Kumaraswamy (Eds.), *Israel, the Hashemites, and the Palestinians: The fateful triangle*. London: Frank Cass.

Perra, A. (2017). *Kennedy and the Middle East: The cold war, Israel and Saudi Arabia*. London & New York: I. B. Tauris.

Raad, Z. (1994). A nightmare avoided: Jordan and Suez 1956. *Israel Affairs, 1*(2), 288–308.

Shlaim, A. (2008). *Lion of Jordan: The life of King Hussein in war and peace*. London: Penguin.

Yitzhak, R. (2017). From cooperation to normalization? Jordan–Israel relations since 1967. *British Journal of Middle Eastern Studies, 44*(4), 559–575.

The Arab Legion

Graham Jevon

The military is a critical component of the state; it is also a vital tool of imperial control. The Arab Legion, therefore, as the Jordanian national army financed by Britain and staffed by British and Arab officers, was a crucial feature of the formative Jordanian state. It was the bedrock of British imperial control, provided security for the Hashemite regime, and formed the basis for the modern Jordanian army.

THE ORIGINS OF THE ARAB LEGION

The Arab Legion was officially established in 1923—that was when the force was given that name, but its origins lay in Britain's earliest attempt to establish control of its new imperial possessions after the collapse of the Ottoman Empire and pre-dated the formal existence of the Jordanian state. In the immediate aftermath of the First World War, Transjordan became a hotbed of inter-tribal politics as the region's tribes sought to establish authority in the political vacuum left behind by the now defunct Ottoman administration. With political uncertainty compounded by the dissolution of Faisal's Syrian administration in the summer of 1920, after the French defeated him, local alliances were built, battles fought, and many villagers lived in fear. From the British perspective, in this period of transition,

---

G. Jevon (✉)
Endangered Archives Programme, British Library, London, UK

anarchy now reigned and the imperial authority would have to re-establish control.

Precisely how Britain should establish law and order over the region was open to debate. High Commissioner for Palestine Herbert Samuel wanted Transjordan to be incorporated into the Palestine administration with a small British military force sent to occupy and secure the region. British Foreign Secretary Lord Curzon, though, did not want to extend direct rule to the area east of the River Jordan. Instead, he authorised the installation of a handful of political advisers tasked with overseeing the establishment of local self-governing institutions. Six British officers—most of whom had previously served in the area after General Edmund Allenby conquered the region in 1918—were sent to set up and advise three local governments in Ajlun, Balqa, and Karak.

When these local governments were established, Arab-led police and gendarmerie forces—remnants of Faisal's Syrian administration—maintained law and order. However, British army Captain Dunbar Brunton appraised that additional security resources were required and proposed a Reserve Force of 2312 men, a small strike force capable of providing mobile support for the existing gendarmerie. Brunton believed that this was essential to maintain the confidence of pro-British elements and assert the government's prestige and authority. He based this force in Amman, which had hitherto been a minor Circassian settlement with a population of approximately 5000 people. Amman was selected because of its access to the Hejaz railway and its relative proximity to Jerusalem, and the establishment of the Reserve Force there was one of the many factors that contributed to this hitherto nondescript village becoming Jordan's capital city.

The Reserve Force's formative existence was rooted in a power struggle between the British authorities and the local tribal sheikhs. The primary purpose of Brunton's Reserve Force was to enforce local governance, collect taxes, and suppress the power of the tribes. In response to the establishment of this force, however, Mithqal al-Fayiz, a leading sheikh of the Bani Sakhr, allied with local tribes in an attempt to consolidate his own authority. A power struggle between Brunton and Mithqal ensued, but Brunton did not have the resources to control Mithqal by force, and so, he sought to defuse the situation by suggesting that Mithqal be appointed as the president of the Tribal Council. Mithqal declined, however, prompting Brunton to focus on strengthening the Reserve Force.

Brunton ideally wanted the ranks of the Reserve Force filled with an equal number of Arabs and Circassians. He was particularly keen to recruit the latter, first, because they would provide a counterweight to Arab nationalism, and, second, because they had experience of combatting the region's nomadic tribes and protecting the settled zones, having served with the Ottoman army before the war. Initially, Circassians were reluctant to enlist for fear that the Reserve Force might have to fight the Bedouin, which might in-turn prompt reprisals against Circassian settlements. However, by 14 October, recruitment was almost complete, and the Reserve Force was composed of a roughly equal number of Arabs and Circassians, former soldiers from the Ottoman and Arab armies with experience fighting in the First World War.

The first test for the Reserve Force came after inhabitants of Sahab, a small village southeast of Amman, refused to pay tithes, defied government orders, and looted telegraph poles. On 7 October 1920, Brunton's deputy, Arif al-Hasan, dispatched 70 men commanded by Lieutenant Abd al-Rahman Areikat. They intended to teach the villagers a lesson and send a message to the rest of the region. However, the offensive failed as Bedouin reinforcements congregated in support of the villagers. The following day, Brunton arrived with his own reinforcements to demand unconditional surrender. There were no reports of any shots being fired, but the threat of violence, particularly the threat of impending air strikes, combined with mediation by local sheikhs, helped Brunton compel the village to accept his terms. This left him with the belief that the region's tribal sheikhs, including Mithqal al-Fayiz, now feared and respected imperial authority. At the very least, it helped establish a communicative relationship between Brunton and Mithqal. However, just three months after establishing the Reserve Force, Brunton resigned his position and left Transjordan.

Peake's Legion

Brunton was replaced as commander of the Reserve Force by Captain Frederick Peake, who had served under T.E. Lawrence in 1918 and been appointed as inspector of the gendarmerie in Amman at the beginning of October 1920. It was not until 1 October 1923 that Peake formally renamed this force as the Arab Legion, but during those intervening years, the Reserve Force was integral to the establishment of the Jordanian state and the Hashemite regime. When the British aligned themselves with

Abdullah to rule Transjordan in 1921, they agreed to provide the Hashemite ruler with military support. As Abdullah began to establish his administration, he believed that the backing of a "military force to maintain internal security and protect the frontiers of the country" was crucial to the stability of his regime.[1] Partly for financial reasons, but also because they feared Abdullah might attack the French in Syria, the British refused to support Abdullah's aim to raise an army of approximately 2400 men. Instead, they offered support primarily from the British army in Palestine but also via the integration of Peake's Reserve Force and Abdullah's military entourage: a force of about 200 infantry men that was under the command of Captain Abd al-Qadir al-Jundi.

One of the determining factors leading to this unity was the impact of a severe tribal rebellion in Kura in May 1921, which decimated the Reserve Force. Eighteen men died and many more deserted, out of either fear or humiliation caused by the force's crushing defeat.[2] The Kura incident was an eye opener for both Abdullah and Britain and consequently had a profound effect on the future of the Jordanian military. It undermined the British authorities' faith in the existing Arab-led security forces and prompted the imperial power to establish more control. Meanwhile, it encouraged Abdullah to seek greater British support to help prop up his regime and establish order throughout the country. Secretary of State for the Colonies Winston Churchill sent T.E. Lawrence to Amman to assess the situation, and he appraised that a weak military was the reason for poor administration. In late 1921, Lawrence advised that a strengthened Reserve Force was crucial towards the assertion of the government's authority. Britain, therefore, agreed to provide Abdullah with further financial assistance to support a reorganised Reserve Force of 750 men, led by Peake. The purpose of this force was to support the static police and gendarmerie in maintaining order and security. This was the start of a lifetime's acceptance of British control of his army, which would ultimately put Abdullah at odds with Arab nationalists.

The enlarged Reserve Force was still relatively weak, and this in itself helped shape contemporary Jordan, as the Reserve Force's limitations helped unify the primary stakeholders in the fledgling Jordanian state.

---

[1] Quoted in: P. J. Vatikiotis, *Politics and the Military in Jordan: A Study of the Arab Legion 1921–1957* (London, 1967), p. 60.

[2] C. S. Jarvis, *Arab Command: The Biography of Lieutenant-Colonel F. W. Peake Pasha* (London, 1942), p. 77.

Designed merely to maintain internal security and tax collection, the Reserve Force was not capable of defending Transjordan's borders against external threats—notably the Ikhwan from Saudi Arabia. To defend against this threat, Abdullah, the tribes, and the British had to work together. The lack of military support thus prompted Transjordan's first ruler to pursue a policy of alignment with the local tribal sheikhs, to assert and protect his authority over his new domain.

Abdullah's coalition building was somewhat at odds, though, with Peake's approach to establishing law and order. Like Brunton, Peake's primary objective was to assert authority over and to suppress the power of the tribes. One of his first tasks was to send the Reserve Force on a tour of the major towns, as a show of force to demonstrate to the Arab population that the government was capable of maintaining law and order.[3] In February 1922, Peake established military control over Karak. He aimed to rid the region of tribal feuds and ensure the collection of taxes. The settled population welcomed this intervention. However, in May 1924, Abdullah and Peake's divergent approaches came to a head when Peake accused Abdullah of paralysing the newly formed Arab Legion—which brought together the police, gendarmerie, and Reserve Force—by dismissing soldiers accused of being heavy-handed towards nomads and preventing it from being strengthened. This was just one of many complaints—some exaggerated—against Abdullah by local British officials, which had a profound effect on the future of Transjordan. In the summer of 1924, Britain issued Abdullah with an ultimatum, which forced him to reform his administration, enabling tighter British control and a reduction of the tribal element. Meanwhile, after a purge of nationalist officers, Peake assumed full control of the Arab Legion. It was now a more cohesive and efficient unit and thereafter became one of the primary tools used to create and maintain a centralised state.

By 1925, the Arab Legion contained nearly 1500 men, but it was deployed mainly in the settled zones, which meant that the desert peripheries remained mostly ungoverned. The main tribal confederacies, such as the Huwaytat in southern Transjordan, were immune from the Arab Legion's authority. In 1926, Britain sought to remedy this and therefore created the Transjordan Frontier Force—which included a higher number of British officers—to protect and police Transjordan's southern and eastern borders against tribal raiding. Consequently, the Arab Legion was

---

[3] Jarvis, *Arab Command*, p. 72.

reduced to just 855 men, lost its artillery, and was restricted to police duties. Britain backed the Transjordan Frontier Force as the most effective means of controlling the tribal areas, but it also failed in this task. While the Frontier Force had some success in preventing reprisals by Jordanian-based tribes, it struggled to prevent raids into Transjordan, principally by the Ikhwan. The Jordanian government, therefore, turned to the man who had proved successful in controlling the Iraqi border with Saudi Arabia: John Bagot Glubb.

Glubb's Legion

Glubb arrived in Transjordan in November 1930 as Peake's second-in-command. The two men did not get along, partly because of their different visions and partly because of their desire to exert independent authority. Their uneasy relationship was eased, however, by the separation of their duties. Despite officially being second-in-command to Peake, Glubb was not involved with the core Arab Legion. Glubb was tasked with bringing order to Transjordan's southern desert and to that end was given "a free hand in raising a Bedouin police."[4]

Left mostly to his own devices, Glubb created the "Desert Patrol," a small force that he intentionally distanced from the main Arab Legion. Consistent with Peake's policy of pacifying the desert peripheries and with the approach of the Transjordan Frontier Force (TJFF), the Bedouin tribes considered the Arab Legion to be their enemy. Glubb, therefore, deduced that to gain their trust, he needed to distance himself from that force. Contrary to Peake's approach, Glubb focused on cooperation. Peake had consistently sought to exclude the Bedouin from the Arab Legion. As he explained: "My policy was to raise a Force from the sedentary, or village, Arabs, which would gradually be able to check the Bedouin and allow an Arab Government to rule the country without fear from tribal chiefs."[5] Glubb, however, sought to bring an end to tribal raiding by integrating the Bedouin. To that end, Glubb invited Bedouin tribesmen with whom he had served in Iraq to help him convince the tribes of Transjordan of his intent and his credentials. Glubb also distributed money

---

[4] Humphreys to Glubb, 9 December 1930, Glubb Papers (2006 accession), Box 4, St Antony's College, Middle East Centre Archive (MECA), Oxford.

[5] Quoted in: Joseph Massad, *Colonial Effects: The Making of National Identity in Jordan* (New York, 2001), p. 106.

during a period of economic crisis—reducing the tribes' need to raid—offered other incentives such as good government pay, and, by enlisting the sons of Bedouin sheikhs, gave the tribal leaders a stake in the central government's authority.

The Desert Patrol created by Glubb was the antithesis of the Arab Legion created by Peake. And when Glubb replaced Peake after the latter resigned in 1939, the new commander immediately began to reshape this force. This year was a pivotal turning point for the Arab Legion and a crucial marker in the shaping of contemporary Jordan. After Glubb assumed full control of the Arab Legion, on 21 March, it experienced two significant changes: one by design, and one by force of circumstance.

The design element was Glubb's integration of the Bedouin, a significant change from the days of Peake. For political scientist Joseph Massad, Glubb's bedouinisation of the Arab Legion was instrumental in the creation of a Jordanian national identity. From Glubb's design of a traditional Bedouin uniform, including the red and white headgear (*shmag*), which later became symbolic of the Jordanian national identity, to the establishment of mansaf as the "national" dish, Massad argues that Glubb consciously bedouinised not only the Arab Legion but also the whole country, intentionally establishing a new Jordanian national identity. This interpretation somewhat overplays Glubb's Machiavellian intentions and his agency. Glubb was not solely responsible for the shaping of a Jordanian national identity, but the military was the pre-eminent institution within the state, and Glubb's shaping of the Arab Legion was undoubtedly an essential factor in the evolution of contemporary Jordan.

The forced change of 1939 was caused by the onset of the Second World War, less than six months after Glubb assumed control of the Arab Legion. Immediately after war was declared, Abdullah pledged his full support for the British war effort. Transjordan was the only Arab country to offer full support to the Allies, and it was a calculated move designed to reap payback when the war was over. Ideally, Abdullah wanted British support for his long-term ambition to expand his rule over a Greater Syrian kingdom, covering Transjordan, Lebanon, Syria, and Palestine. However, as a compromise, he was rewarded with independence in 1946, albeit nominal independence given Britain's continued control of the Arab Legion.

Much to Glubb and Abdullah's frustration, the Arab Legion was not involved in any of the main fighting in Europe. There were plans to that end, which led to an increase in the number of British officers in 1944, but the Arab Legion's role was primarily restricted to guard duties, protecting British military installations and the Iraq-Haifa oil pipeline in Palestine, thus freeing up the British army for duties elsewhere. The most active year for the Arab Legion was 1941 when it was involved in two campaigns. First, in Iraq, where the pro-British government had been overturned by a military coup led by Rashid Ali. In May, the Arab Legion helped the British army restore the status quo ante by cutting communications, sabotaging transport networks, intercepting traffic, obtaining intelligence on enemy forces, and using Bedouin men within its ranks and Glubb's legacy in Iraq to forge tribal alliances. With Iraq secured, the Arab Legion returned to action almost immediately, when it was called upon to help the British army to defeat the Vichy French in Syria. After the fall of France in 1940, the Allied French army in Syria transformed into a hostile one, and with the Germans expected to arrive imminently, the Arab Legion helped British forces capture Palmyra and ultimately secure the country. In 1941, Transjordan was surrounded by hostile neighbours, but with the help of the Arab Legion, Britain's position in the Middle East was secured.

The Arab Legion's involvement in the Second World War had two important consequences, beyond its part in helping Transjordan obtain independence. First, it gave the force some genuine military experience; and second and primarily, it prompted a massive expansion of the force. During the conflict, the Legion's workforce increased from approximately 1000 to 6000 men. Having previously been little more than a gendarmerie, or police force, charged with maintaining internal security of this fledgling political entity, the Arab Legion had been transformed into an ad hoc army. After the war, Britain planned to scale the Arab Legion back to its original size, but the growing turmoil in Palestine combined with the hastily constructed nature of the 1946 Treaty of Independence precluded any reduction. This meant that when conflict erupted over neighbouring Palestine in 1948, Transjordan was now a military force to be reckoned with.[6] The Arab Legion was not the largest, but it was the best trained and most efficient of all the Arab armies.

---

[6] Graham Jevon, *Glubb Pasha and the Arab Legion: Britain, Jordan, and the End of Empire in the Middle East* (Cambridge, 2017), pp. 33–53.

The 1948 War

After the Second World War, the major political and military issue in the Middle East concerned the future of Palestine, and when the United Nations (UN) endorsed partition in November 1947, the Arab Legion's two masters—Britain and Transjordan—both had a vested interested in its future. Despite withdrawing from Palestine, the British were eager that the area remained stable and pro-British to secure their strategic interests in the region. Separated only by the River Jordan, Transjordan also had an interest in the future of neighbouring Palestine, not least because King Abdullah held a long-term expansionist aim to expand his rule over a Greater Syrian kingdom, of which Palestine would be part. Moreover, both were rivals of Palestine's dominant political figure—Grand Mufti of Palestine Hajj Amin al-Husseini—and did not want to see him assume control of the area.

To secure their objectives in post-mandate Palestine, both Abdullah and Britain were wholly reliant on the Arab Legion. A week before the UN partition resolution, King Abdullah and Golda Meir of the Jewish Agency acknowledged a mutual interest and willingness to accept a Hashemite-Zionist partition of Palestine, with Abdullah acquiescing in the establishment of a Jewish state and the Zionists accepting the Jordanian control of the proposed Arab state. To implement this scheme, Abdullah required British support, and at a meeting in London in February 1948 between British Foreign Secretary Ernest Bevin and Jordanian Prime Minister Tawfiq Abu al-Huda, Britain gave tacit approval for plans to use the Arab Legion to occupy the areas of Palestine allocated by the UN to the proposed Arab state, thus creating Greater Transjordan. Thereafter, the conduct of the Arab Legion—which included rapid expansion and reorganisation, the redeployment of troops, secret meetings with Haganah commanders, and negotiations with Palestinian Arab notables—was explicitly designed to prepare the Arab areas of Palestine for occupation by the Arab Legion when the mandate formally ended on 14 May 1948.[7]

As the end of the mandate approached, however, the Arab Legion's intention to occupy Palestine was hampered by inter-Arab politics. Abdullah was put under pressure by appeals for assistance from Palestinians and by the Arab League's efforts to arrange a coordinated response. Thus, when the Arab Legion crossed into Palestine at midnight on 14/15 May,

---

[7] Jevon, *Glubb Pasha and the Arab Legion*, pp. 63–88.

it did so as part of an Arab coalition—including Egypt, Iraq, Syria, and Lebanon—ostensibly intent on aborting the birth of Israel and establishing an independent Arab state in all of Palestine. Days before the invasion, King Abdullah was appointed as the commander-in-chief of this coalition, but this was in name only. In truth, he had no control over the other Arab armies. He was not even fully in control of his own army.

The Arab Legion's conduct in the 1948 War was governed primarily by Glubb's limited autonomy. Despite his dynastic ambitions, Abdullah's support for the Greater Transjordan scheme wavered in response to pleas for help from Palestinians. On 16 May, he, therefore, ordered Glubb to send the Arab Legion into Jerusalem, an order that Glubb initially ignored. Politically, Glubb was concerned that this was contrary to the Greater Transjordan scheme approved by Bevin. Militarily, he did not want the Arab Legion to become embroiled in street combat, for which it was unprepared. Because of the pressure from above and also below—from a frustrated rank and file—two days after the initial order, Glubb eventually relented and adhered to the king's instruction. On 19 May, the Arab Legion entered Jerusalem where it experienced the most intense fighting of the conflict. This was contrary to the pre-war intention to avoid direct conflict with Zionist forces but because Jerusalem was designated by the UN to be an international zone—the fighting in the holy city was broadly consistent with the Greater Transjordan scheme, which dictated that the Arab Legion should avoid encroaching on the proposed Jewish state. In a recent article intent on providing a "revised military history" of the Arab Legion's involvement in the 1948 War, Matthew Hughes emphasised the military realities the Arab Legion faced to explain its limited approach.[8] This was certainly important. But political machinations were also a crucial factor.

When the fighting came to an end with the signing of a series of bilateral armistice agreements between Israel and the Arab states in the spring of 1949, the Arab Legion's efforts had ultimately proved successful. While it had lost some territory since the start of the second round of fighting on 9 July 1948, the Arab Legion had secured much of the West Bank. Although this territory was not formally annexed until 1950, its attachment to Transjordan was enshrined in the armistice agreement it signed with Israel on 4 April 1949, when the expanded country was renamed the Hashemite Kingdom of Jordan.

---

[8] Matthew Hughes, 'The Conduct of Operations: Glubb Pasha, the Arab Legion, and the First Arab–Israeli War, 1948–49', *War in History* (2018), pp. 1–24.

Border Wars and Arab Nationalism

The 1948 War proved a significant turning point in the shaping of contemporary Jordan. Not only did the country incorporate additional territory containing approximately 400,000 inhabitants, but it also had to include an additional 500,000 refugees and deal with an extensive border with a hostile neighbour: Israel. Each of these new factors created problems for the state and the army. The Arab Legion was in an awkward position because it had to defend the border against Israeli incursions. However, on the other hand, it was also responsible for preventing Arab infiltration into Israel, which was often used as a pretext for attacks by the Israel Defence Forces (IDF). Preventing Arab infiltration—which might involve individual acts of sabotage, a refugee returning home, or merely a farmer tending their field—was an almost impossible task. However, to solve the border defence problem, Glubb launched a new initiative. Because the Arab Legion did not have the resources to defend the whole border, Glubb armed and trained West Bank villagers, creating a National Guard to act as the first line of defence before the regular Arab Legion could be deployed. After a few months, Glubb observed that this military training had the added benefit of integrating the new Palestinian population into the Jordanian state. However, neither the National Guard nor the Arab Legion could prevent all Israeli incursions and major attacks such as the 1953 Qibya massacre—in which nearly 70 men, women, and children were killed by an IDF unit commanded by future Israeli Prime Minister Ariel Sharon—led to huge criticism of the Arab Legion and the British connection.

From 1948 onwards, British control of the Arab Legion became an increasingly fraught issue, both inside and outside the force. The first and most prominent anti-British figure to emerge from within the Arab Legion was Abdullah al-Tal, who defected to Egypt in 1949. After joining the Arab Legion in 1942, Abdullah al-Tal rose through the ranks. In March 1948, he was promoted to the rank of Major, and just a few months later, in June, he was promoted again. Against Glubb's advice, King Abdullah promoted al-Tal to the level of Lieutenant-Colonel. Al-Tal spent most of the war in Jerusalem, where the fiercest fighting took place. He was appointed Military Governor of the City and entrusted with negotiating a ceasefire with his Israeli counterpart, Moshe Dayan. King Abdullah placed high trust in al-Tal, but less than two months after the armistice agreement with Israel was signed, Abdullah al-Tal resigned his position and defected to Egypt, where he accused King Abdullah and Britain of betraying the Arabs in Palestine. He handed copies of secret documents to the Egyptian press, and in 1958, he reiterated his criticism of Britain's control of the Arab Legion in his memoirs.[9]

While al-Tal criticised the Arab Legion from without, others championed the nationalist cause from within. Just like in Egypt and Syria, the 1948 War spawned a Free Officers movement in Jordan, which sought to usurp control of the national army. Unlike its Egyptian counterpart, on which it was based, the Jordanian movement was much less effective—in part because of the strong Bedouin component that Glubb had established. However, nationalism became increasingly important as the 1950s progressed. The aims and intentions of this group are described in the memoirs of its leading members, such as Shahir Abu Shahut—one of its founding members—who explained that the movement's aim was "the liberation of the Jordanian army from the influence of British officers."[10] The most prominent figure in the movement—though not one of its founders—was Ali Abu Nowar. In his memoirs, Abu Nowar was adamant that the 1948 War was the catalyst for his politicisation, though it was not until the 1950s—after the assassination of King Abdullah—that he came to prominence. The crucial moment was a chance meeting in 1951 with Abdullah's grandson and Jordan's future king, Hussein. This proved to be the start of a close relationship that helped undermine Glubb's control of the Legion.

Arabisation of the Arab Legion

Ali Abu Nowar became one of Hussein's closest aides, and after his accession as king in 1953, the Arab Legion was at the centre of a power struggle for control, which climaxed with the abrupt dismissal of Glubb and other officers on 1 March 1956, an event that Abu Nowar described as "equal to the Suez Canal nationalisation."[11] For Arab nationalists, both

---

[9] Abdullah al-Tall, *Karithat Filastin, Mudhakkarat Abdullah al-Tall, Qaid Marakat al-Quds* (Cairo, 1958). For a comparison and reconciliation of Glubb's and al-Tal's differing accounts of the 1948 War in their respective memoirs, see: Eugene Rogan, "Jordan and the 1948 War," in Rogan and Shlaim (eds.), *The War for Palestine: Rewriting the History of 1948* (Cambridge, 2007), pp. 104–124.

[10] Shahir Abu Shahut, *Qissat Harakat al-Dubbat al-Urduniyyin al-Ahrar (1952–1957)* (unpublished manuscript, 1993); quoted in: Massad, *Colonial Effects*, p. 169.

[11] Interview with Ali Abu Nowar, 20 June 1990, Geyelin Papers, MECA.

local and regional, Glubb was the personification of imperial control and was often criticised for being the "real ruler" or the "uncrowned king" of Jordan. Glubb was the target of propaganda emanating from Egypt, a thorn in the side of Ali Abu Nowar's political ambitions, and therefore a liability to the personal and political authority of King Hussein, whose reputation was tarnished by association. This provided the background to the dismissal, though the trigger for the decision owed much to a build-up of frustration caused by the British government's failure to heed Hussein's desire for more authority over the Arab Legion and Glubb's refusal to countenance the use of the Arab Legion in the event of a conflict breaking out between Israel and Jordan's Arab allies, Egypt and Syria, in the spring of 1956.

However, if Hussein intended to assert his authority, this was not strictly how things immediately panned out, as his military's new leadership soon threatened his dynasty. Officially, Glubb was replaced by a long-serving police officer Radi Innab. However, he was little more than a stooge. Ali Abu Nowar was now the real power behind the Arab Legion, and on 24 May 1956, he officially replaced Innab, thus formalising his control of the military. Two months later, on 12 July 1956, the Arab Legion was henceforth known as the Jordan Arab Army. The bulk of the British officers did not leave until after the Suez crisis in November, and the British continued to subsidise the force until the termination of the Anglo-Jordanian treaty on 13 March 1957. That marked the formal end of British imperialism in Jordan and British control of the military, but the legacy of the Arab Legion—as designed by Glubb—lived on. When Ali Abu Nowar launched a coup against Hussein in April 1957, it was the Bedouin component of the army that the king relied upon to thwart this attempt.

Conclusion

For almost four decades, the Arab Legion was instrumental to the establishment and consolidation of the Jordanian nation-state. The formal existence of the Arab Legion lasted from 1923 to 1956. During this period, it was arguably the pre-eminent institution within the country and played a pivotal role in the shaping of contemporary Jordan. It was essential to the consolidation of the Hashemite regime; played a significant role in the 1948 War; provided the foundation for the modern Jordanian army; and was an important factor in the creation of a Jordanian national identity. In short, the Arab Legion was integral to the nature of contemporary Jordan.

Muslim Brotherhood and Salafism

Joas Wagemakers

It has become common for some politicians in Western countries to view both peaceful and violent Islamic movements with a certain degree of suspicion, particularly since the radical Islamist al-Qaeda organisation committed the terrorist attacks of 11 September 2001. In the Arab world, such movements have been considered a nuisance or even a threat for a much more extended period. In countries such as Egypt and Syria, regimes have long fought Islamist organisations they deemed a danger to their dictatorships and, as such, have sometimes killed thousands to protect their autocratic rule. An exception in this respect is Jordan, which has had rather cordial relations with at least some of its Islamic movements for decades.

Jordan, unlike the republics in the region, has a regime whose royal family can boast of a strong Islamic pedigree. The present ruler of Jordan—King Abdullah II—is the great-grandson of Hussein b. Ali (c. 1853–1931), the emir of Mecca, and through him, he traces his lineage all the way back to the Hashem clan of the Prophet Muhammad. This claim of prophetic discordance has given the country its official name—Hashemite Kingdom of Jordan—and the royal family's roots in Mecca have ensured that its Sunni Islamic credentials are not in doubt. This can also be said about the

---

J. Wagemakers (✉)
Department of Philosophy and Religious Studies, Utrecht University, Utrecht, The Netherlands
e-mail: J.Wagemakers@uu.nl

© The Author(s) 2019
P. R. Kumaraswamy (ed.), *The Palgrave Handbook of the Hashemite Kingdom of Jordan*, https://doi.org/10.1007/978-981-13-9166-8_16

country as a whole. While Jordan has a small Christian minority, the overwhelming majority of its inhabitants are Sunni Muslims, often heavily influenced by the spiritual paths of Sufism. The state also offers a Sunni Islamic infrastructure with *sharia* judges, a Ministry of Religious Endowments and a Fatwa Department influenced by the Hanafi and Maliki schools of Islamic law.[1]

Apart from the more orthodox form of Islam that the state's institutions represent and the spirituality found in Sufism, Jordan has also witnessed the rise of Islamic movements of various types. One of these is *Jama'at al-Tabligh*, a movement rooted in the teachings of the Indian scholar Mawlana Muhammad Ilyas (1885–1944), which focuses on the transmission (*tabligh*) of a message of personal piety that reached Jordan in the 1950s. A much more political organisation also present in Jordan is *Hizb al-Tahrir al-Islami* (the Islamic Liberation Party), which was founded by the Palestinian scholar Taqi al-Din al-Nabhani (1909–77) in East Jerusalem in 1953 when it was under Jordanian control and which strives for the resurrection of the caliphate in the Muslim world. Because of its explicitly anti-establishment character, this organisation is a controversial one in the Arab world and has been banned in Jordan. While difficult to gauge, it seems to have few followers in Jordan today. Two movements in Jordan that are more popular and whose adherents are far more numerous than either *Jama'at al-Tabligh* or *Hizb al-Tahrir al-Islami* are the Muslim Brotherhood and Salafism. This chapter, therefore, focuses on these two movements, giving special attention to how both have negotiated their relations with the regime throughout their history.

The Muslim Brotherhood: From Cooperation to Confrontation

The Society of the Muslim Brotherhood (*Jama'at al-Ikhwan al-Muslimin*) was founded by an Egyptian schoolteacher called Hasan al-Banna (1906–49) in 1928. He later propagated it as a broad and general message

---

[1] Hasan Abu Haniyya, *Al-Turuq al-Sufiyya: Durub Allah al-Ruhiyya; Al-Takayyuf wa-l-Tajdid fi Siyaq al-Tahdith* [Sufi Orders: The Spiritual Paths of God; Adaptation and Renewal in the Context of Modernization] (Amman: Friedrich Ebert Stiftung, 2011); Muhammad Abu Rumman and Hasan Abu Haniyya, *Al-Hall al-Islami fi l-Urdunn: Al-Islamiyyun wa-l-Dawlah wa-Rihanat al-Dimuqratiyya wa-l-Amn* [The Islamic Solution in Jordan: Islamists, the State, the Contests of Democracy and Security] (Amman: Friedrich Ebert Stiftung, 2012), 39–53.

of Islam that could supposedly provide answers to all questions, including the British colonial occupation of Egypt. Strongly anti-imperialist and focused on making Egyptians embrace Islam as their belief system and lifestyle, al-Banna travelled around the country preaching his ideas, leading the organisation to grow substantially while also being noticed by the authorities. Al-Banna's message, which was often critical of the country's rulers and their unwillingness to confront the British, gained more adherents, and the Muslim Brotherhood also engaged in electoral politics and even fought against Zionist forces in the battle for Palestine in 1948. These led the Egyptian authorities to take an increasingly negative stance towards the organisation, and the regime banned the Muslim Brotherhood in 1948. After one of its members turned out to have assassinated a minister, al-Banna—although he condemned the killing—was murdered in 1949.[2]

Cooperation: Loyalty to the Regime

Although al-Banna was not so much a great scholar or thinker, he had an activist message that was inspiring to many. Local branches of the Muslim Brotherhood were founded in other countries in the Arab world (and beyond), including in Transjordan. There, a merchant called 'Abd al-Latif Abu Qura (c. 1906–67) became strongly interested in the Palestinian cause during the strike against the Zionist presence in Palestine in 1936, and it was there that he first met members of the Egyptian Muslim Brotherhood. Having been impressed by them, he received permission from al-Banna to set up a local branch of the organisation. Thus, Abu Qura set up the Transjordanian Muslim Brotherhood and became the organisation's first leader in 1945.

The fact that such an organisation could be founded in Transjordan and even received an official license in 1946 was perhaps not a coincidence. The first ruler of Transjordan, Emir (and later King) Abdullah I (r. 1921–51), was probably quite aware that his Meccan roots and the fact that Transjordan was a colonial creation did not contribute to his popularity among the local people. He, therefore, used several sources of

[2] For more on the early Muslim Brotherhood in Egypt, see Brynjar Lia, *The Society of the Muslim Brothers in Egypt: The Rise of an Islamic Mass Movement, 1928–1942* (Reading, UK: Ithaca Press, 1998); Richard P. Mitchell, *The Society of the Muslim Brothers* (Oxford, etc.: Oxford University Press, 1969).

authority—including Islam, in the form of his prophetic lineage—to bolster his status as a ruler. His support for the early Muslim Brotherhood may, therefore, have been a strategic move to support Islamic organisations to undergird his own religious credentials and authority.

However, King Abdullah I was also suspicious of the Muslim Brotherhood. He realised that they had developed into a political opposition in Egypt and was aware of their strongly anti-Zionist (and later anti-Israel) views, which clashed with the more conciliatory position he had adopted. He, therefore, supported the Brotherhood as a religious organisation that could act as a counterweight to the nationalist ideas that were increasingly popular in the Arab world but simultaneously kept a close eye on them to see if they did not develop into a political movement. Under Abu Qura's leadership, the Brotherhood mostly stayed away from the political opposition and focused on religious and charitable activities, although it also sent fighters to join the battle for Palestine in 1948, just as the Egyptian Muslim Brotherhood had done.

The Brotherhood took on a more confrontational character when a new generation of members rose to become leaders of the organisation. Consisting mostly of educated professionals from landowning East Bank families, these young men were politicised through their interest in the Palestinian question and, as a result, adopted a more overtly political discourse. First and foremost among them was Muhammad 'Abd al-Rahman Khalifa (1919–2006), who took over from Abu Qura as the Brotherhood's leader in 1953 and remained the group's General Guide (*al-muraqib al-'amm*) until 1994, thereby becoming the longest-serving leader of the organisation. Although Khalifa objected to the aforementioned Taqi al-Din al-Nabhani's decision to split off from the Muslim Brotherhood and form *Hizb al-Tahrir al-Islami* in 1953, he sympathised with al-Nabhani's view that the organisation should take a more political approach and strive to establish an Islamic state.[3]

Despite the more politicised discourse, the Muslim Brotherhood still remained firmly loyal to the regime during Khalifa's leadership, especially in its earlier decades. This was due to several factors. First, the regime and the Brotherhood saw Egyptian President Gamal Abdel Nasser as an enemy. While the Egyptian regime's pan-Arab, republican, and socialist policies, were anathema to Jordan's pan-Arab, monarchical, and conservative

---

[3] Marion Boulby, *The Muslim Brotherhood and the Kings of Jordan, 1945–1993* (Atlanta, GA: Scholars Press, 1999), 39–54.

views, the Muslim Brotherhood criticised Nasser for cracking down on their brethren in Egypt. Thus, the Brotherhood fully supported the Jordanian regime when it prevented a Nasserite coup in 1957. Second, the Jordanian regime often acted in ways—both concerning foreign and domestic policies—that squared with the Muslim Brotherhood's own views. The regime fought (but lost) the war against Israel in 1967, for example, and allowed the Brotherhood to have a parliamentary presence from 1956 onwards. It was partly due to such factors but also because of its non-confrontational approach, that the Muslim Brotherhood—despite being strongly pro-Palestinian—did not protest the regime's crackdown on Palestinian militants during Black September in 1970.

Confrontation: Adopting the Role of Oppositional Force

The fact that loyalty and cooperation characterised relations between the Muslim Brotherhood and the Jordanian regime does not mean that there were no tensions. Members of the Muslim Brotherhood were sometimes arrested, and their first weekly newspaper, *Al-Kifah al-Islami*, was taken out of circulation now and then in the 1950s. Such measures from the regime ensured that the Brotherhood knew who was in charge. After 1967, when Jordan lost the West Bank to Israel, King Hussein (r. 1953–99) suspended parliamentary elections. This meant that from 1967 to 1989, when parliamentary elections were resumed, the Muslim Brotherhood did not really have an avenue of political participation while the enemy they shared with the regime—Nasserism—was no longer a threat. In this context, the Muslim Brotherhood developed a more oppositional character.

When parliamentary elections did take place again in 1989, the Muslim Brotherhood was the only group that was well organised on a national level because political parties were not allowed. Moreover, the extensive charitable and social network that the organisation had built up since the 1940s could now be put to good use to mobilise supporters and attract voters. As a result, the Islamic movement (comprising individual candidates from the Muslim Brotherhood and independent Islamists) won 34 seats in parliament out of a total of 80. The elections were a huge success for the Muslim Brotherhood. To the regime, however, the elections had not so much been an attempt at greater democratisation or liberalisation, but a way of managing the discontent that had erupted over drastic economic reforms that left many people less well off in the short term.

When it saw that the 1989 elections had brought about a parliament—including particularly its Islamist members—that had the potential to be a force of criticism and opposition to its policies, the regime took several measures to ensure that the next elections would result in a more regime-friendly lower house. Through gerrymandering and—most importantly—a change in the electoral law, it ruined the chances of the Muslim Brotherhood achieving such electoral success again, thereby damaging the relations between the Islamist movement and the regime.[4]

Meanwhile, other changes in Jordan occurred that affected the relationship between the Muslim Brotherhood and the regime. In 1992, the Jordanian government adopted the Political Parties Law, causing the Brotherhood to set up a political party called the Islamic Action Front (IAF), thereby consolidating the more politicised direction the organisation had taken. It also meant that the Muslim Brotherhood increasingly became a movement, rather than just an organisation, encompassing charitable activities, hospitals, religious activism, and now also a political party. The Brotherhood could express its contention through all these organisations and activities, and it increasingly felt the need to.

Although it had been grateful to King Hussein for not giving in to American pressure to join the international coalition against Iraqi dictator Saddam Hussein during the Kuwait Crisis in 1990–91, the Brotherhood was adamant in its refusal to accept the 1994 peace agreement between Jordan and Israel. It was also frustrated that, despite its opposition (and that of many other Jordanians), it had been unable to stop this agreement from being adopted, adding to a more general sense of the relative futility of being in parliament. Combined with the disappointing outcome of the 1993 parliamentary elections as a result of the regime's interference in the electoral process, the IAF (as well as other parties) decided to boycott the 1997 elections.

---

[4] Kamel S. Abu Jaber and Schirin H. Fathi, "The 1989 Jordanian Parliamentary Elections," *Orient* 31, no. 1 (1990): 67–86; Hanna Y. Freij and Leonard C. Robinson, "Liberalization, the Islamists, and the Stability of the Arab State: Jordan as a Case Study," *The Muslim World* 86, no. 1 (1996): 8–16; Russell E. Lucas, "Deliberalization in Jordan," *Journal of Democracy* 14, no. 1 (2003): 137–40; Katherine Rath, "The Process of Democratization in Jordan," *Middle Eastern Studies* 30, no. 3 (1994): 538–40; Glenn E. Robinson, "Defensive Democratization in Jordan," *International Journal of Middle East Studies* 30, no. 3 (1998): 390–3; Curtis R. Ryan, "Peace, Bread and Riots: Jordan and the International Monetary Fund," *Middle East Policy* 6, no. 2 (1998): 55–7; Jillian Schwedler, "A Paradox of Democracy? Islamist Participation in Election," *Middle East Report*, no. 209 (1998): 27–8.

The following period brought challenges of a different kind. In 1999, King Hussein died and was succeeded by his son King Abdullah II, who shared his ancestors' suspicion of the Muslim Brotherhood and—on top of that—was perhaps less inclined to be influenced by the close historical ties that the Hashemite regime had enjoyed with the movement. As a result, the growing distance between the two became even wider. This situation was exacerbated by the terrorist attacks in the US on 11 September 2001. Although these attacks had nothing to do with the Muslim Brotherhood, it was relatively easy for uninformed or hostile forces to conflate the movement with al-Qaeda, thereby creating pressure for the Brotherhood to show its ideological "moderation" and its loyalty to the Jordanian regime. Given the fact that the reasons the Brotherhood boycotted the 1997 elections—a toothless parliament, the absence of real reform, no change in the electoral law—were still there, it was probably this increased pressure that caused it to participate in the parliamentary elections of 2003.

The above may give the impression that the Muslim Brotherhood was the passive victim of regime repression and did not play any active role in its plight. Although the Brotherhood was the target of crackdowns by the Jordanian regime, the crisis in the relationship between the movement and the regime was not entirely of the latter's making. One example of this is the visit of Brotherhood members to the mourning ceremony held in honour of Abu Musab al-Zarqawi (1966–2006), the Jordanian leader of al-Qaeda's Iraqi branch who was infamous for killing hundreds of civilians through bomb attacks and beheading at least one person. Although many Jordanians supported al-Zarqawi as someone they believed was fighting the American army that had invaded Iraq in 2003, their opinions about him changed when he claimed credit for the 2005 attack on several hotels in Amman, killing dozens of civilians. One could explain the visit of some Brotherhood members to al-Zarqa', the birthplace of al-Zarqawi, as a courtesy call from politicians who felt obliged to pay their respects to a family from their constituency, but many viewed it as inappropriate and insensitive to honour a man responsible for the deaths of Jordanian civilians.

It is not clear whether the arrest of the Brotherhood members and the eventual imprisonment of two of them for visiting al-Zarqawi's mourning ceremony had any negative impact on their electoral chances. What is clear is that the 2007 elections were a disaster for the movement, and it appears that a combination of internal divisions, election rigging by the regime, an inefficient strategy, sagging popularity, and an uneven record in parliament were responsible for the IAF's worst electoral result so far, winning only 6 out of 110 seats in parliament. Not having achieved much during its time in parliament and still waiting for its demands of real political reform—including changing the hated electoral law—to be met, the Muslim Brotherhood decided to boycott the following parliamentary elections in 2010 and made the same decision in 2013.[5]

Although the Brotherhood was clear in its refusal to participate in the 2013 elections, a lot had changed in both the region and the movement since its previous boycott in 2010. The major regional change was the Arab Spring, a term used for the series of uprisings and protests that unseated dictators in Tunisia, Egypt, and Libya and created unrest in several other Arab states. Although Jordan did not witness anything remotely resembling an uprising, it was affected by it. The regime became less tolerant of the Muslim Brotherhood, which had played a major role in the uprising in Egypt, and arrested and imprisoned several of its members, including the movement's deputy leader, Zaki Bani Irshid, for their alleged engagement in incitement and jeopardising relations with other countries.

At the same time, the Muslim Brotherhood had also undergone internal changes. Although individual members had left the movement at various stages during its history—to protest its boycott of the parliamentary elections in 1997, for example—it had remained intact as a single unit. This changed in the period 2012–15. The roots of this lay in ideological differences, primarily about the regime, political participation, and whether the movement should be exclusively Islamist or be open to extensive cooperation with others. The mostly ill-defined term "hawks" is often applied to those Muslims Brothers who take a sceptical view of the regime and political participation and tend towards Islamist exclusivism, while their ideological opposites are often referred to as "doves."

While the movement had mostly been led by two "doves" since 1989—'Abd al-Majid Dhunaybat (1994–2006) and Salim al-Falahat (2006–08)—the Brotherhood elected Hammam Said (2008–16) as their leader in 2008, a more hawkish figure. His election, as well as that of other hawkish Brothers to other leading positions, indicated the hardening of views

---

[5] Abu Haniyya and Abu Rumman, *Al-Hall*, 63–155; Mohammad Abu Rumman, *The Muslim Brotherhood in the 2007 Jordanian Parliamentary Elections: A Passing "Political Setback" or Diminished Popularity?* (Amman: Friedrich Ebert Stiftung, 2007), 61–72.

among the members of the movement as a result of the regime's tougher policies towards the Muslim Brotherhood.

Despite the growing attitude of inflexibility and scepticism towards the regime within the movement, the "doves" continued to exist, of course, and became increasingly dismayed with the Brotherhood's course. As a result, several initiatives were taken by prominent members that eventually led to major divisions within the movement. The first of these was the 2012 Jordanian Initiative for Building (Al-Mubadara al-Urdunniyya li-l-Bina'), better known as the ZamZam Initiative (named after the ZamZam Hotel in Amman, where its founders met to discuss it). The initiative was led by Ruhayyil Gharayiba, a prominent member of the Brotherhood, and explicitly called for political reform based on a broad coalition of members from all sections of society. To more hawkish members of the Brotherhood, this was a challenge to the character and organisational framework of their exclusively Islamist movement, and its leaders were therefore sceptical of the initiative and eventually fired Gharayiba—as well as two other members—from their ranks.

The dismissal of Gharayiba and the others did not go down well with some of the more dovish members of the Brotherhood who may not have supported the ZamZam Initiative, but who did not believe that firing its leaders was called for either. These "wise men" (as they were often labelled), who initially merely wanted to mediate between the Brotherhood leadership and the ZamZam initiators, became increasingly dismayed with what they saw as the unwillingness of the former to compromise and began venting frustrations over the movement's leadership as a whole that had brewed for a longer period of time but only now came to the surface in a divisive way. The conflicts that developed between the Brotherhood leadership and the "wise men" eventually led to a rupture, and in December 2015, hundreds of Brothers followed the latter in handing in their resignation from the movement. Given the stature of some of those resigning—including Hamza Mansur, a former Secretary General of the IAF, and Salim al-Falahat, the aforementioned former General Guide of the Brotherhood—this was a harsh blow.

The Brotherhood's trouble did not end there because while all of this was happening, another split off was in the making. This one was led by 'Abd al-Majid Dhunaybat, another former General Guide of the Muslim Brotherhood, who was critical of the direction the movement had taken over the past few years and had decided to organise meetings with like-minded members to reform the movement. This slowly grew into a new

Muslim Brotherhood, however, and this group eventually registered with the authorities as the Association of the Society of the Muslim Brotherhood (*Jam'iyyat Jama'at al-Ikhwan al-Muslimin*). Because the government accepted only one Muslim Brotherhood and because it accused the older organisation of not having its registration in order, it eventually banned the original Muslim Brotherhood and only allowed the new one. This new organisation even went so far as to present itself as the real Muslim Brotherhood and claim the assets of the organisation from which it had split off. The original Muslim Brotherhood, currently led by a caretaker leadership, is in a sort of legal limbo and is technically illegal, but still exists.

The relationship between the Muslim Brotherhood and the Jordanian regime has thus gone from cooperation to confrontation, with the former no longer in existence as a single organisational unit. The regime's increased scepticism of the Brotherhood as a result of not just the changing relationship over the past few decades but particularly the movement's role in the Egyptian uprising led it to scrutinise the group's every move. The Arab Spring thus heightened the regime's sensitivity towards any oppositional activities and caused it to crack down on dissent more easily.

The Brotherhood, for its part, was too divided to come up with a single answer to the Arab Spring. Some believed that more opposition was called for; others thought that now was the time to take a less confrontational approach to escape the regime's eventual response. Because the regime exploited these divisions, it ended up with a more dovish official Muslim Brotherhood and an outlawed unofficial one. The latter has, in a sense, been brought to heel; during the parliamentary elections of 2016, the IAF—despite being led by more hawkish members—probably realised that it had better play along with the regime's game to remain legal and decided to participate again. This means that its contention is expressed in parliamentary terms and—most importantly, from the regime's point of view—has become manageable again.

Salafism in Jordan: Between Cooperation, Opposition, and Confrontation

The Muslim Brotherhood in Jordan, but also in other countries, is characterised by a broad and general ideology, and its members do not usually delve into great detail about Islamic law or spirituality, let alone theology. Salafism is, in that sense, the complete opposite of the Muslim Brotherhood because it pays precise attention to such aspects of Islam. Salafis can be defined as those Sunni Muslims who claim to emulate *al-salaf al-salih* ("the pious predecessors," usually associated with the first three generations of Muslims) as closely and in as many spheres of life as possible. Because of their desire to follow the Prophet, his companions, and their early descendants, Salafis pay considerable attention to what these first generations of believers did, said, allowed and forbade through the study of *hadith*s. As a result, references to these traditions relating sayings of the Prophet or his early followers often pervade the discourse of Salafis, keen as they are to adhere closely to Muhammad's lifestyle in all areas of life, including dress, language, and gender relations.

What sets Salafis apart from other Muslims is not just their lifestyle, but—more importantly—their ideology. Concerning theology, they adhere strictly to what they see as the pure ideas on the unity of God (*tawhid*) and the different components of faith (*iman*) they believe were adhered to by the earliest Muslims, rejecting any rational or metaphorical readings of the Qur'an. Instead, they read the sources literally and as they were supposedly revealed. Legally, Salafis differ from other Sunnis, and they state, for instance, that since the four schools of Islamic law (*madhahib*, sing. *madhhab*) that mainstream Sunnis often follow did not exist when the Prophet and his immediate followers were alive, Salafis should not practice blind emulation (*taqlid*) of these schools either. They should instead interpret the Qur'an and the Sunna independently (*ijtihad*) and according to the understanding of the *salaf*, thus underlining their desire to emulate the latter in the legal sphere, too. As this requires a lot of knowledge of Islamic law, many non-scholarly Salafis follow a school of Islamic law—often the Hanbali one—in practice.[6]

Origins and Early Development of Salafism in Jordan

The different tenets of the Salafi ideology as described above have deep roots in the history of Islam. Their appearance in Jordan is of a more recent date. According to some Jordanian Salafis, the earliest signs of the

---

[6] For more on Salafism, see Roel Meijer (ed.), *Global Salafism: Islam's New Religious Movement* (London: Hurst & Co., 2009); Bernard Rougier (ed.), *Qu'est-ce que le salafisme?* [What is Salafism?] (Paris: Presses Universitaires de France, 2008); Behnam T. Said and Hazim Fouad (eds.), *Salafismus: Auf der Suche nach dem wahren Islam* [Salafism: In Search of True Islam] (Freiburg, etc.: Herder, 2014).

Salafi ideology in the kingdom could already be seen under the rule of King Abdullah I, who is said to have been influenced by scholars with Salafi tendencies or was even accompanied by some of them when he moved from Mecca to what is now Jordan.

While this may be correct, one could not speak of a Salafi trend until the 1950s when several important local scholars started adopting Salafism as their religious ideology. Prominent men in this regard are the Turkish-born Ahmad al-Salik (1928–2010) and the originally Palestinian Muhammad Ibrahim Shaqra (c. 1933–2016), both of whom had studied at al-Azhar University in Egypt but had become Salafis upon their return in the mid-1950s. Their Salafi preaching at mosques in Amman created a small following, which was supported by other sheikhs, like Syrian-born Muhammad Nasib al-Rifa'i (1915–92), who joined al-Salik and Shaqra in their missionary activities (*da'wa*) in Amman, and the originally Palestinian Yusuf al-Barqawi (d. 2009), who preached in al-Zarqa'.

Apart from their Salafi beliefs, the men described above had in common that they all had roots outside Jordan. The same applies to the man who turned the budding Salafi trend in Jordan into a far greater movement—Muhammad Nasir al-Din al-Albani (1914–99). Born in Albania but raised in Syria, al-Albani was already a scholar of considerable reputation when he went to work at the Islamic University of Medina in Saudi Arabia in the 1960s. He was later invited to come to Jordan by the aforementioned Jordanian scholar Muhammad Ibrahim Shaqra and, after visiting the country several times, eventually decided to settle there. Al-Albani's considerable knowledge of *hadith*s and his long experience in the Salafi trend, to which Shaqra and his countrymen were relative newcomers, ensured that he naturally became the informal leader of the Jordanian Salafi movement. Through his sermons, fatwas, and publications, he managed to gather a large following.

Al-Albani's followers met and spoke with him mostly through informal meetings at people's homes to avoid attracting too much attention from the authorities. The latter were nevertheless sceptical of this Syrian scholar, who was preaching such an unusual message of personal piety and ritual purity. Although al-Albani's message was focused on "purifying" Islamic tradition and preaching the result to his followers—a strategy he referred to as "cleansing and teaching" (*al-tasfiya wa-l-tarbiya*)—and was thus decidedly apolitical, the Jordanian regime still saw him as a security concern. As a result, al-Albani was temporarily banned from the country but was allowed back in later when Shaqra convinced King Hussein that al-Albani could be relied upon to side against what he saw as the real danger to Jordan: Shias. Afterwards, Salafism was given some more freedom by the regime and was also allowed to become institutionalised, through a journal (*Al-Asala*), mosques, and, after al-Albani's death, a special centre called the Imam al-Albani Centre for Studies and Research.

Divisions Among Salafis: Domestication, Politicisation, and Confrontation

Salafis thus grew closer to the Jordanian regime, particularly after al-Albani's death, but this came at a price. While al-Albani was a-political, he was also independent. As a major sheikh who seemed to reach his scholarly conclusions without taking into account how others felt about it or what political repercussions it would have, he could support his a-political ideas with his actual aloofness from political activism. Some of his students, however, were more inclined to be actively pro-regime (rather than remaining neutral on the state's affairs) and sometimes sought contact with like-minded scholars in Saudi Arabia.

When the Gulf War of 1990–91 brought the more politically engaged Sahwa movement to the fore in Saudi Arabia, some of al-Albani's students—particularly Ali al-Halabi (b. 1960), the most prominent Salafi scholar in Jordan today—actively distanced themselves from this movement and its scholars. This tendency to take sides against enemies of the regimes in the region was strengthened when the regime actively sought to domesticate Jordanian Salafis by incorporating them into its sphere of influence through the Al-Albani Centre mentioned above. This placed the major Salafi scholars in Jordan clearly on the side of the regime, a position they were glad they had taken when several attacks by Salafi-inspired terrorists—especially the 11 September 2001 attacks and the 2005 bombings in Amman—gave Salafism a bad reputation.

All these developments led to the emergence of three types of Salafis in Jordan: quietist Salafis, whose apolitical tendencies are dominant among the Salafi community in the kingdom; political Salafis, who do believe in political activism; and Jihadi-Salafis, who believe in the justification of violent action against their own regime on religious grounds. Because the latter two trends often took a far more critical view of the Jordanian state, quietist Salafis felt the need to condemn them, refute their arguments, and denounce the Arab Spring and the Salafi proponents of this phenomenon. Although they partly did so to show their loyalty to the regime, they also felt a genuine ideological motivation to denounce the revolutions and uprisings in the region, believing that such revolts would only lead to more chaos and civil strife. This overt and explicit loyalty to the regime has resulted in a domesticated quietist Salafi trend that has lost its independence, rarely strays into politics of any kind, and focuses almost entirely on achieving doctrinal and ritual purity through lessons, sermons, and publications.[7]

It was to be expected that al-Albani's aloofist a-politicism—not to mention his students' loyalist quietism—should encounter criticism from other Salafis in Jordan, which did happen indeed. Some of them wondered why their form of Islam, which they saw as relevant and applicable to all aspects of life, should be limited to studying and teaching, at least for the foreseeable future. While al-Albani's philosophy focused on Islamising society through preaching and education to prepare it for the founding of an Islamic state—a process that could take centuries—other Salafis wanted a focus on politics right now. This desire for immediate political action and a wish to think about politics in Salafi terms was helped by the Gulf War. During that conflict, the Palestinian leader Yasser Arafat seemed to side with Iraqi dictator Saddam Hussein, who had just occupied Kuwait. The regime of the latter responded to this by expelling virtually all Palestinians—some 400,000—from its soil after the war. Since many of these Palestinians had come from the West Bank in the 1950s and 1960s when it was Jordanian territory, they were officially Jordanian citizens, and some 250,000 of them, therefore, "returned" to Jordan. Some of these were Salafis and had been influenced by the ideas of the originally Egyptian scholar Abu Abdullah Abd al-Rahman b. Abd al-Khaliq and his organisation, *Jam'iyyat Ihya' al-Turath al-Islami*. The latter was of a strongly political Salafi persuasion before the Gulf War and the Palestinians who came to Jordan and adhered to such ideas as well abetted the already existing criticism of al-Albani's quietism.

Throughout the years, several organisations and associations have been set up promoting a more political—or "reformist," as they call it—interpretation of Salafism. Some of these have focused on charitable work, particularly among Syrian refugees who have fled the civil war in their country since 2011. This may not sound very "political," but it is in the sense that it actively engages with public affairs and bases its activism on this. Political

---

[7] Joas Wagemakers, *Salafism in Jordan: Political Islam in a Quietist Community* (Cambridge, etc.: Cambridge University Press, 2016).

Salafis believe that Salafism is about more than studying and preaching, and they contend that engaging in societal activism—even if it is as uncontroversial as helping refugees—sets them apart from their quietist brethren.

The most prominent political Salafis organisation in Jordan—and one that is also more overtly political—is *Jam'iyyat al-Kitab wa-l-Sunna* (The Association of the Book and the Sunna). Founded in Amman in 1993 by a disparate group of Salafis critical of al-Albani's focus on studying and preaching, it went through several ups and downs (including repression by the authorities, who mistrusted this new group) but eventually—in the early 2000s—re-emerged as an organisation that more narrowly focused on charitable activities. Its discourse, however, is explicitly political. Articles in its magazine *Al-Qibla*, for example, deal with regional conflicts in terms of international relations, geopolitics, and state's interests, rather than seeing them merely as conflicts between Sunnis and Shiites, for instance.

The *Jam'iyyat al-Kitab wa-l-Sunna*'s political awareness has been heightened by the Arab Spring, during which some Salafi groups—most prominently in Egypt—have risen to power and have won a substantial number of seats in parliament. Unlike quietist Salafis in Jordan, who rejected the Arab Spring as a source of chaos and civil strife (*fitna*) and believed it was better to support the rulers (even if they were repressive ones), political Salafis in the kingdom enthusiastically endorsed the uprisings and the Salafi groups who decided to run for public office. The leader of the organisation, Zayid Hammad, and prominent members who regularly write articles for *Al-Qibla*, like Usama Shahada and Ahmad al-Dhuwayb, have openly sided with the protesters against the regimes in Tunisia, Egypt, Syria, and Libya, and particularly, Shahada has been a strong supporter of the Egyptian Salafi political party *Hizb al-Nur*.

Despite the organisation's support for Salafi political activism, it has been somewhat difficult for *Jam'iyyat al-Kitab wa-l-Sunna* to translate its enthusiasm into founding a Salafi political party in Jordan. The reasons for this given by the organisation's members themselves include that the country does not have enough Salafis to make such an effort worthwhile, the existing Salafi community does not have a mature and robust infrastructure, and it would not be clear what such a political party would stand for and how it would differ from the Islamist IAF. Moreover, the parliamentary experiences of the Muslim Brotherhood and the IAF are not exactly encouraging.

Finally, *Jam'iyyat al-Kitab wa-l-Sunna* is given considerable freedom by the regime to pursue its goals throughout the country under its mandate from the Ministry of Culture. Any decision to set up a political party would make the organisation the responsibility of the Interior Ministry, which is unlikely to look favourably towards the establishment of yet another Islamic party in opposition to the regime. As such, setting up a political party could give the organisation a bad name and might even jeopardise all its other activities. The *Jam'iyyat al-Kitab wa-l-Sunna*, while political in outlook, therefore, seems to have no concrete plans to set up a political party anytime soon, and this seems to be even more the case for other political Salafi groups in Jordan.[8]

Whereas Jordan's quietist Salafis are characterised by domestication and its "reformist" ones by politicisation, the third branch—Jihadi-Salafis—have chosen the path of confrontation with the regime. Of course, radical Islamist ideas go back further in time than the rise of Jihadi-Salafism in Jordan. The revolutionary ideas of the Egyptian Muslim Brotherhood member Sayyid Qutb (1906–66), for example, were written in the 1960s, when Jihadi-Salafism did not yet exist in Jordan. It was the mixing of politicised ideas like those of the Muslim Brotherhood (and particularly the radical ones espoused by Qutb) with (radical reinterpretations of) the purity-centred beliefs found in Salafism that produced Jihadi-Salafi ideology. The connection between these two ideologies was made in various places, but perhaps most prominently during the *mujahedeen* (jihad fighters) phase in Afghanistan in 1979–89.

One person who emerged from this period as one of the leading scholars of Jihadi-Salafism was Abu Muhammad al-Maqdisi (b. 1959), a Palestinian sheikh who was born in the West Bank but spent his childhood in Kuwait and who lived in Peshawar (Pakistan) during the war in Afghanistan. When he was expelled from Kuwait after the Gulf War, along with so many other Palestinians, he went to Jordan to spread his views there. Jordan, meanwhile, was going through a tumultuous period at the time. Apart from the aforementioned far-reaching economic reforms, the parliamentary elections and the peace negotiations with Israel in the early 1990s, this period also saw its Arab neighbour and ally—Iraq—invade another Arab country—Kuwait—but was subsequently driven out by an international

---

[8] Ibid., 201–19; *id.*, "The Dual Effect of the Arab Spring on Salafi Integration: Political Salafism in Jordan," in *Salafism After the Arab Awakening: Contending with People's Power*, ed. Francesco Cavatorta and Fabio Merone (London: Hurst & Co., 2016), 119–35, 274–8.

coalition led by the US. This not only brought about a sense of Arab incompetence in the face of overwhelming Western military power but also brought hundreds of thousands of Palestinians to Jordan.

This sequence of drastic changes—economic, political, diplomatic, military, and demographic—led to a sense of insecurity among many Jordanians, who felt they were losing control of their own society. This, in turn, caused some young men to seek more radical Islamist solutions, set up militant groups that engaged in attacking people, and develop a discourse that was strongly anti-regime. It was precisely in this time-frame that al-Maqdisi came to Jordan, where he—as a relatively experienced thinker—could easily provide these radicalised youngsters with an overarching ideology that made sense of their grievances. His own loosely organised group of followers was called *Jama'at al-Tawhid* (the Group of the Unity of God) or *Jama'at al-Muwahhidin* (the Group of the Unifiers of God)—though it became known as *Bay'at al-Imam* (Fealty to the Imam) in the media—and included Abu Musab al-Zarqawi.

The group was involved in making plans to avenge the Palestinians killed by Israeli terrorist Baruch Goldstein in Hebron in 1994, but they were arrested before they could execute the attack, landing the entire group in prison, from which they were released on the occasion of King Abdullah II's ascension to the throne in 1999. Since then, al-Maqdisi has become one of the leading Jihadi-Salafi scholars in the world, although he sometimes clashed with his former student al-Zarqawi, who rejected his teacher's advice to focus on radical *da'wa* in Jordan itself and decided to go abroad, where he eventually became the leader of al-Qaeda in Iraq before being killed in 2006.[9]

---

[9] Muhammad Abu Rumman and Hasan Abu Haniyya, *Al-Salafiyya al-Jihadiyya fi l-Urdunn ba'da Maqtal al-Zarqawi: Muqarabat al-Huwiyya, Azmat al-Qiyada wa-Dababiyyat al-Ru'ya* [Jihadi-Salafism in Jordan after the Killing of al-Zarqawi: The Approximation of Identity, the Crisis of Leadership and the Obscurity of Vision] (Amman: Friedrich Ebert Stiftung, 2009); Beverley Milton-Edwards, "Climate of Change in Jordan's Islamist Movement," in *Islamic Fundamentalism*, ed. Abdel Salam Sidahmed and Anoushiravan Ehteshami (Boulder, CO: Westview Press, 1996), 123–142; Joas Wagemakers, *A Quietist Jihadi: The Ideology and Influence of Abu Muhammad al-Maqdisi* (Cambridge, etc.: Cambridge University Press, 2012), 191–236; id., "A Terrorist Organization that Never Was: The Jordanian 'Bay'at al-Imam' Group," *Middle East Journal* 68, no. 1 (2014): 59–75. For more on al-Zarqawi, see Jean-Charles Brisard (with Damien Martinez), *Zarqawi: The New Face of Al-Qaeda* (New York: Other Press, 2005); Fu'ad Hussein, *Al-Zarqawi: Al-Jil al-Thani li-l-Qaida* [Al-Zarqawi: The Second Generation of al-Qaeda] (Beirut: Dar al-

The ideology guiding the Jihadi-Salafi movement in Jordan is decidedly Salafi in the theological and legal sense, but much more challenging to the state because its adherents hold it against the country's rulers (king, prime minister, ministers, etc.) that they supposedly do not apply Islam at the state level. Other Salafis agree that the *sharia* should be the law of the land, but—whereas quietists seek to achieve this goal eventually through peaceful *da'wa* and politicos want to get to that point through political participation—Jihadi-Salafis believe that the current order should be overthrown and contend that violence against the state is justified. The underlying justification for this anti-state violence is the belief that the kingdom—just like other Muslim countries—is ruled by apostates who, because of their alleged unwillingness to apply Islamic law in full, have ceased to be Muslims. This process of excommunication (*takfir*) of fellow Muslims enables Jihadi-Salafis to place rulers outside the religion of Islam and thereby legitimises waging jihad against them in pursuit of an Islamic state.

As the conflict between al-Maqdisi and al-Zarqawi suggests, Jihadi-Salafis do not agree on everything. Al-Maqdisi represents the more careful and scholar-centred wing of the Jordanian Jihadi-Salafi movement, judging violence against the state as legitimate but unwise because of the regime's overwhelming power. The followers of al-Zarqawi's represent the more action-oriented and fighter-driven wing of Jordan's Jihadi-Salafi movement. They are more likely to wage jihad and care less about the legal and doctrinal niceties that scholars such as al-Maqdisi write and preach. This division between scholar- and fighter-centred approaches has also more or less translated in what has become the most important bone of contention among Jordanian Jihadi-Salafis: whether or not to support the Islamic State (IS), the organisation that took over from al-Qaeda as the most prominent Jihadi-Salafi organisation in the Middle East during 2012–17.

Although al-Maqdisi had been in the forefront of those scholars calling for the establishment of an Islamic state (rather than merely waging jihad for jihad's sake), he became increasingly dismayed with the excessive violence displayed by IS, its exclusive mindset, and its tendency to disavow opponents (even those within the Jihadi-Salafi movement). IS, which could have represented the ideal, scholar-centred state that al-Maqdisi and

---

Khayya, 2005); Loretta Napoleoni, *Insurgent Iraq: Al Zarqawi and the New Generation* (New York: Seven Stories Press, 2005).

his followers dreamed of, turned out—in their eyes, at least—to be the very fighter-centred nightmare that they had feared all along. For a few years, al-Maqdisi has been supported in his anti-IS (but pro-al-Qaeda) views by Abu Qatada al-Filastini (b. 1960), a major Palestinian-Jordanian Jihadi-Salafi scholar who resided in England for a long time before his expulsion to Jordan in 2013. Together they have formed perhaps the most prominent ideological bloc against IS. Many of al-Zarqawi's supporters (as well as some of al-Maqdisi's), however, have enthusiastically supported IS as the heir to al-Qaeda in Iraq, and some have even joined IS in Syria. This division is the most important source of strife between Jihadi-Salafis in Jordan. Ironically, this has led to a situation in which al-Maqdisi and Abu Qatada, who have spent years denouncing the "apostate" regimes in Jordan and the rest of the region, are now seen as relatively non-confrontational because of their opposition to IS.[10]

Conclusion

Islamic movements in Jordan are quite diverse. Some have a quietist, apolitical character, while others are highly politicised; some focus on education or seek to change the political system from within, while others are confrontational and prepared to use violence. Doctrinally, there are significant differences, as well, with both Muslim Brothers and Salafis prominently present in the kingdom; the former are activist but not very specific in theological or legal matters, while the latter are often—though not always—the exact opposite.

One of the things they have in common is that they must, somehow, all deal with and relate to the Jordanian state. Some, like the Muslim Brotherhood, have done this through a close relationship that has gradually deteriorated and has resulted in the original Brotherhood being outlawed altogether. Only the groups willing to play by the regime's rules—either because they split off from the Brotherhood or because they represent a regime-friendly version of the organisation—have survived.

---

[10] Kirk H. Sowell, *Jordanian Salafism and the Jihad in Syria* (Washington, D.C.: Hudson Institute (www.hudson.org/research/11131-jordanian-salafism-and-the-jihad-in-Syria, accessed 21 November 2017), 2015; Joas Wagemakers, "Jihadi-Salafism in Jordan and the Syrian Conflict: Divisions Overcome Unity," *Studies in Conflict & Terrorism* (forthcoming as a hard copy, but available online at http://www.tandfonline.com/doi/full/10.1080/10 57610X.2017.1283197 (accessed 21 November 2017)).

The Salafi movement, on the other hand, started out as an independent trend but slowly grew into a loyalist and explicitly pro-regime current. Two other Salafi trends developed, partly in opposition to these quietists, into a highly politicised "reformist" type of Salafism and a radical and sometimes violent branch labelled Jihadi-Salafism. In the changing political landscape in both the region and the kingdom itself, Islamic movements have thus shown quite a tendency to adapt, split up, and survive (if they were willing to cooperate with the regime) or perish (if they did not). The regime, while often struggling to handle all these different Islamic trends, has generally come out on top.

References

Antoun, R. T. (1989). *Muslim preacher in the modern world: A Jordanian case study in comparative perspective.* Princeton: Princeton University Press.

Boulby, M. (1999). *The Muslim brotherhood and the kings of Jordan, 1945–1993.* Atlanta: Scholars Press.

Clark, J. A. (2004). *Islam, charity, and activism: Middle class networks and social welfare in Egypt, Jordan, and Yemen.* Bloomington: Indiana University Press.

Hamid, S. (2014). *Temptations of power: Islamists & illiberal democracy in a new Middle East.* Oxford, etc: Oxford University Press.

Harmsen, E. (2008). *Islam, civil society and social work: Muslim voluntary welfare associations in Jordan between patronage and empowerment.* Amsterdam: Amsterdam University Press.

Moaddel, M. (2002). *Jordanian exceptionalism: A comparative analysis of state-religion relationships in Egypt, Iran, Jordan, and Syria.* New York: Palgrave.

Schwedler, J. (2006). *Faith in moderation: Islamist parties in Jordan and Yemen.* Cambridge, etc: Cambridge University Press.

Wagemakers, J. (2012). *A quietist jihadi: The ideology and influence of Abu Muhammad al-Maqdisi.* Cambridge, etc: Cambridge University Press.

Wagemakers, J. (2016). *Salafism in Jordan: Political Islam in a quietist community.* Cambridge, etc: Cambridge University Press.

Wiktorowicz, Q. (2001). *The management of Islamic activism: Salafis, the Muslim brotherhood, and state power in Jordan.* Albany: State University of New York Press.

The West Bank Under Jordan

Avraham Sela

During the 1948 war, the Hashemite Kingdom of Jordan completed its takeover of the Mandate Palestinian territory from Jenin in the north to Hebron in the south, including the Old City of Jerusalem and its surrounding Arab neighbourhoods. The takeover of this area, henceforth named the West Bank, coincided with King Abdallah's long-lived aspiration to expand his rule over the historic territory of "Greater Syria" (*suria al-kubra*), which also included Mandatory Palestine. Hence, even before the official unification of the West Bank with the then Jordan in April 1950, the Hashemite monarch steadily applied his symbols of power and practical authority over the Arab population that came under his military rule.

A number of causes and processes explain the creation of the West Bank and Jordan's eventual control of it:

A. It was originally part of the territory allotted to the Arab State by the United Nations (UN) Partition Resolution 181 of 29 November 1947.

A. Sela (✉)
The Department of International Relations and the Harry S. Truman Institute for the Advancement of Peace, The Hebrew University of Jerusalem, Jerusalem, Israel
e-mail: avraham.sela@mail.huji.ac.il

© The Author(s) 2019
P. R. Kumaraswamy (ed.), *The Palgrave Handbook of the Hashemite Kingdom of Jordan*, https://doi.org/10.1007/978-981-13-9166-8_17

B. As of late 1947, Abdallah secretly discussed with the Jewish Agency (JA) and the British government, albeit separately, his intention to incorporate it into his kingdom once the British Mandate expires. Already before the partition resolution was approved, Abdullah and the JA representatives reached a tacit agreement by which the former would take control of the territory allotted to the Arab State without interfering with the JA's intention to establish their own sovereign state on the area assigned to them by the UN. In essence, the two parties aimed at implementing the partition of the country peacefully, though without discussing Jerusalem, which according to the UN Partition Plan was to be *corpus separatum* under the international sovereignty, or any specific implications concerning land and population.
C. Britain gave its secret consent to the king's plan of taking control of the territory the UN allotted to the Arab State though it also dictated that the Arab Legion, the Jordanian army, which was commanded by British officers, should by no means violate the partition lines.
D. The escalation of the Arab-Jewish inter-communal strife parallel to the diminishing British military presence in Palestine towards the end of the Mandate, the Jewish military offensive of April–May 1948 which resulted in hundreds of thousands of Arabs fleeing their homes to a safe haven in the neighbouring Arab countries, all triggered strong responses by the Arab governments, which culminated in establishing an inter-Arab war coalition including King Abdallah of Jordan. Hence, despite their early understanding, a military confrontation between Israeli and Jordanian forces was inevitable, especially in Jerusalem and along the main road from the coastal plain to the city. The heavy battles between Israel and Jordan resulted in the division of Jerusalem between the two states and a Jordanian control of a smaller area of the original mountainous region allotted to the Arab State.

The final borders of the West Bank and divided Jerusalem were thus the products of war, not of a secret agreement between Israel and Jordan. Nonetheless, their tacit understanding before the war and the secret peace negotiations they conducted in late 1949 and early 1950 clearly attested to their common interests, also shared by Britain, to prevent the establishment of an Arab-Palestinian State led by the ex-Mufti al-Haj Amin al-Husseini or his followers. Hence, already before the official end of the 1948 war, King Abdallah invested considerable efforts to mobilise local Palestinian notables in overtly legitimising his rule over the West Bank, many of whom traditionally identified with the opposition to the Husseini clan.

Although the political history of the West Bank during the period under discussion was fraught with alienation and defiance towards the Hashemite establishment, their 19 years of unity with Jordan can be divided into two equal periods namely, 1948–57 and 1957–67. During the first decade, the absolute control of the king and his security establishment over the political system enabled the Hashemite monarchy to maintain some flexibility with the West Bank-based political opposition. Aware of the host of contradictions between the West Bank residents and their administration, the Hashemite rulers adopted a strategy of avoiding brutal repression and reducing frictions with their opponents as much as possible. Such policy was preferable for both earning domestic and Arab legitimacy for the union and diffusing tensions between both parts of the kingdom.

This strategy of walking a tightrope in relation with the West Bank came to an end in April 1957 with the dismissal of the short-lived government of Suleiman al-Nabulsi over crucial differences concerning the international orientation of the Kingdom and the continued authoritarian nature of the monarchic regime. The following decade saw a shift towards more violence and repression in the relations between the regime and Palestinian opposition largely due to the latter's subversion under the Hashemite monarch and the escalating inter-Arab ideological and political rivalries inspired by Gamal Abdal Nasser and his Palestinian adherents in the West Bank.

Politics of East Bank/West Bank Unification

The aftermath of the 1948 war witnessed a broad tendency among Arabs in general and Palestinians in particular to blame King Abdullah and the British command of the Arab Legion (Jordan's army) for the catastrophic results that befell the Palestinians. Specifically, the Hashemite regime was accused of abandoning Lydda and Ramle under the Israeli offensive of July 1948 due to the withdrawal of the token—and militarily inferior Jordanian unit stationed there, which resulted in a massive wave of refugees fleeing to the area under Jordan's military control. Besides, the Jordanian monarch was blamed for surrendering to Israel the Palestinian villages along the western slopes of the Samaria Mountains as part of their 1949 armistice agreement which, again, derived from Jordan's military weakness.

These accusations were indeed unjustified given Jordan's military, financial, and political constraints. In addition to the Arab Legion's relatively small order-of-battle (four battalions and two artillery batteries at entering into Palestine), Jordan's strategy in the war was shaped by its entire dependence on Britain's subsidy since its very inception in the 1920s (until 1956). Britain also instructed Abdullah to strictly avoid attacking the territory allotted to the Jewish State in the Partition Plan, threatening that such violation would cause the withdrawal of the British officers in the Arab Legion.

Accusations of the Hashemite ruler and his British military command as collaborators with the Zionist enemy were ostensibly approved by the secret peace negotiations conducted between senior Israeli and Jordanian representatives in 1949–50. Although the negotiations ended without an agreement between the two states, King Abdallah continued to maintain secret contacts with Israeli officials until his assassination in July 1951.

The formal annexation of the West Bank was conducted in four steps parallel to the tightening of military control over the territory and population:

A. The Palestine Congress opened on 1 October 1948 in Amman in response to the Egypt-backed Palestinian national congress held in Gaza in September and establishment of the "All-Palestine Government" under Haj Amin al-Husseini's presidency. This congress invited King Abdallah to take care of the Palestinians' matters as he wished.
B. The Jericho Conference held on 1 December 1948 led by Hebron's Mayor Sheikh Muhammad Ali al-Ja'bari concluded by calling for unifying the two banks of River Jordan under King Abdullah's throne.
C. Signing an armistice agreement with Israel on 3 April 1949 bestowing international de facto recognition on Jordan's possession of the territory outlined by the "Green Line."
D. Finally, on 24 April 1950, a newly elected Parliament comprised of an equal number of delegates of each of the two banks officially approved the "complete *unity* between the *two* sides of the *Jordan* and their union into one state." The day after, the British government announced its recognition of the annexation and extension of the Anglo-Jordanian Treaty (1948) to the new armistice borders (Madi and Musa 1988, 533–545).

The West Bank: Social and Economic Data

The unification of the West Bank added 5600 square kilometres to Jordan's territory and more than doubled its original population. The West Bank original population at the time of annexation to Jordan was about 490,000. In addition, the West Bank became a refuge to 280,000 Palestinians who had fled from the areas taken by Israel in the war in addition to thousands of Palestinian refugees who had arrived in East Jordan during the war (UN Conciliation Commission for Palestine 1949). According to other sources, the West Bank original population was about 400,000 and the number of refugees nearly 415,000 (Cohen 1986, 85–86).

The immigration into the area of 300,000–400,000 refugees created a high population density—20 times higher than in the East Bank—high rate of unemployment and poverty, pushing many, especially of the refugee population, to migrate to East Bank and also to the Gulf countries later on, where educated and skilled labourers were in high demand for their quickly developing oil economies. The Jordanian government encouraged the migration to the East Bank, especially of skilled labourers and educated peoples, which coincided with the policy of directing most of its development budget to the less developed East Bank. Between 1948 and 1967, more than 155,000 of the West Bank original population and 240,000 of the refugees in this region migrated from this area to East Jordan and the Gulf countries, mostly at the age of 20–39 (Lavie 2008, 6; Cohen 1986, 91).

The continued migration of hundreds of thousands of Palestinians from the West Bank not only weakened its economy but was also apparent in the population growth which remained very low during the period under discussion despite a 3 per cent natural growth annually. Hence, between 1949 and 1967, the population of East Jerusalem remained the same, 60,000 (Cohen 1986, 93). Indeed, the original West Bank population before the 1948 War hardly grew during the years of Jordanian rule, first and foremost due to migration. By 1967, the West Bank represented about 47 per cent of Jordan's population and about 30 per cent of its gross domestic product ("West Bank Region, Palestine," *Encyclopaedia Britannica in:* https://www.britannica.com/place/West-Bank).

Until 1948, the West Bank economy was based primarily on agriculture, mostly dry farming, which employed more than 40 per cent of the labour market. Other vital sectors were tourism to Christian holy places and light industry which mainly consisted of traditional manufacturing of olive oil soap and queries. Almost no industrial development of the West

Bank was noticed during the Jordanian period, and by the mid-1960s, less than a dozen industrial establishments in the area were employing more than 30 per cent employees in the area ("West Bank Region, Palestine," *Encyclopaedia Britannica in:* https://www.britannica.com/place/West-Bank).

Concerning economic growth, between 1945 and 1966, the West Bank economy scored an annual average of 2 per cent, less than the natural population growth. Another estimate maintains that in 1949–67, the West Bank experienced about 4 per cent of average economic growth, mostly thanks to increase in the services. Even this level of growth still lagged behind the population's needs when compared to the East Bank pace of growth (Cohen 1986, 107).

The disconnection of the West Bank from the rest of Mandatory Palestine had far-reaching repercussions on the economy in this region, most saliently the crisis of unemployment. The war resulted in the loss of direct communication to Lebanon and Syria, forcing any movement of people and goods to the neighbouring Arab countries to take a much longer distance through the East Bank. Moreover, the war resulted in the closure of the electricity production by the hydro-electric power plant in Naharayim and disconnected West Bank cities from their electricity and fuel suppliers in Haifa and Tel-Aviv. Similarly, East Jerusalem was disconnected from the city's power plant, which remained in Western Jerusalem. The solution to the crisis of electricity supply to the West Bank and East Jerusalem was employing local low-productive fuel-based generators, which in turn limited the region's economic development.

In 1966–67, the total number of all West Bank school students in the government system of education was 127,000, in addition to 60,000 students in other systems, including 40,000 in United Nations Relief and Work Agency (UNRWA) schools, two-thirds of them in the West Bank. Only 9 per cent of the students in the West Bank were in high schools. Until the establishment of the University of Jordan in 1962, there was no university in Jordan (and students seeking higher education had to study in Lebanon, Syria, or Egypt). In 1965–66, the total number of all sorts of schools and levels in the West Bank was 920, and 105 of them were in East Jerusalem. In that academic year, the total number of students in Jordan was 205,241 in all systems of education, 39.3 per cent of them girls (State of Israel, West Bank Economic Survey 1967, Ch. 13, 1–3).

The rural sector lagged far behind the urban one in education, connection to electricity and water supply, and life expectancy. Still, the state of the West Bank's rural area was largely better than much of the rural sector in East Jordan.

WEST BANK-EAST BANK POLITICS 1948–1957

Despite its formal approval by the West Bank representatives, the West Bank-East Bank unification remained internationally controversial. The Arab States, on their part, were vehemently opposed to Jordan's intentions on two juxtaposed issues namely, signing a five-year non-aggression agreement with Israel and finalising the official annexation of the West Bank to Jordan. Egypt led the campaign against Jordan's policy on both issues employing the Arab League forums to exert pressures on Jordan to refrain from finalising any of the two measures.

Because of the filtering news that Israel and Jordan had abbreviated a five-year non-aggression agreement in February 1950, the Arab League confirmed a set of economic and political punitive measures against any member state signing a separate peace agreement with Israel. In view of these Arab threats, the Jordanian elite refused ratification of the deal though it stood firm in supporting the annexation of the West Bank. Similarly, the Arab States could not formally acquiesce in a formal annexation of the West Bank to Jordan, which effectively confirmed the partition of Palestine and the existence of Israel, the most significant issue on their collective agenda since the Arab League was founded in 1945. Old inter-Arab rivalries, especially between Jordan on the one hand and Egypt and Saudi Arabia on the other, added further impetus to the Egypt-led campaign against the annexation of the West Bank as far as threatening to expel Jordan from the organisation. Once Jordan gave up on its negotiations with Israel, however, the Arab States offered their temporary approval to the West Bank annexation by formulating it as a "trusteeship," which was practically meaningless as far as the Jordanian establishment and its Palestinian supporters were concerned.

Altogether, Jordan became the Arab State with the largest Palestinian population. The Palestinian demographic upheaval indeed defined the tragedy that befell the Palestinians' fledgling political community in the 1948 war. Unlike any other Arab State, Jordan granted full citizenship to the West Bank residents and the Palestinian refugees already in East Jordan. The Hashemite regime, however, saw to administratively and politically repressing the Palestinian identity seeking instead to appropriate Arab Palestine and consolidate a Hashemite Jordanian identity based on the euphemistic slogan of "Unity of the Two Banks" (*wahdat al-daffatayn*). Contrarily, in the occupied Gaza Strip, the Egyptian government adopted a policy of highlighting the Palestinian identity and the temporary nature of the Egyptian military government in this area.

Ruling over the West Bank and East Jerusalem population indeed proved a troubled task for the Hashemite monarchy. This population was exceptionally politicised following decades of struggles against foreign domination and by far more educated and experienced in trade association, administration, and social organisation compared to most East Jordanians. During the Jordanian rule, the West Bank population indeed had an unmistakable impact on the demographic, economic, and infrastructural development of the kingdom in addition to exporting to the Jordanian arena vibrant public debates and party politics. Unusually defiant were the young urban elites of Nablus, Ramallah, and East Jerusalem represented by old (communist) and newly established (the Ba'ath party, the Arab Nationalist Movement, and the Islamic Liberation Party) radical parties.

The post-1948 Palestinian leadership consisted of typical middle-class figures—young urban professionals (lawyers, doctors, engineers, educators, and journalists) who had taken part in national activities during the late-Mandatory years. Unlike the pre-1948 notable elite, the new political leaders were better connected to other social strata and capable of mass mobilisation and conduct of popular protest. The communists' long experience of clandestine activity indeed served as a role model for the newly emerging radical groups, especially the Ba'ath party, the largest in scope and distribution in the country (Sela 1984).

The challenges posed to the Hashemite regime by the newly annexed Palestinians—most saliently by the West Bank political elite—had their causes in the domestic and foreign policies of the Hashemite regime, which often contradicted the attitudes and expectations of the Palestinian population. Shaped by the circumstances of its very inception in the early 1920s and objective political and economic constraints, the Jordanian regime could hardly shift its policies to meet even partly the Palestinians' expectations. The following are the main issues that nurtured the conflict between the West Bankers and the Jordanian regime, especially during the first decade after 1948.

a. Economic Destitution and Border Wars The establishment in late 1949 of UNRWA as an international agency of aid to the Palestinian refugees somewhat mitigated their grave conditions of life along the years, introducing social and economic services, which took some of the burdens from the Jordanian government. In addition to the large population of refugees in the West Bank and Jordan generally, the war and the armistice agreement resulted in severe and prolonged economic difficulties for West Bankers particularly. In addition to losing access to the relatively close harbours of Haifa and Jaffa and large markets before the war, over a hundred thousand Palestinian villagers located along the border lost access to significantly large cultivated land now inside Israel (Sela 1984, 144).

The poor Jordanian economy remained dependent on the foreign financial aid of which only a small part could be dedicated to social and economic development. The dire economic conditions triggered a broad tendency of infiltration into Israel's territory, beginning as attempts to harvest and cultivate previously owned land, then committing property thefts, which soon assumed the form of sabotage and murder. With the broadening phenomenon of cross-border infiltrations, sabotage, and attacks on its citizens, Israel adopted a policy of military retaliation against Palestinian villages—often dragging Jordanian military forces into the fray—and official institutions such as police stations.

In 1951, the Jordanian government established the National Guard in which all men at the age of 20–40 would have to actively serve in defence of the border villages. At its peak in the mid-1950s, the National Guard encompassed 40,000 men organised in 46 battalions armed with only light weapons and maintained under strict control of the Arab Legion (Bar-Lavi 1981, 23). Israel's military retaliations continued until late October 1956 when, following the Suez War, the Jordanian authorities managed to control their border with Israel better. The harshest Israeli retaliation was the raid on the village Qibya in October 1953 in which an Israel Defence Force (IDF) unit killed 69 civilians, many of them women and children, and bombed some 45 homes. Israel's military retaliations resulted in repeated outcries by Palestinian politicians against the passivity of the military, calling for arming the border villagers to enable them to protect themselves. The public criticism against the armed forces was directly aimed at the anomaly of Jordanian army being commanded by British officers.

b. The Status of Jerusalem Versus Amman In the first few years after the 1948 War, Jerusalem remained a bastion of the opposition to and subversion against the Hashemite monarch, represented by supporters of the Husseini clan. The government's suspicions of the opposition materialised when in July 1951 a young Palestinian of a Husseini descent assassinated King Abdallah at the entrance to the al-Aqsa Mosque. Despite the government's efforts to promote the economic and administrative integration between the two parts of the kingdom, during the first decade after 1948, West Bank politicians and public figures kept demanding to establish representations of government ministries and authorities in Jerusalem to save the West Bankers the need to travel to Amman for legal and bureaucratic purposes.

The Hashemite rulers favoured Amman as the kingdom's capital giving it a priority in budget allocations as well as in official status. The Jordanian policy of strengthening Amman's status over Jerusalem represented a general policy of prioritising East Jordan in budget allocations for economic development and infrastructure building. This policy concerning Jerusalem remained unchanged until 1967 though the Hashemite monarchs and their governments publicly glorified Jerusalem's religious and symbolic significance and held well-communicated prayers in the al-Aqsa Mosque.

King Hussein, who came to the throne in 1953, maintained the policy on Jerusalem of his grandfather Abdullah. He took advantage of Jerusalem's symbolic status for legitimising his kingship and highlighting its Arab-Muslim identity but refused the Palestinian demands to equalise its status to that of Amman. At the most, he was willing to declare it a "spiritual capital" and equalise its formal municipal status (*amana*) to that of Amman. The Jordanian policy on Jerusalem thus reflected declarative support for its special Islamic status mixed with practical prudence and suspicion. Hence, in July 1953, the Jordanian government declared the city "Jordan's second capital" and held its first session in Jerusalem after Hussein's coronation in response to Israel's decision to move its foreign ministry to this city. Similarly, Jordan protested Israel's violations of the 1949 armistice agreement by holding military parades in Jerusalem in 1958 and 1961.

c. Palestinian Quest for Democratisation The Palestinians in Jordan sensed political deprivation and discrimination by the Hashemite regime concerning power-sharing in the unified kingdom despite their formal equality to East Jordanians. Indeed, although Palestinians constituted two-thirds of the population in the Kingdom and despite their better education and experience in administration, the central state institutions, especially the security system, remained strictly held by East Jordanians. The sense of political discrimination was strongly expressed by the West Bank representatives of the opposition parties in the Parliament and through the printed media, by repeatedly demanding democratisation of the political system.

Within this context, Palestinian representatives insisted on three significant constitutional changes, namely free political association, making the government accountable to a freely elected Parliament, and the introduction of a general draft to the military. The implementation of these demands would practically shift the political power to the Palestinian majority and reflect its decisive demographic weight in the military as well. The regime, on its part, allowed the opposition, mostly located in the West Bank, to play an active role in the parliamentary system albeit without an official approval of political existence as parties and in strict "rules of the game," employing punitive measures, such as imprisonment of political figures and bans on the opposition printed media for violating those rules. Nonetheless, following years of repression and fraudulent elections, under the growing Nasserist tide (see below) and intense political agitation of the opposition groups in support of "Arabisation of the military" and breaking up with the British patronage of Jordan, the regime held free elections in October 1956.

d. Jordan's Western Orientation and Status Quo with Israel Contrary to the hopes among Palestinians, especially the refugees, for a "second round" of an Arab war against Israel and liberation of Palestine, which had been much trumpeted by other Arab States, the Hashemite monarchy and its armed forces adopted a relatively accommodating policy along the Israeli-Jordanian border. This policy also included efforts to prevent cross-border infiltrations and avoid military clashes with Israel. Especially because of Israel's repeated raids into the West Bank, the early 1950s witnessed increasing rhetorical attacks on the British military command, especially its top commander Glubb Pasha, demanding to "Arabise" the Arab Legion and replace the British subsidy by Arab financial support (see below).

Another bone of contention between the regime and the Palestinian opposition concerned the former's endorsement of plans to be funded by the US and implemented under the UN umbrella for resettling the Palestinian refugees in the countries of their residence. In 1953, the US special envoy Eric Johnston introduced his plan for utilising the Jordan basin's water by Lebanon, Syria, Jordan, and Israel for this purpose. The US plans faced vehement opposition of the Palestinian politicians, claiming that such plans aimed not to resolve but to erase the refugee problem and propagating strict adherence to the refugees' right of return to their original homes as the only option. By 1956, the radical parties' propagation against the US plan scored success when it was finally shelved due to the refusal of the refugees to collaborate with it.

e. The Impact of Nasserism
The mid-1950s witnessed a rising influence of Gamal 'Abd al-Nasser of Egypt, primarily thanks to his resistance to British colonialism in the Arab world. In 1955, this resistance focused on preventing Syria and Jordan from joining the Baghdad Pact, which Turkey and Iraq had signed in February 1955 at the behest of Britain (who later joined the Pact and so did Iran and Pakistan). The campaign against the Baghdad Pact was taken to the public sphere throughout the Arab world by the Egyptian mass media, notably the *Voice of the Arabs* (*sawt al-'arab*) radio broadcasting from Cairo. The Egyptian propaganda, combined with local political agitation, managed to mobilize the Arab masses, especially in the West Bank, for thwarting the Jordanian intention to join the Pact.

Nasser's success in preventing Jordan and Syria from joining the new alliance elevated him to an Arab national hero, reflecting the masses' strive for a daring leader whose defiance of the West instilled a sense of national pride. Nasser's heroic image grew bigger when he broke the Western embargo on arms supplies by signing an arms deal with Czechoslovakia, which became public in September 1955. The Czech-Egypt arms deal boosted the domestic pressures on the Hashemite regime to rid itself from the British officers commanding the Arab Legion. In March 1956, under growing pressures of the opposition parties and popular protests, the king dismissed Glubb Pasha and later on the other British military officers.

f. The April 1957 Crisis The democratic parliamentary election of October 1956 brought about the first government of typical opposition parties, including the leader of the Ba'ath Party, 'Abdallah al-Rimawi from Ramallah and 'Abd al-Qadir al-Saleh from Nablus who was identified with the Communist Party. Prime Minister Sulayman al-Nabulsi's government, however, was short-lived due to foreign policy decisions that collided head-on with the monarchy's traditionally western orientation. The most salient of all was the "Arab Solidarity Agreement" signed with Egypt, Syria, and Saudi Arabia in January 1957 by which the latter Arab States were to cover Jordan's defence expenditures instead of hitherto British aid. This was followed by another agreement signed two months later with Britain on abrogating the 1946 Anglo-Jordanian Defence Treaty.

April 1957 was saturated with growing popular demonstrations in the West Bank cities organised by the opposition parties and escalating tension between the government and the monarchic establishment. The tension reached its peak over the government's declaration on establishing diplomatic relations with the USSR, on the one hand, and the king's welcoming of the Eisenhower Doctrine. The sense of crisis reached its height with the allegedly failed military coup attempt against the king followed by his decisions to dismiss the government, outlaw all parties, and declare a state of emergency, all of which triggered broad popular demonstrations and protests in the West Bank cities and escape of leading opposition leaders and senior military officers to Syria. It is noteworthy that during the April crisis, the Muslim Brotherhood (MB) actively supported the monarchy, including the use of weapons for repressing demonstrations against King Hussein in the refugee camps of Jericho (Bar-Lavi 1981, 31; Shlaim 2007, 129–152).

West Bank-East Bank Politics 1957–67

The events of April 1957 marked a turning point in Jordan's internal and inter-Arab position. The Nasserist tide continued to sweep the Fertile Crescent countries, reaching its peak in early 1958 with the unification of Egypt and Syria in the United Arab Republic (UAR). In the following years, the resistance to the Hashemite regime was led by former Palestinian leaders of the opposition parties, primarily 'Abdallah al-Rimawi, leader of the Ba'ath Party in Jordan since 1950. Rimawi and other opposition figures who fled to Damascus conducted subversive and terrorist activities against the Jordanian regime with unhidden support by the UAR. These efforts escalated because of the US president's declaration in April 1957 that Jordan was "vital to the interests of the United States," heralding a new era of close relationship between the two countries, to the chagrin of the Jordanian-Palestinian opposition and the UAR.

Jordan's posture in the region sustained another blow due to the military coup in Iraq on July 1958, which eliminated the other Hashemite regime and Jordan's closest Arab ally, followed by the arrival in Jordan of a British paratrooper brigade at the king's request (Madi and Musa 1988, 662–680; Shlaim 2007, 161–164). The late 1950s and early 1960s were indeed saturated with growing ideological strife between Arab nationalist regimes and movements led by Nasser and his followers and the Arab monarchies, most vulnerable of which was Jordan. The efforts of Jordan's enemies to undermine its domestic stability included sabotage and terrorist attacks—peaked in the assassination of Prime Minister Hazza' al-Majali in August 1960—and many coup attempts by military officers of East Jordanian descent connected to the Jordanian-Palestinian Ba'ath Party aimed at toppling the regime.

Domestically, the aftermath of April 1957 witnessed a decisively restrictive approach of the Hashemite regime towards any indication of opposition against the regime, especially in the West Bank. This policy grew more repressive parallel to the escalating activities, both domestic and external, of subversion and resistance to the regime's very existence. Henceforth, the regime adopted a tight control over all aspects of political life in the Kingdom. Following the crisis of April 1957, the regime disbanded all political parties in the country, turning the Parliament into a façade of political representation without any real say by the public about the king's appointment of loyalist figures as representatives. The ban on party activity was accompanied by harsh persecution of former and actual members of the opposition parties, including imprisonment and tortures (Bar-Lavi 1981, 31). Similarly, the press came under strict control, and in return for their "good behaviour," the publishers received an official subsidy from the government.

Parallel to repressing the opposition groups, the regime turned to foster traditional patronage relations with local leaders, especially his traditional supporters among the Bedouin population in the southern part of East Jordan. Of all the pre-1957 parties and political movements, the regime allowed only the MB to continue their social and political activities. Though the movement's leaders constantly preached the application of the Islamic law (*shari'a*) and criticised cultural westernisation and the regime's close relations with Britain and the US, the MB traditionally supported the monarch, especially against the tide of Nasserism and its nationalist-leftist supporters (Cohen 1982, Ch. 4). The MB's main areas of support in the West Bank were in Hebron and Nablus, and their senior members served as ministers with many others taking important positions in the Jordanian administration.

In the late 1950s, all government ministries were obliged to establish second offices in East Jerusalem, and the government embarked on a new routine of holding its meetings in the city every second week. In the mid-1960s, the king began constructing the Royal Palace on a hill north of the city (construction remained incomplete by 1967) and stayed in the city overnight once a week. In the late 1950s, King Hussein embarked on a fundraising campaign in the historic Muslim shrines of Jerusalem, al-Aqsa mosque and the Dom of the Rock. The project was completed in 1964 and celebrated in the presence of many Arab and Muslim leaders amidst broad propaganda campaign praising the Hashemite monarchy.

Despite the harsh repression of the political parties in the kingdom, the West Bank population continued to be highly responsive to nationalist events in the Arab arena such as the establishment of the UAR and the military coup in Iraq. The breakup of the UAR caused a deep frustration among many Palestinians, especially in the West Bank, but the tripartite unity agreement between Egypt, Syria, and Iraq in April 1963 once again took thousands of demonstrators to the streets of Jerusalem, Ramallah, and Nablus in support of Jordan incorporation to the newly established Arab union, which turned very short-lived. This time the regime took no risks by harshly repressing the demonstrations by military force (Bar-Lavi 1981, 39–40; Sela 1984, 48).

The Arab summit conference held in January 1964 in Cairo signalled a new era of mitigated inter-Arab tensions and rapprochement between Jordan and Egypt following years of hostility and conflict, not without a cost for the former. In return for Nasser's conciliatory approach, Hussein gave his consent to the establishment in May 1964 of the Palestine Liberation Organization (PLO) by Ahmad al-Shuqayri, as a political framework of the vaguely defined structure of the 'Palestinian Entity'. Shukeiri was a veteran Palestinian politician and diplomat who had just inherited the position of representative of the "All-Palestine Government" (established in September 1948 in Gaza City) in the Arab League. If the Hashemite king assumed he could control the PLO by having many of his Palestinian loyalists participating in the founding conference, the newly established organisation turned into a primary cause of frustration for the Jordanian government. This was primarily due to Shuqayri's demands that challenged Jordan's sovereignty, such as establishing a Palestinian army on Jordan's territory under the PLO's authority, taxation of Palestinian salaries in the Kingdom, and arming the border villages. At the same time, the Jordanian monarch could not ignore the enthusiasm and rising national sentiments among Palestinians, especially in the West Bank, about the newly established organisation.

The establishment of the PLO coincided with the rise of the Palestine Liberation Movement (*harakat tahrir filastin* known in its abbreviations as FaTaH). On 1 January 1965, the organisation launched its first sabotage action in Israel following a few years of clandestine ideological and mobilisation preparations, including in the West Bank. Contrary to the Arab patronage of the PLO, Fatah was a grassroots organisation representing authentic Palestinian nationalist commitment, hence the heated competition between the two. The Fatah attacks against Israel from the West Bank territory once again triggered repeated Israeli retaliations against Jordanian targets though the Jordanian regime made sincere efforts, albeit partly successful, to repress the Fatah and other Palestinian activists and prevent infiltrations across the border with Israel.

The last two years of the Hashemite rule over the West Bank thus saw a rising Palestinian nationalist sentiment which grew stronger along with the growing feud between the Jordanian government on the one hand and Shuqayri and his Egyptian patrons on the other and repression of Fatah's activists in the West Bank. In November 1966, Israel launched a massive raid on the village of Samu' south of Hebron in retaliation for the killing of three Israeli soldiers by a mine explosion within Israel. Fifteen Jordanian Army soldiers were killed, and over 50 homes were destroyed. The responses that erupted in the West Bank cities were the gravest of all in the history of their relations with the Hashemite regime and the most dangerous for the latter's stability indicating the peak of the Palestinisation of the West Bank residents.

The mass demonstrations and strikes assumed an unprecedented scope and organisation, including the sporadic use of firearms by the demonstrators against the Jordanian soldiers sent to repress them. The opposition leaders behind the protest represented primarily local interests of notable families in addition to being strongly encouraged by outside incitement. At the height of the turmoil, they signed a joint "covenant" with a list of far-reaching political demands reminiscent of the grievances and demands of the Palestinian opposition in the early 1950s, especially the democratisation of Jordan. Indeed, had the 1966 demands been accepted, it would have resulted in Palestinian autonomy (Susser 1994, 110–113; Shemesh 2018, 213–220).

The last episode in the tumultuous relationship between West Bank Palestinians and the Hashemite regime was the formers' demonstrations following the escalating events in the second half of May 1967 that culminated in the eruption of an all-out war between Israel and its Arab neighbours in which Israel captured the West Bank. As in the aftermath of the Samu' raid, Palestinian demonstrations in West Bank cities in support of

Nasser apparently played a prominent role in King Hussein's decision to meet with Nasser in Cairo on 30 May 1967 and subordinate his army to an Egyptian commander. The extent of the king being captive of the public in his Kingdom, especially the West Bank Palestinians, was reflected in the king's return from Cairo together with Shuqayri, which further fuelled the atmosphere of enthusiasm for war in the Kingdom.

Epilogue

King Hussein indeed lost the West Bank, including East Jerusalem, in the 1967 war though he saved his throne and sovereignty over the East Bank. Nonetheless, the Hashemite monarch remained committed to retrieve the West Bank to his Kingdom, albeit by sheer diplomacy. However, Israel's annexation of East Jerusalem immediately after the war ended and its intention to maintain full control over the Jordan Valley turned any such option entirely unrealistic from the king's viewpoint. In addition to the Israeli obstacles to the return of the West Bank to Jordan, the post-1967 years witnessed a bitter military struggle between the Hashemite regime and the PLO, now dominated by the Palestinian guerrilla groups. Though Jordan managed to crash the latter and expel them from the Kingdom in two major rounds of military confrontations (1970's "Black September" and July 1971), Jordan lost the diplomatic struggle with the PLO over the right to represent the West Bank following the resolution by the Arab summit conference in Rabat (October 1974) to recognise the PLO as "the sole legitimate representative of the Palestinian people." Even this resolution, however, could not dissuade King Hussein from his efforts to subvert the Arab summit decision, among others by maintaining close and secret relations with Israel and his Palestinian loyalists in the West Bank.

It was the Palestinian uprising (*intifada*) which erupted in December 1987 that forced the king to finally give up his claim over the West Bank. On 31 July 1988, he announced a legal and administrative disengagement from the West Bank following months of mass protests, demonstrations, civil disobedience, and military attacks against the Israeli authorities throughout the West Bank in support of the PLO coupled by collective Arab endorsement of the latter. The disengagement put into effect a long course of Jordanisation of the East Bank that is a process of state-building confined to this territory. The disengagement practically paved the road for the PLO to declare in November 1988 its independent Palestinian

State within the territory allotted for this purpose by the UN Partition Resolution, bringing to closure the history of practical loss and nominal recovery of Palestinian statehood.

References

Al-Madi, M., & Musa, S. (1988). *Tarikh al-'Urdun fi al-Qarn al-'Ishreen*. Amman: Maktabat al-Muhtasib.

Bar-Lavi, Z.'e. (1981). *The Hashemite regime 1949–1967 and its position in the West Bank*. Tel-Aviv: Shiloah Institute, Tel-Aviv University.

Cohen, A. (1982). *Political parties in the West Bank under the Jordanian regime 1949–1967*. Ithaca: Cornell University Press.

Cohen, A. (1986). *The economic development of the territories 1922–1980*. Giv'at Haviva: The Institute of Arabic Studies (Hebrew).

Lavie, Ephraim. (2008). *The Palestinians in the West Bank: Patterns of political organization under occupation and self-rule*. Unpublished Ph.D. dissertation submitted to the Senate of Tel-Aviv University (Hebrew), Tel-Aviv.

Sela, A. (1984). *The Palestinian Ba'ath: The Arab Ba'ath socialist Party in the West Bank under Jordan (1948–1967)*. Jerusalem: Magnes Press (Hebrew.

Shemesh, M. (2018). *The Palestinian national revival. In the shadow of the leadership crisis, 1937–1967*. Bloomingdale: Indiana University Press.

Shlaim, A. (2007). *Lion of Jordan. The life of King Hussein in war and peace*. London: Allen Lane.

Susser, A. (1994). *On both banks of the Jordan. A political biography of Wasfi al-Tall*. London: Frank Cass.

State of Israel, The Authority for Economic Planning. (1967). *The West Bank – Economic survey*. Jerusalem: Prime Minister's Office.

United Nations Conciliation Commission for Palestine. (1949). *Final Report of the United Nations Economic Survey Mission for the Middle East* (Pt. 1, Appendix B). Lake Success: United Nations.

West Bank Region, Palestine. *Encyclopaedia Britannica*. https://www.britannica.com/place/West-Bank. Accessed 11 Oct 2017.

Jerusalem: Hashemite Quest for Legitimacy

Yitzhak Reiter

Jordan's attachment to Jerusalem has two dimensions. The first is the Hashemite role in Al-Quds—the modern name of the city in Arabic and particularly to the third holiest place in Islam—Al-Haram al-Sharif (also known as Al-Aqsa). The second dimension is Al-Quds as a matter of religious and political identity of the Jordanians, of which many are from a Palestinian extraction, while both Jordanians and Palestinians alike are part of historical Al-Sham (Greater Syria) and of the Arab and Muslim Worlds. The Hashemite dimension reflects an identity construction project of the royal family as historical guardians of Islam's holiest places and as descendants of Prophet Muhammad of which they derive their legitimacy to rule. The Jordanian people's dimension links to the Arab-Israeli conflict in the Middle East and particularly to the religious aspect of this conflict.

The two dimensions intertwine. The Hashemite monarch employs Jerusalem as a tool for consolidating legitimacy by emphasising the role of the Hashemite family as guardians of the holy cities in Islam (Mecca and Medina under Sharif Hussein Bin-Ali and Al-Quds since 1948). At the same time Jordanians, mostly opposition factions, such as the Muslim Brotherhood, are using the post-1967 reality in Jerusalem to criticise their Hashemite regime for not doing enough to protect the Islamic nature of the city.

Y. Reiter (✉)
Ashkelon Academic College, Ashkelon, Israel
e-mail: reiter@edu.aac.ac.il

Jerusalem Under Jordanian Rule

The roots of the Hashemite attachment to Jerusalem are traced to the pre-Jordan days. The official websites of King Hussein and King Abdullah II claim that Sharif Hussein Bin-Ali donated money for the restoration of Al-Aqsa in 1924. Indeed, the Mufti of Jerusalem sent a delegation to the Hejaz to collect money for the restoration, but historians debate the sum and the donation of the Sharif of Mecca.[1] Yet, the websites present this donation as no less than "the first Hashemite restoration, 1922–1924" in spite of the fact that the restoration was undertaken by the Mufti Haji Amin al-Husseini, who was also the one who initiated the burial of the Sharif of Mecca at the Haram precinct and did it for his political ends.[2]

Historians of the 1948 War hold that King Abdullah I did not plan to fight over Jerusalem and that he wished to secure those parts of Palestine's territory that were assigned to an Arab state by the 181 UN Partition Resolution to be ruled by the Hashemite Kingdom of Jordan. Jerusalem according to this resolution fell under an international regime as a *corpus separatum*, and Abdullah claims in his memoirs that he objected to the internationalisation of Jerusalem.[3] When the war broke out, he was still loyal to the British and did not intend to challenge their interest. The historians conclude that fighting in Jerusalem was imposed on Abdullah when the Jewish forces invaded the Old City and were deployed in the hills around Jerusalem challenging Jordan's Army—the Arab Legion—positions in the West Bank.[4]

The battle over Jerusalem was victorious for both Jordan and King Abdullah and it opened a new era of Hashemite control of the holy and historic Old City. Two weeks after the surrender of the Jewish Quarter to the Arab Legion, Abdullah arrived in the Old City on Friday to participate in the public prayer at Al-Aqsa Mosque and visited the grave of his father, who was buried inside the holy compound.[5] He negotiated with Israeli officials the terms of the 1949 Rhodes ceasefire and the practical issues of border regime in the divided city.

---

[1] Katz, *Jordanian Jerusalem*, p. 100 and note 44 on p. 175; on the Hashemites' attachment to Jerusalem see also Abdullah, I. a.-H. (1979).
[2] Azaryahu and Reiter.
[3] Abduallah, *Al-Takmila*, p. 88.
[4] Gelber, *Israeli-Jordanian Dialogue 1948–1953*, p. 12.
[5] Musa, *Ayam la tunsa*, p. 347.
[6] Reiter, *Jerusalem and Its Role in Islamic Solidarity*, p. 135.

Until 1967, neither Abdullah nor his successors ever declared the capital of Jordan to be Jerusalem. From time to time, King Abdullah would come and conduct the Friday prayers at Al-Aqsa Mosque, and his visit would be escorted by a military ceremony of the Legion's orchestra.[6] The Palestinians dominated Jerusalem, and it seemed risky to rule the entire Kingdom from the holy city. Among the Mufti faction of the Palestinians, Abdullah was considered a rival and a traitor. When the Hashemite monarch visited Al-Aqsa on 20 July 1951, he was assassinated at the entrance to the mosque by a former follower of the Mufti.[7]

Jerusalem was subordinated to Amman with the aim of weakening the Husseini opposition to the Hashemites. The new Mufti nominated by King Abdullah was situated in Amman instead of Jerusalem, and the Supreme Muslim Council that was formerly headed by Mufti Haj Amin al-Husseini was abolished.

The official Jordanian attitude to Jerusalem between 1948 and 1967 was dual. On the one hand, Jerusalem was destined to be inferior to Amman, but on the other hand, the monarchy invested a lot of energy to emphasise the personal respect of the Hashemite leaders to the holy city and particularly to the Haram. In April 1953, under the Regency Council ruling Jordan a new national holiday was introduced: *Al-isra' wal-mi'raj* marking Prophet Muhammad's Night Journey to Al-Aqsa and his ascension to heaven to underline the regime's respect for Jerusalem.[8] It seems that the new holiday is still celebrated every 27th of the month of Rajab and continues to stress the importance of Jerusalem to Islam and to the Hashemites.

In July 1953, two months after young King Hussein was enthroned in Amman, the government conducted a meeting in Jerusalem and resolved to invest in its economic development.[9] The investment was modest to the needs and the religious importance of the city. King Hussein was criticised for making Jerusalem inferior to Amman and not investing enough in its development. The criticism came mainly from Palestinians who contested the Hashemite leadership.[10] Due to the growing criticism from within Jordan in 1959, Al-Quds was promoted by the Jordanian government from a status of regular mayorship (*baladiyya*) to a metropolitan mayorship

---

[7] *The Guardian*, 21 July 1951.
[8] Katz, p. 113.
[9] Har-Zvi, *From Abdullah to Abdullah*, p. 83.
[10] Later on, Israeli scholars used it to belittle the status of Jerusalem for the Muslims. Reiter, *Jerusalem and Its Role In Islamic Solidarity*, p. 69.
[11] Halabi, *Baladiyyat al-Quds al-Arabiyya*.

(*amana*)—the same municipal status like the capital Amman—and King Hussein declared it as "the second capital of Jordan."[11]

Two major investment projects were carried out by the Jordanian government in Jerusalem during the period under review: developing the Kalandia airport to be capable of receiving tourist flights, mainly Christian pilgrims, and developing the tourism section of Jordanian Jerusalem and the renovation of the Dome of the Rock adoring it with the gold-coated cover beginning in the mid-1950s. The renovations' inauguration ceremony in August 1964 was organised with the participation of distinguished political leaders and religious figures from 24 countries manifesting Muslim recognition of Jordanian sovereignty of the holy city to Islam.[12] With this endeavour, Jordanian officials used to present Jerusalem as the spiritual capital of Jordan.

King Hussein also purchased land in Shuafat neighbourhood on a high hill named Tell el-Ful, one of the highest summits of Jerusalem area and began building his summer palace that due to the June War of 1967 was never completed. Jordanian textbooks emphasised the special Hashemite attachment to the holy city underlying its conquest in 1948 by the Arab Legion by an order of King Abdullah I and King Hussein's role in protecting and developing its holy sites.[13]

Post stamps were one of Jordan's tools in maintaining legitimacy as rulers of Jerusalem. In the mid-1960s, a series of stamps were printed marking the 1964 Pope Paul VI visit to Jerusalem with the aim of revealing the message that King Hussein is the guardian of the holy sites[14] and in the following year, a stamp showing the Hashemite monarch looking towards the Dome of the Rock marking the completion of its restoration was issued.[15]

THE JUNE 1967 WAR AND ITS AFTERMATH

Jordan's involvement in the June War resulted with the loss of the West Bank including the eastern part of Jerusalem to Israeli control. Following the war, King Hussein attempted to negotiate with Israel the return of Jerusalem and the West Bank to Jordan. When the diplomatic attempts

---

[12] Har-Zvi, p. 100.
[13] Ibid., p. 95.
[14] Katz, p. 148.
[15] Ibid. p. 284.
[16] Dumper, *The Politics of Jerusalem*, p. 168.

failed, he made every effort in Arab and Islamic forums to preserve the Jordanian custodianship over the Arab part of the city and in protecting its Arab and Islamic character from Israeli attempts to Judaise its Arab-inhabited areas.

Israel's concern regarding the international arena's reaction to its control of the religious and historical part of the city and building strategic security relations with Jordan resulted in a policy to keep open bridges with Jordan and allow the Jordanian Waqf (Islamic trust) authorities to resume its administration of the Haram al-Sharif (known as the Temple Mount).[16]

Following the incident of setting fire to Al-Aqsa Mosque in August 1969 by an Australian Christian visitor, Jordan formed the Royal Committee for Jerusalem Affairs and issued post stamps commemorating the event. Hussein had to cope with changing realities and in his 1972 Confederation Plan between the two banks of Jordan, he designated Al-Quds as the capital of the Palestinian West Bank district. Until the outbreak of the first Palestinian *intifada* in December 1987, Jordan made efforts to keep some strongholds in the Arab part of the city fearing from a Palestinian Liberation Organisation (PLO) domination and these include: the Chamber of Commerce that functioned also as a mini-ministry of interior issuing Jordanian passports and other notary documents; the Waqf and its school system; the Supreme Muslim Council; and the Jordanian matriculation (*tawjihi*) and school textbooks[17]; newspapers such as *Al-Nahar* and the Jerusalem District Electricity Company. Following the outbreak of the intifada, on 31 July King Hussein announced the disengagement from the West Bank but excluded Jerusalem and its holy places while resuming Jordanian financial support of about 2–5 million dinars annually to about 3500 employees, including 1800 Waqf workers, 200 clerks of the Sharia Courts, 420 teachers, and funding 750 mosques.[18]

Jordan had to cope in the Arab arena with challenges to its custodianship over Al-Quds. In 1987, it fired the pro-PLO imam of Al-Aqsa Mosque, Ikrima Sabri (later on the PLO nominated him as Mufti and today he is the head of the Supreme Muslim Council and preacher in al-Aqsa). In 1977, Jordan undermined a Saudi attempt to operate twin

---
[17] Dumper, *Jerusalem Unbound*, p. 76.
[18] *The Jordan Times*, 6 August 1988; Reiter, *Islamic Institutions*, p. 50.
[19] Merhav and Giladi, p. 189.

cities arrangement of Mecca and Jerusalem, and in 1992, King Hussein had to sell a private house in London to fund the renovation of the Dome of the Rock to prevent a Saudi offer to fund the works. The renovation project was celebrated in a high-profile event in April 1994.

The significant efforts of Jordan regarding Jerusalem were dedicated to preserving its Islamic nature and to object Israeli attempts to change the character of the city. Given the changing reality on the ground following the intifada King Hussein began stressing the religious nature of the city with an attempt to preserve at least Jordan's role in the holy places (mostly the Haram al-Sharif) as a source for legitimacy for the Hashemite rule in Jordan. Jordan worked hard in the international arena to complain against Israeli policies of creating facts on the ground in East Jerusalem such as the demolition of the Mughrabi neighbourhood to make room for the Western Wall Plaza, nationalisation of the Jewish Quarter that included a number of Muslim religious monuments, building Jewish neighbourhoods, Israel's Basic Law Jerusalem of 1980, Israeli Police storming Al-Aqsa compound in October 1990 resulted in the killing of 17 Muslims, and archaeological excavations. Its most significant success was the inclusion of the Old City of Jerusalem among UNESCO's list of world heritage sites in danger.

Hussein's advisor, Adnan Abu Odeh published in 1992 an article in Foreign Affairs titled *Two Capitals in an Undivided Jerusalem* proposing that Arab neighbourhoods of Jerusalem would come under future Palestinian control but that the Old City will have no sovereign (but God) and would be administered by a religious council of the three monotheistic faiths. Experts interpreted the article as conveying the king's view renouncing Jerusalem to the Palestinians while sticking to be involved in the administration of the holy places.

Peace with Israel

The September 1993 Oslo Accords between the PLO and Israel that included a clause regarding Jerusalem to be negotiated between the two parties in the final status agreement surprised Jordan. While negotiating peace with Israel, King Hussein insisted and succeeded to convince Israel to agree to what was enumerated in the Israel-Jordan Peace Agreement of 1994 in article 9(2): "In this regard, in accordance with the Washington Declaration, Israel respects the present special role of the Hashemite Kingdom of Jordan in Muslim Holy shrines in Jerusalem. When negotiations on the permanent status will take place, Israel will give high priority to the Jordanian historic role in these shrines."[19] As a matter of gesture, Israel allowed King Hussein to fly around Al-Haram al-Sharif on his way back from London to Amman. But the agreement and Israeli gestures did not help Jordan when the Palestinian Authority (PA) that was established in 1994 in the West Bank and the Gaza Strip contested Jordan over dominating East Jerusalem and Al-Haram al-Sharif.

The PA established its own Ministry of Waqf headed by a former Jordanian Jerusalem Waqf administrator Hasan Tahboub who placed his office in one of the Waqf assets inside the Old City and the PA also nominated its Mufti to compete with the Jordanian Mufti in Jerusalem until the later retired.[20] Jordan failed to receive recognition of the December 1994 convention of the Organisation of Islamic Conference representing 57 pre-dominant Muslim countries as custodian of the holy places of Jerusalem.[21]

With the Palestinian failures to gain control in East Jerusalem due to Israeli policies, Jordan became the only actor who could use its good relations with Israel, on the one hand, and its standing in the international community, on the other hand, to prevent harsh unilateral Israel measures in East Jerusalem, not always with success. Jordan resisted Israeli land expropriation in Arab neighbourhoods including Jabel Abu Ghneim (Israeli Har Homa) and denounced the 1995 US Congress decision to transfer its embassy from Tel Aviv to Jerusalem.

Following the 1996 Israel's unilateral opening of an exit to the Western Wall tunnel (Hasmonean tunnel) and King Hussein's sharp criticism of Israel, PA President Yasser Arafat was convinced that it would be irresponsible to distant Jordan from protecting Arab East Jerusalem. Hence, he agreed that Jordan will have a temporary custodianship over the holy places (only) and will hand it back to the Palestinian when they establish their capital in the city. In a 1997 public letter written by King Hussein to his prime minister, he said that article 9(2) of the peace agreement with Israel was not aimed at harming the right "of our brothers to establish their capital in Jerusalem." What enraged the Palestinians was that the capital of a future Palestinian state will be "in Jerusalem" instead of "Jerusalem."[22]

---

[20] Dumper, *Jerusalem Unbound*, p. 133.
[21] Klein, *Jerusalem: The Contested City*, p. 173.
[22] Har-Zvi, p. 254; David, Changes in Jordan's Positions.
[23] David.

Abdullah II Reign Since 1999

Like his father, King Abdullah II's policy was focused on sustaining the Hashemite role in the holy places in Jerusalem, notably Al-Haram al-Sharif as a source of legitimacy but he adapted his positions to the changing political realities. During the lifetime of Arafat, Abdullah was less enthusiastic and less emotionally attached to Jerusalem. Jordanian Member of Parliament Abd al-Ra'uf al-Rawabdeh even said in an interview to Jordan's official TV in 1999 that "if our Palestinian brothers will show interest in being responsible on the Waqf affairs [including the Haram, YR], then Jordan will relinquish its responsibility in their favour." King Abdullah even went further by saying that "the Palestinians have the right to take responsibility over their capital during negotiations and undertake the final responsibility. The holy places are under international and Arab responsibility."[23] When he was appointed prime minister, Rawabdeh was in *Newsweek* magazine in June 2000 with the following exchange of Q&A:

> Q: Jordan is currently the guardian of the Muslim holy sites in east Jerusalem. If there is a peace agreement between the Palestinian and the Israelis, would Jordan want to keep that "special status" or give it to the new Palestinian state?
> A: Our view is that in the future, the holy sites, which are the responsibility of Jordan, should be in a free city, open to the three religions – Jews, Christians, and Muslims.
> Q: But would you like to see them remain the property of the Hashemite kingdom?
> A: No, when you talk about Jerusalem's being an open city, you change the equation. In other words: the holy sites need to be run by the three religions.

When in July 2000 peace negotiations between Israel and the Palestinians took place in the Camp David II summit, Abdullah did not insist on a special role for Jordan in Jerusalem because he evaluated the Palestinians as a strong power.[24] He refrained from publicly confronting the PA due to internal Jordanian politics since the Jordanian Palestinians comprise a majority of the population. He even defended the PLO strongholds in Jerusalem and strongly criticised Israel when it closed down the

---

[24] Har-Zvi, p. 289.
[25] David.

PA offices in the Orient House at the heart of Jerusalem as well as denouncing Israel's construction of the security barrier in and around Jerusalem. However, following the weakening of the PA since 2002 and the death of Arafat in November 2004, Abdullah made many efforts to regained power in Jerusalem and particularly over the Haram.

Since 2002, Jordan was involved in physical repairs (such as the bulge in the Southern Wall) and other public works in the Haram. Israel welcomed the Jordanian involvement to weaken the Palestinian and Israeli Islamist strongholds in this holy shrine. In return, it expected a political remuneration from Israel which allowed Jordan to invest four million dinars in infrastructure works inside the Haram (completed) and to build a fifth minaret to be identified with Hashemites (rejected). It was officially presented as marking the five pillars of Islam and reinforcing the Islamic nature of the city. In 2006, King Abdullah even announced a public architectural competition to planning the minaret. He also announced establishing a special fund for the upkeep of the Haram, nominating his advisor for religious affairs, Prince Ghazi Bin-Talal as its director and donated on his own account a new prayer carpet to Al-Aqsa Mosque (installed in 2011). Jordan at that time defined its role in Jerusalem as "religious custodianship" (*ri'aya diniya*).

The website of the Royal Committee for Jerusalem Affairs in a section in Arabic dedicated to "Jordan and Jerusalem" differs between two types of sovereignty in Jerusalem; the political one in which the Palestinians are the sovereigns in the eastern part and the Israelis in its western part and the religious one, the walled city of which the sovereignty belongs to God. Jordan aspires to symbolise and represent this sovereignty. However, the drafters of this page honestly admit that the principle of religious sovereignty disappeared with the passing of King Hussein, and thus, it is no longer discussed. This is said because the "new Jordanian leadership" tends to avoid any Palestinian sensitivity and to call for an Israeli intervention and particularly in order not to poison Jordanian-Palestinian relations. The authors distinguish between the Hashemite spiritual attachment to the city that still exits and the strategic demographic and political aspect that invoked a change in Jordan's policy.[25]

In 2008, Jordan expressed its concerns that Israel continues the process of Judaising the character of Jerusalem that will turn the city into a museum empty of residents. King Abdullah stressed the responsibility of

---

[26] Reiter, *Contested Holy Places in Israel-Palestine*, p. 70.

Jordan as a "historical deposit on our shoulders" until Jerusalem will be liberated from occupation. He emphasised that the sovereignty (*siyada*) on the Islamic holy places is under Jordanian responsibility "and we will protect it to defend Al-Aqsa Mosque and other holy places in Jerusalem until the formation of the independent sovereign Palestinian state with Jerusalem as its capital."

Another important project connecting Jordan to Al-Aqsa was the restoration of the preacher pulpit—Nur al-Din Minbar—that was burned down in the 1969 fire. The restoration work lasted four years at the cost of 1.25 million dinars, and the *Minbar* was installed in the mosque in 2007 and Abdullah's intention to inaugurate the installation in person was nixed by the Palestinians.

To gain Palestinian recognition of its custodianship over Jerusalem's holy places Jordan also resisted in the international arena Israel's plan to replace the Mughrabi Ramp with a new bridge.[26] Bilateral discussions between Jordanian and Israeli officials resulted in an agreement in November 2011, but due to a leak of part of the agreement to the press, the project was put on hold and did not materialise until early 2018. In April 2012, Jordan already felt strong enough versus Palestinian opposition to dispatch Prince Ghazi Bin-Talal to visit Al-Aqsa Mosque together with the Chief Mufti of Egypt. Interestingly, when Jordan realised the 2007 split among the PA between Fatah and Hamas, it named its custodianship over historical Jerusalem "sovereignty."[27]

A remarkable turn symbolising Jordan's status regarding the Arab part of Jerusalem occurred in March 2013 with the agreement signed by the PLO Chairman and PA President Mahmoud Abbas and King Abdullah II. The deal served the interests of both parties after the 2012 UN General Assembly resolution that recognised Palestine as a non-member state and reconfirmed Jordan's special role in the territory of the "Palestinian state."

The preamble of the agreement states:

> D. Recalling the role of King Al-Sharif Hussein Bin Ali in protecting, and taking care of the Holy Sites in Jerusalem and in the restoration of the Holy Sites since 1924; recalling the uninterrupted continuity of this role by His Majesty King of the Hashemite Kingdom of Jordan, who is a descendant of Al-Sharif Hussein Bin Ali; recalling that the Bay'ah (oath of allegiance) according to which Al-Sharif Hussein Bin Ali held the custodianship of the

---

[27] David.

Jerusalem Holy Sites, which Custodianship was affirmed to Al-Sharif Hussein Bin Ali by the people of Jerusalem and Palestine on March 11, 1924; and recalling that the Custodianship of the Holy Sites of Jerusalem has devolved to His Majesty King Abdullah II Bin al-Hussein; including that which encompasses the "Rum" (Greek) Orthodox Patriarchate of Jerusalem that is governed by the Jordanian Law No 27 of the year 1958.[28]

According to the agreement, King Abdullah will: "administer the Islamic Holy Sites and to maintain them so as to (i) respect and preserve their religious status and significance; (ii) reaffirm the proper identity and sacred character of the Holy Sites; and (iii) respect and preserve their historical, cultural and artistic significance and their physical fabric; to represent the interests of the Holy Sites in relevant international forums and competent international organizations through feasible legal means; to oversee and manage the institution of Waqf in Jerusalem and its properties in accordance with the laws of the Hashemite Kingdom of Jordan."[29]

> The Jordanian king has a great interest in retaining the title of "Guardian of the Holy Places," which gives him a status and influence that are also important domestically. The Palestinian Authority, for its part, obtained renewed recognition of the sole right to represent the Palestinian people that is entrusted to the PLO, while making clear that the Jordanian role does not contravene its claim to sovereignty over all of the West Bank without any exceptions.[30] King Abdullah gained recognition as the major Islamic protector of the holy places in Jerusalem and as the Muslim leader who traces his genealogy to the house of Prophet Muhammad and who is legitimated to maintain the Hashemites' historic role as guardians of the holy places of Islam. What could be concluded from this agreement is that Jordan under the leadership of King Abdullah expects in any future settlement regarding Jerusalem no more than a symbolic role in the third holiest place for Islam and that this is aimed only to sustain the Hashemite legitimacy to rule Jordan.

[28] http://jcpa.org/the-agreement-on-jerusalem-between-the-palestinian-authority-and-jordan-initial-implications/
[29] http://jcpa.org/the-agreement-on-jerusalem-between-the-palestinian-authority-and-jordan-initial-implications/
[30] http://jcpa.org/the-agreement-on-jerusalem-between-the-palestinian-authority-and-jordan-initial-implications/

AL-HARAM AL-SHARIF (TEMPLE MOUNT) CONTROVERSY 2014–17

Al-Haram al-Sharif has been a central issue of Jerusalem also in Jordan's relations with Israel. On June 1967, a new era began in the history of the site when for the first time since the destruction of the Second Temple the Jews regained free access to the site, at pre-set visiting times that were coordinated between Israel and the Jordanian Waqf administration on the spot, but without praying. Israel entrusted the Waqf authorities to manage the Haram, which resulted in a new modus vivendi based on the arrangements tacitly agreed upon between Israel and the Jordanian Waqf after 1967 and provided an effective tool for controlling confrontation until September 1996. The routine matters that evolved between 1967 and 1996 proved themselves as a new status-quo that both parties could live with, although neither party fully achieved its desired goals.[31]

Israel's opening of the Western Wall Tunnel exit in September 1996 enraged King Hussein who claimed that Israel surprised him in spite of the good relations between the two governments. Another serious affair took place in September 2000 when Ariel Sharon, then leader of the opposition, demonstratively visited the holy compound. The events following this visit set the trigger for the outbreak of the second Palestinian uprising known as the Al-Aqsa intifada. Although subordinated to Jordan, the Waqf employees are Palestinians and they dictated closing the Haram for visitors. In August 2003, after pre-informing Jordan, Israel unilaterally enforced the reopening of the site to Jewish and other non-Muslim visitors and a gradual process put Jordanians and Palestinians on the same side against Israeli actions.

On the other hand, Israeli Jewish zealots endorsed religious nationalists including many rabbis to visit the Temple Mt./Haram. Their political base assisted in impacting members of the Israeli government and members of Knesset who expressed their support in many ways: visitation, exerting pressure on the police to allow more Jews in bigger groups to ascent the Mount. The Muslims are concerned that this activity intends to take over the Haram from them reacted by organising "study groups" of men and women to harass the Jewish religious groups visitors. When in the summer of 2014 violence broke out at the Haram and the Israeli police stormed the compound Jordan accused the Israeli government for supporting the extremists.[32] King Abdullah was cited by a Jordanian newspaper saying: "As

---

[31] Reiter, *The Eroding Status Quo*, p. 29.
[32] *Al-Rai*, 25 September 2014.

Hashemite custodian of Jerusalem's Muslim and Christian Holy Sites, I will continue to oppose any violation of Al Aqsa Mosque's sanctity," he warned.[33]

A year later, the incidents around the Haram compound accelerated to Palestinian riots, demonstrations, and individual terror actions. They were calmed down only after the involvement of the US administration. In a meeting with Mahmoud Abbas and King Abdulla the Jordanian demanded the stationing of surveillance cameras inside the Haram and US Secretary of State John Kerry publicly announced that Prime Minister Benjamin Netanyahu agreed to this. The Jordanian suggested to establish continuous around-the-clock (24/7) cameras inside the holy compound. Yet, due to disagreement between Israel and Jordan about the responsibility for the camera monitoring and with Palestinian opposition the surveillance cameras were not installed. For the first time since 1967 an Israeli prime minister announced that, "Only Muslims may pray on the Temple Mount and non-Muslims may only visit."[34]

Another example of the delicate situation of both Jordan and Israel vis-à-vis the Palestinians is the metal detectors crisis of July 2017. Two days after a 14 July terror action in which two Israeli policemen were fatally shot by three Palestinian citizens of Israel at the Haram, Israel unilaterally stationed surveillance cameras and metal detectors at its entrances. The Palestinian reaction was a complete resistance by organising mass demonstrations and mass prayers on the streets leading to the Haram and banning the entrance to and their own prayer inside the Haram. Mass violence and warnings from Jordan and other Arab countries resulted by the Israeli withdrawal and dismantling the new facilities, an action that restored order in Jerusalem. More violent actions spread in the West Bank. King Abdullah's request to Netanyahu in a phone call led to the Israeli decision to remove the metal detectors. Here again, like in the early 2000s, Jordan acted as the responsible go-between actor regarding the most sensitive site in Jerusalem contributing to the end of the crisis.

Conclusion

Jordan's policy regarding Jerusalem emanates mainly from the quest of the Hashemite monarchs for legitimacy as rulers of Jordan in light of political challenges from the Palestinians of both banks of the Jordan

---

[33] *Al-Rai*, 25 September 2014.
[34] Reiter, *The Eroding Status Quo*, p. 141.

River, from the Israelis and other competing Arab states. The custodianship over the third Islamic holy site—Al-Haram al-Sharif—serves Hashemite Jordan as a religious symbol of legitimacy, underlining some 700 years of Hashemite leadership of Mecca as servants of the holy shrines of Islam to be complemented with a special attachment to the Nobel Sanctuary in Jerusalem.

Being a vulnerable country, Jordan leaders have had to manoeuvre between different contenders over Jerusalem, and hence, the Jordanian position regarding the future of the city changed over time. King Abdullah I seized Jerusalem and wished to control it to safeguard his rule by the annexation of Jerusalem and the West Bank to Jordan. His grandson, King Hussein opted to maintain Hashemite legitimacy while coping with many internal and regional challenges, Israel, the Palestinians, and Arab neighbours. However, both Hussein and his successor Abdullah II needed to adapt their positions regarding Jerusalem according to the political reality on the ground. When the PLO was strong, the Hashemite monarchs had to renounce sovereignty over the territory and only maintain the symbolic religious attachment to the Haram. However, when the Palestinian Authority was weak, they tried to re-claim political responsibility for the eastern part of the city.

In sum, at the end of the second decade of the third millennium, it seems that Jordan relinquished its claim for sovereignty in Jerusalem and seeks only a symbolic role in its Islamic holy places to sustain its historical and political legitimacy.

References

Abdullah, I. a.-H. (1979). *Al-Takmila min Muzakirrat Hadrat Sahib al-Jalalah al-Hashimiyya al-Malik Abdallah ibn al-Husayn*. Amman: Umar al-Madani.

Azaryahu, M., & Reiter, Y. (2015). The (geo)politics of interment: An inquiry into the burial of Muhammad Ali in Jerusalem, 1931. *Israel Studies, 20*(1 Spring), 31–56.

David, A. (2008, February 2). *Changes in Jordan's positions regarding Jerusalem in the last decade*. Tel Aviv: ECF. [Hebrew].

Dumper, M. (1997). *The politics of Jerusalem since 1967*. New York: Columbia University Press.

Dumper, M. (2014). *Jerusalem unbound: Geography, history & the future of the Holy City*. New York: Columbia University Press.

Gelber, Y. (2004). *Israeli-Jordanian dialogue 1948–1953 – Cooperation, conspiracy or collusion?* Brighton: Sussex University Press.

Halabi, U. (1993). *Baladiyyat al-Quds al-Arabiyya*, Al-Quds: PASSIA. [Arabic].
Har-Zvi, S. (2014). *From Abdullah to Abdullah: Jordan's policy on Jerusalem – The regional and national contexts*. Dissertation submitted for a Ph.D. degree at Tel Aviv University. [Hebrew].
Katz, K. (2005). *Jordanian Jerusalem: Holy places and national spaces*. Gainesville: University Press of Florida.
Klein, M. (2001). *Jerusalem: The contested city*. London: Hurst.
Merhav, R., & Giladi, R. M. (2002). The role of the Hashemite Kingdom of Jordan in a future permanent status settlement in Jerusalem. In M. J. Breger & O. Ahimeir (Eds.), *Jerusalem, a city and its future* (pp. 175–202). Syracuse: Syracuse University Press.
Musa, Suleiman (1982). *Ayam la tunsa: Al-Urdun fi Harb 1948*. Amman. [Arabic].
Reiter, Y. (1997). *Islamic institutions in Jerusalem: Palestinian Muslim administration under Jordanian and Israeli rule*. The Hague/London/Boston: Kluwer Law International.
Reiter, Y. (2008). *Jerusalem and its role in Islamic solidarity*. New York: Palgrave Macmillan.
Reiter, Y. (2017). *The eroding status quo: Power struggles on the Temple mount*. Jerusalem: The Jerusalem Institute for Policy Research.

Jordan-Hamas Relations

Hillel Frisch

The Hashemite Kingdom of Jordan, which in its short history, has been one of the most threatened states in the world; the imperialist puppet that Gamal Abdul Nasser felt had to be removed; the scourge of the radical left Palestinian factions, one of which, the Popular Front for the Liberation of Palestine, even placed its erasure on its logo, is obviously a state that is dedicated to maintaining its existence by keeping its many enemies and rivals off-balance. One of these has been Hamas, the Palestinian sister organisation of the Jordanian Muslim Brotherhood.

Jordan, Hamas, and the Palestinian Movement

The emphasis of the Jordanian state regarding both Hamas and the local sister organisation is to keep enemies off-balance and divide rather than to destroy them. As the Moroccan monarchy dealt with its rivals, the very existence of many rivals offers the opportunity to divide and rule over the Kingdom's foes.

Hamas, in the first decade of its existence, fit the equation perfectly. The Palestine Liberation Organisation (PLO), which the Israeli government of Yitzhak Rabin during the Oslo process enabled to transform from an increasingly weak diaspora entity into a state-in-the-making in the West Bank (and

H. Frisch (✉)
Bar-Ilan University, Ramat-Gan, Israel

Gaza Strip), was a growing threat to the Kingdom with a clear Palestinian majority. Hamas' rise in the first intifada offered not only to be a counterweight to the growing threat posed by the Palestinian Authority under Yasser Arafat, King Hussein's nemesis, but even more bore the possibility of splitting the Palestinian camp in the future both within and outside Jordan.

This explains why in the last decade of the twentieth century and the first of Hamas' existence, Jordan enabled Hamas to set up an office in Amman in 1991, which was in effect the Political Bureau of Hamas, its highest governing body, composed of the organisation's highest ranking leaders outside of Gaza. These included Khalid Masha'al who officially became head of the Political Bureau (PB) in 1996, Ibrahim Ghosheh, the organisation's spokesperson, Muhammad Nazzal, the local Hamas representative, all of whom were Jordanian citizens and later on Musa Abu Marzouk.

Though the Jordanian authorities turned a blind eye to the existence of the Hamas office as the political centre of the movement and described it merely as the Hamas office in the Kingdom, relations were often strained. Hamas' inflammatory statements against the Oslo peace process from 1993 onwards calling for the destruction of Israel and its declaration that it "does not differentiate between the Oslo agreement and the Jordanian-Israeli agreement; we oppose and reject both," (Kumaraswamy 2001). The peace treaty signed between Israel and Jordan in 1994 was one source of continuous tension. The other was the involvement of Hamas activists in Jordan in terrorist acts executed in Israel. In 1992, Hamas activists were arrested along with an unnamed senior member of the Islamic Action Front (IAF), the political party of the Muslim Brotherhood within Jordan.

The political presence of Hamas in the capital aroused the ire of the Palestinian Authority (PA), leading to calls on Amman to withdraw its tacit support of Hamas, which contested Arafat's authority by calling to replace the PLO with a new national body. In April 1996, Palestinians officials even blamed Jordan for allowing the presence of a Hamas activist who was conspiring to assassinate Arafat.

Israel's disapproval was also palpable. In April 1994, Prime Minister Yitzhak Rabin sharply criticised the existence of the office, whose representatives expressed warm support for a massive suicide bombing within Israel at the time. The Jordanian authorities reacted by a demand on Hamas to cease making political declarations. To back up their call, the passports of Nazzal and Ghosheh were withheld. A year later, Jordan expelled 'Imad al-Alami and Abu Marzouk, both foreign nationalists, for their support of suicide bombings.

Combined PA and Israeli pressures were probably responsible for the detention of Ghosheh in September 1997 who had aroused the PA's wrath for threatening the PA with internal strife were it to implement its intent of making mass arrests in Hamas ranks to reduce the organisation's terrorist activities. Israel protested against his declarations, which once again supported suicide bombings.

The Jordanian decision to deny Ahmad Yassin, the founder of Hamas, a visit to the country in late May–early June 1998, reflected by then, an increasingly troubled relationship between the Jordanian state and the movement. After all, it was King Hussein who was responsible for his release from prison as the price Israel paid for the release of two Mossad agents in an attempt to assassinate Masha'al in Amman in September 1997. Yassin's visit to Jordan was to be a part of the tour of several Gulf countries. The king also announced that he "would not have alternatives or hold a dialogue with alternatives," an obvious allusion to attempts to find an alternative to the PLO and the PA, to assuage PLO fears.

The presence of the Hamas office became even more untenable after the signing of the Wye River Memorandum in October 1998, in which Israel agreed to further withdrawals (deployments as they were described in the document) in favour of the PA. The Jordanian authorities warned Masha'al and Nazzal from travelling to Syria at the cost of not being able to come back. Masha'al and Nazzal might have been exploring the possibility of setting up base in Damascus. It is interesting to note that the threat showed that Jordan was still interested in the existence of the Hamas office.

The Turning Point

The year 1999 marks the turning point. From a relationship characterised by intense interaction to a marginal inimical relationship at least directly as stronger states such as Israel, later Saudi Arabia and Egypt increasingly contained and rolled back Hamas power without the need for direct Jordanian involvement. King Abdullah, who had just succeeded his father Hussein, made several swift moves painful to Hamas; on 31 August 1999, five commercial offices in Amman registered under the names of Hamas leaders were closed; many Hamas activists were detained; and arrest warrants were issued against six Hamas leaders, namely bureau chief Khalid Masha'al, 'Izzat al-Rishq, Nazzal and politburo members Musa Abu

Marzouk, Sami Khater, and Ibrahim Ghosheh. Al-Rishq and Nazzal went into hiding. The latter three were on a visit to Iran along with Masha'al.

How swift and unexpected was the move became apparent in an interview Ghosheh gave to the Beirut-based *Al-Nahar* a day after the crackdown when he claimed that Jordan had "not asked any of Hamas leaders to leave the country." A shocking rebuff met Hamas' hopes to restore ties with the Jordanian Kingdom. Masha'al and his colleagues were arrested at the Amman airport when they returned from Tehran on 22 September. Abu Marzouk, who held a Yemeni passport, was quickly deported. Deciding the fate of Masha'al, Khater, al-Rishq, and Ghosheh was more complicated as they were Jordanian citizens of Palestinian origin. In a move legally and constitutionally problematic, they were given the option of either being tried in the security court for membership in an illegal organisation or leaving Jordan.

King Abdullah made it clear that for him, the Hamas presence in Jordan was not a political problem but "a criminal issue." He was responding to fears expressed in the Jordanian press that the deportations established a dangerous precedent "for expelling Jordanians of Palestinian origin who are somehow affiliated with a Palestinian opposition faction."

In moving against Hamas, the Kingdom reinstated a doctrine from the "Black September" era, namely, the State's resolve not to allow "Jordanian citizens to work for a non-Jordanian organisation from Jordanian territory" (Kumaraswamy 2001). There were even veiled suggestions that Hamas posed threats to Jordan reminiscent of the PLO's threat to the Hashemite monarchy in September 1970. One Jordanian official was quoted as saying that "Hamas grew to such an extent that it infiltrated hardliners among Islamists in Jordan and began controlling them, as well as some opposition groups, in a way that brings to mind the tragic events of 1970 Black September" (Kumaraswamy 2001). Similarly, some Hamas leaders alluded to Jordan's "September complex." The authorities also refused to accept Hamas claims that an agreement existed between Hamas and King Hussein which protected the group's "media and information activity" in Jordan.

The fate of the rank and file detainees was no better; though at first they were charged with minor charges such as affiliation with an illegal organisation and possession of light arms, the final charge sheet included charges, some of which were punishable by death. These included running a military training camp, weapons storage, and armed activities against Israel.

Two months of intense negotiations between members of the Muslim Brotherhood and the government ensued, the outcome of which was somewhat of a compromise, though leaning against Hamas. King Abdullah emphatically upheld Prime Minister Abdul Raouf Rawabda's decision to close the Hamas office: "Jordan has made itself quite clear. Hamas offices will be shut down and this is what will happen." The four Hamas leaders were deported to Doha on 22 November after the Emir of Qatar offered "to host" them. After the deportations, Hamas continued its campaign for the reversal of the Jordanian position. It resorted to demonstrations, protest rallies, media criticisms, legal challenges, third-party mediation, and direct appeals to the king. The arrests and deportations were also seen as a setback to King Abdullah's commitments for democratisation.

Both the decision and the timing of the crackdown have been attributed to external pressures, especially from the PA, as well as to the onset of final status negotiations. The crackdown, according to one commentator, was inevitable because Hamas had "antagonised the PA, antagonised Israel and added militancy to the Muslim Brotherhood in Jordan" (Kumaraswamy 2001). Nevertheless, one must agree with yet another Palestinian commentator who remarked: "Irrespective of the analyses and how correct they are, Jordan would not have taken such a big step against the Hamas movement based only on external pressure if this step did not coincide with its political considerations and factors for its internal stability" (Kumaraswamy 2001).

So determined was the monarchy in ridding Jordan of an official Hamas presence that when Hamas spokesman Ibrahim Ghosheh arrived unexpectedly in Amman in the summer of 2001 from exile, defying a November 1999 government decree that banned the militant Palestinian Islamist group's activities, many expected Jordan to accept a compromise formula that would allow Hamas to resume its presence in the Kingdom. Neither a subsequent confrontation with the Qatari government nor the on-going Intifada weakened King Abdullah's resolve. After spending more than two weeks at the Amman airport, Ghosheh was forced to "freeze" his membership in Hamas in return for re-entry into the country, thereby establishing a precedent for other exiled Hamas leaders.

Masha'al and his colleagues after being deported to Qatar, soon found refuge in Syria, yet another political actor with a long record of undermining the Kingdom. Both countries had a shared history of giving shelter to the opposition of the other. As far back as 1949, Colonel Abdullah al-Tal, ex-military governor of Jerusalem, and Musa Abdullah Husseini, accused of plotting an assassination attempt against King Abdullah I, found refuge in Syria. So did Arab nationalist chairman of the Joint Chiefs of Staff, Ali Abu Nuwar, in 1957, after King Hussein accused him of trying to overthrow him. The following year it was the turn of Major-General Ali al-Hiyari, Abu Nuwar's chief rival in the Jordanian army, who was appointed as Abu Nuwar's replacement, and he too fell out with the king and fled to Damascus. In 1963, Abu Nuwar declared from Damascus a government-in-exile in the name of the Jordanian Republic and disseminated propaganda through his own radio station. Jordan responded by providing refuge to Syrian Muslim Brotherhood leaders who ran afoul of the Syrian Baathist regime. This was especially in evidence after the failed 1982 Hama uprising. The expulsion of the Hamas leadership and subsequent welcome in Damascus has to be seen in this vein.

This sharp contrast between the last decade of King Hussein and later the reign of King Abdullah II begs the question why this happened. The thesis presented at the beginning of the chapter provides the answer except that under new circumstances, the divide and rule principle called for passive rather than active behaviour on the part of Jordan. Under Hussein, Jordan felt it had to empower Hamas to play the divide and rule role in the Palestinian camp. In the subsequent two decades, the dynamics outside Jordan's control realised the Kingdom's political objectives without any effort on Jordan's part.

Changing Regional Dynamics in the Twenty-First Century

For the Kingdom, this was a truly auspicious change. Until then, regional dynamics usually worked against Jordan's interests, now they played to its benefit. The al-Aqsa intifada, as opposed to the first, reflected the growing polarisation and growing symmetry of power between the PLO/PA/Fatah and Hamas. The latter became the first organisation since the re-emergence of the PLO in 1964, to surpass Fatah in terrorist activities, mainly with spectacular and deadly suicide bombings. Even more important, the organisation throughout the second intifada maintained its unity. The PA, its security agencies, and Fatah, by contrast, were riven by internal division, especially in the Gaza Strip, where firefights between rival security agencies and Fatah took place almost daily. Israel's unilateral withdrawal from the Gaza Strip in 2005 also played into Jordan's hand by setting in motion the growing geographical division of the Palestinian population between the West Bank and Gaza with almost no physical interaction between the two since the Israeli withdrawal.

By far, the most critical developments in this regard was the decision by Hamas to contest the 2006 elections to the Palestinian Council, its subsequent electoral victory and the establishment of a Hamas government in the Gaza Strip. One of its first moves was to set up a Hamas-dominated security force, the Executive Force, under the Ministry of Interior. The step, rendered illegal by President Mahmoud Abbas' edict, set in motion five rounds of conflict between the PA security forces answering to Abbas in Ramallah, the Fatah al-Aqsa Martyr Brigades on one side, against the Hamas Executive Force, the Izz ad-Din Martyr Brigades, which culminated in the Hamas takeover of Gaza in June 2007 and the division of the Palestinians into two separate entities.

Arab Spring and the Marginalisation of Hamas

Subsequent developments were even more auspicious for the Kingdom. Jordan could only be pleased with the growing security cooperation between Abbas' newly US-trained forces and the Israel Defence Forces and the Israel Security Agency in severely weakening the Hamas terrorist and political infrastructure. Meanwhile, Israel launched its first of three punishing rounds against Hamas in Gaza in December 2008 followed by two more rounds in 2012 and in the summer of 2014, which was by far the most punishing and lasted 50 days. Hamas has increasingly been deterred. Whereas in the two years before the first round, Hamas launched nearly 3000 missiles, in the three years following the third round, only 75 missiles have been launched, mostly by Salafi organisations which defy Hamas authority.

As Hamas was increasingly mauled physically, the PA was also losing domestic political ground as a result of the intensive security cooperation efforts in which Israel apprehended terrorists at night, and PA forces hit at the Hamas civil organisations by day and monitored former Hamas and Jihad al-Islami prisoners. Clearly, at the turn of the new century, the threat the Palestinians posed to Jordan since the re-emergence of the Palestinian national movement in 1964 was receding in its favour as the rival Palestinian entities repressed their respective internal opposition.

Further good fortune for Jordan, at least regarding Hamas, came in the wake of the Arab Spring uprising that broke out in Syria in March

2011. The uprising increasingly pitted a Sunni majority in the suburbs of Syria's major cities, small towns, and villages against an Alawite regime backed by Iran and proxy heterodox (mostly Shiite) militias, the most prominent of which was Hezbollah, the militant Shiite organisation in Lebanon. At first, Hamas adopted a "wait-and-see" attitude towards the civil war rather than coming out in support of the Assad regime as the latter demanded to provide critical financial and logistic support to the movement since 1999. Instead, Hamas emphasised the role of Syria as the host country for the resistance against Israel while stressing the legitimacy of the people's demands.

Its ambiguous stance aroused the ire of the Syrian regime reflected in increasing criticism of the organisation in the Syrian press. At the same time, Syrian undercover agents in the guise of Hamas members were seen suppressing anti-government demonstrations in the Hajar al-Aswad neighbourhood that bordered the Yarmuk Palestinian refugee camp in Damascus in an effort to drive a wedge between the organisation and the Syrian rebels and protestors.

Hamas felt compelled to leave Damascus and set up base in Qatar in February 2012, where they were undoubtedly less innocuous to the Jordanian state than operating from the Syrian capital. As the decision to leave Qatar for Damascus indicated, far-away Qatar was a second choice compared to Lebanon or Jordan. The desire to relocate to Amman was probably one of the reasons for Khalid Masha'al's visit to the Jordanian capital in January 2012. One must assume that Lebanon and Jordan were not willing to allow its political bureau to establish in their countries. In Lebanon, Hamas also feared Hezbollah in light of deteriorating relations with the Syrian regime and Iran, Syria's only ally at the time and the chief backer of Hezbollah.

Hamas was dealt a further blow with the ouster of Egyptian President Mohammad Morsi by the Egyptian military in July 2013 and the assumption of power by Abd al-Fattah al-Sisi who proceeded to outlaw and suppress the local Muslim Brotherhood and imprison its leadership. Egypt also moved against Hamas. The most notable single event is the abduction and disappearance of four Izz ad-Din Brigade members, Yasser Zanoun, Hussein al-Zabda, Abdullah Abu al-Jabin, and Abdel Dayem Abu Labda just outside the Egyptian side of the al-Rafah border crossing in August 2015. Presumably, they were en route to Iran for training. The Egyptian authorities never officially confirmed their arrest and were probably responsible for leaked photos of two of the four, Yasser Zanoun and

Abdulkareem Abulibda, who are seen incarcerated under harsh conditions a year after their abduction. Hamas-linked media sources since their abduction routinely report attempts by Hamas officials to broach the subject with the Egyptian security services and achieve their release but to no avail. According to the Hamas-affiliated *al-Resalah*, any progress on their release was contingent on Hamas' willingness in Sinai to fight the Islamic State, deploy additional security forces along the Rafah-Sinai borders, hand over to Egypt Palestinians who are allegedly involved in Sinai violence and wanted by Egyptian security forces.

Hamas also felt the new regime's iron fist as it systematically destroyed most of the underground smuggling—from which Hamas derived its income to finance its 30,000 strong security force (source) and 22,000 public servants (mostly teachers) it hired since 2007. With so many regional dynamics operating to keep the Palestinians weak and divided, there was no need for Jordan to maintain strong ties with Hamas or extend it a helping hand.

Only briefly during the height of the Arab spring as the Jordanian regime faced the threat that demonstrations for reform would turn into a widespread movement of protest, did it temporarily soften towards Hamas. Masha'al was allowed two visits to the Kingdom in 2012. On the second, he met King Abdullah, Prime Minister Fayez Tarawneh and director of the General Intelligence Directorate Faisal Shoubaki. The January 2013 was also the last to take place between the king and a Hamas leader. Jordan, subsequently, even responded with an indirect attack on Hamas for meddling in Muslim Brotherhood affairs in February 2015. An unprecedented accusation was levelled by Sharaf al-Qudat, head of the Muslim Brotherhood Scholars Council in Jordan, a group of legal scholars independent of the MB's Shura Council and close to the Jordanian monarchy. Qudat said that a secret organisation linked to Hamas is leading the hard-liners in Jordan.

This was vociferously denied by Hamas political bureau member, Sami Khater, who refused "to involve Hamas in the on-going dispute between the leaders of the Brotherhood in Jordan" about the split that took place within the IAF and the Muslim Brotherhood in Jordan. According to Khater, "Hamas has nothing to do with Jordan's internal affairs because it is a Palestinian national liberation movement that contents itself with freeing Palestine and facing the occupation." If a linkage did exist, it was—according to Murad Adayleh, a member of the IAF's executive bureau—at the behest of the Jordanian regime. He claimed that the chairman of the

Hamas political bureau, Masha'al, advised the Brotherhood to run in the parliamentary elections held in January 2013, after Jordan's royal authorities had asked him to do so.

Despite official efforts to curtail relations between Hamas and the IAF and the Muslim Brotherhood, Hamas impacts on Muslim Brotherhood members and relations between them. The hardliners, mostly of Palestinian origin, bolster their efforts to lead the Muslim Brotherhood by claiming an endorsement from Hamas, a claim Ali Abu Sukkar, the deputy head of the IAF, strenuously denied.

Little wonder that in 2015, Masha'al was denied his request to visit Jordan purportedly to congratulate deputy head of the Muslim Brotherhood Zaki Bani Ershaid upon his release from prison for defaming the United Arab Emirates. In other words, once the danger posed by the Arab uprisings passed, Jordanian policy towards the organisation became negative once again.

Even a Weak Hamas Is a Rival

Nevertheless, even a weakened Hamas is an organisation Jordan has to reckon with. Two major tension points in the relationship are Jordan's role on the /Haram al-Sharif/Tempe Mount—Hamas usually sides with the PA to undermine Jordan's role—and continuous Hamas attempts to bring about a mass uprising that would both damage Israel and undermine the PA. Jordan, as a status quo state, is dedicated as much as possible to preserve stability both on the Haram al-Sharif and in the West Bank in general. Jordan always fears that uprisings might lead to attempts of West Bank inhabitants to seek refuge in the Kingdom as they did in the past.

These tensions played out simultaneously during the demonstrations that took place in reaction to an Israeli-Jordanian agreement to place surveillance cameras on the Haram al-Sharif in October 2015, and those on a far larger scale that took place in summer 2017 surrounding attempts by Israel to set up metal detectors at the entrance to the Harem in the wake of a terrorist attack that began on the Temple Mount and ended in the killing of two Israeli Border Police as well as the three terrorists.

At the same time, Hamas tried desperately to transform the demonstrations into violent confrontations. Jordan, by contrast, relatively peaceful worked behind the scenes to keep the demonstrations peaceful and bring about an Israeli decision to rescind the decision after Jordan recalled its ambassador in Israel, Walid Abidat, in protest of the Israeli decision. Jordan was successful and the Israeli authorities dismantled the detectors, but it was also evident in the meeting of religious officials in Jerusalem to announce the victory over Israeli designs that the role of the Jordanian head of the Waqf was marginalised. It was the PA-backed Mufti of Jerusalem, Muhammad al-Husseini, who stood at centre-stage to make the speech. The Jordanian Waqf's "trusteeship" over the Haram, was not only criticised by Hamas but by members of the Jordanian Brotherhood as well.

Another continuous point of tension relates to Hamas' relationship to the Jordanian Muslim Brotherhood. Whereas Jordan's interest is to reduce the relationship between Hamas and the local Muslim Brotherhood if not efface it altogether, Hamas naturally would like to strengthen bonds between two sister organisations. Immediately after the Hamas takeover of Gaza, it was erroneously perceived at the time both within and outside the organisation that the action was a reflection of the organisation's growing strength and hawks of Palestinian origin headed by Hammam Said increased their leadership role of the Jordanian Muslim Brotherhood. Their ascendance reflected a growing bond between the two movements that could have only threatened the movement's leadership of east Jordanian origins.

In retrospect, the Jordanian leadership has succeeded in creating a split in the Jordanian Muslim Brotherhood towards marginalising the hardliners who are mostly of Palestinian origin. In Hamas itself in 2017, the leadership shifted from the "outside" to "inside" as Gaza-based Ismail Haniyeh succeeded Masha'al as the head of the Political Bureau of Hamas, and Yahya al-Sinwar, a former senior commander in the Izz ad-Din al-Qassam Brigades and former prisoner, became the second-in-command. Nevertheless, as a photo of a "victory" rally in Amman staged by the Muslim Brotherhood at the end of August 2014 to mark the termination of the longest round of Israel-Hamas conflict in Gaza, makes clear—a complete separation is difficult to maintain. Demonstrators are seen donning the green Hamas caps waving placards "We are all Hamas."

Preventing Hamas from using Jordan as a base against Israel also remains one of the top objectives in the Kingdom's relationship with Hamas. In December 2014, *Al-Jazeera* reported the uncovering by Jordanian intelligence of formation of a Hamas cell of 20 terrorists that were planning attacks in Israel of which at least two were Jordanian citizens. It later turned out that the group was directed by a Hamas operative and spokesperson, Husam Badran, who operated out of Qatar. The Jordanian members in the cell were involved in smuggling in gold jewellery to be used by the Nablus-based cell to finance their operations instead of cash that the cell members felt was too vulnerable to disclosure.

Occasional reports of failed attempts to plan, establish, and execute terrorist attacks from Jordan must, however, be seen as exceptions to the rule. The very fact that most of these efforts are foiled attest to Jordan's success in preventing Hamas from creating such a base on its soil. Hamas attempts to create such activity testifies equally to the tensions between Hamas and the Jordanian government.

Conclusion

Considerable tension and conflict mark the Jordanian-Hamas relations. Jordan allowed Hamas in the last decade of the twentieth century to operate its most crucial office outside the Gaza Strip and the West Bank, to offset the growing power of the PLO and the PA. As the prospects that the PA would transform into a full-fledged State of Palestine receded, so did Jordanian goodwill to Hamas disappear. In 1999, it expelled the "outside" Hamas leadership, a policy it has maintained ever since despite continuous attempts by Hamas to persuade Jordan to allow an official Hamas presence in Jordan. Tensions between the two sides surface over Hamas attempts to use Jordan as a basis of terrorist activity, over mobilising Palestinians over the Haram al-Sharif and against Israeli and PA rule, and over the relationship between Hamas and the Jordanian Brotherhood.

As marked as these tensions are, the two sides refrain from head-on, zero-sum confrontation with the goal of destroying each other. In the Middle East of today, such restraint cannot be taken for granted. It is also a relationship in which in the long run, Jordan has the upper hand and explicitly so, in the past five years as the PA, Israel, and Egypt joined forces to weaken Hamas.

Reference

Kumaraswamy, P. R. (2001, August/September). The Jordan-Hamas divorce. *Middle East Intelligence Bulletin, 3*(8). http://www.mafhoum.com/press2/60P2.htm

Political Reforms

Artur Malantowicz

Stability has traditionally been Jordan's ultimate objective in both foreign policymaking and domestic politics. Its location in a volatile and crisis-ridden region, multifaceted weakness vis-à-vis its neighbours, and little-to-no natural resources have, in the long term, paradoxically contributed to the regime's survival. Jordan's geopolitical centrality and strategic importance have been skilfully played by the Hashemites to secure political and military support of the global superpowers, resulting in a continuous inflow of foreign aid. Both have also been used in the regime's rhetoric of political reform, when stability was frequently invoked amidst regional threats, slowing down or completely eroding meaningful democratic changes (Malantowicz 2017).

Despite prior experience as a constitutional monarchy (the most liberal period being the early 1950s), the limited political opening in 1989, and subsequent liberalisation of the socio-economic system, the status quo in Jordan has remained mostly intact for the past three decades. It is still an authoritarian regime with the king being the central figure of the system, holding almost absolute power, and several hollow democratic institutions aimed primarily at appeasing the international audience the Kingdom relies on so heavily. Therefore, the Jordanian democratisation process has frequently been described negatively, as "defensive," "elusive," "frozen," "stalled," or "artificial."

A. Malantowicz (✉)
Centre for International Initiatives, Warsaw, Poland

© The Author(s) 2019
P. R. Kumaraswamy (ed.), *The Palgrave Handbook of the Hashemite Kingdom of Jordan*, https://doi.org/10.1007/978-981-13-9166-8_20

The three decades of political reforms in Jordan can be divided into four major phases, each characterised by a distinct international context, different priorities of the ruling family and associated political elites, and different outcomes for the socio-political system of the country. Between 1989 and 1993, an unprecedented opening of the political scene took place as a defensive reaction of the regime to internal and external pressures. It was quickly reverted to its previous state by King Hussein after 1993 when a significant re-orientation in Jordanian foreign policy was accompanied by a crackdown on political freedoms and civil liberties. With King Abdullah II ascending the throne in 1999, hopes were raised that further liberalisation of the political system was possible. However, key stakeholders of the process quickly became disillusioned when the security agenda co-opted democratic rhetoric concerning regional developments. It resulted in the stabilisation of the authoritarian regime, with a new impulse for change, both positive and negative, re-appearing only in the wake of the Arab protests at the end of 2010.

A Prelude to the Reforms: 1980–88

The 1980s economic crisis hit Jordan exceptionally hard. The collapse of the oil markets not only slowed down its economy (from 11.2 per cent in 1980 to 1.5 per cent in 1988) and contributed to the increase in unemployment (from 3.5 per cent in 1980 to 9 per cent in 1988), but also reduced private remittances from the Jordanians working in the Gulf as well as the foreign aid flows from the Gulf Arab states (Abu Rumman 2012). Budgetary constraints pushed the monarchy to seek the support of the international financial institutions to renegotiate its debt. These, in return, imposed an economic reform (structural adjustment) package that introduced numerous austerity measures—for example, new taxes, cuts in subsidies and central expenditures, and increases in the price of basic commodities—supplemented by fiscal and administrative reforms (Brynen 1992).

Soaring prices of food and fuel were met with public discontent and mass riots, initially only in southern Jordan, in Ma'an, Tafilah, and Karak (areas traditionally supportive of the monarchy), but eventually expanded throughout the country. Even though the protesters neither criticised the king nor made explicit requests for democratic reforms, they demanded that the austerity measures be revoked, the government resign, new parliamentary elections to be held, and corrupt officials be punished. This created a serious dilemma for the regime, which essentially had three options to choose from:

(a) Withdraw from the structural adjustment programme to appease the public and risk economic crash;
(b) Respond with force to the demonstrations and restore order at the expense of its own legitimacy; or
(c) Renegotiate the social contract, that is, liberalise the socio-political system in exchange for public consent to undergo the economic reforms (Brynen 1992).

In the face of international pressure, King Hussein eventually decided to dismiss the government and allowed for controlled political liberalisation.

Defensive Democratisation, 1989–93

The royal decision to pursue the democracy agenda is consistent with the concept of "defensive democratisation." This notion explains that in the face of crisis, a state attempts to pre-empt anticipated demands for political reform (Robinson 1998). In the case of Jordan, defensive and paced political liberalisation became a tool to re-establish the regime's authority and to restore stability, but also to limit the opposition's role in the Islamist movement, which had steadily gained momentum since the 1980s. Thus, the democratisation efforts could have served as a way of co-opting the Islamists into the mainstream politics and to strengthen political forces alternative to the religious right. King Hussein announced that the parliamentary elections would be held in November 1989.

The elections were organised on the basis of the amended electoral law of 1986 (the voters could cast several votes for candidates running in multi-mandate electoral districts), but in a rather unfavourable environment: political parties were still formally banned, while the official campaign lasted less than a month. This contributed to a privileged position of tribal candidates with extended patrimonial networks and individuals affiliated with the Muslim Brotherhood, the only political organisation freely operating at the time. Moreover, the electoral law preserved over-representation of predominantly tribal rural areas, as well as quotas for ethnic and religious minorities. Engineered this way, the popular vote was expected to fill the parliament with the traditional support base of the monarchy—the loyalists (Robinson 1998).

The electoral outcome, however, did not meet these expectations. With a relatively low and disappointing turnout (40 per cent), the Islamists became the strongest ideological bloc in the parliament, represented by 21 (out of 80) deputies from the Muslim Brotherhood and 13 independent Islamists. The remaining seats were divided between royal loyalists (22), representatives of the left and nationalist groups (13), and independent candidates (11) (Greenwood 2003). Initially, it was feared that the royal court would not accept such strong opposition in the parliament and would dissolve the body. Nevertheless, King Hussein saw this as an opportunity to co-opt Islamists into government (e.g., by offering them cabinet posts), expecting in return, their support for political pluralism and recognition of the role of the monarchy in the political system of Jordan. At the same time, a royal commission was appointed by the king to draft the Jordanian National Charter, a document meant to redefine the relationship between state and society as well as outline the framework for further liberalisation (Brynen 1992).

In the process of drafting the document, the opposition was presented with a simple offer by the regime: if they recognised the legitimacy of the Hashemite monarchy, political party pluralism would be reinstated in the country (Choucair-Vizoso 2008). The Islamists and the leftists accepted the offer, and the king eventually signed the National Charter in June 1991. On the one hand, the Charter can be regarded as a liberal and progressive document, affirming democratic and private property rights, intellectual pluralism, equality, tolerance, and freedom of political activity (including the right to form political parties). A step towards the demands of Islamists was the recognition of Islam as one of the four equal sources of law and political legitimacy in Jordan, next to *qawmiyyah* (Arab nationalism), *wataniyyah* (Jordanian nationalism), and universal norms (The Jordanian National Charter 1991). On the other hand, the Charter consolidated existing power structures, that is, by emphasising the importance of the institution of the hereditary Hashemite monarchy (Robinson 1998).

Meanwhile, the government of Prime Minister Mudar Badran was reshuffled with the aim to fully reflect ideological divisions of the Jordanian parliament and to neutralise the Islamist opposition (Lucas 2005). Among others, five Muslim Brotherhood deputies were offered cabinet positions, including the education portfolio. Soon after, however, the Brotherhood called for gender segregation in all schools and public offices and criticised

Jordan's involvement in the Middle East peace process. Consequently, both actions triggered a reaction from King Hussein who dissolved the government. Importantly, the royal decision did not reverse the general direction of political change in Jordan at that time. In July 1991, for instance, martial law was abolished, and a year later, the new Political Parties Law legalised political associations. While it remained highly restrictive—de facto prohibiting any financial or organisational foreign support for the parties and banning non-Jordanians from becoming members of political parties—for the first time in over 35 years, it allowed political activism in the public sphere. This has strengthened secular political movements, hitherto unable to challenge the power of the Islamists. By the time of the 1993 parliamentary elections, more than twenty parties had registered, including the Islamic Action Front (IAF), a political arm of the Muslim Brotherhood.

Equally crucial for the liberalisation process was the Press and Publications Law (1993), even though it was far from introducing full freedom of the media. While it lifted several restrictions on the press and allowed for licensing new (also private) media, it also set high registration fees for new media outlets and forced all practicing journalists to register with the Jordanian Press Club. It introduced a set of "red lines" for the press not to cross, de facto imposing (self-) censorship, for example, on the news offending the royal family, armed forces, and heads of states of friendly countries, and news damaging national unity or hurting public morals and ethics (Lucas 2005). Interestingly, the law enacted by the parliament was much more restrictive than the original draft submitted by the government. It was symptomatic of the changing political climate, with the pace of political reforms generally slowing by 1993.

DE-LIBERALISATION, 1993–99

When the US re-launched the Middle East peace process in the early 1990s, it was in the national interest of Jordan to join it. It was a chance to restore good relations with Washington (undermined by the Jordanian position during the 1990–91 Gulf War) and thus the US financial assistance and political support. King Hussein realised that the prospect of making peace with Israel would face strong domestic resistance and that simultaneous negotiations with Israel and increased domestic political opening were incongruous (Lucas 2005).

Hence, the regime introduced several measures meant to curb opposition, such as electoral law reform, and restrictions on public gatherings—to indicate that the liberalisation process has its limits and can be easily reversed. The primary target of these measures was the Islamist movement, with some of the most vocal opponents of the regime (e.g., independent Islamist Laith Shubeilat) subjected to hoaxed charges and imprisonment (Robinson 1998). To add further significance to the situation, King Hussein himself became involved in the campaign of discrediting the Muslim Brotherhood, publicly describing them as supporters of backwardness and as a tool for foreign influence in Jordan's domestic affairs (Robinson 1997).

Furthermore, in August 1993, shortly after the dissolution of the incumbent parliament, the royal decree amended the electoral law to ensure a more favourable stance of the legislature towards the peace process. It introduced the formula of a single non-transferable vote (SNTV), commonly known in Jordan as the "one-person, one-vote" system, aimed to weaken well-organised political movements and strengthen pro-regime independent and tribal candidates. Additionally, before the November 1993 elections, a ban on public rallies was introduced while public sector employees were deprived of the right to participate in the electoral campaign (Greenwood 2003).

As anticipated, the elections led to a reshuffle of the Jordanian political scene. The Islamists obtained only 22 seats in the new parliament, while most deputies—51 out of 80—represented groups loyal to the monarchy. Despite the results being contested due to irregularities in the voting procedure, they provided King Hussein with parliamentary support and a *carte blanche* to engage in the peace process. It was yet another proof that at the time, the monarchy was prioritising its foreign policy course at the expense of the liberalisation process (Lucas 2005).

Despite being weakened, the IAF continued to oppose the normalisation of relations with Israel, in the wake of the final peace negotiations taking place. Given the potential economic benefits of peace (e.g., debt relief, foreign investments, and financial assistance), the new government of Abd Al-Salam Al-Majali—Jordan's former chief negotiator during the Madrid peace process—could not allow it to be sabotaged. The Press and Publications Law of 1993 was used to impose restrictions on the most critical press outlets, while local councils in major cities, primarily controlled by the Islamists, were dissolved. Simultaneously, Crown Prince Hassan organised a meeting with key Islamic leaders in which he indicated that the use of mosques for political purposes would not be tolerated. Besides, the regime imprisoned some anti-Israeli activists and banned opposition rallies. Eventually, the peace treaty between Jordan and Israel was signed on 26 October 1994 and was ratified by the Jordanian parliament two weeks later (Robinson 1998).

As with the re-orientation of its foreign policy, the implementation of a package of liberal economic reforms was more of a priority to the regime than democratic change. At the beginning of 1996, the new head of government, Abd Al-Karim Kabariti, pledged to fight corruption and protect civil liberties. However, the main task of the new cabinet was to implement the economic reforms envisaged in the second structural adjustment plan imposed by the International Monetary Fund (IMF). Introduced in August 1996, they led to a sharp increase in food prices, which, like 1989, triggered demonstrations across the country. This time, however, the regime's reaction was different: a regular army was sent to quell the riots, and several hundred demonstrators were arrested for undermining the state stability. King Hussein himself accused "foreign elements" of meddling in Jordan's internal affairs, criticised the leftist parties for their links with Iraq, and warned against the use of democratic slogans as a cover for anti-state activities (Lucas 2005).

The tensions between the opposition and the regime were further deepened by the anti-Palestinian policies of Benjamin Netanyahu's government (1996–99), especially the expansion of Jewish settlements in the West Bank, the Tunnel Crisis of 1996, and the Masha'al affair. All of them fuelled the anti-normalisation lobby in Jordan that spread throughout professional associations, which, in turn, started to expel members for 'collaborating' with Israeli citizens. It was that moment when the regime realised the threat posed by the institutionalisation of the anti-normalisation movement, including to its very survival. With the parliamentary elections planned for November 1997, King Hussein initiated a series of measures aimed at curbing political freedoms and preventing an electoral success of the opposition. The most important of them was modifying the Press and Publications Law. Under the cover of fighting the abuse of freedom of expression by tabloid media, the government imposed restrictive financial regulations and licensing requirements for all media outlets, as well as draconian penalties for breaking the new rules. As a result, many opposition and independent newspapers were banned while many others were fined (Ryan 1998; Lucas 2005).

The government's actions triggered numerous protests by activists from the entire political spectrum, not only representatives of the left and Islamists but also liberals and groups traditionally supportive of the regime. Together, they called on King Hussein to reject the controversial amendments to the publications law. At the same time, the united opposition decided to boycott the forthcoming elections, arguing that the regime undermined the public's trust and that participation in the elections would only legitimise its actions. With full-fledged censorship of any anti-Israeli content, the popular vote resulted in a predominantly conservative and tribal parliament, willing to pledge full loyalty to the monarchy. Subsequently, many cases of electoral fraud were also reported (Ryan 1998).

The rift between the regime and public opinion widened even further when King Hussein revised his policy towards Iraq. To rebuild Jordan's relations with the Gulf Arab states and establish an alliance with the US, the king was forced to distance himself from Saddam Hussein's regime, despite the prevalent pro-Iraqi sentiment in Jordan. Hence, when the Americans engaged in a political confrontation with Iraq with possible military repercussions in February 1998, King Hussein decided to take preventive measures: pro-Iraq demonstrations were banned throughout the country.

The opposition saw this move as clear evidence of the monarchy's servile attitude to American interests in the region, with the new Press and Publications Law—even more restrictive than the one decreed in 1997—considered a tool to curtail any criticism of the government. Concerning freedom of the press, it meant a full return to the martial law (Lucas 2005). Soon later, however, the democratisation agenda was overshadowed entirely in the public debate, when at the beginning of 1999, King Hussein died following a long battle with cancer. His oldest son, Abdullah, ascended to the throne in February 1999.

Stabilisation of the Authoritarian Regime, 1999–2010

As widely expected, the young and Western-educated monarch initially expressed his full support for political reform in Jordan. To address the public's mistrust, King Abdullah II invited representatives of the opposition and professional associations to take part in a "national dialogue." He also submitted to the parliament a proposal to limit some of the restrictions in the press law and criticised the corruption and inefficiency of the state administration. At the same time, the first years of Abdullah's reign saw an increase in political activity within Jordanian society, manifested in a higher number of demonstrations and strikes. Symptomatic of the change in public discourse was the 1999 municipal elections, where the opposition came to power in several districts. Even the IAF described the polls as free and fair, even though minor incidents occurred during the elections (Ryan 2003).

Nevertheless, Abdullah's drift towards democracy was relatively short-lived, eventually rupturing in the aftermath of a deteriorating security situation in the region. In particular, the Al-Aqsa Intifada—which erupted in September 2000 in response to Ariel Sharon's provocation at Haram Al-Sharif—was a security threat to Jordan. The unfolding unrest in Palestine and its potential spillover into Jordanian streets could have undermined the monarchy's stability and endangered the peace treaty with Israel. Although King Abdullah publicly criticised the Israeli government and declared support to the Palestinian cause, the government also introduced a ban on public demonstrations. It did not stop professional associations from organising the "March of Return" in the Jordan Valley in October 2000. It gathered some 20,000 protesters opposing Israeli actions but was quickly dispersed by security forces (Lucas 2005).

In June 2001, with domestic tensions rising, King Abdullah decided to dissolve the parliament and commissioned the electoral law reform. In the absence of legislative power, the government issued a relevant decree, which increased the number of seats in the parliament to 110 and doubled the number of electoral districts. This move significantly increased the chances of independent candidates with tribal support being elected. Simultaneously, the monarch decided to delay the elections by at least ten months, officially, to provide sufficient time to transition into the new electoral system (Greenwood 2003). However, even though the elections were initially scheduled for November 2001, they did not take place until mid-2003.

The monarchy claimed that the main reason for this delay was an unfavourable political climate in the region, which threatened the stability of the country—albeit the real reason was the lack of checks and balances and the possibility of decreeing temporary laws by the government. Under the pretext of "stabilising" the state, over 250 legal acts were issued, many of which restricted civil liberties. For example, the reform of the Penal Code widened the definition of terrorism and introduced penalties for publishing news undermining national unity and stability, while the temporary Municipalities Law enabled the government to fully control all municipal councils by nominating half of their members. These measures were implemented by the regime to suppress the voices of opposition to its pro-Western policy and its support to US-led "War on Terror"—an opposition that stemmed from both the street (opposition parties, student unions, professional associations, and the Jordanian society at large) and from within the circles of power (the conservative part of the parliament). They all contested the US military expansionism in the Middle East. Irrespective of his reasoning, King Abdullah was also criticised by the opposition for abuse of power and undermining the reform process (Yom and Al-Momani 2008).

To divert public attention from democratisation, security, and foreign policy, the monarchy proposed several socio-economic reform packages, the biggest of them—"Jordan First"—launched in October 2002. The initiative focussed on improving health services and education, combating poverty and unemployment, advancing the status of women in society, civic engagement, and finally, strengthening national unity (Greenwood 2003; Yom and Al-Momani 2008). Although the Jordan First Committee appointed by the king prepared many recommendations for changes in the legal order, only a few of them were ultimately implemented. These included the establishment of a new ministry to oversee the reform process, the introduction of quota for women in the parliament, and new parliamentary elections, which were held in June 2003 (Greenwood 2003). Despite the relatively fair electoral process and high voter turnout (57 per cent), the political status quo did not change, and the parliament maintained its conservative and tribal character.

The hopes of reformist groups were revived in February 2005, when King Abdullah established an expert commission to draft a ten-year comprehensive plan of political reforms and socio-economic modernisation, the National Agenda. The multifaceted work of a diverse group of representatives from all walks of life (government, opposition, civil society, media, and the private sector) resulted in a very progressive and ambitious plan to take Jordan through a transition to a modern and progressive state. As it turned out, the agenda was doomed to fail: the terrorist attacks in Amman in November 2005 and the electoral success of Hamas in Palestine in January 2006 drew the Jordanian attention back to security concerns. Therefore, when the National Agenda was eventually published in December 2005, it was no longer relevant. Additionally, the king distanced himself from the reform plan under pressure from conservative elites who openly criticised the proposed changes, considering them premature and dangerous for the stability of the country (Muasher 2011). Consequently, using the pretext of security concerns, the regime introduced several controversial measures that severely weakened civil society and political parties: the 2006 Antiterrorism Law, with a definition of "terrorism" that was purposely left broad and open for interpretation, and the 2007 Political Parties Law that had more restrictive financial and administrative regulations, which caused several smaller parties to shut down.

It is not surprising then that the 2007 municipal elections were held among an atmosphere of distrust in state institutions. Even though traditionally strong on the local level, the IAF decided to withdraw on election day, accusing the authorities of rigging the electoral process by buying and falsifying votes. Accordingly, the monarchy retaliated with a public campaign portraying the Muslim Brotherhood as undemocratic and unpatriotic and accusing it of collaboration with foreign elements, namely Hezbollah and Hamas. The parliamentary elections that took place only a few months later were equally fraudulent, with local and international non-governmental organisations (NGOs) not allowed to monitor their progress (Susser 2008). As a result, the parliament's composition once again proved to be pro-regime and conservative, with the IAF representatives winning only six seats in the 110-member house.

Similarly, the prioritisation of security served as an argument when the regime decided to introduce regulations aimed at further controlling civil society. The Law of Societies, finally adopted by the parliament in July 2008, drastically limited the freedom of NGOs, including granting the government the right to refuse registration to new entities or to dissolve existing organisations without giving any reason, as well as full control over their finances and activities (Jarrah 2009). Strongly protested by civil society organisations and the international community, the law was eventually amended in September 2009, whereby some financing restrictions were lifted. Nevertheless, the government's power to easily dissolve NGOs remained in place.

Ultimately, owing to the growing dissatisfaction with the work of the Jordanian parliament, however, King Abdullah II dissolved it in November 2009, and then scheduled new elections for the end of 2010. At the same time, he requested the government prepare a reform of the electoral system that would enable a fair and transparent vote, thus contributing to the democratic process and modernisation of the country. In response, several

NGOs formed a coalition to campaign for the improvement of the electoral system. Its recommendations not only suggested scrapping the SNTV system by introducing two electoral lists (local and national) and a possibility to cast two votes but also encouraged the establishment of an independent body to oversee the electoral process and redistricting to ensure equal representation.

On the surface, the new electoral law, finally adopted in May 2010, seemed to adhere to the recommendations provided. Indeed, severe penalties for vote-buying were introduced, while the role of electoral observers was institutionalised to ensure transparency of the elections. In addition, the number of seats in the parliament increased from 110 to 120. Of these extra seats, six strengthened the women quota, while the remaining four were distributed among under-represented urban constituencies. The reality, however, painted a different picture, as the introduction of the single-mandate sub-districts and their geographical distribution still favoured the tribal population, which did not alter the status quo. It was for this reason that the IAF decided to boycott the elections planned for November 2010. Nonetheless, some Islamists, including many prominent Muslim Brotherhood activists, decided to break away from the protest and run on independent platforms (Beck and Collet 2010).

During the weeks preceding the elections, many political incidents took place, including the detainment of young activists and media censorship. It made the Jordanian regime a target for international human rights organisations. Despite it, the elections per se were commonly perceived as free and fair. They also set a precedent: for the first time, the monarchy invited both local and international actors to monitor the electoral process directly.

Hybridisation of the Political System, 2010–17

The Arab Spring reached the Hashemite Kingdom of Jordan as early as January 2011 when numerous protests took place in major cities across the country. The Jordanians were dissatisfied with the deteriorating socio-economic situation and demanded improvements to their living conditions and political reforms. Even though organised frequently, the demonstrations have never gathered more than 8000–10,000 people, therefore lacking a critical mass to pressure the regime. Nevertheless, not willing to escalate the domestic situation any further and being pushed by the US to liberalise the political system, King Abdullah decided to initiate the reform process. He dismissed the cabinet (in January) and appointed the Royal Committee on Constitutional Review (in April). The results of its work became a framework of the discussions about constitutional reform: ensuring an efficient system of checks and balances, strengthening the rule of law, and broader civic engagement (Ryan 2011).

By the end of September 2011, the parliament endorsed most of the Committee's recommendations. It also introduced an unprecedented scale of amendments into the constitution for the first time since 1984. Among others, the new provisions formally recognised the independence of the judiciary and established both the Constitutional Court and an independent electoral commission—two new institutions in the Jordanian legal system. Nevertheless, the reform did not limit the level of royal prerogatives, de facto leaving the political system intact. The legislative was also still subordinate to executive power under the king's leadership.

Similarly, a revolutionary change did not materialise when the Elections Law and the Political Parties Law were both amended in 2012, even though they were positive developments, addressing some of the popular demands. The former slightly reduced requirements for establishing a new political party, allowed for running fundraising campaigns and party-owned media outlets, as well as penalised discrimination in public life due to membership in political parties. The latter sanctioned the role of the Independent Elections Commission (established in December 2011), charged with oversight and administration of parliamentary elections, but it failed to address the main shortcoming of the electoral system itself: the commonly criticised SNTV system. To partly mitigate the problem, voters were granted an additional ballot to cast a vote on the newly introduced national list with 27 seats, based on a proportional representation system. Around the same time, in June 2012, the Constitutional Court was eventually established as an independent legal body tasked with examining the constitutionality of laws and regulations, as well as interpreting the constitution.

In mid-to-late 2012, while facing the escalation of conflict in Syria with the number of refugees entering Jordan on the rise, increasing tensions in Egypt, and the closely linked energy crisis, the regime modified its stance once again. Symptomatic of this fact was the Press and Publications Law reform of September 2012, widely seen as curbing freedom of expression and an attempt to close outlets critical of the regime. The deterioration of both regional security and the socio-economic situation also significantly decreased external pressure to pursue further reforms. Stability and the monarchy's survival, rather than democracy, became the new overarching priority of the international community vis-à-vis Jordan. Therefore, the financial and political support of the West and the Gulf allowed the regime to successfully manage the popular unrest caused by the food and fuel prices increase in November 2012 and swiftly restore public order. At the same time, the security rhetoric intensified, aiming to present all forms of civil disobedience as threats to the monarchy's stability, and all protesters as instigators and revolutionists.

In such circumstances, of a volatile neighbourhood and mutual mistrust between crucial stakeholders of the political process in Jordan, the parliamentary elections took place in January 2013. According to King Abdullah's vision, they were supposed to be a stepping stone into a real constitutional monarchy by initiating the majority-based parliamentary governments. Even if the electoral process was free and transparent (despite minor irregularities), its outcome did not change the status quo: a boycott by the IAF resulted in both a parliament and government largely occupied by loyal and conservative monarchists vesting their interests in the regime's stability rather than any genuine reform (Malantowicz 2013).

The monarchy further demonstrated its disinterest in meaningful reform in October 2013 during the reshuffle of the royally-appointed Senate's seats. First, the Senate's speaker, liberal Taher al-Masri, was replaced by a conservative, Abdel Raouf al-Rawabdeh. Second, and against the tradition of involving all former prime ministers in the Senate's work, there was no place left in the new term for former prime ministers Abd Al-Karim Kabariti and Awn Khasawneh, who both identified with the reformist movement. Finally, despite having significant popular support, the Islamists were not represented in the Senate. Instead, they were marginalised by the regime after they lost an important external ally, Egyptian President Mohamed Morsi, after the coup d'état in July 2013.

What followed was the regime's discourse of democratisation as being more about procedures and capacity-building rather than the redistribution of power. It was in this vein that the procedural reforms deprived of depth and breadth continued to take place in the following years. At the same time, freedom of expression and freedom of the media experienced a severe setback. As a result of controversial regulations introduced in 2013, many independent electronic media outlets were shut down, several journalists were arrested, and many others imposed self-censorship. As a result, Jordan's position on the Freedom of Press Index plummeted to 155th place in 2014 (the worst in the country's history) and only slightly recovered in the 2017 ranking (138th place). The situation was further worsened by the revision of counter-terrorism laws in June 2014, which controversially broadened the definition of "terrorism" to include such acts as "disturbing relations with a foreign state."

In August 2014, the Jordanian constitution was amended for the second time in barely a few years. One of the changes, which was welcomed by all stakeholders, expanded the jurisdiction of the Independent Election Commission to organise and supervise also local and municipal elections. Far more surprising, however, was the amendment to Article 127, which granted the king sole authority to appoint key security positions in Jordan—director of the General Intelligence Department, and chairman of the Joint Chiefs of Staff—without parliamentary oversight. For reform activists, it was a clear sign of concentrating more power in the hands of the monarch vis-à-vis a weakened parliament (Malantowicz 2015).

This move is part of a broader agenda of centralising power and strengthening the role of the security apparatus, but also as a direct response to multiple internal and external threats. Since 2011, the war in Syria has continued to exacerbate the already delicate socio-economic and security environment in Jordan, specifically the intensification of military activity on the ground, the deteriorating humanitarian situation, and the massive influx of refugees into the country. Likewise, the border clashes with jihadists, the territorial expansion of the Islamic State, and an alarming rise in support for extremist Islamism within the Kingdom itself created an unprecedented threat. In response to the latter, the authorities launched a crackdown on supporters of the Islamic State by arresting a few hundred citizens and referring them to the State Security Court on suspicion of intent to support terrorism.

Later reforms, notably ones in 2015 and 2016, should be seen through the lens of ensuring the regime's survival, security needs, and concentration of power as well. The new Political Parties Law, introduced in January 2015, once again restricted functioning of the political parties by tightening funding regulations and banning organisational affiliations with foreign entities. The new Municipalities Law and the Decentralisation Law, which were endorsed in summer 2015 after being touted as a step towards empowering local communities, effectively led to undermining the position of locally elected councils, whose decisions can now be overthrown by centrally nominated governors.

Likewise, the government gained a prerogative to appoint 25 per cent of the new councils. In a similar move, the regime pushed for additional constitutional amendments in April 2016, further consolidating power in the hands of the king and limiting the parliament's authority to oversee the executive branch. On that basis, the king can make appointments to critical posts (e.g., regent, crown prince, chairman, members of Senate, president, members of the Constitutional Court, etc.) by a royal decree, without the approval of the government, thereby removing any form of political accountability. At the same time, the government became involved in a campaign aimed at discrediting the Muslim Brotherhood, primarily by supporting moderate Islamists in their split from a more radical wing of the movement, but also by shutting down their offices in major locations (Bouziane 2016).

Finally, the Elections Law was amended again in March 2016, formally abolishing the widely criticised SNTV voting system, but failed to address the shortcomings of the Jordanian electoral system: over-representation of rural areas, quotas for minorities loyal to the monarchy, and the lack of incentives to vote for candidates representing political agendas rather than tribal affiliations. On the contrary, it eliminated the national list that proved to galvanise support for political parties in the 2013 elections. The September 2016 elections, based on the new law, even if commonly praised as credible, free, and transparent, changed little more than the composition of the parliament where the newcomers took 57 per cent of the seats. Instead, they were used as a tool of legitimacy and as a mean for patronage distribution for the regime, therefore hindering any meaningful reform.

Conclusions

The history of political reform in the Hashemite monarchy after 1989 is closely interlinked with its foreign policy as well as stability and security concerns. Overall, even though Jordan's democratic façade has indeed expanded, the essence of the political system remains rigid. It does not mean, however, that nothing has changed since 1989. The political culture in Jordan has transformed, the number of civil society organisations has steadily increased in the past decades, several democratic procedures such as regular elections have been implemented, and the society itself has opened to modern trends and ideologies. There is slightly more room for the rule of law as well as political and social activism, while the level of state repressions has somewhat declined over time. In other words, the Jordanian authoritarianism of pre-1989 differs quite significantly from the authoritarian regime one sees in the region today. Nevertheless, Jordan is still a political system that does not meet the criteria of democracy: regularity of meaningful competition for all effective positions of government power, a highly inclusive level of political participation, pluralism of the political environment, and widespread civil and political liberties.

References

Abu Rumman, M. A. (2012). The impact of economic factors on democratization: Jordan case. *Journal of Advanced Social Research*, 2, 37–51.

Beck M., & Collet L. (2010). *Jordan's 2010 election law: Democratization or stagnation?* Länderprogramm Jordanien. Konrad-Adenauer-Stiftung e.V.

Bouziane, M. (2016). Jordan – Disquiet at the island of stability. *IEMed Mediterranean Yearbook*, 2016, 214–217.

Brynen R. (1992). Economic Crisis and Post-Rentier Democratization in the Arab World: The Case of Jordan. *Canadian Journal of Political Science*, 25(1), 69–97.

Choucair-Vizoso, J. (2008). Illusive reform: Jordan's stubborn stability. In M. Ottaway & J. Choucair-Vizoso (Eds.), *Beyond the Façade. Political reform in the Arab world* (Vol. 2008, pp. 45–70). Washington, DC: Carnegie Endowment for International Peace.

Greenwood, S. (2003). Jordan's "new bargain": The political economy of regime security. *The Middle East Journal*, 57(2), 248–268.

Jarrah S. (2009). *Civil Society and Public Freedom in Jordan: The Path of Democratic Reform* (The Saban Centre for Middle East Policy at The Brookings Institution Working Paper, No. 3).

Lucas, R. E. (2005). *Institutions and the politics of survival in Jordan. Domestic responses to external challenges, 1988–2001*. New York: State University of New York Press.

Malantowicz, A. (2013). Crisis, chaos, violence – Is that really what we want? A stalled democratization in Jordan. *The Copernicus Journal of Political Studies*, 1(3), 77–96.

Malantowicz, A. (2015). Jordan: Resilience against All Odds. *IEMed Mediterranean Yearbook*, 2015, 194–197.

Malantowicz, A. (2017). Democracy or stability? Everlasting dilemma of the Hashemite Kingdom of Jordan. *Hemispheres. Studies on Cultures and Societies*, 32, 55–65.

Muasher M. (2011). A Decade of Struggling Reform Efforts in Jordan: The Resilience of the Rentier System. *The Carnegie Papers*, May 2011.

Robinson, G. E. (1997). Can Islamists be democrats? The case of Jordan. *The Middle East Journal*, 51(3), 372–387.

Robinson, G. E. (1998). Defensive democratization in Jordan. *International Journal of Middle East Studies, 30*(3), 387–410.
Ryan, C. R. (1998). Elections and parliamentary democratization in Jordan. *Democratization, 5*(4), 176–196.
Ryan, C. R. (2011). Identity politics, reform, and protests in Jordan. *Studies in Ethnicity and Nationalism, 11*(3), 564–578.
Ryan, C. R. (2003). Political liberalization and monarchical succession in Jordan. *Israel Affairs, 9*(3), 129–140.
Susser, A. (2008). Jordan: Preserving domestic order in a setting of regional turmoil. *Middle East Brief, 27*, 1–7.
The Jordanian National Charter. (1991). Source: http://www.kinghussein.gov.jo/charter-national.html. Accessed Jan 2018.
Yom, S. L., & Al-Momani, M. H. (2008). The international dimensions of authoritarian regime stability: Jordan in the post-cold war era. *Arab Studies Quarterly, 30*(1), 39–60.

The Palestinians

Donna Robinson Divine

Whatever havoc erupts in the Middle East typically crosses Jordan's borders. In a region torn by violence, instability, and brutality, staged with pride for an audience riveted with fear, Jordan, a country defined as vulnerable to regional upheaval, has maintained stability seemingly against all the odds and expectations. The qualities that once presumably rendered the monarchy fatally flawed are now viewed, surprisingly, as mechanisms for survival and a reason for its king to seize an ambitious role in the embattled Middle East. The ugly mix of religious, ideological, social, and economic antagonisms that has typically been attributed to colonialism now, ironically, circles around Jordan for a way out of this predicament. It is ironic because, in a country whose capital city is dotted with Palestinian refugee squatter slums, the scars of colonialism are visible.

However, the misery brought to the Middle East from colonialism, once epitomised by the 1948 disaster, can no longer be told as merely a Palestinian story either in its troubling origins or in its disruptive consequences. For events in the Middle East have ensnared every country into a dimension of politics where the familiar vocabulary once regularly deployed by rulers no longer describes the stark choices before them.

D. R. Divine (✉)
Smith College, Massachusetts, MA, USA
e-mail: drdivine@smith.edu

© The Author(s) 2019
P. R. Kumaraswamy (ed.), *The Palgrave Handbook of the Hashemite Kingdom of Jordan*, https://doi.org/10.1007/978-981-13-9166-8_21

From Syria to Iraq, Lebanon, and Saudi Arabia, some developments impart an aura of an apocalypse.

Altered geopolitical circumstances have prompted many Arab regimes to downgrade their attention to the Palestine problem. Even if official rhetoric is familiar, it is uttered with less conviction. In a region where states have collapsed, Iran has replaced Israel as the most immediate danger now able to project its power across the region. More countries have sought military aid from their former colonial masters, making Jordan, a country that never fully subscribed to the axiom that such ties should be severed, a critical ally. With Palestinians increasingly ignored in the region and with their peace process frozen, only Jordan has the geographic and demographic interest not only to take up their cause but also to advance it. Ask Jordan's monarch to describe the country's future, and he would say independence, prosperity, quality education, and society as protective of its religious and tribal heritage as it is open to the opportunities made available by global relationships. Ask him what he does not want, and he will respond: violence, civil discord, and colonialism. However, the society he imagines overlaps with the world he rejects and it is precisely the values and ties they share that now contain an unexpected added value for his regime as well as for the region.

The Hashemite Kingdom of Jordan captures a century of contradictory influences in the Middle East, and perhaps, for the first time, the conflicting imperatives embedded in this regime are working not to undermine it, as in the past, but rather to anchor it. Jordan has always been identified as a symbol of the remnants of colonial power refusing total withdrawal, a proxy for an old traditional order longing to return to the past and a magnet for the destructive radical forces searching for a base from which to launch their attacks. Jordan's fragility has always been served up as a lesson for what can happen to a country if its rulers are tied too tightly to the West and to dated bankrupt ideas of force.

Incorporated into the Palestine Mandate, the very country cannot avoid evoking the tainted history of British colonialism and its decades-long commitment of support for the development in Palestine of a Jewish National Home. No aspect of Jordan's history has drawn more criticism than the country's engagement with Palestinians, a population that has been a vital part of Jordanian political life and a threat to its stability, if not to its existence.

The broad shape of Jordanian history forced the Palestinian issue to the forefront. The claims of Abdullah I on Arab Nationalism—initially as Emir and later as king—could not displace the need to forge a policy of cooperation with Zionists for economic development (joint ventures with Jewish-owned Palestine Electric and Potash companies during the mandate) and for security (ongoing clandestine contacts with Zionist and Israeli leaders essential to keeping at bay the furies periodically unleashed against regime and country). This exposed the contradiction in Abdullah's grand plans because most Arab nationalists opposed contacts, let alone interactions, with the Zionist enterprises. As the 1948 *Naqba* gained its imaginative potency, Abdullah's pragmatic statecraft increasingly appeared as a betrayal. Charges that the Trans-Jordanian Legion waged its battles in compliance with the 1947 UN Partition Resolution that the country had officially opposed created the justification for the Arab League to refuse to recognise the legitimacy of King Abdullah's decision to annex the West Bank territories conquered during the 1948 War. They also generated ambivalence and uncertainty about the very idea of citizenship in Jordan because it was extended to Palestinians by the same act. For that reason, Jordan's periodic confrontations with embedded nationalist forces have been interpreted as stemming primarily from Palestinians holding to their identity as a badge of resistance to an order forcibly imposed on them. As much as Palestinians constituted a threat to Jordan's monarchy, the country's policies posed a dilemma for Palestinians. Where and when Jordan's army was deployed to attack Israel or to defend Palestinians may have aroused bitterness or even been a mark of shame, but forced Palestinians either to take enormous risks for liberation from Jordanian society or to accommodate and gain some access to its benefits. Accommodations were necessarily fragile, continuously punctuated by changes in the regional and domestic political order.

The *Naqba* eventually brought Arabs, of all classes, across the region together in new ways generating a regional political dynamic that no ruler could dismiss. When King Abdullah incorporated the West Bank, he gained a population whose skills may have advanced Jordan's economic development, but whose sheer numbers and urgent needs threatened the country's survival and put the monarchy on notice. Abdullah's assassination in July 1951 in Jerusalem on the Noble Sanctuary left the Kingdom temporarily without a king, but what some thought a fatal blow, ironically allowed the forces craving for order and normalcy—including many in the newly conquered West Bank—to regroup around a new monarch and the idea of state sovereignty.

Because the conflicts unsettling Jordan's polity were never fully resolved, the passions they aroused periodically produced chaos. In a country with a significant number of its citizens[1] longing for a place wiped off the map and living with the painful reminder that force can crush ideals, turbulence might be contained, but never erased. From Palestinian refugees filling the streets in Amman or pressing on scarce resources in other parts of the country, the monarchy had to confront its opponents with all the civil and military instruments at its disposal even drawing on foreign military units or international organisations, like UNRWA, whose initial operations were not fully authorised by the regime and thus deemed to compromise the country's national sovereignty.

However, if Jordan became a testing ground for what liberating Palestine would mean for the Middle East, it was also a battleground for the struggle against colonialism. In creating what became Trans-Jordan in 1921 and then the Kingdom of Jordan in 1949, the British bestowed upon the regime the blessings and curses of colonialism. It trained its army; it provided financial stipends for its public works and gave the country limited access to modern education. It enveloped its rulers in an imperial project held responsible for the region's disunity, underdevelopment, and enduring powerlessness. Before independence, Emir Abdullah's entanglement in Palestinian politics could not be disentangled from what was widely perceived as a favourable disposition to Great Britain's endorsement of a Jewish National Home. Critical financial contributions from imperial overlords sustained the regime's budget and provided a reason for hostility from an array of Palestinian nationalist leaders. That the elements sustaining Jordan's regime were bound to unravel has long been a commonplace assumption because the regime could never presumably escape its compromised beginnings that are always read into contemporary difficulties.

For much of the country's history then, its leaders struggled to reconcile its many different and conflicting affiliations, particularly in an era when its roots in colonial history were so easily turned into a derogatory label by those who saw no common ground to share with their former foreign rulers. While Jordan's kings could build their legitimacy around kinship with the Prophet's family, they also had to present themselves as culturally enough distinctive at home and as sufficiently cosmopolitan abroad to secure their grip on power and to move the nation ahead in a competitive region still haunted, if not paralysed, by the loss of an Arab

---

[1] Seventy per cent of the 9856.950 Jordanians are Palestinian with 2,000,000 of the latter registered as refugees.

Palestine in the 1948 *Naqba*. Here is the structural fact of Jordanian politics that explains why incidents quickly spiral out of control perpetually backing the country's population into stances of aggression and fear.

In some way, Jordan cannot help but remind its people of this tragedy, even as it ironically demands that redemption is based on forgetting rather than on remembering it. While Jordan might claim the country shared the tragedy common to the region, it provided no atonement for the Palestinian lands it incorporated or for the Palestinians it absorbed after the 1948 War. The 1948 War may have forged Jordan's politics, but it could never imprint on the country a national identity that joined two incompatible populations possessing so many clashing interests and goals and such radically different legacies of sorrow. Beneath all the tensions, supposedly lay a profound incompatibility.

The unification of East and West Banks in 1950 ran against the tide of Arab nationalist sentiment sympathetic to the All-Palestine Government set up in 1948 with the blessing of the Arab League. Arab nationalist sentiment demanded a united front against Israel, and this was complicating Jordan's security interests. Because the regime was held accountable by Israel for controlling its side of a very long border, it was forced to deploy its military to try to stop Palestinians dispossessed from home and land from crossing it to return either for food, shelter, or for continuing their war against the Jewish state and its citizens. Border clashes produced bloody conflicts between Israel and Jordan, such as in Qibya in 1953 and Es-Samu in 1966. They deepened Palestinian dissatisfaction with a monarchy seemingly seeking stability instead of pursuing policies its rhetoric seemed to promise. Jordan's attempts to protect its citizens and simultaneously prevent them from provoking Israeli retaliatory raids forced even the Palestine Liberation Organisation (PLO) to declare at its founding in 1964 that it had no claims on territory governed by the monarchy.[2]

The nightmare that joined these two populations—from the East and West Banks of the Jordan River—also had a grim resonance to the anticolonial struggles that ran deeply enough through the country's history to become a defining political impulse in Jordan almost ending the monarchy in the 1950s. The attacks against King Hussein, taken up with fervour by an opposition located in the West Bank, reflected the high expectations in the 1950s, when military coups brought down kings in Egypt and later in

---

[2] Moshe Shemesh, *Arab Politics, Palestinian Nationalism and The Six Day War*, Brighton: Sussex Academic Press, 2008, p. 74.

Iraq and were expected to generate a dynamic capable of returning Palestinians to the homes and villages they left abandoned in 1948. The future claimed by those in the Middle East who seized the instruments of power on behalf of their exploited and impoverished people, and in devotion, at least rhetorically, to what became the sacred cause of Arab unity brought no liberation from the wreckage of 1948 or from the unwavering line of fate it drew around the region's politics.

Despite clear signs that Arab nationalists' promises to return Palestinians to their home could not be kept, the 1967 war losses left Arabs in a state of shock. Israel swept away the strongest and most well-equipped armies that Arabs could send to the battlefield, and moreover, the Jewish state was left in possession of all mandatory Palestine (as well as the Sinai Peninsula and the Golan Heights) and stunned as many men and women in the so-called Arab street as in the palaces. For many, the war's devastations were not only unforeseen, they could not be imagined even after the fighting was halted. Arabs were not only defeated, but they were also humiliated and uncertain about where they should turn for a future. Although the very idea of a Pan-Arabism in ruins seemed unbearable, even when the march it promised from refugee camp to family homes in Palestine was always blocked, people were reluctant to surrender values so fervently celebrated as sacred.

Stepping into the breach was Yasser Arafat, elected to head the PLO in 1968, based on the promise that a new strategy could re-energise the Palestinian cause and save Arab honour. Arafat intended to force the world to see how Palestinian suffering might touch their lives while showing his own people that the only way back home would come from their own personal and collective commitment to what some might describe as a perpetual war for national liberation. Arafat argued that Palestinians could defeat the forces arrayed against them only if they were prepared to unleash the furore they had for too long held in check as refugees. The trouble Palestinians should fear, he contended, was entropy, not chaos.

Jordan quickly became the first staging ground for this new militant strategy where a dreadful history of suffering and abuse became an ordeal of viciousness and victimhood plunging the country into a chaos that seemed to foreshadow, once again, its imminent collapse. Parts of Jordan's cities were turned into armed camps pitting Palestinian armed fighters against official instruments of law and order. The turmoil subtracted power and legitimacy from Jordan's monarch. Once again dreams turned into nightmares where gruesome losses of the past reverberated when

Fedayeen declared a new era for Palestinians who would leave no one at peace until Palestinians were at peace; that terror would be meted out until Palestinians were no longer terrorised and property confiscated, until Palestinian men and women were no longer dispersed and dispossessed. The dispute with Israel would be transformed into conflict with existential consequences for all in firing range, but first and foremost, for Jordan. The attacks launched against the Jewish state from the Jordanian soil threatened to unravel, the regime was so desperate to rebuild after its devastating military defeat. Jordan was in the curious position to be both crucial to the viability of the new-born Palestinian movement and inimical to its full independence.

Standing down radical nationalists in the 1950s had allowed King Hussein to re-establish control over the army, draw on British military resources, and extend benefits to tribal leaders to intensify their connections with and dependence on the regime. When Palestinians in Jordan were drawn into radicalism in the aftermath of the June War and stood in almost open rebellion against the regime, Hussein appealed, once again, to East Bank residents to double down on their tribal and kin networks to bestow on the monarchy sufficient power and legitimacy to confront the threats forcefully. Fighters had to be either tamed into submission or expelled from the country to arrest the chaos.

In post-war Jordan, loss of territory, skilled labour, and East Jerusalem complicated by an additional 265,000 new refugees contributed to one of the country's most painful episodes. Jordan's defeat and military disarray struck a chord for many Palestinians who were animated by the energy shown by Palestinian insurgents but whose towns and villages were burdened by the retaliatory raids the attacks against Israel triggered. No wonder that Palestinian activists and Jordanian citizens, including Palestinians, viewed this violence differently. For Palestinian fighters, these attacks constituted the beginning of a national liberation they would achieve with their own hands. For Jordanian citizens, the violence stopped the economic and political recovery.

With military backing and support from the East Bank tribal leaders, King Hussein confronted the Palestinian fighters. From September 1970 to 1971, he killed and expelled thousands of fighters and destroyed the institutions they had set up. Palestinian activists had plunged the country into a civil war but lost to a monarch with increased authority and legitimacy because most of the population, including Palestinians, craved for order and normalcy.

Palestinian demands for self-rule did not initially stop Jordan from assuming responsibility for negotiating the return of territories lost to Israel in 1967. Jordan also had to give Palestinian sentiment its due—from always insisting on not signing any agreement with Israel that failed to restore all the lost territories, including East Jerusalem, to eventually promising autonomy in a proposed confederation. Ultimately, however, grassroots Palestinian nationalism convinced King Hussein, whose own diplomatic efforts never succeeded, to acknowledge in 1988 that the PLO was the sole legitimate authority for Palestinians.

What appeared a touchstone for Jordanian recognition of a Palestinian identity complicated the kind of support and privileges that had been extended to this population for decades. Jordanian disengagement from the West Bank, announced in July 1988, also denied many Palestinians automatic access to the benefits conferred by citizenship. For some Palestinians, education in Jordanian schools became more expensive. Others were denied access to health care and employment. When the PLO decided, in 1993, to negotiate the resolution of its conflict with Israel, the promise of a new beginning not only for Palestinians but also for the entire Middle East overshadowed the suffering produced by Jordan's recognition of the PLO's legitimacy. The Oslo Process allowed Jordan to sign its Peace Treaty in 1994 with Israel opening up the opportunity for mutually beneficial economic and political ties with the Jewish state. Paradoxically, while Oslo was interpreted, initially, as confirming the Palestinian will to go it alone, whether Jordan shared flag or crown with the Palestinians, their fates could never be entirely separated.

The Arab Spring Protests

Since 2011, the Middle East has condensed the insecurities of globalisation and spread them into almost every country in the region. That it has been contained reasonably well at Israel's border is no surprise. That it has been successfully bracketed in Jordan is astounding given that predictions abound of the country's imminent collapse. Unlike past regional disasters—the *Naqba* of 1948, military coups, the 1967 War—Jordan has kept the violence from seeping across its borders even as the country has had to allow large numbers of refugees—by some accounts, well over a million—

on its lands.[3] An increasingly diverse, fragmented, and distrustful young Arab population, acutely sensitive to the vested interests propping up their countries' governments, and most importantly, standing in the way of their dreams, paid only passing polemical attention to the Palestinian dispossession and exile. While no Arab leader would acknowledge abandoning the Palestinian cause, none claims it as a regional priority, given the turmoil that followed these demonstrations and civil wars. Palestinians have been left without defences in Syria and Lebanon and forced to rely more on Jordan for attention and support. A narrative that once loomed large in the Arab imagination seems to be in retreat.

Anticipating trouble from these regional shifts, King Abdullah II returned to some of the dark times of the past and followed a strategy that his father and even his grandfather would have instantly recognised and approved, namely deploying forces when necessary, elections when possible, and fragmenting the opposition by dividing Palestinians from so-called East Bank Jordanians, because residents continue to fight for access to power and resources. Although he might adopt the popular idioms critical of Israel and its policies, the king persists in expanding economic and security relations with the Jewish State sustaining the long-standing divide between words and deeds.

The monarchy has good prudent reasons not to lean too far against populism—religious or secular—but rather to arrest its momentum whenever it gains significant traction. As a steward of peace, the court has ironically sometimes widened those divisions between Palestinian and East Bank Islamists typically cited as the primary reason for the country's vulnerabilities. East Bank Islamists cannot afford to alienate the monarchy because it offers them access to jobs, funds for investment, and the benefits of entry into the best schools. The more Palestinian and East Bank Jordanian Islamists are reminded of their divergent interests, the wider the gap between them grows.

Most telling of all examples comes from the September 2016 election. The Islamic Action Front split with one faction of mostly East Bank residents participating and one—Palestinian Islamists—boycotting the election. While no faction challenged the monarchy's legitimacy, the decision of some not to compete in the election was less painful than one might imagine for suspicion of the monarchy among Palestinian Islamists is high,

---

[3] Aaron Magid, "Amman's Refugee Waiting Game: The Time Bomb on Jordan's Border," *Foreign Affairs*, May 24, 2017.

if not intense. Deepening the divide between the people who presumably share common theological principles diminishes opposition to the country's structure of power by turning rivalries and suspicions inward and away from the institutions that control election outcomes. While a fractured national identity is often a vector carrying unrest, it has become a means in Jordan of forging a consensus on royal power as essential to stability. That no collective identity has emerged that might form a unified response to any of the country's pressing problems highlights the monarch's centrality in keeping order, sustaining the religious culture, and mitigating the conflicts that have upended so many regimes and turned so many cities into battlefields.

Relations with Israel continue to be a flashpoint triggering national unrest because so often economic interests collide with ideas prevalent in the culture but with baleful consequences if turned into actions. The material incentives for good relations with Israel are ignored by groups who see the Jewish state only as threats against Muslim values and Palestinian ambitions. Conflicts about and with Israel profoundly affect Jordanians at all levels of society, and they are a testing ground for the monarchy. The stakes are made plain as soon as some incident—no matter how seemingly trivial—becomes a cause for either embattled Palestinians or Islamists.

Consider the outrages unleashed after Israel installed metal detectors at the several gateways to the Harem al-Sharif after three Israeli Arabs shot and killed two law enforcement officers with weapons smuggled into the holy site that then became the launching pad for their attacks. Never mind the outbursts of righteous indignation over the metal detectors in Israel, no similar reactions to the same security system stationed outside holy sites in Saudi Arabia, Iran, Syria, Iraq, and in countless other Muslim countries were ever recorded.

There is, of course, nothing like social media for disseminating images and stirring up enough rage for protests to descend into violence. Even before technology opened ways of instantly transmitting fake news, word of mouth rumours could propel riots into prolonged battles. Perhaps the absorption into a grand narrative gives people a reassuring sense of social cohesion even among the radical differences that may divide them. But if the past is any guide, the unity felt in defending an ideal can quickly collapse and the tide of anger can turn in other directions. Urging people to protest the security measures taken in the aftermath of a terror attack coming from the Harem al-Sharif can become the basis for attacks that hold the monarchy accountable for brokering a peace treaty with the very state accused of repeatedly trespassing Islam's holy sites and its religious imperatives. Such transgressions, it is argued, call for martyrdom, not compliance, an act that disregards, if not devalues, the benefits coming from the ordinary and peaceful economic and political interactions with Israel.

Downplaying incitement, renaming acts of violent resistance, Jordanian officials publicly joined the chorus of people who claimed to see menace in Israeli security measures.[4] The king cannot be indifferent to the public will, but he understands that protests initially aimed at Israel can easily be redirected against him. His privileged status as protector of Jerusalem's Harem al-Sharif allows the king to set policies for the religious officials stationed at the holy site, who, in turn, monitor activities and worship, all of which endow the monarchy with a magnetic charge that can keep the peace intact for the sake of worship and spirituality. The king cannot remain silent when a call for resistance is issued despite the risks.

The king claims his policies have stopped Israeli efforts to Judaise the Harem al-Sharif, although he knows that he remains in control over the sites because of Israeli policies that have remained the same since the end of the June War in 1967.[5] Once again, Jordan is tied to Israel—through its peace treaty reconfirming its custodial role—and to Palestinians who claim the city as capital—with its position made extremely difficult by the need to accommodate conflicting imperatives, both with a potent hold on the population.

While the daunting challenge of dealing with the tensions over Israeli security measures persisted and while it was impossible to imagine another crisis, one did erupt adding to the urgency of the situation. In the rented residence of Israel's Ambassador to Jordan, a furniture delivery somehow triggered an attack against her security guard who killed the assailant. The apartment owner, caught in the crossfire, also died. The incident was interwoven in news accounts with the confrontations in Jerusalem between police and Muslim worshippers, but they are connected only by timing and not by the kind of danger each posed for the monarchy. The rage in Jordan over two deaths ramped up the rhetoric of the king but did not ultimately affect his actual decisions. He followed diplomatic protocol permitting Israel's Embassy staff to return to Israel, but the Israeli prime

---

[4] Alan Johnson, "When 'Alternative Facts' Kill", *World Affairs Journal*, August 7, 2017.
[5] Michael Dumper, *Jerusalem Unbound*, New York: Columbia University Press, 2014, pages 183–184.

minister's public welcome of the security guard who had killed two Jordanian citizens was the kind of action that inevitably summoned back the king into the polemical fray.

Because the incident occurred at the same time as the riots and violence in Jerusalem over the security measures taken by the Israelis in the aftermath of the terrorist attack from the Haram al-Sharif, many Jordanians insisted the two were connected, and for Jordan's monarchy, there is this vital difference. In Jordan, the riots provoked by the deaths exposes the dilemmas of sustaining a monarchy in a populist moment when the general will always be viewed as pushing the country towards turmoil. By contrast, the tensions and confrontations in Jerusalem over the holy sites, driven as they were by Palestinians, sent a message to king and to the world about Palestinian national rights and claims to Jerusalem as their capital. Jordan pays the salaries of the Waqf officials who govern the area, but Palestinians still possess considerable leverage over what can be done. Above all, the Jerusalem crisis shows the futility of Jordan's efforts to detach itself from Palestinian political developments and from the toxins that they can unleash in the region.

Jordanian-Palestinian: Entangled Fate and Shared Destiny

The story of the PLO's rise to prominence and power is typically told as a tale of loss for Jordan. One, a symbol of a progressive emancipatory impulse is thought to represent the future; the other, a synonym for the forces of reaction is presumed to bend towards the past and thus in the wrong direction. But the traditions Palestinians claim to have left behind cannot be rejected entirely: they are linked by place, by common religious pilgrimages, by overlapping sacred and national jurisdictions, and most recently, by the potent contradictions produced by a paralysed peace process. While there are differences between Jordanians and Palestinians, mutual needs have brought their politics not so much into alignment as into an intersection gracing King Abdullah with a renewed mandate to shape Palestine's future if not its destiny. Particularly, in an increasingly fragmented but interconnected Middle East, with violence stoked by the confrontation between Shi'a-majority Iran and Sunni-majority Saudi Arabia, King Abdullah has become an ever more critical agent in keeping the insurrectionary forces long associated with Palestinians at bay and now, surprisingly and however slowly, in advancing the project of two states for two peoples.

The Palestinians, torn between ambitions and immediate needs, with an aging leader leaving more pathways to chaos than to a stable transition, do not need to beckon hard for Jordan's help. With Palestinian organisations paralysed and fractured, Jordan is already assuming responsibility for keeping the peace and for charting the course to relief from a long-festering problem. At a time when Jordan is stepping up to the challenge, the country is also stepping into a breach with an aura of risk hovering over it. For a while, hostilities may be encrusted, they typically find vigorous expression when directed at Jordan's ties with Israel or with its former colonial masters. Such antagonism has been heard before without disrupting regional and global relations that Jordan's monarchs considered vital for regime and nation. At this historical juncture, as in the past, Jordanians and Palestinians need friends, not enemies.

References

Anderson, B. S. (2005). *Nationalist voices in Jordan: The street and the state.* Austin: University of Texas Press.

Brand, L. A. (1994). *Jordan's inter-Arab relations: The political economy of alliance making.* New York: Columbia University Press.

Fischbach, M. R. (2000). *State, society and land in Jordan.* Leiden: Brill.

Patel, D. S. (2015). The more things change, the more they stay the same; Jordanian Islamist responses in spring and fall. *Project on United States Relations with the Islamic World.* Washington, DC: Brookings Institution.

Ryan, C. (2002). *Jordan in transition: From Hussein to Abdullah.* Boulder: Lynne Rienner.

Ryan, C. (2017). Hashemite Kingdom of Jordan. In M. Gasiorowski & S. L. Yom (Eds.), *The government and politics of the Middle East and North Africa.* Boulder: Westview.

Schenker, D. (2017, April 19). Taxing times in Jordan. *The American Interest.*

Sowell, K. H. (2016, March 17). Jordan is sliding toward insolvency. *Carnegie Endowment for International Peace.*

Susser, A. (2008). Jordan—In the maze of tribalism, Jordanianism, Palestinianism and Islam. In S. Asher (Ed.), *Challenges to the cohesion of the Arab state.* Tel Aviv: Moshe Dayan Center for Middle Eastern and African Studies.

PART IV

Foreign Policy and Security

Foreign Policy Under King Hussein

Victoria Silva Sánchez

To speak about the reign of King Hussein (1952–99) is to talk about the contemporary history of Jordan. During his 46-year rule, the country has witnessed fundamental changes within its borders and in the whole region, which have tested the endurance of the Hashemite Kingdom. It is not easy to summarise the foreign policy under King Hussein, and a chronological order would address the main events at the regional level and the Jordanian stance towards them, studying its motivations and balancing strategy to survive among more powerful neighbours.

VOLATILE ENVIRONMENT 1952–58

The initial years of Hussein's rule were marked by internal pressures that affected his foreign policy as they faced one of "volatile regional turmoil and backlash against imperialist rule" (Tahboub 2016, p. 67). Hussein was present at Al-Aqsa when his grandfather, King Abdullah I, was shot dead by a Palestinian activist in July 1951, leaving a significant impression on him, but it was also a lesson on how to deal with different regional actors. For Hussein, as for his grandfather, the primary objective was to ensure the continuity of the Hashemite dynasty in Jordan.

V. Silva Sánchez (✉)
Villanueva de Córdoba, Spain

His first moves were aimed at restoring relations with the Arab countries, severely damaged due to the policies of his grandfather towards Israel and Palestine as well as the perceived British domination of the country. Those conditions made Jordan an easy prey for the radical Arab propaganda spread by Damascus and Cairo.

Hussein was a convinced anti-communist (Hussein of Jordan 1962, p. 68) and he viewed favourably the establishment of the Baghdad Pact, a UK-led alliance against communism that also included Turkey, Iraq, and Pakistan. Hussein was under enormous pressure from the Arab nationalist elements within the country and the widespread opposition to the pact was so huge that he had to decline it, despite the military benefits that it would have brought to the Jordanian army. Besides, he believed that the Pact should be an Arab initiative and not undertaken in a unilateral way (Tahboub 2016, p. 79).

Another example of the influence of domestic politics on foreign policy can be seen during the Suez Crisis of 1956. Hussein was the first Arab leader to congratulate Egyptian President Gamal Abdul Nasser on his nationalisation of the Suez Canal. This stance can be better understood in a context where pro-Nasser nationalist forces won the October 1956 parliamentary elections, but also due to "Arab nationalism, albeit of a particular, Hashemite character, [that] was central to his personal ideology" (Ashton 2005, p. 226). As Hussein himself pointed out "Arab nationalism can survive only through complete equality" (Hussein of Jordan 1962, p. 75). In this regard, it is worth mentioning that the security situation between Jordan and Israel had seriously deteriorated on the eve of the Suez Crisis, with daily attacks and casualties on both sides, and Hussein feared a major Israeli strike, especially after the Israel Defence Forces operation in Qalqiliya in October 1956 (Raad 1994, p. 291).

The inevitability of the Suez War led Hussein to ask for the deployment of Iraqi troops in Jordan, thereby giving Israel a *casus belli*. British diplomats, committed to the Anglo-Jordanian Treaty of 1948, moved to avoid an all-out conflict by encouraging an Israeli attack against Egypt, to which they would join French and their forces, with the aim of recovering the management of the Suez Canal. The understanding signed in Sevrès by the three countries was conditioned on the rejection of the use of force against Jordan by Israel. Although the attack on Egypt disappointed King Hussein, who severed relations with France, the fact "that Jordan was not attacked comprehensively by Israel between 15 and 20 October 1956 was principally the result of Britain's resolute support of the Anglo-Jordanian Treaty and France's pressure on Israel" (Raad 1994, p. 300).

The government formed under the leadership of Suleiman al-Nabulsi, a pro-Nasserite, in 1956 sought an end of the Anglo-Jordanian Treaty, which, to the surprise of Nabulsi and Hussein, was welcomed by the British (Ashton 2005, p. 227). General John Glubb Pasha, the British commander of the Arab Legion, was fired from his position due to internal and external pressures and "the presence of a British General presuming to dictate policy to an Arab state supposedly sovereign but in fact in British bondage worked wonders to demonstrate the character of the British connection" (Dann 1989, p. 27). Although these events damaged the relationship with the former colonial power, it was fixed soon as Hussein was anxious to maintain the alliance with Britain (Dann 1989, p. 34).

The creation in 1958 of the United Arab Republic (UAR) by Egypt and Syria was met by the establishment of the Arab Federation between Jordan and Iraq. This union was formally open to any Arab state but it "was, in essence, a 'family compact'" (Maddy-Weitzman 1990, p. 72). However, it was short-lived. The Arab Federation was dramatically interrupted by the military coup against Faisal II in Iraq in July that year, which ended in a bloody termination of the Hashemite rule in the Mesopotamian country. Hussein feared a similar fate by the growing Nasserite opposition in Jordan and sought support from the West, an anxiety that can be identified in his early autobiography *Uneasy Lies the Head* published in 1962. Although the Anglo-Jordanian treaty had lapsed the previous year, Britain committed troops to guarantee the security of the king. During hard negotiations, the British managed to convince the US of the need to sustain Hussein's regime against threats posed by the UAR, revolutionary Iraq, and Israel (David Ben-Gurion had admitted to the US of Israel's intention to seize the West Bank) (Tal 1995, p. 48).

Finally, on 21 August 1958, the UN Security Council unanimously accepted a resolution sponsored by the Arab League calling on all Arab states to respect "the territorial integrity and sovereignty of other states and to observe strict non-interference in each other's internal affairs" (Tal 1995, p. 49). The resolution established a UN observer mission in Amman and allowed the withdrawal of Western forces from the Kingdom. Apart from guaranteeing the territorial integrity of the country, the UN presence allowed Hussein to prove the significant existence of an external threat to his regime (Tal 1995, p. 50). The presence of British troops and, later on, of the UN acted as a deterrent for the ambitions of the surrounding countries, which since that moment, had to come to terms with the long-term presence of Hussein. It also marked the beginning of a period of "cold peace," as labelled by Tal (Tal 1995, p. 52), with Nasser's Egypt.

Towards Arab Unity, 1958–67

The 1958 crisis marked "a new era in Jordanian politics" (Tal 1995, p. 50), since it represented "a significant discontinuity in Jordan's political evolution" (Tal 1995, p. 54). The Kingdom lost Iraq, its major ally, leaving it more exposed to the Arab unity camp. During this period, the Arab world split into two major camps: the "moderates" and the "radicals" and both clashed in the Yemen civil war in 1962. Yemen's ruling Imam was deposed and replaced by a republican government supported by Egypt, which sent part of its army to Yemen. On the other side, Saudi Arabia and Jordan sided with the Imam and declared a military alliance. However, Jordan withdrew this support in 1964, after the Arab summit meetings. As Adnan Abu Odeh, former advisor to the monarch, explains in an interview, "when it became evident that the republican regime in Yemen was in control of the country and that there was no way of changing the new status quo and the Nasserite movement was well established in Yemen, Jordan recognised the republican government right away" (Mutawi 1987, p. 60). After this conflict, Saudi Arabia emerged as a regional rival to Egypt and, although Jordan wanted to remain neutral in this power balance, it meant the end of the era of Arab cooperation. The split between Iraq and Egypt fed the concept of Jordan as a "Third Force," establishing as an independent centre of power in the region (Shlaim 2007, p. 175).

This Arab cooperation started in 1963 with the celebration of Arab heads of state meeting in Cairo to discuss one of the main issues affecting the relations with Israel: the diversion of the Jordan River waters towards the Negev area. The conferences, which lasted until 1964, observed the establishment of different cooperative initiatives, including the Unified Arab Command (UAC), a joint military command of the Arab League states. However, the end of the meetings signified the end of the nascent cooperation among Arab countries. Jordan was a firm supporter of the UAC, but after 1964, the idea was buried, mainly due to the lack of commitment by the members and the hostile actions of Syria, which promoted Palestinian commandos' activity against Israel from the Jordanian soil. As King Hussein stated, "if all those various difficulties had been solved as they occurred, […], the Arab world would have been able to move ahead and realise its programme for common action" (Hussein of Jordan 1968, p. 18).

The Arab summits also saw the establishment in 1964 of the Palestinian Liberation Organisation (PLO) as an umbrella body where all the Palestinian groups would be represented at the highest level. However,

Hussein did not believe in the armed struggle to liberate Palestine because "like his grandfather, he was the king of realism" (Shlaim 2007, p. 611). Under the leadership of Ahmed Shukeiri, the demands of the Palestinians increased, together with the guerrilla activity carried out by the commandos and "the PLO came into existence at a crucial point in the all-encompassing process of integration between the West Bank and the East Bank" (Abu Odeh 1999, p. 112), bringing with it severe consequences to the building of national identity.

The 1966 Israeli aggression against the West Bank town of As-Samu marked a turning point, and it was a response to a previous Fatah assault on Israeli troops. The latter responded by sending thousands of forces that stormed the village, destroying dozens of buildings, and killing 16 Jordanian soldiers, three civilians, and injuring more than 100. The retaliatory attack was widely condemned by the UN Security Council, which passed Resolution 228. During the previous years, King Hussein had maintained secret conversations with Israeli officials to avoid this kind of response to increasing Palestinian guerrilla activities that he was not able to control. The lack of response by the Jordanian regime encouraged the opposition and, together with the failure of Israeli officials to honour their promise of not retaliating against Jordan, meant that the possibility of war became real.

The drums of war sounded in May 1967 when President Nasser requested the withdrawal of the UN troops from Sinai and closed the Strait of Tiran to Israeli shipping on 23 May. Meanwhile, Jordan had cut off diplomatic relations with Damascus on the 21st, due to a car bomb sent by the Syrians to Ramtha, a village on the Jordanian-Syrian border, which killed 17 Jordanians. On the eve of war, Arab disunity was the norm. These considerations made Hussein travel to Cairo to sign a mutual defence pact with Egypt, which added to the one already signed between Cairo and Damascus. However, Hussein was never optimistic about the fate of the conflict and "all we had in Jordan was a plan of defence. An offensive action was out of the question. Particularly, with the limited forces available at that time" (Hussein of Jordan 1968, p. 56). Although Nasser movements were provocative, he did not want a war with Israel, since he believed that "there was very little that Arabs could do" (Mutawi 1987, p. 49).

At the dawn of 5 June, Israel carried out a surprise attack on Egyptian military bases, destroying almost all its aircrafts on the ground. However, Cairo informed that Egyptians had destroyed 75 per cent of Israeli aircrafts, confusing Jordanians and forcing their entry into combat, although by that moment Jordanian troops only counted on the Iraqi support. Syria, despite its defence commitments, delayed the deployment of its forces, which arrived at the Jordanian front once the war was over. As stated by Mutawi, "Syria's role in forcing a confrontation with Israel is even more ironic when one considers its passive stance when war eventually broke out" (Mutawi 1987, p. 182).

The conflict officially ended on 10 June, and within six days, Israel occupied the Sinai Peninsula, the Gaza Strip, West Bank (including East Jerusalem), and the Golan Heights. Jordan was the country most affected by the war, losing the West Bank, and with it, the majority of its agricultural production, supposing a severe blow for the country's economy. As King Hussein states: "at 2 pm, on Tuesday, June 6, the situation was perfectly clear. For me, this so-called war was lost" (Hussein of Jordan 1968, p. 80). Hussein did not believe in a victory in the war, but he was motivated to join due to his commitment to Arab unity and cooperation, but actually he was just expecting to maintain the status quo (Mutawi 1987, p. 183). "If there is anybody who thinks he is a better Arab nationalist than I, let him demonstrate it in his own country, and not by using Jordan as his proving ground"(Hussein of Jordan 1968, p. 151).

In the aftermath of the war, the UN Security Council passed Resolution 242, which established the formula of "land for peace," that is, Israel would return the territories occupied during the war in exchange for borders recognition and peace. Syria and the PLO rejected the resolution, while Egypt, Jordan, and Lebanon were favourable to its implementation. Secret but unsuccessful Israeli-Jordanian diplomacy was established (although supported by Nasser) to achieve comprehensive peace in the Middle East (Ashton 2008, p. 366; Shlaim 2007, p. 612).

Civil War and Survival, 1967–71

The June War marked the end of Pan-Arabism as a political ideal and Palestinians also became conscious that the Arab states would not liberate their land, leading to the radicalisation of the PLO and increasing actions of the *Fedayeen* (Palestinian fighters) commandos. Jordan became the basis from where armed Palestinian groups launched attacks against Israel, leading to the retaliation by the Israeli Defence Forces in a constant cycle of violence. In March 1968, Israeli forces penetrated the Jordanian soil with the aim to crash the Fedayeen force located in the village of Karameh, in the Jordan Valley, which acted as headquarters of the Fatah leader and future chairperson of the PLO, Yasser Arafat. Through secret diplomacy, Hussein tried to stop the attack, but during the battle, the Jordanian army fought alongside the Fedayeen, capturing several Israeli tanks and forcing the IDF to withdraw.

In 1968, Israel considered Hussein's regime as "expendable" (Ashton 2006, p. 98) but the increased activity of the Fedayeen made Israeli politicians change their opinion and understand the need to support the Jordanian monarch. The situation deteriorated following the Karameh battle and "the more Israel punished Jordan for the guerrilla's incursions into either Israel itself or Israeli-occupied territory, the more it undermined royal authority in Jordan and Hussein's ability to rein in the *Fedayeen*. Both the *Fedayeen* and the Israelis were thus partly responsible for the crisis of September 1970" (Ashton 2006, p. 97). Israel and the US reaffirmed their support to Hussein's regime, and they did it through the creation of the Roger's Plan, an initiative to achieve peace in the region.[1] Its acceptance by Egypt in July 1970 meant the end of its War of Attrition with Israel and paved the way for Jordan to crack down on the Fedayeen (Pedatzur 2008, p. 300; Abu Odeh 1999, p. 179).

Karameh became a symbol for the Palestinian resistance and increased the popularity of the Fedayeen. However, the Jordanian army saw itself as the real winner of the battle and felt resented in their pride. Hussein tried to build a common front but failed (Ashton 2006, p. 100), and by 1969, the situation was unsustainable. Forced by the Israeli attacks, Fedayeen moved to the urban centres, where they disregarded the law and authority, establishing checkpoints inside the cities and harassed civilians, and these practices eventually turned the population against them.

Two main events triggered the Jordanian regime's response: the attempt of the Popular Front for the Liberation of Palestine (PFLP) to assassinate King Hussein on 1 September, and the hijacking of three airliners between 6 and 9 which were landed in Zarqa and Azraq airports. The airplanes were exploded by the hijackers after having liberated the hostages.

On 17 September, Hussein authorised the army to root out Fedayeen from Amman, "the toughest decision he had ever taken" (Abu Odeh 1999, p. 180), forcing them to move to the northern areas of the country

---

[1] The Roger's Plan was a framework proposed by the US Secretary of State William P. Rogers in the aftermath of the 1967 war. Launched in 1969, it was aimed at ending the confrontation between the Arab countries and Israel and, especially, the war of attrition between Israel and Egypt.

where they declared Irbid, the second Jordanian city, as a "liberated area." On the 20th, Syria sent armoured brigades that occupied Irbid in support of the Palestinian fighters. This prompted Hussein to ask the Israelis for help through the Americans to attack the Syrian forces from the air. However, Israel considered necessary a ground attack, something unacceptable for Jordan, which put the Israeli effort in standby.[2] During 22–23, the Jordanian forces drove back the Syrians, and the Israeli intervention was not needed, but "what Israel might have done, had the Syrians broken through to Amman, remains an imponderable" (Ashton 2006, p. 115). The contribution of Israel to the Jordanian victory has been exaggerated (Ashton 2006, p. 115) since it only amounted to the strengthening of its forces in the Golan Heights and the supply of intelligence information, while the Jordanian army waged the bulk of the battle.

The role of Jordan and Hussein during the 1970 crisis has been cast in different ways. Some present him as a "skilful manipulator" who portrayed himself as a "man of peace" in a volatile region but whose regime survival has depended on the US since 1952 (Little 1995, p. 513). Others consider that this "'puppet in search of a puppeteer' thesis misrepresents US-Jordanians relations during the crisis. Hussein's reading of the regional balance and the motives of key players proved more supple and sophisticated than the framed in Washington. Perhaps, therefore, the real puppeteer during the crisis was Hussein himself" (Ashton 2006, p. 118). In addition, the process that led to the showdown of the Jordanian army was not only fruit of the king's decisions but of the pressure of his political entourage (Makara 2016, p. 402).

At the Cairo summit meeting that took place on 27 September, Hussein was forced to accept the terms of a ceasefire agreement brokered by Nasser that was more favourable to Arafat, since it forced both sides to a mutual withdrawal, which allowed the Fedayeen to regroup in the northern areas of the country. However, the sudden death of Nasser the following day left the PLO without its greatest protector, paving the way for Hussein for the "final onslaught against the *Fedayeen*" (Ashton 2006, p. 117). On 13 July 1971, most of the Palestinian fighters in the Jerash-Ajloun area were captured or killed, while the rest fled to Syria or Israel. Prime Minister Wasfi al-Tall, considered a hardliner, took responsibility for the operation (Makara 2016; Ashton 2006, p. 117).

---

[2] For an in-depth account of the decision-making process behind the Israeli intervention refer to Pedatzur (2008).

Regional Balance of Power, 1971–91

The consequences of June War and the civil war led Jordan to remain out of the October 1973 War, except for a few units sent to the Syrian border. More critical was the civil war that broke out in Lebanon in 1975 and that was crucial in launching the negotiations between the Jordanian regime and the PLO.

According to the Israeli journalist Ehud Yaari, three main scenarios conflicted in Lebanon. The first one was the Assad Plan, which tried to balance between Syrian-Jordanian cooperation and Syrian domination over the PLO, creating a "con-federal framework which would link Syria to Jordan, the PLO and perhaps also Lebanon" (Institute for Palestine Studies 1976, p. 137). A second scenario was the Jalloud Plan, based on the establishment of a radical Arab bloc with Soviet support and a Northern Front against Israel. Jordan was excluded from this plan despite Assad's request that it should be part of it. A third and final plan was the Sadat one, whose fundamental aim was to push the Syrian regime towards a major change and re-establishing the Arab cooperation regarding the future of the PLO and in general terms.

Although Jordan had approached Syria during that period, the situation the Syrians were facing in Lebanon made Hussein to reassess the value of the Damascus-Amman axis by fear of being dragged into a Syrian-Israeli conflict, and this made Hussein turn to Iraq instead (Sasley 2002, p. 39). The supply of cheap Iraqi oil reinforced the relation to Jordan, and by 1989, Jordan received 17.3 per cent of its imports from Iraq and sent Iraq 23.2 per cent of its exports (Ryan 2000, p. 41). Above all, Hussein saw strong relations with Iraq as a protection against the expansionism of Israel (Hussein's concern about Israel pushing the Palestinians into Jordan) (Mufti 2002, p. 15) and Iran (in case it would win the Iraq-Iran war). In order to balance its interests, Jordan pushed for the creation of the Arab Cooperation Council (ACC) in 1990, which included also Egypt, Iraq, and Yemen, and this "gave Jordan the opportunity to have supporters in case peace with Israel was achieved, or use them as protectors if it was not" (Mufti 2002, p. 15) as well as to face Syria.

In the Arab summit in Rabat in 1974, the PLO was recognised as the sole representative of the Palestinians by all Arab states. This recognition forced Jordan to give up its right to speak as a representative of the Palestinian people and to acknowledge that an independent Palestinian state will be set up apart from Jordan. The December 1978 Arab summit held in Baghdad strengthened the Jordanian-Iraqi alliance (Ryan 2000, p. 40). The signing of the Camp David Accords between Egypt and Israel led to the expulsion of Egypt from the organisation. King Hussein opposed the agreements due to his conviction that this was a treacherous act towards the Palestinians (Ashton 2008, p. 366).

The refusal of Jordan to join the Camp David agreement distanced it from the US. This prompted Jordan to re-approach the UK, which under Margaret Thatcher, saw an improvement of relations between both countries. Four main factors motivated this movement: an interest in altering the US policy towards the Arab-Israeli conflict; seeking a more active role of the European Economic Community (EEC) in the Middle East; ensuring an alternative arms supplier; and defend the position of its Iraqi ally (Ashton 2011, p. 652). Throughout the 1980s, Thatcher gave considerable support to Hussein's position in the Middle East process, backing his initiatives and acting as a mediator with Washington. An example of that was the visit of Thatcher to Jordan in 1985, after Jordan and the PLO had reached the 11 February agreements. The relationship grew further through arms trade, with Jordan becoming a new regional market for the British defence industry, and also thanks to the role played by Hussein in establishing links between the Thatcher administration and Saddam Hussein's regime (Ashton 2011, 670). This British-Jordanian honeymoon ended when Iraq invaded Kuwait and the different approaches both countries took towards the crisis. In a meeting in London on 31 August 1990, the strong relation between Hussein and Thatcher came to an end in an awful discussion that froze the relations between Jordan and the UK until Prime Minister John Major took office at the end of that year (Ashton 2011, p. 671).

In 1980 and 1981, Israel annexed Jerusalem and the Golan Heights, respectively, and launched the slogan that "Jordan is Palestine," a claim that threatened Jordan's existence. Meanwhile, Jordanians and Palestinians reached the 11 February 1985 Agreement, which featured two main points: the convening of an international peace conference, with the participation of the five permanent members of the UN Security Council and the PLO, and the establishment of a confederation between Jordan and Palestine. However, its implementation faced a lot of difficulties, mainly due to the US and Israel opposition and the unreliability of the PLO, and these led to the cancellation of the agreement in 1986. The outbreak of the first Intifada in December 1987 changed the whole picture. Jordan supported the Palestinians politically and economically during this period, and on 31 July 1988, King Hussein, in a broadcasted TV appearance, announced the renunciation of Jordanian rights over the West Bank, while preparing to support the Palestinian authorities in the peace process.

THE POST-COLD WAR ERA, 1991–99

The post-Cold War era emerged in the Middle East in the shape of the Gulf War. Different considerations shaped Jordan's stance in the conflict. First was the firm belief of Hussein against occupation and the need to solve the crisis within an Arab framework (Tahboub 2016, p. 227). Before the invasion took place, Hussein visited both countries and urged to resolve the conflict peacefully, and when the annexation happened, Jordan did not recognise it and asked Saddam Hussein to withdraw while reaffirming the legitimate authority of the Emir of Kuwait (Tahboub 2016, p. 227). However, when the international coalition formed under the US to force Iraqi troops out of Kuwait, Jordan remained outside and opposed the invasion, heavily criticising it (Mufti 2002, p. 15). Hussein visited 25 Arab and Western countries to gather support for his peaceful solution, but he faced massive criticism for his position, misinterpreted as supportive of Saddam Hussein (Tahboub 2016; Mufti 2002, pp. 14–15).

The geographical situation of Jordan placed it in an awkward position. On one side, siding with Iraq meant losing the financial assistance from the Gulf countries as well as jeopardising the employment of 300,000 Jordanians working there. On the other hand, siding with Kuwait will damage Jordanian economy due to the close ties with Iraq and could lead to internal problems, since Arab public opinion, and in Jordan specifically, was supportive of Saddam Hussein. Besides, "the only real threat at the system level was the threat of direct Israeli-Iraqi confrontation, which presumably would be fought in Jordan. Fear of becoming an Israeli-Iraqi battleground did in part lead the Jordanian regime to try desperately to avoid a regional war over the Gulf crisis" (Ryan 2002, p. 74).

Against this situation, Jordan chose a neutral and peaceful approach to settle the differences within an Arab framework. Despite the existence of the ACC as a forum to address these issues, the Iraqi invasion of Kuwait killed the newborn organisation. Once Iraq withdrew its forces from Kuwait on 28 February 1991, Hussein started a new round of diplomacy to rebuild trust and cooperation with Arab and Western countries. However, Jordan suffered a substantial adverse impact from the conflict as its refusal to participate in the international coalition was interpreted as alignment with Iraq. The US and Gulf countries froze US$500 million in financial assistance to the country. Saudi Arabia imposed sanctions on Jordan, banning all Jordanian products from entering Saudi or other Gulf countries, forbidding Jordanian trucks to pick imports from Jeddah port, and banning Jordanian planes from flying over Saudi space (Tahboub 2016, p. 230). Besides, the coalition forces imposed a blockade on ships navigating to Aqaba, Jordan's only port, and international aviation corporations suspended flights to the country (Tahboub 2016, p. 230). Despite this heavy punishment, by 1992, Hussein was again welcomed in Washington since the US once again recognised the role that Jordan was called to play in the Middle East peace process and the strong personal friendship between George Bush and Hussein helped to maintain the ties (Ashton 2008, p. 282; Mufti 2002, p. 16).

In 1991, a joint Jordanian-Palestinian delegation participated in the Madrid conference, an international peace conference sponsored by the US and the Soviet Union. Bilateral negotiations continued between Israel and the joint Jordanian-Palestinian delegation during 1992, but after that, they separated and the Palestinians negotiated on their own. In 1993, the PLO and Israel signed the peace agreement known as the Oslo Accords. The accords took by surprise all Arab countries, including Jordan, which at the beginning was angered at them. However, Jordanian authorities soon realised that it was the moment to step aside as a part of the peace process and pursue its peace treaty with Israel. The result of this change of approach was the 1994 Wadi Araba peace treaty with Israel, signed by "the best of enemies" Yitzhak Rabin and Hussein (Ashton 2008). Apart from the Oslo Accords, the US pressure and the presumably material gains to win from the treaty pushed Jordan to sign it (Ryan 2002, p. 76). Immediately after, foreign debt worth US$1 billion was written off by the US and the Gulf states started to inject money into the Jordanian economy (Ryan 2002, p. 76). Most importantly, the recognition of borders ended the threat of Israel occupying the East Bank.

During the mid-1990s, Jordan became critical of Saddam Hussein, allowing the Iraqi opposition groups to open offices in Amman since 1996, and Hussein even met with the opposition and Kurdish leaders due to his new position towards the West as a peacemaker in the region. This new foreign policy orientation distanced Jordan from Iraq and brought it closer to Israel and Turkey, as shown by the Jordanian participation in joint US-Israeli-Turkish naval exercises and by its designation in 1996 as a "non-NATO ally." Besides, Jordan military cooperation with Turkey "amounted to a Jordanian-Turkish alliance" (Ryan 2000, p. 42) and was admitted to the World Trade Organisation as well as achieved "association status" with the European Free Trade Association (Ryan 2000, p. 42).

Conclusion

Jordanian foreign policy during Hussein's reign is inseparable from the domestic political conditions, but it was also shaped by the regional power competition and global superpower balance. Hussein's primary objective of consolidating Jordan as a new nation in the Middle East was accomplished. Between 1952 and 1970, the Hashemite Kingdom was constantly under threat of disappearing and became part of Israel or Syrian projects due to the expansionist ambitions of Syria, Iraq, Israel, and the Palestinian Fedayeen, but the regime survived and became an important country in the region.

Hussein's foreign policy was characterised by his anti-communist and pro-Western stance, which opposed Jordan, first to Pan-Arabists, and then to Islamists, after the Iranian revolution. The constant external threats forced Jordan's security to rely on external actors, first the British and later the Americans. This was evident during the 1958 crisis and in the 1970 civil war, where British, American, and Israeli support was essential to ensure the continuity of the regime.

The British-Jordanian relations have persisted during this period, although since 1953, the US became the main backer of the regime, both economically and militarily. However, the different approach to the peace process made Hussein come closer to Britain, which acted as a safety net in the face of growing US-Israeli ties. The relations with Israel were characterised by the ambiguity created by the need to cooperate to maintain regional security and stability and the continuous threat that Israel expansionist policy posed to Jordan. Although Hussein sought to establish relations, even in a secret manner, to prevent confrontations with Israel, the constant aggression and threat led him to take part in the 1967 war and to refuse to sign the peace until 1994, once Palestinians and Israelis reached an agreement.

Its particular vision of the Arab unity, based on the cooperation of all Arab countries despite their different ideologies, isolated Jordan at least until the death of Nasser. This stance forced the Kingdom to regularly accept positions that frequently run against its national interest, such as its participation in the 1967 war against Israel. However, its small size and geographical location forced Jordan to choose one or another despite its desired neutrality. Since the Suez Crisis until the Gulf war, Hussein was confronted with this painful reality that, in most of the cases, proved very expensive to the Kingdom, as happened in the aftermath of the 1967 and 1991 wars. Nevertheless, it was also his skilful policymaking and statesmanship that contributed to navigate some of the most complicated crisis of the twentieth century.

References

Abu Odeh, A. (1999). *Jordanians, Palestinians and the Hashemite Kingdom in the Middle East peace process* (322 pp). Washington, DC: United States Institute of Peace.

Ashton, N. (2005). 'A "special relationship" sometimes in spite of ourselves': Britain and Jordan, 1957–73. *The Journal of Imperial and Commonwealth History, 33*(2), 221–244. https://doi.org/10.1080/03086530500123812.

Ashton, N. (2006). Pulling the strings: King Hussein's role during the crisis of 1970 in Jordan. *The International History Review, 28*(1), 94–118.

Ashton, N. (2008). *King Hussein of Jordan: A political life* (431 pp). London: Yale University Press.

Ashton, N. (2011). Love's labours lost: Margaret Thatcher, King Hussein and Anglo-Jordanian relations, 1979–1990. *Diplomacy & Statecraft, 22,* 651–677.

Dann, U. (1989). *King Hussein and the challenge of Arab radicalism. Jordan, 1955–1967* (206 pp). New York: Oxford University Press.

Hussein of Jordan. (1962). *Uneasy lies the head* (233 pp). London: Heinemann.

Hussein of Jordan. (1968). *My war with Israel* (176 pp) (J. P. Wilson & W. B. Michaels, Trans.). London: Peter Owen. English translation 1969 William Morrow and Company, New York.

Institute of Palestine Studies. (1976). The effect of Lebanese events on inter-Arab relations source. *Journal of Palestine Studies, 6*(1 Autumn), 136–138. Published by: On behalf of the University of California Press Institute for Palestine Studies http://www.jstor.org/stable/2535730

Little, D. (1995). A puppet in search of a puppeteer? The United States, King Hussein, and Jordan, 1953–1970. *The International History Review, 17*(3), 512–544.

Maddy-Weitzman, B. (1990). Jordan and Iraq: Efforts at intra-Hashemite unity. *Middle Eastern Studies, 26*(1), 65–75.

Makara, M. (2016). From concessions to repression: Explaining regime survival strategies in Jordan during Black September. *The Journal of the Middle East and Africa, 7*(4), 387–403.

Mufti, M. (2002). A king's art: Dynastic ambition and state interest in Hussein's Jordan. *Diplomacy & Statecraft*, *13*(3), 1–22. https://doi.org/10.1080/714000336.

Mutawi, S. A. (1987). *Jordan in the 1967 war* (228 pp). Cambridge University Press: Cambridge.

Pedatzur, R. (2008). The rescue of King Hussein's regime. *Civil Wars*, *10*(3), 294–318.

Raad, Z. (1994). A nightmare avoided: Jordan and Suez 1956. *Israel Affairs*, *1*(2), 288–308.

Ryan, C. R. (2000). Between Iraq and a hard place: Jordanian-Iraqi relations, *Middle East Report*, *215*(Summer), 40–42.

Ryan, C. R. (2002). *Jordan in transition: From Hussein to Abdullah* (159 pp). Boulder: Lynne Rienner Publishers.

Sasley, B. E. (2002). Changes and continuities in Jordanian foreign policy. *Middle East Review of International Affairs*, *6*(1), 36–48.

Shlaim, A. (2007). *Lion of Jordan. The life of King Hussein in war and peace* (698 pp). London: Penguin Books.

Tahboub, N. (2016). *Jordan under the Hashemites* (418 pp). Amman: University of Jordan.

Tal, L. (1995). Britain and the Jordan crisis of 1958. *Middle Eastern Studies*, *31*(1), 39–57.

Foreign Policy Under King Abdullah II

Faisal Odeh Al-Rfouh

Viewed in a broad perspective, foreign policy of Jordan has been channelised towards meeting three significant challenges: (a) challenges pertaining to the Arab-Israel conflict, the occupation of the West Bank and the question of Palestinian refugees; (b) promoting the survival of the State in the light of its limited natural and economic resources; and (c) safeguarding Jordan's territorial integrity, sovereignty, stability, and security notwithstanding multiple internal and external threats in the region (Rashdan 1989, p. 71). Enthronement of King Abdullah II in February 1999 coincided beneath the cusp of the twenty-first century and the contemporary geopolitical and geo-economic ambiance, having witnessed a decade-long occurrence of developments veering round globalisation and post-Cold War setting at regional and global levels, entailed unpredictable future.

Soon after his enthronement, King Abdullah II did not hesitate in consolidating Jordan's international ties with major world powers such as the US, European Union (EU), Japan, China, France, etc. and cultivated close links with international financial institutions such as International Monetary Fund (IMF), World Bank, and the World Trade Organisation

F. O. Al-Rfouh (✉)
Glendon Political Science, York University, Toronto, ON, Canada

University of Jordan, Amman, Jordan

© The Author(s) 2019
P. R. Kumaraswamy (ed.), *The Palgrave Handbook of the Hashemite Kingdom of Jordan*, https://doi.org/10.1007/978-981-13-9166-8_23

(WTO). At the regional level, he continued the rich legacy, inherited by him, of nurturing cordial and friendly relations with Jordan's immediate neighbours as well as member countries of the Gulf Cooperation Council (GCC).

The King embarked on a series of visits to key foreign capitals to garner support for his regime and these visits were underpinned by his central concern for the economic development of Jordan and reflected his interest and aptitude for engagement with the outside world. Apart from visiting member countries of the Group of Seven (G-7) and European Union (EU), he focussed on fostering close cooperation with Jordan's immediate neighbouring countries and Gulf Arab Countries to elicit political and economic support for his regime.

Jordan's near-landlocked geographic location, sparse natural and economic resources, and relative economic, political, and military weaknesses vis-à-vis its neighbours make an impact on its foreign policy (Ryan 2004, p. 45). While articulating a strong nationalist approach and to counter foreign influences in the domestic politics, King Abdullah came with the slogan of "Jordan First" or *al-Urdun Awalan*. While elaborating his conception of "Jordan First" in early October 2002, the King observed:

> The programmes, objectives, membership, and financing of every party operating in Jordanian territory ought to be purely Jordanian … In recent decades, Jordan has given priority to Arab interests and not to its national interests …We have a right to be concerned first for our own people, as every country in the world does, which is where our "Jordan first" slogan comes from. (Agence France Presse, 11 October 2002, cited in Ryan 2004, p. 56)

King Abdullah's rule, spanning close to two decades, has witnessed growing economic, political, and military cooperation between Jordan and great powers, including immediate neighbours and Gulf Arab countries.

Jordan-US Relations

King Abdullah II had inherited a rich legacy of cordial and friendly relations between Washington and Amman and tragic events of the 11 September terrorist attacks on the US and Jordan being among the first Arab and Muslim countries to extend support to the Global War on Terrorism, brought both countries closer. In recognition of its vital role in the war against terrorism, particularly after the American war in Afghanistan in 2001 and the Iraq war in 2003, the US increased its foreign aid to Jordan from US$228.4 million to US$1.557 billion in 2003. Ostensibly, the objective of this increased aid was to ease the impact of the Iraq war on Jordan's economy and to help Jordan maintain its border security.

Under the terms of an agreement reached between the US and Jordanian governments on 22 September 2008, the former agreed to provide a total of US$660 million in annual foreign assistance to Jordan over a five-year period (2010–2014) and this deal committed the US to provide US$360 million per year in Economic Support Funds (ESF) and US$300 million per year in Foreign Military Financing (FMF). Total bilateral US aid to Jordan through 2016 amounted to approximately US$19.2 billion. In accordance with a nonbinding three-year memorandum of understanding (MOU) signed on 3 February 2015, the US pledged to provide the Kingdom with US$1 billion annually in total foreign assistance from 2015 to 2017. The provision for Jordan under the Consolidated Appropriations Act, 2017, inter alia include about US$1.279 billion in bilateral aid to Jordan and up to US$500 million in funds from the Defence Department's Operation and Maintenance, Defence-Wide account to support the armed forces of Jordan and to enhance security along its borders (Sharp 2017, p. 13).

Within a short span of Abdullah's accession to the throne, Washington and Amman on 24 October 2000, signed a US-Jordanian Free Trade Agreement, which eliminated duties and commercial barriers to bilateral trade in goods and services originating in the two countries, which positively impacted their overall trade. As a direct outcome of this agreement, the US emerged as Jordan's chief market making up nearly one-third of its total exports by 2007 and the latter ranked 74th American trading partners in the volume of trade in 2012. In that year Jordan exported over 1 billion dollars worth of goods and services to the US, a large percentage of which comprised apparel and clothing accessories. In the same year, Jordanian imports from the US reached US$1.6 billion, and the principal commodities consisted of aircraft parts, machinery, appliances, vehicles, and cereals (Sharp 2013, p. 12). In 2014, Jordan became 66th trading partner of the US concerning the volume of trade (Al Sarhan 2016).

Their friendly relations also extend to military and defence cooperation, entailing the supply of American defence equipment, training of Jordanian defence forces, and joint military exercises. Jordan, having been granted the Major non-NATO Ally (MNNA) status by the US in 1996, made it eligible to receive excess US defence articles, training, and loans of equipment for cooperative research and development. Between 2009 and 2012, the Kingdom received excess US defence equipment valued at approximately US$81.69 million (Sharp 2013, p. 13).

In the wake of instability spreading throughout the Arab world, Jordan's likelihood of emerging as the most dependable Arab partner for pursuing US interests in the region have increased. Such an indication could be discerned from the remarks of the US President Barack Obama, who during his visit to Jordan in March 2013, said:

> The reason I'm here is simple. Jordan is an invaluable ally. It is a great friend. We've been working together since the early years of the Kingdom under His Majesty's great-grandfather, King Abdullah I, who gave his life in the name of peace. Today, our partnership in development, education, health, science, technology, improves the lives of our peoples. Our close security cooperation helps keep your citizens and ours safe from terrorism. Your military and police help train other security forces from the Palestinian Authority to Yemen (Sharp 2013, p. 8).

Jordan has acquired Advanced Medium Range Air-to-Air Missiles, upgrades for its fleet of F-16 fighters (approximately 70–80) and Black Hawk helicopters from the US. In July 2017, the US delivered two S-70 Blackhawk helicopters, bringing their total Blackhawk fleet up to 26 aircraft. Proposed arms sales notified to Congress include 35 Meter Coastal Patrol Boats; M31 Unitary Guided Multiple Launch Rocket Systems (GMLRS) Rocket Pods; UH-60 M VIP Blackhawk helicopter; and repair and the return of F-16 engines (Sharp 2017, p. 15).

Jordan's relations with Trump Administration have continued to follow the past rich legacy of friendship and cordiality. During their meeting in Washington on 20 September 2017, President Trump and King Abdullah vowed to keep working together to fight terrorism in the Middle East. While touting the bilateral ties, President Trump said: "Never has the relationship been better than it is now" (*Los Angeles Times*, September 20, 2017). In spite of this deep-rooted friendly relation between Jordan and the USA, there's a difference in political points of views; particularly, regarding the Palestinian- Israeli conflict, the Jerusalem issue, as well as, Iraqi situation.

JORDAN-EU RELATIONS

Jordan's relations with the European Union are characterised by many bilateral agreements, close cooperation, and almost identical views on global issues. Trade relations between Jordan and EU have recorded substantial growth in recent years and trade in goods amounted to €4.4 billion in 2016. The EU imported goods worth €0.3 billion from Jordan in 2016, which mostly comprised chemicals and machinery and transport equipment. The EU exports to Jordan in 2016 accounted for €4.1 billion comprising machinery and transport equipment, followed by agricultural products and chemicals. Two-way trade between EU and Jordan in services amounted to €1.4 billion in 2015 with EU imports of services representing €0.5 billion and exports €0.9 billion (European Commission). The Association Agreement governs the Jordan-EU bilateral trade, entered into force in May 2002, established a Free Trade Area liberalising two-way trade in goods.

Jordan is a partner country within EU's programme of the European Neighbourhood Policy (ENP) since 2004. Political framework for the dialogue between EU and Jordan is envisaged by a joint ENP Action Plan endorsed by the EU-Jordan Association Council. In October 2010, both reached an agreement on a new EU-Jordan ENP Action Plan and this envisaged substance to the "advanced status" relationship between the two. In January 2014, a new programme the European Neighbourhood Instrument (ENI) was introduced as the first multi-annual strategic framework for the EU cooperation with Jordan.

The financial allocation for the period 2014–2020 under the ENI was to vary between €587 million and €693 million depending on the progress made on democratic and socio-economic reforms by Jordan. On 27 January 2014, their representatives met in Amman and deliberated on enhancing security cooperation and joint efforts to combat crime, especially in the wake of international and regional security developments. Extending support to Jordan to handle the impact of the Syrian crisis, the EU has so far provided more than €320 million since 2011 in humanitarian, crisis response, and development support to this aim (*The Jordan Times*, various issues).

Jordan-Russia Relations

Jordan shares cordial and friendly relations with Russia and there were exchange of high-level visits between the two countries, especially in the aftermath of the Syrian crisis. There have been frequent exchanges of top-level visits which have proved instrumental in bringing both countries closer. In September 2000, President Vladimir Putin and King Abdullah had a short talk during the "Millennium Summit" in New York. In August 2001, the King paid his first official visit to Russia and subsequently he visited Russia in November of 2001, July and November of 2002, November of 2003,

September of 2004, and August of 2005. Discussions veered round augmenting bilateral relations and the situation in the region. President Putin visited the Hashemite Kingdom of Jordan in February 2007, and this was followed by the visit of King Abdullah to Russia in April 2014 and August 2015 and the visit of Russian Deputy Foreign Minister in August 2016 to be followed by the visit of Abdullah to Russia in February 2018.

Their growing political interactions during the first decade of the twenty-first century also witnessed trade and economic cooperation moving to a new stage since 2007. The two-way trade grew substantially and amounted to US$169 million, for ten months in 2007, in comparison to only US$64.8 million in 2006. This period also witnessed attempts at developing techno-economic cooperation, and the Russian Railways showed interest in taking part in building Amman-Zarqa railway line and another company Tekhnopromexort reportedly showed interest in building two thermal power plants and hydroelectric power stations on the River Yarmuk (Sharif 2015).

However, the Syrian crisis and the Russian involvement in it brought Jordan's strategic geographic location into focus, and the direct outcome was the coming closer of Russia and Jordan. During 2014 and 2015, Jordan maintained close contacts with Russia for finding a lasting political solution to the Syrian conflict. On 24 March 2015, Jordan concluded a US$10 billion deal with Russia for building the Kingdom's first nuclear power plant, with two 1000-megawatt reactors. The deal, a strategic one for the energy-starved Kingdom, followed many months of negotiations (Ibid.).

During his visit to Moscow in the last week of August 2015, King Abdullah held discussions with Russian leaders, including President Vladimir Putin, on bilateral cooperation as well as developments in the Middle East. The talks emphasised on the need for the expansion of partnerships in the fields of military cooperation, air and railway transportation, as well as religious and medical tourism. While dwelling on contemporary developments especially combating terrorism and extremism as part of a comprehensive approach and with the participation of all stakeholders, both leaders also reviewed the Syrian crisis and other events in the region, in addition to efforts of reviving Palestinian-Israeli peace negotiations (*The Jordan Times*, 26 August 2015).

Undoubtedly, the Russian intervention in Syria had commenced at the end of September 2015 and Jordan's initial silence was an indication of its "tacit approval" of Moscow's role and signified Amman's cautious approach to the Syrian conflict. The Kingdom was trying to keep itself away as far as possible from "axis wars" in Syria and hoped for a solution that could help maintain Syria's territorial integrity and prevent its collapse (Sharif 2015).

The sudden announcement simultaneously made in Moscow and Amman on 23 October 2015 that both countries had agreed on military coordination in Syria through a joint mechanism took the world by surprise. While asserting that both the armies had decided to coordinate their actions, including military aircraft missions over Syrian territory, the Russian side added that such coordination would be effective against terrorists of all shades. The Jordanian spokesperson averred that his country's coordination with Russia was aimed at safeguarding the country's northern borders and stability in southern Syria. The agreement, apart from reflecting a standard approach to Syria, also served Jordan's interests in keeping its northern borders outside the cycle of violence for so long as possible (Sharif 2015).

After the October 2015 agreement, media reports confirmed consistent cooperation between on airline security, exchanging intelligence, including information on people suspected of having ties to extremists and collaboration on ground operations. Defending Jordan's strategy of having an agreement with Russia, Barmin (2017) has opined that the critical factor in Jordan's security equation is the border being shared by Jordan with Syria and Iraq, and it is against this backdrop that cooperation with external powers, "such as Russia and the United States, is motivated solely by Jordan's internal security calculations. It is no coincidence that in this tumultuous region, Jordan has remained one of the few 'islands of stability' …" (Barmin 2017).

Before the Russian military intervention in Syria in the second half of 2015, the contours of the Russian-Jordanian bilateral relationship were mostly confined to nonbinding political deliberations and limited trade and arms deals, despite the frequency of interaction. The past decade has witnessed the signing of many arms deals between Russia and Jordan, which among other things include, Igla portable air defence system, Kornet anti-tank systems and localising production of Russian RPGs in Jordan. However, the Syrian conflict has catapulted this relationship to a new trajectory of growth, and under the prevalent geopolitical scenario in the Middle East, Russia and Jordan need each other politically and militarily.

Jordan-UK Relations

Jordan shares a long-standing and close relationship with Britain and defence relations are an essential part of this. King Abdullah, having inherited a rich legacy, has made efforts to further consolidate this relationship by continuing the conduct of annual joint military exercises between the two armies, and Royal British Navy ships pay regular visits to Aqaba. In September 2001, British Prime Minister Tony Blair visited Amman and early November 2001, King Abdullah paid an official visit to Britain (*The Jordan Times*, 7 November 2001). Jordan was supported by the UK in July 2002 in debt rescheduling as a result of the Paris Club discussions, and this enabled Jordan to reschedule debts to lender states. In 2008, the UK and other member countries of the Paris Club agreed for US$2 billion debt settlement with Jordan. Subsequent period has witnessed frequent exchange of visits by dignitaries and high-level delegations between the two counties.

During his visit to Britain in early March 2017, Abdullah held discussions on wide-ranging issues with Prime Minister Theresa May, including boosting cooperation in the economic, military, and security fields along with the importance of following up on the outcomes of the London donor conference held in February 2016 to aid countries hosting Syrian refugees (*The Jordan Times*, 4 March 2017). Bilateral cooperation, especially in economic and defence areas, Middle East peace process and Syrian crisis were the primary focal points of discussions between Abdullah and May who visited Jordan in early April 2017. While the Jordanian King expressed appreciation of continued British support, the British premier asserted her country's high regard of Jordan's efforts to support peace and stability in the Middle East (*The Jordan Times*, 4 April 2017).

During her visit to Jordan in the last week of November 2017, Prime Minister Theresa May outlined her vision for the post-Brexit relationship with Jordan and the wider region, focusing on a commitment to support national prosperity and regional security. She emphasised on supporting joint bilateral initiatives that promote socio-economic development and enable the Kingdom to achieve economic security through job creation and employment for a bulging youth population. While security and counterterrorism cooperation dominated her approach, she also sought to reiterate her commitment to boost trade and investment opportunities and strengthen long-term support for economic and social reforms in Jordan and its neighbouring region (*The Jordan Times*, 30 November 2017).

The volume of trade between Jordan and the UK is more favourable to the latter. Jordanian exports to the UK in 2015 stood at JD18 million compared to JD200 millions of imports. Jordanian experts and business circles feel that Brexit will have no direct effects on Jordan's economy and bilateral agreements will remain active. It is being argued that Jordan and the UK will start re-negotiating their bilateral trade agreements after Brexit (*The Jordan Times*, 27 August 2016).

Jordan-China Relations

The frequency of high-level visits between Jordan and China has proved instrumental in bringing their bilateral relationship to new heights. In January 2002, King Abdullah visited China and again in July 2004 to be followed by the visit of in October 2004 by the then prime minister of Jordan; and in December 2005, King Abdullah II again visited Beijing. This period also witnessed visits of the Chinese delegations to Jordan and discussions veered round means of boosting bilateral relations and expanding prospects of cooperation, particularly in the fields of investment and trade exchange.

Abdullah's visit to China in September 2013 was followed by a high-level Chinese delegation visiting Jordan in November 2014. However, Chinese President Xi Jinping's visit to Jordan in the second week of September 2015 proved instrumental in further consolidating the friendly level of friendship. This occasion was utilised by both leaders to exchange views on bilateral relations in different fields and developments at the regional and international arenas. Their announcement to establish strategic partnership relations was hailed as a "new chapter" and that it would take bilateral ties to a new level of fruitful cooperation, especially in economic fields. On his part, the Chinese President lauded Jordan's efforts in the war against terrorism and extremism, stressing his country's willingness to help the Kingdom deal with the Syrian refugee crisis. While reviewing the latest developments in the Middle East, with specific emphasis on the need for a comprehensive political solution to the Syrian crisis conflict, both leaders also discussed endeavours to revive Palestinian-Israeli negotiations on the basis of the two-state solution (*The Jordan Times*, 10 September 2015).

A joint statement issued at the end of the talks, while announcing the establishment of a strategic partnership, also stressed the importance of carrying on with efforts to enhance friendship and cooperation ties that would serve the interests of both peoples as well as regional and world peace, stability, and progress. It also reflected both countries' agreement to mutually support their vital interests, with the Kingdom stressing its commitment to the "one China principle," renewing its position on Taiwan as an integral part of the Chinese mainland and supporting "the Chinese government's efforts to achieve peaceful development across the Taiwan Strait and its efforts to reunite the country." For its part, Beijing pledged to support Jordan to maintain its security and stability and enhance its economic and social development. Jordan also highlighted the importance of the Chinese initiative to participate in building "the economic belt of the Silk Road" and "the naval silk road of the 21st century" (Ibid.).

Undoubtedly, the trade volume between Jordan and China reached US$3.6 billion in 2014 but is tilted in favour of China despite Jordan's exports to China having gone up by 200 per cent from 2013. Jordan's exports goods comprised mainly of potash and phosphate, valued at around US$300 million while the imports from China stood at US$3.3 billion. With bilateral trade said to have reached US$3.1 billion in 2016, the number of Chinese tourists coming to Jordan rose by 60 per cent in 2016 (*The Jordan Times*, 3 April 2017). During the visit of the Chinese foreign minister to Jordan in June 2017, both sides reiterated their commitment to further enhance political mutual trust, deepen practical cooperation speeding up the advancement of cooperation projects in economy, trade, investment, infrastructure, and other fields, in a bid to make joint contribution to safeguarding regional peace and security (*The Jordan Times*, 24 June 2017).

Jordan-France Relations

Frequent exchange of high-level visits, sharing identical views on many regional and international issues and holding close and detailed dialogue through regular high-level bilateral meetings have immensely contributed to uniting Jordan and France through ties of friendship and trust. In July 2002, King Abdullah visited France and discussions between the two sides veered round bilateral relations and the situation in the region. Visit of the Jordanian King to France in August 2007 entailed discussion on bilateral relations and to elicit French support for Mideast peace and stability in Iraq.

King's September 2014 visit proved instrumental in eliciting French support for Jordan's development efforts, especially in the aftermath of the influx of Syrian refugees into Jordan and accordingly in early October 2015, France confirmed its support for Jordan through the signing of development agreements totalling US$265 million. During the visit of the French President Francois Hollande in April 2016, six contracts were signed, including a memorandum of understanding between the Agence Française de Développement (AFD) and the Ministry of Planning and International Cooperation concerning the granting of €900 million in additional loans over the next three years.

France ranks sixth concerning foreign investors, with €1.5 billion in Foreign Direct Investment (FDI) stock and is active in the area of telecommunications, which accounts for 66 per cent of French investment, banking services, cement production, water distribution and treatment, fuel distribution, and transport. The French exports to Jordan increased by 9.1 per cent in 2016 compared with 2015 and France has a trade surplus of €308 million, and the total trade volume is €370 million (Diplomatie France).

Visit of the Jordanian King to France in June 2017 culminated in his talks with the French President Emmanuel Macron on the latest regional and international developments and means to enhance cooperation and partnership between the two countries, thereby, highlighting the importance of continuing coordination and consultation between the two countries on issues of mutual interest and expanding participation in the economic and military fields. The joint statements issued for the media during this visit emphasised on historical relations between the two countries (*The Jordan Times*, 20 June 2017). On the Syrian crisis, both sides agreed on the importance of reaching a political solution to the crisis in a way that guarantees the unity of Syria and the security of its people.

The focal points of deliberations between King and the French president, during his visit to France in December 2017 entailed, apart from bilateral issues, regional issues as well, specifically the US announcement to recognise Jerusalem as the capital of Israel. Both sides stressed the importance of continued coordination between Jordan and France on various issues and boosting cooperation in the economic, military, and security fields. Emphasising that the Trump administration's unilateral decision to recognise Jerusalem as Israel's capital was against the international law; from Jordanian point of view, King Abdullah said that both sides agreed that there was no alternative to the two-state solution and that there is no solution without Jerusalem. On his part, the President Macron, while underlining the on-going progress between France and Jordan in different fields, stated that the issue of Jerusalem was of paramount importance for both sides, dictating cooperation between France and coordination with Jordan (*The Jordan Times*, 20 December 2017).

JORDAN-JAPAN RELATIONS

Recognising the importance of political and economic stability of Jordan, which is located in a unique geopolitical position and directly affects the stability of the Middle East, Japan has actively extended support to the Kingdom. This understanding has been furthered by the mutual exchange of high-level visits between the two countries. During his working visit to Japan in December 2004, Abdullah, while exchanging views on bilateral and regional issues, also sought Japanese support and investment for his development programmes. Emphasis on augmenting bilateral cooperation, increase in Japanese investment in Jordan and developments in the Mideast Peace process constituted the central planks of his visit to Japan in April 2010.

During his visit to Japan in October 2014, Abdullah held wide-ranging talks with the Japanese leaders. The Japanese side expected that the bilateral relationship would be further strengthened in a wide range of fields, including politics, security, and economy. On his part, the King thanked Japan for the various kinds of support offered to deal with the Middle East situation. He also explained Jordan's efforts for the Syrian refugee issue and the current challenges and asked Japan for continued cooperation (*The Jordan Times*, 27 October 2014).

In the wake of Jordan's significant role to the Middle East peace process and the sustainable peace in the region, Japan has been implementing economic cooperation to Jordan by providing practical assistance in each area combining requisite modalities, including loan, grants, and technical cooperation. Since 2009 to early 2016, Japan has extended more than US$1 billion in financial assistance to Jordan, including some US$491 million as grants and US$530 million as soft loans (*The Jordan Times*, 5 September 2016). Concerning trade, the overall trade balance is favourable to Japan; in 2016, Jordan's exports comprised mainly fertiliser and phosphorus ore and Jordanian imports consisted mainly of transport machinery and other machinery.

During his visit to Jordan in early January 2015, the Japanese Prime Minister Shinzo Abe while assuring his readiness to extend non-military assistance said that Japan would provide financial help to Jordan, which was struggling financially owing to its efforts to support refugees fleeing from Syria and Iraq. Besides, an agreement was signed between the two private sectors to establish Shams Ma'an, projected to be the largest solar energy project in the Middle East with an investment of up to US$160 million (*Japan Times*, 18 January 2015).

During the October 2016 visit of the King, apart from the exchange of views on bilateral and regional issues, proved instrumental in eliciting a soft loan worth US$300 million to be spent on development projects. Exchange of views also encompassed ways to maintain coordination and communication and boost cooperation in political, economic, and security fields. Japan also evinced its interest to expand its role and build on the "peace corridor" project to promote economic cooperation between Israel, Jordan, and the Palestinians, as well as support the Red Sea-Dead Sea Water Conveyance Project (*Japan Times*, 28 October 2016).

JORDAN-ISRAEL RELATIONS

Jordan's relations with Israel under the leadership of King Abdullah II have been marked by many ups and downs and is described as "semi-cordial official relationship," which is used by him to "improve Jordan's standing with Western governments and international financial institutions, on which it relies heavily for external support and aid" (Sharp 2013, p. 7). The unresolved perennial question of Palestine is the main stumbling block in the full normalisation of Jordan's relations with Israel and for that matter between Israel and other Arab countries. In May 1999, King Abdullah had stated that Jordan was needed as a "fulcrum for the future stability of the region" (*The Jordan Times*, 18 May 1999).

Israeli opposition to two-state solution and its insistence on one-state solution (merging West bank with Jordan), which had been endorsed by Trump administration in February 2017, was viewed with alarm by the Kingdom, which has reiterated in the strongest terms its steadfast commitment—along with of the Arab states during the March 2017 Arab summit in Amman—to a two-state solution that would give Palestinians a homeland in the West Bank and Gaza and King Abdullah in his meeting with President Trump in Washington in April 2017 made this position clear (Muasher 2017).

During his first ever official visit to Israel in April 2001, King Abdullah tried to convince Israeli leadership that to improve the bilateral relations between it was imperative for Israel to make substantial progress with the Palestinians. In early 2004, Prime Minister Sharon visited Jordan at the invitation of the King, and while referring to the nature of talks, Abdullah recalls, "I knew that the true national interest of Jordan and of Israel would be served only by reaching peace between Israel and the Palestinians. I tried to convince him of this, but by the end of the meeting, after a lengthy discussion of Israeli actions in the Occupied Territories and the need to take effective steps to create an environment conducive to the resumption of serious peace negotiations, I was quite certain that Sharon did not share my view" (King Abdullah 2011, Chap. 26).

Israeli action of constructing a wall dividing the West Bank and the continued construction of illegal Israeli settlements in the Occupied Territories, which was already in progress, was opposed by the King during his meeting with Sharon on 19 March 2004 in Negev (Israel), but of no avail. In his memoirs, Abdullah describes briefly about his meetings with Israeli leaders between 2004 and 2010 wherein he frequently raised the issues of illegal Israeli settlements in the West Bank and East Jerusalem, as they were eating away at land that should be part of the future Palestinian state and thereby threaten the viability of a two-state solution. However, the pleadings of the Jordanian King with Israeli leaders failed to bear any tangible outcome, and he was convinced that the proof of the intentions of Israeli leaders was in their actions, not in their words (Ibid.).

The 1994 Jordan-Israel Peace Treaty proved instrumental in opening up some avenues of cooperation, though limited and the post-treaty phase saw the development of Qualified Industrial Zones (QIZs), in Jordan where the companies that used a percentage of Israeli inputs could export duty-free goods to the US. These zones were reported to have generated many jobs, thereby emerging as a potent engine of growth for the Jordanian economy. In 1999, US$2.5 million worth of goods were exported to the US through QIZs, which by 2007 had exceeded US$1.14 billion. In 1999, there were only two companies in the QIZs, and the number of employees in the zones was about 5000, and by 2007, the number of companies increased to over 50 and the zones employed over 46,000 workers (Mitha 2011).

Other examples of Israeli-Jordanian cooperation are agreement on water sharing signed in early December 2013 and an agreement on Israeli natural gas to Jordan signed in 2014. A regional water agreement signed among Israel, Jordan, and the Palestinian Authority entailed the potential of paving the way for Red-Dead-Canal that could provide freshwater to water-scarce countries in the surrounding areas while restoring the Dead Sea. In 2014, Israel signed an agreement with Jordan for the supply of natural gas (Sharp 2015, p. 5).

Despite these overtures of cooperation, the second half of 2017 witnessed brewing up of diplomatic tensions owing to disputes over holy sites in Jerusalem and to an incident at the Israeli Embassy in Amman in which two Jordanian citizens were killed by an embassy employee who claimed to be acting in self-defence (Sharp 2017, p. 7). The US President Donald Trump's announcement in early December 2017 to recognise the disputed city of Jerusalem as the capital of Israel has been opposed by Jordan, and the King in his subsequent meetings with President Trump in 2017 and early 2018 has conveyed his country's opposition to it and this has also led to an unease in Jordan's relations with Israel, particularly after the refusal of the Jordanians to the so-called the American deal of the century.

JORDAN AND PALESTINE

There has been no dilution of Jordan's support to the Palestinian cause and under the leadership of King Abdullah II, time and again Jordan has reiterated its endorsement of the two-state solution that would lead to a Palestinian State in the West Bank and Gaza. Israel is opposed to two-state solution and has been arguing for some time for the Jordanian control over parts of the West Bank that it does not wish to keep and such a proposal essentially promotes a solution that is detrimental to the Palestinians and denies them any control over East Jerusalem as well as undermines Jordan's national interests (Muasher 2017). The divisions within the ranks of the Palestinian leadership, especially between Fatah and Hamas, have further complicated the goal of attaining a two-state solution to the Palestine problem.

Jordan has continued to support Mahmoud Abbas government, despite tense periods on some occasions. However, the emergence of an unexpected trilateral rapprochement involving Hamas, Egypt, and former Fatah strongman Mohammad Dahlan has seemingly added to Jordan's worries. The emergence of Yehya Sinwar as the de facto prime minister of the Hamas-led government in Gaza in early 2017 and alteration by Hamas in its manifesto in May 2017 where it accepted an independent Palestinian State according to the 4 June 1967 borders, but without recognising

Israel are touted as serious developments complicating the already complex issue of Palestine (Sharif 2017).

In Jordan's view, the fate of the two-state solution is intimately linked to the future of Gaza and the West Bank. Articulating Jordan's apprehensions, Sharif (Sharif 2017) writes: "A semi-autonomous Gaza opens the path to unilaterally imposed arrangements by Israel regarding the future of the West Bank—Israeli control of the land with responsibility for the population assigned to Jordan through some form of confederation, in which it is refused by the Jordanian King and people. Amman could be pressured and enticed to accept such a deal. The caveats include giving up on Palestinian refugee rights and awarding citizenships to most, which would upset Jordan's current demographic balance."

During his visit to West Bank in August 2017, King Abdullah held a short meeting with the Palestinian President Abbas and the two leaders discussed recent tension with Israel, and it is a move seen by some observers as an act of unity during a time of heightened tension with Israel. In the wake of US President Donald Trump's assertion in early December 2017 to recognise Jerusalem as the capital of Israel, on 28 January 2018 King Abdullah affirmed his support for establishing a Palestinian capital in East Jerusalem, highlighting his differences with the Trump administration on a central issue in the Israeli-Palestinian conflict (*The Jordan Times*, 28 January 2018).

JORDAN AND SYRIAN CRISIS

In the wake of on-going Syrian Crisis since 2011, according to the data based on preliminary results of the national census conducted in late November 2015 that of the total non-Jordanian population, 1.265 million are Syrians (*The Jordan Times*, 30 January 2016) and according to United Nations High Commissioner for Refugees (UNHCR), as of 31 December 2017, there were 655,624 registered Syrian refugees in Jordan (UNHCR, December 2017). Looking after such a massive number of refugees has impacted profoundly on Jordan's fiscal resources, augmenting government expenditures on subsidies, public services, and security, while further compounding the negative economic consequences of regional instability. However, the regime has sought to meet this challenge despite all odds through the National Resilience Plan (NRP 2014). The government has come out with Jordan Response Platform 2017–2019, a three-year plan that seeks to address the needs and vulnerabilities of Syrian refugees and the Jordanian people.

In February 2016, the government entered into an arrangement with foreign governments and international financial institutions known as Jordan Compact for improving the livelihoods of Syrian refugees already living in the Kingdom. This programme is designed to enable the government to procure low-interest loans from foreign creditors and preferential access to European markets for goods manufactured in special economic zones with a high degree of Syrian labour participation (Sharp 2017, p. 5).

JORDAN AND GCC COUNTRIES

Jordan shares cordial, brotherly, friendly, and close relations with Gulf Arab countries. King Abdullah II has accorded priority in maintaining ties with these countries and harnesses his rapport with heads and the leaders of the Gulf countries to foster close ties and broadly extends his Kingdom's support for the decisions of the Gulf Cooperation Council (GCC) on broader issues.

The proximity between Jordan and the GCC is discernible from the trade relations which have been on ascendance for years now. In 2016, Jordan's exports to Arab Gulf States stood at JD1.32 billion, while imports amounted to JD2.53 billion. Jordan's exports to GCC countries stood at JD455 million in the first five months of 2017, while imports amounted to JD1.11 billion for the same period (*The Jordan Times*, September 28, 2017).

By the end of 2016, the total amount of funds transferred from the Gulf countries' grant to Jordan had reached JD1.661 billion. Jordan has received JD524.94 million from Saudi Arabia, JD721.04 million from Kuwait and JD415.61 million from the UAE. The total sum of the funds spent in 2016 was JD327.17 million, while the value of approved projects reached JD2.469 billion. The GCC Higher Council, in its 32nd session in 2011, approved allocating US$5 billion in grant to support development projects in Jordan over five years provided by Saudi Arabia, the UAE, Kuwait, and Qatar on a share basis of $1.25 billion for each country (*The Jordan Times*, 19 April 2017).

The unexpected eruption of Gulf dispute on 5 June 2017 in the wake of severance of diplomatic relations with Qatar jointly by Saudi Arabia, the UAE, Bahrain, and Egypt presented Jordan with a dilemma. The specific reasons for this extraordinary action were allegations that Qatar was funding terrorist groups and was interfering in the domestic affairs of these countries in clear violation of GCC agreements and international law. It was a litmus test for King Abdullah's diplomatic acumen. On 6 June 2017, the government of announced the downgrading its diplomatic representation with Qatar and asked the Qatari ambassador to leave and revoked the license of *Al-Jazeera*'s office in Jordan (*Al-Monitor*, 22 June 2017). But the relation between Jordan and Qatar resumed its natural path in July 2019.

The Jordanian King adroitly handled the diplomatic crisis by refraining from making any comments or pronouncements in the post-crisis phase and making a choice not to get directly involved in the Gulf spat while extending support to Kuwait's peace efforts. Perhaps the King was reminded of the grave consequences faced by Jordan by having sided with Iraq during the Kuwait crisis in 1990–1991 and asked for an Arabian solution to solve the disputes through negotiations.

Since September 2011, when the GCC formally invited Jordan to submit a bid for membership of the regional forum, speculative reports have been doing rounds in the national and international media about Jordan joining the GCC. As a member state of the GCC, Jordan would receive much-needed financial support and concessional supply of oil. On the other hand, the Gulf States would benefit from the Kingdom's military expertise, competitive workforce, and diplomatic ties to Western powers. Jordan is regarded as a strategic and geopolitical partner by the GCC member states (*The Jordan Times*, 5 November 2017). Once the GCC wriggles out of the diplomatic crisis that erupted in early June 2017, further progress on Jordan's membership of the GCC can be expected.

Conclusion

Under the rule and leadership of King Abdullah II, Jordan has pursued a foreign policy that partly has been the continuity of the rich legacy of the past left by King Hussein and partially it has been characterised by the change that is perhaps required by the prevalent geopolitical compulsions occurring at regional and global levels. Unlike his predecessor's emphasis on "Arab First," Abdullah has emphasised on "Jordan first," a phrase which perhaps has found favour with American President Donald Trump. The adage in Jordan that king is the fountainhead of Kingdom's foreign policy perhaps finds its best articulation in Abdullah's diplomatic acumen of frequently visiting important nations which are significant politically, economically, and strategically to elicit necessary support for Jordan. He possesses appropriate acumen of transforming challenges into opportunities.

Initially focusing on foreign policy, working hard to cement Jordan's relations with many different nations and travelling to visit heads of Gulf

Arab States and the US and other relevant countries, Abdullah took advantage of the "beginning of his reign to make a 'meet and greet' tour of many different nations, using these visits as opportunities to strengthen or build new relationships with a number of countries" (Wagner 2005, p. 87).

Jordan under his leadership has come to regard its alliance with the US and its burgeoning relations with the European Union as crucial strategic interests and sees itself as in sync with both on most foreign policy issues. According to Ryan (2014): "Jordan even views itself as a model for the region regarding policy areas of deepest concern to Western governments and Western-led global institutions: supporting neoliberal economic politics, pursuing domestic political reform, combating militant Islamism and terrorism, stabilizing Iraq, bringing an end to the Syrian civil war and restoring the Arab-Israeli peace process."

REFERENCES

Al Sarhan, A. (2016). *United States' foreign policy towards the Hashemite Kingdom of Jordan: 1990–2014.* Unpublished thesis. Atlanta: University of Atlanta.

Al Sharif, O. (2015, November 3). How will Jordan's pivot to Russia pay off? *Al-Monitor.*

Al Sharif, O. (2017, July 11). *Hamas-Dahlan Détente keeps Jordan on edge.* Middle East Institute. Available at http://www.mei.edu/content/article/hamas-dahlan-d-tente-keeps-jordan-edge

Barmin, Y. (2017, May 31). Russia's Syria strategy hinges on Jordan. *Al-Monitor.*

European Commission, Jordan. Available at. http://ec.europa.eu/trade/policy/countries-and-regions/countries/jordan/

Japan Times. Various issues.

King Abdullah II. (2011). *Our last chance: The pursuit of peace in a time of peril.* London: Penguin Books, e-pub.

Mitha, F. (2011). The Jordanian-Israeli relationship: The reality of "cooperation". *Middle East Policy, XVII*(2 summer).

Muasher, M. (2017, September 8). Jordanian-Palestinian relations. *carnegieendowment.org.* https://carnegieendowment.org/2017/09/08/jordanian-palestinian-relations-pub-73006

Rashdan, A. A. (1989). *Foreign policy making in Jordan: The role of King Hussein's leadership in decision-making.* Unpublished thesis. Texas: University of North Texas.

Ryan, C. R. (2004). 'Jordan First': Jordan's Inter-Arab relations and foreign policy under King Abdullah II. *Arab Studies Quarterly, 26*(3 summer), 43–62.

Ryan, C. R. (2014). Jordanian foreign policy and the Arab spring. *Middle East Policy Journal*, *XXI*(1 Spring).

Sharp, J. M. (2013, April). *Jordan: Background and U.S. relations*. Washington, DC: Congressional Research Service.

Sharp, J. M. (2015, March). *Jordan: Background and U.S. relations*. Washington, DC: Congressional Research Service.

Sharp, J. M. (2017, November). *Jordan: Background and U.S. relations*. Washington, DC: Congressional Research Service.

UNHCR (United Nations High Commissioner for Refugees). (2017, December). *Syria regional refugee response*. Available at http://data.unhcr.org/syrianrefugees/regional.php

Wagner, H. L. (2005). *King Abdullah II*. Philadelphia: Chelsea House Publishers.

Websites of Government of Jordan, Government of France, Government of the United States, Government of Japan, etc. consulted.

Relations with Saudi Arabia

Md. Muddassir Quamar

The Hashemite Kingdom of Jordan and the Kingdom of Saudi Arabia share a sophisticated but friendly relationship. They have many common traits; both are Islamic monarchies named after their ruling families and have been close allies of the US. In both cases, the ruling families consolidated power by gaining the loyalty of the local tribes and adopted a policy of modernisation to gain the confidence of the broader population. At the same time, they are countries with divergent socio-political trajectories. Jordan is recognised as an open, cosmopolitan and inclusive society, especially when it comes to its women and minorities, while Saudi Arabia has struggled with problems of social conservatism, segregation of women and an exclusive approach towards minorities, especially the non-Arab migrant population. Politically Jordan has adopted a policy of gradual opening, has a functioning Parliament with elected representatives and political parties. Saudi Arabia, on the contrary, does not allow political organisation and its Parliament, the *Majlis al-Shura*, remains a nominated consultative body. In terms of economy, the disparity is wider. Jordan is a resource-starved country and relies on international aid for sustenance while petroleum resources make Saudi Arabia one of the wealthiest countries in the world and an Arab financial powerhouse. In fact, in recent

---

Md. M. Quamar (✉)
Institute for Defence Studies and Analyses, New Delhi, India

© The Author(s) 2019
P. R. Kumaraswamy (ed.), *The Palgrave Handbook of the Hashemite Kingdom of Jordan*, https://doi.org/10.1007/978-981-13-9166-8_24

decades, Jordan has become increasingly dependent on Saudi financial aid and investments for economic subsistence.

Notwithstanding the current state of benevolent ties, the origin of relations between the Hashemite and Saudi monarchies is rooted in conflict and rivalry for dominance in the Arabian Peninsula. The Hashemites ruled over Hejaz since the days of early Islam, trace their lineage from the Prophet, and were the custodian of the Islamic Holy sites in Mecca and Medina for centuries. The al-Sauds on the other hand, are rooted in the central Arabian region of Nejd from where they rose to establish a strong state. Riding on the enthusiasm of tribal warriors immersed in the puritanical religious message of Muhammad Bin-Abdul Wahhab, the Saudi State expanded to threaten other family rules in the vicinity.

With declining Ottoman authority, the al-Saud and Hashemite families competed and often clashed for superiority and dominance in the Arabian Peninsula. By the early nineteenth century, the Saudi threat to the Hashemites became overwhelming, and the message reached the *Sublime Porte*. The Sultan then deputed the Egyptian Mamluk ruler Muhammad Ali to protect the Hashemite rule in Hejaz. Ali's army led by his son Ibrahim attacked and destroyed the Saudi State in 1818.

The rivalry was revived in the early twentieth century when Abdulaziz Bin-Abdulrahman al-Saud (Ibn Saud) regained control of Riyadh and capitalising on the disarray in the Ottoman Empire and aided by the British, he sought to expand his rule in the whole of Arabian Peninsula. While the Hashemites were busy exploring the end of Ottoman dominance over Arabia and establishing a Kingdom of Arabia under their tutelage, a struggle erupted between al-Saud and Sharif Hussein of Mecca for dominance and ended with the ousting of the Hashemite family from their traditional base in 1925.

Both the Sharif Hussein and Ibn Saud were harbouring a desire to lead the Muslim *Ummah* after the fall of Ottoman Empire and the dissolution of the Caliphate by the Turkish National Assembly on 3 March 1924. Indeed, Hussein's declaration of himself as the Caliph (Teitelbaum 2001, p. 243) days after the dissolution was the immediate trigger for the military onslaught on Hejaz by Ibn Saud's army as he was also eyeing the vacuum created due to the end of Caliphate. Eventually, al-Saud prevailed due to a variety of factors including the propensity among the Hashemites to ignore the challenge coming from Nejd over the larger goal of attaining the Kingdom of Arabia, not to forget the decisive role played by the British manoeuvres while protecting its interests in the region.

Though the rivalries between the al-Saud and the Hashemites goes deeper in history with ideological and religious dimensions, the events of 1924–1925 left a deep scar between the two families, and it took a long time to heal. It was not until the assassination of King Abdullah I of Jordan in 1951 and the death of Ibn Saud in 1953 that the situation started to change. Saud—the eldest surviving son of Ibn Saud—and Hussein—the grandson of Abdullah I—despite their contrasting personalities established a working relationship mainly due to the geopolitical developments in the region. Nevertheless, the tendency to see each other as rivals and suspecting motives behind any foreign policy measures remained the norm for most of the 1950s. It was the reign of King Faisal (1964–1975) that laid the foundations for the contemporary relations between Jordan and Saudi Arabia. For a brief period in 1990–1991, the Kuwait crisis and Jordan's ambiguous position derailed the relations but soon after the crisis was over the situation returned to normalcy.

The Early Phase

The Emirate of Transjordan, a British protectorate, became an independent Hashemite Kingdom of Transjordan (renamed the Hashemite Kingdom of Jordan in 1949) in March 1946. After the formation of Israel, Jordan along with Egypt, Iraq, and Syria took the lead in launching a military operation to prevent the newly formed Jewish State from establishing effective control over Mandate Palestine. Saudi Arabia too contributed troops that fought under the Egyptian command in the 1948 conflict. Though the Arabs collectively faced a significant setback at the Israeli forces, Jordan's Arab Legion took control of the West Bank and the Old City of Jerusalem. This was to some extent seen as a compensation for the loss of the Hashemites' sovereignty over Mecca and Medina in 1925. The Custodianship of the third holiest site in Islam, the Al-Aqsa and Dome of Rock, became a primary source of legitimacy for the Hashemite rulers.

Despite fighting on the same side, Saudi Arabia and Jordan were not at ease with one another. King Abdullah, "as the self-imposed senior scion of his house, never forgave the Saudis for expelling his family from Mecca. Abd al-Aziz, on his part, suspected that the Hashemites never gave up the ambition to recapture their ancestors' realm" (Nevo 1994, p. 104). King Saud after succeeding his father to the Saudi throne briefly toyed with the idea of accommodating the concerns of Arab Nationalism and formed a coalition with Egypt to oppose external intervention in Arab affairs. When the Baghdad Pact was signed in 1955 between Iran, Iraq, Turkey, Pakistan, and Britain, Jordan came under intense British pressure to join the grouping, but Saudi and Egyptian counsel and anti-Hashemite protests and riots in Amman effectively prevented the Hashemites from joining the military bloc (George 2005, pp. 28–29). During the Suez crisis, both Jordan and Saudi Arabia extended support to Egypt. Jordan's siding with Egypt against Britain eventually led to the termination of the 1922 agreement between the UK and Jordan in March 1957. Saudi Arabia, Egypt, and Syria came forward with financial support to replace the £12 million annual British subsidies to Jordan.

Nonetheless, the Arab solidarity did not last long, and the rising Arab nationalist fervour which targeted monarchies forced Iraq, Jordan, and Saudi Arabia to form a "Royalist Coalition" in late 1957. The quest for dominance in the Arab world became a major cause of friction between the Arab Nationalists led by Gamal Abdul Nasser and the Arab monarchies. Two events in 1958, namely, the formation of United Arab Republic (UAR) in February and the coup d'état in Iraq in July, brought Saudi Arabia and Jordan even closer. Vilified by "the Arab radical regimes as anachronistic, imperialist leaning and unrepresentative the leaders of Jordan and Saudi Arabia found solace with support for each other at those times when the future of their dynasties looked precarious" (Milton-Edwards and Hinchcliffe 2001, pp. 101–102).

The civil war in North Yemen (1962–1970) further strengthened the alliance between Jordan and Saudi Arabia. The conflict had erupted after the coup d'état against Imam Muhammad al-Badr, who proved to be the last Zaidi-Shia Imam of Yemen, led by Abdullah Sallal, a colonel in the army and supporter of a republican Yemen. The coup against the Yemeni royal family alarmed the Saudi and Hashemite rulers as pressures from nationalist forces within these countries were building up. They feared that Nasser's support to the rebellious groups would eventually dethrone their family monarchies. This common threat perception brought the Saudis and Jordanians closer, and the two decided to extend active military support to the Yemeni royal family against the rebel forces.

On the other hand, Nasser committed military and financial support to Sallal, and at the height of the civil war, nearly 70,000 Egyptian soldiers were stationed in Yemen. Even though Jordan withdrew from the conflict in July 1964 under pressure from Iraq and Egypt, Saudi Arabia continued to provide military and financial support to the royalist forces. It was not until the Arab defeat in June War of 1967 that Nasser decided to end Egyptian intervention in Yemen and the Egyptian troops were finally withdrawn from Yemen in December.

THE ERA OF GROWING COOPERATION

The June War had a profound impact not only on the Israeli-Palestinian conflict but also on the broader Arab politics. It marked the end of Nasserism and pan-Arabism and hastened the rise of Pan-Islamism led by Saudi Arabia. This also meant that the centre of gravity of Arab politics shifted from Egypt to Saudi Arabia. Jordan which had at the last minute decided to join the war lost control over the West Bank and East Jerusalem. This was a devastating blow for the Arabs, and the War resulted in a greater Egyptian and Jordanian dependency upon the Saudi financial aid. Saudi Arabia, for example, committed to extending an annual financial aid of US$150 million to Egypt and offered financial assistance and contributed troops for Jordanian security by dispatching a brigade to Amman.

In the changed regional circumstances, Saudi Arabia and Jordan saw it necessary to cooperate. For al-Saud, the stability and security of the Hashemite Jordan were essential for its security, and this was appreciated by the Jordanian royal family. Not that the two agreed on all regional matters. For example, on the issue of recognising the Palestine Liberation Organisation (PLO) as the sole representative of the Palestinian people in 1974, Riyadh went against Jordanian interest (Ashton 2008, pp. 182–184). Nonetheless, they agreed to cooperate and work towards stabilising the region and avoid any internal crisis. Saudi Arabia readily sent troops and military support to Jordan whenever it faced domestic crises. The events of September 1970, often referred as Black September, threatened not only the Hashemite Kingdom but also shook Saudi Arabia that had a significant expatriate Palestinian population that was restive due to lack of any resolution in the conflict with Israel and was under constant incitement by Syrian and other revolutionary regimes.

After efforts for reconciliation failed, many Palestinian factions openly declared their intention to overthrow the Hashemite monarchy, and in response, King Hussein decided to take recourse to force. On 16 September, the Jordanian army entered the Palestinian refugee camps in Amman and pitched battle between the armed Palestinian guerrillas and the security forces began. Saudi Arabia took a position of expressing regret at the loss of lives on both sides but refused to yield to pressures to stop financial aid to the Jordanian monarchy or condemn its actions. King Faisal was worried over possible trouble the Palestinian expatriates could create inside the Kingdom and did not come out openly in support of Jordan. At the same time, he did not cut aid to the monarchy and galvanised military assistance through the Pakistani army that proved to be effective in quelling the Palestinian rebellion saving the monarchy. As the Black September events came to an end, the "cease-fire between the Jordanian army and the Palestinian organisations caused calm to ensue within Saudi Arabia" (Mann 2014, p. 721). It was both a relief in term of the restoration of stability in Jordan and threats from Palestinians expatriates inside Saudi Arabia.

For much of the 1970s, Saudi Arabia extended military and financial aid to Jordan. In addition to annual grant-in-aid, it also committed to providing US$250 million for the Jordanian air defence network (Anthony 1979). Though both were not directly involved in the hostilities during the October War of 1973, both came out in support of the Arab countries and Saudi Arabia spearheaded the oil embargo which received Jordanian support. Under the Camp David Accords (1978) when President Anwar Sadat signed a separate Peace Treaty with Israel in (1979), both Jordan and Saudi Arabia came out against Egypt and took the lead to expel the latter from the Arab League.

The year 1979 had many milestones when it comes to the geopolitics of Middle East; in February Iran had witnessed the fall of Shah; Egypt signed a peace treaty with Israel in March; and in December the Soviet Union invaded Afghanistan. However, the most significant internal challenge for the al-Saud rule came in November due to the siege of Mecca and a test for the Saudi-Jordan relations.

The siege led by hard-line Salafist rebel Juhaiman al-Otaibi and a few hundreds of his supporters declared the "arrival" of Mehdi and establishment of an Islamic state. Otaibi declared his brother-in-law Muhammed al-Qahtani as the Mehdi who according to the rebels was divinely ordained to re-establish Allah's sovereignty on earth. Initially, the Saudi authorities mobilised the military and the National Guards to flush out the rebels but could not succeed despite large-scale bloodshed inside the holy mosque surrounding Kaaba. King Hussein travelled to Saudi Arabia and met King Khaled and Commander of the National Guard Prince Abdullah and offered Jordanian military help to defeat the rebels but was politely declined (Trofimov 2007, pp. 169–172). Gradually, it became clear that the Saudi forces need external help for securing the Kaaba and neutralising the rebels and "nearby Jordan seemed the most natural choice for riding to al Saud's rescue" (Ibid., p. 170). However, there was a catch; the Saudis were conscious that the Hashemite family ruled over Mecca half a century ago and feared that if the "Jordanians come to Mecca, they will never leave!" Eventually, the siege ended with the involvement of the elite French paratroopers and the Kingdom waded through the crisis. The Jordanian offer to help and eagerness to come to the rescue of al-Saud, though did not materialise, reflected the growing ties between the two monarchies.

One of the reasons for growing cooperation between Saudi Arabia and Jordan throughout the 1970s and 1980s was the prosperity in the Gulf Arab countries due to the influx of oil wealth and increasing Jordanian dependence on them for the economic well-being of its population. While Amman was a primary recipient of aid from Gulf countries as a frontline country fighting against Israel, economic cooperation has grown with Jordan exporting agricultural products to the Gulf. Jordan also received cheap oil from Saudi Arabia, Kuwait, and the UAE and sent workers to these countries who in turn sent significant remittances that helped in the sustenance of the local economy. For example, nearly 350,000 Jordanians lived in Kuwait in 1990 who in turn sent nearly US$1 billion per annum in remittances (Milton-Edwards and Hinchcliffe 2001, p. 104). During the Iran-Iraq war (1980–1988), Jordan was one of the main conduits through which Saudi and Gulf military and financial support reached Iraq. The unconditional Jordanian support to Iraq during the war has paved the way for Jordan and Iraq developing close friendly relations. Iraq had emerged as a significant destination for Jordanian industrial and agricultural exports while it imported cheap oil in return.

This became a huge problem for Jordan when Iraq invaded Kuwait in August 1990 as it found itself "in an impossible position: it was closely allied to the US and enjoyed warm relations with its fellow conservative monarchies in the Gulf; but it was also close to Saddam's Iraq" (George 2005, p. 34). It affected not only its relations with Kuwait and other Gulf Arab countries but also the US. Amman's ambivalent position was seen as support for Saddam Hussein, and this led to the expulsion of almost the entire Jordanian expatriate workers population from Kuwait after liberation. Saudi Arabia and the UAE too expelled many Jordanians leading to a sudden decline in the inflow of remittance and an increase in the flow of Gulf returnees. Except for Oman that remained friendly, Jordan's relations with Gulf monarchies were severely affected. Even though soon after the crisis, Saudi Arabia and Jordan resumed friendly relations, the events of the Kuwait crisis underlined the fault lines of inter-Arab politics affecting bilateral ties between the two countries.

Alliance or Dependence?

Despite the disruption in ties at the start of the decade due to the Kuwait crisis, since the mid-1990s Saudi-Jordanian relations have progressively moved in the direction of economic, political and security cooperation. Political asymmetry in ties and increased Jordanian economic dependence on Saudi Arabia have become the norm and "relations between the two countries are not balanced," and the "major reason is their economic asymmetry, the implication of which extend beyond the multifaceted financial aid to Jordan." Concerning economic relations, "one can actually speak of Jordan's dependence on Saudi Arabia" (Nevo 1994, p. 111).

Economic Dependence

The economic relations between Jordan and Saudi Arabia have grown extensively since the 1990s. For Jordan, Saudi Arabia has continuously been one of its highest trading partners. For example, in 2016–2017, Saudi Arabia was Jordan's second largest export destination as well as the source of imports; Jordan imported US$2.33 billion worth of goods while exported US$0.99 billion worth of commodities (The World Bank 2018). This was a many-fold increase from 1993 to 1994 when the bilateral trade was US$0.22 billion, but Saudi Arabia was the largest trading partner for Jordan even then and continues to retain that position. On the other hand, for Saudi Arabia, Jordan is the 12th largest export destination and 33rd in the list of its sources of imports. This means that for Jordan, Saudi Arabia is one of the most significant trading partners but for the latter Jordan is not even among the top ten importers or exporters.

Likewise, Jordan is a primary recipient of financial aid from Saudi Arabia. Though it received assistance even in the 1970s, its dependence on the Saudi largesse has increased in recent decades. For example, since the Arab Spring protests started in 2010–2011, Saudi Arabia has promised to invest millions of dollars in the Jordanian economy. In 2011, Saudi Arabia and other Gulf countries pledged to provide US$5 billion worth of financial support in the form of aid for developmental projects to Jordan

(Obeidat 2014). As protests in mid-2018 again hit the country due to growing unemployment, Saudi Arabia, the UAE, and Kuwait further pledged US$2.5 billion in financial support (*Al-Jazeera* 2018b). According to Saudi Center for International Communication, between 2007 and 2017, Saudi Arabia has spent US$33 billion in foreign aid and out of which US$13 billion has gone to Yemen while Jordan received over US$516 million and ranked ninth in the world in terms of Saudi aid recipients (Center for International Communication 2018).

This extensive financial and economic dependence had an impact on the political ties and reduced Jordan to be a subordinate or junior partner of Saudi Arabia in regional politics. This is evident from the fact that King Abdulla II of Jordan and his ministers and officials undertake several annual official and private visits to Riyadh while the number of Saudi official or high-level visits has been few and far between. "This imbalance in mutual visits is a conspicuous indication that relations with Saudi Arabia are much more important to the Jordanians that vice versa" (Nevo 1994, p. 112). This was also evident from the fact that Jordan was keen to join the Arab federation, an expansion of the six-member Gulf Cooperation Council (GCC) in the wake of the Arab Spring protests. The idea was to bring the only two remaining Arab monarchies outside the Gulf into the GCC fold and create a security-based alliance of Arab monarchies. Though it did not materialise, Jordanian keenness underlined its dependence on Saudi Arabia.

Jordan's foreign policy cooperation with Saudi Arabia is also a product of its economic and political dependence. Many regional developments show that Amman seeks to align its policies with Riyadh. This is evident from its reaction to Saudi actions in Yemen and against Iran and Qatar. For example, Jordan has taken an active part in the Saudi-led coalition military strikes in Yemen against the Houthi rebels who dislodged the Abdrabbuh Mansur Hadi-led government from Sana'a in September 2014. Jordan along with the UAE, Egypt, Kuwait, Bahrain, Morocco, and Sudan is a major partner in the Saudi-led war in Yemen. Amman has committed its military and air force, and despite growing international criticism of the Saudi-led coalition strikes for exacerbating the humanitarian crisis, it has not backed out of the coalition.

Similarly, Jordan has come forward strongly in support of Saudi Arabia in its rivalry and the diplomatic dispute with Iran. As the diplomatic row between Tehran and Riyadh intensified over the execution of dissident Saudi Shia cleric Nimr al-Nimr in January 2016 and the subsequent violent protests in Tehran and Mashhad in which Saudi embassy and consulate were targeted, Jordan decided to downgrade its diplomatic representation in Iran and recalled its ambassador from Tehran. King Abdullah II has been critical of Tehran for its regional interference and meddling in internal Arab affairs. For example, in his conversation with Fareed Zakaria during the World Economic Forum in Davos in January 2018, the King had remarked "We believe in Jordan that dialogue is the best way to solve problems, but the policy of Iran poses major challenges in Syria, Lebanon, and Yemen" (*Al-Jazeera* 2018a). He had also commended Saudi role in countering Iranian regional ambitions, which evoked an angry reaction from Tehran.

Jordan's growing proximity and political association with Saudi Arabia was again visible when the Qatar crisis broke out in June 2017. Though Jordan was circumspect in taking punitive measures due to its domestic political vulnerabilities, it was quick to support the Saudi-led boycott. Within a day after diplomatic, political, and economic boycotts were announced by Saudi Arabia and the UAE, Jordan downgraded its diplomatic ties with Qatar, recalled its ambassador from Doha, and revoked the license of *Al-Jazeera* network to function in the Kingdom. The Hashemite monarchy has also been supportive of other Saudi regional policy measures over Syria, Lebanon, and Palestinian territories. In the Arab Summit in Amman in March 2017, a resolution endorsing the Saudi-backed Arab Peace Initiative for resolving the Israeli-Palestinian conflict was adopted. While there is mutuality of political interests, the economic dependence has been a significant factor in Jordan aligning its regional policy with Saudi Arabia (Eran and Guzansky 2017).

Security Alliance

Notably, the Jordan-Saudi relations are not one-way traffic. The partnership has components where Jordan is seen as a significant contributor and an ally of Riyadh. This is most evident in the domestic security and regional stability. First, for Riyadh, security and stability of the Hashemite Kingdom is of utmost importance for its security and comprises an essential aspect of its national interest. Historically Saudi Arabia and Jordan have seen security and stability of the other as an important component of their domestic security. This was evident when both have come to each other's rescue or have offered support at times of crisis such as the Black September events in Jordan in 1970 and the Siege of Mecca in 1979. Saudi Arabia has been extremely sensitive towards any danger to Arab monarchies including Bahrain, Oman, or even in far-off Morocco. Towards this end, Riyadh has been offering financial and military help to them since the outbreak of Arab Spring protests. Jordan too has been a significant recipient of Saudi largesse in the wake of widespread protests. Undoubtedly, Saudi Arabia sees security and stability of Jordan as an extension of its internal security.

Second, issues related to inter-Arab affairs are an important aspect of mutual interests between the two as they have a similarity of views on matters such as in Palestine, Syria, Lebanon, Yemen and other regional issues. The Saudi-Jordanian views on Israeli-Palestinian conflict significantly overlap, and both have come to see the resolution of the conflict in their interest. They have been cooperating over the civil war in Syria, and Jordan has been a significant conduit for Saudi and the US support to the moderate Syrian rebels. On Iraq and the dangers from Islamic State (IS) both see them as a direct threat to their internal security and have cooperated to stop the expansion and spread of the IS ideology. In Lebanon, they have been collaborating and supporting groups opposed to the growing clout of Hezbollah that represents Shiite resistance and Iranian influence in that country.

Third, Jordan has been a beneficiary of alliance with Saudi Arabia in gaining an international diplomatic voice. For example, in 2013, Jordan took the non-permanent membership of the United Nations Security Council (UNSC) after Saudi Arabia declined to take the seat over differences with the US on Syria and other regional issues. Riyadh was reportedly miffed with the US for not making any diplomatic initiative in the UNSC for international military intervention to remove Bashar al-Assad from power. As a result, it rejected the seat after being elected to the UNSC for the first time and subsequently, Riyadh asked Jordan to take its place, and the latter obliged. In a sign of diplomatic alliance, Amman did not contest the Saudi candidature in the UN Human Rights Council a few months later (Nichols 2013).

Fourth, Saudi Arabia has been sensitive about political reforms in neighbouring monarchies, and it has been argued that Jordan is persuaded by the al-Saud to go slow on its political reforms as it will lead to pressure on Saudi Arabia for a political opening which it is not ready yet. This became evident when King Abdullah II put the onus on his security and intelligence forces for the slowing down of political reforms in the Kingdom (Patrick 2013). This has also been a reason for Saudi Arabia to shower Jordan with economic and financial support. These underline that the relationship between Jordan and Saudi Arabia is not a complete political, economic, and strategic subordination of Hashemite Kingdom. There is no doubt that Saudi Arabia is the dominant partner, mainly due to its economic prosperity and regional leverage but Jordan's significance as a security partner for Saudi Arabia cannot be ignored. Jordan's role as a stable Arab monarchy and an important player in inter-Arab affairs are significant factors in Saudi Arabia seeking partnership with Jordan. Hence, if one looks at the contemporary relationship between Jordan and Saudi Arabia, there is a degree of Jordanian dependence, but there is also a component of mutuality of interest.

Conclusion

For much of the century of their existence, Saudi Arabia and Jordan have shared several ups and downs. The history of rivalry between the two royal families was fresh in the early years and the two founding Kings Ibn Saud and King Abdullah I never came to terms with each others' existence and did not try to establish ties. However, the tumultuous politics of the 1950s and 1960s forced the Saudi and Hashemite leaders to see the benefit of extending a hand of friendship. This did not immediately break the ice between the two royal families and though they continued to cooperate, the relations remained constrained by the past. Gradually, however, the tenacity of the hostile history gave way to the need for an active political, economic and security cooperation based on national interest. The 1970s and 1980s thus saw growing cooperation between the two monarchies, and as Saudi Arabia became economically prosperous while Jordan struggled with a resource crunch, the Saudis became a more dominant partner. This dynamics of relations between Saudis and Hashemites evolved in the 1990s and became firm under the rule of King Abdullah II who ascended the throne in 1999 upon the demise of his father. The situation settled in this way during the 2000s and the outbreak of Arab Spring in late 2010 further stabilised their relations. Jordan shares a complicated but active and friendly relationship with Saudi Arabia. While economically and politically Jordan is dependent on Saudi Arabia, when it comes to internal stability and regional affairs Saudi Arabia seeks Jordanian partnership. This interdependence defines the contemporary Saudi-Jordanian relations.

References

Al-Jazeera. (2018a, January 29). Iran blasts Jordan's king over 'unfair' statement. https://www.aljazeera.com/news/2018/01/iran-blasts-jordan-king-unfair-statement-180129101847328.html

Al-Jazeera. (2018b, June 11). Gulf nations pledge $2.5bn economic aid package to Jordan. https://www.aljazeera.com/news/2018/06/gulf-nations-pledge-25bn-economic-aid-package-jordan-180611055833875.html

Anthony, J. D. (1979). Foreign policy: The view from Riyadh. *The Wilson Quarterly, 3*(1), 73–82.

Ashton, N. (2008). *King Hussein of Jordan: A political life.* New Haven: Yale University Press.

Center for International Communication. (2018, February 28). *Saudi Arabia's aid to the world reaches nearly $33 billion in 10 years.* Press Release. https://cic.org.sa/2018/02/saudi-arabias-aid-to-the-world-reaches-nearly-33-billion-in-10-years/

Eran, O., & Guzansky, Y. (2017, April 2). *Jordan-Saudi relations, in context of the Arab league summit.* INSS Insight, No. 911. http://www.inss.org.il/publication/jordan-saudi-relations-context-arab-league-summit/

George, A. (2005). *Jordan: Living in the crossfire.* London: Zed Books.

Mann, J. (2014). Saudi-Palestinian relations during the run-up to and the aftermath of Black September. *Terrorism and Political Violence, 26*(4), 713–724.

Milton-Edwards, B., & Hinchcliffe, P. (2001). *Jordan: A Hashemite legacy.* London: Routledge.

Nevo, J. (1994). Jordan and Saudi Arabia: The last royalists. In J. Nevo & I. Pappé (Eds.), *Jordan in the Middle East: The making of a pivotal state, 1948–1988* (pp. 103–118). Essex: Frank Cass & Co.

Nichols, M. (2013, November 13). Saudi rejects U.N. Security Council seat, opening way for Jordan. *Reuters.* https://www.reuters.com/article/us-un-saudi-jordan/saudi-rejects-u-n-security-council-seat-opening-way-for-jordan-idUSBRE9AB14720131112

Obeidat, O. (2014, December 8). Jordan received JD1.2b foreign aid in 11 months. *The Jordan Times.* http://www.jordantimes.com/news/local/jordan-receives-jd12b-foreign-aid-11-months

Patrick, N. (2013, July). *Saudi Arabia and Jordan: Friends in adversity.* LSE Kuwait program research paper, no. 31, p. 16, http://eprints.lse.ac.uk/55661/1/__lse.ac.uk_storage_LIBRARY_Secondary_libfile_shared_repository_Content_LSE%20Kuwait%20Programme_PARTRICK%20%28Jan%202015%20update%29.pdf

Teitelbaum, J. (2001). *The rise and the fall of the Hashemite Kingdom of Arabia.* London: Hurst & Co.

The World Bank. (2018). *World integrated trade solutions.* https://wits.worldbank.org/CountryProfile/en/Country/JOR/StartYear/1994/EndYear/2016/TradeFlow/Import/Indicator/MPRT-TRD-VL/Partner/SAU/Product/all-groups

Trofimov, Y. (2007). *The siege of Mecca: The forgotten uprising in Islam's holiest shrine.* London: Penguin Books.

A Century of Israel-Jordan Relations

Meron Medzini

For the past century, separated by the Jordan River, the State of Israel and Hashemite Kingdom of Jordan were destined to live together for better or worse, their fate intertwined and their survival hinged on the relations that developed between these two national entities. Both began as parts of the Ottoman Empire, then came under a British Mandate that in 1921 divided that Mandate in two halves, thus creating the Emirate of Transjordan (Jordan since 1946, and the Hashemite Kingdom of Jordan since 1949). From the early 1920s, the Zionist leadership and the Hashemite Dynasty came to the conclusion that their future survival was closely tied to each other, and that they would have to find ways to co-exist or perish together. The story of the century of their ties is a tale of the attempts to find paths to co-existence in spite of two major wars they fought.

Relations from 1921 to 1947

The first significant contact between the leadership of the Zionist Organisation and the Hashemite dynasty took place in Aqaba, with Chaim Weizmann, then one of the leaders of the World Zionist

---

M. Medzini (✉)
Department of Asian Studies, The Hebrew University of Jerusalem, Jerusalem, Israel
e-mail: mmedzini@zahav.net.il

© The Author(s) 2019
P. R. Kumaraswamy (ed.), *The Palgrave Handbook of the Hashemite Kingdom of Jordan*, https://doi.org/10.1007/978-981-13-9166-8_25

Organisation, who played a significant role in securing the Balfour Declaration from the British Government in November 1917. In this document, the British Government expressed its support for the creation of a national Jewish homeland in Palestine. On the eve of the Paris Peace Conference, it became clear to Weizmann that the Jews would have to find a way to get along with the local Arab population as well as that of the neighbouring Arab countries. In early 1919 in Aqaba, he met Prince Feisal, the oldest son of the founder of the Hashemite Dynasty Hussein Bin-Ali and reached an understanding with him that the Arabs would not hinder the Jewish enterprise in Palestine provided that an Arab Empire would be created as well.

After World War I, the League of Nations awarded the Mandate over Palestine to Great Britain under the condition that it fulfil its promise to the Zionists to implement the Balfour Declaration. But soon after, due to the need to re-organise the British holdings in the Middle East and in view of the failure of an Arab revolt against France, a decision was made in Cairo in 1921 in the presence of the British Colonial Secretary Winston Churchill to create the Emirate of Transjordan and award that territory east of the Jordan River to Feisal's younger brother Emir Abdullah. Jordan comprised of some 90,000 square kilometres (against 28,000 square kilometres of Palestine). This meant that Jewish settlement was barred from Transjordan and limited only to Palestine. Amman became the capital of Transjordan that became a separate administrative unit ruled effectively by a British resident under the overall responsibility of the British High Commissioner for Palestine.

The relations between the World Zionist Organisation and Emir Abdullah were more than cordial. For years, he received a subsidy from the Jewish Agency, the de facto government of the Jewish community of Palestine, and maintained close ties with the leaders of the *Yishuv*. Among them were Chaim Arlozoroff and Moshe Sharett. In 1926, The Palestine Electric Company received a concession to utilise the waters of the River Jordan and River Yarmuk for the generation of hydro-electric powder for both sides of the Jordan. Abdullah was a frequent visitor to Jerusalem, and his troops belonging to the Arab Legion were stationed in Palestine from the beginning of World War II. In March 1946, Britain granted independence to Jordan and Abdullah was crowned as its king. By then he already harboured visions of creating a Greater Syria under his leadership comprising of Syria, Lebanon, Palestine, and Jordan. He realised that he would need the support of the Zionists for this dream and sought to gain it by negotiations.

These came to a head when the United Nations General Assembly was meeting in New York in the fall of 1947 to determine the future government of Palestine and by then Britain had announced its decision to abandon the Palestine Mandate. It was apparent to Abdullah and the Zionist leadership that they would have to reach a *modus vivendi* once the country would be partitioned into Jewish and Arab States. A high-level meeting was held between the king in the facility of the Palestine Electric Company in Naharayim on 17 November 1947 and Golda Meir represented the Jewish Agency. The King proposed that eventually a separate and autonomous Jewish entity would exist as part of Greater Syria and suggested that the Jews be given autonomy with representation in the Jordanian Parliament. The meeting was mostly an exchange of ideas. No agreement was signed, and there was no prepared agenda for discussion.

The Jewish delegation thought that Abdullah would enable the Jews to establish their state within the area allocated to it in the envisaged partition plan. The Jews for their part voiced no objection to Abdullah gaining control of the parts allotted to the Arab State, comprising mostly of today's West Bank. Jerusalem would be an internationalised city under the United Nations. It was assumed that Jordan would not be a party to the Arab military preparations to fight the Jews once the British withdrew from Palestine.[1]

THE 1948 WAR

Contrary to the expectations, based on the Golda Meir-Abdullah meeting, that Jordan would not be actively involved in an attack on the Jewish State, the Arab Legion did become involved in many attacks on Jewish convoys delivering supplies to besieged Jewish settlements mostly in the Etzion Bloc area south of Jerusalem. In February 1948, the British Foreign Secretary Ernest Bevin informed the Jordanian Prime Minister that Britain would not object to Jordan taking control of those parts of Palestine allotted to the Arab State under the United Nations (UN) Partition Plan of 29 November 1947, but warned against invading the area assigned to the Jewish State. King Abdullah felt that the commitments he gave Golda Meir were by now problematic and that he had to join the emerging united Arab front against the future Jewish State. He allowed his Arab Legion (commanded by British officers) to help Palestinian Arabs attack

[1] Report on Talk with Abdullah, 17 November 1947, Central Zionist Archive, S25/4004

Jewish settlements and convoys. He also came under massive pressure to let Iraqi forces to cross into Jordan on their way to Palestine. By early April 1948, refugees from various parts of Palestine were beginning to flock to the West Bank, and many crossed the Jordan River into the East Bank. Abdullah was being pressed daily to help the fleeing Palestinian refugees to resist Jewish attacks, mainly after the Jews were able to occupy Haifa, Tiberius, Safed, and Jaffa (Gelber 1997).

By late April and early May 1948, news arrived from Amman conveyed by British officers that it would be beneficial if a senior Jewish representative would meet the King and learn what his intentions were. It was decided that the person to meet the King would be Golda Meir. Dressed in Arab clothing, she and an aide travelled to Amman and met the King on 10 May 1948. Abdullah admitted that he made a commitment in November, but claimed that then he was alone, now he was one of five Arab nations poised to attack the Jewish State. He proposed that the Jews delay their declaration of independence and agree to become an autonomous part of his Kingdom with representation in its Parliament. Meir rejected these proposals, and he sadly agreed that there would be war. On her way back to Tel Aviv, Meir could see Iraqi forces poised near the Jordan River on their way to Palestine. She reported to David Ben-Gurion that she failed in her mission to deter the King from joining the war and the latter realised that the plans of the *Yishuv* would have to be radically altered to prepare for an attack on the Eastern front including Jerusalem, by then cut off from the coastal plains.[2]

The Arab Legion was deeply involved in attacks that brought about the collapse and destruction of the Jewish settlements in Etzion Bloc, was able to capture the Old City of Jerusalem, the entire West Bank including Lod, Ramle, and the international airport. Israeli attempts to relieve the siege of Jerusalem by attacking the fortress of Latrun failed with the Israeli army suffering many casualties. Israel was forced to accept a UN-imposed 30 days truce (10 June–10 July 1948). This permitted the Israeli army to bring military supplies, add to its growing human resources, and prepare for the resumption of the war. This happened when the Arab States rejected a UN appeal to extend the truce (Bregman 2009).

During the truce the newly appointed UN mediator Count Folke Bernadotte proposed a reworking of the November 29 Partition lines,

---

[2] Report by Golda Meir to Members of the Provisional State Council, Protocols 18 April–13 May 1948, Jerusalem, Israel State Archives, 1978, pp. 40–44.

giving the Galilee to the Jews, the Negev to the Arab State, and Jerusalem to Jordan. Israel rejected the plan out of hand and went on an offensive that drove the Arab Legion from Lod, Ramle, and the international airport but failed to open the road to Jerusalem and capture Latrun and the major cities of the West Bank. The fighting brought hundreds of thousands of Palestinian refugees to the West and East Bank swelling the number of refugees now under Jordanian control. During the second truce, Israel and Jordan negotiated an agreement effectively demilitarising Mount Scopus in Jerusalem.

In September 1948, Ben-Gurion proposed to his cabinet an operation to capture East Jerusalem and parts of the West Bank but failed to gain their approval. Israel did manage to seize additional territory in the southern part of the West Bank. In late September, direct contacts were resumed between Israeli and Jordanian officers, and on 30 November 1948, Israel and Jordan signed a "Sincere Ceasefire Agreement," pledging not to engage in hostilities in the now divided city of Jerusalem. This signalled the end of the fighting between Israel and Jordan. The Jordanian army was not involved when Israel launched its final military operations that drove the Egyptian military from Palestine (apart from the Gaza Strip), the Lebanese from entire Galilee, and the bulk of the Syrian army from certain areas in the Hulah Valley.

Armistice Negotiations and Their Aftermath

Contacts between Israeli and Jordanian officials were resumed in Jerusalem in September 1948. The Armistice negotiations between the parties began in March 1949 and were conducted on the Island of Rhodes, where the two delegations met under the United Nations auspices, but the real talks were held in Amman between senior Israeli negotiators and the King. During the negotiations, Israel launched its final campaign of the war that brought the Israeli army to Eilat on the Gulf of Aqaba. No shots were fired by the Jordanians who were informed in advance. The Israel-Jordan Armistice Agreement was signed on the Island of Rhodes on 3 April 1949 and was the sole legal binding document until it was replaced by a ceasefire on 7 June 1967. When King Abdullah annexed the West Bank to his Kingdom in 1950, Israel gave its tacit agreement (Abdullah 1978).

Negotiations between Israel and Jordan for a peace treaty were held in secret in 1949 and early 1950 and resulted in the initialling of a five-year non-aggression pact. But Jordan recoiled fearing adverse Arab reaction and expulsion from the Arab League. Israel, too, had second thoughts. The talks lapsed after the assassination of King Abdullah in Jerusalem in July 1951. Both countries attempted to reach arrangements that would keep the border areas quiet but these efforts failed and for the next seven years the relations were marked by a growing number of border incidents caused by infiltration of Palestinians from the West Bank into Israel that resulted in the latter adopting a policy of retaliation, with the Israel Defence Forces (IDF) entering the West Bank and blowing up homes, police stations, and military bases. This policy, however, failed to achieve its purpose and the borders were aflame until early 1957.[3]

By the late 1950s and early 1960s, it became evident to Hussein, who was crowned King of Jordan in 1953, that the territorial integrity of Jordan and his survival depended on good relations with Israel. For its part, Israel indicated to Jordan that the entry of Iraqi forces to the Kingdom would elicit an Israeli military response. By then Jordan and Israel had a new common enemy, namely, President Gamal Abdul Nasser of Egypt. From 1963, Hussein engaged in secret meetings with a senior Israeli official in London, during which he was told that Israel considered the existence of an independent Jordan as a significant Israeli interest. Foreign Minister Golda Meir repeated this in a secret meeting with the King in Paris in 1965. Tacit understandings were reached on the division of the waters of River Jordan, intelligence sharing and arms limitations along the borders that were now relatively quiet (Shlaim 2007; Hussein 1962).

All this changed when new developments forced King Hussein to make many strategic decisions. In May 1964, Israel and Jordan were faced with a new entity—Palestine Liberation Organisation (PLO)—that was established in East Jerusalem under Egyptian aegis. That organisation's armed wing began to launch attacks against Israel, initially from Lebanon and since 1965 from Jordan. Israel was forced to revert to its previous policy of retaliation. Hussein also participated in a series of Arab League summits that created a unified command, sought to frustrate Israel's National Water Carrier plan, and he recognised the PLO that challenged his rule over the West Bank. When Israel launched a major military operation against Jordan in the West Bank village of Samua in November 1966, Hussein felt he had to throw his lot with the rest of the Arab world, primarily with Egypt, and participate in their preparations for a forthcoming war against Israel.

---

[3] Morris, Benny, *Israel's Border Wars 1949–1956*, Tel Aviv, Am Oved, 1996 (Hebrew).

As tensions rose in the region in April and May 1967, Egypt, goaded by false Soviet claims that Israel was about to attack Syria, embarked on a series of moves that destroyed the status quo that existed since the 1956 Sinai war. It filled Sinai with Egyptian troops, expelled the United Nations Emergency Force from the Sinai Peninsula and the Gaza Strip, and finally announced the re-imposition of the naval blockade in the Straits of Tiran leading to Israel's southern port of Eilat. Hussein understood that he had no choice but to join Egypt and Syria in their plans to fight Israel lest he becomes isolated from the rest of the Arab world and even lose his throne. At the same time, he also realised that in a future war he would be defeated by the Israelis who could not see Jordan being a lynchpin in an Arab invasion of the country. On 30 May 1967, he flew to Cairo and signed a defence pact with Egypt placing his army under the command of an Egyptian general. When Israel launched its pre-emptive strike on Egypt on 5 June 1967, Hussein was misled by Nasser to believe that Israel was about to be annihilated. Ignoring Israeli warnings that if he would stay out of the war, his Kingdom would not be harmed, he launched an attack on Jerusalem and other Israel cities along the 1949 Armistice Demarcation Line.

In response to the Jordanian shelling, the IDF destroyed the tiny Jordanian air force and its bases and entered the West Bank and began to attack the Jordanian positions in East Jerusalem. Within 48 hours, Israel succeeded in capturing the entire West Bank and occupied East Jerusalem with its holy sites. On the third day of the war, Jordan asked for a cease fire and the remnant of the Jordanian army retreated to the East Bank. A day later Egypt asked for, and on 10 June, after Israel captured the Golan Heights, Syria too agreed to a cease-fire. The defeat of the combined Arab forces was dramatic, but the one who lost most was King Hussein (Bowen 2003).[4]

Hussein resumed talks with Israeli leaders in London in July 1967. His significant demand was the return of the West Bank and East Jerusalem and the restoration of the status quo, but he was not willing to enter into a peace treaty with Israel. When an Arab League summit in Khartoum in late August 1967 decided that the Arabs would not recognise Israel, negotiate with it, or sign peace treaties with the Jewish State, Hussein was bound to honour this dictum. This did not prevent him from negotiating with Israeli officials, among them Defence Minister Moshe Dayan, Deputy Prime Minister Yigal Allon, and Foreign Minister Abba Eban. He was told

---

[4] Vick Vance, and Pierre Lauer, *Hussein of Jordan: My War with Israel*, New York, Morrow, 1969.

that unlike Egypt and Syria, to whom Israel promised the return of the entire territories it captured in the Six-Day War in return for full-fledged peace, it wanted special arrangements in the West Bank and Jerusalem. In any case, on 28 June 1967 Israel effectively annexed East Jerusalem, and many villages around it, imposed its laws and administration on them and made them part of its capital city. It granted Israeli residence to the Palestinians who lived in those places.

Israel was faced with a dilemma: if it annexed the entire West Bank, it would have to grant political and civic rights to the population that then numbered over a million people. That would have shifted the demographic balance in favour of the Arabs and could endanger the Jewish character of Israel. Simultaneously, for strategic, defence and later ideological considerations, Israel did not want to abandon the West Bank hoping it would become a bargaining chip in future negotiations with Jordan. In July 1967, Deputy Prime Minister Allon conceived of a plan whereby Israel would return to Jordan the bulk of the West Bank, keeping entire Jerusalem and a defence strip along the River Jordan, thus leaving the majority of the population under Jordanian rule. The idea was to retain Israel's Jewish character while ensuring its security in the east.

The plan was rejected out of hand by both the US and Jordan. Hussein insisted that Israel withdraw first from the West Bank and then both countries would pursue negotiations based on Security Council Resolution 242 adopted on 22 November 1967. It called for Israeli withdrawal from territories occupied in the recent hostilities and established guidelines for future negotiations to resolve the issue of Palestinian refugees, freedom of navigation in the international waterways, and the right of each country too live in peace and security in agreed, secure and recognised borders.

A new situation prevailed. Israel continued its occupation and even began to establish Jewish settlements, initially in places where there were Jewish settlements before 1948, primarily the Etzion Bloc and several villages north of Jerusalem. Israel embarked on a new policy called the Open Bridges Policy whereby trade and movement of people across the River Jordan were permitted and even encouraged. Jordan continued to pay the salaries of civil servants, teachers, and judges in the West Bank and it also controlled the Waqf, the Muslim religious body in charge of Muslim holy sites, mainly the mosques on Temple Mount. A new co-existence was created: Jordan looked after certain civilian affairs while Israel was responsible for law and order and the prevention of growing acts of terror by the increasingly restive Palestinian population.

In 1968, Yasser Arafat became the Chairman of the PLO, and this marked a vast increase in anti-Israel terror both within the West Bank and from the East Bank, a situation the King was unable to control. One of the primary results of the June War was the growth of Palestinian nationalism and the Palestinisation of the Arab-Israel conflict. In March 1968, Israel launched a major operation against the PLO base in Karame, and the battle expanded and involved the Jordanian army causing considerable casualties to both sides. Once Israel was able to destroy the PLO presence in the West Bank, Arafat moved its military operations to the East Bank from where it launched attacks on Israel and Israeli targets overseas. Arafat and other Palestinian radical nationalist organisations then felt that they had to overthrow the Jordanian Monarchy in favour of a Palestinian State initially in the East Bank, partly because some 60 per cent of Jordan's population is Palestinians (Rabinovich 1991).

Some Israeli leaders, Ariel Sharon among them, felt that a separate Palestinian State in the East Bank under Arafat would be an acceptable solution provided the King would be replaced by Arafat with whom Israel would then negotiate a peace treaty. The concept became known as "Jordan is Palestine." Palestinian efforts to overthrow the monarchy reached their peak in September 1970 known as "Black September." In the course of this attempt, Syrian armoured units crossed the border and invaded Jordan. The King called upon the US to secure Israeli military involvement to save his throne. At the request of the US, the IDF mobilised some units near the Jordan River, and its air force flew reconnaissance missions over Jordan. The Syrians retreated without the need for Israeli military intervention. The monarchy was saved. King Hussein found quiet ways to express his gratitude to Israel mostly through the US. The remnants of the PLO fled to Lebanon from where they launched operations against Israel. A decade later Israel would embark on a war to destroy the PLO presence in Lebanon.[5]

Since the early 1970s, Israel and Jordan held many high-level meetings that involved Israeli Prime Ministers Yitzhak Rabin, Golda Meir, and Yitzhak Shamir. Tacit understandings were reached on matters on the division of River Jordan, prevention of Palestinian terror acts emanating from Jordan, permission for Israeli Arabs to travel via Jordan to the Holy City of Mecca for the Hajj, pest and flood control and other common

---

[5] For "Black September," see Henry Kissinger, *White House Years*, Boston, Little Brown and Co. 1979.

issues. In spite of the absence of a formal peace treaty, the relations between the two nations were described as excellent ties between friendly enemy countries. Therefore, it came as no surprise that Israel objected vehemently when Hussein announced in 1972 a new plan for a federation between Jordan and the West Bank. Golda Meir who met the King in March 1972 asked why there were no advance consultations. He insisted on the return of the West Bank before any meaningful peace talks. Hussein did warn Israel on the eve of the that war was imminent but could not provide dates and other critical information lest he be considered a traitor to the Arab cause. Jordan wisely refrained from actively participating in the 1973 Egyptian and Syrian attack on Israel. However, under mounting pressure, the King was forced to send an armoured division to fight alongside Syria on the Golan Heights and lost some 20 tanks. He did give Israel an advanced warning of his intentions, and hence this did not mar Israel-Jordan ties and trade continued 100 miles down the River Jordan.

At the conclusion of the October War, a series of agreements were signed between Israel and Egypt. In January 1974, they signed a Separation of Forces agreement, and in June 1974, a similar agreement was signed with Syria. In their first meeting, King Hussein asked newly appointed Prime Minister Rabin to accept a separation of forces zone along the River Jordan that would entail a token Israeli withdrawal. Due to domestic political constraints, Rabin was unable to comply. In October 1974, the so-called "Jordanian Option" lapsed as an Arab League summit conference in Rabat proclaimed the right of the Palestinian people to establish an independent state in the West Bank and that the PLO was the sole legitimate representative of the Palestinian people. The latter claim was soon to be adopted by the United Nations General Assembly. This created a major obstacle to both Israel and Jordan, who now had to contend with a new claimant—the PLO. Jordan henceforth could no longer represent or speak on behalf of the Palestinian people. Israel and Jordan then decided to pursue various local arrangements along the border that would enable them to co-exist peacefully.[6]

While Rabin was prime minister from 1974 to 1977 and later as minister of defence from 1984 to 1990, the King had a series of meetings with him to cement the existing status quo between the two countries. Hussein slowly abandoned any hope of reaching an agreement with the PLO to

---

[6] For the events of the 1973 war and its aftermath, see Henry Kissinger, *Years of Upheaval*, Boston, Little Brown and Co. 1982.

enable both of them to maintain a common front against Israel. There was no sense of urgency on the part of Israel to make any territorial concessions to Jordan or to engage in peace negotiations through an international conference that would have to include the PLO. This suited the position of Prime Minister Yitzhak Shamir who rejected an understanding reached between Foreign Minister Shimon Peres and King Hussein in secret talks in London on 11 April 1987.[7] That agreement dealt with the modalities of a peace process including the convening of an international conference.

The final decision to disengage entirely from the West Bank was taken by King Hussein on 31 July 1988, as an outcome of the first Palestinian Intifada that erupted in the Occupied Territories in December 1987. By announcing an administrative disengagement from these areas, Hussein gave up any territorial demands west of the River Jordan. His primary concern now was to ensure that the uprising would not spread to the East Bank. This he successfully achieved by putting down with brutal force any attempts by Palestinians to undermine his rule. Secret contacts with Israel continued to ensure that the many cross-border arrangements would not be harmed.

The Kuwait Crisis (1990–91) placed Hussein in a most challenging position. He had to decide whether to support Saddam Hussein, the Iraqi ruler who invaded and occupied Kuwait in August 1990, a move supported by the PLO but opposed by a US-led coalition that now included Syria, Egypt, and Saudi Arabia. Hussein decided to sit on the fence and lost the sympathy of the US that led to the imposition of American economic sanctions on Jordan. On the eve of the Operation Desert Storm, the King met in London with Prime Minister Shamir and promised him that he would ensure that Iraqi forces would never enter Jordan. The defeat of Saddam Hussein by the Western coalition created for Jordan an additional refugee problem, as at least a quarter of a million Palestinians who worked in the Arab Gulf States were expelled and had to find shelter in Jordan which was ill-suited to deal with this massive inflow of people. Jordan was forced to seek Israeli intervention in Washington to lift the economic Sanctions (Shlaim 1990).

When Present George H.W. Bush announced the convening of an international peace conference in Madrid to seek an Arab-Israel peace

---

[7] For the London Agreement, see Michael Bar-Zohar, *The Phoenix – Shimon Peres, a Political Biography*, Tel Aviv, Yedioth Ahronot, 2006, pp. 573–586 (Hebrew).

(October 1991), Jordan agreed to the inclusion of a Palestinian delegation within the framework of a joint Jordanian-Palestinian delegation. This enabled Yitzhak Shamir to attend the conference and resulted with the commencing of open Israel-Jordanian bilateral negotiations in the framework of the Madrid Peace Conference. Little progress was recorded.

In June 1992, Yitzhak Rabin was again elected prime minister of Israel and resumed his secret meetings with King Hussein, usually held on a boat in the Gulf of Aqaba or in Tel Aviv. However, Jordan was kept in the dark during the negotiations in Oslo that led to the signing of the Israel-Palestinian Declaration of Principles on 13 September 1993 that included among other things mutual Israel-PLO recognition. This enabled the King to pursue peace negotiations with Israel, talks that lasted almost a year and included a highly publicised signing on the White House Lawn of a Joint Jordanian-Israeli proclamation to end of the state of war (25 July 1994). The Israel-Jordan Peace Treaty was formally signed in the Arava north of Eilat on 26 October 1994 in the presence of President Bill Clinton (Horowitz 1996; Rabinovich 2007).[8] The agreement ended the state of war, proclaimed new borders, created full normalisation in the ties between the two countries and dealt extensively with economic and water issues. The Knesset gave its approval to the peace treaty by an unprecedented majority of over 100 members. In the following two years, 16 agreements were signed between the two states in various economic fields. Israelis began to visit Jordan in growing numbers through two border crossing points. Some Israeli industries opened factories in Jordan using cheaper local labour.

The assassination of Yitzhak Rabin by an Israeli zealot on 4 November 1995 brought King Hussein to Jerusalem (the first time since 1967) to attend the funeral and to eulogise Rabin in a highly emotional speech.[9] The relations with Rabin's successor, Benjamin Netanyahu, soon soured. Netanyahu declared that he was committed to the peace treaty, but Israeli opening of a new tunnel on Temple Mount in Jerusalem in October 1996 led to violence and resulted with many victims. Jordan claimed that the peace treaty gave it a special standing in the administering the Moslem Holy Sites in Jerusalem and protested. A year later the relations reached a breaking point when Israeli agents attempted to assassinate a senior Hamas

---

[8] The text of the Israel-Jordan Peace Treaty, see *Israel's Foreign relations – Selected Documents*, Jerusalem, Ministry of Foreign Affairs, Vol. XIV, 1995, pp. 826–854.

[9] Hussein's Eulogy at Rabin's Funeral, *Israel's Foreign Relations, Selected Documents*, Jerusalem, Ministry of Foreign Affairs, 1997, Vol. XV, p. 348.

official Khalid Masha'al, in Amman. The attempt failed, and the Israelis escaped to the Israel embassy in the Jordanian capital. The King threatened to break into the embassy. The impasse was broken with the intervention of Foreign Minister Ariel Sharon and Deputy Mossad head Efraim Halevi. The Israelis were released in return for the release from prison of the Hamas leader Ahmed Yassin but relations sunk to their lowest ebb. They did not improve in spite of the King's intervention in negotiations that led Israel to withdraw from Hebron in February 1997 and further Israeli withdrawal under the Wye River Plantation agreement in October 1998. By then the king was ill with cancer, and when he died in early 1999, his funeral was attended by many Israeli leaders led by Prime Minister Netanyahu.[10]

The peace treaty with Jordan failed to filter into the Jordanian population and remained mostly a government-to-government agreement. But it was effective enough to ensure Israel's security on the River Jordan border, to ensure that Jordan would not become involved in the US-led invasion of Iraq (2003) and to refrain from involvement during Israel's second War in Lebanon (2006). Prime Ministers Ehud Barak (1999–2001), Ariel Sharon (2001–06) and Ehud Olmert (2006–09) established close working relations with King Abdullah II, but the warmth that existed with his late father was absent. There have been no cultural ties or exchanges of any sort due to the open opposition of Jordan's intellectual, media, and academic elite.

As a result of the Arab Spring, Jordan found itself increasingly dependent on the Israeli port of Haifa to import and export some of its goods that were trucked from the Sheikh Hussein Bridge near Beit Shean. Security cooperation continued to be a hallmark in the ties between the two that shared intelligence regarding the intentions of various groups ranging from Hamas, Hezbollah, and other radical Palestinian and non-Palestinian Arab terror groups, some supported by Iran. In 2017, the ties again soured over violent events on Temple Mount in Jerusalem and the killing in Amman in August 2017 by an Israeli embassy security guard of two Jordanian civilians. The entire embassy staff was moved back to Israel and the King expressed his dismay over the warm reception granted to the Israeli security official by the prime minister and the embassy was reopened in February 2018.

---

[10] For the years 1996–99, see Philip Robins, *A History of Jordan*, Cambridge, Cambridge University Press, 2003.

Clearly, Israel had always maintained—and this remains true after almost of a century of ties with the Hashemite rulers of its eastern neighbours—that the Hashemite dynasty must remain in power in Jordan, or as Golda Meir once said to a British foreign secretary: "We pray five times a day for the well-being of the Jordanian King."

REFERENCES

Abdullah, K. (1978). *My memoirs completed*. London: Longman.

Bowen, J. (2003). *Six days: How the 1967 war shaped the Middle East*. London: Simon and Schuster.

Bregman, A. (2000). *Israel's wars 1947–1993*. London: Routledge.

Gelber, Y. (1997). *Jewish-Transjordanian relations 1921–1948*. London: Frank Cass.

Hussein, B.-T. (1962). *Uneasy lies the head: An autobiography*. London: Heineman.

Rabinovich, I. (1991). *The road not taken: Early Arab-Israel negotiations*. New York: Oxford University Press.

Shlaim, A. (1990). *The politics of partition: King Abdullah, the Zionist movement and the partition of Palestine*. Oxford: Oxford University Press.

Shlaim, A. (2007). *Lion of Jordan – The life of king Hussein in war and peace*. London: Allen Lane.

Jordanian-Israeli Relations Under King Hussein

Russell E. Lucas

Most aspects of Jordan's foreign and domestic policies during the reign of King Hussein (1952–99) somehow linked to relations with Israel. Of the Kingdom's many enemies and partners, Israel fell into both camps. One can explain how Hussein dealt with Israel through three different frameworks. First, the international politics of Jordan's general alignment with the West during the Cold War often placed the Kingdom in a problematic position in intra-Arab politics against Israel. Second, Jordan's incorporation of the West Bank after 1948 made the Palestinian question both a domestic and a foreign policy issue that threatened the survival of the regime. Third, Hussein frequently relied on his charisma and charm in handling Jordan's politics. Thus, the King frequently handled relations with Israel personally through secret interactions with Israeli leaders.

The political conditions of Hussein's inheritance defined the early years of his rule when he suddenly ascended to the throne at the age of 17. Hussein was by his grandfather's side when Abdullah I was assassinated in Jerusalem in July 1951. This event touched the young prince deeply as King Abdullah was perhaps more a paternal figure to Hussein than his

---

R. E. Lucas (✉)
Michigan State University, East Lansing, MI, USA
e-mail: relucas@msu.edu

father, Talal. A family council removed King Talal in August 1952 officially for reasons of mental illness. King Hussein quickly faced both the constraints of Jordan's geopolitical position in the post-1948 Middle East as well as the domestic challenges produced by Abdullah's long and Talal's brief reign.

Britain still had considerable sway over Jordan's foreign relations despite granting Jordan's independence in 1946. Alec Kirkbride continued as British Ambassador to Jordan and John Baghot Glubb "Pasha" continued to lead Jordan's Arab Legion. In the transition from Abdullah to Talal to Hussein, both Englishmen seemed to hold as much sway as Queen Zain, Hussein's mother, or Prime Minister Toufiq Abdul Huda. Britain's position in the broader Middle East was fading because of World War II and its withdrawal from Palestine in 1948.

Hussein's most significant and troublesome inheritance from his grandfather was Jordan's acquisition of the West Bank in the War of 1948 with the resulting demographic doubling of Jordan's population of Palestinian refugees and West Bankers. The impression that Abdullah had colluded with the leaders of the *Yishuv* in the partition of Palestine circulated across the region. Palestinian disgruntlement with Abdullah's war effort led to his assassination. One of King Hussein's persistent challenges would be to incorporate this group of reluctant subjects with their legacy of a generally higher level of education and economic development than their East Banker compatriots.

Hussein also inherited his father's 1952 Constitution for Jordan. While the monarchy still held considerable vetoes over all branches of government, the powers of the Parliament and cabinet insured that King Hussein could not rule alone as his grandfather did. The new King inherited a fractious elite divided in numerous directions. The Queen mother's efforts eventually tampered down rivalries within the Hashemite family. However, the broader range of notable politicians reflected rivalries based on social origins, political ideology, foreign policy agendas, and personal relations.

Hussein started his reign with a great deal of uncertainty towards dealing with the Israeli government. Glubb used the Arab Legion to keep unauthorised border crossings contained. Nevertheless, the Israeli retaliation for Palestinian incursions grew through these early years. The massacre in the West Bank village of Qibya in 1953, led by Ariel Sharon, marked Hussein's first real test of managing Jordan's relations with Israel and the Palestinians. In response to public protests and his discomfort with the Arab Legion's British officers, the King began to take an interest in not just reigning but ruling by leading policy as well.

The winds of a rising Arab Nationalism buffeted the Kingdom in the mid-1950s. Jordan's relationship with Israel remained close to the surface during debates about Jordan's participation in the Baghdad Pact and the Suez Crisis. The opening—and then harsh closing—of Jordan's domestic political pluralism reflected the influence of both the Cold War and inter-Arab relations. The rapid series of events from 1955 to 1958 showed King Hussein that he could not remain neutral in Arab affairs in the face of conflicting demands from great power patrons, regional allies and rivals and public opinion. In response to popular mobilisation and demonstrations, Hussein moved out of Britain's orbit by first declining to join the Baghdad Pact and then by sacking Glubb. He also attempted to recalibrate Hashemite family relations vis-à-vis his relatives in Iraq. To large sections of Jordan's public, however, the problems of the Palestinians and Israel's behaviour merged into general anti-colonial anger that Gamal Abdul Nasser's actions and propaganda were able to mobilise. Imperial and Israeli duplicity seemed to be checked with Nasser's "victory" in the Suez Crisis. Hussein could thus not challenge the forces of Arabism on the international stage. He attempted to ride the wave of Arabism at home. A failed coup attempt in 1957 by portions of the newly Arabised Army pushed him to clamp down on domestic unrest. Hussein threaded the needle of threats to Jordan's existence and the Hashemites' rule by knitting diverse coalitions of elites to support his diplomatic manoeuvres. In the process, he changed British for American international backing. Hussein chose regime survival over his desire for democratic legitimation and Arabist inclinations.

Hussein in the 1960s, however, questioned the reliability of American support. This led him to pursue seemingly contradictory foreign policies in his pursuit of security not just for Jordan, but his regime as well. On the one hand, Hussein recognised that Israel was an established fact on the ground and he would need to deal with it pragmatically. This led him to pursue secret direct contacts with Israeli leaders—even with the knowledge of the price his grandfather paid for this practice. Thus, through his British doctor, Hussein in 1963 began to meet regularly with Israeli officials and intended to achieve a peaceful resolution of conflicts with Israel for both Jordan as a state and the Palestinians as a people. These meetings would continue in secret until peace talks become public in the 1990s.

In the mid-1960s, Israeli retaliation raids for incursions by Palestinian commandos launched from Jordan's territory became more severe—in spite of the Jordanian army's attempts to keep the Israeli frontier quiet.

This led King Hussein, in a seeming contradiction to his private Israeli rapprochement, publically to embrace Nasser's regional politics. Part of this policy led Hussein to acquiesce to the creation of the Palestine Liberation Organisation (PLO)—a choice that would lead to long-run competition with the organisation in return for short-run increases in popularity with public opinion. Hussein's relationship the PLO and Nasser, however, would entangle Jordan into commitments that would result in the loss of half the Kingdom during the June 1967 war.

Thanks to Hussein's leadership in 1967, "Jordan's part in the June War was brief, ineffective and inglorious."[1] Most regime supporters, including the King himself, when asked why Jordan joined the ill-fated war effort argued that Jordan faced no choice to engage in the inevitable war. In this narrative, if Jordan had sat out the war, King Hussein would have met a popular insurrection that would have toppled his regime. Moreover, most Arab forces at the time felt that military victory—or at least a Suez-style outcome of political victory—was at hand. Hussein relinquished command of Jordan's military to Egyptian control despite warnings from his advisors. Thus, Jordan had to deal with both misinformation from the Egyptian side and the tactical blunders of Nasser's generals.

The Israelis initially held back from crushing the Jordanian army in the West Bank. Once Jordan's forces were committed to the fight however, the Israelis first eliminated Jordan's air force and then routed its army in the West Bank before the cease-fire took effect. Jordan and Israel continued to send messages via American and British intermediaries. These communications did not prevent Israel from seizing the West Bank, but they probably did keep Israeli air raids from personally targeting Hussein. In sum, King Hussein's fears of Israeli expansion led him to miscalculations that ensured that it happened.

Hussein faced many challenges with the loss of half of the Kingdom's land and population, its economic engine and its holy sites of Jerusalem. An immediate popular insurrection was not one of them. It did not take long for the repercussions of the June War to shake Jordan's stability.

In the wake of the stunning loss, Hussein began to refocus on diplomacy as the only possible route to dealing with Israel. Some forces in the Israeli cabinet favoured a "Jordanian option" in coming to an agreement with Hussein over the West Bank and Palestinian issues. Others in the

---

[1] Avi Shlaim, *Lion of Jordan: The Life of King Hussein in War and Peace* (London: Penguin, 2007), p. 251.

cabinet preferred dealing with the Palestinians in the West Bank and Gaza directly. The September 1967 Arab Summit in Khartoum, reached an Arab consensus on rejecting recognition, negotiations, and peace with Israel. The summit did leave, however, the door open for individual states to explore negotiations with Israel. Hussein explored this track through American mediation while continuing with his secret meetings with Israeli officials in London. With little pressure from the US on Israel, divergent policy preference among the Israeli cabinet resulted in Israeli stalling and the collapse of United Nations and American efforts at peace.

Meanwhile, Palestinian resistance organisations increased their activities in light of the failures of the Arab States in the June War. They also feared that Jordan would follow its state interests, not their interests, at the negotiating table. Thus, PLO groups expanded their guerrilla activities across the Jordan River. Hussein opened the door to greater *Fedayeen* activities in Jordan and against Israel as he grew more disenchanted with the prospects of overcoming Israeli intransigence. The cooperation between the Jordanian Army and the PLO at the battle of Karameh in March 1968 enabled them to repulse an Israeli incursion into Jordan. In the wake of the June 1967 defeat, the meagre victory at Karameh emboldened both the PLO and the Jordanian army. The King, again acquiescing to public opinion remarked, "We may reach the stage when we shall all become fedayeen."[2] The King adopted this stance partly out of his conviction based on frustration with Israeli and Arab foreign relations. He also catered to the popularity of the resistance similarly as he had tried to ride the Arab Nationalist wave of public opinion in the mid-1950s. With the Americans seemingly disengaged, he turned towards gathering domestic and Arab support. A little over two years later, however, the King would instead crush the Palestinian resistance organisations when they threatened his rule.

The cycle of outbidding one another by Palestinian groups pushed the Jordanian regime into a crackdown in September 1970. While the Jordanian military was able to subdue the Fedayeen in reasonably short order, it was only because no external powers came to the Fedayeen's aid. Hussein requested air support from the US and would have even welcomed Israeli intervention when Syrian forces began to intervene in the fighting in the northern city of Irbid. However, the Jordanian air force was

---

[2] Charles Tripp, *The Power and the People: Paths of Resistance in the Middle East* (Cambridge: Cambridge University Press, 2013), p. 29.

able to push back the Syrians without assistance when the Syrian air force failed to support the Syrian armoured divisions. The King signed an agreement with Arafat soon afterwards and over the next few days and weeks the Jordanian army disarmed or liquidated any remaining armed vestiges of the resistance organisations. When the opposition attempted to shove the regime from power, Hussein pushed aside his concerns for popular legitimacy to save his regime's security.

Hussein turned towards reconstruction at home, remedying Jordan's isolation in the Arab world and attempting to prod the Israelis towards peace after Black September. He met with limited success on each of these fronts during the 1970s. Instead, the forces of social division unleashed by the civil war festered at home. Regionally, intra-Arab relations reset with the rise of Anwar Sadat and Yasser Arafat while Israeli strength yielded complacency with the status quo.

Israeli leaders proposed the "Allon Plan" soon after the June War that would hand some of the populated parts of the West Bank back to Palestinian rule with Israel keeping overall security control in the Jordan Valley. However, with changes in the Israeli cabinet and Hussein's victory over the Fedayeen, Israeli government preferences changed to presenting partial rule over the West Bank back to Jordan. Hussein rejected this "Jordanian Option" because it would entail significant changes in the border and would have been unacceptable to the Palestinians.

Hussein instead proposed his vision of a "United Arab Kingdom" in March 1972 in which the East and West Banks would be autonomous regions within a federal system. In other words, he offered a separate Palestinian entity but under Hashemite sovereignty. The plan was roundly rejected across the Arab world. The Israelis also opposed the initiative—unless Jordan altered it into a repackaged version of the Allon Plan. Nevertheless, Hussein continued with his secret dialogues with the Israelis to keep the border quiet as well as to keep options open for the day when an Israeli cabinet would develop a consensus to make a just peace with Jordan.

Hussein tried to return to the Arab fold by attending a summit in Cairo as the region returned to a war footing in September 1973. Both Egyptian President Sadat and Syrian President Hafiz al-Assad ended Jordan's diplomatic isolation from the Arab States. Sadat, however, did not share his plans for an attack on Israel with Hussein. Sadat also had a channel with the US, which he kept secret from Assad as well. Hussein cautioned that the region was slipping towards war when he met again with Israeli leaders later in the month. His warning did not reveal any special knowledge of Sadat and Assad's plans but a general demand for moving peace talks forward. Years later, Israeli officials revealed that Hussein met with the Israeli Prime Minister Golda Meir just before the outbreak of the October 1973 war. While it was perceived that Hussein had warned the Israelis of the impending attack, the meeting—as attested to by many of those involved— remained at the level of a warning of the situation leading to war and not that an attack was imminent.[3]

Jordan did not immediately join the Egyptian and Syrian attack when war did break out in October. Hussein did eventually send Jordanian troops to the Syrian front to save face in inter-Arab relations. Before he did so, however, he sent a message to Israel via the UK and the US to communicate that Jordan's efforts were only a token force and Jordan would not directly target Israel despite Syria's urging. In the wake of the 1973 war, Sadat's wish to open up to negotiations with Israel became clearer. In the process, it relegated Israel's relationship with Jordan to secondary importance.

Jordan's principal foreign policy concern moved from its relationship with Israel to its ties with the PLO after the Arab summit in Rabat in October 1974. With the PLO recognised by the Arab States as the sole legitimate representative of the Palestinian people, Hussein limited his diplomatic activity on behalf of the Palestinians while still trying to keep Jordan's place as a key interlocutor. He continued his secret contacts with the Israelis. Hussein, however, would not agree with Israeli offers to administer the West Bank unless Israel withdrew from it. Failing on this front, Israeli leaders took up Sadat's peace overtures. Because Sadat sought to put Egypt's position ahead of pan-Arab concerns, he succeeded in keeping Hussein out of the Camp David negotiations in 1977. In the end, the peace accords talked about Palestinian autonomy—especially regarding Jordan's role in it—but did not mention the PLO. Hussein rejected the agreements because he was not a party to the negotiations and thus not bound by them. Backed with Saudi Arabia's rejection of Sadat's claims to speak for all Arabs, Hussein felt he could turn down American overtures to join Sadat's peace process.

While the 1980s began with Jordan's relationship with PLO starting from the point of agreement, soon Arafat and Hussein vacillated between rivalry and cooperation. Part of Hussein's difficulties stemmed from his

---

[3] Shlaim, pp. 360–363.

difficult personal relationship with the Palestinian leader. He was also constrained by the functional cooperation that Jordan and Israel had established. Hussein felt more confident about his direct channels with Israeli leaders but not sufficiently so to make them public after Sadat broke the taboo of direct negotiations with Israel.

The 1987 Palestinian Intifada decisively tipped the balance in the Jordanian-PLO relations. The uprising against the Israeli occupation probably would have erupted earlier if it had not been for the functional cooperation of Jordan and Israel keeping the bridges between the West Bank and Jordan open for goods and people.[4] The Intifada threatened that cooperation, however, as more Israeli Likud party elites began calling for the expelling of Palestinians to the East Bank and the creation of an alternative Palestinian homeland in Jordan (*watan al-badil*). Hussein and his supporters feared this outcome. In response to this growing Israeli argument as well as PLO moves towards declaring statehood, King Hussein made a surprise announcement of Jordan's administrative disengagement from the West Bank in July 1988. The decision forced both the Israelis to negotiate directly with the Palestinians while removing Jordan as the PLO's scapegoat for dealing with the Occupied Territories. The disengagement decision, however, caused a fiscal crisis for Jordan. The resulting economic remedies led to rioting in April 1989 and Jordan's decision to open a process of political liberalisation.

The disengagement also crystallised a growing East Bank first sense of Transjordanian nationalism that had its roots in the failure of the United Arab Kingdom plan and the 1970 civil war. The rise of East Bank nationalist groups pushed Palestinian issues away from Jordan's discussions with Israel on the future status of the West Bank towards internal debates about who was a loyal citizen of the Kingdom. The Gulf Crisis following Iraq's invasion of Kuwait in 1990 and both Jordan and the PLO's stance of Iraqi-leaning neutrality papered over these differences. Hussein's policies of political liberalisation and opposition to the US-led anti-Iraq coalition caused his popularity to hit a new height. Like with earlier episodes Hussein faced a choice of popular legitimacy or Western great power backing. In this episode, however, he leveraged domestic support over American displeasure.

---

[4] Yehuda Lukacs, *Israel, Jordan and the Peace Process* (Syracuse, NY: Syracuse University Press, 1997), p. 183.

Hussein, despite his domestic popularity, saw his international position as isolated and facing a precarious financial situation in the wake of the US-led coalition's victory over Iraq in the spring of 1991. Thus, when the Bush administration turned to push Arab-Israeli relations into an American-led "peace process," Jordan quickly joined the initiative for fear of further international marginalisation. The King would have preferred an international conference under UN auspices because he had secretly developed such a plan in the late 1980s with the then Israeli Foreign Minister, Shimon Peres. The bipolar politics of Israel's national unity government at the time, however, eventually scuttled the initiative. In 1991, Hussein agreed to attend an international conference—but one functionally fully under American management.

The King happily sponsored a joint Jordanian-Palestinian delegation to the October conference in Madrid. This met the Israeli demand that the PLO does not directly participate while Jordan was able to continue its involvement in Palestinian affairs despite the 1988 disengagement. In Madrid, the Palestinians sat publically at the negotiating table for the first time with Israelis. The main success of the Madrid Conference was that it opened a period of negotiations in Washington between the Israelis and the various Arab parties, namely, Jordan, Syria, and the Palestinians. After a series of procedural decisions—many of which were solved on a sofa in a corridor of the US State Department[5]—the Jordanian and Palestinian delegations began functionally separate talks with the Israelis.

The negotiations in Washington only incrementally progressed between Israeli and the Palestinians (and the Syrians as well) over the following year and a half. In contrast, the Jordanian delegation was ready by October 1992 to agree with Israel on a common agenda for a peace treaty on bilateral issues. Jordan did not advance any further on agenda while the Palestinian track remained stuck because the Palestinian negotiators rejected Israeli proposals of limited autonomy in the Occupied Territories.

To the surprise of King Hussein—and the Palestinian negotiating team as well—Yasser Arafat and the PLO agreed in secret with the Israelis to accept terms the team in Washington had not. The King was furious with the announcement of the Oslo Accords in September 1993. He, however, quickly recognised the new reality because it allowed him to pursue a separate peace with Israel while not being outside the Arab fold as Sadat and

---

[5] Abdul Salam Al-Majali, et al. *Peacemaking: The Inside Story of the 1994 Jordanian-Israeli Treaty* (London: Garnet Publishing, 2014), pp. 23–50.

Egypt had done. In just 22 hours after the signing of the Oslo Accords, Jordan and Israel initialled an agenda for a peace treaty that had been waiting for almost a year.

The negotiating teams of Jordanian technocrats and Israeli ministers formally held responsibility for finalising the details of a treaty. The longstanding direct communication between the King and his Israeli counterparts, however, provided a shortcut to allow negotiations to move forward rapidly. Hussein and Yitzhak Rabin forged a strong bond as the "personal trust between the king and prime minister was the key to progress on the Jordanian track."[6] Failures from the 1980s plus Peres's attempts to upstage Rabin in the early 1990s troubled Hussein's relationship with the Foreign Minister. When Peres let slip in fall 1993 that secret negotiations at the highest levels were also taking place with Jordan, Rabin sidelined his Foreign Minister from the Jordanian track.

Over the next few months, Jordan and Israel hurried towards a peace treaty. In July 1994, the Washington Declaration ended the state of war between the two countries. The terms of the document practically outlined the future peace treaty. By October, the negotiators finalised the deal between Jordan and Israel. It was signed at the Wadi Araba border just north of Aqaba on 26 October 1994. The agreement established diplomatic relations and committed both sides to respect each other's sovereignty.

The treaty provided for Israel returning occupied Jordanian land in the northern Jordan Valley and Wadi Araba and allowed Israel to "lease" some of the lands so that its farmers could continue to use it. Israel also agreed to supply Jordan with water. Jordan reserved a special status in Jerusalem for its trusteeship of the Muslim holy places. Both Israel and Jordan committed to working together in multilateral talks about Palestinian refugees.[7] Most importantly from the Jordanian view was that Israelis would abandon the notion of Jordan as the alternative Palestinian homeland. Jordan's Parliament, which in elections the year before filled the chamber with pro-government supporters, ratified the treaty on November 7 in a 55–23 vote.

---

[6] Shlaim, p. 527.
[7] "Treaty of Peace between the Hashemite Kingdom of Jordan and the State of Israel" October 26, 1994, http://www.kinghussein.gov.jo/peacetreaty.html, accessed 2 February 2018.

At the signing of the treaty, King Hussein remarked that the peace between Jordan and Israel would be a "warm" peace with much more normal relations than Israel's "cold" peace with Egypt. This desire for normalisation stemmed from his personal relationship with Israeli leaders developed over the years—especially that of the mutual respect between the King and Rabin. Seeking normalisation, however, he also sought to cement Jordan's place in the American-led new Middle Eastern order. In addition to large promised amounts of American aid and debt relief for Jordan's persistent resource-starved budget, plans for economic development through joint Jordanian-Israeli (and Palestinian) investors fed into World Bank and International Monetary Fund models of globalising neoliberal economics. The government's attempts at public persuasion focused on many messages, including that Jordan had little choice in joining the peace camp and that Jordan as a sovereign state achieved all of its demands in the negotiations. However, much of the domestic public relations campaign focused on the massive impending peace dividend. While the regime pledged prosperity through peace based on the economic benefits of normalisation, it was the embrace of normalisation by hugging Israeli leaders that the public found delivered.

The negotiations towards peace with Israel were finalised in private over the course of three years because they had built on the decades of secret contacts between King Hussein and his grandfather with Israeli leaders. The seeming rapid pace of peacemaking and the depth of the desired normalisation with Israel shocked many parts of the Jordanian public, especially Jordan's fractious opposition groups. It was not just Palestinians in Jordan (and the opposition parties that represented them) that were put off by peace with Israel. East Bankers also questioned if Jordan received what it deserved out of peace with Israel. Since the opposition in Jordan's Parliament could not delay—let alone block—the ratification of the peace treaty, they began to attempt to stifle normalisation.

Jordan's opposition attempted to block normalisation in three ways. First, opposition to normalisation helped forge a consensus among a spectrum of opposition politicians and groups. The peace treaty offered Islamists—like the Muslim Brotherhood—and independent personalities—like Laith Shubeilat—and leftists and Arab Nationalists a common rallying point. Independent liberals like Toujan Faisal and disaffected regime stalwarts such as Ahmad Obeidat joined the coalition. Second, opposition personalities began a public process of blacklisting people and companies that worked with Israel—especially those outside the government that visited Israel. Finally, the coalition of anti-normalisation opposition forces began direct actions, such as marches and protests, against signs of normalisation; the most notable example being the march against an Israeli trade fair in January 1997 that drew more than 4000 protesters.

The King's hopes for a warm peace also began to dwindle after Rabin's assassination in November 1995. He began to keep his distance from Peres. With the election of Benyamin Netanyahu in 1996, the King first was heartened by the change in Israeli leadership. He, however, soon grew disappointed that the Likud leader not only undermined the peace process with the Palestinians but seemingly endanger normalisation with Jordan as well. Netanyahu's actions such as the Jerusalem tunnel opening and settlement expansion spurred protests in Jordan leading Hussein to feel betrayed. In the wake of these events in March 1997, a Jordanian soldier, Ahmed al-Daqamisah, shot and killed seven Israeli schoolgirls at the Jordanian-Israeli border. The King condemned the attack and paid condolence visits to the girls' families in Israel. While Israelis were impressed with Hussein's compassion, Jordanians saw little reason for his display of grief. Many questioned if an Israeli Prime Minister would do the same in the reverse situation.[8] With the botched attempted daylight assassination of Hamas leader Khalid Mashal in the streets of Amman in September 1997, only King Hussein's crafty negotiations prevented the treaty from collapsing from Netanyahu's adventurism.

During the 1990s, the peace process rose and fell; Jordan's domestic political liberalisation process, in contrast, trended only downwards. The space for criticism of the peace process shrank with amendments to the election law in 1993, enhanced press restrictions in 1997 and continuing harassment and arrests of opposition politicians. Polls still showed that more members of the public thought that peace would lead to economic benefits than those who did not. Polling of elites, however, showed those percentages reversed. Surveys, moreover, found that most Jordanians—regardless of background—viewed Israelis as remaining enemies.[9] Coupled with the lack of significant dividends of peace and continuing economic hardship, King Hussein attempted to mute grown criticism of domestic, foreign, and economic policies.

---

[8] Russell E. Lucas, "Jordan: The Death of Normalization with Israel," *Middle East Journal* 58:1 (Winter 2004), pp. 97–98.

[9] Ibid., 106–108.

King Hussein took ill with cancer in the summer of 1998 and spent the rest of the year in treatment in the US; yet, Jordan's relationship with Israel remained warmer than that of Egypt. Nevertheless, King Hussein's last days saw mostly only lukewarm security cooperation between Israeli and Jordan intelligence and military services. The King exerted his last efforts in keeping the peace process alive by rescuing Bill Clinton's Wye River summit between Netanyahu and Arafat. Soon afterwards, the King succumbed to cancer.

At King Hussein's funeral in February 1999, commentators noted that the largest foreign delegation to attend the ceremony came from Israel. King Abdullah II inherited a global and regional order that was under a *Pax Americana* in which Jordan served as a key "moderate Arab state." Besides Hashemite rule in Jordan was no longer threatened by the downfall of the regime—neither from an Israeli transfer of Palestinians to an alternative homeland East of the Jordan River nor a popular insurrection. Opposition groups could threaten the government of the day or specific policies but not the monarchy itself. Finally, with King Hussein's death personal relations with high Israeli leaders again retreated to the shadows. Public bilateral relations moved back to the realm of functionaries or through American mediation.

References

Abu-Odeh, A. (1999). *Jordanians, Palestinians and the Hashemite Kingdom in the Middle East peace process.* Washington, DC: US Institute of Peace.

Lucas, R. E. (2005). *Institutions and politics of survival in Jordan: Domestic responses to external challenges, 1988–2001.* Albany: State University of New York Press.

Lukacs, Y. (1997). *Israel, Jordan and the peace process.* Syracuse: Syracuse University Press.

Lynch, M. (1999). *State interests and public spheres: The international politics of Jordan's identity.* New York: Columbia University Press.

Majali, A. S., Anani, J. A., & Haddadin, M. J. (2006). *Peacemaking: The inside story of the 1994 Jordanian-Israeli treaty.* Norman: University of Oklahoma Press.

Mutawi, S. A. (1987). *Jordan in the 1967 War.* New York: Cambridge University Press.

Nevo, J. (2006). *King Hussein and the evolutions of Jordan's perception of a political settlement with Israel, 1967–1988.* Brighton: Sussex Academic Press.

Satloff, R. (1994). *From Abdullah to Hussein: Jordan in transition.* New York: Oxford University Press.

Shlaim, A. (2007). *Lion of Jordan: The life of King Hussein in war and peace.* New York: Penguin.

Rabin and Hussein: From Enemies at War to Partners in Peace

Meron Medzini

It is difficult to find two leaders who started out as bitter enemies and ended up becoming partners and friends who admired each other and were able to establish a relationship based on trust and mutual respect. Their friendship enabled their countries to create a modus vivendi in the 1970s, led to an acceptable status quo in the 1980s, and was finalised in a peace treaty between Jordan and Israel that has survived many vicissitudes since it was signed by both leaders in on 26 October 1994. It even survived the assassination of Prime Minister Yitzhak Rabin a year later and the death of King Hussein in 1999. That treaty was the culmination of hours of negotiations and private conversations that were held in an atmosphere of mutual understanding and growing admiration for each other. In the history of the Arab-Israel conflict, there has been no such precedent and it is unlikely that such a relationship could ever be duplicated.

M. Medzini (✉)
Department of Asian Studies, The Hebrew University of Jerusalem, Jerusalem, Israel
e-mail: mmedzini@zahav.net.il

© The Author(s) 2019
P. R. Kumaraswamy (ed.), *The Palgrave Handbook of the Hashemite Kingdom of Jordan*, https://doi.org/10.1007/978-981-13-9166-8_27

Background and Personality Differences[1]

It is hard to imagine two different personalities with such a disparity in their background. Rabin was the older of the two. He was born in Jerusalem in 1922 to a working-class family who was among the founding members of the emerging Israel Labour Party. His mother, the strongest personality of his parents, was active in the Jewish defence underground called the Haganah. His father was a clerk in the Palestine Electric Company. The family moved to Tel Aviv shortly after Rabin's birth and he remained a Tel Avivian until his assassination in 1995.

Rabin's family was well connected and knew the leaders of the *Yishuv*, the emerging Jewish community in Palestine. His mother briefly worked as a clerk alongside Golda Meir in a Federation of Trade Unions company called Solel Boneh. He attended schools that were run by the Labour Movement and in his early childhood was imbued with socialist ideas and the need for the Jews to establish a land of their own in Palestine. The death of his mother when he was 14 years old left a scar on Rabin and he became shy and withdrawn, and to many, he seemed throughout his entire life to be an introvert, almost autistic, dour, and taciturn. He was not a man of small talk, jokes, or childhood pranks, but a serious and hardworking pupil. He attended a Labour Movement high school away from home, and by the time he was 14 years old, he had to decide his future life and career. He chose to study agriculture focusing on irrigation and toyed with the idea of travelling to the US to attend a college and until such time he enrolled at an agricultural high school called Kadoorie, endowed by the well-known Hong Kong Jewish tycoon family. There, he excelled in his studies and joined the Haganah underground.

By the time Rabin graduated, World War II had broken out and studying in the US was out of question. Like many young men of his age and background, he joined a kibbutz, and in 1941 was recruited by Moshe Dayan to join the newly established shock troops of the Haganah called Palmach. This would be the beginning of a 27-year military career that would be crowned with Rabin becoming Chief of Staff of the Israel Defence Forces (IDF) in 1964.

During the 1948 War, Rabin commanded a Palmach brigade that fought to ensure that the Tel Aviv-Jerusalem highway would remain open and that Jerusalem would become part of the Jewish state. His brigade

---

[1] For the life of Rabin, see Horowitz (1996) and Rabinovich (2017).

suffered a considerable number of casualties and failed to capture the Old City of Jerusalem which fell to the Arab Legion and remained under the Jordanian rule until June 1967. The searing failure would remain with Rabin for years, and he was determined to correct this setback. Another lesson he learned from the 1948 war was that Israel must never be caught unprepared and without the necessary weapons to defend its newly won sovereignty. In July 1948, he was the Operations Officer in a campaign that drove the Arabs from Lod, Ramle, and the International Airport, causing a large number of Palestinian refugees who streamed into the West Bank and the East Bank of Jordan.

After the 1948 War, he rose slowly in the ranks, studied briefly in the Kimberley military school in Britain, and became the Chief of Operations in 1959. In 1964, he was appointed Chief of Staff of the IDF, a position he held during the June War of 1967. In that capacity, he led the IDF to an astonishing military victory that included the capture of the West Bank from Jordan, Sinai Peninsula, Gaza Strip, the Golan Heights, and the crowning achievement—the capture of East Jerusalem from the Jordanians.

King Hussein enjoyed an entirely different childhood and early life.[2] He was born in Amman in 1936 to Crown Prince Talal, the son of the then Emir, and since 1946, King Abdullah I of Jordan. As a child, he was tutored by various teachers, but the primary influence on his life was his grandfather, King Abdullah I. His father Talal was afflicted with schizophrenia and had virtually no impact on the future development of his son. His mother, Queen Zeine, was a forceful personality who did have some sway over Hussein. He was too young to play any role in the 1948 war, but three years later, he was at the side of his grandfather when a Palestinian nationalist assassinated the King on Temple Mount in Jerusalem as he was coming out of Al Aqsa Mosque after the conclusion of Friday morning prayers. That event was to mark the life of King Hussein, who in later years would himself become the target of various attempts on his life.

He studied briefly at Sandhurst Military Academy in Britain and developed a strong liking and admiration for Britain, a country that would become his second home, where he had an estate and often visited there. His father, who succeeded Abdullah in 1951, was too ill to remain a king and was deposed and sent to a sanatorium in Istanbul. Hussein was crowned king in 1953 and would remain the sovereign of Jordan until his death in 1999. As King, he had to deal with a vast number of Palestinian

---

[2] For the best biography of King Hussein, see Shlaim (2007).

refugees, with an increasingly volatile situation along the Israel-Jordan Armistice Demarcation Line, and soon with rising Arab nationalism fanned by President Gamal Abdel Nasser of Egypt.

Above all, King Hussein had to ensure that Jordan survives in this turbulent situation and attempt to create a unified nation. His principal source of support came from the Bedouin part of the population and above all from the Jordanian Army, commanded until 1956 by the British general John Bagot Glubb. Growing demands to dismiss Glubb resulted in Hussein firing the general and assuming charge of the Jordanian army while attempting to retain military and economic aid from Britain and soon from the US.

Jordan did not participate in the 1956 Suez War that resulted, among other things, in lessening tension along the Armistice Lines with Israel. A relative calm prevailed along these lines from 1957. Hussein could then devote more time to the development of his kingdom, preferring to invest his scant resources in the East Bank, rather than in the West Bank populated by Palestinians who by and large resented the Hashemite family. In July 1958, Jordan came under serious threat from Egyptian inspired panArab nationalists who toppled the monarchy in Iraq and threatened the same in Jordan. He was rescued by British troops that were flown to Jordan over Israeli airspace.

By then, it was evident that Israel had a vast interest in the survival of Jordan as it became a buffer state between Israel and its neighbours to the east: Syria and Iraq. In 1963, Hussein established contacts with a senior Israeli diplomat in London. These ties ensured that the relative quiet along the borders would be maintained. Israel did not object to Jordan obtaining tanks from the US in 1965, provided they would not cross the River Jordan. This was an understanding reached in a secret meeting between Hussein and Foreign Minister Golda Meir in Paris in late 1965, but soon the King was forced to renege on that promise.

A new threat loomed from 1964 following the establishment in East Jerusalem of the Palestine Liberation Organisation (PLO) under Egyptian sponsorship. That body began to mount terror operations against Israel emanating from Lebanon and Jordan. This resulted in the renewal of Israeli retaliation attacks, and the situation along the Armistice Lines deteriorated. Hussein was unable to stem the tide that gripped the Arab world when, in May 1967, Nasser embarked on many moves that would bring the region to the verge of another war. He opted to side with Egypt knowing well that in case of a war he would lose the West Bank. On 30 May

1967, he signed a defence pact with Egypt and allowed his army to be commanded by an Egyptian General. On 5 June 1967, he ignored an Israeli warning that he stay out of the war that started that morning by an Israeli surprise attack on Egypt's air force, which was annihilated in less than three hours, and launched an attack on Israel along the entire front including Jerusalem. Within 48 hours, he lost the West Bank including East Jerusalem. On 7 June 1967, Rabin, flanked by Defence Minister Moshe Dayan and senior Israeli army officers, marched into the Old City of Jerusalem and arrived at the sacred Western Wall. There they swore that Israel would never give up Jerusalem and later proceeded to annex the Eastern part of that city. Rabin had avenged the losses of 1948.

Post-June War Era

Rabin was not a party to the many meetings that took place after the June war between King Hussein and Israeli leaders, including Foreign Minister Abba Eban, Defence Minister Moshe Dayan, and Deputy Prime Minister Yigal Allon and was not even informed of their contents. In January 1968, Rabin retired from the IDF and was appointed Israel's ambassador to the US. In that capacity, he was told of the regular meetings that took place in London, Aqaba, or near the Jordanian port city between Israeli leaders who, from March 1969, now included the newly appointed Prime Minister Golda Meir. During her term in office (1969–74), she held nine meetings with the King and reached a modus vivendi with him. This resulted, among other things, in Jordan effectively staying out of the surprise attack by Syria and Egypt on Israel on Yom Kippur Day in October 1973. In September 1970, when Hussein faced a grave danger from being overthrown by the PLO and when Syrian tanks invaded Jordan, the King appealed for Israeli help through the US. Ambassador Rabin was involved in the negotiations between Prime Minister Meir and President Nixon to secure Israeli cooperation in assuring Hussein's hold on Jordan. That was quickly achieved without Israel having to send soldiers to defend Jordan. The monarchy survived and Hussein was aware of Rabin's role in that seminal episode.[3]

Prime Minister Golda Meir was forced to resign in April 1974 due to growing public discontent over the October War and was replaced by Rabin who had recently returned from Washington. He was one of the

[3] Kissinger (1977).

few Israeli leaders not tainted with what the Israeli public perceived as the disastrous Yom Kippur War. He was able to create a fragile coalition that included the increasingly right-wing, nationalist religious party aptly called the National Religious Party. To obtain their support, he promised them that any future Israeli withdrawal in the West Bank would entail a national referendum. Rabin, a very cautious untested politician, needed time for Israel to begin to recover from the October War and adjust to the new regional and international realities.

For his part, Hussein wanted a Separation of Forces Agreement with Israel, similar to the ones Israel had signed with Egypt (18 January 1974) and Syria (31 May 1974). Hussein was encouraged to make this demand by Secretary of State Henry Kissinger. The first meeting between King Hussein and Prime Minister Rabin took place near Aqaba in June 1974 when the King renewed his demand for a separation of forces agreement and Rabin had to explain to him that his shaky coalition government would not survive such a move that would entail a token Israeli withdrawal in the West Bank. Rabin offered instead a condominium arrangement in the Jericho area: Israel would remain responsible for security while Jordan would look after the civilian aspects of that city. No agreement was reached in that meeting, but the two leaders had an opportunity to meet and assess each other's personalities and, above all, what they could both promise and deliver. Israel still aspired for what became known as the Jordanian option—a sort of joint rule over the West Bank by both nations. In all his meetings with Hussein during his first term as a prime minister, Rabin was accompanied by Defence Minister Shimon Peres and Foreign Minister Yigal Allon.[4]

A significant event changed all that. At the end of October 1974, an Arab League summit held in Rabat ruled that the PLO was the sole legitimate representative of the Palestinian people and that any part of Palestine that would be liberated would become an independent national entity under the PLO. Two weeks before the Rabat summit, Rabin and Hussein met and the King once again raised his demand for a unilateral Israeli withdrawal in the Jordan Valley. Their third meeting was held on 28 May 1975. By then, Israel was negotiating with Egypt, through Kissinger, an Interim Agreement in Sinai, and Rabin felt that a long-term agreement with Egypt was at the top of his agenda. Israel could not bear parallel withdrawals on both fronts at the same time and the West Bank would

[4] Shlaim (2007).

have to wait. Another meeting took place in Tel Aviv at the end of March 1977 but failed to achieve any concrete agreement (Quandt 2001).

Hussein's fundamental demand now was for a total Israeli withdrawal from the West Bank and East Jerusalem, while Rabin demanded a full-fledged peace treaty. Hussein recalled that Rabin was polite and cordial but tough and uncompromising. On 17 May 1977, the Israel Labour Party lost the Knesset elections and Rabin was replaced by Menachem Begin, the leader of the Likud Party. It was evident that Jordan would be very low in the order of priorities of Begin's new nationalist government. This became evident when Begin authorised a large-scale settlement programme in the West Bank. The man who would carry out this plan was Agriculture Minister, and later Defence Minister, Ariel Sharon. Throughout his administration (1977–83), Begin chose not to meet King Hussein.

Renewed Contacts 1984–90

Jordan was not involved in the hostilities between Israel and the PLO which culminated in the First War in Lebanon (1982–83), which saw the PLO armed forces being dispersed to various Arab states including Jordan. In 1985, Hussein entered into an agreement with Yasser Arafat, the Chairman of the PLO that the West Bank would be part of a future Palestinian entity, but a year later, Arafat reneged on this agreement. In 1984, a government of national unity was formed in Israel with rotating prime ministers. Peres became prime minister while Yitzhak Shamir—who succeeded Begin as the prime minister and Likud Chairman in 1983—became foreign minister. Rabin was appointed the defence minister for the entire term (1984–88).

The order of priorities of the new government included extricating Israel from Lebanon and rescuing its economy that was on the verge of collapse. This meant that Israel had to maintain peace and quiet along the Jordan River. That required the support of King Hussein who quietly acquiesced with the new status quo along the 1967 ceasefire lines: Jordan would ensure that no hostile elements would cross into Israel from its territory; would bar Iraqi forces from entering Jordan; would maintain the Open Bridges policy to enable Israeli Arabs to travel through Jordan to Mecca for the annual Hajj; would pay the salaries of officials in the West Bank; and there would be an equitable sharing of the waters of the River Jordan. This policy suited the Likud party as well, although it authorised a large-scale Jewish settlement in the West Bank and the expansion of the new Israeli neighbourhoods in East Jerusalem.

In October 1986, Shamir once again became the prime minister and Peres became the foreign minister while Rabin remained the defence minister. Shamir was adamantly against any discussion with Jordan regarding a peaceful solution of the Israel-Palestinian conflict. He felt that time was on Israel's side and never felt that the Jordanians had any historical or other claims to the West Bank let alone East Jerusalem. In any case, in 1980, the Israeli parliament adopted the basic law on Jerusalem that proclaimed the city united under Israel. Foreign Minister Peres was keen on breaking the deadlock and in April 1987 reached an agreement with King Hussein that would, if implemented, end with a peace treaty between the two nations after an international peace conference makes arrangements for the West Bank. Shamir rejected the plan out of hand, and the King realised that Peres had little power and authority to push through such a revolutionary step.[5]

In December 1987, the first Palestinian Intifada broke out and posed new threats for Israel and Jordan. The former was unable to deal with this nationalist rebellion initially carried out by young Palestinians who felt that the Palestinian cause was abandoned by their Arab brethren and the rest of the world and that only through an armed uprising their plight would be addressed. Jordan feared that the Intifada would spread across the river and on one occasion repressed by force a demonstration in Yarmouk University. In the summer of 1988, the King concluded that Jordan must cut off all its ties and terminate its responsibilities in the West Bank, and this he did on 31 July 1988. That paved the way for eventual talks with Israel. As long as Prime Minister Shamir was in power, there could be no discussion involving any Israeli withdrawal in the West Bank. In the summer of 1988, Israel once again went to the polls and the results were inconclusive. The government of National Unity continued to function, with Shamir as the prime minister, Peres as the foreign minister, and Rabin continuing as the minister of defence. In May 1989, Israel issued a peace plan inspired by Rabin and agreed to by Shamir: there would be no separate Palestinian state; instead, the Palestinians would be granted large-scale autonomy. The plan also called on Jordan to sign a peace treaty with Israel, but Jordan and the Palestinians could not accept such a proposal.

---

[5] Bar-Zohar (2006).

Two years later, in March 1990, the government of national unity in Israel collapsed and Rabin was no longer the defence minister. In the summer of 1990, Jordan found itself in a most challenging situation, and following the Iraqi invasion of Kuwait, it had to decide whether it supported Saddam Hussein or join the anti-Iraqi coalition led by the US that now included Syria, Egypt, and Saudi Arabia. On 5 January 1991, Shamir met Hussein in London and secured a promise from him that the Iraqi army would not be allowed to enter Jordan. Hussein chose to sit on the fence while Yasser Arafat openly supported Saddam Hussein. At the conclusion of that war, the US arranged for a Middle East Peace conference in Madrid and Jordan was asked to include a Palestinian representation within its delegation and agreed.

The Madrid peace conference (October 1991) opened the way for direct Israeli-Jordanian talks held in Washington but yielded no results. The situation changed when the Labour Party won the June 1992 elections and Rabin once again became prime minister with Shimon Peres as foreign minister. Rabin opted for a deal with Syria as his first priority but allowed the Israeli foreign ministry to pursue clandestine talks with the PLO in London and later in Oslo. Rabin and Hussein were now older, more experienced, and far more assured of their position as leaders. The signing of the Israel-Palestine Declaration of Principles in Washington on 13 September 1993 opened a new era, the beginning of what became known as the Oslo Process. Hussein was initially insulted by being excluded from the negotiations but soon concluded that now that the Palestinians have recognised the State of Israel and entered into negotiations with its government, there was no longer any impediment for him to enter into direct peace talks with Israel.

Peres initially conducted the talks in early November 1993, but the King soon became upset over what he considered Peres' indiscretion when he told Israeli reporters "remember November 3," alluding to a possible peace treaty with Jordan. Hussein suspended talks with Israel and renewed them on condition that his interlocutor would be Rabin. The chief Israeli go-between was the Deputy Director of the Israeli Mossad (Intelligence Agency) Efraim Halevi, a British born Israeli who was trusted by Rabin. A series of meetings took place mostly in or near Aqaba that eventually led to greater understanding due partly to the new realities in the Middle East but also took into account Israel's new and far more improved international position following the Israel-PLO agreement. Many meetings took place between the King and Rabin.

The King was now aware that Rabin was a major international figure, together with Peres and Arafat, the winner of the Nobel Peace Prize, a highly respected statesman in Washington, a close friend of President Bill Clinton, a well-known and much-respected figure on Capitol Hill, and on good terms with Egypt's President Hosni Mubarak. Rabin was welcomed by the leaders of China, Japan, and even Indonesia in addition to the heads of governments in Western and Eastern Europe including, President Yeltsin of the newly created Russian Federation. Hussein came to respect Rabin's analytical mind, his understanding of regional and international processes, his attention to the smallest details, and his ability to quickly read and absorb documents, but above all he relied on Rabin's discretion and knew that once Rabin had given his word, he would be able to follow through due to his now strong position in Israel. Rabin became a sort of a door opener for Hussein in various capitals, mostly in Washington where Rabin interceded with the Clinton Administration to reduce Jordan's debts. The wives of the two leaders also struck a close friendship. They remained patriots and advanced their nations' interests, but knew when a compromise was necessary (Zak 1996).[6]

For his part, Rabin admired the plucky Jordanian sovereign who managed to survive many attempts on his life and endure in a highly turbulent and hostile environment. Hussein survived Nasser, Saddam Hussein, Arafat, and many other threats and was able to build his country's economy and infrastructure slowly. Rabin liked the simple ways of the king, his way of expressing himself, of making the right decisions, and of the choice of his top aides. Both realised that their nations were destined to live side-by-side and thus concluded that there were no longer any barriers that prevented them from signing a full-fledged peace treaty (Susser 1999).

Since both countries were very much beholden to the US, they wisely decided to give President Clinton some of the honours involved in the Israel-Jordan peace process. On 25 July 1994, they issued on the White House Lawn a joint declaration ending the state of war between the two countries. Later that day, Rabin and Hussein addressed a meeting of both the houses of US Congress where both delivered very emotional speeches. At some point, Clinton was heard saying to them: "You guys have met before, haven't you?" (Ross 2004).

Many meetings were held between the senior aides of both leaders before the signing of the peace treaty that took place in the Arava, north

---

[6] Halevi (2006).

of Aqaba on 26 October 1994.[7] The event was attended by major international figures led by President Clinton. The treaty focused on economic issues rather than on territorial or political points. Israel made a token withdrawal and leased those territories from Jordan and promised an annual grant of 50 million cubic metres of River Jordan water to Jordan. Hussein hoped that the treaty would yield many economic benefits, thus making it easier for him to "sell" the treaty to many still opposed to any contact with Israel. For Israel, the benefits of the pact were evident. The fear of an Eastern front now subsided, and it also opened new markets for Israeli goods. The treaty made no mention of the West Bank nor was it conditioned on the progress between Israel and the Palestinians, and above all, it gave Jordan a special standing in the governing of the Muslim holy sites in Jerusalem. The Knesset approved the treaty by an unprecedented majority of over 100 members, including the Likud opposition.

Hussein and Rabin met innumerable times in Israel and Jordan during 1995, although Hussein still refused to come to Jerusalem, and these meetings only served to deepen and expand their friendship. No wonder that Hussein felt as though he was bodily struck when he heard the news that Rabin was assassinated at the conclusion of a peace rally in Tel Aviv on 4 November 1995. He was one among the more than 80 leaders who attended the funeral of Rabin on Mount Herzl in Jerusalem. His eulogy was probably the most moving of all the tributes paid to Rabin and deserves to be cited in full:

> I never thought that the moment would come like this, when I would grieve the loss of a brother, a man, a soldier who met us on the opposite side of the divide, whom we respected as he respected us, a man I came to know because I realise as he did that we had to cross over the divide, establish the dialogue and strive to leave also for us a legacy that is worthy of him. And he did. And so we became brethren and friends.
>
> Never in all my thoughts would it occur to me that my first visit to Jerusalem would be on such an occasion.
>
> You lived as a soldier. You died as a soldier for peace, and I believe it is time for all of us to come out openly and speak of peace. Not here today, but for all the time to come. We belong to the camp of peace. We believe in peace. We believe that our one God wishes us to live in peace and wishes peace upon us.

---

[7] Refer to the text of the peace treaty available in Medzini (1997).

Let's not keep silent. Let our voices rise high to speak of our commitment to peace for all times to come and let us tell those who live in darkness, who are the enemies of light…this is where we stand. This is our camp.

We are determined to conclude the legacy for which my friend fell as did my grandfather in this very city when I was with him but a young boy.

He was a man of courage, a man of vision and he was endowed with one of the greatest virtues that any man can have. He was endowed with humility.

And, standing here, I commit before you, before my people in Jordan and before the world myself to continue to do the utmost to ensure that we shall continue to do the utmost to ensure that we shall leave a similar legacy.

The peace people in the majority of my country, of the armed forces and who once were your enemies are sombre today and their hearts are heavy. Let us hope and pray that God will give us all guidance each in his respective position to do what we can for the better future that Yitzhak Rabin sought.[8]

References

Bar-Zohar, M. (2006). *Phoenix – Shimon Peres, a political biography*. Tel Aviv: Yediot Sfarim. (Hebrew).

Halevi, E. (2006). *Man in the shadows: Inside the Middle East crisis with a man who led the Mossad*. London: St. Martin's Press.

Horowitz, D. (Ed.). (1996). *Yitzhak Rabin: Soldier of peace*. London: Peter Halban.

Kissinger, H. (1977). *White house years*. Boston: Little Brown.

Medzini, M. (Ed.). (1997). *Israel's foreign relations – Selected documents* (Vols. XIV, XV). Jerusalem: Ministry for Foreign Affairs.

Quandt, W. (2001). *Peace process: American diplomacy and the Arab-Israel conflict since 1967*. Berkeley: University of California Press.

Rabinovich, I. (2017). *Yitzhak Rabin: Soldier, leader, statesman*. New Haven: Yale University Press.

Ross, D. (2004). *The missing peace: The inside story of the fight for Middle East peace*. New York: Farrar, Straus and Giroux.

Shlaim, A. (2007). *Lion of Jordan: The life of King Hussein in war and peace*. London: Allen Lane.

Susser, A. (1999). *The Jordanian –Israeli peace negotiations: The geopolitical rationale of a bilateral relationship*. Occasional Papers No. 73. Jerusalem, Leonard David Institute for International Relations, Hebrew University.

Zak, M. (1996). *Hussein makes peace*. Ramat Gan: Bar-Ilan University Press. (Hebrew).

---

[8] For Text of Eulogy, see Medzini (1997).

The ISIS

Tally Helfont

> *We are fighting a war within Islam against the outlaws of Islam ... On behalf of the international community, Jordan has made its decision and taken on a burden far beyond its size.*
> —King Abdullah II Bin-Hussein of Jordan, December 2015

Since its founding, a steady stream of analysts have portrayed Jordan as being perpetually on the brink. At times, these portrayals rang more genuine than at others. Black September—the 1970 bloody civil war between the Jordanian Armed Forces and the Palestine Liberation Organisation (PLO) that claimed the lives of thousands—comes to mind as an unusually low point in the country's history. Unfortunately, the challenge from the Islamic State in Iraq and Syria (ISIS) may be yet another. To King Abdullah II, the Kingdom now finds itself waging both an ideological and a military battle against the outlaws of Islam—going as far as calling it "a Third World War by other means." While the level of alarmism inherent in the latter part of his characterisation may be exaggerated, it does not mean that this sentiment is not acutely felt within the Kingdom and that expressing it as such does not play a compelling and galvanising role in society. And yet, thus far the Hashemite Kingdom has fared quite well relative to

---

T. Helfont (✉)
Institute for Security Governance, Monterey, CA, USA

© The Author(s) 2019
P. R. Kumaraswamy (ed.), *The Palgrave Handbook of the Hashemite Kingdom of Jordan*, https://doi.org/10.1007/978-981-13-9166-8_28

many of its regional neighbours. Why is that? Is it because ISIS never came at Jordan full-force? Is it because of the support Jordan has received from its strong American and Gulf allies? Or is it because of the unifying national identity that has been cultivated in Jordan against all the odds, and the legitimacy enjoyed by its King due to his prophetic lineage? In reality, it is some combination of the above.

To understand the impact that ISIS has had on Jordan, its security, populace, and role in the region, it is essential to explore the radical landscape in the country that ISIS and other Salafi Jihadists have sought to exploit, the emergence and evolution of the group that became ISIS, ISIS' targeting of the Hashemite Kingdom since 2014, and, finally, Jordan's response to this grave threat to its national security and stability.

Jordan's Fertile Ground

Despite the absence of significant ethnic or sectarian cleavages relative to neighbouring countries, Jordan has seen its fair share of tumult. From tribal unrest to civil war to terror attacks, there have been enough crises over the years for observers of Jordan to question its resilience as a state. Nevertheless, Jordan has persisted. Crises aside, there has been one constant weak point in the Jordanian fabric over the course of its seven decades of existence—the regular influx of refugees from other conflicts and the radicalising effect that their experiences and grievances have had on Jordanian society. The Kingdom has managed to weather many of these storms by employing various carrots and sticks, including granting general amnesties to prisoners, forbidding demographic censuses that would stoke national divisions, and giving a nod to reform initiatives that certain sectors of the population vocally demand. However, neither its monarch nor its government is omnipotent. Regional trends towards activist Islamism and even Salafi Jihadism have permeated the Hashemite Kingdom, giving groups like ISIS fertile ground to exploit.

A conservative estimate would find that Jordan's internal stability has been dramatically challenged by four major external conflicts befalling the Middle East. First, the establishment of the State of Israel and the ongoing Israeli-Palestinian conflict have provided an interminable source of fury and a rallying call for violence among Palestinians living in Jordan, Jordanian Islamists, and global terrorist groups alike. While sympathy and anger are felt among the broader Jordanian population, and across the entire region for that matter, the consecutive waves of Palestinians who now call Jordan their home (and their Islamist champions) have kept this more combustible sentiment alive for decades. This sizable demography of Palestinians in Jordan includes the annexed West Bank Palestinians of 1948, the refugees of the June War of 1967, and the Palestinians who were evicted from Kuwait following the PLO's support for Saddam Hussein's 1990–91 invasion of that country. To be sure, a "highly radicalised Palestinian population resonant with terrorist groups and willing to engage in violent attacks against Israel, have at times threatened to destabilise Jordan as well."[1]

Indeed, the PLO was headquartered in Jordan between 1967 and 1970 until it was expelled for its role in the Black September events. What's more, some of the hundreds of thousands of Palestinians that came to Jordan from the Gulf in the 1990s brought with them conservative Salafi interpretations of Islam from the Arabian Peninsula. The most prominent among them was Abu Muhammad al-Maqdisi—considered one of the most influential jihadi ideologues living today and the intellectual architect of al-Qaeda's global jihad.[2] Since arriving in Jordan, Maqdisi has spent the past several decades in and out of Jordanian prisons due to his role in inciting terrorism. Altogether, the fuel that the Palestinian plight has provided would-be terrorists, the internal unrest among Jordanians and Palestinians often surrounding questions of identity and loyalty, and the sometimes-violent Salafism they imported from the Gulf, have had a significantly destabilising effect on the Kingdom.

Second, the decades-long jihad in Afghanistan against the Soviet Union included many Jordanian citizens among the ranks of its foreign fighters. In addition to the radicalising impact of participating in such activities—something that would have a lasting impact on its participants and their countries upon their return—Afghanistan also provided a networking opportunity for future terrorist collaborations. Moreover, it was there that al-Qaeda was born. More importantly for Jordan's part in these developments, it was there that Jordanian national Abu Musab al-Zarqawi began his career as a global terrorist. Though Zarqawi arrived in Afghanistan in 1989 and was too late to fight the Soviets, he returned to Jordan brim-

---

[1] Anne Speckhard, "The Jihad in Jordan: Drivers of Radicalization into Violent Extremism in Jordan," *International Center for the Study of Violent Extremism*, 25 March 2017, http://www.icsve.org/research-reports/the-jihad-in-jordan-drivers-of-radicalization-into-violent-extremism-in-jordan/

[2] Kirk. H. Sowell, "Jordanian Salafism and the Jihad in Syria," *Current Trends in Islamist Ideology*, Vol. 18 (May 2015): 43.

ming with jihadi zeal. While home, he began helping local militant group *Jund al-Sham* (The Levant Division). However, in 1994, he was arrested for having a cache of weapons and explosives in his home, given to him by Maqdisi, and was sentenced to 15 years in prison. Maqdisi joined Zarqawi in prison, and for a time, the two were allied. Ideological differences, and ultimately Zarqawi's ultra-radicalism, which flourished while he was in a Jordanian prison, ruptured that alliance.

In 1999, Zarqawi, Maqdisi, and other prisoners of the same calibre were released as part of a general amnesty granted by King Abdullah II—a decision the King and his kingdom would soon regret. Later that year, Zarqawi was implicated in the failed Millennium plot to blow up the Radisson SAS hotel in Amman just before New Year's Day. He then fled to Afghanistan via Pakistan, sought out seed money to set up a terrorist training camp from Osama Bin-Laden, and founded *Jama'at al-Tawhid wal-Jihad* (Group of Monotheism and Jihad)—a terrorist group expressly bent on bringing down the "apostate" Kingdom of Jordan. In the coming years, he would be implicated in a series of deadly attacks in Jordan, including most notably the assassination of the United States Agency for International Development (USAID) worker Laurence Foley in 2002, and the simultaneous bombing of three hotels in Amman in 2005.[3] And these are just the terrorist activities that Zarqawi was engaged in related to Jordan. He was equally active in Iraq during the same period. In short, the Afghan jihad episode and those who participated in it went on to plague the Kingdom and its stability for years to come.

Third, the wave of Arab Uprisings that swept the region starting in Tunisia in December 2010 had tremendous potential to destabilise the Kingdom. Not only did the prospect of the newly empowered "Arab Street" threaten to upend the ruling regimes in these countries but they also brought to the fore the constant simmering competition between autocratic rulers and their Islamist opponents. After the ousting of the long-ruling dictators in both Tunisia and Egypt, it looked for a time as if Islamist parties were poised to play an outsized role in politics across the entire region. The Muslim Brotherhood's fortunes were in ascent, and an opening was emerging for those Salafis who opted to participate in politics. However, this trend did not extend to Jordan. Protestors comprised secularists and Islamists alike, called for reforming the regime (*islah al-nizam*) rather than toppling it (*isqat al-nizam*) and a return to the 1952 constitution that more closely resembled a constitutional monarchy.

---

[3] David Schenker, "Terrorist Spillover," *Cipher Brief*, 23 June 2016. https://www.thecipherbrief.com/terrorist-spillover

Partisan politics quickly emerged as it became clear that reform meant very different things to different constituencies. Rather than posing an existential threat to the monarch or the monarchy, the protests led more to internal rifts among competing stakeholders in the Kingdom. The Muslim Brotherhood, which observers might have thought would also vie to increase its role and power in the country, did no such thing. The group, which had long been non-violent and worked within the regime's redlines, did not impact the country's future or stability in any significant way during this period. They did, however, clash with some of their Salafi compatriots. The regional uprisings and the questions they evoked also led to a split within the country's 20,000-strong Salafi contingent, pitting Salafi-Jihadists such as Abu Muhammad al-Tahawi and Saad al-Hunayti against regime-loyal traditionalists like Ali al-Halabi and Mashhur Hassan.[4]

This rift led some Jordanian Salafis to engage in a series of protests and violent clashes against the government in the city of Zarqa, the birthplace of Zarqawi. It also resulted in the arrest of crucial Salafi leaders in April 2011. However, these events were short-lived as the bulk of Jordanian Salafis turned their attention away from internal squabbles in Jordan and began focusing their attention on the civil unrest in Syria. In some ways, Jordan was spared, but in others, the significant role that Jordanians have played in the Syrian conflict has come back to haunt the Kingdom and jeopardise its security.

Fourth, the civil war in Syria and the emergence of *Jabhat al-Nusra* (al-Nusra Front) were real turning points in Jordanian society concerning radicalisation and destabilisation. Though neither "an open declaration of jihad nor a statement of support from the Salafi-Jihadi current's leadership" was possible due to the threat of being arrested, Salafis in the country could barely contain their obsession with Syria, regularly announcing how many of their ranks had died in the Syrian jihad and openly holding martyr's funerals.[5] It soon became apparent that Jordanian support for fighting the neighbouring regime had gone beyond ideological approval. By 2012, Jordanians were traveling to Syria en masse to fight the Assad regime.

As if the human toll of hundreds of thousands of Syrian refugees pouring into its domain was not enough, now the Kingdom had to bear the security threat stemming from the free flow of its citizenry into this war

---

[4] Sowell, "Jordanian Salafism and the Jihad in Syria," 47.
[5] Sowell, "Jordanian Salafism and the Jihad in Syria," 49.

zone, only to return radicalised as they had from Afghanistan. As such, Jordanian Intelligence kicked into high gear, and the Jordanian authorities began arresting people. They focused both on preventing people from going to Syria and on capturing those who had returned radicalised and ready to sow violence. However, despite its constant efforts, a significant portion of Jordanians continued to be radicalised by the events in neighbouring Syria. This vulnerability of the population towards radicalism is coupled with another threat: the ever-growing number of Syrian refugees now living in Jordan who were personally traumatised by the conflict and may still seek retribution. Together, they make a tinderbox that the monarchy strives to contend with on a daily basis.

It is on the fertile ground of these radical threats that ISIS enters the scene in Jordan. What is ISIS and from where did it emerge?

ISIS Enters the Scene

The Islamic State in Iraq and Syria—a militant Salafi Jihadi organisation known at different times and in different places as the Islamic State in Iraq and the Levant (ISIL), the Islamic State (IS), and Daesh, its Arabic acronym for *al-Dawlah al-Islamiyyah fil-'Iraq wal-Sham*—has managed to wreak havoc on a global scale in its few years of existence. By engaging in several particularly gruesome attacks, swiftly gobbling up key territory in conflict-ridden Iraq and Syria, and declaring its creation of a new caliphate under the leadership of Abu Bakr al-Baghdadi, the world had no choice but to take notice. However, it was not always so. For a time, the group in its various iterations was relatively unknown, and the global community was not always so fixated on the terrorist threat. That is not to say that there have not been individuals around the world engaging in terrorist activities to achieve their goals all along—the Israel-Palestine conflict provides all too many examples. However, one could argue that it was only after the rise of al-Qaeda under the leadership of Osama Bin-Laden, the attacks of 11 September 2001, and the subsequent American response that global terrorism entered the lexicon.

It was this extended American response, the *Global War on Terror*, that caused the terrorist threat to metastasise. The 2001 invasion of Afghanistan, the 2003 invasion of Iraq, and the subsequent unending reports of bloodletting, setbacks, troop build-ups, and the rest of it served as a beacon for terrorists around the world. As time passed and the global landscape changed, so did the terrorists. Al-Qaeda metamorphosed from a centralised, hierarchical organisation to a franchise, opening and incorporating local branches to meet local needs—to confront nearer enemies than the Great Satan, the United States. With this franchising came both lone wolves and splintering. At times, the splintering occurred due to ideological and theological differences, and in others, due to national and ethnic cleavages among terrorists. And, in some cases, it happened because key leaders were taken out of play, as was the case when US Special Forces killed Osama Bin-Laden in Abbottabad, Pakistan, in 2011. It was from this genesis that ISIS emerged in the early 2000s.

Following the 2003 invasion of Iraq by the US and other Western forces, Zarqawi's *Jama'at al-Tawhid wal-Jihad* pledged allegiance to al-Qaeda to participate in the Iraqi insurgency. This fealty oath in 2004 transformed *Tawhid wal-Jihad into Tanzim Qaidat al-Jihad fi Bilad al-Rafidayn* (Organisation of Jihad's Base in the Land of the Two Rivers), more simply known as al-Qaeda in Iraq (AQI). Zarqawi, however, had ideological differences with Bin-Laden, which caused tension as AQI's *takfiri* beliefs (Muslims declaring other Muslims as unbelievers), led them to the target civilians, fellow Muslims, and the Shia in particular. Though Bin-Laden and al-Qaeda Central viewed the Shias as heretics, they believed that it was their duty to attack the foreign forces that had invaded Muslim lands. As such, AQI's fortunes waxed and waned over the next decade as it clashed with Iraqi and coalition forces and experienced significant backlash from the local Iraqi population. Zarqawi himself was killed in an American airstrike in 2006, purportedly based on tracking information provided to the Americans by Jordanian Intelligence. By 2011, AQI was being run by a local Abu Bakr al-Baghdadi, and American troops had almost entirely withdrawn from Iraq, having failed to obtain Prime Minister Nuri al-Maliki's signature on the Status of Forces Agreement. Under Baghdadi's leadership, AQI, now known as the Islamic State in Iraq (ISI), incorporated into its ranks the Sons of Iraq—former members of Saddam Hussein's military who had been displaced during the invasion of the country—and took Zarqawi's tactics to a new level of violence.

However, it was ISI's foray into the Syrian Civil War in 2013 that animated its growing ambition and hastened its ascent. Taking advantage of the chaos, and driven by Baghdadi's desire to seek out and destroy the Shia (and their Allawi cousins in Damascus) wherever they may be, the group took control of territory on both sides of the border. This move led al-Qaeda's leader Ayman al-Zawahiri to chastise the group and call for them to leave operations against Bashar al-Assad's regime to the al-Nusra

Front. Uninterested in taking cues from al-Qaeda Central any longer, the group rebranded itself as the Islamic State in Iraq and Syria (ISIS) in early 2014 and formally broke with al-Qaeda.[6] By mid-year, having consolidated his gains, capturing crucial cities like Fallujah, Tikrit, and Mosul in Iraq and Raqqa in Syria, and imposing his strict interpretation of Islamic law, Baghdadi once again renamed the group. It was now known as the Islamic State (IS)—a new caliphate—and Baghdadi, of course, was its caliph.[7]

Having gone from virtual anonymity just a few short years earlier to proclaiming his dominion over a newly created caliphate, Baghdadi had shown that he was cunning and dangerous. It seemed to those studying the group's propaganda and its leader's statements that his territorial ambition knew no bounds. Jordan was squarely in the group's crosshairs as it was undoubtedly within the limits of the historical Sham region described in the group's name. Jordan's ties to the US and its 1994 peace treaty with Israel made it an even more attractive target. For the Hashemite Kingdom, this was a serious national security concern. Its northern and north-eastern borders were now crawling with ISIS fighters. The legitimacy of its statehood and its ruler were being called into question by this radical group. There was the issue of ISIS sympathies taking root among Jordan's own population and wreaking havoc from within. By 2014, Jordan was in real danger.

Jordan in the Islamic State's Crosshairs

One of the first consequences for Jordan of the Islamic State's success in Iraq and Syria was that its borders became extremely vulnerable and even porous. Along Jordan's 180-km border with Iraq, Iraqi Armed Forces had pulled out of border towns as ISIS made deft territorial gains. Along Jordan's 375-km border with Syria, thousands of refugees flowed in daily and would-be foreign fighters flowed out to fight the Assad regime. A Stanford University study estimated that by mid-2014, over 2000 Jordanians had gone to fight in Syria and that ISIS had taken "control of nearly all official border crossings between Iraq and Syria and the only

---

[6] Bobby Ghosh, "ISIS: A Short History," *The Atlantic*, 14 August 2014, https://www.theatlantic.com/international/archive/2014/08/isis-a-short-history/376030/

[7] For consistency, ease of reference, and because of the group's subsequent loss of its so-called state or caliphate, the group will continue to be referred to as ISIS from this point onward.

border crossing between Iraq and Jordan."[8] In a bid to ward off would-be invaders, the Kingdom reportedly doubled its forces along its border with Iraq and beefed up its border patrols full tilt.

In June 2014, reports emerged that ISIS had opened a clandestine, unofficial branch within the Kingdom from which it would prepare to expand its caliphate. These reports were exacerbated by the discovery of a map allegedly posted online by ISIS showing Jordan as part of its territory.[9] At this point, it was estimated by numerous governmental sources and media outlets that somewhere between 800 and 2000 Jordanian nationals were part of ISIS and that there were growing sympathies for the group in restive Jordanian cities such as Zarqa and Ma'an. In fact, at two of the anti-government rallies in Ma'an held that same month, "scores of young men, some in black masks, raised their fists, waved home-made banners bearing the logo and inscriptions of the Islamic State of Iraq and Syria (ISIS) and shouted, 'Down, down with Abdullah.'" ISIS flags were hung in other parts of the city as well. These were the first instances of open public support for ISIS. When asked by reporters on the ground why they were supporting ISIS, some described not trusting the government, while others, like political leader Mohammad Abu Saleh said, "The city has been forgotten. There are no jobs, no development, no dignity." He went on to say that support for ISIS was born out of frustration and that many were using "the threat of ISIS to send a message to the regime." The message, he said, was simple: "We've reached the point where the enemy of my enemy is my friend."[10]

These sentiments, however, were not pervasive across the country. For example, senior Salafi leaders who wished to remain anonymous were quoted as saying that they had previously had an understanding with ISIS via some al-Qaeda interlocutors "to forego expansion into the country in a bid to prevent on-going jihadist civil war in Syria to spill over into the

---

[8] "Mapping Militant Organizations: The Islamic State," Stanford University, http://web.stanford.edu/group/mappingmilitants/cgi-bin/groups/view/1

[9] Taylor Luck, "Jordan Strengthens Security along Iraqi Border as ISIL Makes Gains," *The Jordan Times*, 15 June 2014, http://www.jordantimes.com/news/local/jordan-strengthens-security-along-iraqi-border-isil-makes-gains

[10] William Booth and Taylor Luck, "Jordan fears homegrown ISIS more than invasion from Iraq," *The Washington Post*, 27 June 2014, https://www.washingtonpost.com/world/middle_east/jordan-fears-homegrown-isis-more-than-invasion-from-iraq/2014/06/27/1534a4ee-f48a-492a-99b3-b6cd3ffe9e41_story.html

country."[11] They, similar to al-Qaeda's leadership, disagreed with ISIS' approach to forming a caliphate, and in many cases, rejected its methods as well. They also viewed the Syrian arena as being the most pressing issue of the day. They were, however, beginning to fear that ISIS' emboldened activities portended the abandoning of those understandings. Concerning the wider Jordanian population, polling data conducted by the Centre for Strategic Studies at the University of Jordan in late August and early September 2014 showed that 62 per cent of Jordanians thought of ISIS as a terrorist group. This number rose to 72 per cent by December 2014. The December poll also showed that 84 per cent of Jordanians saw ISIS as posing a threat to the stability and security of Jordan. What's more, 77 per cent of Jordanians saw ISIS as posing a threat to the stability and security of the region, meaning that, in their view, the group posed a graver threat to their own stability than everywhere else.[12]

To meet the growing threat of ISIS, American airstrikes began against the group in Syria in August 2014. Not only was Jordan being used as a multilateral staging ground for these operations and as a base for training anti-Assad Syrian rebels but the Kingdom itself also subsequently joined coalition forces in carrying out *Operation Inherent Resolve*. The result was twofold: first, the Kingdom was now playing a forward role in combating this terrorist threat that plagued its security; and second, by doing so, it made itself a much bigger target. The subsequent capture and killing of a member of its military personnel was a prime example of the latter. On 4 February 2015, ISIS released a gruesome video showing Jordanian pilot Lt. Muadh al-Kasasbeh (26 years old), who had been held by the group since 24 December 2014 after his F-16 crashed in Syria, being burned alive in a cage. This imagery shocked the Kingdom.

Where there had once been a healthy opposition to the Kingdom's military involvement in the war against ISIS on the grounds that #*ThisIsNotOurWar*, as the Twitter hashtag read, or that Amman was

---

[11] Taylor Luck, "Jordan Strengthens Security along Iraqi Border as ISIL Makes Gains," *The Jordan Times*, 15 June 2014, http://www.jordantimes.com/news/local/jordan-strengthens-security-along-iraqi-border-isil-makes-gains

[12] "Public Opinion Survey on Some Current National and Regional Issues," *Centre for Strategic Studies at the University of Jordan*, September 2014, p. 28, http://css.ju.edu.jo/Photos/635478413205219966.pdf [In Arabic]; and "Second Public Opinion Poll About the Government of Dr. Abdullah al-Nsour, a Year and a Half After its Formation and Some Current Issues," *Centre for Strategic Studies at the University of Jordan*, December 2014, pp. 5–6, http://css.ju.edu.jo/Photos/635550104895218464.pdf [In Arabic].

blindly doing the bidding of its patron, the US, the majority of that opposition dissipated after Kasasbeh's execution. Polling data from mid-February 2015 from the Centre of Strategic Studies now showed that 95 per cent of Jordanians viewed ISIS as a terrorist organisation, 92 per cent thought ISIS jeopardised Jordan's stability and security, and 88 per cent supported Jordan's military operations in tandem with Arab and coalition forces.[13] The King spoke out forcibly against the group, calling them the outlaws of Islam and vowing retribution. Jordan significantly stepped-up its number of sorties and air operations against the group and expanded strikes into Iraq, deliberately broadcasting every target hit, and every ISIS fighter killed. A series of images showing King Abdullah suiting up and getting ready to fly was released to galvanise the Jordanian public further and demonstrate their monarch's resolve.

These theatrics did not deter ISIS, but coalition efforts against it impacted it. Still, Jordan was targeted. Throughout 2015, Jordan was plagued by numerous security incidents along its borders with Iraq and Syria. In February of that year, the US Embassy in Jordan issued a warning that ISIS-linked militants could target high-end malls in Amman. In July, Jordanian authorities managed to foil a plot by seven of its citizens and one Syrian citizen to attack the Israeli Embassy in Amman. The following year was worse. On 2 March 2016, a Jordanian officer was killed while raiding an ISIS hideout in the northern town of Irbid. On 6 June, an unidentified gunman opened fire on a Jordanian intelligence services office in the Beqaa refugee camp, killing five people. On 21 March, a suicide bomb attack was carried out at the al-Rukban refugee camp near the Syria-Iraq-Jordan tri-border area, killing seven people.[14] On 4 November, a Jordanian guard opened fire on a vehicle carrying US soldiers as it returned to Prince Faisal Air Base, killing three of them. On 18 December, Jordanian authorities engaged in a fire fight with members of an ISIS cell located in the historically significant city of Karak, killing ten people. On 20 December, Jordanian authorities conducted a second raid of a suspected ISIS hideout in Karak, killing four individuals.

---

[13] "Public Opinion Survey on Some Current National," *Centre for Strategic Studies at the University of Jordan*, February 2015, p. 3, http://css.ju.edu.jo/Photos/635608184642126765.pdf

[14] Jeremy M. Sharp, "Jordan: Background and U.S. Relations," *Congressional Research Service Report*, September 10, 2015, p. 5; and Jeremy M. Sharp, "Jordan: Background and U.S. Relations," *Congressional Research Service Report*, 1 June 2017, p. 4, https://fas.org/sgp/crs/mideast/RL33546.pdf

In comparison, 2017 was relatively quieter for Jordanians, though it was not without incidents. This was presumably because of the significant loss of territory, resources, and casualties ISIS suffered in the three years since coalition forces had been working to degrade and destroy it. However, the on-going fighting in Syria, the unstable situation in Iraq, and the inroads ISIS made into some of Jordan's traditionally restive towns meant that each day a new threat may loomed.

Jordan Pushes Back

To meet this ever-present threat, the Hashemite Kingdom has taken many steps aimed at strengthening its hand. First, Jordan introduced new legal measures to increase its ability to police extremism within its borders. Specifically, this came in the form of amending and expanding its already controversial anti-terror laws in the spring of 2014. The revision added the following as acts of terror: "joining or attempting to join armed or terrorist groups, or recruiting or attempting to recruit people to join these groups" and "acts that would expose Jordan or Jordanians to the danger of acts of aggression, or harm the Kingdom's relations with another country."[15]

These revisions were met with mixed reviews. Some in the country saw them as actively meeting the challenges facing the country at a time when jihadi terrorists virtually surrounded the Kingdom. Others viewed it as a slippery slope to becoming a police state. Nevertheless, Jordan has used its sweeping new powers to interdict any and every person who was suspected of threatening its security and stability.

Second, since 2014, Jordan has sought to keep a tighter reign over religious discourse within the country. The state effectively regulates religion in some ways: "It registers and licenses all organisations, and employs its own Islamic scholars. It monitors preaching inside mosques, and since the November 2005 terrorist bombings maintains a tight watch upon all Salafi activity." When members of the opposition are seen to cross regime redlines, arrests ensue.[16] That is to say that since the traumatic events of

---

[15] Kamal Taha, "Jordan Amends Anti-Terror Law to Face Syria Fallout," *Agence France Presse*, 24 April 2014.

[16] Sean Yom and Wael Al-Khatib, "Inflating the Salafi Threat in Jordan," *The Atlantic Council*, 5 December 2014, http://www.atlanticcouncil.org/blogs/menasource/inflating-the-salafi-threat-in-jordan

2005—which for the Kingdom are an open wound—it has remained vigilant against internal threats of this kind, and against Salafis in particular. Luckily for Jordan, the bulk of its domestic critics view the King, his Hashemite lineage, and the institution of the monarchy itself as legitimate. For other less-patriotic Jordanians, the adage "the Devil you know, is better than the devil you don't know" rings truer as the possible messy alternative is playing out in neighbouring Syria.

Third, Jordan has sought out increasing financial aid from the US and the Gulf Arab States to meet the diversity of strains placed on the Kingdom by its security predicament and its refugee populations. According to the World Bank, more than 630,000 Syrian refugees have surged into Jordan since the start of the Syrian conflict in 2011, costing the Kingdom over US$2.5 billion per year and this "amounts to 6 per cent of GDP and one-fourth of [the] government's annual revenues."[17] That number is growing daily. The US foreign aid to Jordan totalled US$1.5 billion in FY2015, US$1.6 billion in FY2016, and approximately US$1.8 billion in FY2017. Moreover, the 2017 Consolidated Appropriations Act also provided "US$180 million for the governments of Jordan and Lebanon from the Defence Department's 'Counter-Islamic State of Iraq and the Levant Train and Equip Fund' to enhance the border security of nations adjacent to conflict areas, including Jordan and Lebanon, resulting from actions of the Islamic State."[18] One hiccup though is that the Memorandum of Understanding that Jordan has with the US, which provides military and economic assistance, has expired, and has yet to be renewed for 2018. Considering that there is a standing budgetary request for FY2018 consistent with the previous FY2015–FY2017 Memorandum of Understanding levels, the Kingdom has likely little to fear. The US Department of Defence assistance has not been just in the form of dollars and has also included operational equipment, weapons, and ammunition.

As for the Gulf States, in response to the initial wave of Arab Uprisings, in December 2011, the Gulf Cooperation Council (GCC) pledged a five-year, US$5 billion aid package to shore up their fellow monarchs. In

---

[17] "Economic Effects of War and Peace in the Middle East and North Africa," *The World Bank*, 3 February 2016, http://www.worldbank.org/en/news/press-release/2016/02/03/economic-effects-of-war-and-peace-in-the-middle-east-and-north-africa

[18] Jeremy M. Sharp, "Jordan: Background and U.S. Relations," 1 June 2017, pp. 15, 1.

August 2016, Saudi Arabia separately committed to the establishment of a multibillion-dollar investment fund.

In summary, the Hashemite Kingdom of Jordan has been significantly affected by the rise of ISIS, though not as severely as neighbouring states. Whether due to altruism, proximity, or a weaker hand than the Saudis, the Hashemite Kingdom has borne the brunt of the refugee crises from Iraq and Syria. While it must vigilantly combat the spread of radicalism within its borders, its greatest woes still come from its economic situation. Its dependence on external donors and the steep cuts it is now required to make as part of the 2016 International Monetary Fund (IMF) deal the Kingdom signed will cause friction within society. This friction, as seen in the Ma'an protests of 2014, can lead to bad things but as many long-time observers of Jordan will tell, with the help of its regional and global allies, Jordan will likely weather this storm as well.

References

Economic effects of war and peace in the Middle East and North Africa. *The World Bank*, February 3, 2016. http://www.worldbank.org/en/news/press-release/2016/02/03/economic-effects-of-war-and-peace-in-the-middle-east-and-north-africa

Ghosh, Bobby. (2014, August 14). ISIS: A short history. *The Atlantic*. https://www.theatlantic.com/international/archive/2014/08/isis-a-short-history/376030/

Mapping militant organizations: The Islamic state. Stanford University. http://web.stanford.edu/group/mappingmilitants/cgi-bin/groups/view/1

Public opinion survey on some current national and regional issues. Centre for Strategic Studies at the University of Jordan. September 2014. http://css.ju.edu.jo/Photos/635478413205219966.pdf. [In Arabic]

Second public opinion poll about the government of Dr. Abdullah al-Nsour, a year and a half after its formation and some current issues. Centre for Strategic Studies at the University of Jordan. December 2014. http://css.ju.edu.jo/Photos/635550104895218464.pdf. [In Arabic].

Sharp, J. M. (2015, September 10). *Jordan: Background and U.S. relations.* Congressional research service report. https://www.hsdl.org/?view&did=787166

Sharp, J. M. (2017, June 1). *Jordan: Background and U.S. relations.* Congressional research service report. https://fas.org/sgp/crs/mideast/RL33546.pdf

Sowell, K. H. (2015, May). Jordanian Salafism and the Jihad in Syria. In *Current trends in Islamist ideology* (Vol. 18, pp. 41–71).

Speckhard, A. (2017, March 25). *The Jihad in Jordan: Drivers of radicalization into violent extremism in Jordan.* International Centre for the Study of Violent Extremism. http://www.icsve.org/research-reports/the-jihad-in-jordan-drivers-of-radicalization-into-violent-extremism-in-jordan/

Yom, S., & Al-Khatib, W. (2014, December 5). *Inflating the Salafi threat in Jordan.* The Atlantic Council. http://www.atlanticcouncil.org/blogs/mena-source/inflating-the-salafi-threat-in-jordan

National Security Priorities

Hayat Alvi

The Hashemite Kingdom of Jordan has long faced national security problems stemming from three interrelated variables: (a) demographics; (b) political turmoil, both regional and domestic, which have included conflicts and wars, waves of refugees, inter-Arab rivalries, internal crises ("palace intrigue"), and terrorism; and (c) water scarcity. With all of these variables coinciding and colliding simultaneously, Jordan faces the perfect storm. Generally, the kingdom's security forces and apparatuses are designed to protect the king and preserve the monarchy. However, recent decades have proven that its national security issues expand beyond the fundamental challenges to the crown.

Overview of Jordan's Modern History

Since the end of World War I, Jordan (known as Transjordan under the British Mandate at the time) has endured massive waves of Palestinian refugees, particularly with the outbreak of the first Arab-Israeli war in 1948 and subsequent wars and refugee crises. Jordan possesses the largest number of Palestinian refugees since 1948, and to date, it has also received Iraqi and Syrian refugee flows in droves since the Kuwait War (1990–91),

---

H. Alvi (✉)
National Security Affairs Department, US Naval War College, Newport, RI, USA
e-mail: hayat.alvi@usnwc.edu

the US-led invasion of Iraq in 2003, and the Syrian Civil War since 2011. In addition, the "founding father" of the Islamic State (IS, also known as Islamic State in Iraq and Syria [ISIS], Islamic State in Iraq and the Levant [ISIL], and Daesh), Abu Musab al-Zarqawi, was a Jordanian who became radicalised and founded al-Qaeda in Iraq (AQI; also known as the Islamic State of Iraq, ISI) in the wake of the US invasion of Iraq. The ISIS reveres Zarqawi as its ideological and organisational founder and its notorious brutality and genocidal anti-Shia sectarian hatred originated with Zarqawi. Hence, the Jordanian security situation is multifaceted, dire, precarious, and extremely sensitive and complex.

According to the *CIA World Factbook*, the population of Jordan is about 10.2 million (July 2017 estimate), but in January 2016, *The Jordan Times* (30 January) put the total number at 9.5 million with 46 per cent of *non-Jordanians* consisting of Syrians, accounting for 13.2 per cent of the total population; thus, the number of Jordanians is 6.6 million, while the total number of non-Jordanians comes to about 2.9 million, or 30.6 per cent of the population.[1] This means that Jordan's demographic shifts, matrixes, and surges exert increasing pressures and stress on its diminishing resources, particularly water, as well as on the domestic economy. Thus, Jordan relies heavily on foreign aid, especially from the US.

A February 2018 Congressional Research Service (CRS) report provides details about the history of Jordan's relationship with the US, particularly regarding foreign aid. The US aid to Jordan has consisted of primarily economic aid since 1951, and military assistance since 1957. The combined Department of State and Department of Defense aid to Jordan leading to the fiscal year 2016 has totalled an estimated $19.2 billion.[2] The 2017 estimate of the US foreign aid to Jordan is about US$1 billion. The request for Jordan's foreign aid disbursement for the fiscal year 2018 is also US$1 billion, ranking as the third top recipient of US foreign aid after Israel and Egypt.[3] To understand the perspective of Jordan's strategic importance, Afghanistan is fourth in rank and Iraq is tenth. Moreover, Jordan maintains critical strategic security cooperation engagement with the US, particularly in the context of counter-terrorism (CT) strategies.

---

[1] Mohammad Ghazal, "Population Stands around 9.5 Million, including 2.9 Million Guests," *The Jordan Times,* January 30, 2016: http://www.jordantimes.com/news/local/population-stands-around-95-million-including-29-million-guests

[2] "Jordan: Background and U.S. Relations," by Jeremy M. Sharp (see https://fas.org/sgp/crs/mideast/RL33546.pdf).

[3] "Jordan Foreign Assistance," United States Office of Management and Budget Data, https://www.foreignassistance.gov/explore/country/Jordan

Jordan's geopolitically strategic location, with Israel, Egypt, Syria, Lebanon, Iraq, and Saudi Arabia as its neighbours, adds to its value in security interests. Its proximity to the Red Sea and the Gulf of Suez/Suez Canal via the Port of Aqaba gives it maritime importance. Moreover, the Hashemite Kingdom of Jordan made peace with Israel in 1994 following the Israeli-Palestinian Oslo Accords (1993). Jordan remains an important player in Arab politics as well as Arab-Israeli and Arab-West relations. Jordan has hosted and absorbed millions of refugees and migrants over the last few decades. Besides, Jordan brokered peace with Israel (1994) soon after the 1993 Oslo Accords between the Palestine Liberation Organisation (PLO) and Israel. Furthermore, the Kingdom has collaborated with the US and other coalition powers to fight against ISIS in Syria and Iraq. The US continues to train and assist the Jordanian security forces in counter-terrorism and national defence strategies and tactics. King Abdullah's pro-West orientation makes Jordan a trustworthy and reliable Arab actor for Western powers in a highly complex, volatile, and often a very anti-West region. These factors make Jordan one of the most critical regional actors for Arab-Western relations, Arab-Israeli issues, and intra-Arab dynamics, in addition to overall counter-terrorism agendas and strategies.

While Jordan's strategic importance has been highlighted, the complex security issues that plague the kingdom both inside its borders and surrounding it must be viewed from the perspective of the three interrelated variables: demographics, politics, and water/resource scarcity. These are affecting each other in a cycle of traumas caused by both regional and extra-regional actors, waves of migrants and refugees, humanitarian crises, economic hardships, and population-resource ratio disparities.

Seismic Demographic Waves Hit Jordan

Jordan has not only experienced and witnessed numerous conflicts and wars, but is itself a product of colonial enterprises after World War I while the Ottoman Empire was on its last leg and collapsing rapidly. The British and French had forged the secret Sykes-Picot Agreement (1916) in anticipation of the collapse of the Ottoman Empire, and as such, they carved up the Middle East territories to serve as future British and French colonies and mandates. The British Mandate in Palestine resulted in Israel asserting itself and achieving statehood in 1948, upon which the neighbouring Arab countries—Jordan included—attacked the newly formed state. The first significant wave of Palestinian refugees crossed the Allenby Bridge into Jordan, and this signified the first of many refugee flows into Jordan to come. Following the 1948 war, Jordan annexed the West Bank, which includes East Jerusalem, thereby inheriting the Palestinian population within it and assuming responsibility for them.

The June 1967 Arab-Israeli War resulted in Jordan losing the West Bank to Israel. Jordan initiated military attacks only to face Israeli counter-attacks driving the Jordanian forces back. As a result of the 1967 war, Israel captured significant Arab lands, including the Sinai and Gaza Strip from Egypt, the Golan Heights from Syria, and the West Bank with East Jerusalem from Jordan. Jordan received an influx of Palestinian refugees numbering about 300,000, the second primary refugee flow of Palestinians into the Kingdom. Losing the West Bank also led to Jordan's extremely terrible economic losses, since much of the country's GNP, agricultural output, labour, and other economic activities were located in the West Bank.

September 1970 marks one of the most severe internal crises that Jordan has faced, known as "Black September," an uprising that the Palestine Liberation Organisation (PLO) led against the monarchy. The Jordanian Armed Forces surrounded the PLO fighters; the *Fedayeen* and Yasser Arafat barely escaped. Following this uprising, which the Jordanian monarchy survived, the PLO re-settled in Lebanon. These events indicate the consequences of demographic imbalance, in this case with the Palestinians and mainly the PLO operating in Jordan that caused internal turmoil challenging Jordan's monarchy. It has served as the impetus for the Jordanian monarchy to remain vigilant about potential threats to the throne. Given that the PLO's move to Lebanon thereafter served as a pivotal factor in triggering the Lebanese civil war, and specifically the Israeli invasion of Lebanon in 1982, the fact that Jordan has absorbed millions of Palestinian refugees has remained a point of concern for the monarchy. While most Jordanians are sympathetic to the Palestinian cause, the role of the PLO in the Black September uprising seeking to topple the Hashemite monarchy will never be forgotten in Jordanian minds.

With the Lebanese civil war (1975–90), Jordan continued to face regional fallout from the conflict, especially with Israel's invasion in 1982, Syrian agendas and actions, and the proxy support from regional actors of various militias fighting in Lebanon. With the 1979 Islamic Revolution in Iran and subsequently the emergence of Hezbollah in Lebanon, Jordan faced yet another major regional threat. With the Iran-Iraq War (1980–88) breaking out and the rise of the Jordanian Muslim Brotherhood, the ideological competition throughout the region manifested itself in Jordan along with the demographic pressures. The demographic fallout and regional impacts of pervasive conflicts on Jordan have led to intense ideological competition, both regionally and within Jordan. This thread of ideological competition runs throughout the Middle East and North Africa (MENA) region, and it coincides with the proliferation of diverse terrorist organisations. Jordan has not been immune to terrorist attacks inside its borders. The ideological competition among extremists encompasses the rise of the Jordanian terrorist Abu Musab al-Zarqawi, the ideological "founding father" of ISIS. Moreover, Jordan has an active Muslim Brotherhood chapter.

The Islamic Action Front is a political branch of Jordan's Muslim Brotherhood, which won the largest seats in parliament in 1989. The linkage between these domestic political developments in Jordan falls on demographic lines, since the Islamic Action Front, along with a significant proportion of Jordan's population, have been pro-Palestinian and inherently carry a strong affinity to the Palestinian cause. The Islamic Action Front has supported the agendas of Hamas. Therefore, undoubtedly, Jordan cannot divorce itself demographically or politically from the Palestinian-Israeli issue. With the Black September stain in Jordan's modern history, political entities that harbour ideological leanings in favour of the Palestinians, which the Islamic Action Front has illustrated, are viewed by the Palace with great caution. Extremists are also a source of national security concern for the monarchy. Combined with these national security priorities are the impacts of regional conflicts on Jordan's political and economic health. An example of this is the impact of the 1991 Gulf War on Jordan.

Politics, Conflicts, and Terrorism

Leading to the 1991 Gulf War, King Hussein tried to arbitrate a peaceful resolution in the wake of Saddam Hussein's invasion of Kuwait and US President George H.W. Bush's ultimatum for an Iraqi withdrawal, the failure of which would result in the coalition-based war against Iraq. King Hussein did not succeed in his efforts and Jordan, and Yemen became ostracised among the Arab states for opposing the 1991 Gulf War. As a result, Iraqi refugees fleeing the war, along with thousands of Palestinian migrant workers fleeing Iraq and expelled from the Gulf Arab states, flooded Jordan. According to the UN Refugee Agency (UNHCR), by mid-March 1991, an estimated 23,000 Iraqi refugees entered Jordan. A massive wave of Palestinians returned to Jordan after their expulsion by Gulf Arab countries. With the US invasion of Iraq, the refugee flow and by 2009 just under 800,000 Iraqi refugees had fled to Jordan. However, following the devastating 2005 hotel bombings in Amman, by none other than Abu Musab al-Zarqawi, Jordan restricted entry of refugees, that is, until the Syrian civil war broke out in 2011. Since then, Jordan has hosted nearly 700,000 *registered* Syrian refugees. It is almost impossible to configure the unregistered numbers.

Jordan's demographic shifts, flows, and influxes of refugees have led to tremendous economic and resource shocks and stresses. They have required Jordan to rely heavily on foreign aid to assist in accommodating the refugees, dealing with the humanitarian crises, offsetting the economic stagnation and deficiencies and, most importantly, countering terrorism inside and around the Kingdom, and Zarqawi's terrorist attacks have specifically sought out Jordanian targets.

On 9 November 2005, three hotels in Amman, Jordan suffered terrorist attacks: *Radisson SAS Hotel*, *Grand Hyatt Hotel*, and *Days Inn*, resulting in 60 deaths and more than 100 injuries. A wedding party was taking place at the Radisson, and as the bomb went off, it "cut through the ballroom like a swarm of flying razors. Hundreds of steel ball bearings carefully and densely packed around the bomb's core, sliced through wedding decorations, food trays, and upholstery. They splintered wooden tables and shattered marble tiles. They tore through evening gowns and fancy clutches, through suit jackets and crisp shirts and through white, frilly dresses of the kind young girls wear to formal parties."

Jordan's intelligence agency, called *Mukhabarat*, recognised the voice claiming responsibility for the bombings in an audio recording: the voice of Abu Musab al-Zarqawi, who was leading al-Qaeda in Iraq at the time. Zarqawi was known to the Jordanian authorities as a petty criminal and hoodlum. In the 1980s, he had fought the Soviets in Afghanistan alongside the Mujahedeen, where Zarqawi became a hardened religious fanatic and militant. He had a penchant for the leadership of like-minded militants, whom he managed to organise even in a notorious Jordanian prison (Warrick, pages 5–7).

In March 1999, Jordan was observing a mourning period for the passing of King Hussein and his successor, Abdullah, granted amnesty to numerous inmates in the country's prisons, as a gesture to allow nonviolent offenders and political prisoners to gain their freedom. In a series of stages, prisoners' names passed from hand to hand, when the parliament finally approved a list of 2500 names. Joby Warrick describes what happened next:

> The king, then just six weeks into his new job and still picking his way through a three-dimensional minefield of legislative, tribal and royal politics, faced a choice of either adopting the list or sending it back for weeks of additional debate. He signed it.

Many months would pass before Abdullah learned that list had included certain Arab Afghans from the al-Jafr Prison whose Ikhwan-like zeal for purifying the Islamic faith should have disqualified them instantly. But by that time, the obscure jihadist named Ahmad Fadil al-Khalayleh had become the terrorist Abu Musab al-Zarqawi. And there was nothing a king of Jordan could do but berate his aides in an exasperated but utterly futile pique.

'Why,' he demanded, 'didn't someone check?'[4]

Zarqawi was known for his hatred (Warrick, pp. 171–175; 185; 202–204) of Shias and he sought to annihilate them, regardless of their civilian or combatant status. His extremely myopic ideology, based on the already extremely literalist and ultra-orthodox ideology of Wahhabism, has sowed hatred of anyone who does not abide by its own degenerate interpretation of Sunni *tawheed* (strictly monotheistic) and *takfiri* (ability to judge another person as a "non-believer," or apostate and hence making him/her a target of violence/death)-based creed.

Ironically, in November 2004, King Abdullah-II had initiated the Amman Message, which intended to disclaim radical and/or extremist Islamist views and ideologies, proclaimed Muslim unity in the efforts to combat extremism, and denounced concepts like *takfir* and related terrorist violence. Similarly, the Amman Message restricts the average person's ability, or claim to have religious authority, to issue *fatwas* (religious decrees). The three main points of the Amman Message are provided below, and they indicate Abdullah's keen recognition of Islamist extremism as a critical potential threat to Jordan's national security, as well as regional security:

---

[4] Joby Warrick, *Black Flags: The Rise of ISIS* (New York: Anchor Books, 2016), p. 43.

1. Whosoever is an adherent to one of the four *Sunni* schools (*Mathahib*) of Islamic jurisprudence (*Hanafi, Maliki, Shafi'i,* and *Hanbali*), the two *Shi'i* schools of Islamic jurisprudence (*Ja'fari* and *Zaydi*), the *Ibadi* school of Islamic jurisprudence, and the *Thahiri* school of Islamic jurisprudence is a Muslim. Declaring that person an apostate is impossible and impermissible. Verily his (or her) blood, honour, and property are inviolable. Moreover, in accordance with the Sheikh Al-Azhar's *fatwa*, it is neither possible nor permissible to declare whosoever subscribes to the *Ash'ari* creed or whoever practices real *Tasawwuf* (Sufism) an apostate. Likewise, it is neither possible nor permissible to declare whosoever subscribes to true *Salafi* thought an apostate.
2. Equally, it is neither possible nor permissible to declare as apostates any group of Muslims who believes in God, Glorified and Exalted be He and His Messenger (may peace and blessings be upon him) and the pillars of faith and acknowledges the five pillars of Islam and does not deny any necessarily self-evident tenet of religion.
3. According to the four Islamic schools of law, the methodology and authority of issuing fatwas are prescribed, "thereby exposing ignorant and illegitimate edicts in the name of Islam".

The Amman Message goes on to proclaim that there exists more in common between the various schools of Islamic jurisprudence than there is a difference between them. The adherents to the eight schools of Islamic jurisprudence are in agreement as regards the basic principles of Islam. All believe in Allah (God), Glorified and Exalted be He, the One and the Unique; that the Noble Qur'an is the Revealed Word of God; and that our master Muhammad, may blessings and peace be upon him, is a Prophet and Messenger unto all humanity. All are in agreement about the five pillars of Islam: the two testaments of faith (*shahadatayn*); the ritual prayer (*salat*); almsgiving (*zakat*); fasting during the month of Ramadan (*sawm*); and the *Hajj* to the sacred house of God (in Mecca). All are also in agreement about the foundations of belief: belief in Allah (God), His angels, His scriptures, His messengers and in the Day of Judgment, and in Divine Providence in good and evil. Disagreements between the *'ulama* (scholars) of the eight schools of Islamic jurisprudence are only with respect to the ancillary branches of religion (*furu'*) and not as regards the principles and fundamentals (*usul*) [of the religion of Islam]. Disagreement concerning the ancillary branches of religion (*furu'*) is mercy. Long ago it was said that variance in opinion among the *'ulama* (scholars) "is a good affair."

Acknowledgment of the schools of Islamic jurisprudence (*Mathahib*) within Islam means adhering to a fundamental methodology in the issuance of *fatwa*s: no one may issue a *fatwa* without the requisite personal qualifications which each school of Islamic jurisprudence determines [for its own adherents]. No one may issue a *fatwa* without adhering to the methodology of the schools of Islamic jurisprudence. No one may claim to do unlimited *Ijtihad* and create a new school of Islamic jurisprudence or to issue unacceptable *fatwa*s that take Muslims out of the principles and certainties of the *Sharia* and what has been established in respect of its schools of jurisprudence.[5]

Nonetheless, the Amman Message did not immunise Jordan from suffering some of the worst terrorist nightmares. In addition to the bombing of the Jordanian embassy in Baghdad in August 2003, which pointed to Zarqawi, the Amman hotel bombings in 2005, and the rise of ISIS in Syria and Iraq following the outbreak of the Syrian civil war in 2011, one of the most heinous demonstrations of anti-Jordanian terrorism came in the form of a shocking video in early January 2015. On 24 December 2014, a Jordanian fighter jet crashed in Raqqa, Syria, and its pilot, named Muath Safi Yousef al-Kasasbeh, survived but fell captive to ISIS. A series of negotiations ensued between Jordanian officials and ISIS, and the latter demanded the release of Sajida al-Rishawi, sitting in death row in Jordan for her involvement in the 2005 Amman hotel bombings, in exchange for the pilot al-Kasasbeh and a Japanese hostage, journalist Kenji Goto.

However, an ISIS video that was soon released showed al-Kasasbeh being burned alive in a cage, to the horror of all of Jordan as well as the global public. Jordanians were outraged, and King Abdullah ordered al-Rishawi to be executed by hanging. The image of the young Jordanian pilot trapped inside a cage and blanketed in billowing flames will forever remain imprinted in the minds of Jordanians, especially the Jordanian armed forces. For this reason, along with the multifaceted and in some respects interconnected demographic issues prevalent in Jordan, counter-terrorism remains one of the kingdom's top national security priorities.

Some of the most hardened extremists have been Arabs of various national identities who fought in Afghanistan in the 1980s and Iraq in 2000s and more recently in Syria and somehow have found themselves in Jordan. Zarqawi was a home-grown terrorist for Jordan, but his ventures

---

[5] *The Amman Message*, "The Three Points of the Amman Message, v.1": http://amman-message.com/the-three-points-of-the-amman-message-v-1/

in Afghanistan and Iraq solidified his early alignment with al-Qaeda, only to break off later and take a path that seems more divergent and extreme in actions even for al-Qaeda terrorists. The cycle of violence, conflicts, wars, and humanitarian crises throughout the region and particularly those neighbouring Jordan revolves not only around the kingdom but also within it, in the form of refugees, the proliferation of militants, and their ideologies and at times grievances against the political establishment. The scarcity of resources in Jordan has been exacerbated due to these harsh realities.

Water Scarcity

Before Jordan's terrorism headaches, the kingdom was facing a severe water crisis. According to *The Economist*, "Jordan is already one of the world's most arid countries. Climate change will make matters worse. By the end of the century, say scientists from Stanford University, Jordan could be 4° C hotter, with about a third less rain. It needs to rationalise water consumption."[6] That is no easy task, especially when refugees from Iraq, Syria, and Palestine surge into the country, critically stressing the already strained infrastructure and natural resources, specifically water. According to the World Health Organisation (WHO),[7] Jordan finds itself in a dire situation with water scarcity. The impacts of climate change, high population influxes, and very low precipitation have created a water crisis in Jordan. The report adds that water management issues simultaneously stress the government.

The energy costs of pumping water in Jordan have also increased substantially. Therefore, the demographic crisis in the country correlates with the infrastructure and resources variables, which are affected and stressed. The government is scrambling to keep up with water demands and avoid major crises in the near and distant future. *The Jordan Times* reports that the increasing demand for water is "estimated at 21 per cent annually," and as a response, the Ministry of Water and Irrigation is exploring desalination of seawater and drilling into deep aquifers to access water.[8]

---

[6] "Jordan's Water Crisis is Made Worse by a Feud with Israel," *The Economist*, December 2, 2017: https://www.economist.com/news/middle-east-and-africa/21731844-thirsty-kingdom-can-ill-afford-fall-out-its-neighbour-jordans-water

[7] "Water is Life" 2018, http://www.who.int/heli/pilots/jordan/en/

[8] Hana Namrouqa, "Red-Dead Project 'Everlasting Solution' to Water Shortages in Jordan," *The Jordan Times*, May 17, 2017: http://www.jordantimes.com/news/local/red-dead-project-everlasting-solution%E2%80%99-water-shortages-jordan

Specifically, the ministry has announced the *Red-Dead Project*[9] (Quoted from: Hana Namrouqa, "Red-Dead Project 'Everlasting Solution' to Water Shortages in Jordan," The Jordan Times, May 17, 2017), which entails the following:

Considering the project as the 'cornerstone of all efforts to solve Jordan's water scarcity', the ministry sees the Red Sea-Dead Sea Water Conveyance Project (Red-Dead) as its everlasting solution to a shortage of water in Jordan.

Under the first phase, a total of 300 million cubic meters (mcm) of water will be pumped each year. In its following phases, the Red-Dead project will see up to 2 billion cubic meters of seawater transferred from the Red Sea to the Dead Sea annually, according to the ministry.

The Red-Dead project's main components are a seawater intake structure; an intake pump station; a seawater pipeline; a desalination plant with a capacity of 65–85 mcm per year; a desalination brine conveyance pipeline; two lifting pump stations; hydropower plants; and discharge facilities at the Dead Sea.[10]

Many other water initiatives are also in the works, but Jordan's water scarcity problem is precarious; adding influxes of refugees due to wars and conflicts will exacerbate an already stressed resource base and infrastructure inside Jordan. The government is aware of this and hence has considered it another top national security priority in the kingdom.

Conclusion

Jordan suffers from the cascading humanitarian and security crises originating in the Syrian civil war, Iraq's conflicts, as well as internal political and ideological strife. The influx of refugees into Jordan and the prominence of militant ideologies, including ISIS ideology, within the country (stemming from al-Zarqawi's inspiration), aggravate the national and regional security crisis for Jordan and the region. In early 2018, media reports hint at an attempted coup in the palace, but King Abdullah has denied the rumours, while, at the same time, placing two brothers and a cousin in forced retirement from the Jordanian armed forces. King

---

[9] Hana Namrouqa, "Red-Dead Project 'Everlasting Solution' to Water Shortages in Jordan," *The Jordan Times*, May 17, 2017.
[10] Ibid.

Abdullah has described this move as a "restructuring" of the armed forces, rather than a palace coup attempt. Nevertheless, along with all the national security priorities that have been examined, the vital one remains the preservation of the Hashemite monarchy. That has not changed since the inception of the kingdom.

Overall, the Hashemite Kingdom of Jordan has dual simultaneous national security priorities of countering terrorism from external extremists, as well as preventing terrorism from within. With the influx of refugees and migrants throughout the last few decades, managing the populations inside the Kingdom's borders has become extremely challenging. Adding the other variables of resource constraints and stresses only exacerbate the demographic, economic, and political tensions and challenges.

Jordan is locked in a vicious cycle: the country has borne the brunt of waves of refugees mainly due to conflicts and wars in the region. The rise in populations has continuously placed extreme stress on the country's economy, political stability, natural resources, water, and food security, and it has also intensified national security concerns and priorities due to terrorism. Because of these factors, Jordan has had to rely on the US and other Western powers and oil-rich Gulf Arab states to provide it with foreign aid. Besides, Jordan relies on the US for security cooperation, counter-terrorism assistance and training, and intelligence sharing. Therefore, Jordan is stuck in a relationship of dependency on other countries for economic, military, security, and development assistance. Given that the MENA region is continuously suffering from conflicts and wars, the vulnerabilities affecting Jordan's national security will not improve anytime soon.

Undeniably, a dark stain on Jordan's modern history has been the character and role of Abu Musab al-Zarqawi in laying the foundations for ISIS. As the "founding father" of ISIS, Zarqawi sowed and spread the seeds of one of the most bloodthirsty, sinister, and intolerant ideologies driving the most atrocious terrorist organisations in the world, which at one point possessed a sophisticated army, institutions, and infrastructure in parts of Syria and Iraq. Diehard ISIS members have continued to carry Zarqawi's torch, despite significant territorial losses in early 2018. As Joby Warrick aptly puts it, "Zarqawi's children were pursuing the founder's far grander ambitions: the end of Jordan and its king, the erasing of international boundaries and the destruction of the modern states of the Middle East. Then, with black flags raised above Muslim capitals from the Levant to the

Persian Gulf, they could begin the great apocalyptic showdown with the West."[11]

Jordan has experienced nonstop waves of people, security crises, the fallout from regional conflicts and wars, economic hardships, and infrastructure and resource dilemmas, including water scarcity and occasional palace intrigue. King Abdullah's renowned father, the late King Hussein, once said, "I have said this in the past, and I will continue to repeat it as long as I live: Whoever tries to hurt our national unity is my enemy until the day of judgment."

REFERENCES

Jordan. *CIA World Factbook*, August 2017. https://www.cia.gov/library/publications/the-world-factbook/geos/jo.html

Jordan: Federal Research Study and Country Profile with Comprehensive Information, History and Analysis – Politics, Economy, Military. U.S. Government Study, Library of Congress, May 8, 2017.

Warrick, J. (2016). *Black flags: The rise of ISIS.* New York: Anchor Books.

---

[11] Warrick, p. 11.

Annexure

Chetna Kuanr and Rashmi Muraleedhar

Key Information

Ruling family: Hashemite
Ruler: King Abdullah II (since 7 February 1999)
Crown Prince: Crown Prince Hussein since 2 July 2009
National Day: 25 May
Parliament: Bicameral *Majlis al-Umma* comprising the Upper House *Majlis al-Aayan* and the Lower House *Majlis al-Nuwwab*
Last parliamentary election: 20 September 2016
Major group in parliament: Independents primarily of tribal origin and decent

Socio-economic Indicators (2017 Figures)

Area: sq. km; 89,342 sq. km
Population: 10.25 million;
Native: 69.3 per cent
Expats and refugees: 30.7 per cent (Syrian 13.3 per cent, Palestinian 6.7 per cent, Egyptian 6.7 per cent, Iraqi 1.4 per cent, other 2.6 per cent)

C. Kuanr (✉) • R. Muraleedhar
University of Chicago, Chicago, USA
e-mail: ck.knr5@gmail.com; mu.rashmi@gmail.com

Religious groups: Muslim 97.2 per cent (official; predominantly Sunni), Christian 2.2 per cent (majority Greek Orthodox, but some Greek and Roman Catholics, Syrian Orthodox, Coptic Orthodox, Armenian Orthodox, and Protestant denominations), Buddhist 0.4 per cent, Hindu 0.1 per cent, Jewish <0.1, folk religionist <0.1, unaffiliated <0.1, other <0.1 (2010 est.)
Youth: 20.07 per cent (15–24 years)
Population growth rate: 2.05 per cent
Life expectancy at birth: 74.8 years
Major population groups: Arabs 97.6 per cent; Circassian, Armenian and others 2.4 per cent
Literacy rate: 95.4 per cent
National currency: Jordanian Dinar
GDP (ppp): US$ 89.1 billion
GDP per capita: US$ 12,500
Foreign trade: Export-US$ 7.734 billion; Import-US$ 18.12 billion (2017 est.);
Defence budget: 4.8 per cent of GDP (2017 est.);
Sovereign Wealth Fund: NA billion;
External debt: US$ 27.72 billion;
Oil reserves: 1 million bbl.
Gas reserves: 6.031 billion cu m
HDI rank: 95
Infant Mortality Rate: 14.2 deaths/1000 live birth;
UN Education Index: 0.700
Gender Inequality Index: 0.460
Labour force: 2.295 million
Unemployment rate: 18.5 per cent
Urban population: 91 per cent
Rate of urbanization: 2.43 per cent annual
Last National Census: 2015
National Carrier: Royal Jordanian Airlines

BIBLIOGRAPHY

Ababsa, M. (2011a). Citizenship and urban issues in Jordan. In M. Ababsa & R. Daher (Eds.), *Cities, urban practices and nation building in Jordan* (pp. 39–64). Beirut: Presses de l'Institut français du Proche-Orient.

Ababsa, M. (2011b). Social disparities and public policies in Amman. In M. Ababsa & R. Daher (Eds.), *Cities, urban practices and nation building in Jordan* (pp. 205–232). Beirut: Presses de l'Institut français du Proche-Orient.

Ababsa, M. (2013). Changes in the regional distribution of the population. In M. Ababsa (Ed.), *Atlas of Jordan: History, territories and society* (pp. 257–267). Beirut: Presses de l'Ifpo.

Abd-el-Jawad, H. R. (2006). Why do minority languages persist? The case of Circassian in Jordan. *International Journal of Bilingual Education and Bilingualism, 9*(1), 51–74.

Abdullah (I), K. (1978). *My memoirs completed.* London: Longman.

Abdullah (I), K. (1979). *Al-Athar al-Kamilah Lil-Malik Abdullah* (The complete works of king Abdullah). Beirut: al-Dar al-Mutahidalil-Nashr.

Abdullah (I), K. (2011). *Our last best chance: The pursuit of peace in a time of peril.* London: Allen Lane.

Abdullah (I), K. (2012). *Our last best chance: A story of war and peace.* New York: Penguin Books.

Abu Assab, N. (2011). *Narratives of ethnicity and nationalism: A case study of Circassians in Jordan.* PhD Thesis, Coventry, University of Warwick. Available at: http://wrap.warwick.ac.uk/50794/1/WRAP_THESIS_Abu-Assab_2011.pdf. Accessed 25 Sept 2018.

© The Author(s) 2019
P. R. Kumaraswamy (ed.), *The Palgrave Handbook of the Hashemite Kingdom of Jordan*, https://doi.org/10.1007/978-981-13-9166-8

Abu Hammour, M. (2000). Financial policy and structural adjustment in Jordan. In A. al-Jumourad (Ed.), *The evaluation of external economic assistance in Jordan 1989–99*. Amman: Center for Strategic Studies, University of Jordan.

Abu Nowar, M. (2006). *The development of trans-Jordan 1929–1939: A history of the Hashemite Kingdom of Jordan*. Reading: Ithaca Press.

Abu Shair, O. J. A. R. (1994). *Privatization and development: Insights from a holistic approach, with special reference to the case of Jordan*. PhD Thesis, Salford, Center for Development Studies, Faculty of Social Science, University of Salford. Available at: http://usir.salford.ac.uk/14719/1/DX187190.pdf. Accessed 27 May 2018.

Abu-Lebdeh, H. S. (1997). *Conflict and peace in the Middle East: National perceptions and United States – Jordan relations*. Lanham: University Press of America.

Abu-Nimer, M., Khoury, A., & Welty, E. (2007). *Unity in diversity: Interfaith dialogue in the Middle East*. Washington, DC: US Institute of Peace Press.

Abu-Odeh, A. (1999). *Jordanians, Palestinians and the Hashemite Kingdom in the Middle East peace process*. Washington, DC: US Institute of Peace Press.

Abu-Zanat, M. (1995, November 9–10). Production systems of small ruminants within the different agro-ecological zones of Jordan. In *Livestock Research Priorities Workshop*, Amman.

Abu-Zanat, M. (1997, November 12–16). Consultation on setting livestock research priorities in West Asia and North Africa (WANA). In *Livestock research priorities in Jordan* (Workshop), Aleppo.

ACTED. (2017, April–October). Wellbeing of urban refugees: Syrians and hosts in Jordan and Lebanon. Available at: https://www.acted.org/en/projects/wellbeing-of-urban-refugees-syrians-and-hosts-in-jordan-and-lebanon/. Accessed 30 June 2018.

Addison, E. (2004). The roads to ruins: Accessing Islamic heritage in Jordan. In Y. Rowan & U. Baram (Eds.), *Marketing heritage: Archaeology and the consumption of the past* (pp. 229–248). Walnut Creek: Alta Mira Press.

Ahmad, E. (1991). *Jordan restructuring public expenditures and protecting the poor* (IMF Working Paper, 91/82). Washington, DC: International Monetary Fund.

Al Jamal, D. (2018). Jordan. *UNICEF*. Available at: https://childfriendlycities.org/jordan/. Accessed 30 June 2018.

Al Madfai, M. R. (1993). *Jordan, the United States and the Middle East peace process, 1974–1991*. Cambridge: Cambridge University Press.

Al Nasser, H. W. (2016, September). New social enterprises in Jordan: Redefining the meaning of civil society. *Middle East and North Africa Programme, Chatham House*. Available at: https://www.chathamhouse.org/sites/files/chathamhouse/publications/research/2016-09-28-jordan-civil-society-al-nasser-final.pdf. Accessed 10 Apr 2018.

Al Sarhan, A. (2016). *United States' foreign policy towards the Hashemite Kingdom of Jordan: 1990–2014*. Ph.D. Thesis, University of Atlanta, Atlanta.

Al Shalabi, J., & Al-Assad, T. (2012, January 1). Political Participation of Jordanian Women. *Egypte monde arabe*, Center detudes et de documentation économiques juridiques et socials, 9. Available at: ema.revues.org/3033; DOI: https://doi.org/10.4000/ema.3033. Accessed 12 Oct 2018.

Al Sharif, O. (2015, November 3). How will Jordan's Pivot to Russia Pay Off? *Al-Monitor*. Available at: https://www.al-monitor.com/pulse/originals/2015/11/jordan-russia-agreement-military-coordination-syria.html. Accessed 18 Aug 2018.

Al Sharif, O. (2017, July 11). Hamas-Dahlan Détente keeps Jordan on edge. *Middle East Institute*. Available at http://www.mei.edu/content/article/hamas-dahlan-d-tente-keeps-jordan-edge. Accessed 5 Aug 2018.

Aladwan, K. I., & Aldabbas, K. M. (2015). The Jordanian parliamentary institution: A study in political representation. *Dirasat, Human and Social Sciences*, 43(1), 269–290.

Alan, G. (2005). *Jordan: Living in the crossfire*. New York: Zed Books.

Al-Attiyat, I., Shteiwi, M., & Sweiss, S. (2005a). *Building democracy in Jordan: Women's political participation, political party life and democratic elections*. Stockholm: International Institute for Democracy and Electoral Assistance and the Arab NGO Network for Development.

Al-Attiyat, I., Shteiwi, M., & Sweiss, S. (2005b). *Building democracy in Jordan: Women's political participation, political party Life and democratic elections*. Stockholm: International Institute for democracy and Electoral Assistance, IDEA/Arab NGO Network for Development, ANND.

Al-Attiyat, I., Shteiwi, M., & Sweiss, S. (2005c). *Building democracy in Jordan: Women's political participation, political party Life and democratic elections*. Stockholm: International Institute for Democracy and Electoral Assistance and the Arab NGO Network for Development.

Alazzam, A. A. (2008). *Political participation in Jordan: The impact of party and tribal loyalties since 1989*. Ph.D. Thesis, Durham University, Durham. Available at: http://etheses.dur.ac.uk/2183/1/2183_192.PDF. Accessed 25 May 2018.

Al-Bakri, J. T., Ajlouni, M., & Abu-Zanat, M. (2008, February). Incorporating land use mapping and participation in Jordan. *Mountain Research and Development*, 28(1), 49–57.

Al-Bustani, B. (1987). *Moḥeet al-Moḥeet Qāmus Muṭawal li-Lughah l-Arabiyyah* (The circumference of the ocean: An extended dictionary of Arabic). Beirut: Maktabah Lubnan.

Al-Dahdah, E., Corduneanu-Huci, C., Raballand, G., Sergenti, E., & Ababsa, M. (2016). *Rules on paper, rules in practice: Enforcing laws and policies in the Middle East and North Africa*. Washington, DC: The World Bank. Available at: https://openknowledge.worldbank.org/handle/10986/24715. Accessed 12 Sept 2018.

Al-Eisawi, D. M. (1985). Vegetation of Jordan. In A. Hadidi (Ed.), *Studies in the history and archaeology of Jordan* (Vol. II, pp. 45–57). Amman: Ministry of Archaeology.

Al-Hait, S. S., & Basheti, I. A. (2017, March 1–7). A narrative review of smoking cessation practices in Jordan. *Journal of Pharmacology and Clinical Research, 2*(4).

Alhasan, K. (2015). The impact of governmental efforts in the fight against corruption, and Citizen's satisfaction with the Government's performance on the participation of citizens in the social movement (Alherak) in Jordan. *Journal of Arts and Social Sciences, 6*(3), 47–60.

Ali, A., Bulad, A., Kozah, A., Oweis, T., & Bruggeman, A. (2006, December 10–15). Fighting desertification in Jordan and Lebanon. *ICARDA Caravan, 23*. Available at: https://apps.icarda.org/wsInternet/wsInternet.asmx/DownloadFileToLocal?filePath=Caravan/Caravan23.pdf&fileName=Caravan23.pdf. Accessed 12 Oct 2018.

Al-Jaloudy, M. A. (2006). *Country pasture/forage resource profiles: Jordan*. San Saba: Food and Agricultural Organization.

Al-Jazeera. (2018a, January 29). Iran Blasts Jordan's King over 'Unfair' Statement. Available at: https://www.aljazeera.com/news/2018/01/iran-blasts-jordan-king-unfair-statement-180129101847328.html. Accessed 20 Oct 2018.

Al-Jazeera. (2018b, June 11). Gulf nations pledge $2.5bn economic aid package to Jordan. Available at: https://www.aljazeera.com/news/2018/06/gulf-nations-pledge-25bn-economic-aid-package-jordan-180611055833875.html. Accessed 16 Sept 2018.

Al-Khalidi, S. (2018, January 19). Jordan says Israel apologizes for deaths of two Jordanians at embassy. *Reuters*, Amman. Available at: https://www.reuters.com/article/us-jordan-israel-diplomacy/jordan-says-israel-apologizes-for-deaths-of-two-jordanians-at-embassy-idUSKBN1F72PQ. Accessed 30 June 2018.

Alkhdour, R. (2011). *Estimating the shadow economy in Jordan: Causes, consequences and policy implications*. Ph.D. Thesis, Department of Economics, Colorado State University, Fort Collins. Available at: https://dspace.library.colostate.edu/bitstream/handle/10217/70433/Alkhdour_colostate_0053A_10845.pdf?sequence=1. Accessed 2 June 2018.

Allan, J. A. (Ed.). (1996). *Water peace and the Middle East: Negotiating resources in Jordan basin*. London: I.B. Tauris.

Allan, J. A. (2002). Hydro-peace in the Middle East: Why no water wars?: A case study of the Jordan River basin. *SAIS Review, 22*(2), 255–272.

Allen, R. (1980). *How to save the world: Strategy for world conservation*. London: Kegan Paul.

Almadhoun, S. (2015). *Access to information in the Middle East and North Africa region: An overview of recent developments in Jordan, Lebanon, Morocco, and*

Tunisia. The World Bank. Available at: https://openknowledge.worldbank. org/handle/10986/22978. Accessed 10 Aug 2018.

Al-Madi, M., & Musa, S. (1988). *Tarikh al-Urdun fil-Qarn al-'Ishrin*. Amman: Maktabat al-Muhtasib. (Arabic).

Almarzoqi, R., Naceur, S. B., & Scopelliti, A. (2015). *How does bank competition affect solvency, liquidity and credit risk? Evidence from the MENA countries* (IMF Working Paper, 15/210). Washington, DC: International Monetary Fund.

Alnawafleh, H., Al Tarawneh, K., & Alrawashdeh, R. (2013). Geologic and economic potentials of minerals and industrial rocks in Jordan. *Natural Science, 5*(6), 756–769. Available at: https://doi.org/10.4236/ns.2013.56092. Accessed 30 June 2018.

Al-Omari, G., & Fishman, B. (2018, June 13). Jordan's economic protests: repackaging reform. The Washington Institute for Near East Policy, Policy Analysis, Policy Watch 2981. Available at: https://www.washingtoninstitute. org/policy-analysis/view/jordans-economic-protests-repackaging-reform. Accessed 15 June 2018.

Alon, Y. (2004). Tribal Shaykhs and the limits of British Imperial Rule in Transjordan, 1920–46. *The Journal of Imperial and Commonwealth History, 32*(1), 69–92.

Alon, Y. (2005a). *The making of Jordan: Tribes, colonialism and the modern state*. London: I. B. Tauris.

Alon, Y. (2005b, May). The tribal system in the face of the state-formation process: Mandatory Transjordan, 1921–46. *International Journal of Middle East Studies, 37*(2), 213–240.

Alon, Y. (2006). The Balqā' revolt: Tribes and early state-building in Transjordan. *Die Welt des Islams, 46*(1), 7–42.

Alon, Y. (2010, September). British colonialism and orientalism in Arabia: Glubb pasha in Transjordan, 1930–1946. *British Scholar, 3*(1), 105–126.

Al-Qaisi, K. (2016). The effect of the financial crisis on the Jordanian industrial sector. *International Journal of Finance and Banking Studies, 2*(1), 43–47.

Al-Qudah, B., & Sabet, J. (2000). Rangeland management, water harvesting and users' involvement with rangeland and conservation reserves in Jordan. *Dryland Pasture, Forage and Range Network News, 19*.

Al-Ramahi, A. (2008). Wasta in Jordan: A distinct feature of (and benefit for) middle eastern society. *Arab Law Quarterly, 22*(1), 35–62.

Al-Safadi, A. (2018). Personal interview with Minister of Foreign Affairs and Expatriates of Hashemite Kingdom of Jordan in Amman on 10 March 2018.

Al-Shraah, I. (2012). Arab (Jordanian) National Union 1971–1974: Historical analytical study. *An-Najah University Journal for Research-Humanities, 26*(3), 731–766.

Amawi, A. (1994). 1993 elections in Jordan. *Arab Studies Quarterly, 16*(3), 15–27.

Amawi, A. M. (1996, October). USAID in Jordan. *Middle East Policy, 4*(4), 77–89.

Ambrose, S. E. (1984). *Eisenhower: The president* (Vol. II). New York: Simon and Schuster.

Amis, J. (2013, January). The Jordanian Brotherhood in the Arab Spring. *Current Trends in Islamist Ideology, 14*, 38–57.

Amro, R. (2008). Palestinian refugees in Jordan as a successful example of immigrants. In M. Finkelstein & K. Dent-Brown (Eds.), *Psychosocial stress in immigrants and in members of minority groups as a factor of terrorist behavior* (pp. 63–72). Amsterdam: IOS Press.

Anderson, B. S. (2005). *Nationalist voices in Jordan: The street and the state.* Austin: University of Texas Press.

Anonymous. (1983, September). September EEMA region presentation to the Board of Directors of Philip Morris Inc. Tobacco Control Documents, Philip Morris Records. Available at: https://www.industrydocumentslibrary.ucsf.edu/tobacco/docs/#id=xfcj0111. Accessed 28 Oct 2018.

Anonymous. (n.d.-a). Public smoking: Warning levels in Arab countries. Tobacco Control Documents, British American Tobacco Records, Available at: https://www.industrydocumentslibrary.ucsf.edu/tobacco/docs/#id=rfnk0196. Accessed 28 Oct 2018.

Anonymous. (n.d.-b). *Cigarettes: Imports of selected countries by country of origin annual 1981–85.* Tobacco Control Documents, British American Tobacco Records. Available at: https://www.industrydocumentslibrary.ucsf.edu/tobacco/docs/#id=npbc0212. Accessed 20 Oct 2018.

Anthony, J. D. (1979). Foreign policy: The view from Riyadh. *The Wilson Quarterly, 3*(1), 73–82.

Antoun, R. T. (1989). *Muslim preacher in the modern world: A Jordanian case study in comparative perspective.* Princeton: Princeton University Press.

Arab Trade Union Confederation. (2015). *Jordan-Ministry of Labour Deported 6467 Migrant Workers Last Year.* Available at: http://arabtradeunion.org/en/content/jordan-ministry-labor-deported-6467-migrant-workers-last-year. Accessed 28 Oct 2018.

Arneberg, M. (1997). *Living conditions among Palestinian refugees and displaced in Jordan*, Fafo Report 237. Oslo: Fafo Institute for Applied Social Sciences. Available at: http://www.fafo.no/media/com_netsukii/237.pdf. Accessed 20 May 2018.

Aruri, N. H. (1972). *Jordan: A study in political development, 1921–1965.* The Hague: Martinus Nijhoff.

Asher, S. (2008). Jordan: Preserving domestic order in a setting of regional turmoil. *Middle East Brief, 27*, 1–7.

Ashton, N. (2005). A 'special relationship' sometimes in spite of ourselves: Britain and Jordan, 1957–73. *The Journal of Imperial and Commonwealth History, 33*(2), 221–244.

Ashton, N. (2006). Pulling the strings: King Hussein's role during the crisis of 1970 in Jordan. *The International History Review, 28*(1), 94–118.

Ashton, N. (2008). *King Hussein of Jordan: A political Life*. New Haven: Yale University Press.

Ashton, N. (2011). Love's Labours lost: Margaret Thatcher, king Hussein and Anglo-Jordanian relations, 1979-1990. *Diplomacy and Statecraft, 22*(4), 651–677.

Assessment of Development Result. (2007). *Evaluation of UNDP contribution: Jordan*. New York: United Nations Development Programme.

Atzori, D. (2015). *Islamism and globalisation in Jordan: The Muslim Brotherhood's quest for hegemony*. London/New York: Routledge.

Azaryahu, M., & Reiter, Y. (2015). The (geo) politics of interment: An inquiry into the burial of Muhammad Ali in Jerusalem, 1931. *Israel Studies, 20*(1), 31–56.

Azzeh, L. (2017, June 2). Unemployment at highest rate in 25 years – DoS. *The Jordan Times*, Amman. Available at: http://www.jordantimes.com/news/local/unemployment-highest-rate-25-years-%E2%80%94-dos. Accessed 30 June 2018.

Badran, A., & Bishara, K. (Eds.). (1986). *The economic development of Jordan*. London: Croom Helm.

Bank, A., & Valbjørn, M. (2010). Bringing the Arab regional level Back in...— Jordan in the new Arab cold war. *Middle East Critique, 19*(3), 303–319.

Bar'el, Z. (2018, April 17). In Jordan, massive refugee influx and inequality raise Questions on identity. *Ha'aretz*. Available at: https://www.haaretz.com/middle-east-news/jordan/.premium-in-jordan-massive-refugee-influx-raises-questions-of-identity-1.6008848. Accessed 30 June 2018.

Barakat, S. (2014, July 24). Building Jordan's future: The case for targeted investment. *Brookings*. Available at: https://www.brookings.edu/opinions/building-jordans-future-the-case-for-targeted-investment/. Accessed 20 Oct 2018.

Barany, Z. (2013). Revolt and resilience in the Arab kingdoms. *Parameters, 43*(2), 89–103.

Barari, H. (2013, December). The limits of political reform in Jordan: The role of external actors. *Friedrichebert Stiftung, International Policy Analysis*. Available at: https://library.fes.de/pdf-files/iez/10455-20140108.pdf. Accessed 28 Aug 2018.

Bar-Lavi, Z.'e. (1981). *The Hashemite regime 1949–1967 and its position in the West Bank*. Tel-Aviv: Shiloah Institute.

Barmin, Y. (2017, May 31). Russia's Syria strategy hinges on Jordan. *Al-Monitor*. Available at: https://www.al-monitor.com/pulse/originals/2017/05/russia-strategy-syria-jordan-mediator-sunni-us-crisis.html. Accessed 26 Sept 2018.

Barnes-Dacey, J. (2012, November 14). What lies behind the protests in Jordan. *European Council on Foreign Relations*. Available at: http://ecfr.eu/blog/entry/what_lies_behind_the_protests_in_jordan. Accessed 16 Nov 2016.

Baster, J. (1955). The economic problems of Jordan. *International Affairs (Royal Institute of International Affairs), 31*(1), 26–35.

Baylouny, A. M. (2008). Militarizing welfare: Neo-liberalism and Jordanian policy. *The Middle East Journal, 62*(2), 277–303.

Beck, M., & Collet, L. (2010, October). Jordan's 2010 Election law: Democratization or stagnation? *Länderprogramm Jordanien*, Konrad-Adenauer-Stiftung e.V. Available at: https://www.kas.de/c/document_library/get_file?uuid=9744fb17-d33a-72bd-bb8d-d0f9d2e96d64&groupId=252038. Accessed 28 Aug 2018.

Beck, M., & Hüser, S. (2015). Jordan and the 'Arab spring': No challenge, no change? *Middle East Critique, 24*(1), 83–97.

Bergem, K. (2006). The role of the state in the in-migration of domestic workers to Jordan and the GCC countries. In F. De Bel-Air (Ed.), *Migration et politique au Moyen-Orient* (pp. 61–79). Beirut: IFPO.

Bernstein, Z. (2014). *Stuck in a Jordanian Winter: Why the Arab Spring failed to result in lasting regime change in Jordan*. Graduate honours Thesis, University of Colorado, Boulder.

Bhattacharya, R. (2003). *Exchange rate regime considerations for Jordan and Lebanon* (IMF Working Paper, 3/137). Washington, DC: International Monetary Fund.

bin Muhammad, G. (1999). *The tribes of Jordan: At the beginning of twenty-first century*. Amman: RUTAB.

Birdal, M. (2010). *Political economy of ottoman debt*. London/New York: I.B. Tauris.

Blackwell, S. (2013). *The British military intervention and the struggle for Jordan: King Hussein, Nasser and the Middle East crisis, 1955–1958*. New York: Routledge.

Blanche, E. (1997). USA and Jordan hold naval exercise. *Jane's Military Exercise and Training Monitor, 4*.

Blavy, R. (2001). *Trade in the Mashreq: An empirical examination* (IMF Working Paper, 01/163). Washington, DC: International Monetary Fund.

Blench, R. (1996). *The Hashemite Kingdom of Jordan: National programme for range rehabilitation and development, baseline survey of socio-economic and animal production data*. Document of the International Fund for Agricultural Development, *1*(1), Amman.

Bligh, A. (1998). *Jordanian–Israeli strategic partnership in historical perspective*. Ariel Center for Policy Research, Policy Paper 24. Available at: http://www.acpr.org.il/pp/pp045-blighE.pdf. Accessed 18 Sept 2018.

Bligh, A. (2001). The Jordanian Army between domestic and external challenges. *Middle East Review of International Affairs, 5*(2), 13–20.

Bligh, A. (2002). *The political legacy of king Hussein*. Brighton: Sussex Academic Press.

Bligh, A. (2004). Palestinian and Jordanian views on Balfour declaration. In N. Yavari, L. G. Potter, & J.-M. R. Oppenheim (Eds.), *Views from the edge: Essays in honour of Richard W. Bulliet* (pp. 19–26). New York: Columbia University Press.

Borek, A. (1988, May 18). Memo: First Arab anti-smoking symposium. *Tobacco Control Documents, British American Tobacco Records*. Available at: https://www.industrydocumentslibrary.ucsf.edu/tobacco/docs/#id=rmpg0201. Accessed 20 Oct 2018.

Boruszewski, J. (2017, December 18). Palestinian refugees in Jordan not at all keen to return home. *La Croix International*, Al-Husn Palestinian Refugee Camp. Available at: https://international.la-croix.com/news/palestinian-refugees-in-jordan-not-all-that-keen-to-return-home/6593#. Accessed 30 May 2018.

Boulby, M. (1999). *The Muslim brotherhood and the kings of Jordan, 1945–1993*. Atlanta: Scholars Press.

Bouziane, M. (2016). Jordan – Disquiet at the Island of Stability. *IEMed Mediterranean Yearbook 2016*, 214–217. Available at: https://www.iemed.org/observatori/arees-danalisi/arxiusadjunts/anuari/med.2016/IEMed_MedYearBook2016_Jordans%20Disquiet%20Stability_Maika_Bauziane.pdf. Accessed 28 Oct 2018.

Bouziane, M., & Lenner, K. (2011). Protests in Jordan: Rumblings in the kingdom of dialogue. In Center for Middle Eastern and North African Politics (Ed.), *Protests, revolutions and transformations – The Arab world in a period of upheaval* (Working papers 1) (pp. 148–165). Berlin: Centre for Middle Eastern and North African Politics.

Bowen, J. (2003). *Six days: How the 1967 war shaped the Middle East*. London: Simon and Schuster.

Bram, C. (2004). The congress of the international Circassian association: Dilemmas of an Ethno-National Movement. In M. Gammer (Ed.), *The Caspian region* (Vol. III, pp. 63–103). London: Routledge.

Bram, C. (2017, November 23–24). *Identity challenges of a Diaspora minority: Lessons from the case studies of Circassians in Israel and in the U.S.A*. Paper presented at the conference, *Circassians in the 21st century: Identity and Survival*, RUCARR, Malmö University, Malmo.

Bram, C., & Gammer, M. (2013). Radical Islamism, traditional Islam and ethno-nationalism in the North-Western Caucasus. *Middle Eastern Studies, 49*(1), 296–337.

Brand, L. A. (1992). Economic and political liberalization in a Rentier economy: The case of the Hashemite Kingdom of Jordan. In I. Harik & D. Sullivan (Eds.), *Privatization and liberalization in the Middle East* (pp. 167–188). Bloomington: Indiana University Press.

Brand, L. A. (1994a). 'In the beginning was the state...': The quest for civil Society in Jordan. In A. R. Norton (Ed.), *Civil Society in the Middle East* (pp. 148–185). Leiden: E. J. Brill.

Brand, L. A. (1994b). *Jordan's inter-Arab relations: The political economy of Alliance making*. New York: Columbia University Press.

Brand, L. A. (1995). Palestinians and Jordanians: A crisis of identity. *Journal of Palestine Studies, 24*(4), 46–61.

Brand, L. (1998). *Women, the state, and political liberalization: Middle eastern and north African experiences*. New York: Columbia University Press.

Brand, L. A. (1999a). Al-Muhajirin w-al-Ansar: Hashemite strategies for managing communal identity in Jordan. In L. Binder (Ed.), *Ethnic conflict and international politics in the Middle East* (pp. 279–306). Gainesville: University Press of Florida.

Brand, L. A. (1999b). The effects of the peace process on political liberalization in Jordan. *Journal of Palestine Studies, 28*(2), 52–67.

Brand, L. A. (2003). Jordan: Women and the struggle for political opening. In E. A. Doumato & M. P. Posusney (Eds.), *Women and globalization in the Arab Middle East: Gender, economy, and society* (pp. 143–168). Boulder: Lynne Rienner.

Brand, L. A. (2010). National narratives and migration: Discursive strategies of inclusion and exclusion in Jordan and Lebanon. *International Migration Review, 44*(1), 78–110.

Bromberg, G. (2008, September 18). Will the Jordan River keep on flowing? *Yale Environment, 360*. Yale School of Forestry and Environmental Studies. Available at: https://e360.yale.edu/features/will_the_jordan_river_keep_on_flowing. Accessed 30 June 2018.

BRP-NCRD. (2011, November). Securing rights and restoring range lands for the improved livelihoods in the Badia of the Zarqa River Basin-Jordan. *Base Line Study*. Available at: https://www.iucn.org/sites/dev/files/import/downloads/baseline_study___securing_rights_and_restoring_land_for_improved_livlihoohs.pdf. Accessed 25 May 2018.

Brynen, R. (1992). Economic crisis and post-rentier democratization in the Arab world: The case of Jordan. *Canadian Journal of Political Science, 25*(1), 69–97.

BTI (Bertelsmann Stiftung's Transformation Index). (2016). Jordan country report. Bertelsmann Stiftung, Gütersloh. Available at: https://www.bti-project.org/fileadmin/files/BTI/Downloads/Reports/2016/pdf/BTI_2016_Jordan.pdf. Accessed 30 June 2018.

Cammett, M., Diwan, I., Richards, A., & Waterbury, J. (2015). *A political economy of the Middle East* (4th ed.). Boulder: Westview.

Castellino, J., & Cavanaugh, K. A. (2013). *Minority rights in the Middle East*. Oxford: Oxford University Press.

Center for International Communication. (2018, February 28). Saudi Arabia's aid to the world reaches nearly $33 billion in 10 years. Press Release. Available at: https://cic.org.sa/2018/02/saudi-arabias-aid-to-the-world-reaches-nearly-33-billion-in-10-years/. Accessed 18 Oct 2018.

Central Bank of Jordan. (2015). Annual report 2014: Overview of Jordan's economic development in 2014. Available at: http://www.cbj.gov.jo/uploads/chapter1.pdf. Accessed 30 June 2018.

Chadwick, S. (1969). *United States Policy towards Jordan*. Master's Thesis, George Washington University, Washington, DC.

Chatelard, G. (2010). Jordan: A refugee Haven. *Migration Policy Institute*. Available at: https://www.migrationpolicy.org/article/jordan-refugee-haven. Accessed May 2018.

Chedid, A., & Saliba, D. (2017). The Armenian Christian minority in greater Syria and the Arab spring. In K. S. Parker & T. Nasrallah (Eds.), *Middle eastern minorities and the Arab spring* (pp. 79–98). Piscataway: Gorgias Press.

Choucair-Vizoso, J. (2008). Illusive reform: Jordan's stubborn stability. In M. Ottaway & J. Choucair-Vizoso (Eds.), *Beyond the Façade. Political reform in the Arab world* (pp. 45–70). Washington, DC: Carnegie Endowment for International Peace.

Christophersen, M. (2013). *Jordan's 2013 elections: Further boost for tribes*. Norwegian Peace Building Resource Centre, NOREF Report. Available at: https://www.files.ethz.ch/isn/162496/3cfcb191c3644dd32cda0c2c3431d149.pdf. Accessed 25 Apr 2018.

Clark, J. A. (2004). *Islam, charity, and activism: Middle-class networks and social welfare in Egypt, Jordan, and Yemen*. Bloomington: Indiana University Press.

Clark, J. A. (2006). The conditions of Islamist moderation: Unpacking cross-ideological cooperation in Jordan. *International Journal of Middle East Studies, 38*(4), 539–560.

Coady, D., Kpodar, K., Gillingham, R., El-Said, M., Newhouse, D. L., & Medas, P. A. (2006). *The magnitude and distribution of fuel subsidies: Evidence from Bolivia, Ghana, Jordan, Mali, and Sri Lanka* (IMF Working Paper, 06/2247). Washington, DC: International Monetary Fund.

Cohen, A. (1982). *Political parties in the West Bank under the Jordanian regime 1949–1967*. Ithaca: Cornell University Press.

Cohen, A. (1986). *The economic development of the territories 1922–1980*. Givat Haviva: The Institute of Arabic Studies. (Hebrew).

Coogle, A. (2016, October 27). Recorded 'Honor' killings on the rise in Jordan. *Human Rights Watch*. Available at: https://www.hrw.org/news/2016/10/27/recorded-honor-killings-rise-jordan. Accessed 30 June 2018.

Cordesman, A. H. (2003). *Saudi Arabia enters the twenty-first century: The military and international security dimensions.* Washington, DC: Center for Strategic and International Studies.

Cox, H. (2000). *The global cigarette: The origins and evolution of British American Tobacco: 1880–1945.* Oxford: Oxford University Press.

Dann, U. (1989). *King Hussein and the challenge of Arab radicalism. Jordan, 1955–1967.* New York: Oxford University Press.

Day, A. R. (1986). *East Bank/West Bank: Jordan and the prospects for peace.* New York: Council on Foreign Relations.

De Bel-Air, F. (2008). Irregular migration to Jordan: Socio-political stakes. *CARIM Analytic and Synthetic Notes* 2008/78, (Florence, Robert Schuman Center for Advanced Studies), 1–19. Available at: http://hdl.handle.net/1814/10511. Accessed 18 May 2018.

De Bel-Air, F. (2016, November 1–19). Migration profile: Jordan. Migration Policy Centre, Robert Schuman Center for Advanced Studies, European University Institute, 6.

De Bel-Air, F., & Dergarabedian, A. (2006). Migrations internationales, globalisation et politique. Les Zones industrielles qualifiantes (QIZs) de Jordanie. In F. De Bel-Air (Ed.), *Migration et politique au Moyen-Orient* (pp. 37–60). Beirut: IFPO.

Devarajan, S., & Mottaghi, L. (2015). *Middle East and North Africa economic monitor: Towards a new social contract. World Bank.* Available at: https://openknowledge.worldbank.org/handle/10986/21718. Accessed 28 Sept 2018.

Dew, P., Wallace, J., & Shoult, A. (2004). *Doing business with Jordan.* London: GMB Publishing.

Domac, I., & Shabsigh, G. (1999). *Real Exchange Rate Behavior and Economic Growth: Evidence from Egypt, Jordan, Morocco, and Tunisia, IMF working paper, 99/40.* Washington, DC: International Monetary Fund.

Due-Gundersen, N. (2017, January 16). Nationalism in Jordan: King, tribe, or country? *Opendemocracy.* Available at: https://www.opendemocracy.net/north-africa-west-asia/nicolai-due-gundersen/nationalism-in-jordan-king-and-tribe-or-love-of-country-part-on. Accessed 15 Apr 2018.

Dumper, M. (1997). *The politics of Jerusalem since 1967.* New York: Columbia University Press.

Dumper, M. (2014). *Jerusalem unbound: Geography, history and the future of the Holy City.* New York: Columbia University Press.

Dunne, M. (2010, November 17). Jordan's elections: An observer's view. *Carnegie Endowment for International Peace.* Available at: http://www.carnegieendowment.org/publications/index.cfm?fa=viewandid=41954. Accessed 10 Oct 2018.

Dweik, B. S. (2000). Linguistic and cultural maintenance among the Chechens of Jordan. *Language Culture and Curriculum, 13*(2), 184–195.

Edwards, B. M. (2018, June). Marginalized Youth towards an Inclusive Jordan. *Brookings Policy Brief.* Available at: https://www.brookings.edu/wp-content/uploads/2018/06/June-2018_Beverly-Jordan_English-Web.pdf. Accessed 4 Oct 2018.

Eilon, J. B., & Alon, Y. (2007). *The making of Jordan: Tribes, colonialism and the modern state.* London: I. B. Tauris.

El Muhtaseb, L. (2013, April). *Jordan's East banker-Palestinian Schism.* Norwegian Peace-building Resource Centre (NOREF), Expert Analysis. Available at: https://www.files.ethz.ch/isn/162779/746892aacedd3e8fcb1ff7370a77fb67.pdf. Accessed 30 June 2018.

El-Abed, O. (2004). Palestinian refugees in Jordan. *Forced Migration Review, 25,* 1–21. Available at: http://www.forcedmigration.org/research-resources/expert-guides/palestinian-refugees-in-jordan/fmo025.pdf. Accessed 30 June 2018.

El-Abed, O. (2014). The discourse of Guesthood: Forced migrants in Jordan. In A. Fabos & R. Isotalo (Eds.), *Managing Muslim Mobilities: Between spiritual geographies and global security regimes* (1st ed., pp. 81–100). New York: Palgrave Macmillan.

El-Anis, I. (2011). *Jordan and the United States: The political economy of trade and economic reform in the Middle East.* London: I.B. Tauris.

El-Anis, I. (2016). Explaining the behaviour of small states: An analysis of Jordan's nuclear energy policy. *Cambridge Review of International Affairs, 29*(2), 528–547.

El-Emam, D. (2015, February 18). Jordanians spend JD500 Million on tobacco every year. *The Jordan Times.* Available at: http://www.jordantimes.com/news/local/jordanians-spend-jd500m-tobacco-every-year%E2%80%99. Accessed 12 Feb 2018.

El-Harami, J. (2014). The diversity of ecology and nature reserves as an ecotourism attraction in Jordan. *SHS Web of Conferences, 12*(01056), 1–10.

Elias, S., & Helen, B. (1993). *Water resources of Jordan: Present status and future potentials.* Amman: Friedrich Ebert Stiftung and Royal Society for the Conservation of Nature.

El-Said, H., & Becker, K. (2001). *Management and international business issues in Jordan.* Binghamton: International Business Press.

El-Said, M., Abdih, Y., & Kyobe, A. (2012). *Jordan: Selected issues* (IMF Country Report No. 12/ 120). Washington, DC: International Monetary Fund.

Eran, O., & Guzansky, Y. (2017, April 2). Jordan-Saudi relations, in context of the Arab League Summit. *INSS Insight,* 911. Available at: http://www.inss.org.il/publication/jordan-saudi-relations-context-arab-league-summit/. Accessed 5 Aug 2018.

Esber, P. M. (2016). Understanding the logic of regime survival? Conceptualizing state society relations and parliamentary liberation in post 2011 Jordan. *British Journal of Middle Eastern Studies, 45*(3), 337–354.

ETF (European Training Foundation). (2017). *Migrant support measures from an employment and skills perspective (MISMES): Jordan*. Turin: ETF.

European Union. (2014). Strategic action plan of the agriculture sector in Jordan, technical assistance of the programme in support to the employment and TVET reforms. Available at: http://etvetreform.gov.jo/wp-content/uploads/2014/02/Agriculture-sector-plan-JORDAN-2014.pdf. Accessed 30 June 2018.

Eyadat, Z. (2017, May 19). From dependency on international aid to sustainability and global economic equality. *The Jordan Times*. Available at: http://jordantimes.com/opinion/zaid-eyadat/dependency-international-aid-sustainability-and-global-economic-equality. Accessed 20 May 2018.

Fanek, F. (2016a, January 17). Services bloom in Jordan's economy. *The Jordan Times*. Available at: http://www.jordantimes.com/opinion/fahed-fanek/services-bloom-jordan%E2%80%99s-economy. Accessed 30 June 2018.

Fanek, F. (2016b, January 11). Expatriate's remittances still growing. *The Jordan Times*. Available at: http://www.jordantimes.com/opinion/fahed-fanek/expatriates%E2%80%99-remittances-still-growing. Accessed 30 June 2018.

FAO (2011). FAO achievements in Jordan. FAO Representation in Jordan. Available at: http://www.fao.org/3/a-ba0007e.pdf. Accessed 30 June 2018.

Fischbach, M. R. (1994). The implications of Jordanian land policy for the West Bank. *Middle East Journal, 48*(3), 492–509.

Fischbach, M. R. (1997). Settling historical land claims in the wake of Arab-Israeli peace. *Journal of Palestine Studies, 27*(1), 38–50.

Fischbach, M. R. (2000). *State, society, and land in Jordan*. Brill: Leiden.

Fischbach, M. R. (2001). Britain and the Ghawr Abi Ubayda Waqf controversy in Transjordan. *International Journal of Middle East Studies, 33*(4), 525–544.

Fischer, J., Khan, I., Khemani, T., Mak, D., & Najmi, R. (2009). Jordan tourism cluster-microeconomics of competitiveness. *Institute for Strategy and Compositeness*, Harvard Business School, 4–10.

Francis, A. (2015). Jordan's refugee crisis. *Carnegie Endowment for International Peace*. Available at: https://carnegieendowment.org/files/CP_247_Francis_Jordan_final.pdf. Accessed 20 May 2018.

Frisch, H. (2007). Fuzzy nationalism: The case of Jordan. *Nationalism and Ethnic Politics, 8*(4), 86–103.

Fruchter-Ronen, I. (2008). Black September: The 1970–71 events and their impact on the formation of Jordanian National Identity. *Civil Wars, 10*(3), 244–260.

Gallets, B. (2015). Black September and identity construction in Jordan. *Journal of Georgetown University-Qatar, Middle Eastern Studies Students Association (MESSA), 12*, 1–9.

Gamba, A. (2015). *New energy sources for Jordan: Macroeconomic impact and policy considerations* (IMF Working Paper, 15/115). Washington, DC: International Monetary Fund.

Gandalfo, L. (2012). *Palestinians in Jordan: The politics of identity.* London: I. B. Tauris.

Ganich, A. (2003). Circassian Diaspora in Jordan: Self-identification, ideas about historical homeland and impact on North Caucasian developments. *Central Asia and the Caucasus.* Available at: http://www.ca-c.org/journal/2003/journal_eng/cac01/03.ganeng.shtml. Accessed 12 Feb 2018.

Gazit, M. (1988). The Israel-Jordan peace negotiations (1949–1951): King Abdullah's lonely effort. *Journal of Contemporary History, 23*(3), 409–424.

Gehan, A.-Z. (1998). *In search of political power – Women in parliament in Egypt, Jordan and Lebanon, women in parliament: Beyond numbers.* Stockholm: International IDEA.

Gelber, Y. (1977). *Jewish-Transjordan relations, 1921–48.* London: Frank Cass.

Gelber, Y. (2004). *Israeli-Jordanian dialogue 1948–1953 – Cooperation, conspiracy or collusion?* Brighton: Sussex Academic Press.

General Population and Housing Census. (2015). Main results. DoS (Department of Statistics). Available at: http://dosweb.dos.gov.jo/wp-content/uploads/2017/08/Census2015_Eng.pdf. Accessed 30 June 2018.

George, A. (2005). *Jordan: Living in the crossfire.* London: Zed Books.

Ghazal, M. (2017, November 15). Jordan to go ahead with Red Sea-Dead Sea project despite Israel's withdrawal threat. *The Jordan Times.* Available at: http://www.jordantimes.com/news/local/jordan-go-ahead-red-sea-dead-sea-project-despite-israels-withdrawal-threat. Accessed 30 June 2018.

Ginat, J., & Winckler, O. (Eds.). (1998). *The Jordanian-Palestinian-Israeli triangle: Smoothing the path to peace.* Brighton: Sussex Academic Press.

Glubb, J. B. (1957). *A soldier with the Arabs.* London: Hodder and Stoughton.

Gubser, P. (1983). *Jordan: Crossroads of middle eastern events.* Boulder: Westview Press.

Guthrie, B., & Adely, F. (2012, October 31). Is the sky falling? Press and internet censorship rises in Jordan. *Jadaliyya.* Available at: http://www.middleeastdigest.com/pages/index/8102/is-the-sky-falling-press-and-internet-censorship-r. Accessed 7 July 2015.

Hadadin, N. A., & Tarawneh, Z. S. (2007). Environmental issues in Jordan, solutions and recommendations. *American Journal of Environmental Sciences, 3*(1), 30–36.

Hadadin, N., Qaqish, M., Akawwi, E., & Bdour, A. (2010). Water shortage in Jordan – Sustainable solutions. *Desalination, 250*(1), 197–202.

Haddad, H. (2010). Jordan. *Yearbook of Islamic and Middle Eastern Law, 16*(1), 209–214.

Haddad, W. W., & Hardy, M. M. (2003). Jordan's Alliance with Israel and its effects on Jordanian-Arab relations. In E. Karsh & P. R. Kumaraswamy (Eds.), *Israel, the Hashemites, and the Palestinians: The fateful triangle* (pp. 31–47). London: Frank Cass.

Haddad, M., & Kailani, W. (2002). Chechen identity, culture and citizenship in Jordan. In M. Ma'oz & G. Sheffer (Eds.), *Middle eastern minorities and diasporas*. Brighton: Sussex Academic Press.

Haddadin, S. (2008, February 26). Jordanian poll: The ratio of women who voted for women candidates did not exceed 11%. *Al Rai*.

Halevi, E. (2006). *Man in the shadows: Inside the Middle East crisis with a man who led the Mossad*. London: St. Martin's Press.

Hamid, S. (2011). The rise of the Islamists: How Islamists will change politics, and vice versa. *Foreign Affairs, 90*(3), 40–47.

Hamid, S. (2014). *Temptations of power: Islamists and illiberal democracy in a new Middle East*. New York: Oxford University Press.

Hansen, L. F. (2014). *The Circassian revival: A quest for recognition: Mediated transnational mobilization and memorialization among a geographically dispersed people from the Caucasus*. PhD Thesis, Copenhagen University, Copenhagen.

Hansen, L. F. (2018, May 13–14). *Ethnicity and education: Towards a renewed arena of conflict in the North Caucasus?* Paper presented at the Conference, *Russia in the Muslim world*, The Harry S. Truman Research Institute, Jerusalem.

Hanssen-Bauer, J., Pedersen, J., & Tiltnes, A. A. (Eds.). (1998). *Jordanian society: Living conditions in the Hashemite Kingdom of Jordan* (Fafo-report 253). Oslo: Fafo.

Harmsen, E. (2008). *Islam, civil society and social work: Muslim voluntary welfare associations in Jordan between patronage and empowerment*. Amsterdam: Amsterdam University Press.

Harrigan, J., El-Said, H., & Wang, C. (2006). The IMF and the World Bank in Jordan: A case of over optimism and elusive growth. *The Review of International Organizations, 1*(3), 263–292.

Harris, G. L. (1958). *Jordan: Its people its society its culture*. New Haven: HRAF Press.

Hartnett, A. (2011). Entries for energy policy in Egypt, Jordan, Libya, and Qatar. In *Encyclopaedia of energy*. New York: Golson Media.

Har-Zvi, S. (2014). *From Abdullah to Abdullah: Jordan's policy on Jerusalem – The regional and national contexts*. Dissertation submitted for a Ph.D. degree, Tel Aviv University, Tel Aviv (Hebrew).

Hassaan, M. (2016). The influence of corporate governance structures on compliance with mandatory IFRSs disclosure requirements in the Jordanian context. *International Journal of Research in Business and Social Science, 2*(3), 14–25.

Hassan, F. M. A., & Al-Saci, D. (2004). *Jordan: Supporting stable development in a challenging region—A joint World Bank-Islamic Development Bank evaluation*. Washington, DC: The World Bank.

Hasson, N. (2017, June 20). 50 years after six-day war, East Jerusalem's Palestinians remain prisoners in their city. *Ha'aretz*. Available at: https://www.haaretz.

com/israel-news/.premium.MAGAZINE-east-jerusalem-s-palestinians-are-prisoners-in-their-own-city-1.5486255. Accessed 30 June 2017.

Hatough-Bouran, A. M., Duwayri, M. A., & Disi, A. M. (1998). *Jordan country study on biological diversity*. Prepared under GCEP, UNDP and GEF (Project No. GF/6105-92-65 and GF/6105-92-02 (2991)).

Havrelock, R. S. (2011). *River Jordan: The mythology of a dividing line*. Chicago: University of Chicago Press.

Hayajneh, A. M. (2014). US–Jordan relations: The king Abdullah II era: An analytical study. In R. E. Looney (Ed.), *Handbook of US-Middle East relations: Formative factors and regional perspectives* (pp. 189–210). London: Routledge.

Hazbun, W. (2002). Mapping the landscape of the 'new Middle East'. The politics of tourism development and the peace process in Jordan. In E. George & H. Joffé (Eds.), *Jordan in transition 1990–2000* (pp. 330–345). London: Hurst and Co.

Hearst, D. (2016, February 25). Jordan's mixed plans for its Palestinian 'Guests'. *Middle East Eye*, Amman. Available at: http://www.middleeasteye.net/news/west-bank-vs-gaza-jordans-mixed-plans-its-palestinian-guests-1529473549. Accessed 30 June 2017.

Hedges, M. (2018). *The role of minorities in regime security; Case study of the Circassians and Chechens in King Hussein's Jordan* (Durham Middle East Papers, no. 95). Durham: Institute for Middle Eastern and Islamic Studies. Available at: http://dro.dur.ac.uk/24395/1/24395.pdf?DDD35. Accessed 21 June 2018.

Helayel, A. M., al-Khasawneh, A. K., Ghayithan, Y. A., el-Salaheen, A. M., el-Bakri, W. A. W., Mujahed, N. M., & al-Hajjawi, S. A. H. (2006, May 5). Resolution No. (109): Ruling on smoking and selling cigarettes. *Board of Iftaa, Research, and Islamic Studies, the Hashemite Kingdom of Jordan*. Available at: http://aliftaa.jo/DecisionEn.aspx?DecisionId=234#.WkvK19-nFPY. Accessed 16 May 2018.

Helfont, S., & Helfont, T. (2012). Jordan: Between the Arab spring and the Gulf cooperation council. *Orbis, 56*(1), 82–95.

Higgit, D. L. (2001). Impact of rapid urban growth on sustainability of soil and water resources in Jordan. *Options Mediterraneennes: Serie A. Seminaires Mediterraneenes, 44*, 223–231.

Hinchcliffe, P. (1997). Jordan's relations with her Neighbours: Victim of war or casualty of peace? *Asian Affairs, 28*(3), 343–348.

Hinnebusch, R. (2003). Identity in international relations: Constructivism versus materialism, and the case of the Middle East. *The Review of International Affairs, 3*(2), 358–362.

Hinnebusch, R. (2012). Empire and state formation: Contrary tangents in Jordan and Syria. In R. Hinnebusch & S. Cummings (Eds.), *Sovereignty after empire: Comparing the Middle East and Central Asia* (pp. 263–281). Edinburg: Edinburgh University Press.

Hinnebusch, R., & Quilliam, N. (2006). Contrary siblings: Syria, Jordan and the Iraq war. *Cambridge Review of International Affairs, 19*(3), 513–528.

Human Rights Watch (HRW). (2010, February 1). Stateless again, Palestinian origin Jordanians deprived of their nationality. Available at: https://www.hrw.org/report/2010/02/01/stateless-again/palestinian-origin-jordanians-deprived-their-nationality. Accessed 22 June 2018.

Human Rights Watch (HRW). (2014). World report 2014: Jordan, events of 2013. Available at: https://www.hrw.org/world-report/2014/country-chapters/jordan. Accessed 30 June 2018.

Human Rights Watch (HRW). (2017). Jordan: Events of 2016. Available at: https://www.hrw.org/world-report/2017/country-chapters/jordan. Accessed 22 June 2018.

Hunting Technical Services (HTS). (1956). *Report on the range classification survey of the Hashemite Kingdom of Jordan*. Amman: Ministry of Agriculture.

Hussainy, M. (2017, January). Jordan 2016: electoral reform and political continuity. PAL papers, Rosa Luxemburg Stiftung. Available at: http://www.rosaluxemburg.ps/wp-content/uploads/2017/01/Rosa-Luxemburg-Articles-English-Mohammed-Hussainy-Paper.pdf. Accessed 10 May 2018.

Hussein, K. (1962). *Uneasy lies the head*. London: Heinemann.

Hussein, B.-T. (1968). *My war with Israel*. London: Peter Owen. Translated by Wilson, J. P., & Michaels, W. B. (1969). English translation. New York: William Morrow and Company, Inc.

Hussein, B.-T. (1988, July 31). *Address to the nation*. Amman. Available at: http://www.kinghussein.gov.jo/88_july31.html. Accessed 10 Aug 2018.

Hussein, A. a.-S. (2010). Al-Muwātanah fi al-Watan al-Arabi (citizenship in the Arab nation). In H. Ghaṣib (Ed.), *Al-Muwātanah fi al-Watan al-Arabi, (citizenship in the Arab nation)* (pp. 1–30). Amman: Dar Ward.

Hussein, I. A., Abu Sharar, T. M., & Battikhi, A. M. (2005). Water resources planning and development in Jordan. In A. Hamdy & R. Monti (Eds.), *Food security under water scarcity in the Middle East: Problems and solutions* (pp. 183–197). Bari: CIHEAM.

Husseini, R. (2010, March 3). Women's rights in the Middle East and North Africa 2010 – Jordan. Freedom House. Available at: http://www.refworld.org/docid/4b9901227d.html. Accessed 30 June 2018.

Husseini, R. (2018, April 11). Long-awaited women shelter 'to Open in May' – Ministry. *The Jordan Times*, Amman. Available at: http://www.jordantimes.com/news/local/long-awaited-women-shelter-open-may%E2%80%99-%E2%80%94-ministry. Accessed 30 June 2018.

Ibáñez Prieto, A. V. (2018, January 23). 9,448 migrant workers deported in 2017 – Labour Ministry. *The Jordan Times*. Available at: http://www.jordantimes.com/news/local/9448-migrant-workers-deported-2017-%E2%80%94-labour-ministry

BIBLIOGRAPHY   497

Ibanez Prieto, A. V. (2018, March 26). Three-year project to boost private sector's contribution to Jordan's economy. *The Jordan Times*. Available at: http://www.jordantimes.com/news/local/three-year-project-boost-private-sector%E2%80%99s-contribution-jordan%E2%80%99s-economy. Accessed 30 June 2018.

Ibn Hussein, A. (1945). *Muthakarati*. Jerusalem: Beit al-Maqdis.

Identity Center. (2014). Policy paper: The 1988 Disengagement Regulations and their effects on identity and participation in Jordan, 1–21, Available at: http://identity-center.org/sites/default/files/1988%20Disengagement.pdf. Accessed 12 June 2018.

Ijzerloo, V. J. (2016, May 27). Jordan's economy remains in jeopardy. RaboResearch – Country Report. Available at: https://economics.rabobank.com/publications/2016/may/jordans-economyremains-in-jeopardy/. Accessed 20 May 2018.

Independent Election Commission (IEC). (2016, September). 2016 Parliamentary Elections. Available at: https://iec.jo/en/content/2016-parliamentary-election. Accessed 30 May 2018.

International Centre for Agricultural Research in the Dry Areas (ICARDA). (2008). *Jordan and ICARDA: 30 Years of partnership for sustainable agriculture, ties that bind*, No. 25. Aleppo: ICARDA.

International Crisis Group. (2008, July 10). Failed responsibility: Iraqi refugees in Syria, Jordan and Lebanon. Available at: https://d2071andvip0wj.cloudfront.net/77-failed-responsibility-iraqi-refugees-in-syria-jordan-and-lebanon.pdf. Accessed 22 June 2018.

International Crisis Group. (2012, March 12). Popular protest in North Africa and the Middle East (IX): Dallying with reform in a divided Jordan. Available at: https://www.crisisgroup.org/middle-east-north-africa/eastern-mediterranean/jordan/popular-protest-north-africa-and-middle-east-ix-dallying-reform-divided-jordan. Accessed 30 June 2018.

International Finance Corporation. (2015, September). *Gender Diversity in Jordan: Research on the impact of gender diversity on the economic performance of companies in Jordan* (Working Paper). Available at: https://openknowledge.worldbank.org/handle/10986/26050. Accessed 18 Sept 2018.

International Labour Organization. (2012–2014). *Protecting Migrant worker's rights in Jordan*. Partnered with Bureau of Democracy, Human Rights and Labour (DRL), US Department of State. Available at: http://www.ilo.org/beirut/projects/WCMS_213470/lang%2D%2Den/index.htm. Accessed 30 June 2018.

International Labour Organization. (2013). ILO response to Syrian refugee crisis in Jordan. Available at: http://www.ilo.org/beirut/areasofwork/syrian-refugee-crisis/jordan/lang%2D%2Den/index.htm. Accessed 30 June 2018.

International Labour Organization. (2015). Access to work for Syrian refugees in Jordan: A discussion paper on Labour and Refugee Laws and Policies. *ILO*. Available at: www.ilo.org/beirut/publications/WCMS_357950/lang%2D%2Den/. Accessed 20 Aug 2018.

International Labour Organization. (2017a). *Work permits and employment of Syrian refugees in Jordan: Towards formalizing the work of Syrian refugees.* Beirut: International Labour Organization. Available at: http://www.ilo.org/wcmsp5/groups/public/%2D%2D-arabstates/%2D%2D-ro-beirut/documents/publication/wcms_559151.pdf. Accessed 12 Feb 2018.

International Labour Organization. (2017b). *Migrant domestic and garment Workers in Jordan: A baseline analysis of trafficking in persons and related Laws and Policies.* Geneva: ILO.

International Legal Materials. (1988, November). Palestine National Council: Political Communiqué and Declaration of Independence, 27(6), 1660–1671.

International Monetary Fund. (2012, August 3). IMF Survey: Jordan gets $2.0 Billion IMF loan to support economy. Available at: http://www.imf.org/en/News/Articles/2015/09/28/04/53/soint080312a. Accessed 30 June 2018.

International Republican institute (IRI). (2017, January 30). Jordan: Poll reveals increased pessimism, anxiety over economy and refugees. *IRI Polls*, Amman. Available at: http://www.iri.org/resource/jordan-poll-reveals-increased-pessimism-anxiety-over-economy-and-refugees. Accessed 30 June 2018.

Inter-Parliamentary Union (IPU). (2016). Jordan: Majlis Al-Nuwaab (House of Representatives), Full Text. Available at: http://www.ipu.org/parline-e/reports/2163.htm. Accessed 30 June 2018.

Isik, I., Kulalı, I., & Agcayazi-Yilmaz, B. (2016). Total factor productivity change in the Middle East banking: The case of Jordanian banks at the turn of the millennium. *International Journal of Research in Business and Social Science, 5*(3), 1–29.

Isin, E. (2017). Citizenship studies and the Middle East. In R. Meijer & N. Butenschon (Eds.), *The crisis of citizenship in the Arab world* (pp. 511–534). Leiden: Brill.

Iskandarani, M. (2002a). *Economics of household water security in Jordan.* Frankfurt: Peter Lang.

Iskandarani, M. (2002b). Household strategies to cope with institutionally induced supply constraints – The case of Jordan. In S. Neubert, W. Scheumann, & A. Van Edig (Eds.), *Reforming institutions for sustainable water management.* Bonn: DIE-GDI.

Jaber, J. O., Sladek, T. A., Mernitz, S., & Tarawneh, T. M. (2008, March). Future policies and strategies for oil shale development in Jordan. *Jordan Journal of Mechanical and Industrial Engineering, 2*(1), 31–44. Available at: http://jjmie.hu.edu.jo/files/V2/004-v2-1.pdf. Accessed 10 Apr 2018.

Jaimoukha, A. M. (2001). *The Circassians: A handbook* (Vol. 6, 1st ed.). New York: Palgrave Macmillan.
Jaimoukha, A. (2004). *Circassian bibliography*. Amman: Sanjalay Press.
Jaradat, H. (2010, October 31–November 1). Jordan's economy: Crisis, challenges and measures. Third Annual Meeting of Middle East and North African Senior Budget Officials (MENA-SBO), UAE, Dubai. Available at: https://www.oecd.org/gov/budgeting/46382448.pdf. Accessed 28 May 2018.
Jarrah, S. (2009). *Civil society and public freedom in Jordan: The path of democratic reform* (The Saban Centre for Middle East Policy at The Brookings Institution Working Paper, No. 3).
Jevon, G. (2014). Book review: Britain and Jordan Imperial strategy, king Abdullah 1 and the Zionist movement. *The Journal of Imperial and Commonwealth History, 42*(2), 352–355.
Joffé, E., & George, H. (Eds.). (2002). *Jordan in transition: 1990–2000*. London: Macmillan Press.
Jordan, A., Wurzel, R. K. W., & Zito, A. R. (2003). *New instruments of environmental governance: National Experiences and prospects*. London: Frank Cass.
Joseph, S. (Ed.). (2000). *Gender and citizenship in the Middle East*. New York: Syracuse University Press.
Journal of Palestine Studies. (1976). The effect of Lebanese events on inter-Arab relations. 6(1), 136–138.
Jureidini, P. A., & McLaurin, R. D. (1984). *Jordan: The impact of social change on the role of the tribes*. New York: Praeger.
Kailani, W. (1998). *The Jordanian Chechens' identity between the original and host cultures: A field work among the Chechens in al-Sukhnah-al-Zarqa District-Jordan*. Master Thesis, Yarmouk University, Irbid (Arabic).
Kailani, W. (2002). Chechens in the Middle East: Between original and host cultures. *Belfer Center for Science and International Affairs*. Available at: https://www.belfercenter.org/publication/chechens-middle-east-between-original-and-host-cultures. Accessed 22 June 2018.
Kailani, W. (2004). *Jordan: Society and politics*. Jerusalem: Rothberg International School.
Kamrava, M. (1998). Frozen political liberalization in Jordan: The consequences for democracy. *Democratization, 5*(1), 138–157.
Kanaan, T. H., & Kardoosh, M. A. (2002). The story of economic growth in Jordan: 1950–2000. *Economic Research Forum*. Available at: http://erf.org.eg/affiliates/taher-kanaan/. Accessed 30 June 2018.
Kanaan, T. H., Al-Salamat, M. N., & Hanania, M. D. (2011). Political economy of cost-sharing in higher education: The case of Jordan. *Prospects, 41*(1), 23–45.
Kanovsky, E. (1968). The economic aftermath of the six Day war: UAR, Jordan and Syria, part II. *Middle East Journal, 22*(3), 278–296.

Kao, K. (2012, July). Jordan's ongoing Election Law battle. *Carnegie Endowment International Peace*. Available at: http://carnegieendowment.org/sada/48781. Accessed 30 May 2018.

Karsh, E., & Kumaraswamy, P. R. (Eds.). (2003). *Israel, the Hashemites and the Palestinians: The fateful triangle*. London: Frank Cass.

Katz, K. (2005). *Jordanian Jerusalem: Holy places and national spaces*. Gainesville: University Press of Florida.

Kelli, H. M. (2015). *Personal status law reform in Jordan: State Bargains and Women's Rights in the Law*. Thesis, Georgetown University, Washington DC. Available at: https://repository.library.georgetown.edu/bitstream/handle/10822/760898/Harris_georgetown_0076M_12957.pdf?sequence=1and isAllowed=y. Accessed 30 June 2018.

Kennedy, D. L. (2004). *The Roman Army in Jordan*. London: Council for British Research in the Levant.

Kessler, O. (2011, September 12). King Abdullah II: Jordan will never be Palestine. *The Jerusalem Post*. Available at: https://www.jpost.com/Diplomacy-and-Politics/King-Abdullah-II-Jordan-will-never-be-Palestine. Accessed 30 June 2017.

Khammash, A. (1986). *Notes on village architecture in Jordan*. Lafayette: University of Southwestern Louisiana.

Khammash, T. (2012, September 9). *The Jordanian health sector*. Jordan Investment Trust P.L.C. Available at: https://jordankmportal.com/system/resources/attachments/000/000/359/original/The_Jordanian_Health_Sector_Report_2012.pdf?1456219357. Accessed 30 June 2018.

Khan, S., & Karam, J. (2003). Use of reclaimed Water in Jordan: Experience of three pilot projects. *Water Reuse Conference*, Amman.

Khandelwal, P., & Roitman, A. (2013). *The economics of political transitions: Implications for the Arab Spring* (IMF Working Paper, 13/69). Washington, DC: International Monetary Fund.

Klein, M. (2001). *Jerusalem: The Contested City*. London: Hurst.

Knowles, W. (2005). *Jordan since 1989: A study in political economy*. London: I. B. Tauris.

Koch, J., Schaldach, R., & Kölking, C. (2009, July 13–17). Modelling the impact of rangeland management strategies on semi-natural vegetation in Jordan. Eighteenth World IMACS/MODSIM Congress, Australia.

Kocher, E. (1990). *Foreign intrigue: The making and unmaking of a foreign service officer*. Far Hills: New Horizon Press.

Krishna-Hensel, S. F. (2012). Challenging the Hashemites: The Muslim brotherhood and the Islamic action front in Jordan. In S. F. Krishna-Hensel (Ed.), *Religion, education and governance in the Middle East: Between tradition and modernity* (pp. 105–126). London: Routledge.

Kumaraswamy, P. R. (2003). Israel, Jordan and the Masha'al affair. *Israel Affairs, 9*(3), 111–128.

Kumaraswamy, P. R., & Singh, M. (2017). Population pressure in Jordan and the role of Syrian refugees. *Migration and Development, 6*(3), 412–427.

Kumaraswamy, P. R., & Singh, M. (2018). Jordan's food security challenges. *Mediterranean Quarterly, 29*(1), 70–95.

Kutum, I., & Al-Jaberi, K. (2015). Jordan banks financial soundness indicators. *International Journal of Finance and Banking Studies, 4*(3), 44–56.

Larzillière, P. (2016). *Activism in Jordan*. London: Zed Books.

Lavie, E. (2008), *The Palestinians in the West Bank: Patterns of political organization under occupation and self-rule*. Unpublished Ph.D. dissertation submitted to the Senate of Tel-Aviv University, Tel-Aviv (Hebrew).

Lawrence, P., Meigh, J., & Sullivan, C. (2002). The water poverty index: An international comparison. *Keele Economic Research Papers (KERP)*, Issue 19. Available at http://econwpa.repec.org/eps/dev/papers/0211/0211003.pdf. Accessed 30 June 2018.

Lenner, K. (2013). Poverty and poverty reduction policies in Jordan. In M. Ababsa (Ed.), *Atlas of Jordan: History, territories and society* (pp. 335–340). Beirut: Presses de l'Ifpo.

Lenner, K. (2015). Projects of improvement, continuities of neglect: Re-fragmenting the periphery in southern rural Jordan. *Middle East–Topics and Arguments, 5*, 77–88.

Lenner, K. (2016). *Blasts from the past: Policy legacies and memories in the making of the Jordanian response to the Syrian refugee crisis* (EUI Working Papers, Max Weber Red Number Series, 2016/32).

Lenner, K., & Schmelter, S. (2016). Syrian refugees in Jordan and Lebanon: Between refuge and on-going deprivation. Institut Europeu de la Mediterrània (Hrsg.), *IEMed Mediterranean Yearbook*. Available at: https://researchportal.bath.ac.uk/en/publications/syrian-refugees-in-jordan-and-lebanon-between-refuge-and-ongoing-. Accessed 10 Apr 2018.

Lenner, K., & Turner, L. (2018a). Making refugees work? The politics of integrating Syrian refugees into the labor market in Jordan. *Middle East Critique*, 1–31.

Lenner, K., & Turner, L. (2018b). Learning from the Jordan compact. *Forced Migration Review, 57*, 48–51.

Leo, S. (2012). *Jordan budget manual: A guide to policy, process, and analytic techniques*. Amman: United States Agency for International Development.

Lewis, N. N. (1987). *Nomads and settlers in Syria and Jordan, 1800–1980*. Cambridge: Cambridge University Press.

Library of Congress, U.S. Government. (2011). *Jordan: Federal research study and country profile with comprehensive information, history and analysis – politics, economy, military*. Washington, DC: Progressive Management.

Lipton, E. P. (2002). *Religious freedom in the near east, northern Africa and the former soviet states*. New York: Nova Science Publishers, Inc.

Little, D. (1995). A puppet in search of a puppeteer? The United States, king Hussein, and Jordan, 1953–1970. *The International History Review, 17*(3), 512–544.

Lockhart, S. (1971, May 4). Policy Committee: National Tobacco and Cigarette Co, LTD, Jordan, 1–4. *Tobacco Control Documents, British American Tobacco Records*. Available at: https://www.industrydocumentslibrary.ucsf.edu/tobacco/docs/#id=xsmy0196. Accessed 10 Apr 2018.

Long, G. A. (1957). *Bioclimatology and vegetation of Eastern Jordan* (Working paper for FAO, FAO/57/2/1109).

Lowi, M. (1993). *Water and power: The politics of a scarce resource in the Jordan River basin*. Cambridge: Cambridge University Press.

Lucas, R. E. (2003a). Deliberalization in Jordan. *Journal of Democracy, 14*(1), 137–144.

Lucas, R. E. (2003b). Press laws as a survival strategy in Jordan 1989–99. *Middle Eastern Studies, 39*(4), 81–98.

Lucas, R. E. (2004). Jordan: The death of normalization with Israel. *Middle East Journal, 58*(1), 93–111.

Lucas, R. E. (2005). *Institutions and the politics of survival in Jordan. Domestic responses to external challenges, 1988–2001*. New York: State University of New York Press.

Lucas, R. E. (2008). Side effects of regime building in Jordan: The state and the nation. *Civil Wars, 10*(3), 281–293.

Luck, T. (2013, April 21). In Jordan, Tensions Rise between Syrian Refugees and Host Community. *The Washington Post*, Mafraq. Available at: https://www.washingtonpost.com/world/middle_east/in-jordan-tensions-rise-between-syrian-refugees-and-host-community/2013/04/21/d4f5fa24-a762-11e2-a8e2-5b98cb59187f_story.html?utm_term=.a264822dd54e. Accessed 30 June 2018.

Lukacs, Y. (1997). *Israel, Jordan and the peace process*. Syracuse: Syracuse University Press.

Lust-Okar, E. (2006). Elections under authoritarianism: Preliminary lessons from Jordan. *Democratization, 13*(3), 456–471.

Lust-Okar, E. (2009). Reinforcing informal institutions through authoritarian elections: Insights from Jordan. *Middle East Law and Governance, 1*(1), 3–37.

Lynch, M. (1999). *State interests and public spheres: The international politics of Jordan's identity*. New York: Columbia University Press.

Maaiah, B. S.-F. (2014). The consequences of natural crises on tourism destinations: A case study of the City of Petra in Jordan. *SHS Web of Conferences, 12*(01042), 1–8. Available at: https://www.shs-conferences.org/articles/shsconf/pdf/2014/09/shsconf_4ictr2014_01042.pdf. Accessed 2 Apr 2018.

Maani, S. A. (2017). Book review: Knowledge production in the Arab world: The impossible promise. *Middle East-Topics and Arguments, 9,* 149–150.

MacDonald, B. (2000). *East of the Jordan: Territories and sites of the Hebrew scriptures.* Boston: American Schools of Oriental Research.

Maciejewski, E., & Mansur, A. (1996). *Jordan: Strategy for adjustment and growth.* Washington, DC: International Monetary Fund.

Mackey, B. D. (1979). *The Circassians in Jordan.* Thesis, Naval Post-Graduate School, Monterey. Available at: https://calhoun.nps.edu/bitstream/handle/10945/26409/circassiansinjor00mack.pdf. Accessed 30 June 2018.

Maddy-Weitzman, B. (1990). Jordan and Iraq: Efforts at intra-Hashemite unity. *Middle Eastern Studies, 26*(1), 65–75.

Maggiolini, P. (2011). The Hashemite Emirate of Trans Jordan: Politics and tribal culture. *Research Centre on the Southern System and Wider Mediterranean (CRiSSMA)* (CRiSSMA Working Paper, 20).

Maggiolini, P. (2015). *Christian Churches and Arab Christians in the Hashemite Kingdom of Jordan: Citizenship, ecclesiastical identity and roles in the Jordanian political field.* Paris: Archives de sciences sociales des religons. Available at: https://journals.openedition.org/assr/27010. Accessed 18 Dec 2018.

Majali, A. S., Anani, J. A., & Haddadin, M. J. (2006). *Peacemaking: The inside story of the 1994 Jordanian-Israeli treaty.* Reading: Ithaca Press.

Makara, M. (2016). From concessions to repression: Explaining regime survival strategies in Jordan during black September. *The Journal of the Middle East and Africa, 7*(4), 387–403.

Maktabi, R. (2013). Female citizenship in the Middle East: Comparing family law reform in Morocco, Egypt, Syria and Lebanon. *Middle East Law and Governance, 5*(3), 280–307.

Malantowicz, A. (2013). Crisis, Chaos, violence – Is that really what we want? A stalled democratization in Jordan. *The Copernicus Journal of Political Studies, 1*(3), 77–96.

Malantowicz, A. (2015). Jordan: Resilience against all odds. IEMed Mediterranean Yearbook 2015, pp. 194–197. Available at: https://www.iemed.org/observatori/arees-danalisi/arxius-adjunts/anuari/med.2015/IEMed%20Yearbook%202015_Panorama_Jordan_ArturMalantowicz.pdf. Accessed 10 May 2018.

Malkawi, A. H. (2012, December). Digital public sphere within the Jordanian Political Movement: A case study for saving Bergesh forests through Facebook. *British Journal of Humanities and Social Sciences, 8*(1), 16–27. Available at: http://www.ajournal.co.uk/HSpdfs/HSvolume8(1)/HSVol.8%20(1)%20Article%203.pdf. Accessed 7 Apr 2018.

Malkawi, K. (2016, August 20). IAF running on 20 'National' lists in election-official. *The Jordan Times.* Available at: http://www.jordantimes.com/news/local/iaf-running-20-national%E2%80%99-lists-elections-%E2%80%94-official. Accessed 30 June 2018.

Mann, J. (2014). Saudi-Palestinian relations during the run-up to and the aftermath of black September. *Terrorism and Political Violence*, 26(4), 713–724.

Mansour, W. (2012). *The patterns and determinants of household welfare growth in Jordan: 2002–2010* (Policy Research Working Paper, 6249). World Bank. Available at: https://openknowledge.worldbank.org/handle/10986/12091. Accessed 10 Sept 2018.

Mansour, M. (2015). *Tax policy in MENA countries: Looking back and forward* (IMF Working Paper, 15/98). Washington, DC: International Monetary Fund.

Marshal, S., Das, R., Pirooznia, M. & Elhaik, E. (2016, November). Reconstructing Druze population history. *Scientific Reports*, 6, 35837. Available at: https://www.nature.com/articles/srep35837. Accessed 22 June 2018.

Martinez, J. C. (2014, July 22). Wheat subsidies in Jordan may be too little too late. *Al-Monitor*. Available at: http://www.al-monitor.com/pulse/originals/2014/07/jordan-agriculture-wheatproduction-harvest-farmers.html##ixzz3DseWqsRJ. Accessed 30 June 2018.

Martinez, J. C. (2018). Leavened apprehensions: Bread Subsidies and moral economies in Hashemite Jordan. *International Journal of Middle East Studies*, 50(2), 173–193.

Masalha, N., & Hamid, S. (2017, February 6). More than just the Muslim brotherhood: The problem of Hamas and Jordan's Islamic Movement. *The Brookings*. Available at: https://www.brookings.edu/research/more-than-just-the-muslim-brotherhood-the-problem-of-hamas-and-jordans-islamic-movement/. Accessed 10 Oct 2018.

Massad, J. (2001). *Colonial effects: The making of National Identity in Jordan*. New York: Columbia University Press.

Mazar, A. (Ed.). (2001). *Studies in archaeology of the Iron age in Israel and Jordan*. Sheffield: Sheffield Academic Press.

Maziad, S. (2009). *Monetary policy and the central Bank in Jordan* (IMF Working Paper, 09/191). Washington, DC: International Monetary Fund.

McCallum, F. (2012). Religious institutions and authoritarian states: Church-state relations in the Middle East. *Third World Quarterly*, 33(1), 109–124.

Medzini, M. (2008). Israel's midwife: Golda Meir in the closing years of the British mandate. *Israel Affairs*, 14(3), 374–397.

Meijer, R., & Butenschön, N. (Eds.). (2017). *The crisis of citizenship in the Arab world*. Leiden: Brill.

Meisen, P., & Tatum, J. (2011). The water-energy Nexus in the Jordan River Basin: The potential for building peace through Sustainability. *Global Energy Network Institute*. Available at: https://www.geni.org/globalenergy/research/water-energy-nexus-in-the-jordan-river-basin/the-jordan-river-basin-final-report.pdf. Accessed 30 June 2018.

Merhav, R., & Giladi, R. M. (2002). The role of the Hashemite Kingdom of Jordan in a future permanent status settlement in Jerusalem. In M. J. Breger &

O. Ahimeir (Eds.), *Jerusalem, a city and its future* (pp. 175–202). Syracuse: Syracuse University Press.

Migration Policy Centre. (2013, June). *Jordan*. Report by MPC Team, European University Institute-Robert Schuman Centre for Advanced Studies-European Union. Available at: http://www.migrationpolicycentre.eu/docs/migration_profiles/Jordan.pdf. Accessed 30 June 2018.

Migration Policy Centre. (2017, March). Jordanian expatriates: A challenging opportunity. Available at: http://jsf.org/sites/default/files/Jordanian%20Expatriates%20-%20A%20Challenging%20Opportunity_0.pdf. Accessed 30 June 2018.

Milton-Edwards, B., & Hinchcliffe, P. (1999). Abdullah's Jordan: New King, old problems. *Middle East Report, 29*(4), 28–31.

Milton-Edwards, B., & Hinchcliffe, P. (2009). *Jordan: A Hashemite legacy*. London: Routledge.

Mitha, F. (2010). The Jordanian-Israeli relationship: The reality of 'cooperation'. *Middle East Policy, 17*(2), 2.

Mitra, P., Hosny, A., Abajyan, G., & Fischer, M. (2015), *Estimating potential growth in the Middle East and Central Asia* (IMF Working Paper 15/62). Washington, DC: International Monetary Fund.

Moaddel, M. (2002). *Jordanian exceptionalism: A comparative analysis of state-religion and relationships in Egypt, Iran, Jordan, and Syria*. New York: Palgrave Macmillan.

Mohaddes, K., & Raissi, M. (2013). Oil prices, external income, and growth: Lessons from Jordan. *Review of Middle East Economics and Finance, 9*(2), 99–131.

Mohan, H. (2010, August). *Jordanian tribal violence: Historical contexts and current problems*. Centre for Strategic Studies, University of Jordan, CSS Papers. Available at: https://www.files.ethz.ch/isn/139093/107.pdf. Accessed 25 May 2018.

Mohsen, M. S. (2007). Water strategies and potential of desalination in Jordan. *Desalination, 203*(1–3), 27–46.

Moore, P. W. (2004). *Doing business in the Middle East: Politics and economic crisis in Jordan and Kuwait*. New York: Cambridge University Press.

Muasher, M. (2017a, September 8). Palestinian nationalism: Regional perspective. *Carnegie Endowment for International Peace*. Available at https://carnegieendowment.org/2017/09/08/jordanian-palestinian-relations-pub-73006. Accessed 10 Apr 2018.

Muasher, M. (2017b, September 8). Jordanian-Palestinian relations. *Carnegie Endowment for International Peace*. Available at: https://carnegieendowment.org/2017/09/08/jordanian-palestinian-relations-pub-73006. Accessed 12 Sept 2018.

Muasher, M. (2018, June 7). End of the rope. *Carnegie Middle East Center*. Available at: http://carnegie-mec.org/diwan/76551. Accessed 5 Oct 2018.

Mufti, M. (2002). A King's art: Dynastic ambition and state interest in Hussein's Jordan. *Diplomacy and Statecraft, 13*(3), 1–22.

Murad, N. (2018, March 24). A Nation of minorities? *The Jordan Times.* Available at: http://www.jordantimes.com/opinion/nermeen-murad/nation-minorities. Accessed 22 June 2018.

Mutawi, S. A. (1987). *Jordan in the 1967 war.* New York: Cambridge University Press.

Namrouqa, H. (2014, October 22). Jordan world's second water-poorest country. *The Jordan Times.* Available at: http://www.jordantimes.com/news/local/jordan-world%E2%80%99s-second-water-poorest-country. Accessed 30 June 2018.

Nanes, S. (2007). Jordan's unwelcome guests. *MERIP.* Available at: https://www.merip.org/mer/mer244/jordans-unwelcome-guests. Accessed 22 June 2018.

Nassar, L. (2017). *A guidance note for SDG implementation in Jordan: Water, energy, and climate change.* Amman: West Asia-North Africa Institute.

Neff, D. (1994). Israel Syria conflict at the Jordan River: 1949-1967. *Journal of Palestinian Studies, 23*(4), 26–40.

Nemeh, B. (2017, March 21). How can the Kingdom's troubled economy benefit more from Syrian migrant workers? *Carnegie Middle East Centre.* Available at: http://carnegie-mec.org/diwan/68330. Accessed 20 Apr 2018.

Nevo, J. (1994). Jordan and Saudi Arabia: The last royalists. In J. Nevo & I. Pappé (Eds.), *Jordan in the Middle East: The making of a pivotal state, 1948–1988* (pp. 103–118). Essex: Frank Cass.

Nevo, J. (2006). *King Hussein and the evolutions of Jordan's perception of a political settlement with Israel, 1967–1988.* Brighton: Sussex Academic Press.

Nichols, M. (2013, November 13). Saudi rejects U.N. Security Council Seat, Opening Way for Jordan. *Reuters.* Available at: https://www.reuters.com/article/us-un-saudi-jordan/saudi-rejects-u-n-security-council-seat-opening-way-for-jordan-idUSBRE9AB14720131112. Accessed 10 Oct 2018.

Noor, Q. (2003). *Lea of faith: Memoirs of an unexpected Life.* London: Weidenfeld and Nicolson.

Nortcliff, S., Carr, G., Potter, R. B., & Darmame, K. (2008). Jordan's water resources: Challenges for the future. *Geographical Paper No. 185.* Available at http://www.reading.ac.uk/web/files/geographyandenvironmentalscience/GP185.pdf. Accessed 10 Apr 2018.

Nothaft, F. E., & Erbas, S. N. (2002). *The role of affordable mortgages in improving living standards and stimulating growth: A survey of selected MENA countries* (IMF Working Paper, 02/17). Washington, DC: International Monetary Fund.

Nowar, M.'a. A. (1993). *The history of the Hashemite Kingdom of Jordan: The creation and development of Transjordan; 1920–1929.* Oxford: Ithaca Press.

Obeidat, O. (2014, December 8). Jordan received JD1.2b Foreign Aid in 11 Months. *The Jordan Times*. Available at: http://www.jordantimes.com/news/local/jordan-receives-jd12b-foreign-aid-11-months. Accessed 12 Oct 2018.

Obeidat, O. (2015, June 15). Despite Meagre foreign aid, economy showing signs of recovery – Premier. *The Jordan Times*. Available at: http://www.jordantimes.com/news/local/despite-meagre-foreign-aid-economy-showing-signs-recovery-%E2%80%94-premier. Accessed 30 June 2018.

Obeidat, O. (2016a, September 24). New lower house includes 74 new faces. *The Jordan Times*, Amman. Available at: http://www.jordantimes.com/news/local/new-lower-house-includes-74-new-faces. Accessed 30 June 2018.

Obeidat, O. (2016b, October 11). IMF, World Bank Foresee better economic performance by Jordan, differ on rates. *The Jordan Times*. Available at: http://www.jordantimes.com/news/local/imf-world-bank-foresee-better-economic-performance-jordan-differ-rates. Accessed 30 June 2018.

OEC-MIT. (2016). *Jordan imports and exports in 2016*. Massachusetts Institute of Technology and Observatory of Economic Complexities. Available at: https://atlas.media.mit.edu/en/profile/country/jor/. Accessed 30 June 2018.

Orabi, M. M. A., Saymeh, A. A. F., & Mohammad, S. J. (2016). The effect of 2008 financial crisis on Jordan banks profit. *Journal of Management Research, 8*(1), 191–206.

Orieqat, H. M., & Saymeh, A. A. F. (2013). Privatization in Jordan, a critical assessment. *Developing Country Studies, 3*(7), 56–67.

Orieqat, H. M., & Saymeh, A. A. F. (2015). Is tourism a gene sector to Jordan's GDP? *International Journal of Development and Economic Sustainability, 3*(5), 75–84.

Oxford Business Group. (n.d.). Jordan's tourism sector focusing on high-end and niche offerings. Available at: https://oxfordbusinessgroup.com/overview/strong-stand-private-and-public-players-invest-high-end-offerings-and-niche-segments-revitalise. Accessed 30 June 2018.

Parker, J. B. (1964). *The tobacco industry in West Asia*. Washington, DC: United States Department of Agriculture, Foreign Agricultural Service.

Parolin, G. (2009). *Citizenship in the Arab world: Kin, religion and nation-state*. Amsterdam: Amsterdam University Press.

Patai, R. (1958). *The kingdom of Jordan*. Princeton: Princeton University Press.

Patai, R. (1984). *The kingdom of Jordan*. Westport: Greenwood Press.

Patel, D. S. (2015). *The more things change, the more they stay the same; Jordanian Islamist responses in Spring and Fall* (Brookings Working Paper, Project on United States Relations With the Islamic World). Washington, DC: Brookings Institution.

Patrick, N. (2013, July). *Saudi Arabia and Jordan: Friends in adversity*. LSE Kuwait Program on Development, Governance and Globalisation in the Gulf States, Research Paper, no. 31. Available at, http://eprints.lse.ac.uk/55661/1/__lse.

ac.uk_storage_LIBRARY_Secondary_libfile_shared_repository_Content_LSE%20Kuwait%20Programme_PARTRICK%20%28Jan%202015%20update%29.pdf. Accessed 5 Oct 2018.
Peake, F. G. (1939). Trans-Jordan. *Journal of the Royal Central Asian Society, 26*(3), 375–396.
Pedatzur, R. (2008). The rescue of King Hussein's regime. *Civil Wars, 10*(3), 294–318.
Pedersen, J. (2007). *Iraqis in Jordan: Their number and characteristics* (Report). UN High Commissioner for Refugees. Available at: http://www.unhcr.org/en-ie/subsites/iraqcrisis/47626a232/iraqis-jordan-number-characteristics.html. Accessed 22 June 2018.
Pelham, N. (2013, January). Jordan: Democracy delayed. *The New York Daily*. Available at: http://www.nybooks.com/daily/2013/01/25/jordan-democracy-delayed/. Accessed 30 May 2018.
Peters, A. M. (2009). Beyond boom and bust: External rents, durable authoritarianism, and institutional adaptation in the Hashemite Kingdom of Jordan. *Studies in Comparative and International Development, 44*(3), 256–285.
Piro, T. J. (1998). *The political economy of market reform in Jordan*. New York: Rowman and Littlefield.
Poghosyan, T. (2010), *Slowdown of credit flows in Jordan in the wake of the Global Financial crisis: Supply or demand driven?* (IMF Working Paper, 10/256). Washington, DC: International Monetary Fund.
Poghosyan, T., & Beidas-Strom, S. (2011). *An estimated dynamic stochastic general equilibrium model of the Jordanian economy* (IMF Working Paper, 11/28). Washington, DC: International Monetary Fund.
Ponížilová, M. (2013). The regional policy and power capabilities of Jordan as a small state. *Central European Journal of International and Security Studies, 7*(1), 82–102.
Prettitore, P. S. (2013). Gender and justice in Jordan: Women, demand, and access. In *MENA knowledge and learning quick notes series* (Vol. 107). Washington, DC: World Bank.
Prettitore, P. S. (2015). Family law reform, gender equality, and underage marriage: A view from Morocco and Jordan. *The Review of Faith and International Affairs, 13*(3), 32–40.
Pundik, R. (1994). *The struggle for sovereignty: Relations between Great Britain and Jordan, 1946–1951*. London: Basil and Blackwell.
Raad, Z. (1994). A nightmare avoided: Jordan and Suez 1956. *Israel Affairs, 1*(2), 288–308.
Ramadna, A. (2012). Mining sector in Jordan, current situation and investment opportunities. *Report of Ministry of Industry and Trade*, Jordan.
Ramahi, S. (2015). Palestinians and Jordanian Citizenship. *Middle East Monitor*, Special Report. Available at: https://www.middleeastmonitor.com/20151209-palestinians-and-jordanian-citizenship/. Accessed 20 May 2018.

Rannut, U. (2009). Circassian language maintenance in Jordan. *Journal of Multilingual and Multicultural Development, 30*(4), 297–310.

Rashdan, A. A. (1989). *Foreign policy making in Jordan: The role of King Hussein's leadership in decision-making.* PhD thesis, University of North Texas, Denton.

Razzaz, S. (2017). *A challenging market becomes more challenging: Jordanian workers, migrant workers and refugees in the Jordanian Labour Market*, International Labour Organization, Beirut. Available at: http://www.ilo.org/wcmsp5/groups/public/%2D%2D-arabstates/%2D%2D-ro-beirut/documents/publication/wcms_556931.pdf. Accessed 18 Aug 2018.

Reed, S. (1990). Jordan and the Gulf Crisis. *Foreign Affairs, 91.* Available at: https://www.foreignaffairs.com/articles/iraq/1990-12-01/jordan-and-gulf-crisis. Accessed 30 June 2017.

Reiter, Y. (1997). *Islamic institutions in Jerusalem: Palestinian Muslim administration under Jordanian and Israeli rule.* The Hague: Kluwer Law International.

Reiter, Y. (2004). The Palestinian-trans-Jordanian rift: Economic might and political power in Jordan. *Middle East Journal, 58*(1), 72–92.

Reiter, Y. (2008). *Jerusalem and its role in Islamic solidarity.* New York: Palgrave Macmillan.

Reiter, Y. (2010). Higher education and socio-political transformation in Jordan. *British Journal Of Middle Eastern Studies, 29*(2), 137–164.

Reiter, Y. (2017). *The eroding status quo: Power struggles on the Temple mount.* Jerusalem: The Jerusalem Institute for Policy Research.

Rempel, T. (1999). The Ottawa process: Workshop on compensation and Palestinian refugees. *Journal of Palestine Studies, 29*(1), 36–49.

Richmond, W. (2013). *The Circassian genocide.* New Brunswick: Rutgers University Press.

Riedel, B. (2012). Jordan's Arab Spring. *The Brookings.* Available at: https://www.brookings.edu/opinions/jordans-arab-spring/. Accessed 12 Oct 2018.

Riedel, B. (2018, June 12). Saudi Arabia bails out Jordan. *Al-Monitor*, Available at: https://www.al-monitor.com/pulse/originals/2018/06/saudi-arabia-bails-out-jordan-economy-protests.html. Accessed 6 Oct 2018.

Roberts, J. (1998). Lessons to be learned by the Mediterranean: Jordanian development, the MENA process, water and value systems. *The Journal of North African Studies, 3*(2), 187–201.

Robins, P. (2004). *A history of Jordan.* Cambridge: Cambridge University Press.

Robinson, G. E. (1997). Can Islamists be democrats? The case of Jordan. *The Middle East Journal, 51*(3), 373–387.

Robinson, G. E. (1998). Defensive democratization in Jordan. *International Journal of Middle East Studies, 30*(3), 387–410.

Rowland, J. (2009). Democracy and the tribal system in Jordan: Tribalism as a vehicle for social change. *Independent Study Project (ISP) Collection, Paper,*

749. Available at: http://digitalcollections.sit.edu/cgi/viewcontent. cgi?article=1740andcontext=isp_collection. Accessed 25 May 2018.

Ryan, C. (1998a). Jordan and the rise and fall of the Arab cooperation council. *The Middles East Journal, 52*(3), 386–401.

Ryan, C. R. (1998b). Elections and parliamentary democratization in Jordan. *Democratization, 5*(4), 176–196.

Ryan, C. R. (2000). Between Iraq and a hard Place: Jordanian-Iraqi relations. *Middle East Report, 215*(Summer), 40–42.

Ryan, C. R. (2002). *Jordan in transition: From Hussein to Abdullah*. Boulder: Lynne Rienner Publishers.

Ryan, C. R. (2004). 'Jordan first': Jordan's inter-Arab relations and foreign policy under king Abdullah II. *Arab Studies Quarterly, 26*(3), 43–62.

Ryan, C. (2011). Identity politics, reforms, and protest in Jordan. *Studies in Ethnicity and Nationalism, 11*(3), 564–578.

Ryan, C. (2014). Jordanian foreign policy and the Arab spring. *Middle East Policy, 21*(1), 144–153.

Ryan, C. R. (2017). Hashemite Kingdom of Jordan. In M. Gasiorowski & S. L. Yom (Eds.), *The government and politics of the Middle East and North Africa* (8th ed.). Boulder: Westview Press.

Ryan, C. (2018, June 4). Why Jordanians are protesting. *The Washington Post*. Available at: https://www.washingtonpost.com/news/monkey-cage/wp/2018/06/04/why-jordanians-are-protesting/?utm_term=.eeb-2122fec71. Accessed 30 June 2018.

Ryan, C. R., & Schwedler, J. (2004). Return to democratization or new hybrid regime?: The 2003 elections in Jordan. *Middle East Policy, 11*(2), 138–151.

Ryan, C. R., & Schweller, J. (2004). Return to democratization or new hybrid regime?: The 2003 elections in Jordan. *Middle East Policy, 11*(2), 138–151.

Ryers, K. (2014). *Jordan: Conditions, issues and U.S. relations, politics and economics of the Middle East*. New York: Nova Science Publishers, Inc.

Sa'd Abujaber, R. (1989). *Pioneers over Jordan: The frontier of settlement in Transjordan, 1850–1914*. London: I. B. Tauris.

Saadi-Sedik, T., & Petri, M. (2006). *The Jordanian Stock Market: Should you invest in it for risk diversification or performance?* (IMF Working Paper, 06/187). Washington, DC: International Monetary Fund.

Sab, R. (2014). *Economic impact of selected conflicts in the Middle East: What can we learn from the past?* (IMF Working Paper, 14/100). Washington, DC: International Monetary Fund.

Sabaghi, D. (2015, July 17). Born and bred without rights – Gaza strip refugees in Jordan. *Transconflict*. Available at: http://www.transconflict.com/2015/07/born-and-bred-without-rights-gaza-strip-refugees-in-jordan/. Accessed 30 June 2018.

Sadek, G. (2013). *Legal status of refugees: Egypt, Jordan, Lebanon and Iraq*. The Law Library of Congress, Global Legal Research Center. Available at: https://www.loc.gov/law/help/refugees/2014-010156%20RPT.pdf. Accessed 30 June 2018.

Salameh, M. T. B. (2017). Political reform in Jordan: Reality and aspirations. *World Affairs, 180*(4), 47–78.

Saleh, A. (2017). Sustainable development in Jordan: Perspectives. *Ecomena*. Available at: https://www.ecomena.org/sustainable-development-jordan/. Accessed 30 June 2018.

Salibi, K. S. (1998). *The modern history of Jordan*. London: I. B. Tauris.

Salloukh, B. (1996). State strength permeability and foreign policy behavior: Jordan in the theoretical perspective. *Arab Studies Quarterly, 18*(2), 39–65.

Sarairah, I. S. (2017). The adequacy of the general rules on compensation for environmental damage according to the Jordanian civil law. *Journal of Arts and Social Sciences, 8*(2), 5–13.

Sasley, B. E. (2002). Changes and continuities in Jordanian foreign policy. *Middle East Review of International Affairs, 6*(1), 36–48.

Satloff, R. (1994). *From Abdullah to Hussein: Jordan in transition*. New York: Oxford University Press.

Satloff, R., & Schenker, D. (2013, May 15). Political instability in *Jordan. Council on Foreign Relations*, Contingency Planning Memorandum no. 19. Available at: http://www.cfr.org/jordan/political-instability-jordan/p30698. Accessed 30 May 2018.

Satloff, R., & Schenker, D. (2016). Growing stress on Jordan. *The Washington Institute for Near East Policy*. Available at: https://www.washingtoninstitute.org/policy-analysis/view/growing-stress-on-jordan. Accessed 30 May 2018.

Sawyer, J. F., & Clines, D. J. (Eds.). (1983). *Midian, Moab, and Edom: The history and archaeology of late bronze and Iron age Jordan and north-West Arabia*. Sheffield: JSOT Press.

Scham, P. L., & Lucas, R. E. (2001). 'Normalization' and 'anti-normalization' in Jordan: The public debate. *Middle East Review of International Affairs, 5*(3), 54–70.

Schenker, D. (2003). *Dancing with Saddam: The strategic tango of Jordanian-Iraqi relations*. New York: Lexington Books.

Schenker, D. (2007, August 7). The Islamist boycott of Jordanian Municipal Elections: A Victory of Public Relations or Politics? *The Washington Institute for Near East Policy, Policy Watch Paper*, 1269. Available at: https://www.washingtoninstitute.org/policy-analysis/view/the-islamist-boycott-of-jordanian-municipal-elections-a-victory-of-public-r. Accessed 18 Apr 2018.

Schenker, D. (2017, April 19). Taxing times in Jordan. *The Washington Institute for Near East Policy, Policy Analysis*. Available at: https://www.washingtoninstitute.org/policy-analysis/view/taxing-times-in-jordan. Accessed 10 Apr 2018.

Schlumberger, O., & Bank, A. (2001). Succession, legitimacy, and regime stability in Jordan. *The Arab Studies Journal, 9/10*(2/1), 50–72.

Schwedler, J. (2006). *Faith in moderation: Islamist parties in Jordan and Yemen.* Cambridge: Cambridge University Press.

Scott, G. (2003). Jordan's 'new bargain': The political economy of regime security. *The Middle East Journal, 57*(2), 248–268.

Seccombe, I. J. (1987). Labour emigration policies and economic development in Jordan: From unemployment to labour shortage. In B. K. A. Badran (Ed.), *The economic development of Jordan* (pp. 118–132). London: Croom Helm.

Seeley, N. (2014). The battle over Nuclear Jordan. *MER 271 – Fuel and Water: The Coming Crises, 44*. Available at: http://www.merip.org/mer/mer271/battle-over-nuclear-jordan. Accessed 8 Apr 2018.

Sela, A. (1984). *The Palestinian Ba'ath: The Arab Ba'ath socialist Party in the West Bank under Jordan (1948–1967).* Jerusalem: Magnes Press. (Hebrew).

Sha'bān, A. H. (2017). *Al-Huwiyyah Wa al-Muwāṭanah: Al-Badā'il al-Multabasah Wa al-Ḥadāthah al-Muta'atharah (identity and citizenship: Ambiguous alternatives and hampered modernization)*. Beirut: Markaz Dirāsāt al-Wiḥdah al-Arabiyyah.

Shaban, R. A., Abu-Ghaida, D., & Al-Naimat, A.-S. (2001). *Poverty alleviation in Jordan: Lessons for the future.* Orientations in Development Series, World Bank. Available at: https://openknowledge.worldbank.org/handle/10986/13906. Accessed 10 June 2018.

Shami, S. K. (1994). Displacement, historical memory and identity: The Circassians in Jordan. In IDEM (Ed.), *Mobility, modernity and misery: Population displacement and resettlement in the Middle East* (pp. 189–201). New York: Centre for Migration Studies.

Shami, S. K. (1995). Disjuncture in ethnicity: Negotiating Circassian identity in Jordan, Turkey and the Caucasus. *New Perspective on Turkey, 12*, 79–95.

Shami, S. K. (1998). Circassian encounters: The self as other and the production of the homeland in the North Caucasus. *Development and Change, 29*(4), 617–646.

Shami, S. K. (2001). The Little nation, minorities and majorities in the context of shifting geographies. In K. Goldman, U. Hannerz, & C. Westin (Eds.), *Nationalism and internationalism in the post-cold war era* (pp. 103–127). London: Routledge.

Shami, S. K. (2009). Historical processes of identity formation: Displacement, settlement and self-representations of the Circassians in Jordan. *Iran and the Caucasus, 13*(1), 141–159.

Shamir, U. (1999). Water agreements between Israel and its neighbors. *F and ES Bulletin, 103*, 274–296. Available at: https://environment.yale.edu/publication-series/documents/downloads/0-9/103shamir.pdf. Accessed 18 June 2018.

Sharp, J. M. (2013, April). *Jordan: Background and U.S. relations*. Congressional Research Service Report. Washington, DC: CRS.

Sharp, J. M. (2017, November). *Jordan: Background and U.S. relations*. Congressional Research Service Report. Washington DC: CRS.

Shdeifat, O., Mohsen, M., Mustafa, M., Al-Ali, Y., & Al-Mhaisen, B. (2006). Tourism in Jordan. *Zarqa, LIFE Third Countries, 1*, 1–68. Available at: http://ec.europa.eu/environment/life/project/Projects/index.cfm?fuseaction=home.showFile&rep=file&fil=GREEN_TAS_D1.pdf. Accessed 20 June 2018.

Shehori, D. (2018, June 26). Peace and quiet and exports. *Ha'aretz*. Available at: https://www.haaretz.com/1.4727156. Accessed 26 June 2018.

Sheldon, Z. (2018, January 2). Nationality, class, and Iraqi Migrants in Jordan. American Center of Oriental Research. Available at: https://www.acorjordan.org/2018/01/02/nationality-class-iraqi-migrants-jordan/. Accessed 22 June 2018.

Shlaim, A. (1988). *Collusion across the Jordan: King Abdullah, the Zionist movement, and the partition of Palestine*. Oxford: Clarendon.

Shlaim, A. (1990). *The politics of partition: King Abdullah, the Zionist movement and the partition of Palestine*. Oxford: Oxford University Press.

Shlaim, A. (2007). *Lion of Jordan: The Life of king Hussein in war and peace*. London: Penguin Books.

Shlaim, A., & Hussein, K. (1999, July 15). His Royal Shyness: King Hussein and Israel. *New York Review of Books*. Available at: https://www.nybooks.com/articles/1999/07/15/his-royal-shyness-king-hussein-and-israel/. Accessed 15 June 2018.

Shoup, J. A. (2007). *Culture and customs of Jordon*. London: Greenwood Press.

Shwadran, B. (1959). *Jordan: A state of tension*. New York: Council for Middle Eastern Affairs Press.

Singh, M. (2017). Parliamentary elections in Jordan, 2016. *Contemporary Review of the Middle East, 4*(3), 297–318.

Slackman, M. (2006, August 10). Seeking roots beyond the nation they helped establish. *The New York Times*. Available at: https://www.nytimes.com/2006/08/10/world/middleeast/10circassians.html. Accessed 10 Oct 2018.

Sneineh, M. A. (2018, June 30). A refugee camp in Jordan holds the right of return for Palestinians. *Middle East Eye*, Baqaa Refugee Camp. Available at: http://www.middleeasteye.net/baqa%27a-refugee-camp-Amman-Jordan-UNRWA-PLO-Black%20September. Accessed 30 June 2018.

Sondos, A.-A., Jihad, A., & Abu-Kharmeh, S. (2010). The Jordanian worker's remittances impact on the main macroeconomic variables. *International Research Journal of Finance and Economics, 41*(July), 121–135.

Sowell, K. H. (2015). Jordanian Salafism and the Jihad in Syria. *Current Trends in Islamist Ideology, 18*, 41–71.

Sowell, K. H. (2016, March 17). Jordan is sliding toward insolvency. Carnegie Endowment for International Peace. Available at: http://carnegieendowment.org/sada/63061. Accessed 10 Apr 2018.

Sowell, K. H.(2017, November 21). *Reforming Jordan's Labour Market.* Carnegie Endowment for International Peace. Available at: http://carnegieendowment.org/sada/74796. Accessed 18 Oct 2018.

Sowell, K. H. (2018a, June 19). *Razzaz's rough road.* Carnegie Endowment for International Peace. Available at: http://carnegieendowment.org/sada/76632. Accessed 18 Sept 2018.

Sowell, K. H. (2018b, March 22). *Slowing Jordan's slide into debt.* Carnegie Endowment for International Peace. Available at: http://carnegieendowment.org/sada/75865. Accessed 20 Apr 2018.

Speckhard, A. (2017, March 25). *The Jihad in Jordan: Drivers of radicalization into violent extremism in Jordan.* International Center for the Study of Violent Extremism. Available at: http://www.icsve.org/research-reports/the-jihad-in-jordan-drivers-of-radicalization-into-violent-extremism-in-jordan/. Accessed 25 Apr 2018.

Spero, S. (2007). Who authorized Israelite settlement east of the Jordan. *Jewish Bible Quarterly, 35*(1), 60–71.

Susser, A. (1999a). The Palestinians in Jordan: Demographic majority, political minority. In O. Bengio & G. Ben-Dor (Eds.), *Minorities and the state in the Arab world* (pp. 91–109). London: Lynne Rienner.

Susser, A. (1999b). *The Jordanian – Israeli peace negotiations: The geopolitical rationale of a bilateral relationship* (Occasional Papers) (Vol. 73). Jerusalem: Leonard David Institute for International Relations, Hebrew University.

Susser, A. (2000). The Hashemite success story. In J. Kostiner (Ed.), *Middle East monarchies: The challenge of modernity* (pp. 87–116). Boulder: Lynne Rienner.

Susser, A. (2008). Jordan—In the maze of tribalism, Jordanianism, Palestinianism and Islam. In A. Susser (Ed.), *Challenges to the cohesion of the Arab state* (pp. 103–119). Tel Aviv: Moshe Dayan Center for Middle Eastern and African Studies.

Susser, A. (2012). *Israel, Jordan, and Palestine: The two-state imperative.* Waltham: Brandeis University Press.

Sweis, N. J. (2012). *The economics of tobacco use in Jordan.* Ph.D. dissertation, University of Illinois, Chicago.

Sweis, N. J., & Chaloupka, F. J. (2014). The economics of tobacco use in Jordan. *Nicotine and Tobacco Research, 16*(1), 30–36.

Tahboub, N. (2016). *Jordan under the Hashemites.* Amman: University of Jordan.

Tal, L. (1995). Britain and the Jordan crisis of 1958. *Middle Eastern Studies, 31*(1), 39–57.

Tal, L. (2002). *Politics, the military and National Security in Jordan, 1955–1967.* New York: Palgrave Macmillan.

Tamkeen Fields for Aid. (2015). *Invisible women: The working and living conditions of irregular migrant domestic workers in Jordan*. Amman: Tamkeen Fields for Aid. Available at: http://tamkeen-jo.org/upload/web_Invisible_Women_English_Colored_amended.pdf. Assessed 28 Oct 2017.

Tarawneh, M. F. (2013). *Rural capitalist development in the Jordan Valley: The case of Deir Alla – The rise and demise of social groups*. Leiden: Sidestone Press.

Tarawneh, K. (2016). A comprehensive outlook of mining industry in Jordan, opportunities and threats. *Open Journal of Geology, 6*(9), 1137–1148.

Teitelbaum, J. (2001). *The rise and the fall of the Hashemite kingdom of Arabia*. London: Hurst and Co.

The General Corporation for Environment Protection (GCEP). (2001, October). *Jordan's report about sustainable development to Johannesburg Summit 2002*. Amman: GCEP.

The Hashemite Kingdom of Jordan, Higher council for Youth, UNDP and UNICEF. (2004, December). National Youth Strategy for Jordan 2005–2009. Available at: http://www.youthpolicy.org/national/Jordan_2005_National_Youth_Strategy.pdf. Accessed 30 June 2018.

The Jordanian National Charter. (1991). Available at: http://www.kinghussein.gov.jo/charter-national.html. Accessed 24 Jan 2018.

The World Bank. (2002). Jordan – Development Policy Review: A reforming state in a volatile region. Washington, DC: The World Bank. Available at: https://openknowledge.worldbank.org/handle/10986/15327. Accessed 20 Apr 2018.

The World Bank. (2004). *The Hashemite Kingdom of Jordan's poverty assessment* (Report No. 27658-JO).

The World Bank. (2012). *Hashemite Kingdom of Jordan – Development Policy Review: Improving institutions, fiscal policies and structural reforms for greater growth resilience and sustained job creation*. Washington, DC: The World Bank. Available at: https://openknowledge.worldbank.org/handle/10986/12306. Accessed 12 Sept 2018.

The World Bank. (2013). Economic participation, agency and access to justice in Jordan. *Jordan Country Gender Assessment, Hashemite Kingdom of Jordan* (Report No. ACS5158). Available at: http://documents.worldbank.org/curated/en/503361468038992583/pdf/ACS51580WP0P130ox0379850B00PUBLIC0.pdf. Accessed 30 June 2018.

The World Bank. (2016). *Hashemite Kingdom of Jordan promoting poverty reduction and shared prosperity: Systematic country diagnostic*. Washington, DC: The World Bank. Available at: https://openknowledge.worldbank.org/handle/10986/2395. Accessed 18 Oct 2018.

Their News team. (2017, September 27). Jordan to open its schools to Syrian refugee children who don't have official Ids. *Their World*. Available at: https://theirworld.org/news/jordan-lets-undocumented-syrian-refugees-in-state-schools. Accessed 30 June 2018.

Toahmeh, K. A. (2013, June 6). Jordan said threatening to renounce citizenship of senior PA officials. *The Jerusalem Post*. Available at: https://www.jpost.com/Arab-Israeli-Conflict/Jordan-said-threatening-to-renounce-citizenship-of-senior-PA-officials-405206. Accessed 30 June 2018.

Tobin, S. A. (2012). Jordan's Arab Spring: The middle class and anti-revolution. *Middle East Policy Council, 19*: 1. Available at: https://www.mepc.org/jordans-arab-spring-middle-class-and-anti-revolution. Accessed 30 June 2018.

Toukan, A. M. (2016). The economic impact of cigarette smoking on the poor in Jordan. *Value in Health Regional Issues, 10,* 61–66.

Trading Economics. (2018). Jordan unemployment rate. Available at: https://tradingeconomics.com/jordan/unemployment-rate. Accessed 30 June 2018.

United Nations Development Programme (UNDP). (2013). The informal sector in the Jordanian economy. Available at: http://www.undp.org/content/dam/jordan/docs/Publications/Gov/The%20Informal%20Sector%20in%20the%20Jordanian%20Economy-jo.pdf. Accessed 25 May 2018.

United Nations Development Programme (UNDP). (2015). Jordan Human Development Report 2015: Regional disparities. Available at: http://www.jo.undp.org/content/dam/jordan/docs/Publications/NDHR/Jordan%20Human%20Development%20Finalest.pdf. Accessed 30 June 2018.

United Nations High Commissioner for Refugees (UNHCR). (2013). Jordan: Background information and current situation. Available at: http://www.refworld.org/pdfid/513d90172.pdf. Accessed 30 June 2018.

United Nations High Commissioner for Refugees (UNHCR). (2015). Jordan 2015. Available at: http://www.unhcr.org/jordan-2015.html. Accessed 30 June 2018.

United Nations High Commissioner for Refugees (UNHCR). (2017). Syria regional refugee response. Available at: http://data.unhcr.org/syrianrefugees/regional.php. Accessed 25 Apr 2018.

United State Agency for International Development. (2018, March). *Water management initiative: Review of water scarcity ranking methodologies, Jordan*. Available at: http://www.mwi.gov.jo/sites/en-us/Hot%20Issues/Review%20of%20Water%20Scarcity%20Ranking%20Methodologies%20-%20Jordan%20Ranking%20Brief.pdf. Accessed 30 June 2018.

United State Agency for International Development (USAID) – Institutional Support and Strengthening Program (ISSP). (2013, November 19). Jordan. *USAID procurement information bulletin*. Available at: https://procurement.usaid.gov/topic/pib-no-13175-full-spectrum-vibration-analysis-jordan. Accessed 18 Feb 2018.

United States Agency for International Development (USAID). (2012). Jordan: Country development cooperation strategy 2013–2017. Available at: https://www.usaid.gov/sites/default/files/documents/1883/Amended_Jordan_

Country_Development_Strategy_November_2016_1.pdf. Accessed 30 June 2018.
Vandenbussche, J., Watt, S., & Blazsek, S. (2009). *The liquidity and liquidity distribution effects in emerging markets: The case of Jordan* (IMF Working Paper, 09/228). Washington, DC: International Monetary Fund.
Vatikiotis, P. J. (1967). *Politics and the military in Jordan a study of the Arab legion 1921–57*. London: Routledge.
Venot, J.-P., Molle, F., & Courcier, R. (2008). Dealing with closed basins: The case of the lower Jordan River basin. *International Journal of Water Resources Development, 24*(2), 247–263.
Verme, P., Gigliarano, C., Wieser, C., Hedlund, K., Petzoldt, M., & Santacroce, M. (2015). *The welfare of Syrian refugees: Evidence from Jordan and Lebanon*. Washington, DC: The World Bank.
Viorst, M. (1981). Jordan: A moderate's role. *The Atlantic Monthly, 247*(3), 4–11. Available at: https://www.theatlantic.com/past/docs/issues/81mar/hussein.htm. Accessed 30 June 2018.
Wagemakers, J. (2012). *A quietist jihadi: The ideology and influence of Abu Muhammad al-Maqdisi*. Cambridge, MA: Cambridge University Press.
Wagemakers, J. (2016). *Salafism in Jordan: Political Islam in a quietist community*. Cambridge, MA: Cambridge University Press.
Wagner, H. L. (2005). *King Abdullah II*. Philadelphia: Chelsea House Publishers.
Walker, J., Firestone, M. D., & Mayhew, B. (2009). *Jordan*. Lonely Planet Publications.
Walt, A. I. (2015). *Tensions between state boundaries and nations: The case of Jordan*. Dissertation for degree of Bachelor of Arts, Clark Honors College, University of Oregon, Eugene.
WANA Institute. (2014). The status of legal empowerment in Jordan: Evidence to support the post-2015 development agenda, Amman. Available at: http://wanainstitute.org/sites/default/files/publications/StatusOfLegalEmpowermentInJordan_WANA_2014.pdf. Accessed 30 June 2018.
Warrick, C. (2009). *Law in the service of legitimacy: Gender and politics in Jordan*. Farnham: Ashgate Publishing Ltd.
Watt, S., Chami, S., & McGettigan, D. (2007). *Jordan's international reserve position: Justifiably strong* (IMF Working Paper, 07/103). Washington, DC: International Monetary Fund.
Watts, D. (1984). A Circassian quarter in Jerash, Jordan. *Urbanism Past and Present, 9*(1), 21–30.
Whitman, E. (2014, February 22). Jordan's Circassians Balk at Sochi Olympics. *Reuters*. Available at: https://www.aljazeera.com/indepth/features/2014/02/jordan-circassians-balk-at-sochi-olympics-201421972329112257.html. Accessed 18 Aug 2018.

Wiktorowicz, Q. (2000). Civil society as social control: State power in Jordan. *Comparative Politics, 33*(1), 43–61.

Wiktorowicz, Q. (2001). *The Management of Islamic Activism: Salafis, the Muslim brotherhood, and state power in Jordan.* Albany: State University of New York Press.

Wilson, M. C. (1990). *King Abdullah, Britain and the making of Jordan.* Cambridge: Cambridge University Press.

Winckler, O. (1997). *Population growth and migration in Jordan, 1950–1994.* Brighton: Sussex Academic Press.

Winckler, O. (2002). The demographic dilemma of the Arab world: The employment aspect. *Journal of Contemporary History, 37*(4), 617–636.

Wolf, A., & Ross, J. (2012). The impact of scarce water resources on the Arab-Israeli conflict. *Natural Resources Journal, 32*(4), 919–958.

World Finance. (2016, March 3). Jordan's banking industry is leading the way in Islamic finance. Available at: https://www.worldfinance.com/banking/jordans-banking-industry-is-leading-the-way-in-islamic-finance. Accessed 30 June 2018.

World Travel and Tourism Council. (2018, March). Travel and tourism economic impact: Jordan. Available at: https://www.wttc.org/-/media/files/reports/economic-impact-research/countries-2018/jordan2018.pdf. Accessed 30 June 2018.

Wróblewski, B. (2016). The mystery of political stability in the Hashemite Kingdom of Jordan: Monarchy and the crisis of state governance in the Arab world. *Polish Quarterly of International Affairs, 25*(4), 7–29.

Yitzhak, R. (2004). The formation and development of the Jordanian Air Force: 1948–1967. *Middle Eastern Studies, 40*(5), 158–174.

Yitzhak, R. (2007). A short history of the secret Hashemite-Zionist talks: 1921–1951. *Midstream, 53*(3), 9–12.

Yitzhak, R. (2008a). A small consolation for big loss: King Abdullah and Jerusalem during 1948 war. *Israel Affairs, 14*(3), 398–416.

Yitzhak, R. (2008b). Fauzi Al-Qawuqji and the Arab liberation Army in the 1948 war toward the attainment of king Abdallah's political ambitions in Palestine. *Comparative Studies of South Asia, Africa and Middle East, 28*(3), 459–466.

Yitzhak, R. (2008c). The question of Arab solidarity in the 1948 war: Political interests versus military considerations. *Mediterranean Quarterly, 19*(2), 19–46.

Yitzhak, R. (2010). The assassination of king Abdallah: The first political assassination in Jordan: Did it truly threaten the Hashemite Kingdom of Jordan? *Diplomacy And Statecraft, 21*(1), 68–86.

Yitzhak, R. (2015). British military supplies to Jordan during the 1948 war: How the Anglo-Jordanian treaty was put to the test. *Middle East Critique, 24*(4), 345–354.

Yitzhak, R. (2016). The war against terrorism and for stability of the Hashemite regime: Jordanian intelligence challenges in 21st century. *International Journal of Intelligence and Counter-Intelligence, 29*(2), 213–237.

Yitzhak, R. (2017). From cooperation to normalization? Jordan–Israel relations since 1967. *British Journal of Middle Eastern Studies, 44*, 4,559–4,575.
Yom, S. (2018, June 11). Jordan's protests are a ritual, not a revolution. *Foreign Policy.* Available at: https://foreignpolicy.com/2018/06/11/jordans-protests-are-a-ritual-not-a-revolution/. Accessed 30 June 2018.
Yom, S., & Al-Khatib, W. (2014, December 5). Inflating the Salafi threat in Jordan. *The Atlantic Council.* Available at: http://www.atlanticcouncil.org/blogs/menasource/inflating-the-salafi-threat-in-jordan. Accessed 5 Sept 2018.
Yom, S. L., & Al-Momani, M. H. (2008a). The international dimensions of authoritarian regime stability: Jordan in the post-cold war era. *Arab Studies Quarterly, 30*(1), 39–60.
Yom, S. L., & Al-Momani, M. H. (2008b). The international dimensions of authoritarian regime stability: Jordan in the post-cold war era. *Arab Studies Quarterly, 30*(1), 39–60.
Yorke, V. (2013). *Politics matter: Jordan's path to water security lies through political reforms and regional cooperation* (NCCR Trade Regulation, Working paper 2013/19). Available at: https://www.wti.org/research/publications/493/politics-matter-jordans-path-to-water-security-lies-through-political-reforms-and-regional-cooperation/. Accessed 20 Apr 2018.
Yusuf, S. (2014). *Middle East transitions: A long, hard road* (IMF Working Paper. 14/135). Washington, DC: International Monetary Fund.
Zabad, I. (2017). *Middle eastern minorities, the impact of the Arab spring.* New York: Routledge.
Zahran, M. (2012). Jordan is Palestinian. *Middle East Quarterly*, Middle East Forum, *18*. Available at: https://www.meforum.org/articles/2011/jordan-is-palestinian. Accessed 30 June 2018.
Zak, M. (1996). *Hussein makes peace.* Ramat Gan: Bar Ilan University Press. (Hebrew).
Zaqqa, N. (2006). *Economic development and export of human capital. A contradiction?: The impact of human capital migration on the economy of sending countries; a case study of Jordan.* Kassel: Kassel University Press.

Index[1]

A

Abbas, Mahmoud, 304, 307, 317, 387, 388
Abdullah, Emir, *see* Abdullah I, King
Abdullah I, King
  al-Adwan tribe *vs*, 217
  appointment as Emir Transjordan, 4, 70, 98, 216, 217, 219, 220, 408
  Arab nationalism and, 218, 226–230, 342, 395, 438
  assassination of, 14, 23, 198, 203, 220, 226–230, 316
  Bedouin tribes *vs*, 217
  criticism against, 220
  drift towards democracy, 331
  Greater Syria plan, 220, 222
  Jordan-China relations, 381–382
  Jordan-EU relations, 376–377
  as King of Transjordan, 220, 226
  Palestinian support and, 222
  political plan, 220
  relation with Britain, 4, 215–222, 224, 226, 229, 230
Abdullah II, King
  Jordan-France relations, 385–387
  Jordan-Israel relations, 385–387
  Jordan-Japan relations, 385–387
  Jordan-Palestine relations, 385
  Jordan-Russia relations, 385–387
  Jordan-UK relations, 385–387
  Jordan-US relations, 385–387
  policy on Jerusalem, 383, 387, 388
  recognition of Palestinian state, 386, 387
  as *reformist* leader, 124
  visits to foreign capitals, 374
Abe, Shinzo, 385
Abidat, Walid, 320
Abu al-Jabin, Abdullah, 318
Abulibda, Abdulkareem, 319
Adayleh, Murad, 319
Adyghe language, 95, 106
Agadir Agreement, 132

---

[1] Note: Page numbers followed by 'n' refer to notes.

Agence Française de Développement
    (AFD), 383
Al Adasiyah village, 77
Al-Aqsa intifada, 306, 316, 331
Al-Aqsa Mosque incident, 5, 229,
    237, 285, 286, 291, 296, 297,
    299, 303, 304
al-Albani, Muhammad Nasir al-Din,
    268–271
Al-Haram al-Sharif controversy, 23,
    237, 295, 299–302, 306–308,
    320, 322, 331, 352
Al Husun, 81
Ali, Rashid, 250
Ali, Sharif Hussein Ben, 3
Allenby, General Edmund, 244
Allon, Yigal, 413, 414, 439, 440
Allon Plan, 426
All Palestine Government, 23, 226,
    280, 291, 345
al-Qaeda, 257, 263, 274, 449,
    452–456, 472
al-Qaeda in Iraq (AQI), 273, 275,
    453, 464, 468
Amman
    bombing 2005, 72, 269, 450,
        468, 471
    Message, 469, 471
Anglo-Jordanian Defence Treaty
    1946, 288
Anglo-Jordanian Treaty 1948, 280,
    358, 359
Anglo-Jordanian Treaty 1957, 255
Arab Cooperation Council (ACC),
    365, 367
Arab Federation, 359, 401
Arabism first concept, 203
Arab-Israeli relations, 429
Arab-Israeli War of 1948, 4, 7, 75, 83,
    187, 209, 234, 240, 463
Arab-Israel peace, 417
Arabistan, 195, 198, 199

Arab-Jewish inter-communal strife, 278
Arab League, 22, 23, 222, 223, 226,
    240, 251, 283, 291, 343, 345,
    359, 398, 412, 413, 416, 440
Arab Legion
    Abdullah's frustration about,
        249, 255
    as ad hoc army, 250
    Arabisation of, 254–255
    Arab nationalism and, 245, 253–254
    British control of, 246, 247,
        253, 255
    under Captain Frederick Peake, 245
    conduct of, 224, 251, 252
    Desert Patrol, 248, 249
    Glubb's design, 248–250
    intention to occupy Palestine, 251
    involvement in the Second World
        War, 250
    masters of, 251
    origins of, 243–245, 250
    Peake's approach, 245–248
    workforce, 250
Arab nationalism, 218, 226–230, 236,
    245, 248–250, 326, 342, 358,
    395, 423, 438
Arab neighbourhoods, 277, 300, 301
Arab Revolt, 3, 165, 166, 215, 216,
    219, 221, 240
Arab Spring, 40, 41, 46, 126, 144,
    149, 196, 203n12, 209, 213,
    264, 266, 269, 271, 317–320,
    334, 348–352, 400, 403,
    404, 419
Arab union, 291
Arab unity, 195, 198, 202, 346,
    360–362, 369
Arab zeitgeist, 202, 204
Arafat, Yasser, 20, 24, 195, 237, 239,
    241, 270, 301–303, 312, 346,
    363, 364, 415, 426, 427, 429,
    433, 441, 443, 444, 466

INDEX 523

Areikat, Lieutenant Abd al-Rahman, 245
Armistice Demarcation Line
　as a firm supporter of the UAC, 360
　as a 'Third Force,' 360
Ashu, Shukri, 229
al-Assad, Bashar, 403, 453
al-Assad, Hafiz, 426
Assemblies of God, 82
Assyrian massacre 1933, 200
Asylum Seeker Certificates (ASCs), 210
al-Ayubi, Musa, 230
Azarq Camp, 73
al-Aziz, Abd, 395

B

al-Badr, Imam Muhammad, 396
Badran, Abbdul-Razaq, 43, 43n40
Badran, Mudar, 326
al-Baghdadi, Abu Bakr, 452–454
Baghdad Pact (Central Treaty Organisation, CENTO), 234, 288, 358, 396, 423
Balfour Declaration 1917, 3, 198, 218, 408
Baptists, 6, 76, 82, 88, 89
Barak, Ehud, 419
al-Batush, Bassam, 211
Bay'at al-Imam, 273
Bedouins
　population of Jordan, 74
　tribes, 4, 9, 70, 96–100, 188, 213, 217, 248
Begin, Menachem, 24, 441
Bernadotte, Count Folke, 410
Bethany, 6, 7, 89, 90
Better Work Jordan (BWJ), 55
Bevin, Ernest, 221, 222, 222n9, 251, 252, 409
Bin Ali, King Al-Sharif Hussein, 3–5, 198, 207, 215, 216, 295, 296, 304

Bin-Laden, Osama, 450, 452, 453
Bin-Talal, Prince Ghazi, 303, 304
Bin-Talal, *see* King Hussein
Black September event, 23, 24, 239, 242, 398, 402, 449
Blair, Tony, 380
Boneh, Solel, 436
Booklet for Migrant Women Workers in Jordan, 55
Bread riots, 17, 131
British American Tobacco (BAT), 168, 169, 171, 173
Brunton, Captain Dunbar, 244, 245, 247
Brzezinski, Zbigniew, 240
Bush, George H.W., 417, 429, 467
Bush, George W., 368

C

Camp David Accords, 239, 240, 398
Caucasian minority in Jordan, 95
Chechens, 7, 9, 16, 30, 70, 74, 75, 77, 84, 95, 95n3, 95n4, 101, 102, 104n11, 107n13, 182
Chechen war, 107, 107n13
Christian and Missionary Alliance, 82
Christianity, 6, 8, 75, 83, 84, 89, 90, 95n5
　history of early, 83
Christians in Jordan, 76, 81–91
Churchill, Sir Winston, 198, 217, 218, 221, 246, 408
Cigarette and tobacco laws, 175
Cigarette market in Jordan, 169, 171
Circassian Charity Association, 104
Circassian ethno-national movement
　post-Sochi period, 109
　role of activists, 108, 109
　and Syrian refugee crisis, 109

Circassians
  ethos, 95, 100, 105
  genocide of, 96, 106, 108
  groups, 7, 74, 76, 93–95, 98–103, 104n11, 105, 109, 110
  identity of, 102, 104, 106
  influence in Jordanian politics, 98
  in Jordan, 94–95, 99–102, 104, 107, 109, 110
  refugees, 96, 109
  republics, 108, 109
  settlements, 99, 244, 245
  trend amongst younger generation, 101
  world estimate, 95
Circassiansas *Adyghe* and *Apsua*, 94
Citizenship
  constitution and, 182, 185–186, 188, 189, 193
  definition, 182–185, 188, 189, 189n1, 191–193
  jinsiyyah, 181, 183–185
  muwātanah, 181, 183–185
  Nationality Law and, 187–188
  in practice, 188–192
  role of religious affiliation, 189
  voting practices, 191
Civil code, 189
Civil legal system
  civil courts, 86
  denomination-specific courts, 86
  religious court, 86
  Sharia Court, 86
Clinton, Bill, 170, 418, 433, 444, 445
Committee on the Elimination of Racial Discrimination Jordan, 73
Council of Church Leaders (CCL), 82
Cunningham, Sir Alan, 200, 200n10
Curzon, Lord, 244

D
al-Daqamisah, Ahmed, 432
Dayan, Moshe, 253, 413, 436, 439

Dead Sea, 3, 90, 127, 128, 136, 387, 473
Dead Sea-Red Sea project, 24, 154, 159, 385, 473
Dhunaybat, Abd al-Majid, 264, 265
al-Dhuwayb, Ahmad, 271
Disi Aquifer water conveyance project, 129
Druze, 7, 9, 10, 30, 74–76, 82

E
East Bank
  Islamists, 349
  Jordanians, 38, 205, 208, 349
  nationalism, 202, 204, 208–212
  Palestinians, 206, 207
East Bankers, 19, 197, 202, 206, 208–213, 422, 431
Eban, Abba, 413, 439
Efendi, Shaikh al-Islam Bahai, 167
Egyptian Muslim Brotherhood, 259, 260, 272
Eisenhower Doctrine, 289
Emirate of Transjordan, 1, 3, 4, 6, 15, 98–99, 198, 216, 395, 407, 408
Emirates Jordan Camp, 73
Environmental campaigns
  following Arab Spring, 144
  impact on decision makers, 143–144
  save Bergesh Forest campaign, 145
  save Jordan's Trees campaign, 143
Environmental challenges
  desertification, 135, 137–139
  energy scarcity, 138
  land degradation, 135, 139
  loss of agricultural lands, 139
  loss of biodiversity, 137, 139
  rapid urbanisation, 137, 139–140
  soil salinisation, 139
  water scarcity, 137, 138
Environmental NGOs, 141–150
  impact on decision making, 144

Environmental Protection Law for
    Jordan, 141
Ershaid, Zaki Bani, 320
Ethnic minorities, 9, 30, 70, 74–75,
    77, 100
Etzion Block, 224
EU-Jordan ENP Action Plan, 377
European Economic Community
    (EEC), 366
European Neighbourhood Instrument
    (ENI), 377
European Union (EU), 41, 57,
    57n10, 66, 124, 132, 192,
    196n3, 373, 374, 376, 377, 391

F
FAIRWAY project, 55
Faisal, King of Iraq, 4, 216, 395, 398
Faisal-Weizmann Agreement, 218
al-Falahat, Salim, 264, 265
al-Fayiz, Mithqal, 244, 245
Fedayeen, 22, 238, 347, 362–364,
    425, 426, 466
    foray into Syrian civil war, 453
al-Filastini, Abu Qatada, 275
Free Evangelical Church, 82
Fuheis, 81

G
Gender equality, 16, 44, 152, 156
Gharayiba, Ruhayyil, 265
Ghosheh, Ibrahim, 312–315
Glubb, John Bagot (Glubb Pasha),
    220, 225n15, 227n16, 234, 235,
    248–250, 252–255, 254n9, 287,
    288, 359, 422, 423, 438
Goldstein, Baruch, 273
Greater Arab Free Trade Area
    agreement (GAFTA), 132
Greater Syria plan, 220, 222

Greater Transjordan scheme, 252
Group of Seven (G-7), 374
Gulf Cooperation Council (GCC)
    countries
    labour emigration to, 38
    socioeconomic problems in, 39
Gulf war of 1990–1991, 83, 241,
    327, 467

H
Hadi, Abdrabbuh Mansur, 401
Halevi, Efraim, 419, 443
Hamas
    Arab Spring and, 317–320
    Egyptian move against, 237
    impact on Muslim Brotherhood, 320
    inflammatory statements against
        Oslo agreement, 312
    -linked media sources, 319
    relationship with Jordanian Muslim
        Brotherhood, 321
    role on Haram al-Sharif/Tempe
        Mount, 320
    takeover of Gaza, 317, 321
Haram al-Sharif/Temple Mount,
    229, 299, 300, 306–307,
    320, 322, 331, 352, 414,
    418, 419, 437
Hashem clan, 7, 10, 257
Hashemite Jordanian identity, 283
Hawari, Dr. Feras, 176
Herzog, Yaacov, 170, 237
Hezbollah, 318, 333, 403, 419, 466
al-Hiyari, Major-General Ali, 316
Howeitat Tribe, 165
al-Huda, Tawfiq Abu, 221, 222, 251
Huda, Toufiq Abdul, 422
Husan, Dr. Abdul Qader, 83
Hussein, Saddam, 41, 241, 262, 270,
    330, 366–368, 399, 417, 443,
    444, 449, 453, 467

Hussein, Sharif, 3–5, 198, 207, 215, 216, 295, 296, 304, 305, 394
Hussein Bin-Ali of Mecca
  Anglo-Jordanian Treaty of Alliance, termination of, 236
  Arabism first concept, 203
  Arab nationalism and, 358, 438
  challenges of securing regime, 236
  childhood and early life, 437
  civil war and survival 1967–1971, 362–364
  commitment to Arab unity, 362
  convinced anti-communist, 358
  custodianship of al-Aqsa Mosque, 237
  death, 5, 242, 433, 435
  funeral, 242, 418, 433
  idea of nationalism, 197, 236
  and Jordanian disengagement from West Bank, 20, 237, 299, 348, 428
  and Jordan-Israel Peace Treaty, 386
  and June war and, 24, 170, 237, 238, 298
  legacy, 198, 242, 390, 422
  measures aimed at curbing political freedoms, 329
  and October 1973 war, 427
  on Oslo Accords, 241
  Palestinian refugees and, 41, 209, 239, 397, 437
  personality, 395, 437
  policy towards Iraq, 330
  post-Cold War Era, 1991–1999, 367–369
  reading of regional balance, 364
  regime as "expendable," 363
  relations with Britain, 234, 235
  relations with Iraq, 241, 365
  relations with Israel, 100, 234, 421
  relations with PLO, 424
  relation with Arafat, 22, 237, 239
  relation with US, 236, 241
  and Suez crisis, 235, 236, 370, 423
  volatile regional turmoil and, 357
  See also Sharif Hussein, Hussein, King
al-Husseini, Mufti Haji Amin, 22, 90, 218, 221, 222, 226, 229, 278–280, 296, 297
al-Husseini, Muhammad, 321
Husseini, Musa Abdullah, 315

I
IAF, *see* Islamic Action Front
Ibn Saud, of Saudi Arabia, 4, 168, 217, 394, 395, 404
IDF, *see* Israel Defence Forces
Ihsan, Major General Shurdom, 100
Ilyas, Mawlana Muhammad, 258
Innab, Radi, 255
International Circassian Association (ICA), 105, 107, 109n14
International Covenant on Civil and Political Rights (ICCPR), 87
Iran-Iraq War (1980–1988), 240, 399, 466
Iraq
  civil war, 3, 209, 212, 391, 473
  invasion of Kuwait 1990, 123, 209, 367, 428, 443, 467
  occupation of Kuwait 1990–1991, 241
Iraqi refugees, 12, 30, 41, 72, 74, 84, 118, 155, 209, 212, 467, 468
ISIS, *see* Islamic State of Iraq and Syria
al-Islami, Hizb al-Tahrir, 258, 260
Islamic Action Front (IAF), 10, 11, 18, 262, 264–266, 271, 312, 319, 320, 327, 328, 331, 333, 334, 336, 349, 467
Islamic jurisprudence, 470, 471
Islamic State (IS), 260, 270, 274, 275, 319, 337, 398, 403, 452, 454–459, 464

INDEX 527

Islamic State of Iraq and Syria (ISIS), 12, 447–460, 464, 465, 467, 471, 473, 474
Islamist extremism, 469
Ismail Haniyeh, 321
Israel
  after Rabin's assassination, 432
  Armistice negotiations, 411–420
  economic cooperation, 385, 399
  under King Hussein, 421–433
  1948 war and, 71, 99, 437
  pre-state from 1921 to 1947, 407
  security cooperation, 317, 433, 464
Israel Defence Forces (IDF), 253, 285, 317, 358, 363, 412, 413, 415, 436, 437, 439
Israel-Hamas conflict, 321
Israeli-Jordanian cooperation, 386
Israel-Jordan Peace Treaty, 7, 23, 418
Israel-Jordan relations, 411–420
Israel-Palestine Declaration of Principles, 443
Israel-PLO agreement, 443
Israel's annexation of East Jerusalem, 293
IS, *see* Islamic State
Izz ad-Din al-Qassam Brigades, 321
Izzat al-Rishq, 313

J

Jabhat al-Nusra, 451
Jalloud Plan, 365
Jama'at al-Muwahhidin, 273
Jama'at al-Tabligh, 258
Jama'at al-Tawhid, 273
Jama'at al-Tawhid wal-Jihad, 450, 453
Jam'iyyat al-Kitab wa-l-Sunna, 271, 272
Jam'iyyat Ihya' al-Turath al-Islami, 270
Al-Jazeera, 176, 321, 390, 401, 402
Al-Jeel Al-Jadeed club, 105

Jericho Conference, 201, 280
Jerusalem, 386
  Jordanian policy on, 207, 224, 286
  under Jordanian rule, 225, 296–298, 414, 437
  status of, 285–286, 297n10
Jewish Agency (JA), 200, 218, 219, 223, 251, 278, 408, 409
Jihadi-Salafis, 269, 272–275
Jinsiyyah, 181, 183–185
Jordan
  acquisition of military weapons, 280
  annexation of Palestine, 218
  anti-terror laws, 458
  Arab Spring experience, 126
  attitude to Jerusalem, 297
  budgetary-deficit problem, 121
  citizens/citizenship, 11, 30, 31, 33, 43, 50, 64, 71, 83, 160, 181, 182, 187, 189–193, 206n16, 211, 228, 270, 312, 314, 321, 347, 352, 387, 449
  civil wars and terror attacks, 448
  confrontations with nationalist forces, 343
  consequences of Islamic State, 454
  counter-terrorism (CT) strategies, 119, 464, 465, 471
  demographic shifts, 464, 468
  demography, 11–13, 77, 449
  domestic politics, 14–19, 171, 323
  economic challenges of, 2, 13
  economic issues of Jordan, 118, 157–158
  economic tussle between Palestinian leadership and, 7
  economy of, 13–14, 23, 38, 40, 47, 52, 99, 119, 124, 125, 149, 158, 171, 176, 228, 285, 368, 375, 381, 386, 400
  education, 45, 73, 104–106, 156, 162, 275, 282, 342, 348, 376

Jordan (*cont.*)
  electoral system, 84, 338
  energy insecurity, 118, 125–128
  environmental, social and economic challenges, 153, 159
  equal citizenship rights, 190
  evolution of, 3–7, 249
  exports and imports to US, 132, 133, 375, 386, 400
  foreign immigrants in Jordan, 50
  foreign workers in Jordan, 13, 14, 33, 39, 53, 58–62
  formalisation of borders, 119
  GCC countries and, 389–390
  geopolitically strategic location, 465
  historical claims and legacies, 6
  identity, 19, 21, 78, 93, 107, 110, 197, 201, 204, 205, 211–213, 283, 448
  impact on Jordan's population, 49, 191
  independence, 8, 15, 123, 168, 195, 198, 199, 217, 408, 422
  inflation in, 13
  inter-Arab tensions and rapprochement between Egypt and, 291
  internal and inter-Arab position, 289
  Islam in, 10
  Islamist extremism in, 469
  Major non-NATO Ally (MNNA) status, 375
  military, financial and political constraints, 280
  military involvement in war against ISIS, 456
  modern history, 176, 463–465, 467, 474
  as most dependable Arab partner, 376
  natural resources, 2, 13, 119, 139, 141, 233
  "open door" policy for labour immigration, 39
  Pan-Arabism political inheritance and inflows of refugees to, 63
  peace treaty with Israel, 3, 40, 100, 331, 368, 398, 442, 454
  poverty in, 121, 133
  protection of asylum seekers and refugees, 209
  raiding of ISIS hideout, 457
  relationship with PLO, 427, 428
  relations with Israel, 5, 22–25, 71, 129, 299, 301, 306, 369, 385–387, 407–433
  relations with Trump Administration, 376
  religious sites, 89–91
  rights and duties, 182, 193
  role in Middle East peace process, 24, 154, 327, 368, 380, 384
  against Salafis, 459
  social landscape, 87–89
  society and population, 7–10
  strategy in war, 280
  Syrian crisis and, 12, 377, 378, 388–389
  terrorist attacks in, 290, 322, 374, 467, 468
  trade between EU and, 192, 376, 377
  unemployment *and* underemployment in, 120, 121
  US Department of Defence assistance, 459
  water scarcity, 137, 153, 472, 473, 475
  waves of refugees, 463, 474
  Western orientation and status-quo with Israel, 287
  women, 11, 34, 43–45, 156, 189
Jordan Arab Army, 255
Jordan-Canada FTA, 132
Jordan-China relations, 387–388
Jordan Electric Power Company, 3
Jordan Environment Society, 142, 143

INDEX   529

Jordan-EU Association Agreement (JEUAA), 132
Jordan-EU Mobility Partnership, 66
Jordan-EU relations, 387–388
Jordan-Europe Free Trade Association free trade agreement, 132
Jordan Family Planning and Protection Association (JFPPA), 42
"Jordan First" or al-Urdun Awalan, 374
Jordan-France relations, 387–388
Jordan-Hamas relations, 311–322
  turning point, 313–316
Jordanian Armed Forces, 146, 203, 238, 447, 466, 471, 473
Jordanian Federation for Environmental NGOs, 143, 144
Jordanian-Israeli agreement, see Israel-Jordan Agreement
Jordanian labour market
  balance between local and foreign workforce, 65
  control operations, 56
  distribution of work permits, 60
  entry and recruitment of foreign labourers, 53–58
  foreign immigrants, 50
  foreign workers, 51, 67
  human resource needs vs segmentation of labour market, 64–65
  irregular status of immigrant workforce, 65
  Jordanian job-seekers, 52, 53, 62, 66, 67
  labour law 1996, 54
  labour migration policies, 52
  labour permits, 51
  Ministry of Labour's Strategic Plan for 2006–2010, 56
  3D activities, 63
Jordanian Muslim Brotherhood, 311, 321, 466

Jordanian National Guard, 234
Jordanian nationalism
  composite nationalism, 195–213
  concept of "all living on the East Bank are Jordanian," 208
  of East Bank Jordanians, 208
  King Abdullah's activities, 201
  Palestinian refugees as Jordanian citizens, 206
  pan-Arab legacy, 198
  stages of, 197–212
  state nationalism, 197, 201–204, 209
  territorial-primordial brand of nationalism, 212
  zeitgeist approach, 196
Jordanian National Society for Anti-Smoking, 174
Jordanian option, 424, 426, 440
Jordanian-Palestinian, 6, 20, 24, 289, 290, 302, 303, 352–353, 368, 418, 429
Jordanian population
  1952–2015, 32
  assimilation of Palestinians in, 228
  average age, specific fertility rate (ASFR), 34
  Christians, 7, 74, 81
  Chechens, 7
  crude birth rate (CBR), 34, 35, 38
  Druze, 7
  early age of marriage for women, 45
  estimate 2015, 209
  ethno-religious composition, 30
  family planning, 42–44, 46
  foreign workers, 29–31, 33
  growth rate of, 11, 31, 49, 136
  high birth rate characteristics, 154
  infant mortality rate and life expectancy, 11, 34, 35, 37
  influx of foreign labour, 38–41
  influx of Palestinians, 30–33, 38, 42, 83

Jordanian population (*cont.*)
  labour immigration and, 39
  minorities, 30
  Muslims, 30
  national population, 29–32, 34–41, 63
  natural population increase rate, 30, 34–41
  non-Palestinian refugees, 29, 33, 41
  overall density, 136, 137
  proportion of Palestinian-Jordanians to the Jordanian-Jordanians, 155
  refugees, 11, 29, 33, 212
Jordanian Salafis, 267–269, 451
Jordanians of Palestinian origin, 19, 21, 192, 314
Jordanian Tobacco Company (JTC), 168–171
Jordanian "vague anti-natalist policy," 43
Jordanian workers, in GCC countries, 38, 39, 41
Jordanian zeitgeist, 212
Jordan-Israel Peace Treaty 1994, 386
Jordan-Israel relations, 385–387
Jordan-Japan relations, 384–385
Jordan-Palestine relations, 387–388
Jordan River, 425
Jordan-Russia relations, 387–388
Jordan's economic development
  bilateral free trade agreements, 132
  challenges and limitations, 118–123
  ending of subsidies, 131
  energy insecurity and, 118, 125–128
  Energy Master Plan, 127
  exports, imports and trade deficit, 133
  focus on desalination of seawater, 129, 130
  freshwater scarcity, 118, 128–130, 133
  under King Abdullah-II, 117, 131
  macroeconomic indicators, 122
  macroeconomic restructuring, 131, 133
  migration to oil-producing states, 52
  neoliberal economic policies, 121, 122, 130–133
  nuclear energy programme, 127
  privatisation of government-owned enterprises, 131
  renewable energy sector, 127
  trade liberalisation programme, 132
  Wastewater Management Policy, 129
Jordan-Singapore FTA, 132
Jordan-Turkey FTA, 132
Jordan 2025, 152, 156, 160, 161
Jordan-UK relations, 387–388
Jordan-US relations, 374–376
Jordan-USA FTA, 132
Joshua Project, 76
JTC, *see* Jordanian Tobacco Company
Jund al-Sham, 450
al-Jundi, Captain Abd al-Qadir, 246
June 1967 War, 7, 29, 33, 42, 298–300, 424

K
Kabariti, Abd Al-Karim, 329, 336
Kafala (sponsorship) system, 53, 64
Karak, 76, 81, 91, 216, 244, 247, 324, 457
al-Kasasbeh, Muath Safi Yousef, 456, 457, 471
Kenji Goto, 471
al-Khalayleh, Ahmad Fadil, 469
Khalifa, Muhammad 'Abd al-Rahman, 260
al-Khaliq, Abu Abdullah Abd al-Rahman b. Abd, 270
Khasawneh, Awn, 336
Khater, Sami, 314, 319
Al-Kifah al-Islami, 261

al-Kilani, Rashid Ali, 220
Kirkbride, Alec, 222n9, 422
Kura incident, 246
Kuwait Crisis (1990–1991), 52, 212, 262, 390, 395, 417

L

Labda, Abdel Dayem Abu, 318
Lawrence, T. E., 165, 166, 215, 245, 246
Lebanese civil war (1975–1990), 5, 466

M

Madaba, 76, 81, 82, 91
Madrid Middle East Peace Conference, 241
al-Majali, Hazza, 290
Major, John, 366
al-Maliki, Nuri, 258, 453, 470
Mansur, Hamza, 265
al-Maqdisi, Abu Muhammad, 272–275, 449, 450
March of Return, 331
Marzouk, Imad al-'Alami and Abu, 312
Marzouk, Musa Abu, 312–314
Masha'al affair, 329
Masha'l, Khalid, 312–315, 318–321, 329, 419, 432
May, Theresa, 380
McMahon, Henry, 198
Mediterranean Arab Free Trade Area agreement (MAFTA), 132
Meir, Golda, 223, 251, 409, 410, 410n2, 412, 415, 416, 420, 427, 436, 438, 439
Millennium Development Goals (MDGs), 151
Minbar, Nur al-Din, 304
Ministry of Environment (MoE), 140–143, 149, 152, 160
 establishment of, 140

Minorities, categories of, 70
Mirza Pasha, 98
Modern Middle East, formation of, 215
al-Muasher, Marwan Jameel Essa, 84, 155, 333, 385, 387
Mujahedeen (jihad fighters), 272
Mukhabarat, 468
Murad IV Sultan, 166
Muslim Brotherhood (MB), 10, 13, 17, 18, 257–276, 289, 295, 312, 315, 318–321, 325–328, 333, 334, 338, 431, 450, 451, 467
Muwātanah, 181, 183–185

N

al-Nabhani, Taqi al-Din, 258, 260
al-Nabulsi, Suleiman, 201, 236, 279, 288, 359
al-Naksa, 191
al-Naqba, 187, 191, 343, 345, 348
Nart, 105
Nasser, Gamal Abdul, 10, 195, 234, 260, 279, 311, 358, 396, 412, 423, 438
National Employment Strategy (NES), 53
National Resilience Plan, 388
National Tobacco and Cigarette Company (NTC), 168, 170, 171
National Water Carrier plan of Israel, 412
Nazarene Church, 82
Nazzal, 312–314
Netanyahu, Benjamin, 307, 329, 418, 419, 432, 433
North Yemen civil war (1962–1970), 396
No Sochi campaign, 108
Nuwar, Ali Abu, 316

O

Obeidat, Ahmad, 431
October 1973 War, 239, 365, 398, 427
Odeh, Adnan Abu, 155, 156, 300, 360, 361, 363
Olmert, Ehud, 419
"One-person, one-vote" system, 328
Open Bridges policy, 414, 441
Operation Desert Storm, 417
Operation Inherent Resolve, 456
Oslo Accords, 241, 300, 368, 429, 430, 465
Oslo peace process, 170, 241, 312
Ottoman rule, 70

P

Palestine Royal Commission (Peel Commission), 219
Palestinian armed fighters, 346
Palestinian identity, 182, 283, 348
Palestinian *Intifada*, 33, 299, 417, 428, 442
Palestinian Islamists, 315, 349
Palestinian Liberation Organisation (PLO)
  Rabat formula of recognizing, 206
  rise of, 291
Palestinian movement, 206, 311–313, 347
Palestinian nationalism, 212, 348, 415
Palestinian refugees, 14, 20, 21, 29, 31–33, 41, 42, 51, 71, 72, 74, 75, 83, 90, 155, 168, 206, 206n16, 208–210, 213, 227, 229, 234, 239, 281, 283, 284, 287, 341, 344, 373, 397, 410, 411, 414, 422, 430, 437–438, 463, 465, 466
Palestinians
  Aarafat stand on, 346
  cause and save Arab honour, 346
  demand for self-rule, 348
  differences between Jordanians and, 352
  division between East Bank Islamists and, 349
  Jordanian recognition of, 348
  on Jordan's monarch, 342, 343, 346, 352, 353, 466
  King Abdullah and, 343, 352
  national rights and claims to Jerusalem, 352
  as a threat to Jordan's monarchy, 343
Palestinian uprising (*intifada*), 293
Pan-Arabism, 10, 17, 19, 51, 63, 346, 362, 397
Pasha, General John Glubb, *see* Glubb, John Bagot (Glubb Pasha)
Pax Americana, 433
Peake, Major General Frederick G, 215, 215n1, 245–249
Peres, Shimon, 417, 429, 430, 432, 440–444
Political reforms in Jordan
  agenda of centralising power, 337
  amendment of constitution, 335, 338
  authoritarian regime, 1999–2010, 330–334
  defensive democratisation concept, 325–327
  de-liberalisation, 1993–1999, 327–330
  electoral law, 325, 328, 331, 334
  hybridisation of political system, 2010–2017, 334–338
  Law of Societies, 333
  Municipalities Law and Decentralisation Law, 337
  1980s economic crisis and, 324
  Political Parties Law, 327, 333, 335, 337
  political reforms in, 124, 323–339

INDEX 533

Press and Publications Law,
　327–330, 335
Political Salafis, 269–272
Popular Front for the Liberation of
　Palestine (PFLP), 239, 311, 363
Population Momentum
　phenomenon, 47
Press and Publications Law (PPL),
　188, 327–330, 335
Pro-Hashemite movement, 215
　public support for, 215
Putin, Vladimir, 108, 377, 378

Q

al-Qahtani, Muhammed, 398
Al-Qibla, 271
Qibya massacre, 234, 253
al-Otaibi, Juhaiman, 398
al-Qudat, Sharaf, 319
Al-Quds, 295, 297, 299
Quietist Salafis, 269–272
Qura, Abd al-Latif Abu, 259, 260

R

Rabin, Yitzhak, 170, 241, 311, 312,
　368, 415, 416, 418, 430–432,
　435–446
　education, 436, 437
　family, 436
　June War and, 437, 439, 449
　Palmach brigade and, 436
　personality, 436–440
Rawabda, Abdul Raouf, 315
al-Rawabdeh, Abdel Raouf, 336
Red Sea Dead Sea Water Conveyance
　Project, 385, 473
Refugees of Jordan, 11, 12, 14, 20, 21,
　32, 41, 47, 57, 63, 66, 71, 72, 77,
　84, 121, 155, 156, 168, 192,
　206, 209, 383, 388, 468, 473
Religious minorities, 70, 75–77, 325

"Repatriation to Circassia,"
　idea of, 107
Reproductive Health Action Plans, 44
al-Resalah, 319
Reserve Force, 244–247
al-Rifa'i, Muhammad Nasib, 268
al-Rimawi, Abdullah, 288, 289
al-Rishawi, 471
River Jordan, 1, 3, 4, 6, 7, 33, 70, 120,
　128, 138, 153, 167, 187,
　200–202, 244, 251, 280, 308,
　345, 360, 407, 408, 410, 412,
　414–417, 419, 433, 438, 441, 445
River Yarmouk, 138, 153, 158
River Zarqa, 138, 140, 153
Roger's Plan, 363, 363n1
Royalist Coalition, 396
Royal Society for the Conservation of
　Nature (RSCN), 141–143
Russian military intervention
　in Syria, 379

S

Sadat, Anwar, 239, 240, 365, 398,
　426–429
Sahwa movement, 269
Said, Hammam, 264, 321
Sajida al-Rishawi, 471
Salafism
　al-Albani's philosophy, 270
　division among Salafis, 269–275
　in Jordan, 266–275
　political Salafis organisation, 271
　preaching in mosques, 268
　types of Salafis, 269
Sallal, Abdullah, 396
Samuel, Herbert, 217, 244
San Remo Conference, 216
al-Saud, 4, 23, 217, 394, 395,
　397–399, 403
al-Saud, Abdulaziz Bin-Abdulrahman,
　see Ibn Saud

Saudi Arabia-Jordan relations
    Black September events and, 23, 24, 239, 398, 402, 449
    cooperation, 400–404, 419
    on diplomatic dispute with Iran, 401
    during Arab Spring, 400
    during Qatar crisis, 402
    early phase, 402–404
    economic relations, 400
    foreign policy cooperation, 401
    Jordanian dependency of Saudi financial aid, 397
    security alliance, 402–404
    siege of Mecca and, 402
    trade relations, 389
    views on Israeli-Palestinian conflict, 403
"Save Jordan's Trees" campaign, 143
September 11 attacks, 10
Shahada, Usama, 271
Shamir, Yitzhak, 24, 415, 417, 418, 441–443
Shaqra, Muhammad Ibrahim, 268
Sharia, 9, 10, 86, 87, 258, 274, 290, 471
Sharon, Ariel, 253, 306, 331, 386, 415, 419, 422, 441
Shias, 41, 72, 76, 269, 453, 469
Shishans, 30, 76, 77
Shlaim, Avi, 130, 200n7, 223n12, 238–240, 254n9, 360–362, 424n1, 427n3
Shoubaki, Faisal, 319
Shubeilat, Laith, 328, 431
Shukeiri, Ahmed, 291–293, 361
Shura Council, 319
Shurdom, Tahseen H. (General), 100
Sinai violence, 319
Single non-transferable vote (SNTV) system, 328, 334, 335
al-Sinwar, Yahya, 321, 387
al-Sisi, Abd al-Fattah, 318

Six Days War, *see* June 1967 War
Social issues in Jordan, 153–157
Social sustainability, 157
Society of the Muslim Brotherhood
    against Nasser, 260, 261
    Al-Banna's message, 259
    character of, 260, 261, 265, 266, 272
    crackdowns by Jordanian regime, 263
    during Khalifa's leadership, 260
    internal changes, 264
    in Jordan, 258, 266
    King Abdullah I's Support, 252, 260
    political participation, 261, 264, 274
    split off, 260, 265, 266, 275
    ZamZam Initiative, 265
Special Working Contract for Non-Jordanian Domestic Workers, 55
Structural Adjustment Plans (SAPs), 52, 329
Suez crisis of 1956, 235, 236, 255, 358, 370, 396, 423
Sunni Muslim, 30, 72, 76, 258, 267
Sustainable development
    aspirations of country, 160
    challenges in implementing, 157, 159
Sykes-Picot Agreement (1916), 198, 465
Syrian-Israeli conflict, 365
Syrian refugees
    crisis, 58, 109, 155, 156. 211, 381
    employment privileges, 192
    in Jordan, 47, 57, 84, 121, 383, 388
    livelihoods to, 66, 389

T
Tahboub, Hasan, 301
al-Tal, Abdullah, 253, 254, 315
al-Tall, Mustafa Wahbi, 217
Tanzim Qaidat al-Jihad fi Bilad al-Rafidayn, 453

INDEX 535

Tarawneh, Fayez, 319
Thatcher, Margaret, 366
Theeb, 165, 166, 168
Tobacco industry in Jordan
   cigarette smuggling, 172
   control initiatives, 174
   history of, 166
   Hussein's diplomacy
      and smoking, 170
   market, 167, 172, 174
   smoking in modern Jordan, 169, 171
   smuggling of tobacco products, 167
TransJordanian entity, 199
Transjordanian Muslim
   Brotherhood, 259
TransJordanian Palestinians, 199
Treaty of Independence 1946, 250
Tunnel Crisis of 1996, 329
Turkish republic, 1

U

Ubaydat, Ahmad, 142
Ummah, 184, 394
Umm Al-Jamal, 82
Unified Arab Command (UAC), 360
Unified standard contract for migrant
   domestic workers (MDWs), 55
United Arab Republic (UAR), 203,
   289, 291, 359, 396
United Nations Development
   Programmes (UNDP), 152, 160
United Nations High Commissioner
   for Refugees (UNHCR), 12, 57,
   62, 72–74, 77, 84, 192, 206n16,
   210, 388, 467
United Nations Relief and Works
   Agency (UNRWA), 20, 21, 71,
   75, 155, 191, 228, 282, 284, 344
UN Partition Resolution 1947,
   277, 343

UN Resolution 242, 238
UNRWA, *see* United Nations Relief
   and Works Agency
US
   Jordan-USA FTA, 132
   Jordan-US relations, 65, 374–376
   US-led "War on Terror," 332
US-Jordanian Free Trade Agreement,
   171, 375

V

Voluntary National Review report
   (VNR), 156, 161

W

Wadi Araba peace treaty 1994, 368
Warrick, Joby, 468, 469, 469n4, 474
Washington Declaration, 300, 430
Wataniyyah, 184, 326
West Bank
   April 1957 crisis, 288, 290
   borders of, 278
   creation of, 277
   demography and economy, 281–282
   economic destitution and border
      wars, 284–285
   formal annexation of, 227, 280, 283
   Hashemite rule over, 202, 292
   impact of Nasserism, 288
   Israeli capture of, 71, 292
   legal and administrative
      disengagement, 293, 428
   political history of, 279
   repression of Fatah's activists in, 292
   unification with East Bank,
      279–280, 345
West Bankers, 19, 202, 205, 206,
   284–286, 422
Wye River Memorandum, 313

X
Xi Jinping, 381

Y
Yaari, Ehud, 365
Yassin, Ahmed, 313, 419
Yemen
  civil war in 1962, 360
  unification of, 1
Yom Kippur War, *see* October 1973 War

Z
Zaatari Refugee Camp, 73, 127
al-Zabda, Hussein, 318
Zaidi-Shia Imam of Yemen, 396
Zain, Queen, 422
Zakaria, Fareed, 402
ZamZam Initiative, 265
Zanoun, Yasser, 318
al-Zarqawi, Abu Musab, 263, 273–275, 273n9, 449, 464, 467–469, 473, 474
al-Zawahiri, Ayman, 453
Zionist movement, 218

Printed in the United States
By Bookmasters